CHILDREN & YOUNG PEOPLE'S WORKFORCE

EARLY LEARNING & CHILDCARE

3

DIPLOMA

MIRANDA WALKER

NKC
NORTH KENT COLLEGE

Learning Technology Centre
Gravesend Campus

Direct Telephone Line: 01322 629615
Direct e-mail address: LTC_Gravesend@northkent.ac.uk

This book has been issued for **four weeks**
Fines will be charged for late returns

7/10/2020		
- 3 NOV 2020		

Nelson Thornes

Published in 2011 by:
Nelson Thornes Ltd
Delta Place
27 Bath Road
CHELTENHAM
GL53 7TH
United Kingdom

11 12 13 14 15 / 10 9 8 7 6 5 4 3 2 1

A catalogue record for this book is available from the British Library

ISBN 978 1 4085 0883 1

Cover photograph © Jasper Cole/Getty
Page make-up by Fakenham Prepress Solutions

Index created by Indexing Specialists (UK) Ltd

Printed and bound in Spain by GraphyCems

Contents

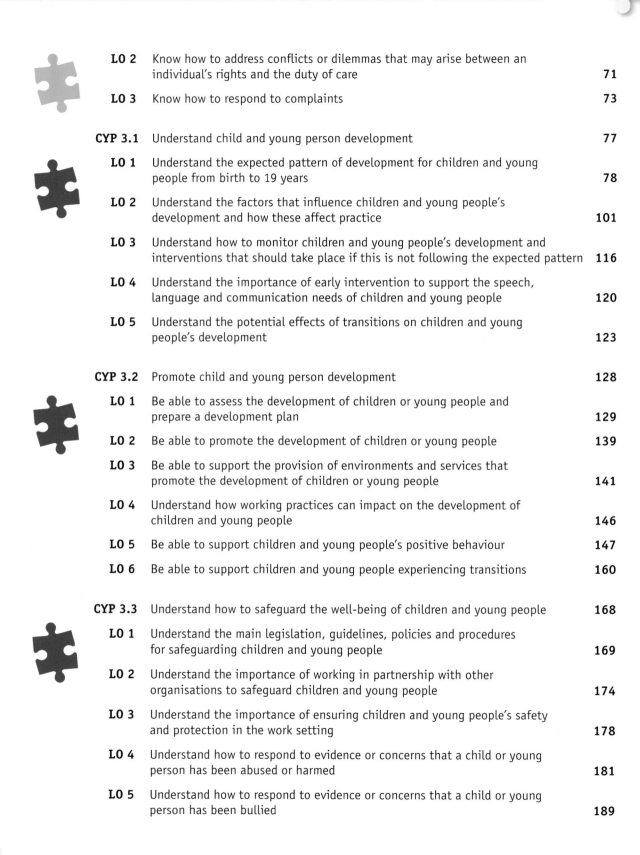

ABOUT THE AUTHOR

Miranda Walker has worked with children from birth to 16 years in a range of settings, including her own day nursery and out-of-school clubs. She has inspected nursery provision for Ofsted, and worked at East Devon College as an Early Years and Playwork lecturer and NVQ assessor and internal verifier. She is a regular contributor to industry magazines and an established author.

INTRODUCTION

The Level 3 Diploma for the Children and Young People's Workforce is a brand new qualification. Before it was introduced, people wanting to work in various jobs within the workforce would undertake completely different qualifications. The government wanted to address this as part of its work to create a unified workforce which shares a common identity and values. The qualification will also help to ensure that a common professional language is shared by practitioners – this will overcome some difficulties which occurred in the past when words such as "observation" and "assessment" had different meanings to different practitioners.

Structure

The structure differs to that of previous qualifications, because there are three different pathways (study routes), which meet the needs of learners wishing to work in three different areas of specialism within the children and young people's workforce. The three pathways are:

- Early Learning and Childcare Pathway
  This is the pathway you have selected, suitable, for example, for those working in a day nursery

- Children and Young People's Social Care Pathway
  Suitable, for example, for those working in children's residential care

- Learning, Development and Support Services Pathway
  Suitable, for example, for Connexions advisers and learning mentors

The qualification has three "shared core units." These are mandatory units that will also be included in other Level 3 qualifications across the children and young people and adult social care workforce. There are then seven "children and young people workforce core units" which must be undertaken by all learners studying for this Diploma. These reflect the knowledge and skills of the common core. (The common core describes the skills and knowledge that everyone who

works with children and young people is expected to have. You can read about this at www.cwdcouncil.org.uk/common-core). There are also mandatory units for each of the pathways, and learners will also select some optional units to study.

The shared units of this new qualification makes it much easier for practitioners to transfer into other areas of work within early learning and childcare during their careers, as it will be possible to undertake additional pathway and optional units rather than starting another different qualification from scratch.

Learning and assessment

How you will be taught and assessed will be explained to you fully by your college or training centre. There will be differences in the learning methods offered by colleges and centres. There are also differences in the way in which the three awarding bodies – CACHE, City & Guilds and Edexel – assess the qualification. Specific advice on preparing for assessment by each of the awarding bodies is given in every chapter of the book, so you can be confident that you'll know what to do – you'll learn more about this on page 12. All learners must be assessed in the workplace as they carry out practical work. Additional commonly used assessment methods include discussion with a tutor or assessor, answering oral or written questions, completing assignments and projects, completing tests and reflecting on your own practice.

Credits and level

Each unit has a credit value which reflects how long it is expected to take the average learner to achieve. This time includes private study and guided learning hours (time spent in lessons or tutorials) time spent undertaking practical work (at work or on placement) and time spent on assessment (including completing tasks and assignments, and being observed). As a rough guide, a unit is equivalent to approximately ten hours of learning. You must gain 65 credits across the qualification in order to gain the Diploma. Once you have completed all of the mandatory units required you will have accumulated 50 credits, so you must select optional units to study with a combined total of 15 credits to complete the qualification. There are more than 40 to choose from in the "option bank." Your college or training centre will advise you on your selection of optional units – they may not offer them all.

The Diploma is ranked at Level 3 on the Qualification and Credit Framework, making it broadly equivalent to 'A' level. Some of the available optional units are ranked as Level 4. These are ideal for those who want to go on to study higher level qualifications in the future, however, many learners will solely choose optional units ranked at Level 3.

Structure of units

Each unit consists of a number of learning outcomes. These specify what you will know and understand in order to achieve the unit. Learning outcomes also tell you what you will be able to do competently in practice to achieve the unit - or in other words, what practical skills you will have.

All learning outcomes must be assessed. Assessment criteria is provided for each learning outcome. This specifies and breaks down the standard/level of knowledge and understanding and practical competence that must be demonstrated.

The content of this book covers all of the knowledge and understanding required for the units included.

HOW TO USE THIS BOOK

Welcome to the *Level 3 Diploma for the Children and Young People's Workforce* student book. This section explains the features of this book and how to use them as a tool for learning. It's important that you read this section.

Throughout the book, there are references to the home countries, e.g. 'You should follow the curriculum framework that applies in your home country'. This is because there are some differences in laws, requirements, curriculums and procedures in England, Wales, Scotland and Northern Ireland.

Learning outcomes
All units are divided into learning outcomes. The first page of each unit lists the relevant learning outcomes.

LEARNING OUTCOMES

The learning outcomes you will meet in this unit are:

Focus on...
This feature appears at the beginning of each learning outcome to explain the focus of the outcome. It also makes a link to the Assessment Criteria.

FOCUS ON ...health and safety

Link Up!

The Link Up! feature frequently appears in the text to direct you to other units in the book that relate to the subject currently being covered.

Did you know?

This feature provides interesting and useful facts that will be valuable to your learning and will enhance your knowledge.

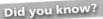

Key terms

During your course you'll come across new words and new terms that you may not have heard before. When these words and terms are first used in the book the key terms feature appears. This gives you a clear definition of the word or term.

Have a go!

The Have a go! feature asks you to do small tasks based on the text you have read. The tasks will help you to understand and remember the information. Some tasks are linked to your placement. These will help you to apply your learning to your practical work.

Good practice

It's important that you always work to high standards and do the best for the children in your care. This feature highlights good practice.

Practical example

Practical examples (case studies) are included to help you understand how theory links with practical work in real settings. After each Practical example a question or two is provided to help you think about how you can use your learning in real situations.

Practical example

Stars Out of School Club interprets legislation

Ask Miranda!

Your expert author, Miranda Walker, answers all the burning questions you may have as you work through the units and supports you on your way to success!

Ask Miranda!

Progress Check

At the end of each unit you will find a list of questions. Answering these will confirm that you have understood what you have read.

▶ Progress Check

Are you ready for assessment?

This feature offers advice on preparing for the different types of assessment you will be required to complete for each unit. The feature is divided into three sections: CACHE, City & Guilds and Edexcel, so you can be confident you will know exactly what you have to do. A tip on how to prepare for assessment is also given. If your Awarding Body does not have a set task or an assignment for you to do for a specific Unit, the tip will relate to gathering evidence or preparing to be observed.

Are you ready for assessment?

Reflective Practice

A key component of professional development is learning from past experience. This is known as 'reflective practice'. You need to demonstrate that you can think about your practice, notice areas for development and plan how to improve your knowledge, understanding and skills, as you work through your qualification. To help you achieve this, a Reflective Practice section is included at the end of the book. It provides suggestions to help you focus on relevant aspects of your professional development.

SHC 31

UNIT 31

Promote communication in health, social care or children's and young people's settings

LEARNING OUTCOMES

The learning outcomes you will meet in this unit are:

1 Understand why effective communication is important in the work setting

2 Be able to meet the communication and language needs, wishes and preferences of individuals

3 Be able to overcome barriers to communication

4 Be able to understand principles and practices relating to confidentiality

INTRODUCTION

All successful practitioners are able to develop good relationships. We build relationships through communication and interaction, so it's important for you to learn how to communicate effectively.

The way in which you talk with children communicates much more than just the words that you say. By communicating well, you demonstrate good use of language and show children that you value what they say and feel. Children also learn from their conversations with adults.

Communicating well will also enable you to establish positive relationships with the adults within your setting, including parents and carers, colleagues and other professionals.

LEARNING OUTCOME 1

FOCUS ON

...understanding why effective communication is important in the work setting

In this section you'll learn about the reasons why people communicate. You'll also learn about how communication affects relationships within the work setting. This includes relationships between children, young people, practitioners and parents and carers. This links with Assessment Criteria 1.1, 1.2.

What we mean by communication

When many people think about communication, the first thing that comes to mind is conversation, and perhaps more specifically, talking. However, it's important to remember that listening is just as important to conversation as speaking! The spoken word is a key method of communication, but others are just as important, as shown in the following diagram.

You'll learn more about these in Learning Outcome 2.

Reasons for communicating

Within a setting, children, young people and adults communicate via a range of these communication methods, and for all sorts of reasons as follows:

■ **Establishing a relationship**
Communicating is how we establish (start) all our relationships. We begin by acknowledging another person – we make eye-contact, we smile, we say hello, we introduce ourselves, we may shake hands. Already we're using body language, facial expression, the spoken word, gesture and touch, and we've only just met someone! We're letting the person know that we're friendly and interested in them, and we're striking up a rapport. Effectively establishing relationships is a crucial part of a practitioner's role, and there will always be new children, families and colleagues to meet. When it's the practitioner who is new to a setting, good communication skills allow them to establish many relationships quickly, and to begin fulfilling their new role. This also applies to learners on placement.

■ **Maintaining relationships**
Once established, all relationships need maintaining. On the most basic level, we do

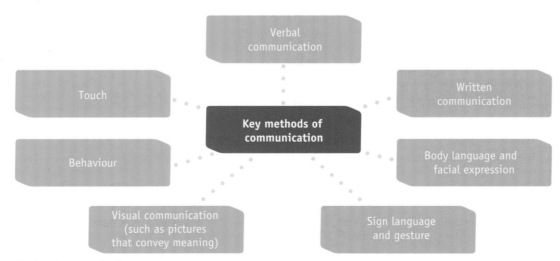

Key methods of communication.

this each time we have another communicative interaction with someone who we have already established a relationship with – for instance, each time you say hello or wave to someone you've already met. If someone you know fails to maintain a relationship in this way, it can lead to feelings of insecurity – have you ever felt unsettled when someone you know has failed to acknowledge you when you've passed by? It's important to avoid this within the setting, as long as it is appropriate to communicate. For instance, it will not always be possible or appropriate to talk to a parent who is being attended to by another member of staff, but you may be able to smile across the room to them, or call goodbye when they leave.

■ **Small talk**

'Small talk' is also an important part of maintaining relationships. For instance, if a parent tells you on Friday that they're looking forward to a trip out at the weekend, you might ask them on Monday whether they had a good time. Small talk with colleagues is generally best kept for break times.

Small talk.

■ **Giving and receiving information**

Much information is given and received every day in settings, verbally, on paper and in electronic files. Some of this will be confidential, and treated in line with your setting's confidentiality policy (see Learning Outcome 4). But whether it's a short informal, verbal message or a detailed written report, it's important that information exchanged is shared appropriately and given clearly, so that it is properly understood. Many settings will have procedures in place to ensure this, such as a system for passing on day-to-day information at the end of a practitioner's shift, or whiteboards recording when sleeping babies were last checked, or message forms to fill in when taking phone messages.

■ **Giving and receiving acknowledgement, reassurance, encouragement and support**

Acknowledgement, reassurance, encouragement and support are important to the emotional well-being of people. This particularly applies to children and young people, for whom life is full of new experiences and situations. They need to know that the adults in their life care for them, take an interest in them and support them in their concerns and activities. Practitioners meet these needs constantly in varied ways, including gentle touch when attending to physical care, verbal praise, encouraging nods and smiles, eye contact and behaving appropriately around children and young people. Interestingly, management studies have shown that adult workers are most satisfied with their jobs when their own need for acknowledgement, reassurance, encouragement and support are met effectively in the workplace.

■ **Expressing needs and feelings**

This is another key to the emotional well-being of both children and adults. Babies and young children in particular have limitations in terms of how they express their needs and feelings, and so practitioners need to become experts in interpreting their communications. For instance, a cry from a baby could mean 'I'm hungry', 'I'm tired', 'I'm uncomfortable', 'I'm in pain', and so on. Children and young people need opportunities to express their needs and feelings, or they may become frustrated or overwhelmed. In time, they will learn to recognise and deal with their feelings in more sophisticated ways. Creative activities are a common way to encourage expression.

■ **Expressing ideas, thoughts and opinions**

Settings function best when practitioners work effectively as a team, and regularly 'put their heads together' to achieve best practice. Good team members contribute their ideas, thoughts and opinions within the group, and also learn from the contributions made by others. It's important that children and young people are also encouraged to express their own ideas, thoughts and opinions, in their play and conversations. We learn much about children and young people's development when we pay attention to these expressions, and we also demonstrate that we value what they think and say.

Observe how experienced practitioners engage in small talk with parents while remaining professional. You'll see that it is just as important to know when to stop as it is to know when to start! It can take time and practice to develop this skill.

How communication affects relationships in the work setting

As we've discussed, communication is at the heart of establishing and maintaining positive relationships with parents, carers and colleagues.

Positive working relationships with adults lead to a pleasant, comfortable atmosphere in the working environment. This is beneficial not only to the adults, but also to the children and young people, because the practitioner's working environment is the child's play and learning space.

When positive relationships are formed, it is easier for colleagues and parents to give and receive trust, information, support, help, advice and encouragement.

This makes it more likely that any problems arising between adults will be positively approached and resolved. It's also more likely that skills and knowledge will be shared. In short, good team work and the effective shared care of children and young people depend on positive working relationships, which in turn depend on effective communication.

Children and young people's experience of a setting will largely depend on the relationships that they make and maintain with practitioners and their peers. However, you need to remember that children and young people are still learning about communication, and about how relationships work. In particular, it takes time and life experience to learn how to deal with and communicate feelings and impulses appropriately. All children and young people can be expected to fall out with those close to them many times as these lessons are learned, as we did when we were that age – but eventually we learn to ask before we take something that belongs to someone else, and to recognise and explain our feelings if we're upset. Whether a toddler is making their first friend, or a teenager is getting together with their first boyfriend or girlfriend, there is a lot to think about!

All children and young people can be expected to fall out...

Also see Unit CYP 3.5 Learning Outcomes 1 and 2, and Unit CYP 3.6 Learning Outcome 2

LEARNING OUTCOME 2

FOCUS ON

...being able to meet the communication and language needs, wishes and preferences of individuals

In this section you'll learn about methods and styles of communication, and how these relate to communication and language needs, wishes and preferences. You'll also learn about responding to reactions from others. This links with Assessment Criteria **2.1, 2.2, 2.3, 2.4.**

Communication and language needs, wishes and preferences

During your career, you will work with children, young people and adults with a range of communication and language needs, wishes and preferences. Part of the practitioner's role is to establish (find out about) these, and to respond accordingly, so that effective communication occurs and good relationships are built and maintained. You need to remember that, when communicating, all parties need to express themselves and also to understand others. Often the best way to find out about needs, wishes and preferences is to ask the people concerned directly – this includes the children and young people. If this is inappropriate, remember that families will generally know their children better than anyone else, and are usually extremely happy to help.

The wishes and preferences of adults

You should always communicate and behave politely and courteously with the adults within your setting. This means that you need to address people appropriately. People's names are part of their identity and their individuality, and it is important to respect that. Find out how people would like to be addressed – you should not assume that it is acceptable for you to use a parent's first name, even though it may be given on the registration form. Also, do not make assumptions about people's titles. Not all parents share the same last name as their child, and not all mothers go by the title 'Mrs'. You should not shorten the name of an adult (or a child) unless you are invited to do so.

Remember your manners whenever you are communicating – good manners show respect for other people. More importantly, a lack of manners is often interpreted as a lack of respect for other people. Demonstrating good manners plays an important part in establishing and maintaining positive relationships, and it influences the behaviour of children too. You must always remember that you are a role model.

Have a go!

Recall a time when you have been offended by someone else's lack of manners. Perhaps someone asked you to do something without saying 'please', or talked over you when you were speaking, or brushed past you without saying 'excuse me'. How did you feel?

When appropriate, also consider the communication methods preferred by other people. For instance, unless there's an urgent matter to discuss, some people prefer email to phone messages.

Link Up!

You'll learn more about this in the next section and in Unit CYP 3.6

Ask Miranda!

Q One of our parents always asks to take paperwork home. Should I ask her whether she has a problem with literacy?

A Reading and writing can be daunting for some people, and not everyone who experiences this feels comfortable drawing attention to it. While some people may ask the setting for direct assistance, it is not uncommon for parents to ask to fill out forms at home, and to return them to the setting the next day, or to request to borrow information displayed in the setting to read in their own time at home. You should always respect this. There is no need to ask her about it.

Communication methods and styles

There are of course many different methods by which we can communicate. Some of these are verbal and others are non-verbal, as shown on the diagrams below.

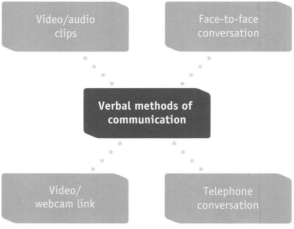

Verbal methods of communication.

You should always aim to communicate clearly, in a way that is appropriate for individual adults, and appropriate to the situation. To do this, consider the methods of communication available to you and what you need to say. (You'll find further information about the advantages and disadvantages of communication methods in Unit CYP 3.6 Learning Outcome 2.)

For instance, is your communication urgent? If you want to make a parent aware that their child has been coughing on and off throughout the afternoon, it would be appropriate to wait and tell them in person

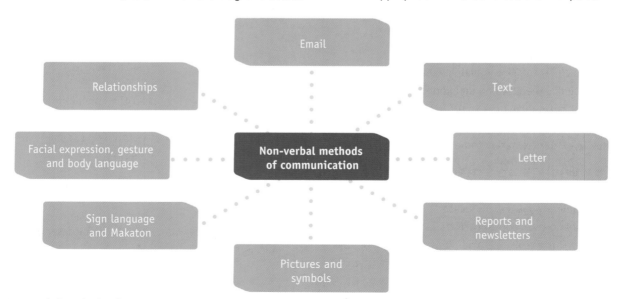

Non-verbal methods of communication.

when they collect their child. However, if a child has vomited and they need to be collected, it will be appropriate to telephone a parent straightaway at their workplace.

Also give due consideration to the issue of confidentiality. For instance, it may be appropriate to put a general, round-robin note in children's bags for them to take home. But you will need to put a formal, confidential letter sealed in an envelope, addressed and marked 'confidential'. It should then be posted, or handed, to the appropriate adult. (You'll learn more about confidentiality in Learning Outcome 4.)

We all have our own natural styles of communication, and this is an intriguing way in which we are all unique. But at the same time, you need to consider whether your approach should be formal or informal. Much of this will depend on the tone and circumstances of what you have to say, and who you are communicating with. This will also impact on the tone and pitch of your voice.

Tone and pitch

Tone of voice has a lot to do with the way in which human beings interpret the communications made to them. Many studies have indicated that people often take more notice of tone than they do of what someone actually says to them. This is also shown in the behaviour of babies, who will often cry if they hear harsh, angry tones, despite having no understanding of the words that are being spoken.

So as a practitioner, make sure you use warm, friendly, respectful tones when communicating on a day-to-day basis with children, colleagues and parents and carers. This applies in person and on the phone. It is good advice to smile when on the phone as you would in a face-to-face conversation, because a smile 'shows' in your voice.

'Pitch' refers to how high or how low your voice is. When engaging a group of children, try to ensure that your voice rises and falls, as this is interesting to listen to. Pay attention to a skilled practitioner reading a story aloud and you will soon see how effective this can be. Babies in particular respond

well to a high-pitched voice – many people naturally adopt a higher pitch, and perhaps a sing-song tone, when they interact with a baby. A low pitch can be effective when we want to adopt a serious tone, and can be useful if we need to step in to stop inappropriate behaviour.

A smile 'shows' in your voice.

Good practice

Some forms of communication, such as face-to-face conversation, for example, can be either formal or informal. However, other methods, such as texting or messages left on sticky notes, are generally regarded as strictly informal and inappropriate in certain circumstances. Be sure to follow any rules your setting has about the methods of communication used to contact parents, carers and outside professionals.

Actively listening to children and young people

Listening well is important because it impacts on the quality of the communication between you and the children and young people in your care. It demonstrates that you value what they say and feel. This in turn impacts on children and young people's levels of confidence and self-esteem. Practise active listening by employing the following strategies:

■ **Let children and young people see that you are interested in what they are saying**

Establish eye contact, getting down to the children's level whenever necessary.
Smile and nod encouragingly if appropriate.

■ **Give children time**

Children need time to formulate their ideas as they speak. Listen for long enough to let them finish what they have to say, even if they need to pause for thought.

■ **Ask children and young people questions about their topic**

This encourages them to talk further (and to think). They will know you are interested if you are asking for more information.

■ **Clarify and confirm**

You can also ask questions to check that you are following what a younger child is telling you. Making sure you are interpreting correctly is part of listening well. You can repeat the essence of what a child says, asking afterwards, 'Is that right?' Or you can ask clarifying questions, for instance, 'So you borrowed three books from the library on Saturday?'

■ **React to what children say**

Show empathy for children's feelings when they are expressed. Be aware of your facial expressions – look happy for children, or concerned, or whatever is appropriate.

■ **Respond**

Make sure that you answer children and young people when they talk to you. Even if they have not asked you a direct question, you should still respond appropriately, perhaps just to say, 'That's interesting' or 'That sounds like fun'. These acknowledgements are important. They let children and young people know that you have received their communication, and that you appreciated their message.

The following types of behaviour could indicate to children and young people that you do not value their ideas and feelings:

■ not really listening

■ not making eye contact

■ looking bored

■ not contributing to the conversation

■ not responding

■ not acknowledging or answering

■ interrupting

■ rushing them to get to the point

■ not acting upon their ideas

■ not thanking or praising them for their contributions.

Sometimes, particularly in group discussions, children and young people will be keen to share their thoughts and may interrupt one another. Allowing interruptions sends the message that one person's thoughts are more important than another's. When a child interrupts, try acknowledging them, but encourage them to wait. You might say for instance, 'Hold on to that idea Maria. Let's finish listening to Declan, and then we'll hear from you.'

Listening well shows that you value what children say and feel.

Communication and language needs

You will learn in detail about meeting and supporting children's communication and language development in Unit EYMP 5. It's recommended that you read this information (which begins on page 407), as part of your study towards this unit.

Adults can experience the same communication difficulties as children. This means that practitioners may have to adapt their communication techniques to meet the needs of other adults. It's important that you are as sensitive to the communication difficulties of adults as you would be to those of children. Otherwise, adults may become isolated or feel excluded within the setting, and may ultimately leave. In the case of parents, if the partnership with practitioners is hampered by communication difficulties, there may be implications for both the adult and their child as information may be missed or misunderstood.

Factors to consider when promoting effective communication

Practitioners can adapt their communications in a number of ways to suit adults' needs and the circumstances of the communication. Strategies may include:

- learning some signs (sign language), or arranging for a signer to interpret

- talking clearly and facing anyone who is lip reading

- talking more slowly

- arranging for an interpreter (for adults for whom English/Welsh is an additional language)

- translating signs, letters and other written communications into the languages required (this can often be done via computer)

- arranging to talk in a quiet area free from background noise

- taking the time to give key information verbally as well as in writing (for adults who have difficulty reading).

You'll learn more about translation and interpretation services in Learning Outcome 3.

Did you know?

Most settings will have a Special Educational Needs Coordinator, or **SENCO** for short. SENCOs are specially trained to oversee the support given within the setting to children and young people with special needs. They should be your first port of call if you need related advice, guidance or information.

key term

SENCO Special Educational Needs Coordinator.

Ask Miranda!

Q I sometimes feel a bit flustered when I go to the office to talk to senior staff. Then afterwards I worry that it stopped me communicating properly. What can I do?

A **Be really clear about the point of your message before you go to the office. It can help to think through/write down key points in advance. You might like to have a practice by yourself, or seek advice from colleagues if you are unsure what to say. Also think about whether a certain response or answer is required before you leave the office.**

It is important that you are clear about the communications that you receive. Whenever you are unsure about any information you are given, or unclear about what is being asked of you, you must check to avoid making mistakes. Ask questions, and clarify key points to ensure that you have understood correctly. You should practise the principles of active listening with adults, just as you would when talking with children and young people (see page 19).

Responding to reactions of others when communicating

When communicating face-to-face, you should always make eye contact. This not only shows interest and attention, it also enables you to read people's facial expressions. This will help you to interpret how your message is being received – or in other words, to judge the person's reaction to what you are saying. Body language is also a good indicator of this, and of course, what people say and the tone and words they use provides us with plenty of 'reaction' feedback.

However, people do not always express how they are feeling in words, as the Practical example on page 23 shows. Once you are aware of someone's reactions, you can modify how you are communicating accordingly. For instance, it may be necessary to adjust the tone or pitch of your voice, to simplify the language you're using to get your message across, or to further explain what you mean. When you are not communicating face-to-face, pay extra attention to the tone of the person you're talking to, and react accordingly.

See Unit CPY 3.5, Learning Outcome 2, for information about handling conflict professionally

Good eye contact shows interest and attention.

Your reaction to others when they are communicating

You must also ensure that you respond with appropriate facial expressions, body language and tone of voice when someone is communicating to you. Remember that these things are just as important as what you say. It may be appropriate to show empathy or concern, or perhaps that you are pleased for someone. Luckily, we often do this naturally! If you are talking to someone who becomes upset, you will probably drop the tone of your voice and speak more softly and slowly. You may also find that you naturally mirror people when interacting – smiling at someone who's happy to be telling you their good news, repeating the babblings of a baby back to them in their own tone, or frowning in concern when a worried child approaches you.

Have a go!

Just think about body language and facial expressions for a moment. What reactions might you notice if a) someone doesn't follow the information you are giving them, b) someone disagrees with something you've said, and c) someone isn't paying attention to you.

Body language and facial expressions help you interpret how a person is feeling.

Practical example

Mareka responds to a reaction

Pre-school worker Mareka has been waiting to talk to a parent, who has volunteered to help out at the forthcoming summer fête. When the parent comes to collect her son, Mareka approaches and starts to tell her about some arrangements made for the fête at last night's staff meeting. The parent seems interested and replies politely, but at the same time she packs up her son's things and inches towards the door. Mareka notices this, and realises that the parent may be in a hurry. She asks if it would be better to talk about the fête at another time. The parent smiles and says she'll have much more time tomorrow. They agree to pick up the conversation then.

Question

Give another example of body language that might indicate that someone doesn't have the time to engage in conversation.

LEARNING OUTCOME 3

FOCUS ON

...being able to overcome barriers to communication

In this section you'll learn about the impact background has on communication. You'll be introduced to strategies to avoid and rectify misunderstanding. You'll also learn about services to support speech and communication needs. This links with Assessment Criteria 3.1, 3.2, 3.3, 3.4, 3.5.

Interpretation and different backgrounds

We are all different, but people who have a shared experience of a particular background will often interpret communication methods in similar ways. This could be to do with a shared culture, experience, knowledge, childhood or family background. This gives you a kind of shorthand when it comes to communicating with others who have a similar background to your own, and may lead you to assume that people in general will interpret your communications as you intend.

However, you shouldn't expect this as a matter of course, as people from different backgrounds may use and interpret communication in different ways, as the following section explains. The experience young children have of communication in the home will have a particularly strong impact on their own communication methods and style, as their communications outside of the home and family will be limited.

■ **Home language and culture**

There may be a complete or partial language barrier. Different forms of the same language may be spoken in different regions of the same country, and accents and pronunciation may vary. Words that have more than one meaning in English can be particularly misleading. People who do not have English as their first language may use and interpret tone and pitch in a different way, for example they may not use rise and fall in their tone. Gestures and body language may be interpreted differently, for instance, eye contact may rarely be established in some cultures. Subjects considered sensitive or unsuitable for 'polite conversation' may differ greatly. There may be different sensibilities in terms of things that are considered rude or offensive.

■ **Home and family background**

Different families interact and communicate in very different ways. Some homes are busy and noisy and calling to one another from two rooms away is the norm. Others are quieter and calmer, and voices are rarely raised. Some children will hear and perhaps use more than one language at home. Swearing may be heard in the home or on TV, or it may not be tolerated at all. Adults may be highly communicative or relatively quiet – they may engage in banter with one another and with

children, or such banter may be rarely heard. Individual children may be used to interacting with other children at home, or they may spend most of their time with adults.

■ **Personality, confidence and self-esteem**

These are closely linked. Some children are naturally more outgoing, while others are more reserved. Some children approach practitioners frequently with something to say, but it's important to also initiate communication with the children less inclined to do so. Avoid pressurising those who are reluctant to speak in group activities or when someone new is present, or there's a danger they may avoid certain situations and become isolated. Negative experiences can seriously impact on children's confidence and self-esteem; if a child is ridiculed for the way they communicate or for mistakes that they make (written or verbal), it can affect them for years to come. They may grow up believing they are no good at writing for instance, and this could become a block to their learning. Personality also influences the way in which children and young people respond. Some are an 'open book' – they may vocally express excitement, enthusiasm, unhappiness or anger. Others communicate this more subtly, but the intensity of their emotion may be the same.

■ **Literacy and technological ability**

As discussed in Learning Outcome 2, literacy skills vary in adults as well as in children and young people. This could be due to a negative/unsuccessful learning experience or lack of learning opportunity, a learning difficulty, or learning English as an additional language. Confidence can also be an issue – some people do not feel confident about expressing themselves in writing, or they may fear making a mistake if reading aloud. Practitioners should provide information verbally as well as in writing when necessary. When working with young children, the provision of activities that promote literacy skills and confidence are valuable. People who

Never assume that everyone is familiar with modern technology.

do not have fluent literacy skills may also be at a disadvantage in terms of technological knowledge or ability, as sending emails and browsing websites relies on these skills. Written instructions for technology, such as the use of a digital camera or a smart phone, can use unfamiliar and complicated language. But people who are highly literate may

also struggle here – they may not have learned how to use modern technology (or may not have access to it), so you should never assume that everyone will sign up to the setting's blog, or check the website for updates.

Barriers to effective communication

Information on common barriers to communication, and strategies for overcoming them, is included on page 261.

Strategies to clarify misunderstandings

To avoid misunderstandings, it helps to think through what it is you want to communicate beforehand (see the Ask Miranda! section on page 21), and to ensure that you are clear about the communication you receive (see the Good practice section on page 22). This is particularly important when you are training.

Practical example

Asner's misunderstanding

Asner is on placement at a holiday club. The play leader asks him to clear away the paint table as it's time for lunch. Asner takes the paint pots out to the 'messy play' sink. He empties all the paint down the drain, washes out the pots and brushes and puts them away.

During lunch, he hears the play leader talking to one of the children about the afternoon's activities. He says that the paint table will be set up again later.

Asner has a sinking feeling as he realises what has happened. He immediately tells the play leader that he misunderstood – he says he's sorry, but he got the wrong end of the stick and threw the paint away. He offers to make up some more. The play leader accepts this and says, 'Never mind, I expect the children would like to choose some new colours. Who wants to help Asner?'

Question
Asner was right to be keen to help by washing up the paint things, but what should he have done first?

Speaking clearly and listening carefully are also always priorities, of course. However, misunderstandings are bound to occur from time to time. As soon as you realise there has been a misunderstanding, it's good practice to let the other person know, with a polite apology, and then to establish clearly the intention of the original communication. If you have taken any inappropriate action as a result of the misunderstanding, be entirely open about it, and willing to rectify the situation if at all possible.

Misunderstandings are sometimes due to the fact that the communication method or style isn't working for the individual or the situation, in which case the practitioner needs to find a more effective way to communicate. Your knowledge of communication barriers and strategies to overcome them will help you here. Something simple such as talking at a slower pace may be all that is needed. However, if the strategies available to you within your setting are not working, or they are inappropriate to your needs, you may need to access extra support or services to enable effective communication.

Accessing extra support and services

The diagram shows the services that can be called on when extra support is required to meet communication needs.

Translation services
Translators are **bilingual** or **multilingual**. They

will translate writing/text into other languages for people who cannot understand English. They will also translate writing/text in other languages into English. For instance, a setting may arrange for their policies to be translated into Polish to meet the needs of a family new to the setting. Writing/text can also be translated to or from Braille. Braille is a series of raised dots. Some people who have a visual impairment read Braille by feeling the dots with their fingertips.

key terms

bilingual fluent in two languages.

multilingual fluent in three or more languages.

Interpretation services
Interpreters are bilingual or multilingual. They will attend a setting to facilitate a conversation between two people who do not speak the same language, by interpreting what each is saying. They are trained to interpret exactly what is said in the way it is said, and not to bring their own personal style of communication to the proceedings. Even if a family has some understanding of English, many settings find it helpful to use the services of an interpreter when something important or formal is being discussed, to ensure that everyone fully understands all the details.

A 'signer' is another sort of an interpreter. He or she will facilitate conversation between a deaf person who uses sign language and someone who does not, by interpreting what each is saying. If a deaf person is attending a meeting where there will be discussion among several people, two signers may be booked. In this case, one will sign what everyone else is saying so the deaf person can understand. Meanwhile, the other signer will translate what the deaf person is communicating via sign language into the spoken word, so everyone else can understand.

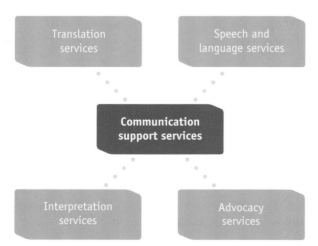

Extra support services.

Did you know?

It is helpful for interpreters and signers to see any documents that will be referred to in advance of scheduled meetings, and to be informed of any jargon or terms that they may not usually use – 'Early Years Foundation Stage profile' is a good example of an unfamiliar term.

Good practice

When a setting first begins working with someone for whom English is an additional language, or someone who uses sign language, it can be particularly helpful to discuss future communication needs via an interpreter or signer to avoid misunderstandings about this important topic. This smoothes the way for successful communications in the future.

Speech and language services

When a problem with speech or language has been identified, a speech and language therapist will meet with a child or young person to work on ways in which their speech and language can be developed and supported. An important part of this role is providing advice and guidance on how families and settings can effectively communicate with children and young people. Suggestions may include activities to promote engagement in communication, as well as advice in the use of specific methods of communication, such as using Makaton, or AAC methods (as described on pages 418–419).

Advocacy services

Advocacy means supporting or representing the interests of people who are thought likely to be disregarded or to have difficulty in gaining attention.

Under the UN Convention on the Rights of the Child, children have a right to be consulted about matters that are important to them. The role of an advocate is to talk to children and young people who may not otherwise have their opinion listened to, about things that are important to them and their lives, and to represent their best interests. Through the advocate, a child or young person's opinions and feelings are passed on to the appropriate person or authority.

Advocates have an extremely important role to play in ensuring the voices of children are heard, and are likely to work with children and young people who are looked after by their local authority, as well as those with communication or learning difficulties. You'll learn more about the UN Convention on the Rights of the Child on pages 57 and 69.

Did you know?

Your setting's SENCO will generally hold contact information for support services available in your local area.

LEARNING OUTCOME 4

FOCUS ON

...being able to apply principles and practices relating to confidentiality

In this section you'll learn about what confidentiality means, and how to handle and treat confidential information appropriately. You will also be introduced to the Data Protection Act of 1984/1998. This links with Assessment Criteria 4.1, 4.2, 4.3.

What does confidentiality mean?

The term 'confidentiality' refers to the rights of people to have information held or known about them kept both privately and safely.

Practitioners are often aware of many personal details about the families that they work with. You may be given confidential information verbally, and you may have access to confidential files and records, depending on your position. These may be paper-based or electronic.

Respecting confidentiality is extremely important, and thanks to the Data Protection Act of 1984/1998, it is a legal requirement for settings to appropriately handle the confidential information that they collect and hold about people.

Good practice

Passing on information when you should not do so can have serious consequences. As well as breaking the rules, trust may be lost, causing damage to working relationships and upset to individuals. Your professional reputation can be affected, and disciplinary action may be taken by employers.

Have a go!

Make sure that you read and understand your setting's confidentiality policy. It will explain your organisational confidentiality procedures. Speak to your supervisor if there is anything that you don't fully understand.

Types of confidential information

You should treat any personal information about the people at your setting as confidential – that includes information relating to children, parents, carers, other family members and colleagues. Types of confidential information include:

- personal details such as those recorded on the registration form, including addresses, telephone numbers and medical information

- information about children's individual development and individual needs, including observations and the type of information held in development reports and on special educational needs registers

- letters, emails or reports from outside professionals working with children or families

- details about family or social relationships or circumstances, including things you may know about the current or past relationships within families, or details about people's jobs or events in their lives

- financial information, including details about how children's places are funded, and how any fees are paid

- information relating to past incidents or experiences of a sensitive nature (for instance, a family may have suffered a traumatic event, or perhaps you know that social workers, therapists or other professionals are working within a family).

Sensitive information should be made available to practitioners on a 'need-to-know basis'. That means that different practitioners in the same setting will not necessarily have access to the same information. Therefore, you should not discuss confidential matters with colleagues unless you are sure that it is appropriate to do so, and that it can be done privately. If you find yourself wondering whether it's acceptable to say something to someone – **don't say it!** If you

are not sure about any issue of a confidential nature, always check with your supervisor before disclosing information to anyone else.

Good practice

It is never good practice to gossip in the workplace!

Practical example

Holly passes on information selectively

Holly works as team leader of the nursery's toddler room. Parent Mr Jacobs confides in Holly. He tells her that he and his wife are spending time apart after some family problems, but that this is not to be made 'common knowledge'. He says that that he and his son Tom are staying with Tom's grandparents and that the grandparents will be collecting Tom for a few days.

Holly checks the registration form. The grandparents need to be authorised to collect Tom, and so they are added to the form. Holly tells her staff that Tom will be collected by his grandparents, but as there is no need for staff to know the reason why, Holly does not mention the family's problems.

Question
Why does Holly not mention the family problems?

Confidential records

A large amount of confidential information is contained within the records of a setting. These could be paper-based or kept electronically – on computers, laptops, discs, memory sticks and so on. This data must be handled with care and stored securely. You should never leave sensitive paperwork or electronic files where people who do not need to know will have access to them. Parents and carers should be aware of,

and party to, information held about them and their children.

Link Up!

You can find out more about the safe storage of paper and electronic files on pages 32 and 33, and in Unit CYP 3.6, Learning Outcome 3

Making sure records remain confidential.

Data Protection Act of 1984/1998

As confidentiality is such an important issue, there is **legislation in place to ensure that people's right to confidentiality is protected.** In accordance with the Data Protection Act of 1984/1998, any organisation that collects and stores personal records must be registered on the Data Protection Register. To summarise, those registered must only collect information that is:

- accurate at the time it is collected

- obtained legally and without deceit

- relevant for its purpose and not excessive.

Collected information should:

- only be used for the purpose explained when it was collected

- be kept confidential from anyone who does not have the right to see it

- be kept up to date

- be made available to the person it is about, meaning that individuals are entitled to see information held about them or their children

- be kept securely – there must be security measures in place protecting against unauthorised access

- only kept as long as is necessary.

You can find more information about the Data Protection Act at **www.ico.gov.uk**.

Did you know?

Confidential electronic files can include photos, video clips and audio clips, as well as email and documents.

Discussing confidential matters

When it's necessary to discuss a confidential matter with a colleague or outside professional either in person or on the phone, always make sure that you can talk privately without being overheard. In a busy setting, this can be achieved by scheduling a conversation at a time when you are free to go to a private space, such as the office, where the door can be closed.

Sometimes, confidential information needs to be discussed with a parent or carer. As it is your responsibility not to reveal private matters to others who do not need to know, you should once again arrange to talk privately, ideally in another room. You should also consider whether it is appropriate for the parent's child to hear the discussion, which may well be about them or about an issue that affects them.

Sharing confidential paper-based or electronic files

Settings routinely share some of the information they collect and hold, such as information about children's achievement as recorded in the Early Years Foundation Stage (EYFS) profile. Further statistical information, such as the ethnicity of families, may also be collected and passed on to local authorities. This must always be done in accordance with your setting's confidentiality policy. Families should be aware of the exchange of information and give their consent.

Link Up!

Further information about the EYFS profile can be found on page 331

Have a go!

Find out what information your current setting routinely shares with parental permission, and who they share it with. You may find the answer in the setting's confidentiality policy, or you may need to ask the supervisor.

Potential tension between maintaining confidentiality and disclosing concerns

You must respect confidential information about children and young people and their families, as long as doing so will not affect their welfare. If, for example, you suspect that a child or young person

Ask Miranda!

Q I work in an area with a high crime rate, and I worry that families would never forgive me if I had to disclose information about a parent.

A **It can be uncomfortable for a practitioner to find themselves in a situation where disclosure is necessary. It may feel as though you are betraying the trust of someone you know well. However, following your setting's confidentiality policy is an extremely important part of your role, and it is essential to the safeguarding of children and young people. It's good practice for settings to make their policies known to those they work with, including families. Should the need to make a disclosure arise, this will certainly help everyone involved to understand the responsibilities and duties of the practitioner.**

is being abused or committing abuse, you have a duty to **disclose** your concerns and the information they are based on, but **only to the relevant person or authority**. Practitioners may also need to breach confidentiality if a crime has been committed, in which case it may be necessary to give information to the police. For further details, see Unit CYP 3.3 Understand how to safeguard the well-being of children and young people.

key term

Disclosing/disclosure the process of passing on confidential information in certain circumstances, in line with confidentiality procedures.

Maintaining confidentiality in day-to-day communication

As we've discussed, understanding your setting's confidentiality policy and good everyday working practices will enable you to maintain confidentiality, and treat confidential documents, files and conversations with respect. The diagrams in the sections on pages 32–33 show ways in which you can maintain confidentiality in your day-to-day communications and handling of information in three key categories:

- paper-based information and communication

- electronic-based information and communication

- verbally shared information and communication.

Paper-based information and communication

While many settings increasingly keep confidential electronic files, some information such as observations and children's drawings or work, generally remain paper-based. As paper documents are easily moved and read, it is important to ensure that they are looked after appropriately to prevent them from becoming lost, damaged, inappropriately accessed or photocopied. Settings generally keep confidential paper-based items in lockable filing cabinets or cupboards. It's important that relevant staff members have keys so they can access the information without difficulty. These keys must be kept securely.

Electronic-based information and communication

Settings are increasingly keeping electronic-based information on computers, laptops, discs, memory sticks and external hard drives. This may include emails, electronic documents, photos, video clips, audio clips and so on. Passwords can be used to protect access not only to computers, but to particular files. This system can effectively allow practitioners sharing a computer to access different files on a need-to-know basis.

Computers should have security in place to prevent them being accessed externally. They should be adequately protected against viruses, and virus checks should be frequently completed. Back-up copies of electronic files should be made to prevent the loss of information. Technology moves quickly, but before any new systems or ways of collecting or storing information are introduced by a setting, security of confidentiality must be addressed.

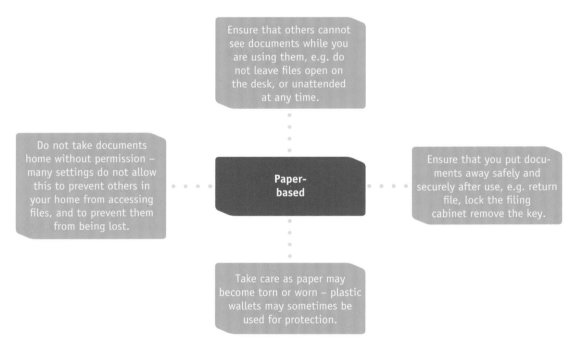

Paper-based information and communication.

Ensure that others cannot see confidential information displayed on computer screens etc. while you areaccessing the files.

Ensure that files are backed up securely to ensure important information isn't lost if files are damaged. Computers should have virus protection and be regularly screened.

Electronic-based

Always be sure to close files securely as soon as you are finished with them. Store discs, memory sticks, external drives etc. securely.

Ensure that files are protected by appropriate means such as secure (not obvious) passwords. Do not display these anywhere.

Electronic-based information and communication.

Verbal information and communication

Practitioners, parents and carers exchange confidential information verbally all the time, so it is important not to become complacent about this. Stop and think about whether the things you are told should be kept to yourself. If it is appropriate and necessary to pass confidential information on to someone else, make sure you do so privately. Give some thought to whether you can be overheard – this also applies when you are on the phone. As we've already discussed, it is never good practice to gossip. If you make it your rule not to gossip in the workplace, you will be less likely to accidently reveal or to hear confidential information inappropriately in your casual conversations.

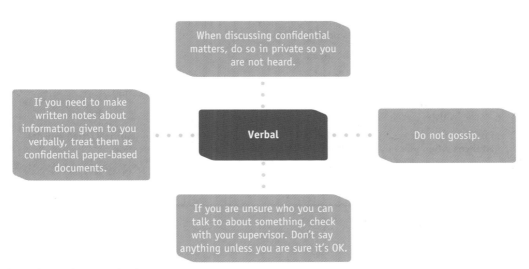

When discussing confidential matters, do so in private so you are not heard.

If you need to make written notes about information given to you verbally, treat them as confidential paper-based documents.

Verbal

Do not gossip.

If you are unsure who you can talk to about something, check with your supervisor. Don't say anything unless you are sure it's OK.

Verbal information and communication.

How are things going?

▶ Progress Check

1. Give four reasons why people communicate. (1.1)

2. How do good communication skills assist you in establishing relationships? (1.2)

3. Name three factors to consider when promoting effective communication. (2.2)

4. Name three types of support services that can help enable individuals to communicate effectively. (3.5)

5. Give five examples of confidential information held by settings. (4.2)

6. Give an example of a situation when a practitioner has a duty to breach confidentiality. (4.3)

Are you ready for assessment?

CACHE

Set task: To establish the context of your practice, you must do some research to provide:

■ an identification of the different reasons people communicate

■ an explanation of how communication affects relationships in the work setting.

It's suggested that you may want to present your written response as a formal report with an introduction. You can prepare by re-reading pages 14–16 and making relevant notes. You can also read about writing reports on page 265.

Edexel

In preparation for assessment of this Unit, it will be helpful to record in your reflective journal instances when you have identified and overcome barriers to communication.

City & Guilds

In preparation for assessment of this Unit, it will be helpful to record in your reflective journal instances when you have identified and overcome barriers to communication.

UNIT 32

Engage in personal development in health, social care or children's and young people's settings

LEARNING OUTCOMES

The learning outcomes you will meet in this unit are:

1 Understand what is required for competence in own work role

2 Be able to reflect on practice

3 Be able to evaluate own performance

4 Be able to agree a personal development plan

5 Be able to use learning opportunities and reflective practice to contribute to personal development

INTRODUCTION

It is important that practitioners continue to develop their skills and professional knowledge throughout their career. This promotes improvement in practice, and positively impacts on the quality of children and young people's care, learning and development. A key component of professional development is learning from past experience – practitioners think about their practice, notice areas for development and plan how to improve their knowledge, understanding and skills. This is known as 'reflective practice'.

LEARNING OUTCOME 1

FOCUS ON

...understanding what is required for competence in own work role

In this section you'll learn about the duties and responsibilities of your work role. You'll also learn about the expectations of your work role, as expressed in relevant standards. This links with Assessment Criteria **1.1, 1.2.**

Duties and responsibilities of your own work role

This qualification will enable you to learn and develop the fundamentals of being a Level 3 practitioner. But there is a huge range of jobs within the early years sector, and the duties and responsibilities of these roles vary enormously. So it is important that you understand what is required of you in your own specific job role.

This will be set out in the job description issued by your setting. The duties and responsibilities will often be expressed as tasks. For instance, if you are working in the baby room of a nursery, tasks listed on your job description may include:

- meet the emotional and physical care needs of babies sensitively

- make regular observations and assessment of the development of babies.

Often, there is an additional 'person specification' section of a job description. This details the knowledge, experience and attributes that the practitioner will need to fulfil the duties and responsibilities. In our example, this may include:

- the ability to interact with babies with sensitivity and respect

- experience of meeting the emotional and physical care needs of babies

- excellent knowledge and understanding of the development patterns of babies.

Have a go!

If you're already employed in a setting, revisit your job description. Consider whether it represents the actual duties and responsibilities of your current role. It's usual for job roles to evolve over time, so you'll find it valuable to repeat this activity periodically. If you're not yet employed, ask your placement supervisor if you could have a look at a job description for a Level 3 post. It's a great way to see what is likely to be expected of you when you finish your course and apply for jobs.

Read job descriptions carefully.

Ask Miranda!

Q Do I need to keep my job description as well as my contract of employment?

A Once appointed, you should always keep a copy of your job description so you can refer to it in the future, and it's essential to be able to refer back if your employer wants to make changes to your usual work. It will also come in handy if you want to apply for a new job. Job application forms will require you to give details about your responsibilities in past positions, and job descriptions will help you to give correct information succinctly.

Work role expectations as expressed in relevant standards

When settings are devising their job descriptions and person specifications, they will consider the relevant standards that they expect their new staff member to meet. Settings will not reach the minimum standards required of them if the practitioners they employ are not up to scratch. The types of standards that will be considered are shown on the diagram below.

This includes standards relating to the ethos or principles of the setting. This would apply to Montessori groups or Steiner schools for instance, or a setting may perhaps place strong emphasis on a certain area, such as developing creativity. You'll learn more about this on pages 297–302.

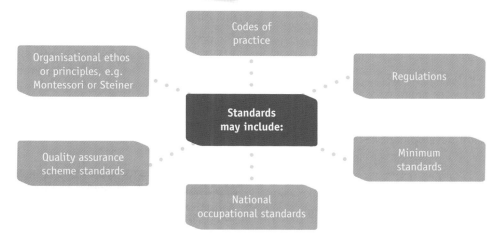

Standards new staff members will be expected to meet.

LEARNING OUTCOME 2

FOCUS ON

...being able to reflect on practice

In this section you'll learn about the importance of reflective practice in continually improving the quality of the service provided. You'll also learn about how to reflect on your own practice, and about how your values, belief systems and experiences may affect working practice. This links with Assessment Criteria 2.1, 2.2, 2.3.

The importance of reflective practice in improving the service you provide

Reflecting on how you do things, what you do and what you achieve (known as your **processes,**

practices and outcomes) effectively helps you to see how well you are working in practice. **Reflective practitioners** regularly:

- think about their practice
- analyse their actions
- evaluate their personal effectiveness
- record their reflections, perhaps in a journal
- discuss their reflections with others
- use feedback from others to improve their own evaluations.

This helps them to do the following:

- **Identify their strengths**
  Practitioners may ask themselves: 'What do I do well or to a high standard?'

- **Identify their weaknesses**
  'What don't I do all that well? What don't I feel confident doing?'

- **Notice their achievements**
  'Where have I made progress? What targets or goals have I reached?'

- **Identify their development needs**
  'Which areas of my work or knowledge should be developed? What new information and/or skills should I learn? How can I address my weaknesses?' (All practitioners benefit from **continuing professional development** in the form of on-going learning and professional updating.)

- **Solve problems**
  'What problems do I currently have, and how can I tackle them?'

- **Improve practice**
  'What can I do to improve my practical work with the children, parents, carers, my colleagues?'

Reflection also helps you to see which of your practical strategies and techniques are successful, and where a fresh approach would be beneficial. This increases your professional knowledge, understanding and skills. With the benefit of hindsight, you can take time to think through an event or an issue, gaining deeper insight or a clearer idea of the impact of your actions. You can share your reflections with others, using their feedback to further inform your evaluation. In the interests of high quality, it's advisable for practitioners to measure how well they are doing by the **best-practice benchmarks**, and not by the minimum standards.

The importance of reflective practice in improving the service the setting provides

When individual practitioners improve their own practice, this impacts on the quality of the service provided by the setting as a whole. In addition, when working as part of a team, practitioners will also be involved in jointly reflecting on and evaluating organisational practices, policies and procedures, as shown in the Practical example on page 39. This analysis of effectiveness allows the setting to make improvements where necessary.

key terms

Reflective practice/reflecting the process of thinking about and critically analysing your actions with the goal of changing and improving occupational practice. *(National Occupational Standards)*

Reflective practitioner a worker who uses reflective practice regularly.

Processes, practices and outcomes how you do things, what you do and what you achieve. *(National Occupational Standards)*

Continuing professional development ongoing training and professional updating. *(National Occupational Standards)*

Best-practice benchmarks widely agreed as the most up-to-date thinking and practice against which you can measure what you are doing – not minimum standards. Benchmarks can be statutory/regulatory or based on other requirements or research. *(National Occupational Standards)*

Practical example

Caris plans a policy review

Caris is the supervisor of a pre-school. There's a meeting next week for all the staff and committee members. It's time for the annual review of the setting's equal opportunity policy, so Caris decides to include this on the agenda that she's planning to send out via email today. So everyone is prepared, Caris also attaches a copy of the current policy. Before coming to the meeting, Caris asks everyone to spend some time reflecting on the quality of the policy, and the effectiveness of the setting's actual equal opportunity practice. That way, they will all be ready to contribute to the important discussion.

Question
How is the preparation Caris makes likely to impact on the quality of the policy review?

The ability to reflect on practice

Several methods can be used to reflect on your practice, as the following section explains. These are known as 'reflective analysis techniques'.

- **Questioning what, why and how**
  Imagine a practitioner has experienced previous difficulty keeping children seated at story time. Today, one child got up and took another's cushion, causing them to cry. The practitioner may question, 'What actually happened, and why did the event occur? How did I respond and why?'

- **Seeking alternatives**
  'How else could I have handled things?'

- **Keeping an open mind**
  'There could be a better way to handle or prevent such situations.'

- **Viewing from different perspectives**
  'How might colleagues have responded? How were the children involved feeling at the time?'

- **Asking 'what if?'**
  'What if I'd given children more time to settle in their seats?'

- **Thinking about consequences**
  'A colleague came to deal with the situation while I tried to carry on with the story. But what would have happened if I'd stopped reading the story to the rest of the group until the situation was resolved?'

- **Testing ideas through comparing and contrasting**
  'What similar events have I experienced, and were they handled effectively? Could techniques used then work in this situation? Did my actions compare or contrast with the policies and values of my setting?'

- **Synthesising ideas**
  'I've thought about the issue myself, and discussed it with a colleague. I remember reading that it is good to take time to settle children at story time. It can help them to concentrate and feel engaged during the session.'

- **Seeking, identifying and resolving problems**
  'On reflection, I think the problem was that the children had not settled before I started reading. Next time I will try giving them more time, and I will ask if they are comfortable and can see the book.'

Good reflective practitioners learn to use all of these techniques, applying one or more of them to each situation or issue they reflect on. They keep a record of their processes and outcomes, often in a reflective journal.

Observation of other practitioners is a good way to become inspired, and visits to other settings are also valuable. Question why and how things are done, and if appropriate reflect on how this could influence your own practice.

Reflective practice can improve the service provided by settings.

key term

Synthesising ideas the process of gathering different ideas from different sources. These are reflected upon, and in a considered way they are blended or joined together to form a new idea.

When should you reflect?

Personal development should be continuous, and practitioners should plan regular non-contact time for reflection. This ensures that the process is not forgotten and that you have the time to think. Records that you keep, perhaps in a reflective diary or journal, will build into a helpful account of your development. Reflection may also be planned in response to the following:

■ **A naturally occurring event**
   This is when a practitioner has come across a new

situation, or when he or she feels something has gone particularly well or badly.

■ **Feedback received**
   This includes feedback from colleagues, supervisors, assessors/tutors, parents, carers or children – also see page 45.

■ **Emerging new best practice/changes to regulations**
   As new discoveries are made and new theories are developed, what we consider to be best practice changes and evolves. You may be able to see how this has happened in your lifetime – think back to how you learned and played in various settings when you were a child, and compare this with how children are encouraged to learn and play now. Regulations are often changed to reflect what is newly considered to be best practice. Practitioners must adapt and develop their own practice in accordance with regulations. This may mean that they need to learn new information or skills, which they will integrate into their practice. (See 'Policy/procedure reviews' below.)

■ **Annual appraisals**
   This is a one-to-one meeting with senior staff at which the practitioner's work performance is discussed – also see page 45.

■ **Policy/procedure reviews**
   Most settings review their policies and procedures annually. Staff members consider how effective the policies are. They also evaluate how well their practice promotes the policies. It may be decided to develop a policy or an aspect of practice in the interests of improvement. Alternatively, if regulations alter, it may be essential to change policies and practice to stay in line with them. (See 'Emerging new best practice/changes to regulations' above.) This may also mean that practitioners need to learn and integrate new information or skills.

■ **Organisational evaluations**
   Settings may regularly review a number of

aspects of their provision, such as the success of activities, or the partnership with parents and carers. Staff, children, parents, carers and outside agencies may all be involved in the evaluation process.

- **Taking part in quality assurance schemes**
Quality assurance schemes state the best-practice benchmarks for settings to aim towards. They are then externally assessed on the achievement of the benchmarks – see also page 43.

Practitioners must find a way of recording their reflections that works for them personally. Why not ask some experienced practitioners at your setting how they do it? You could pick up some ideas to use in your own journal.

How your own values, belief systems and experiences may affect working practice

Reflection is an effective tool for comparing and contrasting what we say we do and what we actually do. It is important to think about this periodically, because although principles, values and policies may be known and understood, there can be times when practice does not promote them. Reflection allows practitioners to identify this, and indicates when it may be necessary to challenge their own practice.

This can be difficult to do. It can be hard to admit that personal beliefs, values, experiences or feelings may be prejudiced or otherwise negative in some way, and that personal development is necessary. But we are all influenced to some degree by the way we were brought up and educated, by what happens to us and by what we believe. This can manifest itself in many ways – for instance, if you dreaded having to play team games in PE as a child, you may avoid including them in your activity programme for young people. Or if you were brought up to finish everything on your plate as a sign of respect for the person who prepared your meal, you may find yourself expecting the children in your care to do the same. To address weaknesses and improve practice, honest reflection is required. Remember that everyone has room for improvement and the capacity for continuing professional development.

Ask Miranda!

Q Won't focusing on my weaknesses undermine my confidence?

A **Focusing on strengths and achievements can increase confidence and self-esteem. But the identification of any weaknesses is also a positive thing, as it helps informed practitioners to take steps to develop their practice. It can improve their confidence to see their work performance improving.**

Practical example

Naomi has reason for reflection

Naomi understands her nursery's policies and values. She would say that she always treats the children fairly and consistently in line with these policies.

Yesterday, 4-year-old Joe deliberately poured a jug of water from the water tray onto the floor. The day before, Naomi saw him deliberately throw his drink to the ground. Today she notices a lot of water on the floor with a jug next to it. Joe is at the water tray with several other children. Naomi heads towards the water tray to remind Joe once again how dangerous it is to pour liquid on the floor, and to see that Joe cleans up the water himself.

However, Naomi's colleague reaches the water tray first. He saw the whole incident – another child had in fact accidentally dropped the jug, and Joe had told her to tell a grown up, because someone could slip up. Having realised she was about to jump to the wrong conclusion and take inappropriate action, Naomi resolves to reflect on the incident later.

Questions
1. **Which reflection method would be appropriate in this instance?**
2. **How can the process of reflection help Naomi to both challenge and improve her future practice?**

LEARNING OUTCOME 3

FOCUS ON

... being able to evaluate own performance

In this section you'll learn how to evaluate your own knowledge, performance and understanding against relevant standards. You'll also learn how to use feedback to evaluate your performance and inform development. This links with Assessment Criteria **3.1, 3.2.**

Evaluating knowledge, performance and understanding

In Learning Outcome 1, we looked at the duties and responsibilities of your own work role, and the expectations of that role as expressed in relevant standards. Once you are aware of these, you can begin evaluating your performance against them.

This requires thinking carefully about your practice and considering:

■ what you can already do well

■ areas for further development.

You will need a way to structure and record your evaluations. Your setting may have set self-evaluation forms for practitioners to complete periodically, or if you're on a course, your tutor or assessor may provide you with forms to fill in.

Evaluating yourself against relevant standards helps you to ensure that your knowledge, performance and understanding meets (and continues to meet) the adequate professional levels that are both expected and legally required. You may like to look back at the diagram on page 37 to refresh your memory of the standards.

Good practice

You should note that while it's essential to fulfil all minimum requirements and legal obligations and requirements, it is considered best practice to aim towards meeting the current **best-practice benchmarks** (see page 38 for key term definition).

A quality assurance assessor will observe the setting's practice.

To help both the setting as a whole and the practitioners as individuals to achieve this, settings may elect to undertake a quality assurance scheme. Such schemes state what they consider to be best practice by expressing 'benchmarks'. These are similar to the welfare requirements expressed by Ofsted (see page 329 and page 210). However, Ofsted states the minimum standards that settings must not fall below. Quality assurance schemes state the best-practice benchmarks for settings to aim towards. When undertaking quality assurance, settings are generally required to compile a portfolio of evidence. When the setting is ready, the portfolio will be assessed by a representative of the scheme, and an observation visit will be made to the setting. The assessor will observe what is going on, in a similar way to an Ofsted inspector. Gaining quality assurance is an achievement for settings. It demonstrates that the setting provides a service that is better than the minimum standard legally required.

Did you know?

Many organisations have their own quality assurance schemes available, including the National Day Nurseries Association, Pre-School Learning Alliance and 4Children. (Some now call these 'quality improvement' schemes.) Self-evaluation will take place against the standards set at the beginning of the scheme. Many settings find it necessary for staff to undertake new learning as part of the quality assurance process, and this helps to raise the quality of the provision as a whole.

Practical example

Scott's self-evaluation

Scott is a trainee at a large children's centre. When he joined, he was given a personal development file. It contains information about how the setting supports personal development, and includes a self-evaluation document for Scott to complete over time. Each section focuses on a different area of professional knowledge, performance and understanding. Scott is required to give himself a score and to record evidence to back it up. He can also make notes about any development he feels he needs. Today he's filling out the 'working with others' section. Here's an extract:

Knowledge, performance and understanding	Competency score 0–5 (Score 0 if you have no knowledge, understanding or practical experience)	Evidence	Future development notes
Liaise with parents and carers on a day-to-day basis when their child is received into the setting and when they are collected.	2	I shadowed Caitlyn when her key-children arrived/departed. I now liaise myself under Caitlyn's one-to-one supervision.	Continue to get experience with Caitlyn's support, then do the task independently.
Meet with parents and carers to discuss their child's learning and development, referring to observations and assessment.	0		Ask Caitlyn whether I can sit in on a meeting in the future to observe how a child's development is discussed.
Provide parents with information about forthcoming events.	3	When I planned a visit to the library with a small group of children for my training course, I told the parents about it and asked them to sign the permission slips.	Next time I would like to plan ahead better so I can also have information put in the parents' newsletter in advance.

Scott's 'Working with others' section.

Use of feedback to evaluate your performance and inform development

When you are evaluating, it helps to consider the feedback you receive from others on your performance alongside your own self-evaluations, and to use this to inform your future development. This can help us to overcome the difficulty of being objective about ourselves. We may sometimes be 'too close to see' things clearly. For instance, we may worry we're not doing something properly when in fact we're doing a great job, or we may not be aware that there is something that we need to improve on or to learn.

Feedback on your performance may come from a number of sources, including colleagues, supervisors, assessors/tutors, parents, carers or children. It may be given formally or informally. For instance, an assessor will give formal feedback during an assessment, while a parent may make an informal passing comment about their child's care.

Most settings have an appraisal system that officially facilitates giving workers feedback on their performance, usually once a year. Generally, senior staff will make an appointment to talk with each worker individually. The staff member's work performance will be jointly discussed. Strengths and weaknesses will be considered, and as a result, a personal training/development plan will be agreed. Practitioners get the most out of an appraisal when they reflect on their own strengths, weaknesses and development needs prior to the meeting, and

contribute their own thoughts during the meeting. It's common for settings to give practitioners a self-appraisal form to complete in advance, to help them with this reflection. Once completed, this is handed in to an appraiser and informs the appraisal discussion.

Appraisals are an important part of personal development.

LEARNING OUTCOME 4

FOCUS ON

...being able to agree a personal development plan

In this section you'll learn about sources of support for planning and reviewing your own development, and how to work with others to review and prioritise key aspects of your continued professional development. You'll also learn how to work with others to agree a personal development plan. This links with Assessment Criteria 4.1, 4.2, 4.3.

Planning and reviewing your own development

Once you have evaluated your knowledge, performance and understanding and identified areas for development, the next step is to draw up a personal development plan.

Personal development plans

A personal development plan should be a written plan of action, against which progress made can be monitored. Plans can take many formats and can be given different names by different organisations – your setting may call your development plan a 'personal profile' for instance. All plans should include clear objectives that are specific, measurable, achievable, realistic and time-bound

– or in other words SMART – as shown in the table below.

Table SHC 32.1: SMART

Specific
State exactly what you are planning to achieve and how you will achieve it so that you can focus clearly on your objective.

Measurable
Decide in advance how you will know when you are on the way to meeting your objective. How will you know when you have achieved it?

Achievable
Make sure that your objective is achievable. Large goals are sometimes best broken down into several achievable objectives. The task then feels more manageable and you can see that you are making progress.

Realistic
Worthwhile objectives can be challenging, but be realistic about how and when you can achieve things or you may become disheartened and discouraged.

Time-bound
Timescales help you to get on with working towards your objectives, and can motivate you effectively. Set dates for when each objective should be met and monitor your progress.

Ask Miranda!

Q I'm interested in an aspect of my role that I'm good at, but should I focus all my energies on addressing my weaknesses?

A **It's important to identify your learning needs and to plan how to meet them. This will help you to improve your knowledge and skills in areas that you may need to strengthen. However, your professional interests are also important. If you are particularly interested in a certain area – such as speech and language development, children's creativity or working with disabled children, for instance – you may want to learn more about it, even if it is an area of strength for you. If so, include this in your personal development plan. In time, some practitioners go on to develop a specialism in an area that began as an interest.**

Sources of support for planning and reviewing your own development

In Learning Outcome 3, you learned about using feedback to evaluate your own performance and to inform development. The people who provide this feedback are often also sources of support when you are planning and reviewing your own development. The diagram on page 47 shows common sources of support. This includes people working both within and beyond your own organisation.

Supervising staff responsible for delivering your setting's appraisal process are a particularly good source of formal support for planning and reviewing your development. They're experienced in working with staff to identify and plan to meet development needs. If you are relatively new to a setting and have not yet been appraised, the information the appraiser learns about your development while supporting you can be used to inform your first appraisal. If you have already been appraised, the staff member will already be aware of your performance, knowledge, skills and development, and are therefore well placed to support you.

Did you know?

Often, the setting's supervisor or manager conducts appraisals, in consultation with each member of staff's immediate superior, e.g. the baby room team leader.

Colleagues can also often informally recommend ways in which they've successfully made and actioned their own personal development plans, and suggest learning activities you might want to look into. If you are on a course, tutors, assessors and mentors are an excellent resource, and will have secure knowledge about your necessary learning and development. If you're interested in developing your current practice in a new area or undertaking training or qualifications so you can progress up the career ladder, careers advisors and the admission tutors of training centres, colleges and universities can offer advice and support.

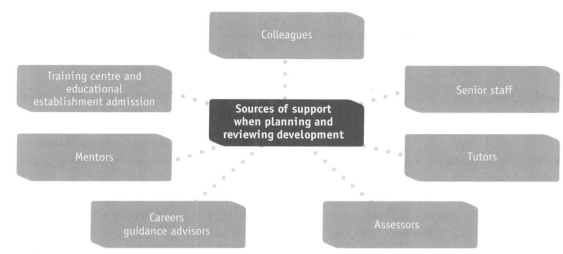

Sources of support when planning and reviewing development.

Ask Miranda!

Q What if I want to plan or review my development in between appraisals?

A Many settings carry out formal appraisals annually. However, this doesn't mean that you need to wait 12 months to access further support from your setting when it comes to the planning and reviewing your own development. Ask for support whenever you need it.

Working with others to review and prioritise

Once you have drafted a personal development plan, it's good practice to review it in conjunction with the other people involved in your personal development, working together to prioritise your learning needs and professional interests. Within the setting this may include your supervisor, line manager or employer. Outside professionals such as tutors, assessors and mentors may also contribute, and if applicable, carers and advocates.

Prioritising is sometimes purely a matter of timescales. For instance, if your first aid certificate will be expiring shortly, it will be a priority to renew it. If a new piece of legislation is coming in, it may need to be researched as soon as possible. Or, you may want to take advantage of an opportunity coming up soon – a seminar series at the local university, for example, or a short course starting at the local college.

Professional seminars can help to meet training needs.

If your workplace will be supporting your personal development financially, they may tell you how and when they'd like you to meet your personal development needs. If they feel there is a weakness in a certain area that affects performance – a lack of knowledge about the Early Years Foundation Stage (EYFS) for instance – they may require you to address this as a matter of priority.

You should also agree how and when you will review your development and monitor your progress towards your plan. (See SMART objectives on page 46.)

Working with others to agree own personal development plan

Once your plan has been reviewed and prioritised, you can produce a final draft. Many settings will require staff to hand this in to the supervisor or manager, who will keep a copy for the setting's records. If the setting will be supporting your development financially (by paying for training perhaps), it is usually at this stage that the money is officially allocated in the budget. Once a plan is agreed, make sure that you understand who has responsibility for any organisational details – for instance, should you make a booking for yourself to attend a course, or will the supervisor do it and make payment at the same time?

Identifying further learning opportunities

There will be times when you need to identify and seek out further learning opportunities as part of your continuing professional development. There is a range of ways to learn either full or part-time, including:

■ distance learning via mail or the internet

■ workplace learning

■ attending tutored courses

■ attending training workshops

■ attending seminars and conferences

■ research via books, articles, internet and training materials, including DVDs

■ observing or shadowing other practitioners

■ visiting other settings.

You can find out about the options and access learning by:

■ enquiring about in-house learning opportunities at work, and ensuring that the appropriate people at your workplace know the type of development opportunities you are looking for

■ contacting the local authority and Sure Start (they may also have details of funding for learning)

■ requesting details of learning opportunities from colleges, other training organisations and membership associations (specific enquiries can also be made to Learn Direct – advisers will help you to find appropriate local learning opportunities)

■ reading about and researching up-to-date developments and thinking in the field, making use of resources such as the internet, the public library and your workplace reference information. (When undertaking web-based research, the sites of national organisations are often a good starting point. Ofsted, National Day Nurseries Association, Pre-School Learning Alliance, National Child Minding Association and 4Children all have websites, and useful links are provided to further informative sites.)

Local colleges provide a range of short courses.

LEARNING OUTCOME 5

...being able to use learning opportunities and reflective practice to contribute to personal development

In this section you'll learn about evaluating the effect of learning activities on practice. You'll also learn about demonstrating how reflective practice has led to improved ways of working, and about the recording of progress made in relation to personal development. This links with Assessment Criteria 5.1, 5.2, 5.3.

The next part of the process

In Learning Outcome 1, you learned that an important part of your role is to identify your learning and development needs. In Learning Outcome 2, you learned how to become a reflective practitioner. In Learning Outcome 3, you learned how to effectively evaluate your performance, and in Learning Outcome 4, you learned how to agree a personal development plan. Once you have completed the planned learning, you are on the way to achieving your objective, but there are still two critical parts of the process left – integrating (incorporating) your learning into your practice, and evaluating the effect that this has.

Integrating new information and learning

If you fail to integrate your learning into your practice, your new knowledge and skills will be wasted, and you will not progress as planned in terms of professional development. To change your practice, you need to put in some thought and effort after the learning has taken place.

Ask Miranda!

Q I've just been on a short course. What can I do to help me integrate my learning into my practice?

A When you have completed something on your personal development plan, get into the habit of reflecting on what you've learned in your reflective journal, giving emphasis to how your learning will impact on your practice. For instance, if you'd been on a short course in promoting positive behaviour, you would reflect on the key learning points. Then you might think about how you'll introduce some of the new behaviour management strategies you've learned into your practice, and plan accordingly. You might also consider how well you responded to the learning activity – was the level right for you? Did the type of learning (attending a course with others, distance learning at home, research, etc.) suit you? This information will help you to improve your learning activity choices in the future.

Good practice

Current best practice, regulations and requirements constantly evolve. Those who don't keep up their professional development or fail to integrate their learning will soon be left behind, and this will impact on the quality of their practice.

Evaluating how learning activities have affected practice

You'll need to evaluate the effect your learning activities have had on your practice. However, you should first give yourself a reasonable amount of time to allow newly integrated learning to become embedded in your practice. It may take you a while to get used to new ways of working, and this may also apply to the children, young people and colleagues that you're working with. When you are ready to evaluate, the previous techniques you have learned can be applied.

Demonstrating that reflective practice has led to improved ways of working

If you embrace working as a reflective practitioner as described in Learning Outcome 2, the notes that you make in your reflective journal will build into a record documenting how your reflection has led to improved ways of working.

Recording progress in relation to professional development

It's very important to record your progress in relation to professional development. If you are currently studying for this qualification on a course, your progress will be recorded on the Individual Learning Record (or an equivalent document). Some settings provide professional development files for practitioners, in which they keep all related information (see the Practical example on page 44). If you don't have access to these, start your own file – it will be with you throughout your career. Take good care of qualification certificates, and also file away certificates of attendance (such as those issued on local authority training courses). These are your proof of learning and evidence of your professional development progress. Should you wish to change jobs or apply for training or study, potential employers and admissions tutors will want to see them. You can also file any written feedback you receive on progress made in your practice as a result of implementing your learning.

Good practice

It's a good idea to also keep another file containing the notes you make and any handouts you're given during learning activities, so you can refer to them in the future.

Did you know?

Your setting will usually want copies of certificates for their own files, as these can be used as evidence during Ofsted inspections and quality assurance assessments.

How are things going?

▶ Progress Check

1. Where would you expect to find written details of your work role? (1.1)

2. How does reflective practice contribute to continuously improving the quality of a setting? (2.1)

3. How might your own values, belief systems and experiences affect your working practice? (2.3)

4. What is the advantage of using feedback when you're evaluating your own performance? (3.2)

5. Give four possible sources of support for planning and reviewing your own development. (4.1)

6. Why is it important to implement learning into your practice following learning activities? (5.1)

7. Give an example of how you can demonstrate that your reflective practice has led to improved ways of working. (5.2)

Are you ready for assessment?

CACHE

Set task:

■ Write a description of the duties and responsibilities of your own job role.

■ Prepare an explanation of the expectations about your own work role as expressed in relevant standards.

You can prepare for this by sourcing the standards relevant to your role, e.g. codes of practice, minimum standards (for registration in your home country) or national occupational standards.

Learning Outcomes 2, 3, 4 and 5 must be assessed in real work environments.

Edexel

In preparation for assessment of this Unit, it will be helpful for you to find out about the appraisal system at your setting, and if possible, to arrange for your own appraisal to take place.

City & Guilds

In preparation for assessment of this Unit, it will be helpful for you to find out about the appraisal system at your setting, and if possible, to arrange for your own appraisal to take place.

UNIT 33

SHC

Promote equality and inclusion in health, social care or children's and young people's settings

LEARNING OUTCOMES

The learning outcomes you will meet in this unit are:

1 Understand the importance of diversity, equality and inclusion

2 Be able to work in an inclusive way

3 Be able to promote diversity, equality and inclusion

INTRODUCTION

Equality and inclusion are both extremely important issues. The effects of discrimination are serious and far reaching – once experienced, children and young people may suffer the impact of them throughout their lives.

Practitioners have a key role to play in promoting equality and inclusion for all of the children, young people and families that they work with.

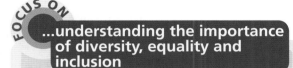

FOCUS ON

...understanding the importance of diversity, equality and inclusion

In this section you'll learn what is meant by diversity, equality and inclusion. You'll also learn about the effects of discrimination, and about how inclusive practice promotes equality and supports diversity. This links with Assessment Criteria **1.1**, **1.2**, **1.3**.

Terminology

There are several terms you need to understand in relation to equality and inclusion:

Prejudice

The word 'prejudice' means to pre-judge. People who are prejudiced make unfair judgements about others based on a 'group' they believe a person to 'belong to'. They already have a negative view before they even meet the person or find out anything about them.

Discrimination

Discrimination occurs when people act on prejudice. For example, a prejudiced person might believe that playing with dolls is only for girls. They will be discriminating if they don't allow boys to play with dolls in the setting.

Anti-bias practice/anti-discriminatory practice

Anti-bias practice (sometimes called anti-discriminatory practice) describes the ways settings work and the steps they take in order to challenge and overcome prejudice and discrimination.

Equality/equal opportunities/equal concern

Equality is achieved when everyone has equal opportunities to participate within a setting. Some children and families have traditionally experienced discrimination. To ensure that this does not happen

in settings, all settings are required to have an Equal Opportunities policy, which you must work in line with. When you take the same care to promote opportunities for every child, you are showing 'equal concern' for everyone. There are also laws about equality and discrimination, which you'll learn more about in Learning Outcome 2.

Diversity

Diversity is the acknowledgement and respect of differences between individuals and within and between groups of people in society. These arise from social, cultural or religious backgrounds, ethnicity (ethnic origin), disability, gender, sexuality, appearance and family structure or background.

Inclusion

Inclusion occurs when a setting embraces diversity and ensures that all children, young people and families are able to fully participate – or in other words, they ensure that everyone is fully included. You'll learn more about inclusive practice on page 56.

Good practice

While the aim of practitioners is to make sure that all children and families have equal opportunities within the setting, that doesn't mean that everyone should be treated the same. It means that we should meet the needs of all children and families. Their needs will be different, so we will need to work in different ways with different children and families to give them equal opportunities. Although some children may need to be given more time and attention than others, everyone should be equally valued and treated with the same concern.

The diagram on page 54 shows ways in which you can work with children and young people fairly.

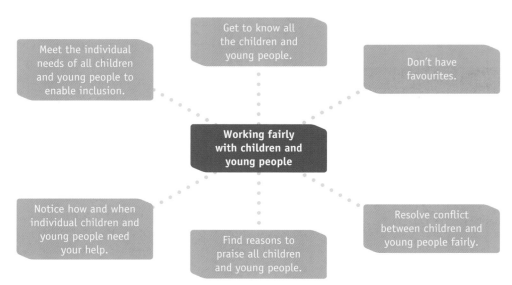

Working fairly with children and young people.

Occurrences of discrimination

Discrimination occurs when people are treated unfairly because of stereotypical views held about a group they belong to or are perceived to belong to. There are many different kinds of stereotypes, and people treat others unfairly based on a broad range of these. However, discrimination is commonly based on:

■ disability

■ ethnicity

■ culture

■ race

■ religion

■ gender

■ age

■ sexuality

■ low socio-economic group.

Inequalities are embedded in our society, in all geographical areas. It is not possible to identify where, for example, within the home countries

certain prejudices or stereotypical beliefs are held because they are widespread and complex. Assumptions that this is not the case may in fact be based on stereotypes. However, we have more equal opportunities legislation and awareness now than ever before, and children are growing up in settings that are required to promote equal opportunities.

Your setting's equal opportunity policy is a public declaration of commitment to equality. However, practitioners can provide additional information about this on the advertisements and leaflets that promote your setting, so that families and communities can easily see that you adhere to these values.

Did you know?

It is advisable for settings to implement 'transparent procedures' about admissions. This means making it clear how places are allocated to children, demonstrating that this is done fairly. Many settings have admissions policies stating that places are allocated on a first-come-first-served basis.

All children and families must have equal opportunities within the settings.

Types of discrimination

There are four types of discrimination:

■ **Direct discrimination**
This occurs when obvious action is carried out to the detriment of a person, because of their age, sex, race, religion, ethnicity or disability. For instance, a setting refuses a child admission because they are Asian.

■ **Indirect discrimination**
This occurs when a condition is applied that will favour one group over another unfairly. For instance, a multilingual setting offers extra places to parents on completion of forms, but only supplies the forms in English.

■ **Segregation**
This is when people are unfairly separated when there is no reason for this. For instance, a setting has a separate area set aside for disabled children to eat in.

■ **Victimisation**
This occurs when people are intentionally treated unfairly after complaining about previous discrimination. For instance, a parent complains that they were not given a chance to book an extra session for their child because they could not understand the form. As a result, the practitioner says there has been a double booking, and their child will not be able to come at all.

If discrimination occurs because an organisation will not meet the needs of someone, or because workers are jointly discriminating, the term 'institutionalised discrimination' may be used.

Effects of discrimination and inequality

Within families that experience it, discrimination can lead to:

■ missed opportunities that may affect a child or young person's experiences and therefore impact on development

■ low self-esteem

■ low confidence

■ little sense of self-worth or self-value

■ confused identity

■ fear of rejection.

In addition, inequality has a negative effect on all children and families, even if they have not been the target of discrimination. If one child or family is stopped from participating within a group, then the rights of all the children and families to participate equally, alongside one another, are affected.

Children and young people should not be exposed to inequality, regardless of whether they are the target of it. They should not be introduced to discrimination – this is introducing children and young people to what is, after all, criminal behaviour. But sadly some children and young people do pick up this behaviour and may go on to inflict discrimination, which is damaging not only to their victims but to themselves and the wider society.

Practical example

Tara discriminates

Practitioner Tara thinks it will be too much trouble to have disabled children in the setting. Whenever a parent or carer of a disabled child enquires about a place, she lies and says the setting is full. Tara is directly discriminating against the disabled children and their families. But this inequality affects the children who do attend too. She is not allowing them to play and make friends with disabled children. She is keeping them segregated from disabled children. This is unacceptable.

Question
What effects may Tara's discrimination have?

Inclusive practice

Inclusive practice promotes equality and supports diversity, and should be evident in every setting. When inclusive practice is employed, practitioners take equal concern to ensure that all children, young people and families have their needs and rights met. You'll learn about the legislation that supports these rights in Learning Outcome 2. You'll also learn about inclusive practice in Learning Outcome 3.

key term

Inclusive practice the practice of embracing diversity and ensuring that everyone can participate.

It is important to support diversity and challenge all forms of discrimination.

LEARNING OUTCOME 2

FOCUS ON ...being able to work in an inclusive way

In this section you'll learn about the importance of multi-agency and integrated working, and how this can deliver better outcomes for children and young people. You'll learn about the barriers to working in this way and how they can be overcome. You'll also learn about assessment frameworks, and how and why referrals are made between agencies. This links with Assessment Criteria **2.1, 2.2.**

Legislation and codes of practice

There is legislation in place covering children's rights, equality and inclusion. Your setting will have its own Equal Opportunities policy in place, which must be in line with the relevant requirements of your home country. You must understand these, and work in accordance with them. An outline is given here.

Have a go!

As you read the outlines below, consider how each applies to you on a daily basis as you fulfil your own work role. You may find it helpful to make notes.

UN Convention on the Rights of the Child

The UK Government made this Convention law in 1991. It contains Articles that refer to the rights and needs of children including the following:

■ **Children have the right to non-discrimination.** All the rights within the Convention apply equally to all children regardless of their race, sex, religion, disability or family background. Children also have a right to be aware of their rights. You should let children know (within the context of your setting) that they have equal rights, and will be accepted for who they are, and respected when they are there. They also have the responsibility to respect other children and adults within the environment. This will be communicated by your actions and attitudes towards young children, but it is appropriate to be more direct as children mature.

■ **Children have the right to rest, play and leisure, and opportunities to join in with activities including those that are cultural and artistic.** Practitioners should ensure that disabled children have full opportunities to join in, as they may experience inequality in this area. A range of different cultural activities should be provided for all children, whatever their own culture.

■ **Children have the right to freedom from exploitation.** Practitioners must ensure that

children are not abused, bullied or used (see Unit SHC 4 and CYP 3.3).

■ **Children have the right to a cultural identity.** Settings should recognise, respect and value the cultural identity of individual families, and celebrate diversity throughout the group.

■ **Disabled children have the right to live as independently as possible, and to take a full and active part in everyday life.** Practitioners must consult with families to support disabled children's independence in the most effective way.

■ **Parents and guardians have the right to support in carrying out their parental responsibilities.** Practitioners must work in partnership with all families.

■ **Children have the right to have their views heard.** Practitioners should consult with children, particularly about decisions affecting them, and take notice of what they say. They should seek out and respect the views and preferences of children. This may be achieved through discussion, 'All About Me' theme work, or even through artwork. Practice should be adapted to suit the child or young person's age, needs and abilities.

■ **Children need a strong self-image and self-esteem.** Children should feel valued and accepted for who they are within the setting. This is achieved through showing children respect.

Disabled children have the right to live as independently as possible, and to take a full and active part in everyday life.

Every Child Matters

Every Child Matters: Change for Children is a programme that aims to improve outcomes for all children and young people. As many disabled children's needs are complex and cross traditional service boundaries, they are one of the groups who stand to gain the most from this programme of change. *Every Child Matters* is supported by a number of policies and strategies that should work together to improve outcomes for disabled children, young people and their families. You can find out more about Every Child Matters at **www.education.gov.uk/ childrenandyoungpeople/sen/earlysupport/ esinpractice/a0067409/every-child-matters**

For more on *Every Child Matters*, see Unit CYP 3.6

The Equality Act 2010

At the time of writing, this new Act is bringing together and harmonising equality law with the aim of making it more consistent, clearer and easier to follow, in order to make society fairer. The new Act will replace existing equality legislation. However, the legal implications for practitioners will essentially stay the same. The government is looking at ways in which the Act can best be fully implemented, and announcements will be made in due course. You can read further up-to-date information at www.equalities.gov.uk, where you can also access a guide for voluntary and community sector service providers.

Disability Discrimination Act 1995 and 2005

The Disability Discrimination Act (DDA) was devised to support the rights of disabled people to take a full and active part in society. It gave them equality of access, or in other words, the same opportunities to participate in society as non-disabled people. This important piece of legislation gave disabled people (adults and children) rights regarding the way in which they received services, facilities or goods. This included education, care and play services.

The DDA was introduced in three stages:

- In 1996 it became illegal for service providers to discriminate against disabled people by treating them less favourably than non-disabled people.

- In 1999 service providers became required by law to make reasonable adjustments for disabled people, such as providing extra assistance.

- In 2004 service providers became required by law to make reasonable adjustments to their premises. This means that it mustn't be unreasonably difficult for disabled people to access the provision because of physical barriers, such as narrow doorways or steps. If a premise's physical features cause a barrier for a disabled person, that feature may be removed or altered. Or a service may provide a reasonable way of avoiding the feature or may make their service available in a different way, for example, a pre-school may replace steps into the front of their building with a ramp, or they may open a fire door around the side to let a wheelchair user in.

A disabled person is defined in the DDA 1995 as someone who has a physical or mental impairment that adversely affects their ability to carry out normal day-to-day activities. This will be long-term – it will have lasted for 12 months or be likely to last for more than 12 months. This includes some chronic illnesses, such as ME, which affect some people's ability to carry out normal day-to-day activities. ME is a chronic illness. The symptoms include chronic fatigue.

Also see page 512 for details of The Special Educational Needs Code of Practice

Human Rights Act 1998

This Act was brought into force in 2000. It allowed people in the UK to enforce rights given under previous laws in the British courts. Before the Act, it was necessary to take cases to the European

Court in Strasburg, which incurred time, expense and inconvenience. The previous laws included the European Convention on Human Rights, which was ratified by the UK in 1951. It guaranteed rights and freedoms for all as identified in the United Nations Declaration on Human Rights.

Race Relations Act 1976

This Act stated that racial discriminatory practice is unacceptable, and defined in law what that means. The Act was introduced to make discriminatory practice illegal in the UK, and came about due to substantial ingrained discrimination within our society.

Racial and Religious Hatred Act 2006

The main provision of this Act was to create a new offence of stirring up hatred against persons on religious grounds, for which people can be prosecuted.

Equality Act 2006

This made it unlawful to discriminate on grounds of religion or belief:

- in the provision of goods, facilities and services
- in the disposal and management of premises
- in education
- in the exercise of public functions.

Children Act 1989

This Act requires all settings to have an equal opportunities policy that is regularly reviewed and to take account of children's:

- religion
- racial origin
- cultural background
- linguistic background.

Children Act 2004

The overall aim of this Act is to encourage integrated planning, commissioning and delivery of services as well as to improve multi-disciplinary working. This

Diwali celebrations.

was part of a wider reform programme that included *Every Child Matters:* Change for Children (see page 321). The Act also placed a duty on local authorities to promote the educational achievement of looked-after children.

Link Up!

For further legislation relating to Special Educational Needs, see Unit CYPOP 6. Settings must also meet the Welfare Requirements – you'll find details of this on page 513

Respecting beliefs, culture, values and preferences

As a practitioner you will work with people with a wide range of beliefs, culture, values and preferences.

Chinese New Year celebrations.

An important part of your job role is to show equal concern and respect for these, and to meet any needs that arise because of them. You cannot show respect for people's beliefs, culture, values and preferences unless you are **aware** of them in the first place. Building a strong relationship with families is the foundation stone to this, as it means you will get to know them well.

Did you know?

Inclusive practice is another key way of demonstrating that you respect a wide range of beliefs, culture, values and preferences.

Good practice

Whenever a new family joins a setting, it's generally the appointed key worker who will complete the registration form with them and have the opportunity to talk about their beliefs, culture, values and preferences. It's good practice for the practitioner to then pass on relevant information to the rest of the team who will be working with the child or young person.

Whenever a new practitioner starts work at a setting, it's important that they too are given appropriate information. If the new practitioner will become a key worker for some existing families, it's good practice for him or her to begin finding out about the families' beliefs, culture, values and preferences as soon as possible. A practitioner would normally look at children's or young people's registration forms, talk to their new colleagues and then arrange to meet with parents and carers.

LEARNING OUTCOME 3

FOCUS ON
...being able to promote diversity, equality and inclusion

In this section you'll learn about actions that model inclusive practice. You'll also learn about supporting others to promote equality and rights, and about challenging discrimination in a way that promotes change. This links with Assessment Criteria **3.1, 3.2, 3.3.**

Inclusive practice

To have a truly inclusive setting, practitioners must identify barriers to inclusion and find effective ways to overcome them.

Barriers to participation are factors that can cause difficulties for families, children and young people, who then experience discrimination, preventing them from accessing services. Practitioners must welcome families from all backgrounds, ensuring that barriers to participation are identified and removed. Barriers fall into three categories:

■ environmental

■ attitudinal

■ institutional.

Attitudinal and institutional barriers are often based on practitioners' worries and anxieties. They may be concerned that they will not adequately be able to meet the needs of a disabled child, or that they will not understand how to give the right cultural respect to a family. These things can be overcome with equality training and support. There is no place in this sector for attitudinal or institutional barriers based on prejudice to go unchallenged – you'll learn more about this on page 64.

Environmental barriers can be identified and removed with procedures and practices to overcome the negative effects. Here are some examples:

■ **Steps:** A parent who uses a wheelchair cannot get into the setting.
A ramp could be built from concrete, or a free-standing ramp could be used.

■ **Poor lighting:** A child with a visual impairment is experiencing more difficulty than usual due to inadequate light.
In consultation with the family, practitioners can find out what lighting works effectively for the child and introduce it.

■ **Lack of space:** A setting does not have enough space for a child who uses crutches to manoeuvre between activities.
The furniture can be altered to a better position. It may be necessary to put out fewer activities at one time, but change them more frequently.

■ **Language:** A child and her family speak so little of the setting's home language that practitioners cannot explain the admissions procedure clearly.
Find out the family's home language and translate

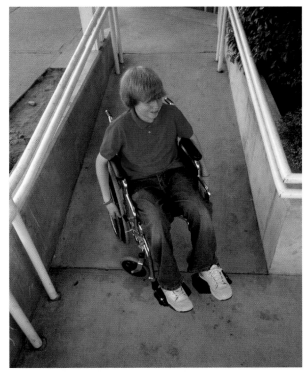

Environmental barriers can be identified and removed.

documents, while arranging to bring in an interpreter.

An effective way to break down barriers is to find appropriate ways to reach families that have found services hard to access, and provide them with information about your setting and the equality of access that you offer. Your local Sure Start will have information to help you target families appropriately within your area. They will also hold details of community resources and support that are available within your locality to assist with equality of access. This may include funding in some circumstances. This may be valuable to you, and it is helpful to have this information at hand for families who may need it. There may also be scope for referral if necessary (see page 259).

It is also valuable to involve all relevant community groups in your setting or service. If you have a committee, 'friends', 'supporters' or 'partners' scheme, you can invite appropriate groups to link up with you by joining. This adds to the diversity of your group, and helps to ensure that your practices and activities are appropriate and accessible to everyone in the community. You can also provide information on local community groups to the families at your setting, perhaps via posters and leaflets.

Assessing children and young people's needs

All children and young people have a right to high-quality childcare provision that meets their individual needs. So it is essential that practitioners undertake assessment of children's needs when they begin at the setting. This will require particular focus if a child has individual needs. The child's appointed key worker and the setting's appointed person taking responsibility for inclusion are likely to work together on this. (The appointed person is known as the SENCO or Special Educational Needs Coordinator.) Where appropriate, there must be regard to the Special Educational Needs Code of Practice 1994 and Assessment of Special Educational Needs.

Practitioners may also contact outside professionals for support, and/or draw on resources available locally to help them meet children and young people's needs – this may include funding. Talking with parents and carers should be the first step. A child's family will know them better than anyone, and parents and carers are generally very pleased when practitioners show

commitment to finding out how best to support their child. This sets the tone for working in partnership together from the outset, which is valuable for practitioners and families. Practitioners will want to discuss the following, recording notes on the registration documents:

- the details of children and young people's individual needs

- how the needs impact on the child or young person

- what strategies the child/young person/family currently uses to meet these needs

- if there are any potential barriers within the setting

- how barriers should be overcome (an action plan and a date of completion should then be drawn up by practitioners and acted upon)

- what support the child or young person may need on a daily basis and how this will be facilitated. (The information may be quite detailed depending on the needs. It is important to get everything down so that needs are not overlooked. If the child or young person will need personal assistance that is not usually consistent with

Children and young people have a right to high-quality provision that meets their individual needs.

Good practice

Once the needs of a child have been assessed, practitioners need to follow up by completing the action points that were identified. This may entail making physical changes to the premises, such as moving furniture to ensure a wheelchair user can manoeuvre with ease. Practitioners will also want to check the setting's future activity plans, some of which are likely to have been drawn up already. The purpose is to identify any adaptations or support that will be necessary to ensure the child can fully participate in all of the activities and experiences on offer, as is their entitlement.

their age, such as help with toileting for a young person, practitioners must arrange for this to be done with regard to their right to privacy. Details of any special equipment, extra staffing and so on should be recorded, and practitioners must action this accordingly.)

Where appropriate, practitioners may also arrange for CAF (see page 259), or activate Early Years Action or Early Years Action Plus. This is explained in Unit CYPOP 6.

Promoting diversity through positive images of people

Within the setting, practitioners should promote positive images of all people, reflecting the wider society. That is, they should seek to show, through the way they portray people, that all different kinds of people are valued positively in the setting. This can be done by ensuring that the pictures children and young people see in books, displays, on puzzles and so on show males and females, people of all sizes, ethnicities and cultures, and people who have impairments.

Positive images should also be reflected in the toys that you choose whenever these represent people. For instance, within the setting's collection of baby dolls you may include dolls of different ethnicities, and within your puppets you may have different ages represented. Your doll's house may feature a ramp and a doll with a wheelchair, or perhaps crutches, or a hearing aid. The purpose is to represent society's diversity overall. It is of course unrealistic to attempt to cover every eventuality in each collection of resources.

You should also ensure that people are shown in a positive light. Strong images of those people who may be discriminated against are particularly important. Some examples of strong image resources on the market are:

- a set of jigsaw puzzles that each show a family of a different culture eating a meal together

- a poster on the theme of celebrations, that shows six families of different religions celebrating

- a set of picture postcards showing athletes competing in the Paralympics

- a set of doll's house dolls, featuring four elderly couples of different ethnicities

- a set of puppets with the theme of 'People who help us' – including a female police officer and an Asian doctor

- a set of jigsaw puzzles showing children helping, including a child with special educational needs washing a car

- stories that are not about a child's disability, but the lead character just happens to be disabled.

Be wary of images that are not positive – in stories or pictures, disabled people are sometimes shown as

Positive images should also be reflected in the toys that you choose.

being dependent on non-disabled people, perhaps by being cared for or pushed in a wheelchair. Similarly, females may be shown as the underdogs to male characters.

To weave the thread of diversity throughout your setting, you should extend this further wherever you have the opportunity. For instance, you can ensure that different styles of clothing are represented in the dressing-up clothes, and that cooking utensils and food in the home corner (an area that mimics the children's home environment) are also representative of the wider world. You can purchase crayons in a range of flesh tones for art activities. There are many possibilities.

Practical example

Nina's choice

Nina is planning to buy some toys to promote positive images. She comes across a doll for a doll's house that she initially likes the look of. It is a woman sitting in a wheelchair. Then she notices that the whole thing is made out of one piece of plastic. It occurs to Nina that this may be a problem. The woman cannot be taken out of her wheelchair. Also, the wheels of the chair do not go around. Nina wonders if this toy promotes positive images, and if it would give good play value.

Question
What do you think? Should Nina buy the toy with the money earmarked for promoting positive images? Why/why not?

Supporting the promotion of equality and challenging discrimination

As a practitioner, you should promote your setting's equal opportunities policy in your own work at all times. But you should also think of yourself as a guardian of the policy. This means that if you come across discrimination of any sort, it is your responsibility to challenge it professionally.

Colleagues
You may on occasion find yourself working with colleagues who have not fully grasped the principles and practice of promoting equality and inclusion. If the setting's equal opportunities policy is not being consistently implemented, you must raise the issue.

If you feel that a colleague is not acting fairly – perhaps what they say does not show respect for a child's beliefs or culture for instance, or they do not give a young disabled person equal opportunities to participate – it is easy to become angry. However, it is important to remain calm and professional, and to tackle the situation in a non-confrontational manner – refer to the guidelines for resolving conflict positively on page 248. Your aim is for the person to listen to you and to think about what you are saying.

Did you know?

Anger usually only results in the other person becoming defensive – it does not pave the way for an open professional discussion.

It helps to remember that attitudinal and institutional barriers are often based on practitioners' worries and anxieties. It may be appropriate for the colleague to undertake equality training, and it may be useful for the setting as a whole to dedicate time at a staff meeting to reflecting on how well the equal opportunity policy is implemented in practice, and how work could be improved.

Children and young people

As you've learned, it's a sad fact that some children and young people pick up negative attitudes towards diversity, and may say or do things that upset others in the setting – this is true even in the pre-school years. It's important to comfort the person on the receiving end of such negativity. Reassure him or her that the behaviour is not acceptable in the setting and that you will deal with the issue. When you talk with the child or young person who has acted inappropriately, you have an opportunity to educate them about equality, in line with their level of maturity. Make it clear that such behaviour will not be tolerated. It may be appropriate to speak to the parents/carers of both children when they are collected, and to record it in the incident book.

Good practice

The old adage 'sticks and stones may break my bones, but words cannot hurt me,' couldn't be more wrong. They do hurt people, even though comments may be laughed off, particularly by teenagers who are feeling humiliated. Never dismiss it as 'acceptable teasing'. A hurtful comment about someone's appearance – based on the fact that they wear a brace on their teeth for instance – can be just as upsetting as a racist comment.

Parents and carers

Parents and carers sometimes hold views that do not respect diversity. If a parent or carer makes a comment or a request that does not promote equality, it may be necessary for staff to explain the policy of the setting and to let them know where they stand. For instance, a parent may say that they do not want their child playing with a boy who has learning difficulties, in which case, the practitioner will need to explain that children are not segregated within the setting. It will also be helpful to talk through the reasons for such a request and to address any underlying worries and concerns. In our example, the parent may have seen the child rocking back and forth, and may be afraid that their child could pick up the same behaviour. If a parent is unable to accept the setting's policy, they can of course leave the setting.

How are things going?

▶ Progress Check

1. Explain what is meant by the following terms:
   - diversity
   - equality
   - inclusion
   - prejudice
   - discrimination. (1.1)

2. What are the potential effects of discrimination? (1.2)

3. How can your work practices demonstrate respect for an individual's beliefs, cultures, preferences and values? (2.2)

4. What is inclusive practice? (3.1)

5. How can your work practices promote inclusion? (3.1)

6. What would you do to challenge discriminatory remarks from:
   - a colleague
   - a young person
   - a parent? (3.3)

Are you ready for assessment?

CACHE

Set task:

Produce information for the workplace stakeholders (this could include children, young people and staff) that supports understanding and raises awareness of diversity, equality and inclusion, including:

- what is meant by diversity, equality and inclusion
- the potential effects of discrimination
- how inclusive practice promotes equality and supports diversity.

You can prepare for this by re-reading this Unit and making brief notes of the key relevant points.

Edexel

In preparation for assessment of this Unit, you may find it helpful to observe the way in which colleagues work in an inclusive way. You may also like to talk to your setting's SENCO about how this is successfully achieved.

Learning Outcomes 2 and 3 must be assessed in real work environments.

City & Guilds

In preparation for assessment of this Unit, you may find it helpful to observe the way in which colleagues work in an inclusive way. You may also like to talk to your setting's SENCO about how this is successfully achieved.

UNIT 34

Principles for implementing duty of care in health, social care or children's and young people's settings

LEARNING OUTCOMES

The learning outcomes you will meet in this unit are:

1 Understand how duty of care contributes to safe practice

2 Know how to address conflicts or dilemmas that may arise between an individual's rights and the duty of care

3 Know how to respond to complaints

INTRODUCTION

Practitioners have a 'duty of care' towards the children and young people that they work with. This means that practitioners take on legal responsibilities to safeguard the welfare and well-being of the children in their care. This is a big responsibility that should not be taken lightly.

In order to fulfil your duty of care, you will need to learn about the rights and needs of children and young people, and the rights and responsibilities of their parents. This unit closely links with Unit EYMP 3 and Unit CYP 3.3. You may find it helpful to refer to these as part of your study towards this unit.

 **Link Up!**

Unit EYMP 3 Promote children's welfare and well-being in the early years
Unit CYP 3.3 Understand how to safeguard the well-being of children and young people

LEARNING OUTCOME 1

FOCUS ON

...understanding how duty of care contributes to safe practice

In this section you'll learn about what it means to have duty of care in your work role. You'll also learn about how duty of care contributes to the safeguarding or protection of individuals. This links with Assessment Criteria **1.1, 1.2**.

What it means to have a duty of care

In the *Dictionary of Law*, a duty of care is defined as 'the legal obligation to take reasonable care to avoid causing damage ... there is a duty of care in most situations in which one can reasonably foresee that one's actions may cause physical damage to the person or property of others.' If due care isn't taken

and any damage is caused to others or their property, a negligence claim may be made.

This means that as we go about our daily lives, we all have a duty of care towards other people – we must take reasonable care not to do things that would harm others. This of course also applies in the workplace.

How duty of care contributes to the safeguarding or protection of individuals

When we're working with children and young people, our duty of care towards them is a huge responsibility, as we also take on what's known as 'loco parentis'. This means that while a child or young person is in our care, we take on the same responsibilities to ensure their safety and well-being as their own parents. This includes the responsibility to see that children's rights are promoted and their needs are met. The following sections explain more about the legal responsibilities of parents.

Children Act 1989

When it was introduced in 1989, this law enforced a big change in the way parents' roles were regarded. The emphasis is now on parents having a responsibility to their children, rather than rights over them. It recognises that children themselves have rights, and that they should be treated with respect. Under the Act, children have rights to:

- be protected from harm (see 'Did you know?' on page 69)

- discuss their concerns

- be listened to

- be told what their rights are

- have their wishes considered when decisions that affect them are being made

- have details about their age, culture, race and gender considered when decisions are made

- be told about the decisions that are made

Exercising duty of care in the workplace.

- be heard if they are involved in a court case, and to have their own solicitor to represent them

- refuse a medical examination if they understand what that entails and do not want to have it done.

Did you know?

The Law describes 'harm' as the 'ill treatment or the impairment of health or development'.

- 'Ill treatment' includes physical abuse, sexual abuse and forms of abuse that are non-physical such as emotional abuse.
- 'Health' means mental health and physical health.
- 'Development' means social, physical, intellectual or behavioural development.

Ask Miranda!

Q What is safeguarding?

A Protecting the rights and needs of children and young people is known as 'safeguarding'. Safeguarding the right to be protected from harm is perhaps the most important responsibility of all for a practitioner.

UN Convention on the Rights of the Child

The UK Government ratified this convention in 1991. It contains Articles that refer to the rights and needs of children. These acknowledgements include:

- children have the right to protection
- children have the right to a family life
- parents and guardians have the right to support in carrying out their parental responsibilities

- children have the right to have their views listened to
- children's views should be given due consideration
- children need to receive good physical care
- children need to be shown love
- children need to feel secure
- children need a strong self-image and self-esteem.

Children have the right to a family life.

Link Up!

For more on the UN Convention on the Rights of the Child, see Unit SHC 33 Promote equality and inclusion in health, social care or children's and young people's settings

Safeguarding children and young people in practice

Children and young people are vulnerable because they have limited ability to:

- recognise and avoid potentially dangerous situations
- handle danger when it occurs
- attend to their own health, care and physical needs
- recognise and avoid behaviour that may cause harm or upset to others

- communicate about ill health and the harm others may be causing them.

Generally speaking, the younger the child, the more vulnerable they are. Babies and younger children rely on adults entirely to keep them safe and to take care of their physical and emotional needs. As their immune systems are not yet robust, their vulnerability in terms of health is also increased.

There are many ways in which practitioners and settings safeguard the vulnerability of the children and young people in their care, as the following table shows:

Table SHC 34.1: How practitioners and settings safeguard children and young people

Purpose	Example of actions taken
To provide a healthy and hygienic environment	Establishing and following health, safety and hygiene policies. Key points will include the following. Cleaning the setting, including daily vacuuming, sweeping, washing of floors, careful cleaning of kitchen and toilets, etc., preventing cross-contamination by storing and handling food safely, handling and disposing of waste products and bodily waste safely. Provision of a well-stocked first-aid box and access to a first aider. Providing high-quality physical care and nutrition. Establishing and following a care of sick children policy.
To provide a physically safe environment	Completing risk assessments of premises, and keeping the setting secure in terms of who enters and exits. Using safety equipment such as stair gates, finger guards, socket covers, etc. Establishing and following emergency procedures including the provision and checking of fire alarms and extinguishers and keeping fire exits clear. Ensuring appropriate temperatures and ventilation.
To provide safe activities and play opportunities	Completing activity risk assessments, ensuring activities are suitable for the individual children and young people taking part. Ensuring that toys and equipment have safety markings and are appropriate (clean, not broken, suitable for the age range, etc.). Providing the appropriate level of adult supervision to ensure safe play and use of equipment.
To ensure that behaviour remains within safe boundaries	Establishing and following a behaviour policy, ensuring that behaviour that is likely to harm or upset others is not permitted and is handled effectively if it occurs. Expectations are appropriate to children and young people's age and stage of development.
To ensure that children and young people's development is supported	Regularly observing and assessing development of individual children and planning an appropriate programme of activities and opportunities to support development and meet individual needs. Taking appropriate action to gain support for a child if developmental progress presents cause for concern.
To prevent harm being caused to a child	Establishing and following a child protection policy. Understanding and remaining vigilant to the signs and symptoms that indicate that a child may be experiencing abuse, and taking appropriate action if abuse is suspected.

You'll learn more about all of the above as you work through this book.

Practical example

Abbey-leigh feeds Lenny

Abbie-leigh is a student on placement in a nursery baby unit. The nursery nurse has 7-month-old Lenny's lunch ready. Abbie-leigh watched him eat his breakfast earlier, and now the nursery nurse asks her whether she'd like to feed him his lunch. Abbie-leigh is keen! She goes to the kitchen and washes her hands, and also fetches a clean bib for Lenny. When she gets back, she finds that the nursery nurse has already cleaned Lenny's hands (he likes to hold his own spoon), and strapped him into a high chair. Abbie-leigh allows Lenny to eat at his own pace. She makes lots of eye-contact with him and talks to him often.

Question

What has been done by Abbie-leigh and the nursery nurse to promote a) good health, safety and hygiene, b) good physical care and c) a good emotional experience for Lenny?

LEARNING OUTCOME 2

FOCUS ON

...how to address conflicts or dilemmas that may arise between an individual's rights and the duty of care

In this section you'll learn about the potential conflicts or dilemmas that may arise. You'll also learn about how to manage the risks associated with conflicts or dilemmas, and where to get additional support and advice about them. This links with Assessment Criteria **2.1, 2.2, 2.3.**

Potential conflict and dilemmas between the duty of care and individual rights

Legislation and the individual rights of children, young people and adults are often complex, and there are times when aspects of them seem to conflict. When this happens, a practitioner may find themselves in a dilemma between the duty of care they have for a child or young person, and individual rights of their parents or carers.

For example, in Unit SHC 31 Learning Outcome 4, you learned about the potential tension between maintaining confidentiality (a parent's right) and disclosing your concerns about a child's welfare if you suspect ill treatment (as you must as part of your duty of care). However, the Children's Act gives priority to the rights of children over the rights of the parent. As a result, in most instances, the legal interests and rights of a child will be put before the legal interests and rights of a parent. In our example, this means that the child's right to protection overrides the parent's right to confidentiality.

Balancing the duty of care with challenge and risk can also present potential conflict. This is because we have a duty of care to keep children and young people safe. But children and young people have a right to play and to develop in line with their age and stage of development. This means that we must allow them to take on appropriate risks and challenges, and to have a sense of freedom and autonomy (self-rule) in their play.

Link Up!

Unit SHC 31 Promote communication in health, social care or children's and young people's settings

Good practice

We can't 'wrap children up in cotton wool', and it would be wrong to try. But there can be disagreements between adults when it comes to deciding what constitutes an acceptable level of challenge or risk. Risk assessments and a good knowledge of individual children and young people's development and skills help practitioners to strike the right balance between their duty of care and promoting appropriate challenge and risk.

A balance must be struck between duty of care and promoting appropriate challenge and risk.

Managing risks associated with conflicts and dilemmas

When it comes to conflicts and dilemmas between the duty of care and individual rights, it's essential to find the appropriate level of balance. It's important for practitioners to put personal feelings aside and to look at the situation objectively. The right action should always be taken, even if it is emotionally difficult for the practitioner to carry out. (There's more about handling the discomfort of making a disclosure on page 31.)

Duty of care must never be taken lightly and must

be exercised if necessary. But practitioners should always remember that they are not the primary carer of children and young people. Parents have a deep, life-long bond with their children – their responsibilities to their child endure, while yours are temporary. Parents and carers are responsible for making many decisions which affect their entire family, and may well live their life in a way that is different to you and yet entirely within their rights and responsibilities. If you exercise your duty of care, ensure that you do so sensitively and with the greatest regard for the rights and responsibilities of the parent, as this will help you to avoid becoming embroiled in a conflict or dilemma.

Unit SHC 31 Promote communication in health, social care or children's and young people's settings

Ask Miranda!

A What should I do if I think I should exercise my duty of care and intervene?

Q If you feel that the duty of care should be exercised, make sure that you follow organisational procedures and chains of reporting. In most settings, practitioners will be required to report their concerns to senior staff before taking further action, such as contacting outside agencies. Respect confidentiality at all times (see Unit SHC 31 Learning Outcome 4). If you are a student on placement, you must always refer concerns to the qualified staff member supervising you – never take it upon yourself to raise an issue with a parent directly.

Good practice

Think carefully about intervening before you act. Kneejerk reactions can undermine parents and you may regret them later. It is absolutely a practitioner's role to exercise their duty of care if necessary, but this must be balanced with the risk of excessive intervention or interference. It can help enormously to talk the situation over with the setting's supervisor, who may be more objective if less closely involved with the family.

▶▶Link Up!◀◀

Unit SHC 31 Promote communication in health, social care or children's and young people's settings

Additional support and advice about dilemmas

If you do find yourself in a dilemma over your duty of care and the rights of a child or their parent, you may feel stressed or under pressure. But remember that your setting's policies and procedures are there to guide you, and senior colleagues are there to offer advice and to give you support. In child protection cases, practitioners can also access additional support and advice from Social Services professionals and the NSPCC (National Society for the Prevention of Cruelty to Children). There is more about this is Unit CYP 3.3.

▶▶Link Up!◀◀

Unit CYP 3.3 Understand how to safeguard the well-being of children and young people

LEARNING OUTCOME **3**

FOCUS ON ...how to respond to complaints

In this section you'll learn about how to respond professionally to complaints from parents and carers. You'll also learn about the main points of agreed procedures for handling complaints. This links with Assessment Criteria **3.1, 3.2.**

Complaints

As we've discussed, having duty of care is a huge responsibility, and conflicts and dilemmas may arise.

There may be times when a parent or carer feels that the setting has not sufficiently fulfilled the duty of care that they have for their child, or when their child's rights have not been prioritised or protected.

Did you know?

Families have every right to make a complaint if they feel that this is appropriate. In fact, as they are responsible for safeguarding their child's welfare and well-being, it could be said that parents are not fulfilling their own obligations to the child if they fail to complain when necessary.

Responding to complaints

All complaints must be recorded and taken seriously. Settings will have an agreed formal complaints procedure in place to ensure that all complaints are recorded and then handled professionally. It's helpful if staff involved view complaints as an opportunity to fully identify any problems and to put them right for the future, which will help the setting to improve as they move forward.

The value of agreed complaints procedures

An agreed formal complaints procedure is an extremely important document because it:

■ makes parents and carers aware of their right to complain

■ explains to parents and carers how to make their complaint

■ explains to parents and carers what will happen as the setting handles the complaint

■ makes parents and carers aware of how they can also complain to external agencies (such as Ofsted) if they see fit

■ makes parent and carers aware of their next step if they are not satisfied with the outcome of the complaint

■ sets out clear procedures for staff to follow when a complaint is received, which both protect and guide them as they handle the issue

■ ensures all complaints are taken seriously and handled fairly and consistently

■ ensures that the rights of families and the responsibilities of the setting/practitioners are protected and promoted.

The main points of agreed complaints procedures

The content of agreed procedures will vary from setting to setting. However, the main points covered will generally include:

■ who the complaint should be raised with in the

All complaints must be taken seriously.

first instance – usually the key-worker or the manager, and how it will be recorded

■ what will happen as a result – usually a discussion between the key-worker, manager and the parent

■ how progress will be documented throughout and how the parents will be kept informed

■ if actions to rectify an aspect of the service are to be taken, details of how this will be done, documented and evaluated, and who will take responsibility for this

■ the accepted timescales for handling a complaint. (If the matter isn't resolved, there may be an investigation by the manager, the results of which are discussed with the parent. If the matter isn't successfully resolved, it may be referred to the management committee, if the setting has one, for further discussion/investigation. If the issue is still not resolved satisfactorily, it may be referred to the appropriate body so they can look into it – for many settings, this body will be Ofsted (see below). Registered settings display an Ofsted complaints poster giving the telephone number for complaints – 0300 123 1231.)

Ofsted complaints and enforcement

Parents and carers are entitled to raise concerns about the quality of a service via a complaint to Ofsted. Ofsted will look into any concern or complaint that a provider is not meeting the requirements of the registers they are on, or their conditions of registration (see page 321). Ofsted also look into concerns that a person is providing child care without obtaining the required registration.

Did you know?

The role and procedures of Ofsted are explained in their document *Concerns and complaints about childcare providers*, which you can access using the search field at **www.ofsted.gov.uk**

How are things going?

▶ Progress Check

1. What does the term 'duty of care' mean in terms of your work role? (1.1)

2. How does duty of care contribute to the safeguarding and protection of children and young people? (1.2)

3. Why is there potential for conflicts and dilemmas between the duty of care and children and young people's rights? (2.1)

4. Give a strategy for managing the risks associated with conflicts or dilemmas between the duty of care and an individual's rights. (2.2)

5. Where can you get additional support and advice about conflicts and dilemmas? (2.3)

6. When a setting has an agreed complaints procedure, what are the benefits for staff when required to respond to a complaint? (3.1)

7. Give three main points of an agreed complaints procedure. (3.2)

Are you ready for assessment?

CACHE

Set task:

■ An in-depth task in which you prepare an information document on fulfilling the duty of care in your own setting, to be used in the induction of a new member of staff.

Prepare by ensuring that you fully understand the duty of care requirements of your specific job role, and your setting's own organisational procedures for meeting the duty of care. It will be helpful to refer to a job description and the setting's safeguarding policies.

Edexel

In preparation for assessment of this Unit, you may like to make notes in your reflective journal about the impact duty of care has on your work practices.

City & Guilds

You must complete the mandatory Assignment 055. This has three tasks, each one relating to one of the three Learning Outcomes. It entails answering questions and completing the tables provided. You can prepare by ensuring that you follow the links provided in this Unit, enabling you to read all the relevant information.

UNIT 3.1
Understand child and young person development

The learning outcomes you will meet in this unit are:

1 Understand the expected pattern of development for children and young people from birth to 19 years

2 Understand the factors that influence children and young people's development and how these affect practice

3 Understand how to monitor children and young people's development and interventions that should take place if this is not following the expected pattern

4 Understand the importance of early intervention to support the speech, language and communication needs of children and young people

5 Understand the potential effects of transitions on children and young people's development

INTRODUCTION

It is essential for practitioners to have a good understanding the development of children and young people. It informs all of the everyday aspects of your work, from how you pitch your interactions with young children, to what you expect young people to be interested in doing.

Also, a key part of the practitioner's role is to monitor and assess development. This enables you to recognise how you can best support and promote the development of the individual children and young people that you work with.

LEARNING OUTCOME 1

FOCUS ON

...understanding the expected pattern of development for children and young people from birth to 19 years

In this section you'll learn about the factors to take into account when assessing, and about assessing development in a number of areas. You'll also learn about assessment methods and developing a plan to meet the needs of a child or young person. This links with Assessment Criteria **1.1**, **1.2**.

Key aspects of understanding child development

Children's development is holistic. In other words, although we refer to different areas of children's learning for convenience, in practice children don't learn in a compartmentalised way.

Link Up!

There's information about adopting an integrated, holistic approach to providing activities to stimulate children's learning and development in the section 'An integrated approach to planning' in Learning Outcome 2, Unit EYMP 2 Promote learning and development in the early years

Expected rates of development

Tables within this unit give an approximate guide as to when babies, children and young people are likely to achieve certain milestones in their development (such as learning to walk). These are the accepted **expected development rates**. But it

is important to understand that children develop at **different** rates – this is entirely normal and should be expected. Always remember that the guides are **approximate**.

Children of the same age will not reach all of the milestones at the same time – some children will achieve milestones earlier than the expected rates of development and some will achieve them later. The same child may well be ahead of expected rates in some areas and behind them in other areas. For example, a child may crawl and walk early but begin to talk a little late.

key term

Expected development rates the approximate age at which most children will achieve key developmental milestones.

Sequence of development

Children generally develop in broadly the same **sequence** (order) – babies will learn to roll over before they sit up, for example, and children will say single words before they string two or three together in early sentences. However, there are exceptions to this – disabled children and young people and those who have specific needs may develop differently. You'll learn about this in Learning Outcome 3. Also, some children and young people are gifted and/or talented. Being gifted or talented is outlined by the Government as follows:

'Gifted and talented' describes children and young people with an ability to develop to a level significantly ahead of their year group, or with the potential to develop those abilities. Gifted learners are those who have abilities in one or more academic subjects, like maths and English. Talented learners are those who have practical skills in areas like sport, music, design or creative and performing arts. Skills like leadership, decision-making and organisation are also taken into account when identifying and providing for gifted and talented children.'

Sequence of development rates the expected order in which most children will achieve key developmental milestones.

Talented learners are those who have practical skills in areas such as sports.

All schools have a Leading Teacher for Gifted and Talented Education (or share one in the case of some primary schools), who are responsible for coordinating differentiated learning for gifted and talented pupils as appropriate, and maintaining a Gifted and Talented Register. Children may move on and off the register over time – especially in primary schools – as they develop at different rates to their peers. In settings, practitioners should also ensure that play and learning opportunities and experiences meet the needs of children who are ready for additional challenge.

Practitioners must have a good understanding of the child development rates they can do the following:

- **Carry out observation and assessment effectively**
  Practitioners are required to evaluate individual children's development by making comparisons between a child's actual developmental stage and the expected development rates.

- **Offer appropriate activities and experiences for individual children**
  This will be informed by observation and assessment of individual children. You'll learn more about this in Learning Outcome 3.

- **Anticipate the next stage of a child's development**
  This allows the practitioner to provide activities and experiences that will challenge and interest children, stimulating their learning and development.

- **Notice when children are not progressing as expected**
  Although children develop at different rates, significant delays in one area or many delays in several areas can be an indication that children need intervention and extra support.

Nature and nurture

There are two key factors that influence how development occurs:

- **Nature**
  Development occurs in response to the way children are genetically programmed from birth to be able to do certain things at certain times. This is referred to as 'nature'.

- **Nurture**
  Development occurs in response to the experiences that individual children have from the time they are born onwards. This is referred to as 'nurture'.

It's generally accepted that individual children develop as they do because of a combination of these two factors – nature and nurture. Language is a good example of this. Studies have shown that babies all over the world make coos, gurgles and other sounds that are very similar. The potential to speak and a common ability to make similar pre-language sounds would seem to be down to nature. But children learn to speak the language they are exposed to – this is down to nurture.

This means that practitioners must understand that individual children's development and levels of maturity will depend in part on the experiences they have had (or the way they have been nurtured).

To have realistic expectations about children's development and maturity, practitioners must take into account that children develop within unique families and different families influence children in widely different ways.

Families exist within a social and cultural system. Social and cultural systems interact with and influence the family, and therefore the child's development. Children have different experiences at different times and so they develop at different rates. Children cannot be expected to achieve aspects of development that are largely attributed to nurture if they have not yet been exposed to experiences that encourage this development. Practitioners must keep this in mind. The diagram below shows how nature and nurture influence aspects of children's development.

Nature	Nurture
Genetically programmed to make sounds from birth	Will learn the language to which they are exposed

Language development of babies.

Did you know?

When discussing development, the term 'neonate' is used to refer to a newly born baby. 'Prone' is the term used to describe the position of a baby lying on his or her front. 'Supine' is the term used to describe the position of a baby lying on his or her back.

Good practice

You need to have detailed knowledge about the expected development rates for babies, children and young people. There are many books available dedicated solely to the topic of child development. It is advisable for practitioners to read widely about the subject. The tables on pages 83–101 give an overview of the expected rates of development from the age of 0–16 years, in the following areas:

- physical development
- communication development
- intellectual/cognitive development
- social, emotional and behavioural development
- moral development.

Physical development

Physical development is about how children master physical control of movements made with their bodies.

The **neonate** (newly born baby) has **reflexes**. These are physical movements or reactions that neonates make without consciously intending to do so. For example, neonates will move their head in search of the mother's nipple or the teat of a bottle when their lips or cheek are touched (known as rooting), and they will also suck and swallow milk. These reflexes help babies to feed, and therefore survive. You may have experienced the grasp reflex – babies will clasp their fingers around yours if you touch their palm. You will have probably seen the startle reflex too – startled babies will make a fist and their arms will move away from their body. This can often be seen if there is a loud noise, or if babies wake up suddenly. The standing and walking reflex can be seen if babies are held upright in the standing position with their feet resting on a firm

The grasp reflex.

surface, such as the floor. They will make stepping movements with their legs.

Gross motor skills

Gross motor skills are an aspect of physical development. The term 'gross motor skills' is used to refer to whole-body movements such as sitting up, crawling, walking or kicking a ball. These skills develop rapidly during a child's first five years.

Locomotive movements

Sometimes, practitioners separate out an additional category of physical development – locomotive movements. They use this to describe activities relating to balance and travelling, such as walking,

Crawling

Sitting from lying down

Bear-walking

Walking with two hands held

Walking with one hand held

Walking alone

Gross motor skills involved in the development of walking.

running and standing on one leg. Others include these in the gross motor skills category as described above.

Fine motor skills

Fine motor skills are also an aspect of physical development. The term 'fine motor skills' is used to refer to the delicate, manipulative movements that are made with the fingers. Fine motor skills and the development of vision are linked. This is often referred to as 'hand/eye coordination'. Fine motor skills and hand/eye coordination are used when a child is threading cotton reels for example – the child will look carefully at the position of the hole in the reel, and manipulate the string accordingly.

key terms

Gross motor skills (sometimes called 'large motor skills') whole-body movements, such as walking.

Fine motor skills (sometimes called 'small motor skills') the delicate, manipulative movements that are made with the fingers.

Communication development

Communication development is the way in which children master speech, language and communication with others. There are a range of communication methods, including talking, body language (including gesture), reading, writing and sign language. There are close links to intellectual/cognitive development, because children need to think about and understand the communications that they receive from others as well as what they want to communicate themselves. Acquiring language also helps children's thinking processes.

▶▶Link Up!◀◀

You'll learn more about language development in Learning Outcome 1 Unit EYMP 5 Support children's speech, language and communication. It's a good idea to read this as part of your study towards this unit

Holding and exploring objetcs

Palmar grasp using whole hand

More delicate palmar grasp involving the thumb

Inferior pincer grasp

Exploring with the index finger

Delicate/mature pincer grasp

Fine motor skills involved in the development of manipulation.

Intellectual/cognitive development

Intellectual/cognitive development is concerned with developments in the way the brain processes the information that children constantly receive from their surroundings and from people. It is a vast area of development, with coverage including memory, concentration, imagination, creativity, problem solving, knowledge and understanding. There are close links between cognitive development and communication development, as explained above.

Social, emotional and behavioural development

This is about the way in which children experience and handle their own emotions, which gives rise to behaviour – frustration at not being able to do something is a good example of this. Children gain increasing control of their emotions as they develop. This area is also concerned with children's attachments to key people in their lives and how they relate with others. This has strong links to cognitive and communication development, as communication and understanding is at the heart of all relationships, as is the act of expressing feelings and emotions.

Moral development

Morality describes the values and principles that we have. These inform our behaviour and decisions. This includes values and principles that are enforced by society – that stealing is wrong, for example – and those that are considered subjective, such as whether we have sex before marriage. There are strong links to social, emotional and behavioural development, because morality encompasses social acceptance, the control of feelings and the impact that this has on behaviour (e.g. a child may know that it's wrong to hit someone, but controlling anger and behaviour so as not to do so is another matter). There are also strong links to intellectual/cognitive development, because developing values and principles requires the ability to think about issues and make decisions about them (e.g. whether or not to eat meat).

The development tables

On the following pages, a concise overview of each stage of development is given in the **rate and sequence of development tables** – this is a snapshot in time, representing the **big picture** of a child's expected development at any given age. Within this, the expected **development milestones for each of the areas of development** appear in colour-coded segments. This enables you to track specific aspects of a child's development within the big picture, as you would do in reality. For example, if you want to track physical development from 0 to 19 years, follow just the blue segments on every page.

Table CYP 3.1: Rates and sequence of development 0–19 years

BIRTH–3 WEEKS

OVERVIEW

Full-term babies are born at around 40 weeks. If born more than three weeks before the due date, babies are premature. They will then be expected to take a little longer to meet the early development milestones. Newborn babies need to begin bonding with their primary carers from birth. Babies spend more time sleeping than they do awake.

PHYSICAL DEVELOPMENT

Reflexes as described on pages 80–81

Usually holds hands tightly closed

In supine position, lies with head to one side

In prone position, lies with head to one side and tucks knees up under the abdomen

COMMUNICATION DEVELOPMENT

Cries to communicate hunger, tiredness and distress

INTELLECTUAL/COGNITIVE DEVELOPMENT

Recognises mother's voice

SOCIAL, EMOTIONAL AND BEHAVIOURAL DEVELOPMENT

Begins to bond with primary carers from birth. Needs close physical contact with them for security and when care needs are met

Totally dependent on others

1 MONTH

OVERVIEW

Babies will have developed rapidly in the four weeks since birth. They will be sleeping a little less frequently and some may be settling into a sleeping and feeding routine. They begin to communicate through sounds as well as crying, and will begin to smile.

PHYSICAL DEVELOPMENT

When sitting: head falls forwards (known as head lag), and the back curves

Posture more 'unfurled'

Reflexes persist, startle reflex is seen less frequently

Gazes attentively at faces, particularly when fed and talked to

COMMUNICATION DEVELOPMENT

Communicates needs through sounds

Communicates needs through crying

Communication occurs through physical closeness

Begins to coo and gurgle in response to interaction from carers

INTELLECTUAL/COGNITIVE DEVELOPMENT

May be soothed when crying by a familiar voice or music

Senses are used for exploration

SOCIAL, EMOTIONAL AND BEHAVIOURAL DEVELOPMENT

Smiles from about 5 weeks

Begins to respond to sounds heard in the environment by making own sounds

Engaged by people's faces

3 MONTHS

OVERVIEW

Babies will now be far more alert, and some may have settled into a routine that includes sleeping through the night. Being more settled and engaging and interacting more with carers and the world, generally results in babies crying less often.

PHYSICAL DEVELOPMENT

Turns from side to back

In supine: head in central position

In prone: head and chest can be lifted from the floor, supported by the forearms

When sitting: little head lag remains, back is straighter

Arms can be waved and brought together

Legs can be kicked separately and together

Alert, the baby moves head to watch others

Engages in hand and finger play

Holds rattle briefly before dropping

COMMUNICATION DEVELOPMENT

Recognises and links familiar sounds such as the face and voice of a carer

Will hold 'conversations' with carer when talked to, making sounds and waiting for a response

Can imitate high and low sounds

Returns a smile when smiled at – may smile often

INTELLECTUAL/COGNITIVE DEVELOPMENT

Through use of senses, begins to understand he/she is a separate person

Begins to notice objects in immediate environment

SOCIAL, EMOTIONAL AND BEHAVIOURAL DEVELOPMENT

Begins to discover what he/she can do, and this creates a sense of self

May cry if a primary carer leaves the room, not yet understanding that person still exists and will return

Shows feelings such as excitement and fear

Reacts positively when a carer is caring, kind and soothing

If a carer does not respond to a baby, the baby may stop trying to interact

6 MONTHS

OVERVIEW

Rapid development will have continued. Babies are physically stronger and very alert. They can now clearly express enjoyment and excitement through smiling, laughing and squeals of delight, which encourages carers to interact with them playfully. They can also reach for objects they're interested in, allowing them a new degree of autonomy in exploration. (The items must be within their reach.)

PHYSICAL DEVELOPMENT

Turns from front to back, and may do the reverse

In supine: head can be lifted and controlled when pulled to sitting position

In prone: head and chest can be fully extended supported by arms, with the hands flat on the floor

Sits unsupported for some time, with back straight, and plays in this position

Uses hands to play with feet, and may take them to the mouth

Weight-bears when held in standing position

Uses palmar grasp to pick up objects

Takes objects to the mouth for exploration

Passes objects from hand to hand

COMMUNICATION DEVELOPMENT

Sounds are used intentionally to call for a carer's attention

Babbling is frequent. The baby plays tunefully with the sounds he/she can make

Rhythm and volume explored vocally

Enjoys rhymes and accompanying actions

INTELLECTUAL/COGNITIVE DEVELOPMENT

Interested in bright, shiny objects

Very alert

Watches events keenly

Takes objects to mouth for exploration

SOCIAL, EMOTIONAL AND BEHAVIOURAL DEVELOPMENT

Shows a wider range of feelings more clearly and vocally

May laugh and screech with delight, but cry with fear at the sight of a stranger

Clearly tells people apart, showing a preference for primary carers/siblings

Reaches out to be held, and may stop crying when talked to

Enjoys looking at self in the mirror

Enjoys attention and being with others

9 MONTHS

OVERVIEW

Mobility makes a huge difference at this stage. Babies can now explore the environment, and increased strength means that they will also sit up and play for extended periods of time. Cognitive development and communication development are coming on hand in hand, with babies understanding some familiar words. There's an important emotional milestone as babies begin to understand that carers who leave the room will return (object permanence).

PHYSICAL DEVELOPMENT

Sits unsupported on the floor

Will go on hands and knees, and may crawl or find an alternative way to move around

Pulls self to standing position using furniture for support

Cruises around the room (side-stepping, holding furniture for support)

Takes steps if both hands are held by carer

Uses an inferior pincer grasp to pick up objects

Explores objects with the eyes

Points to and pokes at objects of interest with index finger

COMMUNICATION DEVELOPMENT

Initiates a wider range of sounds, and recognises a few familiar words, including 'no'

Knows own name

Greatly enjoys playing with carers and holding conversations

Makes longer strings of babbling sounds

Intentionally uses volume vocally

INTELLECTUAL/COGNITIVE DEVELOPMENT

Likes to explore immediate environment (as long as a primary carer is within close proximity)

Begins to look for fallen objects (object permanence)

SOCIAL, EMOTIONAL AND BEHAVIOURAL DEVELOPMENT

Enjoys playing with carers, e.g. peek-a-boo games and pat-a-cake

Offers objects, but does not yet let go

Increasing mobility allows baby to approach people

Begins to feed self with support

Understands that carers who leave the room will return

12 MONTHS

OVERVIEW

Babies are becoming increasingly mobile and are beginning to walk. Fine motor skills are also developing with the emergence of a sophisticated pincer grasp and the ability to feed themselves with a spoon. Other key milestones include increased babbling leading to speaking the first words, and the development of memory, which opens up a whole new world of learning.

PHYSICAL DEVELOPMENT

Sits down from standing position

Stands alone briefly and may walk a few steps alone

Throws toys intentionally

Clasps hands together

Uses sophisticated pincer grasp, and releases hold intentionally

Feeds self with spoon and finger foods

COMMUNICATION DEVELOPMENT

Increasingly understands the basic messages communicated by carers and older siblings

Can respond to basic instructions

Babbling sounds increasingly like speech, and leads to the first single words being spoken

Shows understanding that particular words are associated with people and objects, by using a few single words in context

INTELLECTUAL/COGNITIVE DEVELOPMENT

Looks for objects that fall out of sight, understanding they still exist although they can't be seen

Memory develops

Remembering past events enables the anticipation of future familiar events (e.g. a baby may show excitement when placed in their high chair ready for lunch)

Begins to anticipate what comes next in the daily routine, e.g. a nappy change before nap time

SOCIAL, EMOTIONAL AND BEHAVIOURAL DEVELOPMENT

The sense of self identity increases, as self-esteem and self-confidence develop

Waves goodbye, when prompted at first, and then spontaneously

Content to play alone or alongside other children for increasing periods of time

15 MONTHS

OVERVIEW

At this stage, language is really developing, with children understanding more and using an increasing number of single words. Walking is steadier, and as independence develops, there will begin to be frustration when the child is prevented from doing certain things, or when they are unable to do something they want to do themselves. As they are 'into everything' and fully mobile, careful supervision is necessary.

PHYSICAL DEVELOPMENT

Walks independently

Crawls upstairs. Crawls downstairs feet first

Sits in a child-sized chair independently

Tries to turn the pages of a book

Makes a tower of two blocks

Makes marks on paper with crayons

Holds own cup when drinking

COMMUNICATION DEVELOPMENT

Understands the concepts of labels such as 'you', 'me', 'mine', 'yours'

Use of single words increases, and more words are learned

INTELLECTUAL/COGNITIVE DEVELOPMENT

Will put away/look for very familiar objects in the right place

Uses toys for their purpose, e.g. puts a doll in a pram

Shows a keener interest in the activities of peers

SOCIAL, EMOTIONAL AND BEHAVIOURAL DEVELOPMENT

Curious. Wants to explore the world more than ever, as long as carers are close by

May show signs of separation anxiety (e.g. upset when left at nursery)

May 'show off' to entertain carers

Can be jealous of attention/toys given to another child

Changeable emotionally. Quickly alternates between wanting to do things alone and being dependent on carers

May respond with anger when told off or thwarted. May throw toys or have a tantrum

Can be distracted from inappropriate behaviour

Possessive of toys and carers. Reluctant to share

Child 'is busy' or 'into everything'

18 MONTHS

OVERVIEW

Children are increasingly keen to have independence, and become frustrated easily if incapable of doing something. This may lead to asserting will strongly, showing angry defiance and resistance to adults. Children cannot yet control their emotional responses, and need sensitivity from their carers when they become overwhelmed by their feelings. They will understand a lot of what is said to them, so communicative stimulation is important. Children will begin to enjoy mark-making and use trial and error in exploration, for example, trying to post several shapes in the hole of a shape sorter.

PHYSICAL DEVELOPMENT

Walks confidently. Attempts to run

Walks up and down stairs if hand is held by carer

Bends from the waist without falling forwards

Balances in the squatting position

Pushes and pulls wheeled toys

Propels ride-on toys along with legs

Rolls and throws balls, attempts to kick them

Uses delicate pincer grasp to thread cotton reels

Makes a tower of three blocks

Makes large scribbles with crayons

Can use door handles

COMMUNICATION DEVELOPMENT

Understands a great deal of what carers say

More words spoken. Uses people's names

INTELLECTUAL/COGNITIVE DEVELOPMENT

Uses trial and error in exploration

SOCIAL, EMOTIONAL AND BEHAVIOURAL DEVELOPMENT

Has a better understanding of being an individual

Very curious, and more confident to explore

Becomes frustrated easily if incapable of doing something

Follows carers, keen to join in with their activities

Plays alongside peers more often (parallel play), and may imitate them

Still very changeable emotionally

May show sympathy for others (e.g. putting arm around a crying child)

Can be restless and very determined, quickly growing irritated or angry

May assert will strongly, showing angry defiance and resistance to adults

Can still be distracted from inappropriate behaviour

2 YEARS

OVERVIEW

By now, children's individuality and uniqueness is evident, and emerging more all the time. The long journey of learning to express this in words as well as behaviour will begin as short sentences are spoken. More confident physical movements lead to new experiences such as running, climbing and sliding, and appropriate outside apparatus will be enjoyed. Children still struggle with their overwhelming emotions, but are beginning to understand that actions have consequences. This is an important cognitive and behavioural development.

PHYSICAL DEVELOPMENT

Runs confidently

Climbs low apparatus

Walks up and down stairs alone holding hand rail

Rides large wheeled toys (without pedals)

Kicks stationary balls

Makes a tower of six blocks

Joins and separates interlocking toys

Draws circles, lines and dots with a pencil

Puts on shoes

COMMUNICATION DEVELOPMENT

Will often name objects on sight (e.g. may point and say 'chair' or 'dog')

Vocabulary increases. Joins two words together, e.g. 'shoes on'

Short sentences used by 30 months. Some words used incorrectly (e.g. 'I *goed* in')

INTELLECTUAL/COGNITIVE DEVELOPMENT

Completes simple jigsaw puzzles (or 'play-trays')

Understands that actions have consequences

Builds towers of bricks

SOCIAL, EMOTIONAL AND BEHAVIOURAL DEVELOPMENT

Beginning to understand own feelings. Identifies sad and happy faces

Experiences a range of changeable feelings, which are expressed in behaviour

More responsive to the feelings of others

Often responds to carers lovingly, and may initiate loving gestures (a cuddle)

Peals of laughter and sounds of excitement are common for some

May use growing language ability to protest verbally

May get angry with peers, and lash out on occasion (e.g. pushing or even biting them)

3 YEARS

OVERVIEW

As children gain the ability to express themselves with language, behaviour related to frustration (e.g. tantrums) decreases. This facilitates moral development. Many children start pre-school. This is timely, as at this stage interest in being with peers increases, and most children will enjoy playing with others of a similar age. This is also easier, thanks to an increasing ability to share and take turns. Many children will experience planned learning activities for the first time.

PHYSICAL DEVELOPMENT

Walks and runs on tip-toes

Walks up and downstairs confidently

Rides large wheeled toys using pedals and steering

Kicks moving balls forwards

Enjoys climbing and sliding on small apparatus

Makes a tower of nine blocks

Turns the pages of a book reliably

Draws a face with a pencil, using the preferred hand

Attempts to write letters

Puts on and removes coat

Fastens large, easy zippers

COMMUNICATION DEVELOPMENT

Enjoys stories and rhymes

Vocabulary increases quickly

Use of plurals, pronouns, adjectives, possessives and tenses

Longer sentences used

By 42 months, most language used correctly

INTELLECTUAL/COGNITIVE DEVELOPMENT

Child is enquiring. Frequently asks 'what' and 'why' questions

Use of language for thinking and reporting

Can name colours. Can match and sort items into simple sets (e.g. colour sets)

Can count to ten by rote. Can only count out three or four objects

Begins to recognise own written name

Creativity is used in imaginary and creative play

SOCIAL, EMOTIONAL AND BEHAVIOURAL DEVELOPMENT

Can tell carers how he/she is feeling

Empathises with the feelings of others

Uses the toilet and washes own hands

Can put on clothes

Imaginary and creative play is enjoyed

Enjoys company of peers and makes friends

Wants adult approval

Is affected by mood of carers/peers

Less rebellious. Less likely to physically express anger as words can be used

MORAL DEVELOPMENT

Increasingly able to understand consequence of behaviour and the concept of 'getting in trouble'

Understands the concept of saying sorry and 'making up'

4 YEARS

OVERVIEW

Many children will make the transition to school during this year, which marks a huge change in their lives. They will also be fluent talkers, confident movers and increasingly adept socially. Their play will contain definite ideas, which they can now verbalise. Their concentration span will be increasing all the time, and many children will now be experienced in taking part in planned learning activities.

PHYSICAL DEVELOPMENT

Changes direction while running

Walks in a straight line successfully

Confidently climbs and slides on apparatus

Hops safely

Can bounce and catch balls, and take aim

Makes a tower of ten blocks

Learning to fasten most buttons and zips

Learning to use scissors. Cuts out basic shapes

Draws people with heads, bodies and limbs

Writes names and letters in play as awareness that print carries meaning develops

COMMUNICATION DEVELOPMENT

Uses language fluently

As an understanding of language increases so does enjoyment of rhymes, stories and nonsense

Speech is clear and understood by those who don't know the child

INTELLECTUAL/COGNITIVE DEVELOPMENT

Completes puzzles of 12 pieces

Memory develops. Child recalls many songs and stories

Attention/concentration span increases

Fantasy and reality may be confused

Imagination and creativity increases

Problem solves ('I wonder what will happen if…'), and makes hypothesis ('I think this will happen if…')

Sorts objects into more complex sets

Number correspondence improves

SOCIAL, EMOTIONAL AND BEHAVIOURAL DEVELOPMENT

May be confident socially

Self-esteem is apparent

Awareness of gender roles if exposed to them

Friendship with peers is increasingly valued

Enjoys playing with groups of children

Control over emotions increases

Can wait to have needs met by carers

As imagination increases child may become fearful (e.g. of the dark or monsters)

Learning to negotiate and get along with others through experimenting with behaviour

Experiences being in/out of control, feeling power, having quarrels with peers

Some considerate, caring behaviour is shown to others

Distraction works less often, but child increasingly understands reasoning

Co-operative behaviour shown

Responds well to praise for behaviour, encouragement and responsibility

MORAL DEVELOPMENT

Experiences being blamed, blaming

Has a good understanding of familiar, basic rules

If exposed to swearing, is likely to use these words in their own language

5 YEARS

OVERVIEW

Children will now be in formal schooling. Many will enjoy the cognitive stimulation and challenge of the classroom and the independence they have at playtimes. But for some there may be a negative experience, particularly if reading and writing do not interest them, or they experience difficulties with these areas of learning. Friends are very important to children now. Physical development has now slowed, but coordination increases.

PHYSICAL DEVELOPMENT

Coordination increases

Controls ball well. Plays ball games with rules

Rides bike with stabilisers

Balance is good, uses low stilts confidently

Sense of rhythm has developed. Enjoys dance and movement activities

Controls mark-making materials well (e.g. pencils). Writing more legible

Writes letters and short, familiar words

Learns to sew

COMMUNICATION DEVELOPMENT

Learning to read. Recognises some words

Vocabulary grows

INTELLECTUAL/COGNITIVE DEVELOPMENT

Options/knowledge of subjects are shared using language for thinking

Enjoyment of books increases as child learns to read

Thinking skills and memory increase as vocabulary grows

Spends longer periods at activities when engaged

Shows persistence

Children learn from new experiences at school

Learning style preferences may become apparent

SOCIAL, EMOTIONAL AND BEHAVIOURAL DEVELOPMENT

The school transition may be unsettling

Enjoys group play and co-operative activities

Increasingly understands rules of social conduct and rules of games, but may have difficulty accepting losing

Increasing sense of own personality and gender

Keen to 'fit in' with others. Approval from adults and peers desired

Friends are important. Many are made at school

Many children will have new experiences out of school (e.g. play clubs, friends coming for tea)

Increasingly independent, undertaking most physical care needs for themselves

May seek attention, 'showing off' in front of peers

Often responds to 'time out' method of managing behaviour

MORAL DEVELOPMENT

Feels shame/guilt when adults disapprove of behaviour

Keen to win and be 'right'

6–7 YEARS

OVERVIEW

Children are strongly influenced by what they learn at school, and can increasingly consider this alongside what they learn at home, and draw their own conclusions. This contributes to personality being established more firmly and attitudes developing. Development slows now (it is most rapid in the 0–5 years period), but confidence increases, and so does learning in terms of the school curriculum. Many children will be developing wider interests, and may attend club and classes outside of school hours (e.g. dance, music, drama).

PHYSICAL DEVELOPMENT

Can hop on either leg, skip and play hopscotch

Rides bicycle without stabilisers

Confidently climbs and slides on larger apparatus in school and in parks

Can catch a ball with one hand only

Sews confidently and may tie shoe laces

COMMUNICATION DEVELOPMENT

Language refined and more adult-like

Enjoys jokes and word play

INTELLECTUAL/COGNITIVE DEVELOPMENT

Imagination skills are developed

Fantasy games are complex and dramatic

Many children read and write basic text by age 7, but this varies widely

Ability to predict and to plan ahead has developed

Understands cause and effect well

Can conserve number

Does simple calculations

Understands measurement and weighing

SOCIAL, EMOTIONAL AND BEHAVIOURAL DEVELOPMENT

Enjoys team games and activities

Towards age 7, a child may doubt their learning ability ('I can't do it')

May be reluctant to try or persevere, becoming frustrated easily

Personality is established more firmly as attitudes to life are developed

Solid friendships are formed. The relationship with 'best friends' is important

More susceptible to peer pressure

Cultural identity also established

Has learned how to behave in various settings and social situations (e.g. at school, play club, a friend's house)

MORAL DEVELOPMENT

Attitudes to life beginning to be developed – these are the basis of future moral codes

Can understand increasingly complex rules, impacting on the sense of right and wrong

8–12 YEARS

OVERVIEW

Children will now be reading and writing well. They will know what they like and don't like, and feel they know how and what they learn best. However, an emotionally rocky period can be expected with the transition to secondary and the onset of puberty (although the age at which this occurs varies widely). An interest in TV, computers, console games, DVDs may mean child is less active, so a balanced, active lifestyle should be encouraged.

PHYSICAL DEVELOPMENT

Physical growth slows at first, so fewer physical milestones reached

Puberty generally begins between 11–13 years (see 13–19 years table)

Coordination and speed of movement develops

Muscles and bones develop. Has more physical strength

Begins to run around less in play

Interest in TV, computers, console games, DVDs may mean less active

Does joined-up writing, which becomes increasingly adult-like

Has computer skills. May type well and control the mouse as an adult would

Can sew well, and may be adept at delicate craft activities such as braiding threads

COMMUNICATION DEVELOPMENT

May read for enjoyment in leisure time

Can make up and tell stories that have been plotted out

Verbal and written communication is fluent, often with correct grammar usage

Enjoys chatting to friends/adults

INTELLECTUAL/COGNITIVE DEVELOPMENT

Range of new subjects may be learned at secondary school

Child may follow their interests, learning outside of school

Sense of logic develops. Thinking in abstract by 10 (can consider beliefs, morals and world events)

SOCIAL, EMOTIONAL AND BEHAVIOURAL DEVELOPMENT

May feel unsettled when making the transition from primary school to secondary school, and as puberty approaches

Stable friendships are relied upon. These are generally same-sex, although children play in mixed groups/teams

May be reluctant to go to a play club or event unless a friend will be there too

More independent

Makes more decisions

May play unsupervised at times

May travel to school alone by end of age band

Mood swings may be experienced during puberty (see 13–19 years table)

MORAL DEVELOPMENT

Conflict with parents due to desire for increasing independence ('Why can't I stay home alone?')

May feel rules are unfair ('But all my friends are allowed to do it!')

May refuse to go along with some decisions made by parents (e.g. refusing to wear certain clothes purchased for them as they feel they have the right to choose for themselves)

Thinking in abstract by age 10 (see intellectual/cognitive development)

13–19 YEARS

OVERVIEW

There's a huge variation in terms of when young people mature in this age band. There's a lot happening too – puberty, relationships based on attraction, exams, leaving school, making career choices, establishing one's own ethics and morals – all of which happen in response to many new experiences. Practitioners need to be responsive to how young people respond to pressure at this age, while allowing increasing independence.

PHYSICAL DEVELOPMENT

The bodies of both boys and girls change throughout puberty. Variation in age at which this occurs

Girls generally enter puberty by 13 years, becoming women physically by 16 years

Boys generally enter puberty by 14 years, becoming men physically by 16 or 17 years

Sporting talents may become more apparent

May learn/refine new manipulative skills (e.g. drawing, stitching, carpentry, woodwork, playing an instrument)

Talent in the arts or crafts may become more apparent

COMMUNICATION DEVELOPMENT

May be reluctant to directly ask adults for the advice or information they need. May prefer to access it anonymously

INTELLECTUAL/COGNITIVE DEVELOPMENT

Academic knowledge increases as exam curriculum is followed

Towards age 16, decisions made about the future (college course/career)

SOCIAL, EMOTIONAL AND BEHAVIOURAL DEVELOPMENT

Desire to express individuality, but also a strong desire to fit in with peers

Becomes interested in own sexuality and feels attraction to others

Develops romantic relationships

Develops sexual relationships

May express self creatively through art/music/dance or creative writing

May worry about aspects of physical appearance

May express self/experiment with identity through appearance (e.g. dress, hairstyles, piercings, tattoos)

Pressure at school mounts as exam curriculum is followed

Young people may feel overwhelmed or anxious

A balance of school work/leisure time is important, especially if young people take on part-time jobs

Likely to communicate innermost thoughts and feelings more frequently to friends than to adults

May prefer to spend more time with friends than with family. May stay in bedroom more at home

May swing between acting maturely, and saying/doing 'childish' things (e.g. may watch a young children's TV programme, or sit on a swing in the park)

May experiment with smoking, alcohol, drugs or early promiscuity. This behaviour is linked with low-self esteem

May experience mood swings. Tense atmospheres are lightened when adults remain in good humour

MORAL DEVELOPMENT

Developing own morals, beliefs and values outside of parents' influence

May disregard the opinions/values of parents if they conflict with those of the peer group

Acting on own values may cause conflict at home (e.g. becoming a vegetarian)

Towards end of age band, may protest to make their feelings known and to act on a desire to change the world (e.g. online petitions, student protests)

LEARNING OUTCOME 2

The factors that influence children and young people's development

The factors that influence children and young people's development are divided into two categories:

- personal factors
- external factors.

FOCUS ON

...understanding the factors that influence children and young people's development and how these affect practice

In this section you'll learn about the factors to take into account when assessing, and about assessing development in a number of areas. You'll also learn about assessment methods and developing a plan to meet the needs of a child or young person. This links with Assessment Criteria 2.1, 2.2, 2.3.

We'll look at each in turn.

Personal factors

Personal factors are things that are intrinsic to the child, and they start to influence a child's development at the moment of conception. All cells in our bodies contain 46 chromosomes, which are made up of 23 pairs. Each chromosome consists of long chemical threads, which we know as DNA. Each of the threads contain genes. The father's sperm and the mother's egg each carry their genetic information, and when the sperm and egg fuse, the chromosomes pair off, with the baby getting half of their chromosomes from the mother, and half from the father.

A number of factors are decided genetically, including aspects of health and appearance – hair colour and eye colour for instance, along with face shape and height (although external factors such as a poor diet can also affect growth). The reason that children from the same parents aren't all the same, and the reason we all have our own unique DNA – sometimes called our 'genetic fingerprint' – is that the selection of chromosomes in the sperm and the egg is completely random. Identical twins are the exception to the rule, because in their case, one fertilised egg splits into two sections.

Did you know?

As the science of genetics advances, we're learning more about personal factors all the time. Experts now think we have in the region of 50,000 genes.

Further personal factors can arise during pregnancy and birth. If the mother picks up certain infections, they can affect the baby's development. Harm can also be caused by the mother drinking alcohol or taking drugs during pregnancy. If a baby is born prematurely, the usual full-term development will not be complete, and this can also have long-term effects. Physical impairments or learning difficulties can be caused by all of the above. There can also be difficulties at birth

that can impact on development, including a lack of oxygen, which can cause learning difficulties.

Link Up!

You can learn more about the potential effects on development of pre-conceptual, pre-birth and birth experiences in Learning Outcome 1, Unit CYPOP 1 Work with babies and young children to promote their development and learning. However, it's important to stress that the majority of pregnancies and births are healthy

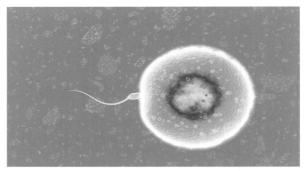

Personal factors influence a child's development from the moment of conception.

Health status

Children's health can have a big impact on their development. If ill health causes them to miss time at school, at a setting or simply being with family and playing with friends, experiences that contribute to development will also be missed. When at school or the setting, children may not have the energy or stamina to fully participate, which can again be detrimental. In these cases, practitioners can devise strategies to support the child. For instance, if there's a pattern to fatigue, quieter whole-group activities such as story time can be scheduled to coincide, so the child needn't miss out while they rest.

There are various causes to health problems. Some health conditions, such as certain heart problems, are present at birth, and the child will be affected by them to some extent from the start of their lives.

There can be a disposition for other conditions, but a child will only develop them if they are triggered by external factors – asthma can be triggered by living in a damp house, for instance, or in an area with high levels of traffic pollution. Other health conditions for which there is no genetic disposition can also be caused by external factors, including a poor diet, poor health care and poor living conditions.

Disability, including sensory impairment and learning difficulties

These can result from genetic make up, pre-birth experiences and birth experiences, as we've discussed. However, external factors can also play a part – for example, a non-disabled child may become disabled in an accident. Any aspect of children's development can be affected by disability, sensory impairments and learning difficulties, for example physical development, social and emotional development, cognitive development, speech, language and communication development. It's up to practitioners to work in inclusive ways to ensure that all children can participate, and that all children have the support they need. This can limit the effect of impairments on future development, and it supports the social model of disability.

Link Up!

You'll learn about this, and the effects of disability and attitudes on positive outcomes for children and young people in Learning Outcome 3, Unit CYP 3.7 Understand how to support positive outcomes for children and young people

External factors

External factors affect development from when a child is born onwards. All children and young people are constantly experiencing these.

Poverty and deprivation

Poverty shapes children's development. Living in poverty is extremely stressful for families. There may be constant worries about having enough food to eat, clothes to wear, heat in the winter and so on. This can have an effect on everyone's mental health, as well as an impact on physical health. Poor-quality food and poor housing are particularly common problems. These can lead to a lack of opportunities to play safely, impacting on learning experiences. Children and young people may also experience the stigma of poverty, which affects their self-esteem and self-respect, impacting on social and emotional development. In turn, the child's expectations for their own outcomes in life may be low – this is worrying because our expectations are a key factor in what we actually go on to achieve. Statistics show that by the time a child from a poorer family is 2 years old, they are more likely to show a lower level of attainment than a child from a better-off family. By the age of 6, a less-able child from a rich family is likely to have overtaken an able child from a poor family.

Link Up!

You'll learn more about poverty and deprivation in Learning Outcome 1, Unit CYP 3.7 Understand how to support positive outcomes for children and young people, which also explores what can be done to improve outcomes for children and young people living in poverty and deprivation

Living in poverty is extremely stressful for families.

Family environment and background

How a child is brought up has a significant impact on their development. In most homes, children are well cared for by a parent/family that loves them. They do their best to feed them well, to keep them safe and to give them the emotional support and encouragement that they need. Many parents respond well to the 'working in partnership' approach of settings, and value being involved. They want their child to do well in life, so when they start at school, they help with homework and take an interest in events. Children have things to do and places to play in their leisure time. This all has a positive effect on development, and on children's life outcomes. This links with what you will learn in Unit CYP 3.7.

However, this is not the experience of every child. Parents, carers or other family members may have issues in their life that affect their parenting and therefore the child's development. This could include drug or alcohol abuse, domestic violence, depression or other mental health issues. It's also a sad fact that some people deliberately harm their own children. There is more about this in Unit CYP 3.3.

Unit CYP 3.7 Understand how to support positive outcomes for children and young people
Unit CYP 3.3 Understand how to safeguard the well-being of children and young people

Personal choices

Part of growing up is having increasing independence and the opportunity to make more and bigger decisions. Some of these can impact on development. For instance, young people make personal choices about taking physical risks, having sex, drinking alcohol, smoking, taking drugs (which can damage the development of young brains as well as causing health and mental health problems) and skipping school. However, they can also make positive choices that impact on development, such as applying themselves at school. There's more information about the effect of both positive and negative personal choices on outcomes for children and young people in Unit CYP 3.7, Learning Outcome 3.

Unit CYP 3.7 Understand how to support positive outcomes for children and young people

Choices made by children and young people can impact on development.

Looked after children/care status

Attachments to primary carers are important to children and young people, who have a deep emotional need to be loved and nurtured by someone who treats them as special. Children who are looked after by their local authority/have care status are most likely to be lacking this stable, consistent, secure person in their life. These children and young people may also be experiencing the effects of disability, family breakdown, youth offending or unsatisfactory parental care. They may live in residential care or foster care, and will perhaps be moved around throughout their childhood.

Education

When we think of education, we tend to first think of schools. These will of course be the places where a vast amount of learning that can impact on development is done, and a lot of children and young people's time is spent there. Children will learn to read and write, to do maths, and about the wider world, to mention just a few subjects. And they will of course be socialising with large numbers of peers. But children and young people also learn throughout their lives in a range of other places – at home for instance, and at groups they may belong to – everything from church, to Brownies, to youth club.

Did you know?

Some children's development will be positively impacted through receiving private one-to-one tuition such as piano lessons or horse riding, or going to group classes such as gymnastics, ice-skating or street dance.

In terms of all sorts of education, the quality of the opportunity is recognised as being of key importance to development (which is why our schools are regulated and inspected). But the level of children and young people's engagement is another prime indicator of how the experience is likely to benefit their development. If a child or young person is actively engaged, the positive impact on their development can be considerable, and they are likely to be interested in extra-curricular activities (such as sports or drama) extending their learning further. If a child or young person experiences education opportunities in a negative way, negative outcomes are likely to follow. For instance, if a child struggles and comes to feel that they're not a good learner, self-esteem and self-confidence will be affected, as well as future aspirations. If a young person experiences bullying, they may be frequently anxious and unable to concentrate or to perform well, affecting their ability to benefit from the learning opportunities that others may be seizing.

Theories about how children learn and develop

Practitioners should understand theories about how children learn and develop. This allows them to support children effectively when planning to meet their needs and when working with them in practice. Some key theories about this are outlined here, but there are many books dedicated to the subject of learning, development and play theories. You may find it interesting to learn about additional theories and the research and experiments that underpin them. Psychologists and other theorists have been making observations on this subject for hundreds of years. They often have conflicting ideas as you'll read below.

Traditionally, the approaches of theorists have been divided into types. These are three key types of approach to cognitive development:

■ **Constructivist approach**
Constructivist theorists focus on children as active learners. They're interested in how children learn from their experiences, and how they learn to understand the world around them.

■ **Behaviourist approach**
Behaviourist theorists focus on the way children respond (behave) in response to the various stimuli and reinforcements. They're particularly interested in the pattern of responses over time.

■ **Social learning approach**
Social learning theorists focus on how children learn through observation and imitation (role modelling).

Three key types of theories on cognitive development are as follows:

■ **Psychoanalytical approach**
Psychoanalytical theorists focus on the unconscious mind. They're interested in how this develops in childhood, and the effect that it has on personality and the way people behave (actions) throughout life.

■ **Humanist approach**

Humanist theorists focus on the basic human needs. They're interested in the motivations people have to get their needs met, and how this links with personality.

■ **Attachment theory approach**

Attachment theorists focus on the need of babies and young children to have strong emotional attachments in their lives. They're interested in how this links to social and emotional development, and the on-going effects of having experienced strong or low-quality attachments.

Some key theories from prominent theorists belonging to each of these types are given below.

Good practice

The ideas of key theorists can be instrumental, and you will recognise how some of those outlined below still influence our practices today. Other practices are left behind as current thinking moves on and new practice emerges as a result. The way behaviour management has changed drastically over the years is a good example of this.

Piaget (constructivist theorist),1896–1980

Jean Piaget developed 'constructivist' theories that have been influential, although they have been challenged over the years. Piaget was the first to say that when children play they can make discoveries for themselves without being taught. He observed that children generally shared the same sequential pattern of learning, and he noted that children of the same age often made the same mistakes.

This led him to believe that children's cognitive development (their ability to think, reason and understand) developed through a series of sequential stages of development. He believed that children should not be hurried through these stages as that

would be detrimental – he said they should be allowed to pass through them naturally. Piaget focused on children's cognitive development in isolation – he did not consider other areas, such as social and emotional development. He referred to children as 'lone scientists', believing that adults should seek to provide environments where children could make their own discoveries. The idea that adults should intervene only sensitively in children's play stemmed from Piaget.

Piaget said that adults should provide environments where children could make their own discoveries.

Piaget referred to children at play as 'active participants in their own learning'. He believed that children use their first-hand and previous experiences to learn. He thought that children make assumptions based on experiences – he called these 'schemas'. Piaget called the process of applying one schema to another circumstance 'assimilation'. For example, imagine that a child had only ever poured water through a funnel. They then discover that dry sand will also pass through the funnel. They have assimilated a new concept into their existing schema – sand and water can both pass through funnels.

Piaget believed that when children cannot fit a new experience into an existing schema, they create a new schema that will fit. He called this process 'accommodation'. For example, a child who has only ever eaten one type of biscuit may believe that all biscuits taste the same. When they find out this is not the case, they accommodate a new schema – different biscuits have different tastes. To take our first example, accommodation may take place if a child discovers

that wet sand will not pass easily through a funnel in the same way as dry sand or water. Piaget believed that children pass through four stages of cognitive development. He did not believe that everyone would attain every stage, particularly stage four:

Piaget's stages of cognitive development

Stage One: Sensory-motor. Child's Age: 0–2yrs
Key Aspects: Babies use their sense to learn. They can only see things from their own point of view – they are 'egocentric'. They do not know that something they cannot see still exists, e.g. if a ball rolls out of view, they will not look for it. At about 18 months this changes. They have then achieved 'object permanence'

Stage Two: Pre-operational. Child's Age: 2–7yrs
Key Aspects: Children are still 'egocentric'. They believe animals and inanimate objects have the same feelings as people – they are 'animalistic'. They use language to express their thoughts, and use symbols in their play, e.g. they pretend a length of string is a snake

Stage Three: Concrete Operations. Child's Age: 7–11yrs
Key Aspects: Now children 'decentre' – they can see other points of view and understand that inanimate objects do not have feelings. They are establishing complex reasoning skills, and they can use writing and other symbols, e.g. mathematical symbols – this is called 'conservation'

Stage Four: Formal Operations. Child's Age: 11–adulthood
Key Aspects: Children can use logic and work methodically. They can think 'in abstract' – doing mental arithmetic and thinking things through internally. They can problem solve thoughtfully

It's generally agreed that while adults can enhance children's play experiences, they should only intervene sensitively, particularly during imaginative play when they should take their cues from children, only joining in when invited, when play is flagging or when children are about to do something inappropriate or unsafe. The idea that children can make discoveries for themselves through play is very much still promoted.

Piaget's influence today.

Vygotsky (constructivist theorist), 1896–1934

Lev Vygotsky was one of the first academics to disagree with Piaget. He died when in his thirties, so his career was short, but he has had a major impact on current thinking. He believed that children learn through social interaction and relationships, through the social tool of language. His theory is called the 'social constructivist theory'.

Interested in children's play, he was of the opinion that all play contains an imaginative element, and that this is freeing for children. He agreed with Piaget that children at play are 'active participants in their own learning'. However, he felt that the emotional aspect of play was as important as the learning aspect. He believed that play was a good way to learn, but he did not think it was the only way.

He developed a concept known as 'the zone of proximal development', which centres around the idea that adults can help children learn, and that children can also help one another. This idea has become known as the 'Vygotsky tutorial'. The Russian word 'proximal' translates to the word 'nearby'. He used the term 'the zone of actual development' to describe the things that children can do without any help at all, and the term 'zone of proximal development' to describe the things that children could potentially do with assistance – the learning that was next or 'nearby'.

He believed that children should always be challenged by some activities that are just beyond them and in their current zone of proximal development, as this would motivate them and move their learning forward. The process of offering activities that will slightly stretch children in this way is referred to as 'scaffolding learning'. In summary, through scaffolding learning with some challenging activities just beyond what a child can do, children can move from the actual zone of development to the proximal zone of development. This contrasts with Piaget's view that children should be allowed to pass through the stages of development naturally with little intervention.

You may group children of different skill levels together for an activity, and encourage children to help one another – this is the 'Vygotsky tutorial' in action. He believed that all children would benefit – the 'learner' by learning the new skill or concept and the 'teacher' by developing a deeper understanding of their existing skill or concept.

Vygotsky's influence today.

Bruner (constructivist theorist), 1915–

Jerome Bruner extended Vygotsky's theories, and called his new theory the 'spiral curriculum'. This makes reference to his belief that children learn through discovery with the direct assistance of adults who should provide opportunities for them to return to the same activities (in terms of materials and ideas) again and again. He believed that by doing this, children would extend and deepen their learning of the concepts and ideas that adults introduce to them.

He observed how children like to return to activities over a period of some years, and felt they are motivated to learn through the spiral curriculum. You may have noticed children who enjoy building the same model time and again, or drawing the same pictures. Resources like interlocking bricks can be a favourite of children for some years.

It is generally accepted that children should have plenty of opportunities for free play and child-initiated activities. This allows them to revisit previous experiences or ideas if they would like to. In addition, it is widely believed that children should be provided with activities to consolidate existing learning and new opportunities to challenge and motivate them.

Bruner's influence today.

Pavlov (behaviourist theorist), 1849–1936

After observing that dogs salivate when they see their food coming, Ivan Pavlov did experiments to see whether they could be classically conditioned. Over a period of time, he rang a bell before he fed two dogs. Eventually, the dogs would salivate at the sound of the bell alone, as this had become a conditioned response. He later stopped sounding the bell before he fed the dogs, and found that they gradually stopped responding to it with salivation. The conditioned response was 'extinct'.

Watson (behaviourist theorist), 1878–1958

John B Watson was born in 1878. He carried on where Pavlov's work left off, but applied it to humans to show how it's possible to classically condition humans as well as dogs. His experiments to create a phobia in a child – 'Little Albert' – to prove that fear of animals is learned and not inherent, are very well known. Albert was fond of a white rat in the laboratory and would happily be with him. Watson discovered that he could scare Albert and make him cry by hitting a steel bar with a hammer behind his head. He began putting Albert on a table with the rat, then hitting the steel bar. After seven cycles of this, he began putting Albert on the table and introducing just the rat. Albert was afraid of the rat and would be desperate to get away. He had learned to associate the rat with his fear and terror of the loud noise, and he was now also afraid of rats. There was debate about how ethical this experiment was at the time and his mother removed him from the hospital where the experiments took place shortly after. These days, of course, such traumatic experiments would clearly be considered unethical and unacceptable.

Skinner (behaviourist theorist), 1904–90

Burrus Skinner developed a theory known as 'operant conditioning'. He demonstrated how this worked in experiments conducted with rats. He gave rats food as a reward when they displayed behaviour he wanted, in this case pressing a lever. He did not feed them otherwise. The rats learned to repeat the rewarded behaviour. They would systematically press the lever and then wait at the position in the cage where the food was dispensed. He called this 'positive reinforcement'. He also taught them not to display behaviour he did not want – he gave them electric shocks when they entered a specific area of a maze he created. They learned to avoid the area.

Skinner's theory of positive reinforcement is still widely used today in the behaviour management of children. We reward children with praise, attention and sometimes tangible items such as stickers when they behave well, to encourage them to repeat the desirable behaviour.

Skinner's influence today.

Bandura (social learning theorist), 1925–

Albert Bandura's social learning theory is that people learn from one another, via observation, imitation, and modelling. He believes that this applies to observing other people's attitudes as well as their behaviour (actions). He said, 'Learning would be exceedingly laborious, not to mention hazardous, if people had to rely solely on the effects of their own actions to inform them what to do. Fortunately, most human behaviour is learned observationally through modelling: from observing others, one forms an idea of how new behaviours are performed, and on later occasions this information serves as a guide for action.' Bandura identifies certain conditions as conducive to effective modelling, including these:

1. **Attention:** various factors increase or decrease the amount of attention paid, including distinctiveness, complexity, functional value.

2. **Retention** (remembering what was paid attention to): including mental images, motor rehearsal (doing an action, e.g. if you try folding a nappy yourself when you see it done, you're more likely to remember how to do it later).

3. **Reproduction:** including physical capability to copy what has been seen, and own opinion of the reproduction.

4. **Motivation:** having a good reason to imitate.

Bandura's work interestingly links behaviourist and cognitive learning theories, because it draws together attention, memory and motivation.

Practitioners are expected to be good role models for children, and children are encouraged to 'learn through doing'. It's generally agreed that by changing existing aspects of negative influence on children, positive outcomes can be realised. For instance, if an angry parent shouts around the house, a child is likely to exhibit similar behaviour when frustrated. But if the adult can learn better anger management strategies and model those instead, this may have a positive impact on the child's behaviour.

Bandura's influence today.

Have a go!

You can watch a five-minute film online, in which Bandura outlines his famous 'Bobo doll' experiment. It shows actual clips from the experiment of children imitating aggressive behaviour they saw modelled on the doll. It's fascinating to watch. Visit **www.youtube.com** and search for 'Bobo doll'.

Freud (psychoanalytic theorist), 1856–1939

Sigmund Freud grew up in Vienna before moving to England. He developed the 'psychoanalytical theory'. This theory was the most influential theory of the 20th century.

Freud thought that the experiences we have in childhood are stored in our unconscious minds. He believed that these experiences are so significant that they influence the way we feel as adults and that these feelings unconsciously direct our behaviour. In other words, according to Freud, we may not know why we behave in certain ways, but it will be due to unconscious feelings that stem from our childhood experiences. Freud's theory gave us the idea that childhood experiences are key factors in the development of personality, particularly if traumatic events occur in childhood.

Freud developed what he called 'psychoanalysis'. This was a talking therapy, through which he believed he could help people to identify their unconscious feelings, and to understand them. He came to believe that his therapy could help people to change the way they feel and behave.

Freud believed that humans have three separate and conflicting aspects to their minds as follows:

- **Id**

  The id is someone's animal instinct, responsible for their need to satisfy basic desires. In other words, it is the part that demands 'I want...'.

- **Superego**

  This represents someone's ideal of what sort of person they would like to be. This is based on demands from parents (currently or from childhood), and demands from society.

- **Ego**

  The ego is the force that regulates between the id and the superego. It tries to resolve conflicts so that the id is satisfied within the limits of what the superego will allow. The ego is sometimes called the 'reality force'.

Freud said that a person needed to have a mental balance between id, ego and superego in order to behave normally. He also believed that people go through 'psychosexual stages of development' called oral (aged birth–18 months), anal (aged 18 months–3 years), phallic (aged 3–6 years), latency (aged 6 years–puberty) and genital (aged puberty–adulthood). Freud believed that problems in passing through these stages could lead to problems in adulthood; for example, if a child didn't receive sufficient nourishment in the oral stage they may grow up to be overly dependent on others, as a nursing infant would be.

Have a go!

You can find out more about Freud from the Freud Museum in London by visiting **www.freud.org.uk**

Freud's theories have been much criticised over the years, although they are still some of the best known. Some of his key working methods have stood the test of time though. We highly value 'talking therapies' to help people deal with feelings and traumatic events that stem from their childhood, for example, many child abuse victims don't disclose the abuse until they are adults (some never disclose at all). His work on the way in which the unconscious mind is expressed is also interesting, and dovetails with more modern work on body language.

Freud's influence today.

Maslow (humanist theorist), 1908–70

Abraham Maslow was born in 1908. He studied people's motivation to do things, and developed a theory that humans are unable to fulfil their potential (which he called 'self-actualisation') unless their basic needs are met. He developed a 'hierarchy of needs', which is shown below. It has five layers, and starts at the bottom with the most basic of all, the 'physiological needs' – the main needs of the body as he saw them. Maslow concluded that until the basic needs identified in his hierarchy are met, a person

Self-actualisation: acceptance of facts, acceptance of self, non-prejudice, morality, creativity, problem solving, objectivity

Aesthetic needs: beauty in art and symmetry, order, balance, form

Cognitive needs: knowledge and understanding, exploration, meaning

Esteem needs: self-esteem, confidence, respect for others, self-respect, achievement

Love and belonging: giving and receiving love, affection, trust and acceptance – family, friendship, sexual intimacy

Safety needs: physical safety, a home, safety from psychological threat (e.g. fear of the dark or the unknown), health, routine/familiarity, employment

Physiological needs: food, water, air, rest, sleep, activity, sex, excretion, temperature

Maslow's hierarchy of needs.

is unable to achieve the pinnacle of the chart, self-actualisation. He said that not having basic needs met created a 'deficiency' in the person. He did not expect the majority of people to fully reach their potential.

> Maslow's hierarchy of needs is represented in the accepted ethos that children's basic needs have to be met before they can fulfil their learning and development potential. This includes physical needs such as good food to eat and warmth, as well as their emotional needs, such as love and protection, which we recognise as leading to good self-esteem and self-confidence, which boost children's outcomes in many other areas. You'll learn more about how positive actions can lead to positive outcomes in Unit CYP 3.7.

Maslow's influence today.

Unit CYP 3.7 Understand how to support positive outcomes for children and young people

Bowlby (attachment theorist), 1907–90

John Bowlby carried out extensive research into attachment, which he defined as a lasting 'psychological connectedness between people'. Bowlby thought that the experiences children have of attachments when they're young would influence their development and also their behaviour in later life, particularly in terms of their relationships.

He identified four characteristics of attachment:

1. **Proximity maintenance**: babies and children (the attached) want to be near the people they're attached to (the attachment figures).

2. **Safe haven**: the attached will return to an attachment figure for comfort and safety if they feel threatened.

3. **Secure base**: an attachment figure acts as a base of security. The attached feels confident to leave the base to explore the surrounding environment.

4. **Separation distress**: anxiety felt by the attached when the attachment figure is absent.

Bowlby also noted that attachments have a survival component – children's attachments to adults who love them generally keep them safe from harm.

> The attachment theory has been accepted. This is evidenced by the EYFS Welfare requirement that early years settings must operate a key worker system so that young children form key attachments to meet their emotional needs when they are away from the care and reassuring presence of their parent or primary carer.

Bowlby's influence today.

Neuro-scientists

New theories about the way in which human beings think, remember and learn are being developed in light of new technology that has emerged in recent years. Using advanced imaging techniques, neuro-scientists (brain scientists) can now look directly inside living, functioning brains. They can actually watch what happens when people are thinking, remembering and learning. Interesting new research is being carried out around the world. Practitioners are advised to keep themselves up to date with developments. Professional journals are a good source of new information as it is released.

See also Learning Outcome 1, Unit CYPOP 1 Work with babies and young children to promote their learning and development

Frameworks to support development

In recent years, frameworks to support children's learning and development (such as the Early Years Foundation Stage that applies in England), have brought together a range of theories in a combined, modern approach. For example, there's clear influence here from Bowlby's attachment theory as mentioned above, as well as shades of Piaget (e.g. that children should have opportunities to make discoveries for themselves through child-initiated play).

You'll learn more about frameworks that support learning and development in:
Unit EYMP 1 Context and principles for early years provision
Unit EYMP 2 Promote learning and development in the early years

Social pedagogy

Social pedagogy is a term used to describe a holistic way of working, originally founded on humanist values. It combines core theories, concepts and approaches from sociology, psychology, education, philosophy, medical sciences and social work. A core value is that bringing up children is a responsibility to be shared by the parents and society as a whole. There's a strong concern with learning, well-being and inclusion into society for all families. Social pedagogy promotes children as 'active agents' in learning, and competent, resourceful human beings.

You can find out more at **www.thewhocarestrust.org.uk** and search for 'social pedagogy'. You can also follow the links on the left of the web page to 'Sam's story' to read a practical example of a child's journey through the care system.

Play theory history

There are many additional theories on play, and some fascinating research and experiments underpin them. Learning more about these is beneficial to any practitioner. An overview of the following is given in Unit EYMP 1 Learning Outcome 1:

- Friedrich Froebel, who opened the very first kindergarten in 1837.

- Rudolf Steiner, who encouraged his students to learn for the pleasure of learning, rather than for tests or exams.

- Margaret McMillan, who worked in the inner city when there was widespread poverty. She campaigned tirelessly for children, for improved health care and nursery education.

- Maria Montessori, the first woman in Italy to qualify as a physician, who worked with children who had learning difficulties.

- Susan Isaacs, who was interested in what effect leaving her nursery and starting school had on children – she concluded that young children need to move around freely.

- Reggio Emilia, a town in Italy, where a programme of early childhood education was developed, based on 'socio-constructivist' theories, including those of Vygotsky, Piaget and Bruner.

- High/Scope, an educational approach founded in the USA that grew from a programme for students who were gifted and/or talented.

Parten's five stages of play

In 1932, researcher Mildred Parten was studying the play of children aged between 2 and 5 years of age. Despite her research being carried out almost 80 years ago, Mildred Parten's findings are still valid today and are generally accepted. She focused on the children's social interactions during their play. She identified five stages of play that children pass through:

- solitary play

- spectator (or 'onlooker') play

- parallel play

- associative play

- co-operative play.

Further details about each of the play types are given on page 113.

Practical example

Felix wants to watch

Shobna is a new learner practitioner on placement. She's at the water tray with a group of children. She notices 2-year-old Felix watching nearby. She invites Felix to come and play. He doesn't. Shobna doesn't want to just leave him there. She thinks he must want to join in but is too shy. She tries hard to persuade him again but he wanders off.

Question
Shobna inviting Felix to play was fine. But what should she have done when he didn't want to join in? Give the reason for your answer.

Solitary play
Solitary play occurs when a child plays alone, completely independent of others. Very young children only play alone.

Spectator play
The word 'spectator' means someone who is watching. Spectator play occurs when a child watches another child or children at play but does not join in. The spectator either will not be playing themselves, or will be doing a different activity to the one they are watching. This is sometimes called 'onlooker play'. Toddlers can often be observed watching others from a distance.

Parallel play
This stage occurs from approximately 2 years of age. At this stage, children play alongside others and may share resources, but they remain engrossed in their own activity. Children have companionship but, even in the middle of a group, remain independent in their play. They do not look at other children.

Associative play
This stage generally occurs from between the ages of 3 and 4 years. During the associative play stage, children share resources and talk to each other. But they each have their own **play agenda** (their own idea of what they want to do). The children don't coordinate their play objectives or interests. This

means there will be trouble! Conflicts arise when children have separate ideas that others do not share. Children especially have trouble when trying to play imaginatively together.

key term
Play agenda what a child wants to achieve in their play.

Co-operative play
The co-operative play stage occurs when children fully interact, and can participate together in play with specific goals in mind. They can play their own imaginary games, organising themselves into roles, and so on; for example: 'You be the doctor and I'll be the patient...'. The older children in Parten's study were capable of co-operative play from the ages of 4 to 5 years.

Although Parten's work was with children aged 2 to 5 years, you will find that you can observe older children playing in the ways she describes. Once children achieve the next stage of play, they will still at times play in the ways they have before. For instance, all children like to have the personal space to play alone sometimes. Most children will also stand back and watch others without joining in at times, especially in new circumstances. Older children will be seen playing alongside each other with little interaction when engrossed in an art or craft activity, such as drawing or making jewellery. Because of this, some people like to think of the stages of play more as 'phases' of play, because children phase in and out of them.

Bob Hughes is a leading modern theorist who studied older children and young people's play extensively, and identified different types of play, known as the 'taxonomy of play types'. It's widely used within play work and youth work. You can find out more with a quick web search.

Current accepted thinking on play

Here's a brief summary of play theory that's broadly accepted and promoted in the majority of modern UK settings today.

Play provides children with the opportunity to interact with both adults and children, at whatever level is appropriate for them. This helps children gain the social skills they need to get on with others and become part of a group. Children learn and practise a wide range of skills when they're playing – how ride a tricycle for example. They also make discoveries and learn concepts – for example, at the water tray, they may learn that pebbles sink. The activity, game or experience will finish when children stop playing, but the learning will eventually be remembered. These are all long-term benefits of play, which develop over time. Other long-term benefits gained through play include increasing:

- independence
- self-esteem
- knowledge and understanding
- well-being, health and development
- creativity
- capacity to learn.

Children make discoveries and learn through their play.

The short-term benefits of play occur at the time a child is playing. They include the opportunity to:

- enjoy freedom
- have fun
- test boundaries
- explore risk
- exercise choice
- exercise control over their body
- exercise control over their actions and emotions.

Social skills and relationships

Play acts as a bridge to social skills and relationships. Young children need to gain skills such as:

- sharing
- taking turns
- cooperating
- making and maintaining friendships
- responding to people in an appropriate way.

By grouping children thoughtfully and being a good social role model, adults can enhance children's learning about how to behave sociably when they play. Socialising opportunities include: circle games; rhymes and songs; packing-away time, with all children encouraged to participate; snack/meal times, with children helping to set up, serve and clear away; pretend play in pairs or groups; any activity where there are limited resources that the children need to share (e.g. painting at easels or playing at water and sand trays, board games and table top activities).

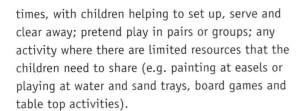

The stages of child development influence children and young people's play needs and behaviours. Practitioners must remember that all children develop at different rates and so their play needs and behaviours will also vary. For example, children tend to have different interests and be drawn to different types of play as they grow up and develop, and the amount of independence that children are comfortable with increases over time. A good knowledge and understanding of children's development is essential to the provision of good, appropriate play opportunities.

Barriers to access

Some children and young people may experience barriers that affect their access to play. Practitioners must take action to identify and remove barriers to ensure that all children are given equal opportunities to play. Adaptations may be made to the way an activity is offered to allow everyone to participate. For instance, other children may play parachute games kneeling down so a child who uses a wheelchair can join in.

Identifying play needs and preferences

It's important for practitioners to identify the play needs and preferences of the children and young people they work with. This enables practitioners to provide play opportunities that will meet the needs of children and young people and promote their development. It also enables practitioners to provide experiences that all will enjoy and will find engaging and interesting. This increases children

and young people's motivation to participate in play experiences. Practitioners can collect information on play needs and preferences by using the following methods:

■ researching theory and practice

■ observing children/young people at play

■ interacting with children/young people.

Ask Miranda!

Q At my holiday club, the children can already get out any of the resources and play as they want to with them. Do I still need to worry about their play needs and preferences?

A **All settings should consult with children and young people about their play needs and preferences. This becomes increasingly important as children grow up. Through consultation, practitioners can interact with children and young people, finding out what they want and need from their play. It's also useful to draw out their own ideas about resources and materials they'd like to experience that aren't currently available, and activities they're interested in that aren't already offered. They may surprise you with their creativeness!**

The relationship between play and learning

Children learn through play. Play is an effective vehicle for children's learning because:

■ children enjoy playing

■ children are intrinsically motivated to play (they are internally driven)

- children can make their own discoveries through play

- children can initiate their own activities and explore their own thoughts and ideas through play

- children can actively learn through play – the learning is a real, vivid experience

- play is necessary for children's well-being – under the UN Convention on the Rights of the Child, children have a right to play.

LEARNING OUTCOME 3

FOCUS ON

...understanding how to monitor children and young people's development and interventions that should take place if this is not following the expected pattern

In this section you'll learn about the factors to take into account when assessing, and about assessing development in a number of areas. You'll also learn about assessment methods and developing a plan to meet the needs of a child or young person. This links with Assessment Criteria **3.1, 3.2, 3.3, 3.4.**

Monitoring and assessment

Monitoring and assessing children and young people's development enables us to notice when children are not progressing as expected. In Learning Outcome 1, you learned that although children develop at different rates, significant delays in one area or many delays in several areas, is reason for concern. Checks should be made to see whether there are underlying causes for the delay, such as an impairment. This enables appropriate support for the child's development and welfare to be put into place. When practitioners and professionals take action in this

way, it's referred to as 'intervention'. You'll learn more about this below.

Types of monitoring and assessment

There are several methods used for monitoring development, as we'll explore below.

Observation and assessment

In early years settings, practitioners observe children's play and behaviour. They use their observation findings and their knowledge of the expected rates and sequence of development to assess children's progress in terms of learning and development. This is recorded on observation and assessment documents. Over time, these build into a good picture of the children's learning and development trajectory. Because all areas of development will be covered, specific aspects of development, such as fine motor skills, can be tracked within the bigger, holistic picture. This is important, because it helps to pinpoint areas of difficulty for children.

Link Up!

You'll learn about methods of child observation and how these inform assessment and planning in Unit CYP 3.2 Promote child and young person development

Assessment frameworks

Assessment frameworks set out how learning and development should be assessed in relation to curriculum frameworks. Examples that apply in

England include the National Curriculum and the EYFS. Detailed information about assessing in line with assessment frameworks is given in Unit EYMP 2, Learning Outcome 1.

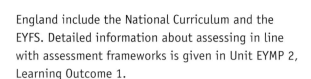

Unit EYMP 2 Promote learning and development in the early years

Standard measurements

Standard measurements are used by some professionals when monitoring and assessing children's development, in a similar way to how practitioners use the rates and sequence of development. The usage of standard measurements includes:

- growth assessments (e.g. height, weight, head circumference)
- auditory assessments (e.g. levels of response)
- cognitive aptitude tests (widely carried out in schools)
- reasoning assessments (carried out by psychologists).

Information from parents or carers and colleagues

It's good practice to collect as much information as possible when monitoring and assessing children's learning and development. Parents or carers generally know their child best, and have much to contribute. They'll usually spend the most time with the child, and will also be aware of the learning that takes place outside the setting, and how the child behaves in a range of contexts, including, crucially, at home. The way a child plays and interacts will be different when they're at home compared to when they're in a busy setting, with lots of peers around them. It's also a good way of involving parents in both the setting and the child's learning.

Key workers generally take the lead in monitoring and assessing their key children, but colleagues who also work with the child should also be consulted, as they may have different perceptions.

It's good practice for colleagues to occasionally contribute to child observations, as they will have more objectivity than the person who knows the child well. There's value in both familiarity and objectivity, so this combined approach is beneficial.

Reasons why development might not be following expected patterns

In the vast majority of cases when a child's development isn't following expected patterns, it is due to one or more of the influences shown on the diagram on page 118:

We'll look at these in turn:

- **Disability**
  This may prevent development in one or more areas. You'll read more about this on page 118.

- **Emotional influences**
  If children are not emotionally settled and secure, their development can be affected. Children need secure, loving attachments with key people in their lives in order to thrive emotionally. Good self-esteem and self-confidence are also important as they affect children's participation and levels of engagement with learning activities. If children are depressed, emotional development can be severely affected.

■ Physical influences

As you learned in Learning Outcome 2, genetics impacts on children's development, including their physical growth and physical strength. For instance, some children take extra time to develop the strength they need in their legs to be able to stand alone.

■ Environmental influences

These link with your learning in Learning Outcome 2 about the external factors that can affect development, both positively and negatively. These include poverty and education.

■ Cultural influences

Cultural beliefs and values influence the way that families bring up their children, and this in turn can have an impact on development. For example, different cultures have differing ideas about what it is acceptable for young people to experience and what decisions they may make for themselves. This can have an impact on social development in terms of independence and confidence. Or, in some

Link Up!

This is explored in more depth in Unit CYP 3.7 Understand how to support positive outcomes for children and young people

cultures, education for girls isn't highly valued, and so girls may not have the same learning opportunities as their peers.

■ Social influences

The type of upbringing received by children and young people can influence development. Whether a child has positive role models to learn from and whether a family supports learning and development through helping with homework or simply playing and talking with a child frequently, all plays a part. Learning and development can also be affected for a period by family circumstances such as divorce.

■ Learning needs

Children and young people with specific learning needs may require a range of additional support with certain aspects of their learning and development – with reading, writing or mathematics for instance. Dyslexia is an example of a specific learning need for which support is required.

■ Communication skills

As we established in Learning Outcome 1, communication development is strongly linked to social, emotional and behaviour development, and intellectual/cognitive development. So if children experience

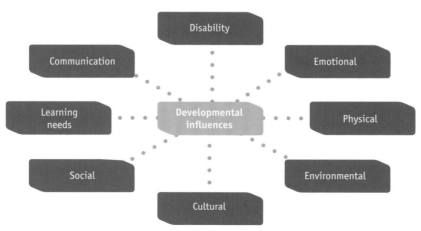

Developmental influences.

difficulties with their communication, there can be a wide-ranging impact on their overall development. As children grow up, problems can increase if frustration at not understanding others, or not being able to express themselves, continues to build and to affect behaviour. Additional problems with reading and writing may also become apparent.

Did you know?

It isn't common, but occasionally a reason for a child not attaining the usual pattern of development cannot be identified, even after professionals have investigated the influences on development thoroughly. One possibility is that it's in the child's genetic makeup to have a slow start to their learning.

Models of and attitudes to disability

The 'social model of disability' and the 'medical model of disability' are explained in Unit CYP 3.7 and Unit CYPOP 6. The benefits of positive attitudes to disability are also explored.

Unit CYP 3.7 Understand how to support positive outcomes for children and young people

Unit CYPOP 6 Support disabled children and young people and those with specific requirements

Different types of interventions

A number of professionals may intervene to support children's development, including:

- social workers
- speech, language and communications therapists
- psychologists
- psychiatrists
- youth justice services
- physiotherapists
- nurse specialists
- additional learning support workers
- health visitors.

You can read more about these key roles on page 256, and pages 369–371. Also see the role of the SENCO within settings, which is outlined in Unit CYPOP 6 page 512.

Assistive technology

For information about how technology can assist disabled people to carry out functions or tasks that may otherwise be difficult or impossible for them, see page 288.

Unit CYPOP 6 Support disabled children and young people and those with specific requirements

LEARNING OUTCOME 4

FOCUS ON

...understanding the importance of early intervention to support the speech, language and communication needs of children and young people

In this section you'll learn about the importance of early identification of speech, language and communication (SLC) delays and disorders. You'll also learn how multi-agency teams work to support SLC, and about activities that can be used to support SLC development. This links with Assessment Criteria **4.1, 4.2, 4.3.**

The developmental importance of speech, language and communication

Speech, language and communication (SLC) is a fundamental part of children's cognitive development, because language helps us to think. It's also key to children and young people's social and emotional development, as it's the foundation of their relationships with others, and the primary way in which they express themselves.

▶▶Link Up!◀◀

This is fully covered in Unit EYMP 5 Support children's speech, language and communication

Effects of SLC delays and disorders

SLC delays and disorders are not just about children being held back with their speaking and listening skills. Such delays and disorders can potentially affect children in different, wide-reaching ways, as outlined in Unit EYMP 5, Learning Outcome 1. Because SLC underpins children's cognitive development and their social and emotional development, the knock-on effect on their development as a whole is considerable. If children don't receive adequate support, they're at risk of serious long-term problems developing, including those shown on the diagram below.

Early identification

Early identification of SLC delays and disorders enable children to get the professional support they need

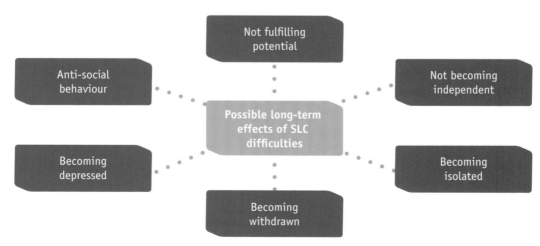

Possible long-term effects of SLC difficulties.

as soon as possible, limiting the effect on their development and everyday experiences. In some cases, support can enable a difficulty to be partially or entirely overcome – stammers are a good example of this, as are some SLC delays. In cases where the difficulty is likely to continue, support can enable different communication methods to be introduced early on, such as using Makaton (a basic form of sign language often used with those who have learning difficulties, and with younger children). The earlier children start communicating, the better.

Good practice

SLC delays are often linked to other problems, such as learning difficulties. So early identification of SLC can lead to the early identification of other problems too if they have not already been detected, and the child can receive the support they need.

The support of multi-agency teams

Once a SLC difficulty has been detected (often by parents or practitioners), the first port of call is usually the family GP, or health visitor. Hearing and/or visual tests are often carried out. Sometimes this will be because hearing and/or visual impairments are suspected, but often it is just to rule them out. It's at this stage that children are referred on to a speech, language and communication specialist, who will make an assessment. In some cases, particularly if the SLC difficulties are linked with learning difficulties, the child will also be referred to an educational psychologist for an assessment.

Once the initial assessments have been carried out, the professionals involved will make recommendations for the best way to support the child. To ensure that the child receives the best possible support, this will involve a partnership (in other words, multi-agency) approach. Professionals, parents and practitioners will

agree how they'll work together, and how the support will be provided.

This may include a SLC therapist advising the setting on activities they can plan to support the child, as well as how to adapt their working practices to utilise any alternative forms of communication that are put in place. You can read about these in Unit EYMP 5.

Good practice

Practitioners may share their observations and assessments of the child with professionals, or a professional may visit the setting to observe the child interacting with peers themselves. Full information on multi-agency working is given in Unit CYP 3.6.

▶▶▶ Link Up! ◀◀◀

Unit EYMP 5 Support children's speech, language and communication
Unit CYP 3.6 Working together for the benefit of children and young people

Supporting SLC development through activities and play

Humans learn SLC through interaction, and for children that means plenty of opportunities for speaking and listening and lots of stimulating play. We can offer a range of activities that promote SLC development (remember that this is strongly connected to social, emotional and cognitive development). It's important that the activities are fun and play-based, so that children are motivated to participate. SLC therapists will often recommend that parents make sharing rhymes and songs part of their everyday activities. This can be a fun, playful, shared experience, carried out frequently – at bath time, in the car and so on. It's much better than just getting children to repeat sentences in isolation, which in terms of giving them practice making certain sounds, would fulfil the same purpose.

Many activities can be used to successfully encourage communication through play.

Some encourage talking, others listening, and some encourage non-verbal communication.

Touch, mark-making and pretend play are all valuable ways to encourage children to communicate through different media. The list of possible activities is extensive, but some ideas are listed here:

- role play with dressing-up clothes, a home corner and other props

- play opportunities with dolls, puppets and soft toys

- small-world play with resources such as a farmyard and animals, or a garage and vehicles

- books and stories

- nursery rhymes and songs

- musical instruments

- basic playground and circle games such as 'Ring-a-ring-o-roses'

- use of toy phones and walkie-talkies

- art activities featuring mark-making, such as painting and colouring

- playing side by side at the water tray, sharing resources

- interesting objects to explore, such as items that scrunch, squelch, rattle or jingle

- ball games between two or more players (rolling, kicking, throwing, etc.).

You can find further play activities to encourage communication in Learning Outcome 2, CYPOP 1 Work with babies and young children to promote their development and learning

How an adult works to support a child can bring a whole new SLC focus to an activity. Providing a good range of activities to stimulate all areas of development allows children to explore a range of interests. Practitioners can share these with children, using the interests as a topic of conversation. Joining in alongside and talking with children about their activities helps to develop relationships as well as communication skills. It also assists cognitive development. With experience, it becomes a very natural, intuitive part of a practitioner's role.

You can read about running commentary in Learning Outcome 4, Unit CYPOP 1 Work with babies and young children to promote their development and learning

Practical example

Scrunching and squelching!

Cooper works at a pre-school. Today, he's filled up the tray usually used for water with a range of interesting items that scrunch or squelch. The activity will be available for all the children to explore, and Cooper's got a feeling that it will be a big hit! He's also planning to spend some time at the tray with his key child Lexy, who has a SLC delay. He knows she loves sensory play, and he's planning to join in alongside her, to both introduce descriptive language and draw it out from her, all while she's playing.

Question
What sort of language might Cooper use with Lexy?

Ask Miranda!

A Will I have to do any special sort of planning to support children with SLC delays and disorders?

Q Strategies to support a specific child's SLC will be recorded on their Individual Education Plan (IEP), which will be devised by the setting with input from the SENCO, key worker, parents and carers and professionals who are also part of the partnership supporting the child. In early years settings, the Early Years Action and Early Action Plus intervention frameworks will also be used.

▶▶Link Up!◀◀

You can read about all of these strategies in detail in Unit CYPOP 6 Support disabled children and young people and those with specific requirements

 LEARNING OUTCOME **5**

FOCUS ON
...understanding the potential effects of transitions on children and young people's development

In this section you'll learn about the factors to take into account when assessing, and about assessing development in a number of areas. You'll also learn about assessment methods and developing a plan to meet the needs of a child or young person. This links with Assessment Criteria 5.1, 5.2.

Different types of transitions

Transitions are periods of change that generally involve a loss of familiar people, and associated anxiety. This includes:

- **Emotional transitions, affected by personal experience**
  For example, bereavement, entering or leaving care

- **Physical transitions**
  For example, moving to a new educational establishment, or a new home/locality

- **Physiological transitions**
  Puberty, or long-term medical conditions

- **Intellectual transitions**
  Moving from pre-school to primary school, or from primary school to secondary school.

To learn about the effects of these types of transitions and the strategies practitioners can initiate to help children and young people cope with them, please read Unit CYP 3.2, Learning Outcome 6 now.

Unit CYP 3.2 Promote child and young person development

The effect of positive relationships during periods of transition

Because children and young people can be expected to feel the effects of stress and anxiety during transitional periods, the care and support of those closest to them is of key importance. Close, positive **existing** relationships will support transitioning children and young people through:

- providing them with security – some things might be changing, but they'll always have some key, stable relationships to rely on and to return to emotionally

- giving them someone to talk to and express their feelings with – this is hugely helpful as you will read in Unit CYP 3.2

- understanding that there may be some changes in the child or young person's behaviour due to stress, and making allowances as appropriate

- bolstering their confidence in advance of the transition, especially if strategies to help prepare the child or young person are carried out together (e.g. a visit to a new setting)

- providing them with moral support at the actual time of transition (e.g. taking them to school on the first day, staying overnight at the hospital with them).

Forming **new** positive relationships connected with the transition (e.g. making new friends, getting to know their new key worker or teacher) will also be hugely beneficial, because:

- fear of 'not knowing anyone' and being isolated or lonely is often a central concern for children and young people who are transitioning

Did you know?

You can help children and young people to adjust to transitions by introducing them to relevant new people early on. Teachers often visit new children starting school at home first of all, so there's a chance for some one-to-one 'getting to know you'.

As you've learned, transitional periods often involve the loss of people who are familiar to the transitioning child or young person's life. Some relationships will change significantly, but would not be expected to end, as in the Practical example on page 125.

- it's reassuring to feel that they have people they can turn to for help and support in the new situation

- once they have a friend, some transitions can start to feel fun, or like an adventure

- in the case of practitioners/professionals, someone will be monitoring how the child or young person is coping with the transition, and will be on hand to help them adjust.

Practical example

Sean goes to college

Sean will be leaving home for the first time to go to college in a different area. This marks entry into a completely new phase of life. He'll be making a big shift from dependence in terms of having his basic needs met by his parents (food, shelter, care, protection) to self-reliance. The dynamic between Sean and his parents will change in response. Sean's looking forward to his college course, but he's got mixed feelings about the transition. He intends to spend the college holiday back at home with his parents.

Question

What do you think Sean's 'mixed feelings' might be?

In the next example, the children involved may arrange to stay in touch via phone or perhaps email, but adult support will be needed for them maintain a friendship in which they spend time together.

Practical example

Sammie and Kayla

Sammie and Kayla have been best friends since they started primary school. Sammie lives in town and Kayla lives in an outlying rural area, so the girls don't see much of each other outside of school. But five days a week, they're virtually inseparable. In eight weeks' time, they'll start different secondary schools. Kayla gets tearful when she talks about it. Sammie doesn't want to talk about it at all.

Question

What would you suggest their parents do to help the girls cope with the transition?

In the following example, a nursery nurse has put plans in place to enable her relationship with a key child to tail off gradually.

Practical example

Cherry's plan

Jayden is 4. He's been going to his nursery for four days a week since he was 3 months old. His key worker, Cherry, has worked with him since he was 2, and Jayden loves her. He's leaving the setting in August, then he's having a holiday at home with his mum. In September, he'll start primary school. He's only going to go in the morning for the first week, then he'll start full-time. During his holiday, Jayden's going to go to buy his school uniform. Cherry and his mum have agreed that he'll pop into the nursery to say hello and to show it to her. So on his last day at nursery, Cherry and Jayden can say 'see you soon' rather than 'goodbye'. Next, they're planning for Jayden to pop in during his first week at school (on one of the free afternoons) to tell Cherry all about it. After this, they'll play things by ear. It's likely they'll leave the ending flexible, with Cherry saying something like 'Come and see us again some time, won't you?' Then, perhaps Jayden will pop in to give her a Christmas card in a couple of months' time.

Question
Why is this better than Jayden saying goodbye on his last day at nursery and leaving it at that?

How are things going?

▶ Progress Check

1. What is the difference between the expected rate of development and the expected sequence of development, and why is this important? (1.2)

2. Explain how development is influenced by three of each of the following:

   a) personal factors and b) external factors. (2.1)

3. Explain how three learning and development theories of your choice influence modern practice today. (2.3)

4. What are assessment frameworks? (3.1)

5. What are standard measurements, and who might use them? (3.1)

6. Explain how disability may affect development. (3.3)

7. Why is early identification of speech, language and communication delays and disorders important? (4.1)

8. Give an example of four different types of activities that can be used to support children's speech, language and communication. (4.3)

9. What is likely to be the effect on children and young people of having positive relationships during periods of transition? (5.2)

Are you ready for assessment?

CACHE

Set task:

■ An in-depth task covering fourteen assessment criteria, in which you prepare a folder on development to be used for reference purposes within your setting.

You can prepare by following all the links given in the Unit and reading the additional material – you will need to draw on this knowledge to complete the assignment.

Edexel

In preparation for assessment of this Unit, you may like to collect together documents you have completed when monitoring children's development, to use as evidence.

City & Guilds

You must complete the mandatory Assignment 023. This has five tasks, each one relating to one of the five Learning Outcomes. It entails completing the tables provided, writing brief reports and answering questions. You can prepare by revisiting the development tables in this Unit, to ensure you fully understand the sequence and rate of development for children and young people.

UNIT 3.2
Promote child and young person development

LEARNING OUTCOMES

The learning outcomes you will meet in this unit are:

1 Be able to assess the development needs of children or young people and prepare a development plan

2 Be able to promote the development of children or young people

3 Be able to support the provision of environments and services that promote the development of children or young people

4 Understand how working practices can impact on the development of children and young people

5 Be able to support children and young people's positive behaviour

6 Be able to support children and young people experiencing transitions

INTRODUCTION

Much of a practitioner's work is connected with promoting the development of children and young people. So your learning in this unit is central to your qualification. As such, there are many links to other units throughout the following pages, which you will need to dip into as part as your study towards this unit.

LEARNING OUTCOME

FOCUS ON

...being able to assess the development needs of children or young people and prepare a development plan

In this section you'll learn about the factors to take into account when assessing, and also about assessing development in a number of areas. You'll also learn about assessment methods and developing a plan to meet the needs of a child or young person. This links with Assessment Criteria **1.1, 1.2, 1.3, 1.4.**

Assessing development of children and young people

There are number of factors to take into account when assessing development, including the following:

- **Confidentiality and parental permission**
  As the primary carers and guardians of their children, parents have the right to decide what personal information is collected and recorded about their child. It is essential that practitioners obtain written permission from parents authorising them to carry out observations and to keep relevant documentation on record. Many settings ask for parental permission on the registration form that parents complete prior to their child attending the setting. This must be signed and dated. The details of observation should be kept confidential unless withholding information would affect the well-being of the child. So it's important that you handle and store assessment documents and notes in line with the setting's confidentiality policy. This links with your learning about confidentiality in Unit SHC 31. It's essential that students also gain permission

from workplace supervisors *before* carrying out observations. Supervisors will probably ask to see your completed observation and the child's family may also want to have a copy. You must also protect the child's identity. This may be done by changing the name, or using another way of identifying them, e.g. 'target child' or 'child A' or 'child 1'.

▶▶▶Link Up!◀◀◀

SHC 31, LO 4 Be able to apply principles and practices relating to confidentiality

- **Children's wishes and feelings**
  You should respect children's wishes and feelings throughout the assessment process. They should not be made to feel under pressure to 'perform' or get things right. If they become reluctant or upset, it is often appropriate to delay the assessment to another time. You should also be respectful in terms of the tone and language that you use when recording your assessments. It can help to think about how the parent is likely to feel when they read it. However, this is not intended to prevent you from making accurate assessments.

Respect children's wishes and feelings throughout the assessment process.

■ **Ethnic, linguistic and cultural background**

You need to consider these factors in your assessments in order to ensure their accuracy. For instance, a child may not participate in completing a task or activity, not because they don't understand the concept or because they're not interested in it, but because they don't understand the language being used. For instance, a child learning English as an additional language may not join in when number operations are performed during songs, (e.g. 'We had five little monkeys, and we took away one, so how many are left?') because they are unfamiliar with the mathematical terms. If they were asked the same question in their home language, they may be keen to work out the answer. Ethnic and cultural background may have a similar impact on a child's experiences. For instance, many of the older children you work with may be used to a lively, vibrant learning environment within which they're encouraged to ask questions and put forward their opinion. But in some cultures it's considered socially unacceptable for children to question adults about the things that they say. However, it doesn't necessarily follow that a child lacks critical thinking skills.

■ **Disability or specific requirements**

You should take disability or specific requirements into account when you're planning your assessment methods, and ensure that children and young people have the support that they need. This may influence a) the assessment methods that you select, b) whether specific support of yourself or another adult is provided, c) whether adaptations or special equipment are made available. If these things are not addressed, there's a danger that the assessment findings will not do the child justice. For instance, a school-aged child with dyslexia may receive adult support to write down answers in class, while a disabled child with a physical impairment that affects their fine motor skills may have someone scribe (write) for them. A younger child in a nursery may need a demonstration of a task they're being asked to do, or reassurance and encouragement to participate in an activity.

A younger child may need a demonstration of a task they're being asked to do.

Reliability of information and avoiding bias

Assessments should be accurate and fair, or there's little point in doing them. So when practitioners carry out observations, they aim to be objective. In other words, they aim to record exactly what is happening without interpreting events from their own point of view. If this is not the case, the observation is not valid.

Some assessment methods are 'open'. This means that it's up to the practitioner to record what they see as being significant – this is by nature subjective. We might unintentionally focus on what we already believe to be true about a child, rather than looking at the whole picture, or we might be drawn to focus on areas of development that hold particular interest for us. It's good practice for key workers to occasionally have a colleague carry out assessments on their key children as this can bring a fresh objective perception. Thinking carefully about which assessment method to use and using a range of methods over time can also help to counteract this. 'Closed' assessment methods prompt practitioners to record particular things, for example 'counts by rote up to ten'. This is not open to interpretation in the same way, but it's hard to notice any development that falls outside the parameters of the prompts when assessing, and there's often nowhere to record it on pre-printed forms.

Ask Miranda!

A But what if a child's close to doing something – can't I write it in?

B Practitioners may sometimes be tempted to record that a child can do something, perhaps because the child can *nearly* do it, and the practitioner wants them to have a favourable outcome. Or, perhaps the practitioner thinks they *might* have seen the child do something before, and so they want to give them the benefit of the doubt. However, once again the practitioner must only record what they see. It's important to remember that we plan what children should learn next and how they should be supported from their assessments, and so we will not be helping them by recording anything that is less than truthful and accurate.

Good practice

Sometimes there are factors outside of the practitioner's control that may affect the reliability or outcome of an observation. If it is a very hot and sticky day, for example, children may be feeling fractious and irritable and they may behave differently than they usually do. This means that an observation may not give a reliable picture of the children's general behaviour. Alternatively, children may be excited or they may be feeling a little unsettled as they get to know a new child or adult who has joined the setting. If you identify a factor that is likely to affect the reliability of the observation, you should record it on the observation record. Failing to do so could make the observation misleading as adults reading it may believe that the behaviour recorded is representative of the way in which a child generally behaves. The outcome would then be compromised.

Areas and methods of assessing development

Practitioners need to assess children and young people's development in the following areas:

- physical
- communication
- intellectual/cognitive
- social, emotional and behavioural
- moral.

There is a range of assessment methods, and it's important for you to become confident in using them. You can then select the most appropriate assessment method for the type of information that you want to collect, and for the purpose for which the information will be used. Using a selection of methods over a period of time helps to build up a differentiated picture of the child's learning and development. (This means a picture that has been built up via different sources).

Assessment methods

Through observation, practitioners can assess children and young people's development in the areas identified above.

Observation is carried out in a cycle. Firstly, baseline information is collected, which tells practitioners about a child's current stage of development (see 'Checklists' later in this section). Later, observations are carried out. These help practitioners to monitor the progress made since the baseline assessment information was collected. Regular observations continue, and an ongoing record of a child's development is built up. Observations are then used to inform planning.

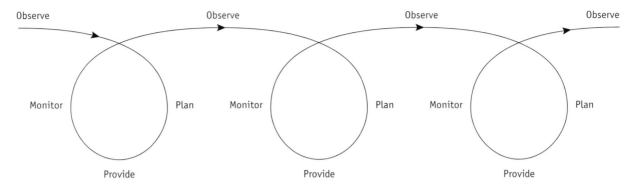

The planning cycle.

There's further information about summative and formative assessment in Unit EYMP 2.

Unit EYMP 2 Promote learning and development in the early years

Sometimes practitioners will carry out general, broad observations of whatever children happen to be doing. But other observations are more focused. For instance, a practitioner may decide to observe a child playing outside with peers because they are particularly interested in observing the child's gross motor skills and social skills. This is referred to as the 'objective' of the observation.

Settings will have their own policies and procedures about the way in which observations are carried out. Practitioners must work in line with these at all times.

The planning cycle

In addition to monitoring general developmental progress, observation is particularly helpful for building up a picture of the social relationships and bonds that children are making with their peers and with adults. It can also reveal whether children are provided with a stimulating environment, interesting activities and appropriate routines. Regular observations can also help to highlight changes in children's behaviour patterns. This can be very helpful if a child has become quiet and withdrawn, or perhaps unsettled or angry, as there is a record of the change to refer to. Records are also helpful for reporting to parents, carers and other professionals if appropriate.

Being a non-participant observer

During observations, the behaviour of children can change. If they are aware of being watched, some children may feel anxious or excited, or they may try harder than usual.

To counteract this, the practitioner may decide to be a 'non-participant observer'. This means that the practitioner will be unobtrusive – they will settle themselves somewhere suitable to watch the child without alerting them to the fact they are being observed. The practitioner will not interact with the children during this time. They will not speak and so there will be no need to make a record of their own actions or words during the observation.

It's easier to be objective and to record what is happening when you are not involved in events. However, it can be hard to find somewhere unobtrusive that still allows you to see and hear everything that occurs. Although you can use any method of observation as a non-participant observer, if you are looking to observe certain aspects of development or behaviour, you may not see them if you do not encourage children to carry out particular activities or tasks. However, this technique is well suited to the 'free description' and 'target child' methods of observation, which are explained below and on page 135.

A non-participant observer will be unobtrusive.

Being a participant observer

Alternatively, the practitioner can be a 'participant observer'. The participant observer can directly ask or encourage children to do things. This technique works well with the 'checklist method' of observation described on page 134, which is often used with babies and young children. Participant observers can ask questions to find out the reason for a child's behaviour, for example, 'Why are you doing that?'

Planning and presentation

Practitioners must plan their observation time with colleagues to ensure that it fits in with the overall plans of the setting. Sometimes practitioners find it necessary to abandon an observation, for example if they see something unsafe about to happen or if a child in search of assistance cannot be redirected to another adult. Whatever method of observation is used, the following key pieces of information are always needed:

- the name of child (or alternate method of identifying them – initials perhaps)
- date and timing of the observation
- where the observation was carried out
- name of the observer
- activity observed/objective of observation
- other children present
- other adults present.

The presentation of observations differs from setting to setting. However, this key information is often recorded on a separate piece of paper, which accompanies the observation itself. The key methods of observation are outlined below.

Free description (also known as written or narrative description)

The observer focuses on the activity of the child, writing down everything seen during the allotted time. Free description observations are generally short, lasting for perhaps five minutes or less. They are helpful for focusing on areas of difficulty for children, for instance working out exactly what is happening when a child struggles to feed him- or herself. These observations are often recorded in a notebook and written up afterwards.

You will need:

- a notepad
- a pen.

What to do

Write a detailed description of how the child carries out the activity being observed.

Note the child's actions and behaviour, including their facial expressions. Record what the child says and any non-verbal communication such as gestures. This is intensive work, which is why this type of observation is usually used for just a few minutes. Observations are usually recorded in the present tense.

Example

Ben is sitting at the painting table next to Jessica. He picks up his paintbrush and looks at her. She looks back. He smiles and holds his brush out to her. Jessica takes it and smiles back. Ben says, 'Thank you'.

Checklists (also known as tick lists)

A form prompts the observer to look for particular skills or reflexes that a child has. The observer ticks these off as they are seen. This method is frequently used for assessing a child's stage of development and to collect baseline information. It is well suited to the observation of babies, whose physical development will typically progress rapidly. The observations may be done over time or babies and children may be asked to carry out specific tasks.

You will need:

■ a prepared checklist (these can be purchased or developed by practitioners)

■ a pen.

What to do

The checklist tells you what to observe and record. As a participant observer, encourage the child to carry out the necessary tasks, ticking the relevant boxes to record the response – generally whether he or she could carry out the task competently. As a non-participant observer, tick the boxes as you see evidence of children's competence naturally occurring.

Example

Table CYP 3.2.1: Checklist

Activity	Yes	No	Date	Observer's comments
Rolls from back to front				
Rolls from front to back				

Time samples

The observer decides on a period of time for the observation, perhaps two hours or the length of a session. The child's activity is recorded on a form at set intervals – perhaps every 10 or 15 minutes. This tracks the child's activity over the period of time. However, significant behaviours may occur between the intervals and these will not be recorded.

You will need:

■ a prepared form giving the times for the observations

■ a pen

■ a watch.

What to do

Keep an eye on the time to ensure that you observe the child at regular intervals. At each allotted time, observe the child and record their activity in the same way as in the 'free description' method.

Example

10.00am

Ben is sitting at the painting table next to Jessica. He picks up his paintbrush and looks at her. She looks back. He smiles and holds his brush out to her. Jessica takes it and smiles back. Ben says, 'Thank you'.

10.15am

Ben gets down from the table. He goes to the nursery nurse. He looks at her and says, 'Wash hands'.

Event samples

This method is used when practitioners have reason to record how often an aspect of a child's behaviour or development occurs. A form is prepared identifying the aspect being tracked. Each time the behaviour or development occurs, a note of the time and circumstance is recorded. Samples may take place over a session, a week or in some circumstances longer. Practitioners may want to observe how frequently a child is physically aggressive, for instance.

You will need:

■ a prepared form adapted for the objective of the observation

■ a pen.

What to do

Watch a child, and each time the aspect of behaviour or development being observed occurs, record the circumstances along with the time.

Example

Table CYP 3.2.2

Event no.	Time	Event	Circumstances
1	2.30pm	Joshua pushed Daisy over	Joshua had left his teddy on the floor. He says Daisy pick it up. He went over to Daisy and tried to take the teddy. She did not let go. Joshua pushed her over. Daisy gave Joshua the toy and started to cry. Joshua walked away quickly with the teddy.

Target child

The observer will record a child's activity over a long period of time but unlike the time sample method, the aim is not to have any gaps in the duration of the observation. To achieve this, the observer uses a range of codes to record, in shorthand on a ready prepared form, what is happening.

You will need:

- a prepared form with a key to the abbreviations that will be used

- a pen

- a watch.

What to do

With this type of observation, the observer has to make decisions about which things are significant and should be recorded because it is impossible to record every detail over a long period. (It is interesting for two people to observe the same target child over the same period and then compare their forms. They are likely to have recorded different things.) Language and activity are recorded in separate columns for ease. It takes practice to get used to using the codes.

Example

See table CYP 3.2.3 below.

Additional codes will be used. Codes vary within settings. Refer to your organisational procedures. (Further information is given in Hobart, C. and Frankel, J. (1999) *A Practical Guide to Observation and Assessment*, Nelson Thornes Ltd, Cheltenham).

Baseline information

Before practitioners can evaluate the progress that children are making, they must get a picture of their current level of development. This is known as 'baseline information'. It is the information on which future observation is based and so it must be documented carefully. Baseline information also informs the way in which practitioners approach their work with individual children. This is because

Table CYP 3.2.3

Time	Activity	Language	Social grouping	Involvement Level
11.30	TC goes to the box of blocks. Uses both hands to tip the box up and get the blocks out	_TC_ 'Out'	SOL	1
11.31	TC sits down. Using right hand he places one block on top of another. He repeats this, building a tower of four blocks		SOL	1

Key:

TC = target child

_TC_ = target child talking to self

SOL = solitary grouping

1 = target child absorbed in his/her activity

the activities that practitioners offer, and the way in which they will relate with children, will depend on individual children's abilities.

Baseline and continuing information can be collected from several sources including:

- discussions with parents and carers

- discussions with the child or young person

- records that parents may have if their child has been to another setting previously

- information from assessments made by other professionals, such as health visitors, GPs or speech therapists

- baseline assessment carried out by the practitioner.

Although information will be gathered from the sources above, practitioners often conduct their own baseline observations to fill in the gaps. For instance, parents may not know whether their child can stack bricks or sort shapes because they may not have the relevant resources at home. So the practitioner will observe the child playing with these resources at the setting in order to inform the baseline assessment.

Standardised tests

These tests are generally used with older children and young people and will typically test basic skills such as literacy or mathematics. You may have taken such a test when you started this course, to see whether you'd benefit from learning support. Overall development can also be tested in this way. Practitioners would usually receive some training before using this type of test, which is most commonly used by teachers.

Photos, film clips, audio clips

These can provide a helpful record of children's activities. Photos are useful for recording things a child has created that can't usually be saved – a sand sculpture for instance, or a Lego™ creation. In the case of film, more information than it's possible to record on paper can be recorded with complete

Standardised tests are generally used with older children and young people.

accuracy. There's also the advantage of replaying it to ensure that nothing is missed, and showing it to parents, carers, colleagues, other professionals and the child or young person for discussion. Audio clips can be used in a similar way, and although the visual element is of course lost, this technique is particularly well suited to recording language development. Ensure that you have permission to record assessments in these ways from all children present, as you never know who will wander into range.

Assessing and evaluating observations

Once an observation (or series of observations) has been completed, a practitioner will consider the observation carefully and then draw conclusions. The consideration aspect is known as 'assessment', and the conclusions drawn are known as the 'evaluation' or the 'outcome'. Some people refer to the whole process of assessing and evaluating as the 'interpretation'.

Settings will have developed their own techniques for interpretation and for the way in which the interpretation is presented in written format. You should follow your setting's guidelines. However, generally speaking, practitioners will follow an assessment procedure similar to the one outlined on the chart below:

Sharing information

It's appropriate to share information gained through observation with colleagues who work directly with the child in question, and with senior staff (in a group setting). Discussion between practitioners can help to build up a well-rounded picture of a child. Information may also be shared with **other professionals** working with the child, in line with confidentiality procedures.

Ask Miranda!

Q What should I do if I've got a concern about a child following the assessment?

A **If you become concerned about a child following observation, it's important that you don't delay in reporting your concerns in line with your setting's policies and procedures. This means that children can get the help and support they may need as soon as possible. Early intervention can often make a difference to how a child continues to progress in their development.**

Go through the observation, noting sections that seem significant in terms of behaviour or development. Significant events could reflect achievement, progress, difficulty or the child's feelings. Unusual behaviour will also be of interest

↓

Reflect on the significant events, considering what conclusions can be drawn. For example, if a 2-year-old has been observed getting out a box of blocks for himself, you may conclude that a level of independence has been achieved in selecting and accessing materials

↓

Consider if the behaviour observed is consistent with what you know about the child development norms. Although it is not required by most settings, your assessor may ask you to make reference to the child development theories on which you are basing your conclusions. This demonstrates that you have a sound knowledge base from which to make assessments

↓

Consider what you already know about the individual child from baseline assessment and prior observations. Are they making progress? If so, how is this evident? If not, is this currently a cause for concern?

↓

Once these assessments are finalised, practitioners will write up their evaluations, generally in a free-flowing style. It is essential to ensure that the final evaluation:
• Is firmly based on what was recorded at the time of observation
• Makes links between the development norms and the child's actual stage of development

↓

The last stage is to use the information gathered to inform the setting's planning

Observation.

It's good practice to share with parents or carers information about the development and progress of children. This should be done in an open, positive way – key workers often arrange a meeting with families for this purpose. The information given by the practitioners should be used a starting point for discussion. It is important to remember that the parents are generally a child's primary carers and that they know their child best. Families have much to contribute to a discussion about the progress of their child and this information should be valued. It can also be recorded in the child's records.

Assessment frameworks

For information about assessing in relation to curriculum frameworks, see Unit EYMP 2.

Unit EYMP 2 Promote learning and development in the early years

Developing a plan to meet the development needs of a child or young person

What practitioners plan and provide for children to promote their development needs should be based on what is known about them, and so observations of children inform the planning. It's now usual for practitioners to involve children and young people in planning for their own development, and in particular, they tend to respond well to thinking about activities that they'd enjoy. This should be a positive, motivating experience, which encourages children to look forward to what they'll learn next. It helps them to take ownership of their own learning and development, and young people are likely to have strong feelings about the ways in which they'd like to learn. Parents and carers should also be involved. This is a great way to encourage and enable them to actively focus on and participate in their child's learning.

Different settings will have their own methods of recording, reviewing and updating plans. It is important that you understand your setting's methods and work in line with them. General guidelines on what to include are given below.

Information to record on plans

The following will usually be recorded:

- child's name and date of birth

- date the plan is made

- name of practitioner completing the plan

- timescale the plan relates to (e.g. four weeks, the following term)

- the purpose of the plan (this may be called the aim or focus)

- specific goals/targets

- achievement criteria (how you will know when the goals/targets have been successfully achieved)

- suggested activities to promote the learning/ development needed to achieve the goals/targets (If specific information is necessary, you can record details of where these will take place and what resources/materials/special equipment will be needed – in this case, record who will source it, from where, and by when.)

- adult support (specific support to be given during activities) – it should be clear who will take on what roles and responsibilities

- date set for review

- roles and responsibilities – who has responsibility for effective implementation and management of the plan.

As part of your study towards this unit, you should also read the additional detailed information on devising learning and development plans given in Unit EYMP 2.

Link Up!

Unit EYMP 2 Promote learning and development in the early years

LEARNING OUTCOME 2

FOCUS ON

...being able to promote the development of children or young people

In this section you'll learn about implementing development plans for children and young people, and revising plans in the light of implementation. You'll learn about the importance of a child-centred, inclusive approach. You'll also learn about listening and communicating with children and young people and encouraging them to participate in decisions and services. This links with Assessment Criteria 2.1, 2.2, 2.3, 2.4, 2.5.

Roles and responsibilities

In Learning Outcome 1, you learned that plans must identify roles and responsibilities. It should be clear:

- who has responsibility for effective implementation and management of the plan

- what adult support will be given, and whose role this is.

It is important that you fully understand your own roles and responsibilities in relation to the implementation of all plans.

Incorporating individual plans

In group settings (including classrooms), the child or young person's individual plan will need to be incorporated into the overall planning of activities for the setting. The usual approach is for all activities to be available to everyone. Within this, particular opportunities are targeted at specific children, and they will be supported in specific ways, as identified on their plan. In early years settings, it will usually be the key worker who carries out the targeted work. He or she may carry out more than one targeted activity with more than one key child in any session, so personal organisation and a focused approach is important.

Development is holistic and interconnected

Children and young people's learning is not compartmentalised, even though practitioners may focus on the different areas of learning and development separately when they assess and make plans. This means that when you're implementing plans, you can pull together different areas of learning into activities. This allows you to maximise the potential learning opportunity for children and young people. It also enables you to follow their interests and make the learning fun. To do this, you must recognise that the activities you provide will generally promote more than one area of learning and development.

Evaluating and revising development plans

Once you've started to implement a plan, you'll get a feel for how well it's working in practice. Plans are working documents, so if planned methods of working are not as effective as it was hoped, or if new ideas are presented, the plan can be amended. This should always be done in consultation with the person who has overall responsibility for the management of the plan, and with the participation of those involved in devising it, including children and young people.

The progress the child or young person is making towards the goals or targets specified should also be monitored. If they have not yet reached them but are progressing well, the time period identified in the plan may be extended. If they have achieved the targets or goals, there should be a celebratory acknowledgement of this, assessment should be reviewed and new goals or targets identified for the next cycle of planning. If progress is not being made as hoped, alternative ways of meeting the development needs should be identified. But if there are persistent difficulties and/ or children are not developing as would normally be expected in a certain area, there may be a specific requirement and a necessity to implement Early Years Action.

You can read about this in Unit CYPOP 6 Support disabled children and young people and those with specific requirements

Within your setting's planning processes, there's likely to be a checklist of factors to consider at the evaluation and monitoring stage, including these:

- Is the child making good progress towards goals/ targets?

- Do the goals/targets still appear to be realistic?

- Does the timescale still appear to be realistic?

- Are the activities providing effective opportunities for the planned learning?

- Is the child enjoying the activities?

- Are resources/materials/special equipment working effectively?

- Is the child enjoying the resources/materials/ special equipment?

- Is the planned adult intervention supporting learning effectively?

- Is the child enjoying the adult support?

- Have the activities provided any additional learning benefits?

- Has the adult support provided any additional learning benefits?

- Are there any suggested extension or follow-up activities?

- What are the child/young person's views on the above?

Unit CYPOP 6 Support disabled children and young people and those with specific requirements

A child-/young person-centred and inclusive approach

Plans should be focused on the needs of the child or young person concerned, rather than what is convenient for the setting or individual practitioners. This means that they are 'child-centred' or 'young person-centred.' Earlier, we discussed the process of incorporating individual plans into the overall plans for the setting. The model described promotes a child-centred, inclusive approach, because children don't have to be separated from the rest of the group or given something different to do in order for them to have their planned learning experience. (In the model described, all activities are available to everyone, within which particular opportunities are targeted at specific children).

Children don't have to be separated from the rest of the group to have their planned learning.

Listening and communicating with children and young people

It's always the aim of a practitioner to encourage children and young people to be interested in their own learning, and to get the most out of the learning activities and experiences. Our way of listening to and communicating with children and young people has a huge impact on how valued and respected they feel during these processes, and whether they enjoy them.

▶▶▶Link Up!◀◀◀

To learn more about this, turn to Unit CYP 3.5 Develop positive relationships with children, young people and others involved in their care

Active participation

As you learned above and in Learning Outcome 1, children and young people should be involved in the devising and monitoring of their development plan, as well as participating in its implementation. This empowers them to begin to take ownership of their learning, and it also builds motivation to learn and achieve.

LEARNING OUTCOME 3

FOCUS ON

...being able to support the provision of environments and services that promote the development of children or young people

In this section you'll learn about features and organisation of an environment or service that promote the development of children and young people. This links with Assessment Criteria **3.1, 3.2.**

There are several links to other units in this section. You are advised to follow these and read the relevant information.

Features of an environment that promote development

In this context, the term 'environment' refers to more than just the physical surroundings of children and

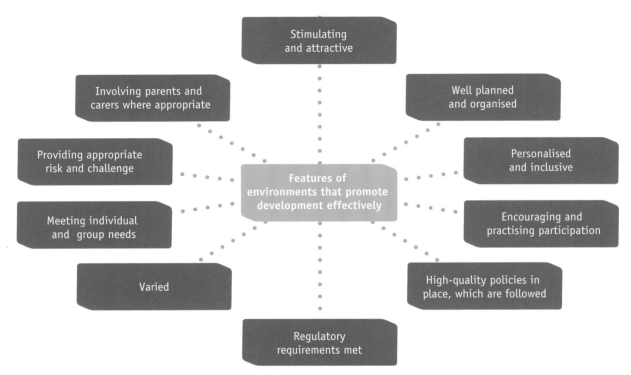

Features of environments that promote development effectively.

young people. It also encompasses the opportunities available to them, and the overall ethos and effectiveness of the services provided. Features of environments that promote development are shown on the spider diagram.

We'll look at these in turn:

■ **Stimulating and attractive**
Adults appreciate attractive, welcoming environments, and this applies to children and young people too. Environments should be stimulating both in terms of the way they look, and in terms of the activities and experiences provided.

You can learn more about this in Unit CYPOP 7 Promote creativity and creative learning in young children and Unit EYMP 1, LO 2 Be able to provide environments within the work setting that support and extend children's development and learning in the early years

■ **Well planned and organised**
You learned about effective planning for assessment and the devising and implementing of development plans in Learning Outcomes 1 and 2.

Information about working efficiently with regard to a curriculum framework is given in Unit EYMP 1 Context and principles for early years provision. Details of well organised layouts are given in Unit EYMP 1

■ **Personalised and inclusive**
'Personalisation' is about the provision of activities and experience being personally relevant to children and young people. This is a requirement of the Early Years Foundation Stage. You can read more about this in Unit EYMP 1 and Unit EYMP 2. You can find out about consulting with children and young people in Unit CYP 3.7, Learning Outcome 1. Details

of inclusive working can be found in Unit SHC 33, Unit CYP 3.7 and Unit CYPOP 6.

Unit EYMP 1 Context and principles for early years provision
Unit EYMP 2 Promote learning and development in the early years
Unit CYP 3.7 Understand how to support positive outcomes for children and young people
Unit SHC 33 Promote equality and inclusion in health, social care or children's and young people's settings
Unit CYPOP 6 Support disabled children and young people and those with specific requirements

- **Encouraging and practising participation**
  You can find out about consultation and participation with children and young people in Unit CYP 3.7, Learning Outcome 1.

Unit CYP 3.7 Understand how to support positive outcomes for children and young people

- **High quality policies in place and regulatory requirements met**
  For details of requirements of regulatory bodies (including the Welfare Standards), see Unit EYMP 2. Information relating to health and safety is included in Unit CYP 3.4. Safeguarding information can be found in Unit SHC 34 and Unit CYP 3.3.

Unit EYMP 2 Promote learning and development in the early years
Unit CYP 3.4 Support children and young people's health and safety
Unit SHC 3.4 Principles for implementing duty of care in health, social care or children's and young people's settings
Unit CYP 3.3 Understand how to safeguard the well-being of children and young people

- **Varied and meeting individual and group needs**
  For information about a varied and balanced approach to the setting's activities and experiences, see Unit EYMP 1, Learning Outcome 2.

- **Providing appropriate risk and challenge**
  Risk, challenge and risk assessment is covered in Unit CYP 3.4, Learning Outcomes 2 and 3.

Unit CYP 3.4 Support children and young people's health and safety

- **Involving parents and carers**
  Information on working in partnership with parents and carers and encouraging their participation in the setting is included in Unit CYP 3.5 and Unit EYMP 1, Learning Outcome 3.

Unit CYP 3.5 Develop positive relationships with children, young people and others involved in their care
Unit EYMP 1, Learning Outcome 3 Understand how to work in partnership with carers

Organising your own work environment

It's good practice for practitioners to evaluate how they organise the work environment. This is important, because the way in which the environment is organised and experienced underpins all other aspects of your work. We'll explore the factors you should reflect on below. You'll also find it helpful to refer to your learning about reflective practice in Unit SHC 32.

Link Up!

Unit SHC 32 Engage in personal development in health, social care or children's and young people's settings

Taking into account personal and external factors

The organisation of your work environment will in part depend on external factors, including the sort of service offered, organisational policies and requirements and the physical location and features. But as you gain experience in different settings during your training and/or career, you'll be exposed to different methods and approaches to the way

Eventually, you'll discover your own personal preferences and style.

environments are organised. Eventually, you'll discover your own personal preferences and style, and perhaps even areas of specialism. This is a really constructive thing as we all bring something different to the way we work, and this allows settings to become melting pots of influences. However, this needs to be managed so that organisation doesn't become chaotic.

Providing specific activities such as play, learning, home visiting

You can look back over your own activity plans, the setting's overall plans (such as curriculum plans) that you will have contributed to delivering, individual children's or young people's development plans. Depending on the type of setting, you may have conducted home visits as part of the induction process for new children due to join.

Providing services

Your setting provides a service to the children or young people that attend, as well as their parents and carers. Some settings clearly offer more than one service – a day nursery and an out-of-school club for instance, and these can be considered separately. However, lots of settings diversify or provide supplementary services in other subtle ways. For instance, a pre-school might keep a database of registered childminders who'll babysit for families in the evenings, or run occasional learning opportunities for parents, such as paediatric first aid or baby massage. Does anything similar apply to your service?

Measuring outcomes

Measuring outcomes is about the way in which the setting collects information that demonstrates how the service is performing in different areas. There's likely to be information from a range of sources, including feedback from parents and carers, feedback from children and young people, progress made by children and young people (an indicator of how effective the learning programme is), external assessments (such as those by quality assurance schemes), inspections from regulatory bodies (such as Ofsted), statistics (e.g. relating to the current child occupancy figures), and finances (e.g. funding received and applied for).

Have a go!

If your setting has a separate committee, ask the chair about the outcomes they measure too.

Communicating effectively and showing appropriate empathy and understanding

As you learned in Unit SHC 31, communication is at the heart of your relationships with children and young people, and the quality of relationships has a big impact on how children and young people experience the environment. This is particularly true of key relationships.

Supporting participation

This is about how you encourage children and young people to actively have their voice heard. What do you do to consult them about their ideas, thoughts and feelings? How do you ensure that they have a say in decisions that affect them? And what do you do with the information once you have it?

Involving parents and carers

It's important for settings to establish and maintain a strong working partnership with parents and carers. The key worker relationship is particularly important. What do you do to contribute to a strong partnership? It's also good practice to encourage parents and carers to become actively involved in the setting. Events such as family socials and open evenings are often well attended, and parents may be interested in serving on a group's committee or parent advisory board/steering group. How are they involved at your setting?

Supporting children and young people's rights

It's a key part of your role to promote children's rights. This includes the right to be cared for and protected, and the right to have their say about decisions that affect them. This should be threaded throughout the ethos of the setting, and will be reflected in the policies and procedures. It's now increasingly common for children or young people to be part of the staff recruitment process, for instance. In a school, they may be consulted about the job description, so they can express their views about the kind of adults they'd like to work with them. One or two might be invited to join the interview panel, or applicants may be asked to work with a group of children for a short period. The children and young people will then give their feedback when the decisions are being made.

Curriculum frameworks

For key information about the organisation of environments following curriculum frameworks, see Unit EYMP 1 and Unit EYMP 2.

Creative environments

For detailed information on providing exciting, vibrant environments that promote creativity, see Unit CYPOP 7.

Link Up!

Unit EYMP 1 Context and principles for early years provision
Unit EYMP 2 Promote learning and development in the early years

Link Up!

Unit CYPOP 7 Promote creativity and creative learning in young children

LEARNING OUTCOME 4

FOCUS ON

...understanding how working practices can impact on the development of children and young people

In this section you'll learn about how working practices can affect children and young people's development. You'll also learn about how institutions, agencies and services can affect this development. This links with Assessment Criteria **4.1, 4.2.**

You'll be driven to strive for the very best practice in all that you do.

How working practices can affect children and young people's development

Most people would instantly agree that the education children and young people receive has a huge impact on their learning and development – it generally seems quite an obvious statement. However, not everyone is so sure about the effect of the **care** that's received on children's development. But the care is equally as important.

The standard of your working practices – or in other words, what you do to fulfil your role, and how you go about doing it – will influence how much of a positive affect you personally have on the development of the children and young people that you'll work with. Most practitioners say they enjoy their work because it's rewarding to contribute to children and young people's lives, and so it stands to reason that you'll be driven to strive for the very best practice in all that you do, for the best possible effect.

It's a good idea for you to read Unit CYP 3.7 at this point, where the difference you can make to the outcomes of children and young people's lives is explained in full. You can also refer to Unit SHC 32, for

information about reflecting on your working practices, and how to develop and improve as a practitioner.

Unit CYP 3.7 Understand how to support positive outcomes for children and young people
Unit SHC 32 Engage in personal development in health, social care or children and young people's settings

How institutions, agencies and services can affect development

A range of institutions, agencies and services can affect children and young people's development through positive support. 'Multi-agency working' is the term used when institutions work together in partnership to meet the needs of children, young people and families in a joined up, coordinated way. This is covered in full in Unit CYP 3.6 – you should refer to this as part of your study towards this unit.

Unit CYP 3.6 Working together for the benefit of children and young people

LEARNING OUTCOME 5

FOCUS ON

...being able to support children and young people's positive behaviour

In this section you'll learn about encouraging positive behaviour and evaluating different approaches to supporting positive behaviour. This links with Assessment Criteria **5.1, 5.2**.

Supporting positive behaviour – current thinking

There's been much debate over the years about the best way to promote positive behaviour and to manage inappropriate behaviour. This is likely to always be the case. But in recent years, there's been something of a shift in focus. This began when debate turned to the fact that children's behaviour is linked directly to their needs.

In the past, the spotlight was on children who presented challenging behaviour, who were seen as the 'problem'. The action taken to manage them by the adult was seen as the 'solution'. However, the spotlight has now turned to the adult, and if children's behaviour is challenging, we're encouraged to think about whether we are responding to the child's needs in the most effective way.

Something that is generally accepted is that children need to be given boundaries to keep to and goals to reach to help them learn how to behave in acceptable ways. A practitioner should encourage children to reach goals, while managing inappropriate behaviour (that oversteps the boundaries) when it occurs.

Realistic expectations

The goals set for children's behaviour should be realistic. They should take into consideration children's age, needs and abilities. If expectations

are too high and children cannot achieve them, they are likely to be in trouble frequently. This is not good for a child's self-esteem and in the long term, it isn't good for their behavioural prospects. Children who are often in trouble may start to feel they are incapable of being good, and they may stop trying to reach behaviour goals. This starts a self-fulfilling cycle – such a child is likely to display more unacceptable behaviour, leading to more disapproval from adults, which reinforces the feeling that they cannot behave well or do the right thing. This is a good example of the clear links between behaviour, self-esteem and children's relationships with others. It is important to always be clear that it is a child's behaviour that is unacceptable, not the child themselves. Never label a child as 'naughty' or 'a troublemaker'.

If expectations are too high and children cannot achieve them, they are likely to be in trouble frequently.

If expectations aren't high enough, children will not learn how to behave appropriately, and this is also likely to affect their progress. For instance, a school-aged child who has not learned how to take turns, share fairly and handle winning and losing is likely to have difficulties with their peers. As a result, the child may dislike and avoid group activities such as playground games.

Just as a child who is encouraged to reach goals is likely to work towards them and eventually attain them, a child who feels that no one expects them to be able to reach goals is unlikely to achieve. This is also true of children who are not given sufficient goals and boundaries.

A range of techniques that can be used to promote positive behaviour are outlined below.

Least restrictive principle

This is about the setting's general ethos and approach to behaviour. The theory is that children who experience an authoritarian approach – who are likely to be aware of strict and often plentiful rules – do not have the opportunity to regulate behaviour for themselves. This means that they are learning to behave as expected in certain settings, but not really internalising a personal code of behaviour conduct because they don't need to take responsibility for what they should and shouldn't do. The least restrictive principle model encourages more behaviour freedom, and getting rid of unnecessary rules (which may seem quite petty under close examination). But with the freedom comes the responsibility to self-regulate behaviour, and to be accountable for actions.

Reinforcing positive behaviour

Practitioners can promote positive behaviour by rewarding children when they behave in acceptable ways. Children enjoy being rewarded, so they are encouraged to behave in the same way again. When children repeat behaviours, over time they become an ingrained, natural part of what the child does. The more a child is given positive attention for behaving appropriately, the less inappropriate behaviour they are likely to display.

Tangible and intangible rewards

Rewards that can be given to children fall into two categories: tangible and intangible.

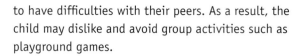

Did you know?

Research has found that when it comes to reducing inappropriate behaviour and increasing appropriate behaviour, rewards are much more effective than punishments in terms of long-term behaviour change.

Tangible rewards are real items that physically exist and can be seen. Intangible rewards are not physical items, but something that children can experience. Some examples are shown in the table below:

Tangible and intangible rewards

Tangible rewards	Intangible rewards
Prizes	Praise
Stickers	Smiles
Certificates	Cuddles
Stars/ink stamps	Round of applause/cheers
Trophies/awards	A 'thank you'
Toys	Public acknowledgement (praise given in front of other people to draw their attention to an achievement)
Money	Pats on the back
Allowed to choose something tangible from a shop	Opportunities to pick a game or story for the group
Work displayed/published (in a newsletter for instance)	Special trips or the provision of favourite activities (e.g. going to the park or baking cakes)

Practitioners use mainly intangible rewards and they are extremely valuable. These rewards show children that they are earning approval from adults and they also demonstrate how to interact positively with other people – how to thank them, for example. They can be used to encourage children throughout an activity or task, showing them that they are behaving correctly and giving them the confidence to continue. You can give children warm praise, thanks and smiles frequently throughout every day, but it would be impractical to do the same with tangible rewards. However, tangible rewards do have their place.

Stickers in particular work well, as children can wear them with pride but they don't break the bank! Tangible items are often used in individual behaviour programmes to reward individual children who are working towards specified behaviour goals that have been identified for them (see page 151). They're also effective for rewarding and celebrating occasional achievements that are out of the ordinary and they can be kept as a reminder of that time. Some tangible rewards, such as money, may be given by parents and carers, but in most settings it would be considered inappropriate to use such rewards.

It's also important to consider how children feel about the rewards being given to others. Tangible rewards in particular may lead to jealousy or a feeling of being treated unfairly if they are not handled carefully. For instance, if one child is given a sticker for sitting quietly at story time because this is one of their individual behaviour goals, children who generally sit quietly at story time and are not rewarded may be unsettled by this.

Certificate of Achievement

Awarded to: .... On: ....

For: Helping a friend

Signed .... Well done!

A certificate rewarding achievement.

Good practice

Generally speaking, rewards should be given soon after the behaviour occurs, when they have relevance and meaning. You should always say why the reward is being given – children can't repeat the positive behaviour if they don't know what it was! Research shows that intermittent rewarding works best. This means that children don't need a reward every time in order to repeat behaviour. However, if a behaviour you haven't rewarded for a while begins to slide, you may like to try increasing the frequency of reward for a short period. Make sure that tangible rewards are small, appropriate and not over used. However, lots of intangible praise and positive attention given at the right time is never a bad thing.

Good practice

Remember, a reward is only a reward when a child likes it! It is important to reward children in a way that values them as an individual. For instance, some children feel uncomfortable with public acknowledgement or being physically touched – they may not appreciate a pat on the back. Also, while it is natural for a practitioner to cuddle a young child, it is not considered to be appropriate in all environments (such as the classroom) or with all children, particularly as they get older. You must adhere to the accepted policies and procedures of your setting.

Modelling positive behaviour

It's important that adults model positive behaviour, as children naturally learn some of their own behaviour from what they see happening around them. Treating people with respect, being polite, not raising voices in anger, showing patience, being kind and considerate – this is the type of behaviour children should see from their role models. If adults behave in this way, it sets the tone for a positive culture within the group.

Looking for reasons for inappropriate behaviour and adapting responses

Challenging behaviour is often a response to a child's immediate feelings and emotions, or an event in their life. Finding the reason helps practitioners to approach the behaviour in the best way. Sometimes causes are easy to spot and short-lived. Examples include the following:

- A child is tired or unwell, and they may feel fractious and irritable. They may fall out with friends easily as a result.

- Children may be bored, or feel they are not being supervised.

- Jealousy may prompt a child to take a friend's toy away, or to hurt them.

- Frustration/anger at not being able to have what they want may cause a child to have a tantrum, for example in the supermarket.

- Frustration/anger at not being able to achieve something may prompt a child to behave inappropriately. For example, a child who is 'out' during a game may protest verbally, get cross and cry.

- Children may show anxiety/stress at being in unfamiliar circumstances, such as the first day at a new school.

- A child may be due for a nap, have had an unsettled night, or it may be the end of a busy day.

- A heightened sense of excitement – a lively activity or special event – may make normal behaviour hard for a child to maintain.

- Changes may have occurred in routine (e.g. different timings or layout of environment).

- There may be a lack of opportunity for physical play and exercise, leading to pent up energy.

Challenging behaviour may be due to overexcitement.

More serious factors may lead to prolonged periods of challenging behaviour:

- bereavement

- the child becoming disabled or seriously/chronically ill

- a close family member becoming disabled or seriously/chronically ill

- parents' relationship breaking down

- parents becoming separated or divorced

- parent/s beginning new serious relationships

- the child becoming part of a step family

- changes at home (living circumstances within the home or moving home)

- having new carers.

Sometimes reasons for inappropriate behaviour are hidden, unconscious or in the past. This is complicated further by the fact that different children may respond to the same events or the same feelings by behaving in very different ways. For instance, one child who has been abused may become very quiet and withdrawn as a result, while another may become aggressive or violent. In these cases, challenging behaviour may be presented over a longer period of time, and professionals such as counsellors or psychologists may also work with the child. (See also attention deficit and speech, language and communication difficulties on page 159.)

Can you come up with a positive way to respond to challenging behaviour caused by each of the reasons in both lists above?

Individual behaviour planning

Sometimes, in consultation with parents, it's necessary to plan a behaviour programme for an individual child. This is in line with, but in addition to, the behaviour policy that applies to all (the policy should cover individual behaviour programmes as one of the strategies used for managing children's behaviour). This means that particular behaviour goals are identified to suit an individual child, and strategies are planned to help them achieve the goals. The practitioner (usually the key worker), child/young person and parent/carers should work together on devising the plan.

Individual behaviour programmes may be necessary if:

- a child frequently/persistently displays challenging behaviour

- a child's behaviour is inconsistent with their age

- a child's behaviour has changed recently

- a child has been identified as in need of specialist help and practitioners are asked to work in partnership with parents, carers and specialists. This could be due to an impairment such as a learning difficulty, communication difficulty or attention deficit.

Link Up!

For more on such impairments see Units EYMP 5 Support children's speech, language and communication, and CYPOP 6 Support disabled children and young people and those with specific requirements

If practitioners suspect an individual behaviour plan may be necessary, it is important that it is based on evidence of the child's behaviour. Practitioners should start to build up a picture of the child's current behaviour patterns. This is done by observing and recording what inappropriate behaviour the child exhibits, when it occurs and the circumstances, as well as through talking with the child, if appropriate to their age and stage of development. It is important to notice how the behaviour is responded to by adults and other children, and what effect this has. Much can also be learned by noting when a child displays positive behaviour.

Practitioners should work in partnership with parents and carers to gather evidence as they will generally know their child better than anyone else. Talking with

Good practice

Depending on age, needs and abilities, practitioners may be able to discuss the planned approach with the child concerned. It is important to take the opportunity to do this where appropriate. A programme has a better chance of success when a child fully understands what is going to happen and is in agreement with the plan. Listen to children's points of view and negotiate with them where possible, checking their understanding. When they feel a sense of ownership and involvement and they are looking forward to rewards (tangible or intangible), children are generally motivated to work towards their goals.

them also enables the practitioner to understand the child's behaviour at home.

Reviewing and discussing the record of a child's behaviour will help practitioners to identify the primary goals to address. The best way to support children to reach their goals should be planned, along with the best strategies for managing inappropriate behaviour. (Also known as '**planning interventions to reduce inappropriate behaviour.**') Practitioners, parents and carers (and where appropriate other specialists) should discuss the programme to ensure consistency, giving the programme the best chance of success. The details of the agreed programme should be recorded.

Once the programme is under way, practitioners should continue to monitor and record children's behaviour patterns as before. Over time, practitioners will be able to see the impact of the programme by considering this evidence. If the measures taken seem to be working, they can be persisted with until the child reaches their goal or until their behaviour is effectively managed. If the measures are not successful, new strategies may need to be introduced. Once a child has adopted a new behaviour and it has become ingrained, it may be appropriate to end the programme or to focus on a new goal.

Phased stages of behaviour planning

An example of this is the use of a sticker chart. A child may receive a sticker for reaching behaviour goals throughout the day – for sitting at the table at mealtimes for instance. When a child has earned a set number of stickers, this may lead to a further reward – a small toy or a trip to the park perhaps. There may also be planned strategies for dealing with inappropriate behaviour from the child, again tailored to suit them.

Days of the week	Morning	Lunch-time	Afternoon
Monday ⭐	⭐		
Tuesday ⭐		⭐	
Wednesday ⭐	⭐		
Thursday ⭐			⭐
Friday	⭐		

A sticker chart.

De-escalate and diversion

Diversionary tactics are particularly helpful when working with young children, whose behaviour tends to be very 'of the moment' and reactionary. Diverting their attention or finding a way to avoid a likely flashpoint or to take the heat out of a situation (de-escalation), helps to keep a calm, pleasant environment. Once this is achieved, you can praise the positive behaviour.

Practical example

Marley diverts

Marley is a childminder for 18-month-old Noah and 24-month-old Lily. Noah has brought an old lunchbox from home with him today that he likes to carry a favourite soft toy around in. Lily has shown some interest in the box and contents, and as soon as Noah drops it, Lily picks it up. Noah snatches it back, and Lily protests vocally. Marley gets Lily's special doll from home out of her bag. Lily reaches for it immediately, and Noah's belongings are forgotten.

Question
Where do you think this behaviour may have led if Marley hadn't diverted Lily?

Containment

This term is used by legal services to refer to action taken to prevent a young offender from offending in the same way again. It can also apply to less formal situations, and can be an effective technique to avoid a child or young person getting into further trouble. For instance, if a child has been removed from a situation, their behaviour can be contained by preventing them from re-entering the situation. Or an adult may stay close by to actively support or provide a watchful presence that serves as a deterrent.

Boundary setting and negotiation

Boundaries set appropriate limits for children's behaviour. In other words, children are not permitted to behave in certain ways because to do so would be unsafe or socially unacceptable. For instance, children are not allowed to climb up on tables to play because it would be unsafe. They are not allowed to tease one other because this is socially unacceptable. Goals for behaviour identify the way children are expected to behave. For instance, children are expected to sit at the table to eat their meals, and to wait their turn when playing a game.

What children know and understand about boundaries will depend on their age, abilities and experience. Younger children may be just starting to learn about boundaries through repetition – they will need to be reminded of boundaries frequently. Children of school age are likely to have a good understanding of boundaries. Many out-of-school clubs involve the children in establishing a simple set of ground rules that are agreed by everyone. This helps children to accept the boundaries and appreciate their purpose. Young people may be involved in agreeing behaviour contracts in settings such as youth groups. Boundaries are most effective when they're set with children and young people themselves.

Young people may be involved in agreeing behaviour contracts.

Children and young people's reflecting on their own behaviour

It's helpful to talk about positive behaviour and to draw children's attention to when they're doing well, particularly in situations that they sometimes find challenging. For instance, you might say, 'You listened really carefully to that story, didn't you? What was it that you liked about it?' Focusing too much on negative behaviour doesn't fit in with current thinking, particularly for young children. However, it is appropriate to talk through some issues, and it can be an effective way to get the bottom of the cause of behaviour, particularly with older children and young people, and particularly if individual behaviour plans are being devised or reviewed. Thinking about how they could handle a similar situation more positively in the future may also be helpful.

Anti-bullying strategies

Young children need to learn how to get along with one another, and it's up to adults to step in without delay if children are behaving in dominating or aggressive ways towards others. In early years settings, there will be lots of focus on being kind, helping each other and so on, and these positive social skills will be the focus of many story times, circle times and so on. Saying sorry when you have upset someone is another key early message. Schools will have a more formal programme of activities aimed at preventing bullying and empowering children to seek assistance if they do experience it.

Have a go!

Visit **www.kidscape.co.uk** and explore the range of advice and activities to promote the anti-bullying message.

Link Up!

See also Unit CYP 3.3 Understand how to safeguard the well-being of children and young people

Time out

Time out should not be used as a punishment. The purpose is to allow children and young people the chance to calm down and take stock of a situation by removing them from the source of conflict or temptation. Children should feel that this is the purpose of time out – they should not be made to feel that they are being rejected from the group. Time out is not recommended for young children who cannot yet understand this concept.

Time out is particularly effective with older children and for handling aggression. In the case of aggression, it is preferable to take children somewhere quiet away from others if possible, and to stay with the child until they calm down. You must remain calm and in control yourself – this is particularly important when children have lost control of themselves as this can be frightening for them and for you. After a period of time out, practitioners should talk to children, resolving any remaining issues if necessary and smoothing their transition back into the activities of the group.

Use of physical intervention

Rarely, and in extreme circumstances, it may be necessary to physically restrain a child to prevent them from hurting themselves or somebody else. If such an event occurs, you must use the minimum force possible. If possible, have someone else with you to protect yourself from allegations of abuse. You should record the incident in the setting's incident book and report it to your superiors and the child's parents or carers as soon as possible. Reins and harnesses must only be used to keep young children safe – when they are in a high chair for instance. Children should NEVER be restrained for punishment, either physically or by using reins or harnesses.

Policies and procedures

A clear behaviour policy is beneficial to practitioners, parents, carers and children. The document should be tailored to meet the needs of the setting, and promote the overall values, ethics and aims of the organisation.

A good policy will explain the setting's philosophy and strategies for promoting acceptable behaviour and dealing with inappropriate behaviour when it occurs. These must be in line with legislation. **Practices that physically hurt, frighten, threaten or humiliate children must *never* be used. Practitioners must *never* use physical punishments such as smacking. It is *illegal*.**

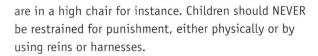

Did you know?

New practitioners should be introduced to the behaviour policy as part of the induction process, and all practitioners must work in accordance with it at all times.

Some parents and carers may question aspects of a setting's policy. For instance, they may feel that the expectations of behaviour are either too high or too low, or perhaps they would deal with inappropriate behaviour differently themselves at home. They may at times be unhappy with the way a situation has been handled. In these circumstances, it is important that issues are discussed openly. Practitioners should explain the thinking or reasoning that underpins a statement, action, approach or ethos rationale behind their policy and their actions. However, it is important for practitioners to listen carefully to what parents and carers have to say, and to monitor and adapt their procedures when appropriate to do so.

Good practice

You should make sure that you know and fully understand your setting's policy so that you can approach children's behaviour appropriately in your practical work. Best practice requires all practitioners to share the same approach to promoting appropriate behaviour and dealing with inappropriate behaviour. When boundaries are consistently applied, children can learn what is expected of them, and knowing this gives children a sense of security. It also helps them to see that they are being treated fairly. Children generally want to have the approval of the people around them, and when they understand what is required of them they have a tendency to behave accordingly.

Responding to inappropriate behaviour

Additional tips on managing challenging behaviour at the time it occurs are given below:

A firm and respectful approach

You must always maintain a respectful approach when you are interacting with children and young people, even if they are in trouble. The well-being of children is paramount. You must never seek to control a child by intimidating them, instead you should intervene sensitively. Remember that you are a role model for children. You do not want children to lose their temper with people or to shout at them, so you must not behave like that yourself. You must remain calm and controlled. However, when you are setting boundaries and when you are dealing with instances of inappropriate behaviour, you should be firm and clear about the behaviour you want.

Practical example

Deepak's dilemma

The dad of 4-year-old Deepak tells key worker Keirra that his son was upset this morning and that he did not want to come to pre-school. This has stemmed from the fact that he was told off towards the end of the last session, just before he went home, for pushing another child. He has been unduly worried that he is still in trouble with the practitioner. Although practitioners must be consistent in their approach to dealing with unacceptable behaviour whenever it occurs, Keirra is concerned and wants to make sure that Deepak does not experience these ongoing feelings again. She tells Deepak's dad that she will explain the situation to her colleagues, so that the adults can ensure that even if Deepak is told off towards the end of a session, he has the opportunity to make restitution (i.e. make up for it) before he goes home. He can then feel that the matter is over with, and end the session on a positive note. Keirra and Deepak's dad agree to talk again to monitor the situation. When his dad has left reassured, Keirra asks Deepak to help her set out some toys. She is then able to thank him and praise him for his efforts, clearly giving him her approval.

Question

The new adapted procedure should ensure that Deepak's behaviour is managed in a consistent way that will not be detrimental to his well-being. What may have happened if Keirra had not responded to the parent's concern?

Clearly define boundaries

It is up to practitioners to help children understand boundaries while also communicating to them that the boundaries are firm. This is known as defining boundaries. It is done through a consistent approach. When children are about to overstep a boundary, practitioners can take the opportunity to remind them of the boundary and why it exists. For instance, a practitioner may say, 'Remember that we all need to wait our turn. That way the game is fair, and everyone has fun.' Children learn from this, and often it is enough to stop them in their tracks and deter them from inappropriate behaviour.

Consistency

If consistency is lacking, children will become confused. For instance, if some practitioners let children have extra turns during a board game to keep the peace, a child will learn that it is worth trying to get an extra turn rather than waiting for theirs because sometimes they are rewarded. The same applies if one practitioner varies their approach, sometimes allowing certain behaviour and sometimes not allowing it. This can make children feel insecure – they are not sure what is required of them, and they never know what reaction their behaviour will get.

Children need to learn rules and boundaries.

Facial expressions

A disapproving look (maintaining a few seconds of eye contact if need be) is an effective way of showing children that they are overstepping a boundary and diverting them. It can be used in conjunction with other strategies. If a child is already aware of a boundary, a look may be enough on its own to prompt them to think about what they are doing, causing them to alter their behaviour accordingly.

No

A firm, simple no is an appropriate way to make even very young children aware of a boundary. It is also useful to halt a child's behaviour quickly – for example, it can stop them from doing something dangerous (the consequences of their action can be discussed once they are safe). If 'no' is to have this effect, it should not be used all the time, so that children take notice when they do hear it. Phrase your instructions positively whenever possible. Instead of 'No running in the corridor!' try the more pleasant, 'Please walk in the corridor'.

Did you know?

No must also mean no. If you say no and then give in to children, it teaches them that it's worth not complying because they may get their way if they resist you for long enough. Similarly, never say you will carry out a consequence unless you mean it.

Consequences

Children need to be aware of the consequences of their actions. This helps them to learn why boundaries are in place and to accept them. Children may not understand why their behaviour is unacceptable unless they are told. A practitioner may say, for instance, 'You must not run up the slide because the children coming down will bang into you, and people will get hurt. Please go up the steps instead.' Sometimes it is necessary to point out that if a child continues to behave that way, a consequence (such as limiting his

or her choices) will have to be applied. Children often need to be told why swear words or name-calling is inappropriate and hurtful.

Limiting children's choices

If children continue to behave inappropriately it may be necessary to limit the choices available to them by taking away the resource or equipment they are using. Alternatively they may be redirected to another activity (perhaps something calmer). This course of action can be effective and called for, but it should be used sparingly as it does limit the opportunities for play and learning that are available to that child. A practitioner might say, 'I have asked you to stop running up the slide. If you carry on doing it, you will have to go and play with something else, otherwise someone will get hurt.'

When it comes to defining boundaries and dealing with behaviour, you should make sure that you communicate information in a way that children can understand. You must take their age, needs and abilities into consideration. Unclear (or ambiguous) directions can confuse children. If they do not do what is required of them due a misunderstanding, they may get into further trouble. Rather than saying to a young child, 'You upset Callum so you should go and make friends again', a practitioner could say, 'Callum was upset when you took his toy away. Please go and say sorry to him.' This is a clear instruction, and the child will know what to do.

Children should learn to say sorry.

Rewarding compliance

When a child **complies** by altering their behaviour, practitioners should respond immediately by demonstrating their approval – a smile, nod or a 'thank you' would all be appropriate. It is important to acknowledge compliance so that a child can see that he or she is valued as an individual – it was only the behaviour that was disapproved of, and now he or she has altered it, the child can feel acceptance once again. This protects children's self-esteem. Children will also be more likely to comply again in the future.

key term

Compliance children co-operating with requests. *(National Occupational Standards)*

Selective ignoring

If an adult does not notice or reward positive behaviour, but does take notice of inappropriate behaviour, children may begin to behave inappropriately to seek attention. They may feel that even negative attention is better than no attention at all. If this occurs, practitioners can try rewarding children with plenty of attention when they are behaving appropriately, while ignoring inappropriate behaviour as much as possible unless it is dangerous or upsetting for other children.

Problem-solving between children

All children will have problems with other children at some time. Learning to get along and cooperate with other people is an important life skill for everyone. Practitioners can help children to learn how to handle disagreements and disputes positively. The extent to which children are able to do this will depend on their age, needs and abilities. When working with younger children, practitioners can ask questions to prompt children to identify their problems and to come up with their own solutions. This is important as there will not always be adults on hand to step in as children grow and become more independent.

When working with older children, practitioners need to resist the temptation to intervene in children's problems right away, giving them the opportunity to resolve things for themselves as long their behaviour is not dangerous or so inappropriate that it should be stopped immediately (in the case of bullying for example).

Practical example

Resolving conflict

Four-year-olds Jordon and Toby are playing with the sand. There is only one sieve. Each has hold of it and both children are attempting to pull it away. This is a familiar scene in any setting. By the time they are 4, most children will have had plenty of experience of an adult settling this type of dispute for them. These children are likely to know how this is done. Marcus, a practitioner, intervenes. He asks the children to put down the sieve and to tell him what the matter is. Both say they want to play with the item. Marcus says, 'Oh, and there's only one. What can we do?' Jordon suggests that they take it in turns to play with the sieve. Marcus says, 'That sounds like a good idea. What do you think Toby?' Toby agrees.

Question

Why is it good for Jordon and Toby to think about how they can solve their dispute for themselves?

Attention seeking

Children may throw tantrums, cry frequently or refuse to settle at activities for long unless an adult is beside them. Children may be hostile or jealous towards another person receiving attention. Children displaying this type of behaviour may be feeling insecure and in need of adult reassurance. However, they may simply be used to lots of adult attention.

Strategy: Go out of your way to praise positive behaviour, and try to ignore inappropriate behaviour when possible. Otherwise, you reward the inappropriate behaviour with the attention the child is seeking.

Aggressive/destructive behaviour

Children may hurt others, by hitting or kicking. They may throw or kick over equipment or furniture. Children may be experiencing frustration, and may have been feeling unhappy for some time. This behaviour has often 'built up' with older children, but may be more spontaneous in younger children.

Strategy: Be firm and in control, to stop the child becoming out of control. Calm the child quickly, in a quiet place if possible. Children who have lost control may be quite scared, and eventually tearful. When the child is ready, find out the source of the upset and resolve the issue. Talk with children about the consequences of their behaviour.

Offensive comments

Children swear or use offensive words or comments that they have heard. They may not understand what they are saying.

Strategy: Tell children why their words are unacceptable within the setting, making it clear that they cause hurt and upset. This also applies to name calling, which should also be regarded as completely unacceptable and should be taken seriously. In all cases, it is important to encourage children to acknowledge the feelings of other people they may have hurt, and for them to apologise. They can also do what they can to make up for it if appropriate (known as 'making restitution').

Communication difficulties, learning difficulties and attention deficits

Communication difficulties, learning difficulties and attention deficits are likely to impact on children's behaviour. All children are different though, and much will depend on the degree of the difficulty or deficit. Children with communication difficulties, learning difficulties and attention deficits may have an Individual Education Plan (IEP) (see Unit CYPOP 6). In this case, behaviour programmes must complement and fit in with the IEP.

Unit CYPOP 6 Support disabled children and young people and those with specific requirements

Communication difficulties may impact on behaviour because:

- children may have difficulty understanding the meaning and structure of language and therefore understanding boundaries and instructions

- children may have difficulty expressing themselves, leading to frustration when other people do not understand their feelings.

In addition, children with learning difficulties may have difficulty understanding and learning to comply with behaviour boundaries and goals.

Children with attention deficits may have a range of traits that make it difficult for them to behave as their peers do (see the diagram on page 160). The majority of the traits are either rooted in difficulties with inattention or difficulties with impulsivity (being impulsive). Some children may display only one or two traits, others may have many. The degree of the traits may also vary. Some children take medication that helps them – some children's behaviour can start to change as their medication wears off. There may be a time gap before the next dose is due to be taken.

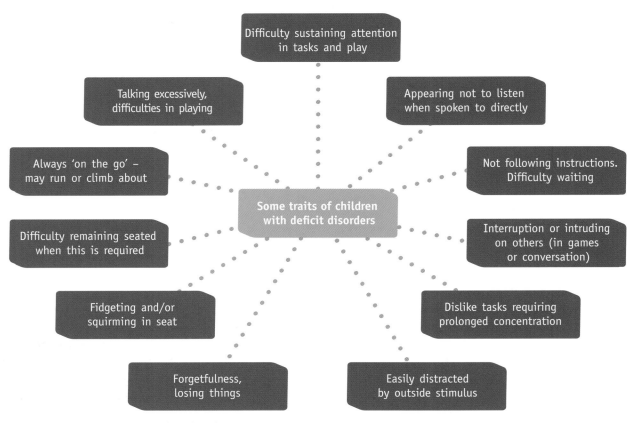

Difficulty sustaining attention in tasks and play

Talking excessively, difficulties in playing

Appearing not to listen when spoken to directly

Always 'on the go' – may run or climb about

Not following instructions. Difficulty waiting

Some traits of children with deficit disorders

Interruption or intruding on others (in games or conversation)

Difficulty remaining seated when this is required

Fidgeting and/or squirming in seat

Dislike tasks requiring prolonged concentration

Forgetfulness, losing things

Easily distracted by outside stimulus

Some traits of children with deficit disorders.

LEARNING OUTCOME **6**

FOCUS ON

...being able to support children and young people experiencing transitions

In this section you'll learn about supporting children and young people experiencing different types of transition. You'll also learn about providing them with structured learning opportunities for exploring the effects of transitions in their lives. This links with Assessment Criteria **6.1, 6.2.**

Support children and young people through transitions

Transitions are times of change. All children and young people will experience a range of transitions of different types as they grow up. Practitioners can initiate effective strategies to help children and young people cope with transitions, as detailed below.

Physical transitions

These occur when a child or young person moves from

one physical place or setting to another. For example, these transitions occur when:

- children attend a setting for the first time – a nursery, pre-school, crèche, childminder's home, primary school, out-of-school club or secondary school

- children move within a setting – from the baby room to the toddler room, or from class to class

- children have new living arrangements (this includes young people who are preparing to leave home or children preparing for a stay in hospital)

- young people leave school and prepare for work/college.

Transitions that involve moving on to the next phase of education can also be referred to as 'intellectual transitions'.

Physiological transitions

These occur when changes happen to the body, and include:

- puberty

- long-term medical conditions

- experiencing an impairment.

Emotional transitions

These occur when children and young people are deeply affected by a personal experience. This includes:

- bereavement (experiencing the death of a loved one)

- entering care

- leaving care

- the breakdown of the family unit (e.g. due to parents separating).

Starting school is a transition.

Smaller transitions

These minor changes happen during the course of a day, and include:

- the daily handover of care from a parent to a practitioner within a daycare setting

- the changeover of staff who work shifts in a residential home

- transitions between lessons in primary school

- transitions between lessons, rooms and teachers in secondary schools.

Younger children are generally affected the most by these smaller everyday changes.

The effects of transitions

So as you have seen, transitions are periods of change that generally involve a loss of familiar people in a child's life. As an adult, you may be familiar with feeling unsettled and under pressure at a time of transition – perhaps when starting a new job or living somewhere new. Children experience the same feelings and they may find them hard to cope with.

Different children respond differently to transitions. The scale of the transition is certainly a significant factor in how it will be experienced – that is, a child who is bereaved would certainly be expected to experience more emotional difficulty than a child who is moving home – however, individual children's responses will be influenced by their previous experience of change, their age, ability and their personality.

Did you know?

Practitioners can assist children in their care by helping them to prepare for the transitions ahead of them. The value of preparing children for transitions is widely accepted.

Practical example

Jamal prepares for school

Four-year-old Jamal will be leaving pre-school in July and starting primary school in September. His future teacher, Mr Evans, has been invited to attend the pre-school during May to read stories to the children. In the same month, Jamal's dad will attend a meeting for new parents at the school. He has already been sent a booklet called 'Starting school: a parent's guide'.

In June, Mr Evans will visit Jamal and his family at home. In July, the pre-school children are going on two visits to the school to join in with music activities. Jamal will also attend a story session at the school with his dad. In September, Jamal will only attend school in the morning for the first week. From the second week onwards, he will attend full time.

Question
What benefit will each of these activities have?

Preparing children and young people for onward transitions

Some transitions are predictable – for instance, children will start school by the statutory age of 5 – this is known to all involved with supporting a child early on. So schools and early years settings now routinely prepare children for this known transition. Policies and procedures are generally in place to outline how this will be done. In many cases the early years setting, school and family will work together to prepare a child, as in the Practical example above.

The following strategies can be used to prepare children for a variety of transitions:

■ Communicating with children about the transition. This means talking about what will happen, but also listening to children's concerns. It's crucial for them to have opportunities to explore how they're feeling about the effect of the transition on their lives. It is important for practitioners to be honest and open as well as reassuring. It can be helpful to teach children strategies to deal with their biggest concerns. For instance, if a child is worried about getting lost at secondary school, you can talk about what they should do if they actually become lost.

■ Arranging visits to a new setting prior to the transition. Depending on the child's age, this may be in the company of parents or carers or with a current practitioner. For example, young children will generally visit a nursery school with their families. Children in their last year of primary school will often spend a day at secondary school escorted by their current teachers.

■ Books, leaflets/brochures, stories, watching DVDs or CD-ROMs that deal with the subject of their future transition all help children and young people to become more familiar with the process of change ahead of them (e.g. starting school, puberty, going into hospital). This helps to minimise a fear of the unknown.

■ Allowing plenty of opportunities for children to express their feelings through conversations, imaginative and expressive play/arts. These opportunities should continue during and after the transition, as children and young people may be dealing with the emotions connected to it for some time afterwards.

■ When smaller transitions (which tend to affect younger children) will occur throughout the day,

Children can express their feelings through expressive arts.

be ready to offer support where needed. It can help to remind children that a transition will be happening ahead of time, for example, 'Ten more minutes, and Carol will be here. Then it will soon be time for me to go home, and I'll see you again next time.'

■ Giving children and young people opportunities to experience increasing independence in line with their needs and abilities, as this better equips them to handle change and the transitions that relate to maturing.

■ Ensuring that all documentation about a child is organised and ready to be passed on to parents/carers or other professionals as appropriate to the situation.

Specialist support for emotional transitions

When children or young people have experienced an intensely emotional transition such as a bereavement, they're likely to benefit from support given by a specially trained counsellor. A structured programme of activities may be devised to help the child or young person to explore the effects of the transition on their lives. Acknowledging and exploring what has happened and how it makes them feel can help children and young people to come to terms with the situation. These activities may take place in support groups for children and young people experiencing similar trauma in their own lives. Here are two examples of common structured activities that may be used with a child who has lost a parent:

■ **Creating a memory box**
A special box is chosen by the child and decorated by them. They choose really special, significant items to put in the box, that remind them of their loved one and how they feel about them. This might include photos of them together, an item of jewellery that belonged to them, a poem that the child has written, a drawing they have made, the order of service from the funeral.

■ **Balloon message**
If a child has something they wish they had said to the person, they may be encouraged to write it down (or have it written down for them). It can then be attached to a special helium balloon, chosen by the child. This can be released. It signifies letting go of the regret, and for some families, there is religious significance to the balloon floating heavenwards. Support groups often do this activity jointly, releasing their balloons simultaneously.

Good practice

It's good practice for practitioners and professionals supporting children and young people through transitions, to work together in partnership.

Link Up!

You'll learn more about this in Unit CYP 3.6 Working together for the benefit of children and young people

Preparing to receive a transitioning child or young person

The following guidelines can help practitioners preparing to receive a transitioning child or young person (on their first days at a new setting, for example):

- Ensure that all registration information has been received before the child attends, so that practitioners are prepared to meet the child's needs.

- Have a key worker allocated to the child.

- If appropriate to the setting, allow the child to adjust to the setting/situation slowly through a combination of visits with parents/carers and one or more short stays alone before the child attends for a longer period.

- Tell children and adults that the new child is coming and encourage them to make him or her welcome. Tell them the child's preferred name – Nicholas may prefer to be called Nick, for example.

- Give the child a warm welcome – the key worker should be available to receive the child.

- Encourage the child and parents/carers to say goodbye to one another (if parents are present). Provide honest reassurance for the child – never lie about when children will be reunited with their family. When appropriate, families should ideally have access to children. If a child is away from home overnight (perhaps during a stay in hospital), personal reminders of families, such as photographs, are helpful. Regular communication can also be established in the form of phone calls, letters, text messages and emails, as appropriate to the child and family.

- If children have comfort objects brought from home, ensure that the child has easy access to them.

- Take the child to hang up their outside clothes and to store their personal belongings. If possible, provide each child with their own pegs, drawers and/or lockers. Younger children can have a picture/word label to help them recognise their own space.

- Show the child around so that the environment becomes familiar. Help him or her to understand routines and/or timetables.

- Provide interesting activities, appropriate to the child's age, needs and abilities. In the case of younger children, it is helpful to include an activity they specifically enjoy – building with bricks, for example. The provision of imaginative/creative activities can encourage children to express their feelings.

- Provide positive images of people. Reminders of the child's home culture should also be promoted.

- Remain supportive while allowing the child time to adjust to the new situation. Make sure that the child knows who to go to if he or she needs help. Even if there is a key worker designated, children should know who to go to if the key worker is not available.

Provide children with their own space for their belongings.

- Advise families that children may experience unsettled feelings while they adjust to the transition. This may include temporary regressive behaviour (when children go back to an earlier stage of development for comfort, for example a 3-year-old may want to be fed).

- Provide ways to involve families in the child's experience, to assist the transition from the setting to home. This is as important for children starting nursery or school as it is for children away from home for longer periods. Daily reports or home-to-setting diaries are helpful.

Common anxieties about transitions

Children and young people often have common anxieties about transitions, as outlined in the diagrams below and on page 166. It's helpful for practitioners to anticipate these and to help children and young people to prepare for them. For instance, the diagram below shows that young people preparing to leave home may be anxious about looking after themselves in terms of shopping, cooking and laundry. By encouraging young people to take some responsibility for these things prior to leaving home, families and practitioners can help them to feel more confident and better prepared.

Young people also need plenty of information and support as they make career, further education (FE) and training choices. Appointments to see careers advisers can be made. Careers advisers have access to a range of information about careers, FE and training.

Many colleges and training centres provide taster days when young people can visit, meet key staff and find out more about courses and training. Some young people will need basic skills support. Careers advisers, colleges and training centres are used to meeting people's basic skills needs. Practitioners can assist by providing information about a young person's needs where appropriate, and by ensuring that the young person has support in handling information given to them in the form of brochures, leaflets and so on.

Multiple transitions

Some children and young people experience multiple transitions. This may be due to frequent family breakdowns or perhaps the nature of a parent's work. In these circumstances, children sometimes become accustomed to change, but they may find it difficult to relate closely with carers and peers. They may become distrustful of adults. Practitioners should persevere and allow a relationship to form gradually with such children, taking care not to overwhelm them. Social Services recognise the problems of multiple transitions – social workers try to make long-term or permanent plans for looked-after children whenever possible.

Leaving home.

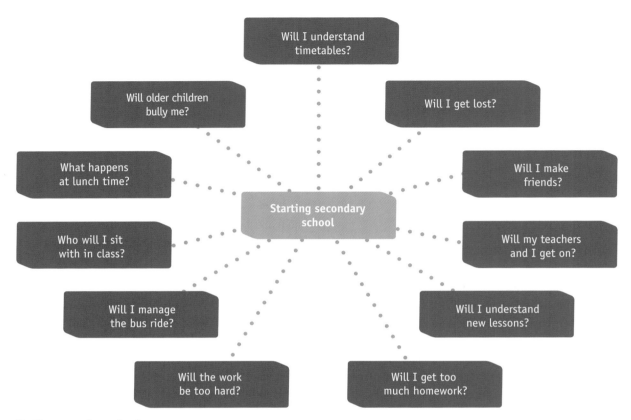

Starting secondary school.

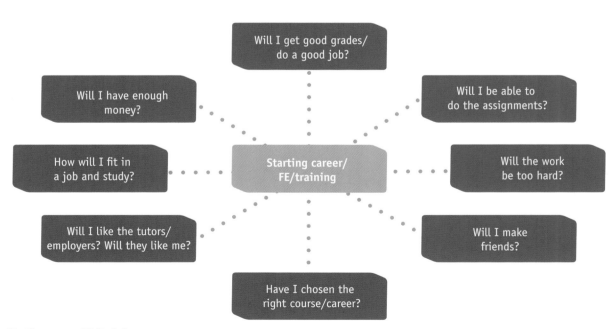

Starting career/FE/training.

How are things going?

▶ Progress Check

1. Explain how to use three observation methods of your choice. (1.3)

2. What is the purpose of a development plan? (1.4)

3. Explain three factors to consider when evaluating a development plan. (2.2)

4. Why should you encourage children and young people to actively participate in decisions about their lives? (2.5)

5. Explain three ways in which your own working practices can positively affect the development of children and young people. (4.1)

6. Explain the following techniques for promoting positive behaviour:

   a) least restrictive principle, b) reinforcing positive behaviour, and c) containment. (5.2)

7. Give two examples of:

   a) physical transitions, b) emotional transitions, and c) physiological transitions. (6.1)

Are you ready for assessment?

CACHE

Set task:

- Explain how your working practices affect children and young people's development.

- Explain how institutions, agencies and services affect children and young people's development.

You can prepare by looking through the notes you've made to date in your reflective journal, and considering what they reveal about the affect of your own working practices.

Edexel

In preparation for assessment of this Unit, you may like to gain practical experience of using the full range of assessment methods introduced in this Unit.

City & Guilds

In preparation for assessment of this Unit, you may like to gain practical experience of using the full range of assessment methods introduced in this Unit.

UNIT 3.3

Understand how to safeguard the well-being of children and young people

LEARNING OUTCOMES

The learning outcomes you will meet in this unit are:

1 Understand the main legislation, guidelines, policies and procedures for safeguarding children and young people

2 Understand the importance of working in partnership with other organisations to safeguard children and young people

3 Understand the importance of ensuring children and young people's safety and protection in the work setting

4 Understand how to respond to evidence or concerns that a child or young person has been abused or harmed

5 Understand how to respond to evidence or concerns that a child or young person has been bullied

6 Understand how to work with children or young people to support their safety and well-being

7 Understand the importance of e-safety for children and young people

INTRODUCTION

Safeguarding and child protection are both extremely important issues. The effects of child abuse are serious and far reaching – once experienced, children may suffer the impact for many years to come.

Practitioners have a duty to safeguard children and young people effectively. This requires secure knowledge and understanding encompassing legislation and policies, signs that may indicate harm and abuse, what to do if abuse is suspected, and how to comply with safe working practices.

LEARNING OUTCOME 1

...understanding the main legislation, guidelines, policies and procedures for safeguarding children and young people

In this section you'll learn about legislation, guidelines, policies and procedures, and how these affect day-to-day work with children and young people. You'll learn about the concept of child protection within the wider concept of safeguarding children and young people, and about inquiries and serious case reviews. You'll also learn about data protection, and information handling and sharing. This links with Assessment Criteria 1.1, 1.2, 1.3, 1.4, 1.5.

1. universal safeguarding, involving work to keep all children and young people safe and to create safe environments for them

2. targeted safeguarding to reduce the risks of harm for vulnerable groups of children and young people

3. responsive safeguarding, involving responding effectively when children are harmed.

This is a good example of the use of safeguarding as an umbrella term, as area 1 above relates to general safety, while areas 2 and 3 clearly relate to child protection.

key terms

Safeguarding umbrella term describing measures taken to keep children and young people safe from a wide range of dangers.

Child protection the measures taken to keep children and young people safe from abuse and harm caused by others.

Safeguarding and child protection

Safeguarding is an umbrella term used to describe any measures taken to help to keep children and young people safe from a wide range of dangers, from accidents in the home to substance abuse and unprotected consenting sex. **Child protection** is covered within this umbrella term. Child protection is about the measures that we take to keep children and young people safe from abuse and harm intentionally caused to them by another person.

In 2007, the Government carried out a major consultation with parents, children and young people, members of the general public and practitioners about their concerns in relation to children's safety. This contributed to the drawing up of the Staying Safe Action Plan, which set out the work the Government would do to drive improvements in children and young people's safety. This covers three areas:

Everyone who works with children has a duty to keep them safe from harm and abuse. There are laws, guidelines, policies and procedures in place that make this a legal requirement. You must know and understand those relevant to your own home country.

Everyone who works with children has a duty to keep them safe.

Children Act 1989

When it was introduced in 1989, this law enforced a big change in the way parents' roles are regarded. The emphasis is now on parents having a responsibility to their children, rather than rights over them. It recognises that children themselves have rights, and that they should be treated with respect. Under the Act children have rights to:

- be protected from harm
- discuss their concerns
- be listened to
- be told what their rights are
- have their wishes considered when decisions that affect them are being made
- have details about their age, culture, race and gender considered when decisions are made
- be told about the decisions that are made
- have a right to be heard if they are involved in a court case, and to have their own solicitor to represent them
- refuse a medical examination if they understand what that entails and do not want to have it done.

The table on page 171 provides further details.

Protection of Children Act 1999
This Act includes clauses that set out the child protection duties of local authorities. It also defines the term 'significant harm'. A summary of the relevant points is given in the table on page 171.

UN Convention on the Rights of the Child
The UK Government ratified this Convention in 1991. It contains Articles that refer to the rights and needs of children. These acknowledgements include:

- children have the right to protection
- children have the right to a family life
- parents and guardians have the right to support in carrying out their parental responsibilities
- children have the right to have their views listened to

- children's views should be given due consideration
- children need to receive good physical care
- children need to be shown love
- children need to feel secure
- children need a strong self-image and self-esteem.

Children Bill 2004
Prior to this bill, there had been concerns that children's services were not working together effectively to protect vulnerable children from abuse. This was highlighted by an independent inquiry into the death of Victoria Climbié, who died tragically at the hands of her carers. The inquiry and subsequent report by Lord Laming led to Every Child Matters (a Green Paper – see page 321 for details) and then to the introduction of the Children Bill. (This applies in England. Equivalent legislation was also established in the other home countries.) The Bill was passed to improve child protection for children and to ensure better coordination of services. This included the introduction of a tracking system recording information on all children, including whether they are known to the police or social, welfare or education services, the appointment of national children's commissioners who must protect the rights of all children, and the appointment of lead councillors for children's services who have local political child welfare responsibilities.

Working Together to Safeguard Children 2006
Working Together to Safeguard Children provides statutory guidance on how organisations and individuals should work together to safeguard and promote the welfare of children and young people in accordance with the Children Act 1989 and the Children Act 2004. It was revised in 2006, and in 2010, guidance in Chapter 8 was changed, which affects the way in which serious case review reports are published. You'll learn more about this in 'Serious case reviews' on page 173.

Vetting and Barring Scheme
The Vetting and Barring Scheme applies to England,

Table CYP 3.3.1: Significant harm

Legislation says...
There must be provision of services for children and their families. Every local authority has a duty to safeguard and promote the welfare of children within their area who are in need. They should promote the upbringing of such children by their families by providing services appropriate to those children's needs.
Local authorities have a duty to investigate if they are informed that a child who lives, or is found, in their areas: ■ is the subject of an emergency protection order ■ is in police protection. They must also investigate if there is reasonable cause to suspect that a child who lives, or is found, in their area is suffering, or is likely to suffer, significant harm. Enquiries must be undertaken to enable the authority to decide whether they should take any action to safeguard or promote the child's welfare.
'Harm' is defined as ill treatment or the impairment of health or developments: ■ 'Ill treatment' includes physical abuse, sexual abuse and forms of abuse that are non-physical, such as emotional abuse. ■ 'Health' means mental health and physical health. ■ 'Development' means social, physical, intellectual or behavioural development.

Did you know?

Local authorities have flexibility in terms of the ways in which they to deliver safeguarding services, so you should be aware of the guidelines, policies and procedures that apply in your own local area.

Wales and Northern Ireland. Scotland is bringing in its own parallel equivalent. The Scheme aims to protect children and young people by ensuring that people who are judged to present a risk of harm are not allowed to work with them. Since July 2010, the Scheme has been phased in – it will be fully implemented at the end of a five-year period. It's now law for anyone wanting to work or volunteer with children, young people (or vulnerable adults) to register with the Independent Safeguarding Authority (ISA). Employers will have a legal duty to check that employees are registered.

Everyone who applies will be vetted by the Criminal Records Bureau (CRB), which is taking responsibility for processing the applications to the ISA. They will check to see whether a person is already barred from working with vulnerable children and young people.

If not, the applicant will be given an ISA reference number, and they will be able to start their work under supervision. The CRB will continue to make checks to see whether there is information held about the person that indicates that they may pose a risk to vulnerable groups. This will include searching police databases, and seeing whether other organisations have reported concerns about the person. If no information is found, a CRB Disclosure can be issued – this is a document that proves to employers that the person has been fully approved to work with children or young people.

The ISA will step in to consider cases where 'relevant information' on presenting a risk is found. The applicant will be informed that they are under investigation, and may subsequently be barred from working with children, young people and vulnerable adults. Decisions are legally binding, and that person cannot be employed for certain roles under any circumstances. Their name will be added to the list of people who are barred, which will be maintained by the ISA.

Crucially, the CRB will also undertake continually to monitor people working with children and young people against new information about them. This means that any offences against children or young people by an existing worker, or any concerns raised by another organisation, should be picked up, and the worker can then be investigated and barred if necessary.

In November 2010, it became mandatory for all new workers or volunteers to apply for registration. As the Scheme continues to phase in, those already working with children and young people will also have to be registered. Applications for existing workers opened in April 2011.

Ask Miranda!

Q I've heard there are different sorts of CRB checks – Standard and Enhanced. Which one will I need?

A **Enhanced checks are for posts working with children, young people or vulnerable adults, including caring for, supervising, training or being in sole charge of them.**

How this affects day-to-day work with children and young people

Both local and national guidelines, policies and procedures affect day-to-day work with children and young people in each of the home countries. There are clearly established lines of responsibility and accountability as in England, for example:

1. The Department for Children, Schools and Families (DCSF) has overall responsibility for safeguarding (including child protection). It is up to them to issue statutory and non-statutory guidance to the country's local authorities.

2. The local authorities interpret the guidance, and develop procedures, which are issued to children and young people's services and practitioners.

3. Services and practitioners develop their own policies and procedures, which explain the ways

in which they will work to safeguard children and young people in practice, in line with national and local requirements. (This is sometimes called the 'childcare practice'.)

The setting's safeguarding policies and procedures must include the following:

- child protection (including supporting children, young people and others who may be expressing concerns)

- health and safety (see Unit CYP 3.4)

- risk assessment (see Unit CYP 3.4).

▶▶▶Link Up!◀◀◀

Unit CYP 3.4 Support children and young people's health and safety

Good practice

You should be familiar with the frameworks that apply in your home country, e.g. in England, you are advised to read in full the EYFS Welfare Requirements for Safeguarding and Promoting Children's Welfare in full as part of your study towards this unit. You can find these online at **http://nationalstrategies.standards.dcsf.gov.uk**

Did you know?

Settings should also be ensuring that children and young people's voices are heard, and many now have consultation policies and procedures in place.

Serious case reviews

Under Regulation 5 of the Local Safeguarding Children Boards Regulations 2006, Local Safeguarding Children Boards (LSCBs) must undertake serious case reviews (SCRs) when a child dies and abuse or neglect is known or suspected to be a factor in the death. This includes death by suspected suicide. The primary purpose of a SCR is for agencies and individuals involved (including social services, the police, education and health services) to learn lessons to improve the way in which they work both individually and collectively to safeguard and promote the welfare of children.

LSCBs can also decide for themselves to conduct a SCR whenever a child has been seriously harmed and the case gives cause for concern about the way in which local professionals and services worked together to safeguard and promote the welfare of children.

The purpose of serious case reviews

The prime purpose of a SCR is for agencies and individuals to learn lessons to improve the way they work both individually and collectively to safeguard and promote the welfare of children. A report of the findings must be written, and a summary must be made public. This must contain details about the key concerns arising from the case, and the recommendations and the action plan to address them.

Public inquiries

A public inquiry may be ordered by the Government after a serious incident. Evidence is presented by organisations and members of the public. Evidence may be document-based, and it may also be heard verbally. Like a SCR, a report of the findings must be written, and must be made public. This is generally expected to make recommendations on how to improve the public organisation to prevent a repeat of the serious incident.

Did you know?

Public inquiries into cases of abuse that result in the release of information about mishandling or mismanagement by public organisations result in high-profile media attention. The Laming inquiry into the death of Victoria **Climbié** and the Bichard inquiry into the death of two girls at the hands of a school caretaker are recent examples of this.

Information handling and sharing

For details on information handling and sharing in line with data protection requirements, see Unit SHC 31, Learning Outcome 4.

Link Up!

Unit SHC 31 Promote communication in health, social care or children's and young people's settings

Information handling and sharing must be in line with data protection requirements.

LEARNING OUTCOME **2**

FOCUS ON

...understanding the importance of working in partnership with other organisations to safeguard children and young people

In this section you'll learn about the importance of safeguarding children and young people, and of a child-centred or young person-centred approach. You'll also learn about partnership working, and the roles and responsibilities of different organisations that may be involved when a child or young person has been abused or harmed. This links with Assessment Criteria **2.1, 2.2, 2.3, 2.4.**

The importance of safeguarding children and young people

We don't know the exact numbers of children and young people who experience child abuse. Statistics are based on the number of cases **recorded** rather than the number of cases that **occur.** Abuse is generally hidden from view, and as the NSPCC explain, some children and young people are too young, too scared or too ashamed to tell anyone about what is happening to them. However, we do know that a significant minority of children and young people suffer serious harm and abuse, and that they may carry the effects with them for a lifetime.

The following NSPCC statistics really do bring home the importance of safeguarding children and young people. According to research:

- every week in England and Wales, one to two children will die following cruelty

- there are on average 80 child homicides recorded in England and Wales each year

- every 10 days in England and Wales, on average, one child is killed at the hands of a parent. This is an average of 35 a year over the past 5 years

- the people most likely to die a violent death are babies less than a year old, who are four times more likely to be killed than the average person in England and Wales

- three-quarters of sexually abused children did not tell anyone about the abuse at the time, and around a third still had not told anyone about their experience(s) by early adulthood

- over a quarter of all rapes recorded by the police are committed against children under 16 years of age

- 31 per cent of children experienced bullying during childhood.

In 2000, a national NSPCC survey of 3,000 young people aged 18–24 years found that:

- 4 per cent had been sexually abused

- 6 per cent had experienced serious physical neglect

- 7 per cent were physically abused by a parent or carer and of these, 80 per cent had also lived in a home where domestic violence took place

- 6 per cent had experienced emotional/ psychological maltreatment.

Have a go!

You can read more about the facts and figures of child abuse at **www.nspcc.org.uk/news-and-views/media-centre/key-information-for-journalists/facts-and-figures/Facts-and-figures_wda73664.html**

Did you know?

The statistics of children on child protection registers has been climbing. Some say this is because awareness campaigns are working, so more concerns are reported. However, we cannot be sure of the reasons. In 2006, 26,400 children were on child protection registers in England.

Did you know?

WTSC states that anyone who has a concern about a child they are in contact with has a clear responsibility to report the concern to the appropriate agency. For practitioners, this means following the chain of reporting outlined in their setting's child protection policy.

Partnership working

To safeguard children and young people effectively and to meet their often complex needs, a range of professionals and agencies with different responsibilities and expertise must work together in partnership.

In Learning Outcome 1, you learned that inquiries and serious case reviews are sometimes conducted when there has been a failure to safeguard a child or young person. Over the years, a lack of partnership working has been regularly highlighted as a root cause of failure to safeguard. There have been many cases in which professionals and/or organisations have not communicated well with each other with regard to a family about which concerns have been made. This prevents a bigger picture of what is happening within a family from emerging, and leads to failure to take sufficient action to prevent harm or abuse.

The Government document 'Working Together to Safeguard Children' (WTSC) sets out how individuals and organisations should work together to safeguard and promote the welfare of children and young people, in accordance with the Children Act 1984 and the Children Act 2004. It was updated in 2010 to reflect recommendations made in Lord Laming's 2009 report, 'The Protection of Children in England: A Progress Report'. What you must do to work in accordance with WTSC will be outlined in your setting's child protection policy.

Good practice

WTSC is aimed at organisations that have a 'particular responsibility for safeguarding and promoting the welfare of children and young people'. This means that it's good practice for all practitioners to read the document fully to understand their roles and responsibilities.

Have a go!

You can read WTSC at **http://publications. education.gov.uk**. On page 22 of the document, you'll find a useful introduction. On page 23, you'll find a table that explains which parts of the document are relevant to your job role. There's no need to read the remaining sections.

'Multi-agency working' is another term used to describe what happens when a range of practitioners and professionals from different agencies, services and teams work together in partnership to meet the needs of children, young people and/or their families.

You can read more about multi-agency working in Learning Outcome 1 of Unit CYP 3.6 Working together for the benefit of children and young people

A child-/young person-centred approach

Every Child Matters makes it clear that the individual needs and interests of the child or young person should always be paramount in the approach of practitioners, professionals and agencies. Working together to meet the needs and interests of individual children and young people is at the heart of partnership, multi-agency working.

In addition, children and young people have the

You can read more about this, and the implication for practitioners' duty of care, in Unit SHC 34 Principles for implementing duty of care in health, social care or children's and young people's settings

right to have their views listened to and given due consideration under the UN Convention on the Rights of the Child. This is of key consideration when important decisions about a child or young person's future will be made.

Roles and responsibilities of different organisations

When a child or young person has been harmed or abused, workers from social services and health

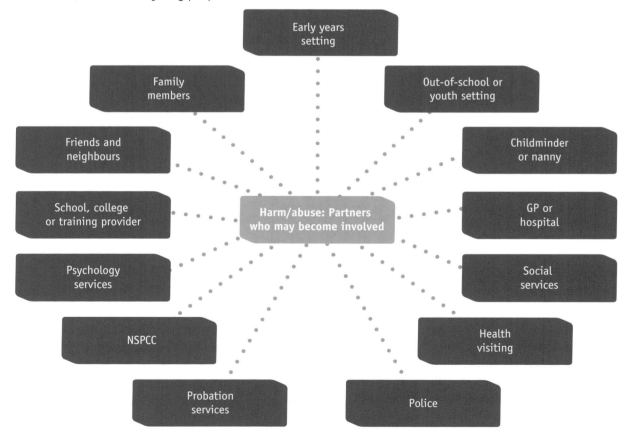

Partners who may be involved when a child or young person has been harmed or abused.

Roles and responsibilities of key organisations

Organisation	Role and responsibilities
GP or hospital	GPs are usually the first port of call for patients, and as such, they are often the first to pick up possible abuse when examining a child or young person at their surgery. In emergency situations, children and young people may be taken or may go to the accident and emergency unit at a local hospital. Hospitals keep a record of patients' visits, and if a child or young person is repeatedly seen with certain sorts of injuries, staff may identify possible abuse.
Social services	Social services have a statutory duty to support vulnerable families. They must also respond appropriately to referrals regarding concerns that a child or young person is suffering or likely to suffer significant harm, and work within the legal framework and local procedures to safeguard children and young people. Social workers must work sensitively with parents while simultaneously ensuring that their children are protected.
Health visitors	Health visitors have responsibilities relating to the health and development of children under the age of 5. They also provide guidance and support to their families. This means that parents who are not coping may turn to them for help. As health visitors go into the family home, they are well placed to notice environmental causes for concern (e.g. if a child is being neglected or is otherwise living in unacceptable circumstances).
Police	The harm or abuse of children or young people may lead to criminal proceedings, which the police will have responsibility for. It is not uncommon for police officers to identify possible abuse when called to attend a domestic disturbance. Police officers may also be involved with social workers should a child or young person be removed from the family home as a safeguarding measure.
Probation services	Probation services are involved when someone is found guilty of harming or abusing a child or young person. Probation officers have a number of duties, including making assessments to advise courts, managing and enforcing community orders, and working with prisoners during and after sentencing. In an effort to rehabilitate offenders, they also have a duty to enforce the conditions of court orders and release licences. In an effort to protect the public, they conduct offender risk assessments and ensure that offenders are aware of the impact of their crime on their victims and the public.
NSPCC	The NSPCC provide advice services for adults worried that a child or young person may be being harmed – parents, professionals and members of the general public can call to help protect children. They also provide a free, online, specialised child protection resource for practitioners, researchers, trainers, policy-makers and other professionals working to protect children. They provide direct services to children and families, concentrating on important issues and groups of children most at risk. The NSPCC also support ChildLine, where trained volunteers are on hand to provide advice and support 24 hours a day to children who make contact by phone or online. A primary schools service is also being developed. It aims to teach children aged 5–11 in every community: ■ what abuse and bullying are ■ how to protect themselves ■ where to get help if they need it.
Psychology services	Child psychologists support children or young people who have been harmed or abused. Clinical or forensic psychologists are often asked to contribute to child risk assessments, which assess the level of risk that a parent may pose to a child or young person. This must be carefully considered when decisions are to be made about where a child or young person will live, and under what circumstances they will be able to see a parent who has caused harm or abuse.

sectors will be involved, along with the police. However, all children and young people are known to a number of organisations, who may be potentially involved in partnership working to support the child or young person and/or their family, as the diagram show on page 176.

The roles of children and young people's practitioners and settings (early years /out-of-school/youth settings, schools and colleges, childminders and nannies) is initially to be vigilant in terms of safeguarding, and to report any concerns appropriately. The roles and responsibilities of the other organisations identified in the diagram are explained in the table on page 177.

Professionals are also there to support you. If you are feeling distressed after or during involvement in a case of suspected or actual abuse, you will need the opportunity to talk through your feelings. But because of strict confidentiality, you must not talk to anyone who does not 'need to know'. However, it is appropriate for you to talk to your supervisor, or to ask your supervisor for the name of the outside professional you should contact to talk things over. This is generally a social worker, or a worker from the NSPCC.

FOCUS ON

...**understanding the importance of ensuring children and young people's safety and protection in the work setting**

In this section you'll learn about why it's important to ensure that children and young people are protected from harm in work settings, and about the policies and procedures to protect children, young people and the adults who work with them. You'll also learn about how to report concerns about poor practice and how practitioners can take steps to protect themselves in their practice. This links with Assessment Criteria **3.1, 3.2, 3.3.**

and it should be at the heart of your own professional values.

Unit SHC 34 Principles for implementing duty of care in health, social care or children's and young people's settings

Policies and procedures to protect children, young people and adults

Policies and procedures must be in place to protect children and young people, as you learned in Learning Outcome 1. They also protect the adults who work with children and young people. You can read more about safe working practices below.

Whistle blowing

Whistle blowing is the term used to describe when a practitioner alerts superiors or outside professionals to their concerns relating to their own setting. All those within the sector have a duty to safeguard children, and as such they must take action to blow the whistle if necessary, even though it may be uncomfortable.

You must report concerns about colleagues to superiors if you suspect them of abuse, causing harm or poor

The importance of ensuring that children and young people are protected from harm

As you learned in Unit SHC 34, practitioners have a firm duty to ensure that children and young people are safe and protected from harm while in their care. It's generally the most important thing to the parents and carers who entrust their children to you each day,

practice. If you have reported concerns to superiors but feel they have not acted appropriately by taking your concerns seriously or by taking the appropriate action, you must report this. If the concern relates to abuse or harm, you should call Social Services without delay. If it relates to other areas of poor practice, you can call the appropriate inspectorate (e.g. in England, this is Ofsted). This applies if you feel there's a lack of action being taken to investiagte suspicions you have raised about a child or young person being harmed or abused outside of the setting, as well as concerns you may have made about colleagues.

Did you know?

In 2009, there was a case involving a nursery worker in Plymouth, who sexually abused toddlers in her care within the workplace. She took over 100 photos of her victims, which she shared with other paedophiles via the internet. It serves as a reminder that we MUST ACT if we are concerned about a colleague's practice.

Good practice

If you need to whistle blow, write down as much information as possible about your area of concern. Include specific information where possible – names, places, dates, times and so on. Think through your concern and make notes to help you explain it clearly. Managers must support whistle blowers under the 1998 UK Public Interest Disclosure Act. There's also a duty to make sure that those who have allegations made about them are protected while these are investigated.

Ask Miranda!

Q Does whistle blowing only apply to concerns about deliberate harm or abuse of children or young people within the setting?

A **No, it applies to any safeguarding issue. For example, you may need to report concerns about risk assessments being disregarded, or about a lack of care taken with procedures to ensure that children and young people are collected by authorised people only.**

Safe working practices

The term 'safe working practices' refers to the way practitioners work to protect children and to protect themselves from allegations of abuse. Your organisation's guidelines will be included within the Child Protection policy, and based on the requirements of your home country. You must make sure that you know and understand these, and always work in accordance with them.

It's the role of the person in charge to check that the safe practices are adhered to, and to monitor their effectiveness. Regulative bodies (such as Ofsted) will also want to be satisfied that these practices are observed. Practitioners need to be open and accepting about being accountable to children, parents, families and other agencies – it is part of holding a position of power and trust. The following are typically included within 'safe working practice' guidance:

■ All adults working/volunteering/living on the premises of the setting must be registered with the Independent Safeguarding Authority (ISA) (see Learning Outcome 1) and undergo a Criminal Records Bureau (CRB) check, known as a CRB Disclosure, to see whether they are regarded as fit to work/live on premises with children. Any prior convictions must be disclosed on the relevant form – none are considered spent in this case.

You have a duty to report concerns to the appropriate person.

- Adults in group settings who have been given a reference number by ISA but have not yet had their disclosure processed may not be left alone with any children, or carry out personal assistance such as toileting or changing nappies.

- At least two adults must always be present at a setting, however many children are there. This applies even if there is one child left who is late being collected – at least two staff must stay. If the parents/carers/alternative adults authorised to collect the child have not contacted you, and cannot be contacted, you may need to take action. After an hour or more has elapsed since the setting officially closed, practitioners should ring the Duty Social Worker (listed under Social Services in the telephone directory) for support. A practitioner must not take the child to the child's home or to their own home. Practitioners have a duty to stay with the child until the situation is resolved, only passing the child on to a person authorised to collect them, a police officer or a social worker.

- Adults must follow guidance on physical contact with children and young people. Babies and young children need close physical contact to feel cared for, safe and secure, and to meet their care needs. But as children mature, less physical contact is needed, and working practices need to be adjusted accordingly. Adults must know what is acceptable contact for the children or young people they are working with. To protect yourself and the child when carrying out physical care tasks (such as changing a young child's nappy or clothes) do so with the door open, and stay within sight of your colleagues. Open plan settings assist practitioners to work 'transparently' at all times, and help them to avoid being alone and out of view with a child or young person.

- Adults should not invite children into their homes, or in the case of childminders, they should not do so out of the normal childminding hours arranged with parents or carers.

- Adults should not offer children lifts in their car, or take them anywhere if they should accidentally meet them outside of the setting.

- Adults must record and report any incidents when they have had no choice but to restrain a child, for instance to protect them from seriously harming themselves or others. (See Unit CYP 3.7.)

- Adults must record and report all accidents, injuries and incidents. A child being bullied is an example of an incident. (See Unit CYP 3.4.)

- There are guidelines in place about what should happen if an allegation of abuse is made about a member of staff.

Open plan settings assist practitioners to work transparently.

- The registered person must ensure that all staff are aware of the possible signs and symptoms that indicate a child or young person is at risk. They should also know their responsibilities to report all concerns according to procedures without delay, and to restrict their concerns to as few people as need to know about them.

- Adults must ensure that off-site visits are carefully planned in terms of risk assessment and supervision, including any journeys. (See Unit CYP 3.4.)

- Adults must ensure that written permission has been obtained before children and young people are photographed, videoed or recorded. The products must only be used for the purpose for which the permission was granted. For example, if a setting has permission to keep a photo of a child playing in their development records, they must not use it to publicise the setting, or put it in the newsletter without getting further written parental permission.

See also Unit SHC 34, Learning Outcome 1.

Link Up!

Unit CYP 3.7 Understand how to support positive outcomes for children and young people
Unit CYP 3.4 Support children and young people's health and safety
Unit SHC 34 Principles for implementing duty of care in health, social care or children's and young people's settings

LEARNING OUTCOME 4

FOCUS ON

...understanding how to respond to evidence or concerns that a child or young person has been abused or harmed

In this section you'll learn about the possible signs, symptoms, indicators and behaviours that may cause concern in regards to safeguarding. You'll learn about the actions to take if a child or young person alleges harm or abuse, and the rights that they have in this situation. This links with Assessment Criteria 4.1, 4.2, 4.3.

Indicators of abuse

For children's welfare, it is important that you learn how to recognise the possible signs, symptoms and behaviour that can indicate abuse. Practitioners learn this so that if they come across these indicators they will realise that abuse could be taking place, and will take the appropriate action. Experts sometimes use more categories to describe the specifics of abuse, but essentially there are four main types:

- physical abuse

- emotional abuse

- sexual abuse

- neglect.

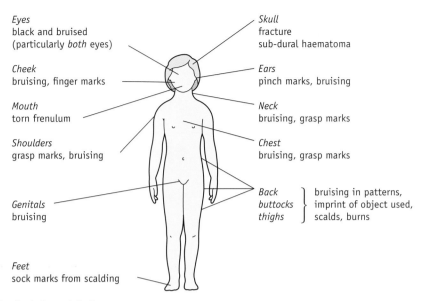

Eyes
black and bruised
(particularly *both* eyes)

Cheek
bruising, finger marks

Mouth
torn frenulum

Shoulders
grasp marks, bruising

Genitals
bruising

Feet
sock marks from scalding

Skull
fracture
sub-dural haematoma

Ears
pinch marks, bruising

Neck
bruising, grasp marks

Chest
bruising, grasp marks

Back
buttocks } bruising in patterns,
thighs } imprint of object used,
scalds, burns

Sites of common physical abuse injuries.

Physical abuse

Physical abuse occurs when someone deliberately causes physical harm to a child. It includes the actions of hitting, kicking, shaking, biting, squeezing, burning, scalding, throwing, attempting suffocation or drowning, giving children poisonous substances or inappropriate drugs or alcohol.

Signs

Signs of physical abuse include bruises, cuts and abrasions. Because children frequently have minor accidents and therefore often have bumps and bruises, it is important to take account of where on the body bruising or marking occurs – the diagram above shows parts of the body that are likely to become bruised or marked when abuse is taking place. (This is called a 'body map'.) In addition, consider how often a child has bruises and marks. If frequency is a concern, you can keep a dated record of the marks you observe, to see if a pattern emerges.

Bruises made by abuse may be in the shape of hands, fingers or other implements. A torn frenulum (web of skin inside the upper lip) is often a sign of abuse. The injury may occur if a child has something forced into their mouth, for instance if they are forcibly fed

with a bottle or spoon. Injuries to this area rarely occur accidentally.

Blank body maps are often used to record the marks actually seen on a child. Remember that physical signs are not always left by physical abuse. Common sites for bruising that occurs as a result of play

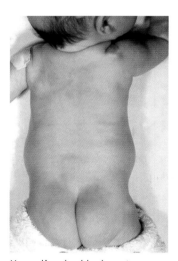

Mongolian (or blue) spot.

and/or accident include marks to the legs and arms, particularly below the knees and elbows. Mongolian spots (or blue spots) are birthmarks that may occur on the lower spine or buttocks of children of southern European, African or Asian descent. They are smooth, with the bluish grey tone of a bruise, and can be quite large. They should not be confused with a bruise or a sign of abuse.

Behavioural/emotional signs

Children who are being physically abused may show signs of changed behaviour in addition to physical signs (or in the absence of physical signs). These may include:

- being withdrawn
- avoiding physical contact
- lack of trust
- afraid to go home or go with abuser
- aggressive behaviour
- acting out aggression in play
- signs of stress such as bedwetting
- seeming sad/preoccupied/unable to have fun
- lack of confidence
- watching others carefully but not participating (sometimes called 'frozen watchfulness').

Emotional abuse

Emotional abuse occurs when children are harmed emotionally. When children's emotional needs, which include love and affection, are not met, then children's development is seriously damaged. They are likely to experience difficulties with social and emotional development, finding it particularly hard to relate to adults and to make friends with children. This can have the effect of putting a child at further risk of bullying.

Children often have low self-esteem, and may develop poor emotional health (mental health). Children who are emotionally abused may live with constant threats, shouting, ridiculing, criticism, taunting and repeated rejection. The signs of emotional abuse are listed opposite.

However, when children experience an emotional upheaval in their life, such as bereavement, divorce or a new baby in the family, they can also show some of those signs of stress for a period of time. You're advised to record instances and share the information with parents and carers. You will have notes in case the signs persist.

Signs

Children who are being emotionally abused may show signs of changed behaviour.

They may include:

- low self-esteem and lack of confidence
- difficulty making friends
- being very wary of their parent's mood
- behaviour difficulties – aggression (may be towards self, e.g. head banging, biting), attention seeking, demanding, stealing, lying, tantrums (in children over 5)
- indiscriminately affectionate – may cuddle or sit on lap of any adult, even if they do not know them
- poor concentration leading to learning difficulties
- inability to have fun
- toileting problems after previously being dry
- overly upset by making a mistake
- behaviour associated with comfort seeking in children over 5 – sucking thumb, rocking, masturbation.

Sexual abuse

Sexual abuse is defined as the involvement of dependent and developmentally immature children in sexual activities. It also includes behaviour that may not involve any physical contact – exposing children to pornography via any media, for instance photographs, videos, DVDs and the internet, or having them witness the sexual acts of others.

Sexual abuse happens to both girls and boys, and to babies. Both men and women sexually abuse children. The majority of children who are sexually abused are abused by someone they know who is in a position of trust, such as a family member or family friend. A minority of sexually abused children go on to become abusers. Sexual abuse frequently causes lifelong emotional damage and serious difficulties in forming relationships. Sometimes children do not show signs of abuse until much later, when they have reached

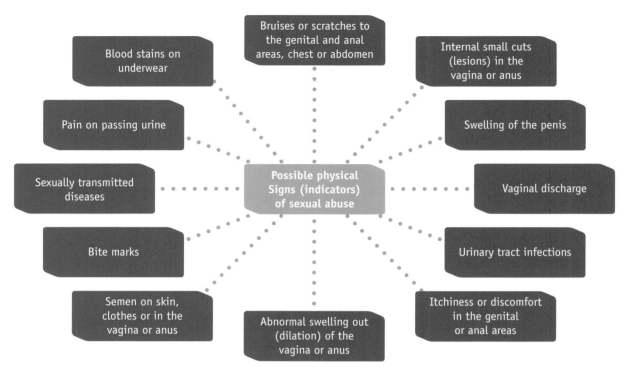

Possible physical signs of sexual abuse.

puberty for instance. It may be that the child had not previously realised that what was happening to them was wrong and abusive.

Signs

There are few physical signs that are likely to be noticed after a child is independent in terms of caring for their own body, so the behaviour signs are particularly important. Over-sexualised behaviour is when children act in sexual ways that are inappropriate for their age – they may say or know things you would not expect, or role play or act out sexual situations.

Did you know?

Over-sexualised behaviour is also called pseudo-sexual behaviour.

Neglect

Neglect occurs when a family does not provide for a child's basic, everyday, essential needs. This can include a lack of supervision (such as leaving the child alone inappropriately), supervising a child while the adult is under the influence of alcohol or drugs, not protecting a child from danger and not providing stimulation. Children who have been neglected are often said to be 'failing to thrive'. Because of a lack of care and attention to their most basic needs, they may not be able to grow and develop as they should. These children are deprived.

Signs

Signs of neglect may include the following:

- Lack of food, or lack of healthy food. This can lead to malnourishment, obesity (being overweight), hunger.

- Clothes uncared for, may be dirty, smelly, worn, may have clothes that are not suitable for the

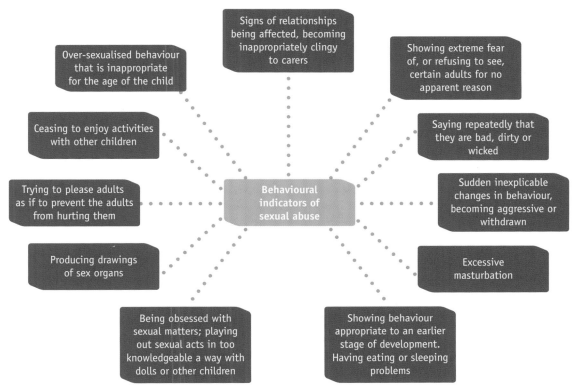

Possible behavioural indicators of sexual abuse.

weather. This can lead to bullying. (In addition there may not be adequate heating at home.)

- Lack of care hygienically. Children may be dirty and they may smell. They may have skin infections and infestations that go untreated (such as head lice). This is also likely to lead to bullying. The child may live in an unhygienic environment and frequently be unwell. Food poisoning is common.

- Inadequate supervision and lack of safety features at home. This may lead to frequent accidents, children having too much freedom (e.g. out alone in the street or garden late at night, or a younger child may be out unsupervised). Children may play truant from school, leading to a lack of stimulation and education. There may not be a child's safety seat in the car.

- Poor medical care. Illnesses and injuries may go untreated; impairments may go unchecked; developmental checkups, immunisations and dental appointments may be missed, possibly leading to serious or prolonged health problems and disability.

- Lack of love, care, affection and moral guidance. This can lead to isolation and possible early smoking, drinking and substance abuse.

Children may appear to be:

- nervous, attention-seeking or clingy

- sad, unpopular with peers

- caring for siblings or other family members, including parents

- angry, and may tell lies

- streetwise – they look after themselves.

Actions to take if a child or young person alleges harm or abuse

Your setting will have clear policies in place to tell you what to do if a child or young person alleges harm or abuse, and it's extremely important that you follow these. However, general guidelines on disclosure are given below.

Disclosure

'Disclosure' is the term that is used to refer to a child revealing to an adult that they have been abused. This may be in the following forms:

- **A full disclosure**

  This is when the child says who has abused them, and goes into the history and nature of the abuse.

- **A partial disclosure**

  A child may begin to tell of abuse, and then shy away and not continue. Or he or she may reveal only some details, leaving out what exactly has happened, or the name of the abuser.

- **An indirect disclosure**

  This occurs when a child indicates abuse indirectly, through their play (often in a role-play or imaginary situation), their artwork or, in the case of older children, through letters, stories or school work. Children may choose to disclose in this way if they are too afraid to tell directly, too embarrassed or ashamed, or if they find it too painful to discuss. They may fear that they will not be believed, or that they will be punished or sent away from home. They may not know the right words to explain what has happened to them. Children sometimes disclose in this way unintentionally – they may not be aware that what is happening to them is wrong, or they may have tried to block out or disguise the abuse, but have inadvertently revealed it in their play or conversation.

When the child is disclosing

- Look at the child, maintaining eye contact if the child is choosing to look directly at you. Aim to be on the same level as the child (or lower) so that you do not appear intimidating. Do not look away from the child – this can be interpreted by them as disapproval. Do not show any signs of disgust on your face, whatever the child says, or they are likely to feel that they disgust you because they were involved in the abuse.

Ask Miranda!

Q I don't know how I'd handle it if a child told me they'd been abused. I'd be so shocked.

A When a child discloses abuse, it can be quite a shocking experience for a practitioner. However, your response is very important in terms of the welfare of the child, so you must stay calm, let the child see that you are in control of yourself, and follow the guidelines below for dealing with the situation.

- Let the child do the talking, allowing them to tell you spontaneously and in their own way.

- Listen and follow carefully. Try to remember exactly what the child is saying and the language they are using, rather than interpreting what it all means.

- Do not ask the child questions or prompt them for more information. This may lead to confused information. It is not helpful for the child to have been 'led' should evidence be needed legally later on. If appropriate, a trained specialist will interview the child at another time.

What to say to the child

- Let the child know that telling you was the right thing to do. ('I'm so glad you've told me.')

- Tell them that the abuse was not their fault.

- Praise them for having told you, and for surviving their ordeal.

- If the child asks whether you believe him or her, say yes.

- All allegations of abuse must be reported and taken seriously. It has been shown that children do not often lie about abuse. Even if the story seems confused or improbable, you must let the child see that you accept it. Your role is not to investigate, but to record and report. Never ask questions such as, 'Are you telling me the truth?' or, 'Are you sure that's what happened?'

- If the child asks you to comment on the abuser, tread carefully. You should not be judgemental. Remember that the child may love the abuser. It is acceptable to say that the abuser was wrong to do the things they have done.

- If a child asks you what will happen to the abuser, say that they will need some help.

- Tell them that you will have to tell someone else. You should never promise not to tell. It is your duty to report suspicions and disclosures of abuse, and the child will lose their trust in you when you do report it if you have not explained this.

- Tell them what you are going to do next.

- Say that you will talk to them again to let them know what has happened.

- Reassure them that they can speak to you again about the abuse if they want to talk about it.

You should record and report a disclosure as soon as possible. See opposite.

Recognising, recording and reporting signs and symptoms

You should read this section in conjunction with information on avoiding premature judgements on page 188.

By recognising signs of abuse, practitioners can take the first steps that may ultimately stop the abuse happening to a child. It is very important to learn the signs and symptoms. Having a good knowledge of children's expected development and behaviour is key, as you will then be more likely to spot behaviour that is inappropriate for a child's age – tantrums or wetting themselves in children generally too old for this, or streetwise or overtly sexual behaviour in children generally too young.

This is informed by the regular observations and assessments that practitioners make on children in their care. Observations can reveal and record how the child forms relationships, how their behaviour or mood may change over time, and recurring themes in their play or conversation. Always date your observations. This is good practice in any case, but it is also important if the information is required as evidence.

If you suspect that a child may be being abused, you should write down all the information as soon as you can, while it is fresh in your mind. It is easy to forget details later, particularly those that do not seem to have much significance at the time but may prove to be important. You must record your observations, and you must inform your supervisor of your concerns, following your setting's procedures and the requirements of your home country. Make sure that you know and understand these. Your setting will have a Child Protection policy that sets out how you should report concerns, and what will happen next. Broadly, you will need to include the following information:

- The date the report is made.

- Child's name, address and date of birth.

- Name of the child's parents or carers.

- Your name and job title.

- Whether you are reporting your own concerns or those that have been reported to you by someone else.

- Concise description of your concerns.

- Incidents leading to your concerns, if applicable (for instance, you may have noticed a behaviour or bruising before, but did not record it until now because you were not concerned until a repetition of the behaviour or bruising occurred).

- Accurate description of physical signs, if applicable, recorded on a body map. Do not make assumptions about the cause of the signs, just record facts.

- Accurate description of behaviour signs if applicable. Again, only record facts.

- If concern has been caused by something a child has said, or if disclosure has taken place, again record only facts, using their exact words as much as possible, not your interpretation of them. You must also record what you said to the child, even if you are concerned that you may not have handled the situation effectively. This is important detail.

- If a parent or carer has given you any explanation for the signs or symptoms you are concerned about, record the facts, again using their exact words as much as you can.

Sign the record and store it safely and confidentially in a locked filing cabinet or cupboard to which only appropriate staff members have access. Only those who **need to know**, that is your superiors and those who work closely with the child, should be able to access such files. Under the Data Protection Act, parents and carers have a right to see records kept about them and their children if they ask to do so.

Your concerns should be reported in private to the appropriate person or agency, in line with the setting's policies and procedures. In group settings, it's usual for practitioners to report concerns to the supervisor or manager, who will then take responsibility for reporting to the appropriate outside agency (e.g. Social Services).

key term

Need to know basis the process of only disclosing confidential information to those allowed to have access to it and at times when they have reason to be informed.

Avoiding judgements

If you notice signs and symptoms that cause you to suspect abuse, it is very important that you remain objective. You must follow procedures closely without making judgements. Remember that there could be other reasons for the child's behaviour or physical signs. You must ask parents or carers if they have noticed the signs and symptoms, and ask them why they think they have occurred. There may be a simple explanation, and you should note what you are told.

You must not make judgements even if actual abuse is confirmed. In the case of either suspected or actual abuse, it can be hard for a practitioner who cares about children not to become upset and/or feel angry. However, as a professional, you will want to help the child by doing what is best for him or her. In the past, children who were being abused were frequently removed from their families. However, it has been found that this is often not the best thing for the child. Some children who were removed have felt that they were being sent away as punishment for 'telling on' their families. The threat that children will be sent away if they tell is often used by abusers – it is often an effective threat because children may desperately want to stay within their family. The Children Act 1989 says that what is best for children should be paramount.

The modern approach is often to keep children within the family, while helping them by preventing further abuse. Families need support if this is to happen, and that requires a multi-professional, multi-agency approach, which includes practitioners. You must continue to treat the parent as you would any other,

and work in partnership with them. If parents feel as though they are being judged or treated differently, they may ultimately stop bringing the child, which would be detrimental to the child and the family. Partnerships with parents and families can be developed and supported by:

- making sure that the key worker has opportunities to get to know the family

- being available at dropping off and collection times, and being sure to greet adults and make general conversation (this need only be brief but regular for parents to see that you are approachable, and to feel that you are not judging them)

- regularly sharing information about the child's progress and achievements

- asking the family to share information about the child's progress and activities at home

- encouraging parents to get involved with their child and the setting, by bringing resources such as empty boxes for making models, for example.

Rights

Children, young people and their families have rights, and it's important that these are observed in situations where harm or abuse is suspected or alleged. Children and young people have the right:

- to protection from harm or abuse

- not to be subjected to medical examinations if they understand the procedure and do not wish to have it carried out

- not to be subjected to repeated questioning following allegations or suspicions of abuse

- to have processes and procedures explained to them, including legal processes

- to be consulted and to have their views taken into consideration when decisions about their future are to be made.

Family members have the right:

- to be informed about what is said about them, and to see relevant reports

- to be consulted and to have their views taken into consideration when decisions about their future, and that of their children, are to be made.

LEARNING OUTCOME 5

Bullying

It's a sad fact that many children and young people are affected by bullying to some extent in their lives, and that the fear of being bullied affects many more.

Research for ChildLine found that just over half (54 per cent) of both primary and secondary school children thought that bullying was 'a big problem' or 'quite a big problem' in their school. Just over half (51 per cent) of Year 5 students (aged 9–10) reported that they had been bullied during the preceding term compared with just over a quarter (28 per cent) of

FOCUS ON

...understanding how to respond to evidence or concerns that a child or young person has been bullied

In this section you'll learn about the different types of bullying and the potential effects. You'll also learn about the policies and procedures that should be followed in response to concerns, and how to support a child, young person and their family when bullying is suspected or alleged. This links with Assessment Criteria 5.1, 5.2, 5.3.

Year 8 students (aged 12–13). Fifteen per cent of primary school students, and 12 per cent of secondary school students said that they had both bullied other children and been bullied themselves in the last year.

Kidscape is a national charity dedicated to preventing bullying and protecting children. They have issued the following worrying statistics:

- 1 in 12 children are badly bullied to the point that it affects their education, relationships and even their prospects for jobs in later life

- each year 10–14 youth suicides are directly attributed to bullying (Home Office figures)

- bullied children are six times more likely to contemplate suicide than their non-bullied counterparts.

Fifty-four per cent of pupils say bullying is a problem in their school.

Types of bullying

Bullying usually falls into one or more of the following types:

- physical – pushing, kicking, hitting, pinching and other forms of violence or threats

- verbal – name calling, insults, sarcasm, spreading rumours, persistent teasing

- emotional – excluding, ignoring, tormenting, ridicule, humiliation

- cyberbullying – using information and communication technology deliberately to upset someone else, particularly mobile phones (upsetting texts, taking humiliating photos or video clips and circulating them) and the internet (often via social networking sites and email, and can include setting up 'hate websites').

Have a go!

You can learn more about cyberbullying online at **www.direct.gov.uk/en/YoungPeople/ HealthAndRelationships/Bullying/DG_070501**

Kidscape has carried out research into bullying. They define bullying as usually including deliberate hostility and aggression, a victim who is less powerful than the bully or bullies, and an outcome that is always painful and/or distressing. Their identified potential effects of bullying are shown on the diagram on page 191.

Reasons for bullying

There are numerous reasons why victims are bullied, but bullies tend to target children or young people who are different to them in some way. The bullying can be homophobic or gender-based, racist, relating to special educational needs or disabilities. It can also be based on other physical characteristics, such as being short, or even being classed as pretty. It could relate to socio-economic factors, such as being perceived as a 'snob', or as coming from a 'poor' family. Being perceived as a 'swot' can also be a factor. Children or young people with low self-esteem and self-confidence are particularly at risk of bullying. (You'll learn about supporting these children in Learning Outcome 6.)

Policies and procedures

All schools have a legal requirement to put an effective policy in place to prevent bullying. This must include consequences for bullying behaviour. Other settings may incorporate the policies and procedures on bullying into their behaviour policy, child protection policy or safeguarding policy.

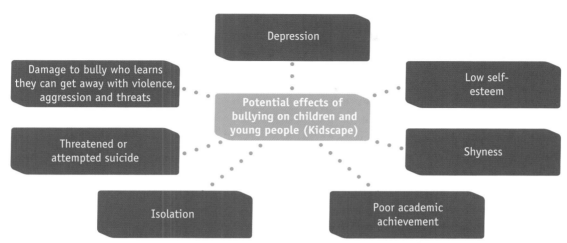

Potential effects of bullying on children and young people.

Childline provides information on bullying for children. You can view this online at **www.childline.org.uk** in the Explore section.

What children and young people should do if they are bullied

The anti-bullying policy should also address what children and young people should do if they are bullied. The setting should regularly communicate this to children and young people. Children and young people should:

■ know who to tell, and to tell them immediately

■ resist at the time of bullying, saying firmly or shouting 'NO!'

■ know that friends should stick together as there is safety in numbers.

Kidscape issue the following advice to professionals:

Kidscape: Dealing with Bullying and Bullies

■ Tell the children from Day One that bullying (verbal or physical) is *not* tolerated in the school. Everyone is expected to ensure that it does not happen and has the responsibility to tell – this is not telling tales.
■ In class, have the children discuss bullying; what it is, what can be done, etc.
■ Have the children do a school survey to find out what children, teachers and staff think about bullying. Is it a problem, should it go on, should children tell if they are being bullied?
■ Have the children compile the survey and allow them to call a school assembly to announce the results.
■ Have the classes make up rules for behaviour. Agree a class/school set of rules.
■ Agree possible solutions (or consequences if necessary).
■ Have the children discuss ways to help the bullies become part of the group.
■ If bullying is happening, find out the facts, talk to the bullies and victims individually. If the bullying is about a particular issue (e.g. death, divorce, disfigurement), mount an education programme about the problem, but not focused on a particular child. Call in parents, ask their suggestions and solicit their support.
■ If necessary, break up the group dynamics by assigning places, keeping bullies at school at the end of the day, etc. Most bullying groups have a leader with other children being frightened of not bullying. Turn peer pressure against bullying and break up groups.
■ Teach children to be assertive using programmes such as Kidscape. Differences should be acceptable and never a cause for bullying. Reward and encourage children for individuality.

Dealing with bullying and bullies.

Good practice

All settings should have clear procedures that tell practitioners what to do in response to concerns or evidence of bullying. These will enable practitioners to act swiftly and appropriately to prevent potential or on-going bullying. They will also be able to support the victim (see page 193), and take action to tackle the bully's behaviour. Written procedures also ensure that a consistent approach is taken, and that a single, clear stance on bullying is promoted at all times.

Did you know?

Kidscape have devised leaflets and advice for children and young people. These are especially helpful for those who have experienced bullying and may be afraid of it happening again. There are also online scenario quizzes.

Have a go!

Have a look at the advice for children and young people at **www.kidscape.org.uk** in the Advice section.

Have a go!

You can view a sample anti-bullying policy online at **www.kidscape.org.uk** (select Advice, Downloads).

Supporting families

When a child or young person has been bullied, their parents and carers are also likely to need support.

Parents will understandably be upset for their child, and may feel angry that it has happened. If bullying was an issue for the parents in the past, this may especially be the case.

Did you know?

Children and young people may tell their parents or carers they are being bullied, or someone who has witnessed bullying may inform them. In this case, it will be the parents or carers who report it to the school or setting.

Good practice

It's important for practitioners to give parents the time to express their feelings, and to assure them that the setting is committed to dealing with bullies and preventing further bullying. You should go through the anti-bullying policy with them, explaining what will happen next (e.g. the victim and the bully will meet separately with a practitioner to discuss the issues). You should also explain what their child should do if they feel scared, or if they are bullied again.

It's hard for parents to know what to advice to give to their children – they are often torn between telling them to physically stand up to the bully, and telling them to run away.

Supporting children and young people

If a child or young person tells you they are being bullied, it's important to respond appropriately. Most will not only be upset, but also worried that telling will result in even more bullying as punishment for getting the bully into trouble. It may be that you are concerned about bullying that has not been reported to you by the victim. In this case, you will need to raise your concerns with them with extreme sensitivity, as they have not decided for themselves to challenge what the bully is doing to them. However, the bullying should still be addressed – some children have committed suicide rather than tell anyone, so you should not wait for them to come to you.

Remember that many children and young people feel humiliated when they are bullied. They are embarrassed that they are disliked to such an extent, and may think it's their own fault for being 'unlikeable' or for having 'something wrong with them'. They may not want their teachers or parents to know that they are 'unpopular' at school or at the setting.

When bullying has taken place, the process of supporting the child or young person who has been the victim is similar to the process of handling a disclosure, which you learned about in Learning Outcome 4. This is what you should do:

■ Talk to the child or young person in private. Remember that they may be anxious about the bully finding out that they have told.

■ Maintain eye contact if the child or young person is choosing to look directly at you. Do not look away as this can be interpreted by them as disapproval.

■ Let the child or young person do the talking, allowing them to tell you in their own way.

■ Listen and follow carefully. Try to remember exactly what they are saying and the language they're using, rather than interpreting what it all means.

■ Believe what they say to you.

■ If a child or young person asks you what will happen to the bully, say they will need some help to stop behaving in that way, because it is unacceptable.

■ If you aren't in authority, tell the child or young person that you will help them by telling someone who is in authority – you should never promise not to tell.

■ Say that you will talk to them again when you have done this to let them know what is happening.

■ Reassure them that they can speak to you again if they want to talk about it.

■ Remind them what to do if the bully attempts to upset or hurt them again.

You should write down what has happened/what you have been told without delay. Make a note of who was there, as there may be a group dynamic to the incident. Witnesses to the bullying may be important if different accounts of the event are given by those involved.

LEARNING OUTCOME 6

Reducing vulnerability

Research has shown that children and young people are less vulnerable to harm and abuse if they:

■ feel self-confident

■ have high self-esteem

■ have self-awareness

■ can be assertive.

We'll explore ways to encourage children and young people to develop these attributes over.

FOCUS ON

...understanding how to work with children and young people to support their safety and well-being

In this section you'll learn about supporting children and young people's confidence and self-esteem, and the importance of supporting resilience in children and young people. You'll also learn about working with children and young people to ensure that they have strategies to keep themselves safe, and empowering them to make positive, informed choices. This links with Assessment Criteria 6.1, 6.2, 6.3, 6.4.

Children can be particularly vulnerable because of the following factors:

- disability
- being a loner
- being the result of an unwanted pregnancy
- being the opposite gender to the one a parent wanted
- being the eldest child
- being a step-child
- being a child who does not feed well or does not like eating (particularly as a baby).

Children are also more likely to be abused if they do not meet a parent's expectations – this can be for a range of reasons. Statistics have shown that a child who has been abused is more likely to be abused again, even at the hands of a different person.

Social factors can also lead to abuse. If parents or carers are abusing substances, the focus of their life may shift. Someone who is addicted to alcohol or drugs may not notice the needs of their child, or be aware that they are being abusive. People dealing with addiction may find that it takes over their lives, frequently or at times leaving them unable to deal with other things. It is hard for someone whose own needs are not being met to meet the needs of someone else.

Did you know?

It can be very frightening for a child to see their parent or carer under the influence of substances. If drugs or alcohol are kept in the home, young children may ingest them accidentally or as a result of copying a parent.

Those with high self-esteem are less vulnerable to harm and abuse.

Self-esteem and self-confidence

It should be the aim of every practitioner to encourage the children in their care to develop independence. This is essential for children's well-being. Children gradually learn to take more responsibility for themselves and others as they mature. It is the job of practitioners to allow children levels of independence appropriate to their age, needs and abilities. This must of course be in line with legislation, the setting's procedures and families' preferences.

Independence also affects children's self-esteem and confidence. Children feel good about being self-reliant, and gain personal satisfaction when they are able to do things for themselves. Gently encourage even the youngest children to try new things, and praise their attempts.

You can provide opportunities for children and young people to participate in activities that foster high levels of confidence and self-esteem, including:

- team activities
- trust games
- games that give all children the opportunity to be the leader
- consultation
- displays of art/craft work.

You can also ensure that you offer children plenty of praise in general terms, and specifically for having a go or trying hard. This links with the information on emotional risk taking on page 221, and the information on supporting future learning and children's achievements on pages 351–352.

Unit CYP 3.4 Support children and young people's health and safety
Unit EYMP 2 Promote learning and development in the early years

Resilience in children and young people

When we talk about children and young people being resilient, we mean that they are able to cope with life's ups and downs. It's an important attribute for them to develop, because resilient young people mature into resilient adults, who are able to cope with the demands and the occasional knocks of the adult world. Feeling you are able to cope in the world underpins good mental health.

Resilience is linked to self-esteem and self-confidence, because it depends on how children and young people feel and how they view themselves. For instance, if a child who has high self-esteem is called 'stupid' by someone else, they will be best equipped to take little notice. Even if they do feel a bit upset or annoyed that someone has called them a name, if they don't believe that they are stupid, they're unlikely to take that label to heart. If they are also confident and able to be assertive, they may stand up for themselves and let the other person know that they most certainly aren't stupid at all.

However, a child with low self-esteem may react completely differently. If they already feel that they're no good at things and that they don't measure up to other people, being called 'stupid' may be altogether more damaging. They may believe the comment, play it over and over again in their mind, eventually

Team activities can help to foster high levels of confidence and self-esteem.

internalising it. They may then carry it with them, taking them further down an emotional spiral.

Good practice

Children and young people's resilience can be positively influenced by a sense of security. Living in a home where they are loved and looked after as an important part of a family, feeling secure attachments to carers and having good relationships with friends and wider family members (e.g. grandparents), all contribute greatly. A feeling that others trust them can also be influential. This can be developed by encouraging independence in children and young people, and by giving them appropriate responsibilities.

Giving children and young people strategies to protect themselves

When children and young people know how to protect themselves, and are aware of the way in which they should and should not be treated, they are empowered to act to stop abuse by disclosing it to an appropriate adult. You can help by teaching them about their rights in respect of their bodies, what to do in

Practical example

Laurence's pet rabbit

Nine-year-old Laurence has wanted a pet rabbit for ages. His dad has read a book on looking after rabbits with him, and they've been to talk to a member of staff at the pet shop about what has to be done. Laurence's dad has asked him to think about the responsibility of caring for a rabbit this week. If he's really sure that he's prepared to help look after it properly, Laurence will be allowed to get one this weekend. He will need to contribute some of the birthday money he's been saving, as the hutch is quite expensive.

Question

How is Laurence's experience of being trusted to take on responsibility likely to impact on his self-esteem, self-confidence and self-reliance?

emergency situations when they are vulnerable, how to identify and express their feelings and what to do if they are bullied. Practitioners should support children in learning about the following.

Children's bodies
Children's bodies are their own.

- Children do not have to show physical affection if they do not want to, including kissing, hugging or sitting on people's laps.

- Children can have help if they need it when toileting, but they have a right to privacy if they want it. For older children, the same applies to bathing/showering and dressing/undressing.

- Adults should ask children whether they would like some help before opening a toilet or bathroom door.

- It is wrong for them to be touched in a way that hurts them, frightens them or feels rude.

Emergency situations
- **What to do if they are lost**
  Stop, look around carefully for the adult they were with. If they cannot see the adult, approach a safe person – a police officer, crossing-patrol

guard (lollipop person), cashier at a till in a shop, or lastly a parent with children. They should wait outside until their adult, their parent or a police officer comes to look after them. They should not go anywhere with strangers, not to a phone, workplace or to a house.

- **Who to go home with**
  When at a setting, both the child and practitioners should know who the child is allowed to leave with.

- **Answering the door**
  They should never answer the door unless an adult is with them (in the case of younger children).

- **Personal details**
  The child should know their personal details: full name, address and telephone number.

- **Stranger danger – who strangers are, what to do if approached**
  If an unknown person talks to them, they need not be rude – they can pretend they haven't heard and walk away quickly, telling an adult if they feel worried. But if a stranger asks or invites the child to go with them, they should run away and tell a safe adult immediately. They must learn to

'Say no and never go!' If children are touched, grabbed or feel otherwise frightened or worried they might be in danger, it is alright to break the usual behaviour rules. They should attract attention by shouting and screaming, and punch, kick, and so on if they feel they need to. Police officers often visit settings to talk to children about being lost and stranger danger, which helps to establish the police as safe people in the minds of children.

Identifying and expressing feelings

- Children can express their feelings, including worry and fear, knowing they will be taken seriously, and not dismissed or ridiculed. Children learn this through experience of being respected. General activities that encourage naming, thinking about and expressing feelings are good for all children.

- Children do not have to keep secrets unless they want to, even if it is an adult's secret. Using the word 'surprise' is often better than using the word 'secret' with young children. Surprises are usually thought of as pleasant things that are only secret for a little while before everyone finds out about them – birthday presents and treats are good examples of this. Older children can learn that they should not keep 'bad' secrets. A touch, kiss and so on should never be a secret.

Activities that involve thinking about feelings are good for all children.

See Learning Outcome 5 for details of what children and young people should do if they are bullied. See Learning Outcome 7 for details of staying safe online and when using mobile phones and video games.

Empowering children and young people to make positive choices

Children and young people need to develop the ability to make positive and informed choices that support their well-being and safety. This is a crucial life skill that will help to keep them safe when adults aren't around, and which young people will rely on entirely when they're ready to strike out on their own in the world. So it is essential that children learn to recognise and manage risk for themselves. Experience of doing this should increase as children mature. Involve children in thinking about safety, and encourage them to tell an adult if they see something unsafe.

'Moral dilemma' games and role plays can also be an effective way to encourage older children and young people to think about how they should handle potentially dangerous situations. For instance, what should they do if their lift home from a disco doesn't turn up? Or if someone were to offer them alcohol or drugs?

Age appropriate information

Children and young people need age appropriate information to help them make safe choices. They need to know about potential dangers or risks, and what to do to minimise them. This should include, in line with the setting's policies and procedures:

- Information about adults, and in the case of young people, those of a similar age to their own, who may pose a danger to them. For young people, this should include information about keeping their drinks safe when they are out to prevent these from being spiked. They should know to stick with friends and to plan a safe journey home together before setting out. Money for their return journey home must always be kept back. Taxis should be booked in advance; they should never get into an unlicensed minicab in the street.

- Sex education, including ways of promoting sexual health and methods of contraception. They should know how to access impartial advice and support quickly should they need it, for instance, if they have had unprotected sex.

- Alcohol, including the immediate risk to health of binge drinking, the long-term effects of becoming addicted and the increased vulnerability of someone who is under the influence of drink. (Young people are more vulnerable to the effects of alcohol than adults because it is concentrated in a smaller body.)

- Drugs. The dangers of substance abuse, including the immediate risk to health, the long-term effects of becoming addicted and the increased vulnerability of someone who is under the influence of drugs.

- Information about keeping themselves safe in everyday life, including everything from road safety to using protective equipment and following instructions carefully if taking part in a higher-risk activity – outdoor pursuits for instance, or a contact sport.

For full and frank information about alcohol and drugs, older children and young people can visit the Frank website at **www.talktofrank.com**. They can also call, text or email a question 24 hours a day, 365 days a year.

Road safety

It's crucial for children and young people to learn road safety. It will usually be the job of parents to decide when their child is ready to begin crossing roads alone (unless, for instance, the child is looked after by Social Services). But practitioners have a big role to play in preparing children for that time. Road safety games, activities and role play are all helpful. It's very important to always set a good example when crossing roads yourself. When crossing with children, talk through the process in a similar way each time, as children learn through repetition (e.g. 'We've stopped at the kerb, and we're looking both ways and listening carefully…').

For more information about safety, visit the Royal Society for the Prevention of Accidents (ROSPA) at www.rospa.com/roadsafety

Did you know?

Young people in particular need reminding to stay self-aware and to take notice of their situation and environment. Listening to MP3 players and using mobile phones can result in paying little attention to the external world, increasing the risk of having an accident when crossing the road, or failing to notice dangers.

LEARNING OUTCOME 7

...understanding the importance of e-safety for children and young people

In this section you'll learn about the risks and possible consequences of being online and of using a mobile phone. You'll also learn about the ways to reduce to this risk. This links with Assessment Criteria **7.1, 7.2.**

Risks and possible consequences of being online and of using a mobile phone

Advances in technology have changed the lives of children, young people and adults in all sorts of positive ways. Most children and young people will use computers at home and at school, and some may well own their own computer or laptop. In 2009, the Government set a target for every home in Britain to have Broadband internet connection by 2012. Many children and young people own their own mobile phone, or will have easy access to one – they may borrow a parent's for instance, or use a friend's. Children and young people who do not own their own computers, games consoles or phones often have these at the top of their wish lists.

However, being online, playing video games and using a mobile phone does present some risks, as follows:

- **Physical danger/contact with paedophiles**
  Paedophiles may pose as a child or young person online. They may target a child by pretending to have similar interests, and use this to establish an online 'friendship'. When trust has developed, they may entice the child to meet up with them in person. This is known as 'child grooming' or 'child procurement'. Studies have shown that this threat is parents' biggest online worry.

- **Exposure to inappropriate material**
  Material may be pornographic, violent or hateful (e.g. promoting extreme political, racist or sexist views). It may promote dangerous or illegal behaviour, or may simply be age inappropriate.

- **Divulging personal details**
  Children and young people may inadvertently disclose personal details, which may be used to facilitate identity theft or con tricks. The details may also fall into the hands of people who may harm them.

- **Illegal behaviour**
  Users may become caught up in behaviour that is illegal, anti-social or otherwise inappropriate. This includes downloading copyrighted material illegally.

- **Bullying**
  Cyberbullying may occur via internet, video games or mobile phones. It can leave victims extremely upset, scared and humiliated. See Learning Outcome 5 for further details.

Mobile phones have both advantages and risks.

- **Online gambling**
  The internet gives easy access to gambling sites.

- **Wrong information**
  Children and young people may believe incorrect information they come across online.

The Byron Review

In 2007, the Government ordered a review to look at the risks to children from exposure to potentially harmful or inappropriate material on the internet and in video games. This was carried out by Professor Tanya Byron, who went on to highlight three strategic objectives for e-safety in the report. These are:

■ **Availability**

We should focus our efforts on reducing the availability of harmful and inappropriate material on the most popular areas of the internet.

■ **Access**

Children's access to harmful material should be reduced. It's not just a question of what the industry can do to protect children (e.g. by developing better parental control software), but of what parents and carers can do to protect children (e.g. by setting up parental control software properly) and what children can do to protect themselves (e.g. by not giving their contact details online).

■ **Resilience**

Just like in the off-line world, no amount of effort to reduce potential risks to children will eliminate those risks completely. We cannot make the internet completely safe. Because of this, we must also build children's resilience to the material to which they may be exposed so that they have the confidence and skills to navigate these new media waters more safely.

Visit **www.direct.gov.uk/en/YoungPeople/ HealthAndRelationships/Bullying/DG_070501** to read the review in full.

Suggested steps towards meeting the three objectives are given in the Government advice issued to parents and carers, which is summarised below.

Ways of reducing risk to children and young people

Parental controls

Use the parental controls available on computers and other digital technologies like games consoles and mobile phones. These allow adults to:

■ block websites and email addresses by adding them to a filter list

■ set time limits for use

■ prevent children from searching certain words.

The equipment's user manual or the manufacturers' websites should give advice on the controls available. Internet service providers and mobile phone operators will also advise about the child safety measures they offer.

Rules

Parents and carers are also advised to create rules with the child. Examples of acceptable use include:

■ The internet-connected computer must be in a family room with the screen facing outward so you can see what's going on.

■ If your child accidentally goes to an unsuitable website they should tell you – you can delete it from the 'history' folder and add the address to the parental control filter list.

■ It's never OK to use abusive or threatening language in any online communication.

■ You child should take breaks from the computer every 30 minutes for health and safety reasons.

■ Your child shouldn't download unknown files from the internet without you agreeing – it's best to never download unknown files at all.

■ Children should not download or share files illegally (e.g. music, films).

■ Children should not attempt to buy or order things online.

Personal safety online

Parents and carers are advised to explain to children that people online might not be who they say they are and could be dangerous, and that any personal information they give out can be used in financial scams or for bullying. Children should be told not to:

■ give out personal information to people they only know online - this includes name, home address, landline and mobile numbers, bank details, PIN numbers and passwords

- supply details for registration without asking for permission and help from you

- visit chat websites that aren't fully moderated/supervised

- sign up to social networking sites without asking for permission and help from you

- arrange to meet an online friend in person without parental knowledge and permission (if a parent agrees to let them, the parent should always go along with them)

- give any indication of their age or sex in a personal email address or screen name

- keep anything that worries or upsets them online secret from you

- respond to unwanted emails or other messages.

It's advisable to monitor children's internet use by checking the history folder on the browser, which contains a list of previously visited sites. Children should be made aware of child-friendly search engines, which filter out inappropriate internet sites. Alternatively, safe search settings can be turned on to allow safe use of traditional search engines.

Cyberbullying

Parents and carers should ensure that children understand that they should never be afraid to tell parents and carers about frightening or bullying emails or messages they get with unacceptable content. It's not their fault that they have received them and the addresses can be added to the parental control filter list.

If there's a problem

If there's a problem, parents and carers are advised to:

- contact their internet service provider if a child comes across inappropriate content or is subjected to any inappropriate contact while online

- install and regularly update filtering software to protect against inappropriate internet access.

If they are worried about illegal materials or

suspicious online behaviour, parents can report this to the Child Exploitation and Online Protection Centre.

For more information about cyberbullying, see Learning Outcome 5.

Ensure that children and young people know how to stay safe online.

Did you know?

Many parents say they are less able to understand and use technology than their children. So educating parents must not be overlooked in ensuring children's safety online.

What does this mean for practitioners?

All children and young people's settings must take adequate steps to ensure that access to technology within the environment is safe. This means following the strategies you learned about above. It's also important for practitioners to be vigilant about the appropriate use of the resources that children and young people bring with them into the setting from home. This includes mobile phones, handheld game consoles and laptops.

How are things going?

▶ Progress Check

1. Explain what is meant by child protection within the wider concept of safeguarding. (1.2)

2. What is:

   a) a serious case review, and b) an inquiry? (1.4)

3. Why is a child-/young person-centred approach important? (2.2)

4. What should you do if you're concerned that a colleague may be harming a child? (3.2)

5. Name three signs of each of the following types of abuse:

   a) physical abuse, b) sexual abuse, c) emotional abuse and d) neglect. (4.1)

6. What are the different types of bullying? (5.1)

7. Why is it important to support resilience? (6.2)

8. What measures can you take to protect children and young people online? (7.2)

Are you ready for assessment?

CACHE

Set task:

■ An in-depth task covering twenty five assessment criteria, in which you prepare a folder on all aspects of safeguarding children and young people.

You can prepare by reviewing your own setting's safeguarding policies, and by becoming familiar with your local guidelines on safeguarding (your setting will have these).

Edexel

In preparation for assessment of this Unit, you may like to access the policies and procedures within your setting which protect children and young people, and those who work with them. You can practice explaining these to colleague or classmate.

City & Guilds

You must complete the mandatory Assignment 026. This has seven tasks, each one relating to one of the seven Learning Outcomes. It entails completing the tables provided, writing reports/briefing notes and answering questions. You can prepare by accessing the policies and procedures within your setting which protect children, and those who work with them.

UNIT 3.4

Support children and young people's health and safety

The learning outcomes you will meet in this unit are:

1 Understand how to plan and provide environments and services that support children and young people's health and safety

2 Be able to recognise and manage risks to health, safety and security in a work setting or off-site visits

3 Understand how to support children and young people to assess and manage risk for themselves

4 Understand appropriate responses to accidents, incidents, emergencies and illness in work settings and off-site visits

INTRODUCTION

The health and safety of children is of paramount importance to all practitioners. It's essential for you to learn how to establish and maintain healthy and safe services and environments for children, both indoors and outdoors.

You must take a balanced approach to risk management. It's a fact of life that accidents, injuries and illnesses happen to all children on occasion, regardless of the precautions that you take. Although this is concerning, it's reassuring for practitioners to know that they have followed the appropriate health and safety guidelines and procedures, and that they've learned how to respond in the event of an emergency.

LEARNING OUTCOME 1

FOCUS ON

...health and safety

In this section you'll learn about the factors to consider when planning healthy and safe environments and services. You'll be introduced to health and safety legislation and guidance. You'll also learn about health and safety policies, and how these are put into practice within settings and services. This links with Assessment Criteria 1.1, 1.2, 1.3, 1.4.

Factors

There are some important factors for practitioners to take into account when planning healthy and safe environments and services for children and young people. We'll look at each of these in turn.

Age, needs and abilities of children and young people

As you learned in CYP 3.1, development milestones tell us the approximate age at which most children and young people are likely to develop certain skills and to behave in certain ways. However, individual needs and abilities will vary from child to child and from young person to young person, particularly if an impairment, such as a learning difficulty or a physical disability, is present.

The age, needs and abilities of children and young people impact greatly on what it is safe for them to do and to come into contact with. For instance, a 6-month-old baby will be expected to pick up objects within their reach independently and take them to their mouth, so it will be important to keep small objects which present a choking hazard out of their reach, including some toys (such as Lego™ bricks) that are only suitable for older children. With this in mind, practitioners must always select toys and materials safely, as explained below.

Selecting toys, equipment and materials safely

Before buying toys or equipment, practitioners must check that the items carry a recognised safety mark (see page 205). Safety marks give assurance that products are safe for use as directed by the manufacturer. So it is important that you only use toys and equipment in line with manufacturer's instructions. You should ensure that all items are assembled according to the directions, and that you follow age guidelines specified

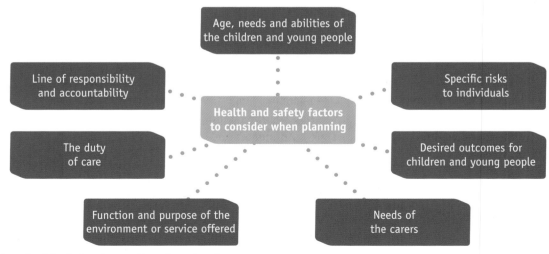

Health and safety factors to consider when planning.

A 6-month-old baby will take objects within reach to their mouth.

– these will appear on boxes and other packaging. You may, for example, find the following statement on the box of a toy car – 'not suitable for use by children under 36 months due to small parts'.

However, sometimes it is necessary to exercise extra caution. For instance, imagine that you are working with a child who is 5 years of age. He has a substantial developmental delay. He still takes toys to his mouth in the manner of a much younger child. It would be necessary for you to think carefully about the toys that can be given to him safely. The toy car we mentioned earlier would not be suitable for him, because despite his age, he has not yet reached suitable maturity in terms of his stage of development

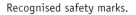
Recognised safety marks.

to enable him to play safely with small parts. You must always consider the needs and abilities of children (along with their age) when selecting toys, equipment and materials.

Selecting good-quality items that are durable (made to last) is practical, as they are most likely to stand up well to group use. This means that there is less chance of the items breaking, and therefore becoming potentially dangerous, during play. It's also important to ensure that consumable materials are suitable, particularly those that may be collected and brought in by families. Items such as 'junk' (household items such as cereal boxes and yoghurt pots brought in for making recycled models) should be clean, free of sharp edges and should not have contained anything unsuitable, such as medication or cleaning products.

Specific risks to individuals

Some activities or circumstances present specific risks to individuals. It's important to have good knowledge and understanding of the individual children and young people with whom you work, so that you recognise these types of risk when they occur. You can then find ways to reduce the risk to acceptable levels, or to offer suitable alternatives. Here are some examples:

■ If a young person is pregnant, some activities that would normally be considered safe for her may present a risk to her own health and/or that of her baby – trampolining at a sports club for instance. However, one of the many alternative methods of exercise that are recommended during pregnancy may be offered.

■ If a child experiences sensory difficulties such as a visual impairment, the risk generally associated with certain activities may be higher – learning to use sharp tools, for instance. Advice can be sought from an outside professional such as an occupational therapist, who may recommend the use of specially designed tools or suggest suitable methods of teaching.

■ A child or young person who experiences health conditions such as asthma or allergies may be

Tired out – you may need to build in times for rest and recuperation.

at risk in ways that other children are not from contact with a range of substances, including dust, pollen and certain foods. It may be necessary to 'damp dust' the setting when cleaning (by using a damp cloth rather than a dry duster to prevent dust flying around), to avoid bringing certain flowers inside or to ensure that everyone in the setting is aware of a child's allergies, the warning signs of an allergic reaction and what steps to take if they occur. (You'll learn more about this in Learning Outcomes 2 and 3.)

■ A child with a long-term illness (such as ME – see page 58) may be at increased risk of exhaustion during certain activities or during the course of a usual day at a setting. It may be necessary to pace activity and to build in times for rest and recuperation.

The needs of carers

Where relevant, the needs of carers are also a factor to consider when planning healthy and safe environments and services. For instance, a carer who is a wheelchair user will need sufficient space to move around safely, and this should be factored into the layout of furniture and facilities. A carer with a visual impairment may need to be informed if the layout of the environment is changed, to prevent them and others from harm caused by tripping, bumping into things or becoming disorientated, particularly if there is an emergency.

The function and purpose of environments and services

Practitioners should take into account the function and purpose of their environments and services. Activities and experiences that are well suited to one environment or service may be less suited, and even ill-advised, in another.

For instance, many sports centres offer holiday activity clubs for children and young people. The environment is specially designed for the provision of sporting activities and, typically, some staff will have received sports specific training, such as coaching. Specialist equipment will also be on hand. This will allow the setting to safely offer some activities that it would be inappropriate to offer in an after-school club that meets in a school classroom.

Likewise, a forest school – which operates outside in woodland and has been specially set up to do so – will also be able to offer specialist activities in a safe manner, such as building a camp fire.

Did you know?

Most children's settings operate a no nut policy – this means that no one must bring nuts or nut products into the setting. For instance, a child would not be permitted to bring peanut butter sandwiches in their lunchbox, even if they do not have a nut allergy themselves. This is because nut allergies can be extremely serious. A child with a severe nut allergy could die of anaphylactic shock as a result of skin contact with a nut product – they do not necessarily need to eat a nut in order to trigger a reaction.

Did you know?

You can find out more about forest schools at **www.forestschools.com**

Desired outcomes for children and young people

The desired outcomes for children and young people are among the factors that influence what it is appropriate, safe and healthy for them to do within your setting or service. In Learning Outcome 2 you will learn about how the potential benefits of an activity or experience must be considered against the likelihood of harm when conducting risk assessments.

This also links closely to the function and purpose of environments and services. For instance, if one of the purposes of your service is to assist looked-after young people to prepare for adulthood, a common desired outcome for young people using the service may be for them to become competent in assessing and managing risk for themselves when in the outside world. Therefore, it may be appropriate for the service to give the young people more freedom to make their own decisions than they may receive in another setting, such as a holiday club based in a sports centre.

Duty of care

You may have heard of the Latin term *in loco parentis*. Translated, this means 'instead of a parent'. When parents leave their child or young person at the school gates or within a care setting, they are in effect agreeing for staff to act *in loco parentis*. This means that staff have a **duty of care** to look after the child or young person, in line with the provisions set out in the Children Act 1989. The Act requires those acting *in loco parentis* to promote the safety and welfare of the children in their care. The level of this duty of care must be that of a 'reasonable parent'. If you do not act as a reasonable parent would do to keep a child or young person safe, you are failing to meet your duty of care – this is known as being 'negligent'. The Health and Safety at Work Act 1974 also obliges the setting or service as a whole to safeguard the safety and well-being of children and young people in its care. Read on to learn more about both of these Acts.

Link Up!

There's more about this in:
Unit SHC 34 Principles for implementing duty of care in health, social care or children's and young people's settings
Unit CYP 3.3 Understand how to safeguard the well-being of children and young people

key terms

In loco parentis being responsible for a child or young person's safety and welfare instead of their parents.

Duty of care term used to describe the responsibility to act at the level of 'a reasonable parent' when *in loco parentis*.

Did you know?

If you put a child or young person in danger or are negligent in the way you care for them, you may be sued by the child's parents for damages. In these circumstances, you should seek professional legal advice immediately.

Lines of responsibility and accountability

It's crucial for practitioners in all settings and services to be crystal clear about their own responsibilities relating to health and safety, or standards will slip and important welfare requirements may not be met.

Link Up!

You can read more about this in Learning Outcome 1, Unit EYMP 3 Promote children's welfare and well-being in the early years

Maintaining and monitoring health and safety

As you know, it's important that healthy, safe settings and services are established. It's also important for practitioners to monitor and maintain health and safety on an on-going basis. You'll learn about how this can be achieved in Learning Outcome 2.

Health and safety legislation and guidance

When providing environments and services for children and young people, you must comply with the laws and regulations relevant to your home country. All of the laws and regulations referred to in this unit apply in England. However, health and safety legislation is fairly universal. You can find out more about the specifics for your home country online:

Scotland: **www.scotland.gov.uk**

Wales: **www.wales.gov.uk**

Northern Ireland: **www.deni.gov.uk**

England: **www.direct.gov.uk**

There are several regulations and requirements that apply to all workplaces in the UK, in addition to those that apply specifically to environments and services for children and young people. Settings have to comply with these by law. Key health and safety regulations and requirements that settings must meet are as follows:

Health and Safety at Work Act 1974 and 1992

This Act is relevant to all places of employment, not just children's settings. Employers have a duty of care to ensure that the workplace and equipment within it are in a safe condition that does not pose a risk to health. Employees (and volunteers) also have a responsibility to take care of themselves and others in co-operation with the employer. The Act also requires employers to use the basic principles of risk management – which are risk assessment, balanced control measures and training. You'll learn more about these in Learning Outcome 2.

Health and Safety (First Aid) Regulations 1981

While most children and young people's settings will have several members of staff qualified to carry out first aid (and must have at least one trained first-aider), these regulations set a minimum standard that applies to all workplaces. Under them, employers must appoint at least one person to be a designated first-aider, responsible for first aid if an accident occurs. Employers must also keep a stocked first aid box. Also see Learning Outcome 4.

Food Safety Act 1990, and Food Handling Regulations 1995

This Act and the Regulations cover how food should be prepared and stored, how food areas must be maintained, and how staff who prepare food must be trained. See EYMP 3 Learning Outcome 4 for further details.

The Control of Substances Hazardous to Health Regulations 1994 (COSHH)

Under these Regulations, settings must assess which substances used on the premises are potentially hazardous to health (e.g. chemicals such as bleach). Practices to manage and store these safely must be devised and recorded. Further information is included in Learning Outcome 2.

Fire Precautions (Workplace) Regulations 1997

These Regulations apply to all workplaces. Under these Regulations, settings must carry out a fire risk assessment addressing seven key areas:

1. fire ignition sources and risk from the spread of fire

2. escape routes and exits

3. fire detection and early warning of fire

4. fire fighting equipment

5. fire routine training for staff

6. emergency plans and arrangements for calling the fire service

7. general maintenance and testing of fire protection equipment.

You'll learn more about this in Learning Outcome 4.

Reporting of Injuries, Diseases and Dangerous Occurrences Regulations 1995 (RIDDOR)

Under RIDDOR, workplaces must have an accident book. All accidents that occur at the workplace should be recorded in the book. In addition, some types of accidents that occur at work – serious ones, or those that result in an employee being absent from work for more than three days – must be reported to the Health and Safety Executive. Some diseases that may be contracted by employees must also be reported.

Personal Protective Equipment at Work Regulations 1992

Under these Regulations, employers must provide all protective equipment their employees need to do their job safely. For instance, settings will provide disposable gloves and aprons to be used when dealing with bodily fluids and waste.

Protection of Children Act 1999

This Act covers child protection. See Unit CYP 3.3 for details.

Children's Act 1989

This Act covers equality of access and opportunity for all children, in addition to health and safety. Further details are included in Unit CYP 3.3.

Health and Safety (Young Persons) Regulations 1997

These Regulations require employers to conduct special risk assessments for employees or volunteers under the age of 18, as they may be less aware of health and safety issues than more experienced workers.

Children Bill 2004

Prior to this Bill, there had been concerns that children's services were not working together effectively to protect vulnerable children from abuse. The Bill was passed to improve child protection for children and to ensure better coordination of services. You'll read more about this in Unit CYP 3.3.

Unit CYP 3.3 Understand how to safeguard the well-being of children and young people

Every Child Matters

Every Child Matters is the government agenda which sets out five major outcomes for all children:

1. being healthy

2. staying safe

3. enjoying and achieving

4. making a positive contribution

5. economic well-being.

The Early Years Foundation Stage (see below) aims to meet the *Every Child Matters* outcomes.

The Early Years Foundation Stage (EYFS) welfare requirements

Settings to which the Early Years Foundation Stage applies must meet the EYFS welfare requirements. These fall into the following five categories as shown in the table on page 210:

See Unit EYMP 2 for more on the EYFS

In addition, the Childcare Act 2006 was passed to introduce the EYFS and to support settings in providing high-quality, integrated care and education for children aged 0–5 years. It also gave local authorities the responsibility to improve outcomes for all children under 5.

Table CYP 3.4.1: EYFS welfare requirements

Safeguarding and promoting children's welfare	The provider must take necessary steps to safeguard and promote the welfare of children. The provider must promote the good health of the children, take necessary steps to prevent the spread of infection, and take appropriate action when they are ill. Children's behaviour must be managed effectively and in a manner appropriate for their stage of development and particular individual needs.
Suitable people	Providers must ensure that adults looking after children, or having unsupervised access to them, are suitable to do so. Adults looking after children must have appropriate qualifications, training, skills and knowledge. Staffing arrangements must be organised to ensure safety and to meet the needs of the children.
Suitable premises, environment and equipment	Outdoor and indoor spaces, furniture, equipment and toys must be safe and suitable for their purpose.
Organisation	Providers must plan and organise their systems to ensure that every child receives an enjoyable and challenging learning and development experience that is tailored to meet their individual needs.
Documentation	Providers must maintain records, policies and procedures required for the safe and efficient management of the settings and to meet the needs of the children. Also see Unit EYMP2 Promote learning and development in the early years.

Manual handling

Information on how to lift children and equipment safely is given in Unit EYMP 3.

Link Up!

Unit EYMP 3 Promote children's welfare and well-being in the early years

Good practice

You should note that requirements are updated over time, and it is important that you remain well informed. This can generally be done effectively by subscribing to industry magazines and journals and regularly visiting government websites.

Have a go!

As part of your study towards this unit, you are advised to visit **www.hse.gov.uk/contact/faqs/manualhandling** Here you'll find a list of requirements for settings, which is regularly updated. There are also links to further relevant information.

Did you know?

Most settings keep one accident book for children and young people and a separate one for employees and other visiting adults.

Health and safety policies and procedures

Regulations and requirements tell settings what they must do, and what standards they must meet. But generally they are not *prescriptive* – they do not tell practitioners how things should be done. It is up to settings to interpret the law and the regulations that apply to them. Settings do this by devising policies that explain how they will work in line with the law and the regulations.

Take the Health and Safety at Work Act 1974 and 1992, for example. It says that employers must ensure that the workplace and equipment within it are in a safe condition. But it doesn't tell settings how to achieve this. In order that everyone involved knows how to keep the workplace and equipment safe, settings draw up their own policies and procedures explaining what should be done. The policy will probably explain when and how equipment should be cleaned, for instance, and what to do if equipment becomes damaged. Sometimes, extra information is needed to explain how areas of a policy will work in action, so settings may devise additional written procedures that explain what to do in more detail.

Good, clear policies and procedures are important because they communicate how the staff must work. Policies also let other professionals, parents, carers and children know how your setting operates. You must make sure that you understand all of your setting's policies, and you must work within them.

The table on page 212 shows some of the key issues that will be covered within a setting's health and safety policy. General details about each issue are included.

Reviewing policies and procedures

Practitioners should check that their policies and procedures still reflect current legislation and regulations, because these are updated from time to time. Practitioners should consider whether the ways of working outlined in the policies and procedures have been followed effectively. If so, these ways

Good practice

To make sure that policies and procedures are effective, it is good practice for settings to review them regularly – at least once a year.

of working have proved successful. This should be done in consultation with colleagues and, when appropriate, with parents, carers, children, young people and outside professionals.

It is important to make sure that practice reflects the policy – there is no benefit in having good policies and procedures if they are not followed. Sometimes, practice and policy do not match up because practice has evolved (progressed effectively) over time. In this case, it will be appropriate to change policy/procedures to reflect the new ways of working. However, if it is the practitioners' work that is not up to appropriate standards, further explanation of the policy/procedures will be necessary and perhaps further training.

The date and outcome of reviews should be documented, and policies/procedures should be amended in writing if they are changed. It is good practice to plan the next review date and make a note in the setting's diary, so that it is not forgotten. Some settings review one or more policies at meetings that

Reviewing policies and procedures.

Table CYP 3.4.2: Key health and safety issues

Key health and safety issues likely to be covered within a health and safety policy	General details likely to be given
Registration	**Registration forms** All families must complete forms, giving children and young people's personal and medical details, before children can attend the setting. **Daily registers** All children, young people and adults attending a session must be registered on arrival and signed out on their departure.
Safeguarding procedures	What the setting does to safeguard children and young people, for instance, the use of safety equipment such as high chair harnesses, and procedures for ensuring that young children cannot wander off the premises/older children cannot leave undetected.
Risk assessment	When risk assessment will be carried out and how often assessments will be reviewed. What staff training is given on risk assessment.
Emergency procedures	**Drills** Where the details of drills are displayed on the premises (who does what, where the meeting points are, who will call 999, etc.), and how often drills are carried out. **Maintenance of equipment** When equipment such as fire extinguishers and alarms are tested, and by whom. Where records/certificates of testing are displayed. **First aid** Who the qualified first-aider is, how they were trained, and where their certificate is displayed. How first aid supplies are checked and replenished. The procedures for calling an ambulance and the family should a child need medical treatment urgently. **Care of sick children and young people** How sick children and young people cannot be cared for at a group setting. How arrangements will be made for the collection of sick children and young people. The procedure for calling an ambulance and the family should a child need medical treatment urgently.
Substances harmful to health	How the setting will identify substances harmful to health, and ensure their safe use and storage.
Food and drink	**Drinking water** How the setting makes water constantly available to children and young people. **Dietary requirements** How dietary requirements are met with regards to families' beliefs/religions/preferences, and regard to individual children and young people's allergies or medical requirements. **Healthy foods** How the setting will provide healthy meals and/or snacks. **Hygiene** How hygiene will be ensured with regards to food and drink preparation areas. How staff preparing food will have a Food Hygiene Certificate.
Hygiene	**Cleaning arrangements** How the setting will be kept clean and hygienic. Procedures for each room and the outdoor space may be referenced. Waste disposal. How all waste is handled and disposed of safely.
Child Protection	Settings will have a separate Child and Young Person Protection Policy, but it may be referenced in the Health and Safety Policy.

they hold monthly, or perhaps quarterly, so that the task of reviewing all of them is spread out across the year.

Settings will have cause to review policies/procedures before the next set review date if:

- practitioners become aware of a change in law or regulations

- it becomes apparent that an aspect of a policy/procedure is not being followed

- it becomes apparent that an aspect of a policy/procedure is not working effectively

- a suggestion for improvement is made, which practitioners would like to implement as soon as possible.

Settings must also legally develop and maintain systems and procedures for risk assessment. See Learning Outcome 2 for further details.

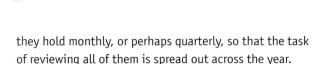

Practical example

Stars Out-of-School Club interprets legislation

Stars Out-of-School Club mentions in its health and safety policy that suitable toys are sterilised once a month. This is one of the ways in which the club complies with legislation about health and hygiene.

A separate set of procedures gives practitioners a four-week timetable of sterilising – some of the toys get sterilised each week. The practical steps of sterilising are explained, including where to carry out the task and how to make up the sterilising solution.

Question
Why is it important for settings to interpret legislation and regulations in written policies and procedures?

Further guidance

Healthy lives, bright futures: The strategy for children and young people's health

This strategy was published in 2009. It presents the Government's vision for children and young people's health and well-being. The strategy sets out how Government will build on existing progress through:

- world-class outcomes for health

- high-quality services

- excellent experience in using those services (for children, young people and families)

- minimising health inequalities.

Annex A of the strategy sets out the National Service Framework, you can also turn to page 559 for a copy. You can read more about the strategy, including progress updates at **www.dh.gov.uk**

Involve children in awareness of healthy eating, by encouraging them to make their own selection from a range of healthy snacks.

Aspects of children's and young people's health

For further published guidance on various aspects of children's and young people's health, including the promotion of health for looked-after children, accident prevention and drug and alcohol education, visit **www.education.gov.uk/publications/standard/ publicationDetail/Page1/DCSF-RR125** and select from the menu in the centre of the webpage.

Guidance for schools

Information and guidelines on aspects of health and safety that affect schools, including the medical needs of children, emergencies and school security can be found at **www.direct.gov.uk/ en/Parents/Schoolslearninganddevelopment/ YourChildsWelfareAtSchool/index.htm**. You can also visit **www.education.gov.uk/schools/pupilsupport/ pastoralcare/health/a0075278/healthy-schools**, where you can read about the Healthy Schools toolkit.

Food safety and healthy hygiene practices

Links to guidance on food safety and healthy hygiene practices can be found in Unit EYMP 3. This information is also relevant to provision for young people.

Unit EYMP 3 Promote children's welfare and well-being in the early years

LEARNING OUTCOME 2

FOCUS ON ...hazards and risks

In this section you'll learn about identifying and dealing with potential hazards to health, safety and security. You'll also learn about health and safety risk assessments and reviews. This links with Assessment Criteria 2.1, 2.2, 2.3, 2.4.

This unit relates closely to EYMP Unit 3 Promote children's welfare and well-being in the early years. Several links are given throughout this unit.

Risk assessment

The process of risk assessment makes settings safer places for children and young people. However, no setting or activity can be completely safe. Children and young people need to be able to take acceptable levels of risk in their play and activities, or their development will be stifled.

Good practice

Think of a child who is just starting to walk. They will fall down many times before they master the skill, and they might hurt themselves on occasion. But we wouldn't dream of stopping them from walking. It would be overreacting. The risk of injury from a fall is acceptable when a child is learning to walk. But we may decide to take some steps to reduce the chance of injury; perhaps we will move the rug they may slip on, and make sure that there is plenty of clear floor space. Risk assessment is simply a formal version of this process.

You will need to risk assess premises, both indoors and outdoors, and also the activities that you plan. As shown on the diagram below, you must identify potential **hazards** to the health, safety and security of all those within your setting or service.

A hazard is the actual item or situation that may cause harm. Potential hazards are all around us in the world, and include the following:

- physical hazards (e.g. unsafe objects, things that may be tripped over)

- security hazards (e.g. insecure exits and windows)

- fire hazards (e.g. heaters, electrical appliances)

- food safety hazards (e.g. faulty refrigerator, unsafe produce)

- personal safety hazards (e.g. stranger danger, busy roads).

First steps.

key term

Hazard an item or situation that may cause harm.

Have a go!

Considering hazards that may occur both inside and outside a setting or service for children and young people, think of at least six more hazards to add to the list above.

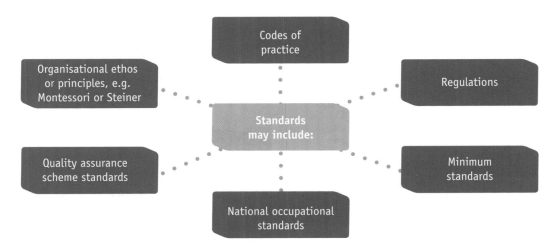

Potential hazards to health, safety or security.

How to risk assess

There are six key risk assessment steps to follow:

1. **Identify hazards.** Remember that a HAZARD is the actual item or situation that may cause harm – a stack of chairs for instance.

2. **Decide on the level of risk posed by the hazards – low, medium or high.** The RISK is the likelihood of the hazard causing harm. How 'risky' would you rate the stack of chairs? It would all depend on the circumstances. A stack of chairs in a baby and toddler room would be high risk. It's likely that a child will pull themselves up on the chairs causing the chairs to tumble. A young child could be badly injured.

3. **Evaluate the risks.** What measures, if any, could/should be taken to minimise or remove the risk? Are there any safety precautions already in place? If so, are they adequate? Is the risk acceptable given the ages, needs and abilities of the children? What levels of supervision will be required? Consider the benefits of activities against the potential for harm. Finally, decide whether the risk can be taken.

4. **If measures are to be taken to minimise or remove the risk, they should be carried out at this stage.** In our example, we can either remove the chairs from the room altogether, or simply un-stack them. The risk is then removed.

5. **Record your assessment.** You should record the whole process, and note your findings. Detail any measures you have taken, and enter the date. You should also set a date on which the risk assessment should be reviewed.

Child near a potentially dangerous electric socket.

6. **Monitor the risk assessment and review at a later date.** Monitoring the risk assessment means paying attention to how effective your measures are in practice. If the level of risk is still unacceptable, revise the assessment immediately (see below).

Monitoring and reviewing risk assessments

You learned about the importance of reviewing policies and procedures regularly with colleagues in Learning Outcome 1 – this also applies to risk assessments. You should review assessments periodically as a matter of good practice, in line with your organisational policies. But you must also reassess whether there are significant changes to premises or activities that impact on the original assessment. Record, date and sign all reviews, and enter in the setting's diary when the next review is due to take place.

Considering stages of development

A sound knowledge of child development will help you when you are carrying out risk assessments and planning security arrangements. You will be able to consider how aware children are of danger at various ages, their skill levels, and the things they are likely to do – pulling themselves up on a chair for example. Examples of this are given in the table on page 217. Further information is also included Learning Outcome 1.

A toddler who has managed to reach the gas hob.

Table CYP 3.4.3: Development indicators for planning health, safety and security developments

Approximate age	Development indicator	Implications for health, safety and security arrangements	Measures to be taken
4–5 months	Will roll from their back to their side	May roll when on a high changing unit	Use units with side bars and anticipate that baby may roll
6 months	Fascinated by small toys within reaching distance, grabbing them with the whole hand	Will pick up objects within their reach independently. This could include safety hazards such as sharp objects, unsafe substances and small objects which present a choking hazard	Ensure that nothing unsuitable is left in the vicinity of the baby
9 months	Starts to crawl and pull itself up to standing position	Crawling means a baby may independently move anywhere – to the stairs for instance. Standing up gives access to a whole new level – may be able to reach heaters, etc	Install safety equipment such as stair gates, socket covers, cupboard locks, heater guards. Assess safety of the objects now on the baby's new level. Baby may pull objects onto themselves, and push less sturdy items of furniture over
15 months	Walking alone. Explores objects using trial and error	May want to walk alone instead of riding in a buggy when out and about. May wander off to explore	Use reins for safety. Supervise carefully on the stairs
2 years	Runs safely. Starting to understand consequences of own behaviour	May disappear from sight quickly	Keep a close eye on child's whereabouts. Be prepared to deal with more minor grazes and bumps
3 years	Walks upstairs, one foot on each step. Rides tricycle. Children are impulsive. May resent adults limiting their behaviour. Asks lots of questions	Learning to use stairs without supervision. May suddenly do something dangerous on impulse, like jump from a slide. May be reluctant to heed safety warnings	Ensure there is a handrail of appropriate height on stairs. Give child safety information as appropriate. Be prepared to be firm on matters of safety. ('No means no')
4 years	Climbs play equipment. May confuse fantasy and reality	Uses bigger, higher equipment. May become engrossed in fantasy play and forget the safety limits of the real world. (We cannot fly, even if we jump from somewhere high)	Ensure safety playground covering is suitable for the higher equipment. Gently remind about safety limits if necessary, but try not to disturb imaginary play unnecessarily
5 years	Balances on beam. Greater levels of independence achieved	Will want less adult support	Encourage child to think about their own safety for themselves
6–7 years	Rides a bicycle, makes running jumps. Increasingly mature	Spends more time alone at home, playing in the bedroom or garden perhaps, or riding bike on own street if it is in a residential area	Continue to support awareness of safety. Ensure cycle helmet is worn

| 8–11 years | Rides scooters, bigger bicycles and skateboards/skates. May play sports. Increasingly independent | May ride a bicycle on the road. Goes out to play with friends without adult supervision. Children become more aware of risks, but may misjudge their abilities. May cross local roads alone | Continue to support awareness of safety. Ensure that helmets and padding designed for safety are used with skateboards, etc. Ensure that children have access to safe, good-quality sports equipment, and encourage them to warm up/cool down before/after sports. Ensure that children learn road safety (and cycle safety if appropriate) |
| 11 onwards | Independence grows as children enter teenage years, and time spent unsupervised by adults increases greatly. Peer pressure may affect young people, and they may experiment with new experiences | Often, young people will not have an accompanying adult to point out risks to them, and they may not have an adult to turn to if they are in an unsafe or difficult situation. Children may try alcohol, drugs (including cigarettes) and engage in sexual behaviour | Ensure that children/young people can recognise risks for themselves. Teach them what to do when hazards occur (role plays, quizzes and moral dilemma games can all be used for this purpose). Teach children/young people about the dangers of alcohol and drugs. Support young people who ask questions about relationships and sex (see Unit CYP 3.7 How to support positive outcomes for children and young people) |

Link Up!

See also Unit CYP 3.1 Understand child and young person development

Have a go!

There are many pieces of equipment on the market that can help to keep children and young people safe, and new products are developed all the time. It's good practice to be aware of these, so spend some time on the internet or with an appropriate catalogue researching safety equipment for yourself.

Cupboard safety locks.

Levels of supervision

Practitioners must supervise children and young people safely at all times and maintain the minimum staff to child ratios, although many settings aim to exceed these ratios in the interests of quality. In day care settings in England (without a qualified teacher) the minimum ratios are:

■ children under 2 years: one adult to three children (1:3)

- children aged 2 years: one adult to four children (1:4)

- children aged 3 to 7 years: one adult to eight children (1:8).

Everyone must be checked by the Criminal Records Bureau as part of the Vetting and Barring Scheme. There's more about this in Unit CYP 3.3. Settings must also be staffed by practitioners with the acceptable qualifications, as specified by the Children's Workforce Development Council. You can see a full list of these online at **www.cwdcouncil.org.uk** – follow the links to 'Areas of work' and then 'Qualifications'.

Unit CYP 3.3 Understand how to safeguard the well-being of children and young people

Staff deployment

For safety, the deployment of staff should be carefully considered throughout the session. Generally, the younger children are, or the more challenging an activity, the closer the supervision will need to be. For some activities, children and young people can safely work and play independently, as long as there are adults in the room keeping a general eye on things – children and young people can approach them

if they need assistance. Other activities would be unsafe without one-to-one support from an adult – for example when a child is learning to use woodworking tools such as hacksaws. Levels of supervision required can change as problems occur, the mood of children and young people changes, or when children and young people master skills. Practitioners learn through experience to adjust the supervision they give accordingly.

You can find out more about safe supervision in Unit EYMP 3 Promote children's welfare and well-being in the early years

Security

Settings must make suitable security arrangements in the interests of the children and young people's safety. There should be clear systems and procedures in place for their arrival at the setting, their departure from the setting, and their security when on outings.

For full details on this, see Unit EYMP 3 Promote children's welfare and well-being in the early years

LEARNING OUTCOME 3

FOCUS ON

...a balanced approach to risk management

In this section you'll learn about the importance of taking a balanced approach to risk management, and the dilemma between the rights and choices of children and young people and health and safety requirements. This links with Assessment Criteria **3.1, 3.2, 3.3.**

This learning outcome links with Unit EYMP 3 Promote children's welfare and well-being in the early years

Challenge and risk

Part of providing children with adequate challenge is permitting them to take appropriate risks. With physically active play there is always a risk of children getting hurt – most setting's accident books are likely to show regular minor playground injuries such as grazed knees and hands from children's falls while simply running. However, it would be inappropriate of practitioners not to allow children to run in case they fell and hurt themselves. In fact *not* running would potentially harm children, affecting their physical development, fitness, confidence and general well-being. In this case, the benefits justify the risk – and the risk is not significant – there may be a high incidence of playground injuries, but they are generally only very minor.

However, it is sensible to minimise risk, for example by making sure that children have sufficient space to run around in without bumping into each other. The use of apparatus such as a climbing frame is another example of an activity that has an element of risk. But practitioners take a number of steps to minimise

This young person is taking an acceptable age appropriate risk by skateboarding in full safety gear.

the risk by, for instance, providing a safety surface underneath and around the apparatus, and restricting the number of children permitted on at any one time.

The risks that are appropriate for children and young people to take increase in intensity as they develop and grow up, and practitioners must allow for that. Remember, if children and young people are not allowed to take age appropriate risks, they will not be sufficiently challenged.

A balanced approach to risk management

Sometimes children and young people may want to take risks that are wholly inappropriate for safety reasons, or inappropriate for a child or young person of their age, needs or abilities. While practitioners should not be **excessively risk adverse** (prone to avoiding risk altogether), they should not allow children and young people to do things that are dangerous and likely to hurt them.

There is a difference between allowing children and young people to take appropriate risks that are worthwhile in terms of development when compared to the likelihood of injury, and allowing children and young people to do things that are likely to seriously hurt them, or injure them without a justifiable developmental gain or experience. This is known as **excessive risk taking**.

Good practice

If a child or young person is attracted to an activity that you consider to be too dangerous, think about whether there's a safer, alternative way to give them a similar experience, as this will be a good compromise.

key terms

Excessively risk adverse prone to avoiding risk altogether.

Excessive risk taking taking inappropriate risks.

To decide what risks are acceptable and unacceptable, and to see what can be done to minimise risk, practitioners should carry out risk assessments, as outlined in Learning Outcome 2. It's important that you know and understand your own setting's policies and procedures for risk assessment and that you follow them closely. Guidelines are generally included within a setting's health and safety policy.

Rights and choices verses health and safety

There's a tricky dilemma between the rights and choices that belong to children and young people in terms of the freedom to play,

Preparing for the thrill of the zip wire.

and the health and safety requirements of settings and services. However, children and young people should be allowed to experience and explore **appropriate** risk during their play.

Good practice

It is helpful if organisations also include information about risk and challenge in their health and safety policy. This is an opportunity to clearly agree and communicate the setting's approach to risk and challenge, which will benefit practitioners, families, children and young people.

There are four types of hazard/risk that should be considered in terms of play. These are:

- physical
- environmental
- emotional
- behavioural.

You learned about physical hazards (tangible items, such as a stack of chairs) and environmental hazards/ risks (such as water, or stairs) earlier in this unit.

Emotional risk

Emotional risk taking is a life skill. Children and young people (and adults) take emotional risks whenever they pluck up the courage to do something that stretches them emotionally, or that risks personal failure or rejection. Examples of emotional risk taking include:

- speaking in front of a group of peers or adults
- performing in public (singing, acting, dancing, playing musical instruments)
- auditioning
- trying to make a new friend
- saying no to friends or refusing to give in to peer pressure
- showing others own creative work (e.g. art or creative writing)
- entering a competition
- suggesting own ideas to peers/adults
- telling a joke
- applying for a college course or a job
- doing something independently for the first time (e.g. using public transport, living alone)
- taking a physical risk in front of others (e.g. going on a skateboard ramp for the first time).

Activities that feel like a risk to one person may come easily to another. Children and young people are individuals who are comfortable doing different things. The things children are comfortable with are sometimes referred to as being within their 'comfort zone'. But if children and young people are to continually move on and progress in their development, they need to 'step out of their comfort zone' every so often, and take an emotional risk.

Those with good levels of self-esteem and confidence are generally more willing to take emotional risks. You can help children and young people to feel equipped for emotional risk-taking by providing opportunities for them to participate in activities that foster high levels of confidence and self-esteem, including:

- team activities

- trust games

- games that give everyone the opportunity to be the 'leader'

- activities that involve a physical challenge

- consultation

- displays of art/craft work.

You can also ensure that you offer children plenty of praise in general terms, and specifically for 'having a go' or 'trying hard'. This helps to communicate that there is value in being prepared to step out of one's comfort zone, whatever the result of taking the risk.

For more on self-esteem issues, please see Learning Outcome 1, Unit CYP 3.7 Understand how to support positive outcomes for children and young people, and pages 194–195.

Behavioural hazards

Behavioural hazards occur when children and young people behave in a ways that could cause harm to themselves or others. For instance, practitioners may provide clay and tools for modelling. Although the tools may be pointed, this would generally be considered a relatively low-risk activity. However, if a young person should begin throwing these tools at 'targets' in play, or even deliberately using them as a weapon during a disagreement, the risk is significantly raised to an unacceptable level. Practitioners would need to intervene quickly (step in and take action) to curb the behaviour and therefore the risk. A child or young person's behaviour can also harm others emotionally.

Always judge if and when to intervene.

Monitoring risk levels

Although risk assessments will be carried out prior to activities, the level of risk can change during play. This is due to the way in which children and young people choose to play and use the resources over time. Practitioners must continually monitor the changing levels of risk. There is no need to intervene in play unless the level of risk becomes unacceptable. If it does, it is the duty of practitioners to intervene and bring the level of risk back to an acceptable level.

It's good practice to involve children and young people in thinking about safety, and encourage them to tell an adult if they see something unsafe. One of the most effective and simple ways to teach children about safety is to explain to them why you feel that an activity, a situation or someone's behaviour is potentially dangerous. (See the Practical example on page 223.)

Young people may help adults to check appropriate parts of the premises for safety, and assist in carrying out risk assessment informally. Moral dilemma games and role plays can also be an effective way to encourage young people to think about how they should handle potentially dangerous situations. These are best done in small groups of three or four.

Did you know?

An effective technique to keep intervention at a minimum is to encourage children and young people to develop an awareness of hazards and how to manage risk themselves. This is also an important life skill.

Supporting children and young people to assess and manage risk

Children and young people will not always be under the close supervision of adults, and as they grow older, they will become entirely independent. So it is essential that they learn to recognise and manage risk for themselves. Experience of doing this should increase as children and young people mature.

 **Have a go!**

Try designing your own moral dilemma game to help young people to consider how to handle potentially dangerous situations. Here's what to do:

■ Compile a list of appropriate dilemmas, e.g. what should a young person do if their lift home from a disco or club doesn't turn up? Or if someone should offer them alcohol or drugs? If you're currently working with young people, why not consult them and include their dilemma ideas too?

■ Write or print the dilemmas onto individual pieces of card.

■ Try the game out with a small group of young people. (Players will take it in turn to choose a card at random. They must then read it out and tell the group what they would do in the situation they have selected.)

■ Reflect on the game and make notes in your reflective journal.

Practical example

Amir's learning opportunity

Amir and his colleague Lola are taking a group of children to visit the nearby local park. They walk along the pavement, but Amir notices that every so often, 4-year-old Kenna gets up onto the raised kerb and walks along for a couple of steps, before returning to the pavement. Amir has told her not to do this before. He is about to remind her when Lola beats him to it. She says, 'Please don't walk up there Kenna, it's dangerous. Do you know why?' Amir is surprised to learn that Kenna has no idea that she's getting dangerously close to the road. With hindsight, he realises that in the past he has not explained the reason why Kenna must not stray onto the raised kerb.

Question
What can Amir do to ensure that he doesn't miss such learning opportunities in the future?

LEARNING OUTCOME 4

FOCUS ON
...accidents, incidents, emergencies and illness

In this section you'll learn about the policies and procedures for the response to and the reporting of accidents, incidents, emergencies and illness. You'll also learn about how these are recorded. This links with Assessment Criteria **4.1, 4.2.**

▶▶▶ Link Up! ◀◀◀

Unit EYMP 3 Promote children's welfare and well-being in the early years

The importance of policies and procedures

The policies and procedures for the response to and the reporting of accidents, incidents, emergencies and illness are hugely important. They can literally mean the difference between life and death should a serious situation occur.

Good practice

It's crucial that you spend plenty of time familiarising yourself with the emergency procedures of your setting or service, as this will help you to recall how to respond should an emergency occur. It's reassuring to know procedures inside out, and it will help you to think clearly if you suddenly find yourself under pressure to take the appropriate action.

Evacuation procedures and fire safety

It may be necessary to evacuate a setting for a number of reasons, including:

■ fire

■ flood

■ gas leak

■ identification of a dangerous substance.

To ensure that premises can be evacuated effectively in an emergency, the following points are essential:

■ **All staff must know how to raise the alarm, where the exit points are, and where the assembly point is**

■ **All staff are aware of their individual roles**
Such as taking the register, dialling 999, checking that rooms are empty.

■ **There are regular opportunities to practise evacuation drills**
These should be taken seriously, and any difficulties should be resolved. The sound of the alarm may upset some children or young people, so be sensitive, and help them to settle after the drill.

■ **Evacuation drill notices should be displayed for visitors to refer to**
These should give details of where the fire extinguishing equipment is kept.

Fire drill.

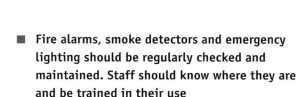

- **Fire alarms, smoke detectors and emergency lighting should be regularly checked and maintained. Staff should know where they are and be trained in their use**
  Details of checks should be recorded in the setting's evacuation log.

- **Emergency exits must not be obstructed.**

One person often takes the responsibility for overseeing evacuation procedures and fire safety.

Missing child procedures

All registered settings must have written procedures addressing what practitioners would do if it was discovered that a child was missing. You should know and understand these procedures, as in such an emergency it will be important to act quickly.

In most situations it would be appropriate to organise a full initial search of the setting, including outdoor areas, and to check when the child was last seen. If the child cannot be found, the search should be widened to the local area. The person in charge should raise the alarm, contacting police and the missing child's parents or carers. Later, if the setting or service is registered, Ofsted should also be informed. Sufficient staff must remain on the premises to care for the remaining children, but surplus staff may join the search. Police will take charge of the search when they arrive. Practitioners should log events in the setting's incident book, while these are fresh in their minds. There will need to be an urgent review of the setting's security.

Common childhood illnesses

All children and young people experience illness from time to time. It is important that you learn to recognise the signs and symptoms of illness in a child or young person. When you notice that a child or young person is feeling unwell, you should promptly take the appropriate action in line with your setting's policies and procedures. It is a legal requirement that all registered settings have written guidelines for the management of illness within the setting.

It is not your job to diagnose diseases or illnesses – that is the role of health professionals such as doctors. It is also not your job to care for sick children or young people, and those who are ill should not attend the setting. However, there will be times when a child or young person's illness will develop while they are in your care. Your job is as follows:

- **Recognise promptly when a child or young person is ill**
  See the diagram on page 226.

- **Respond to symptoms if appropriate, in line with policies**
  This could be cooling down a child with a temperature, for instance, or administering a child's asthma inhaler.

- **Monitor the condition**
  This is in case it becomes worse. Record appropriate details such as temperature readings, or inhalers given.

- **Arrange for the child or young person to be collected as soon as possible, in the case of minor illness**
  The child's parent, carer or alternative contact person (as stated on the registration form) should be called. Be calm and supply the facts. A parent may initially become very anxious about their child, even if symptoms seem minor. If symptoms are more serious, a parent may understandably panic. You must stay in control. Sometimes, a parent may need to call you back to confirm collection arrangements, as they may need a few minutes to organise things, such as leaving work, or seeing whether an alternative contact person is free to come in their place. Parents or carers may ask you what they should do for their child. You are not a doctor, and so you should simply advise them to seek medical attention if they are unsure what to do, or if they are worried by any symptoms.

- **Get emergency assistance urgently if necessary,**

and know which signs and symptoms indicate that immediate medical help is needed

Do not wait for parents or carers if it is an emergency. Dial 999 and request an ambulance. If the child or young person needs to go to hospital before a parent or carer arrives, a practitioner should accompany them and meet parents at the hospital.

Do all you can to make a child or young person comfortable until they leave your care. Children or young people who are ill may be upset or embarrassed. Be sensitive and caring to soothe them. Stay with a child in a quiet area, and carry out a quiet activity, such as sharing a book, if the child is interested.

- **Record the illness**
  See 'Record keeping' on page 227.

- **Do what you can to stop the spread of infection**
  See 'Preventing cross-infection' in Unit EYMP 3, Learning Outcome 2.

Signs and symptoms of illness

Children or young people who become ill at the setting may display the common signs and symptoms of illness shown on the diagram below.

The following signs and symptoms of illness indicate that you may need to call for urgent medical attention:

- breathing difficulties
- convulsions

Unit EYMP 3 Promote children's welfare and well-being in the early years

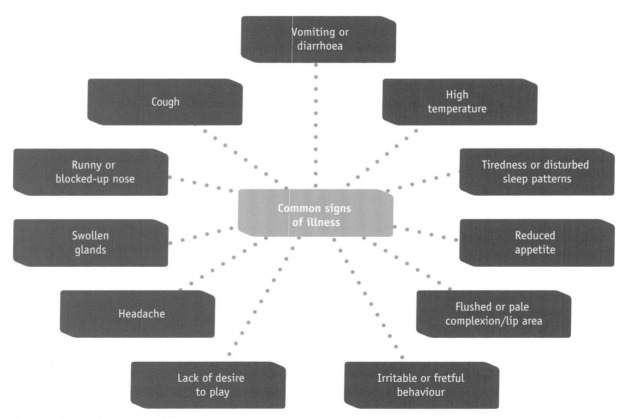

Common signs and symptoms of illness.

- child/young person seems to be in significant pain

- child/young person cannot easily or fully be roused from sleep, or a state of drowsiness

- baby becomes unresponsive and/or their body seems to be floppy

- severe headache, which may be accompanied by a stiff neck or a dislike of light

- rash that remains (does not fade) when pressed with a glass

- vomiting that persists for over 24 hours

- unusual, high-pitched crying in babies

- high temperature that cannot be lowered

- will not drink fluids – this is most worrying in babies.

High temperatures

The normal temperature reading for a child is between 36.5 and 37.4 degrees Celsius. Children may have a higher temperature when they are ill. Taking a child's temperature with a thermometer helps you to monitor their illness. Most settings will use a fever scan thermometer (placed on the forehead) or a digital thermometer (either placed in the mouth or the ear). These come with directions for use. They are safer than clinical thermometers, which are made of glass and contain mercury.

You should take steps to lower a temperature by:

- seeing that warm clothing is removed so that just a cool layer is worn

Taking a child's temperature with a digital thermometer.

- providing a cool drink either of water, or diluted by water

- cooling the environment (opening windows, turning off heat sources, using a fan)

- providing a cool wipe for the face and forehead.

Some children may be given paracetamol syrup by parents or carers, or with parental consent, but this depends on the circumstances and the policy of the setting. (For instance, a child may be prone to febrile convulsions, brought on by a high temperature. Parents may, therefore, bring paracetamol syrup to the setting, giving written permission for it to be administered if their child runs a temperature, in the hope that convulsions may be avoided.)

Did you know?

Children may also have a high or higher temperature after physical activity such as running around, or after they have taken hot food or fluids.

Medication and written permission

Some children and young people may take medication regularly to treat conditions they have. For instance, a baby with asthma may take inhalers, and a child with ADHD may take tablets, or a young person with eczema may use creams.

For further information on medications, see Unit EYMP 3 Promote children's welfare and well-being in the early years

Record keeping

Settings must keep a record of illness, accidents and incidents that occur.

When a child or young person becomes ill at a setting, the practitioner should record the time and date,

Table CYP 3.4.4: Childhood infection

Disease and cause	Spread	Incubation	Signs and symptoms	Rash or specific sign	Treatment	Complications
Common cold (coryza) Virus	Airborne/droplet, hand-to-hand contact	1–3 days	Sneezing, sore throat, running nose, headache, slight fever, irritable, partial deafness		Treat symptoms. Vaseline to nostrils	Bronchitis, sinusitis, laryngitis
Chickenpox (varicella) Virus	Airborne/droplet, direct contact	10–14 days	Slight fever, itchy rash, mild onset, child feels ill, often with severe headache	Red spots with white centre on trunk and limbs at first; blisters and pustules	Rest, fluids, calamine to rash, cut child's nails to prevent secondary infection	Impetigo, scarring, secondary infection from scratching
Dysentery Bacillus or amoeba	Indirect: flies, infected food, poor hygiene	1–7 days	Vomiting, diarrhoea, blood mucus in stool, abdominal pain, fever, headache		Replace fluids, rest, medical aid, strict hygiene measures	Dehydration from loss of body salts, shock; can be fatal
Food poisoning Bacteria or virus	Indirect: infected food or drink	30 mins–36 hours	Vomiting, diarrhoea, abdominal pain		Fluids only for 24 hours; medical aid if no better	Dehydration – can be fatal
Gastro-enteritis Bacteria or virus	Direct contact. Indirect: infected food/drink	Bacterial: 7–14 days Viral: 30 mins–36hrs	Vomiting, diarrhoea, signs of dehydration		Replace fluids – water or Dioralyte; medical aid urgently	Dehydration, weight loss – can be fatal
Measles (morbilli) Virus	Airborne/droplet	7–15 days	High fever; fretful, heavy cold – running nose and discharge from eyes; later cough	Day 1: Koplik's spots, white inside mouth. Day 4: blotchy rash starts on face and spreads down to body	Rest, fluids, tepid sponging; shade room if photophobic	Otitis media, eye infection, pneumonia, encephalitis (rare)
Mumps (epidemic parotitis) Virus	Airborne/droplet	14–21 days	Pain, swelling of jaw in front of ears, fever; eating and drinking painful	Swollen face	Fluids: give via straw, hot compresses, oral hygiene	Meningitis (1 in 400), orchitis (infection of testes) in young men
Pertussis (whooping cough) Bacteria	Airborne/droplet, direct contact	7–21 days	Starts with a snuffly cold, slight cough, mild fever	Spasmodic cough with whoop sound, vomiting	Rest and assurance; feed after coughing attack; support during attack; inhalations	Convulsions, pneumonia, brain damage, hernia, debility

Rubella (German measles) Virus	Airborne/droplet	14–21 days	Slight cold, sore throat, mild fever, swollen glands behind ears, pain in small joints	Slight pink rash starts behind ears and on forehead. Not itchy	Rest if necessary. Treat symptoms	Only if contracted by woman in first 3 months of pregnancy – can cause serious defects in unborn
Scarlet fever (or Scarlatina) Bacteria	Droplet	2–4 days	Sudden fever, loss of appetite, sore throat, pallor around mouth, 'strawberry tongue'	Bright red pinpoint rash over face and body – may peel	Rest, fluids, observe for complications, antibiotics	Kidney infection, otitis media, rheumatic fever (rare)
Tonsillitis Bacteria or virus	Direct infection, droplet		Very sore throat, fever; headache, pain on swallowing, aches and pains in back and limbs		Rest, fluids, medical aid – antibiotics, iced drinks relieve pain	Quinsy (abscess on tonsils), otitis media, kidney infection, temporary deafness

and describe the signs and symptoms of illness. They should record their response to the child or young person's condition, making a note of details such as temperature readings, if appropriate. The parent or carer should be asked to sign the record.

If an incident or accident occurs, practitioners must record the time, date, location and circumstances. Details of any injuries must also be recorded along with any action taken, including first aid treatment. The parent or carer must sign the log, as well as the practitioner who dealt with the incident/accident. Further information about the recording of incidents can be found in Unit CYP 3.3.

Your setting may also have additional procedures for reporting illnesses, accidents and incidents to superiors. If so, you should follow your organisational policies.

A medication log also be kept – see page 390.

Every setting must have a first aid kit. These now come with a list of content inside, often on a sticker inside the lid. Kits should be stored somewhere accessible for staff, but out of the reach of children and young people, in a dry place so that items will not perish. It is crucial that as items are used, the box is replenished. Systems should be devised to ensure that is the case. Often, one person takes responsibility for overseeing the first aid kit. It is good practice to keep

First aid kit.

'guidance cards' within a first aid kit; these contain brief notes (reminders) on how to carry out life-saving procedures – many kits now come with cards.

Link Up!

Unit CYP 3.3 Understand how to safeguard the well-being of children and young people
Unit EYMP 3 Promote children's welfare and well-being in the early years

Good practice

It is good practice to wear gloves when carrying out first aid procedures, to protect yourself and the casualty from cross-infection. Gloves should be kept in the first aid kit.

First aid in emergencies

Accidents will happen, however carefully you carry out risk assessment and supervise children. That is why it is recommended that practitioners take a first aid course. There has to be at least one first-aider present at all registered settings. The aims of first aid are often remembered as 'the three ps', that is to:

- preserve life
- prevent the condition worsening
- promote recovery.

Sometimes first aid is all that is necessary – common minor injuries such as grazes can be sufficiently treated for instance. However, it is important to recognise when medical assistance is urgently required. Whenever you are dealing with an accident, incident or illness, you must stay calm. You should reassure casualties, and children or young people who are bystanders, as they may be very frightened. You should ensure that you and others are not put at unnecessary risk. **Often the most qualified person at the setting will take responsibility for administering first aid, so you may just be required to inform them, depending on the circumstances.** Think through your actions carefully, and make safety your priority. When you first respond to a first aid emergency, you should follow the advice on the diagram below.

How to examine a casualty will be taught on a first aid course. But essentially, you should:

- check for a response – call the casualty's name, pinch their skin
- open the airway and check for breathing
- check the pulse.

Managing an unconscious child who is breathing

An unconscious child **who is breathing and has a pulse** should be put into the recovery position. This will keep the airway clear. Keep checking the airway and pulse until help arrives.

How to manage an unconscious child who is breathing.

Keep calm

Assess the situation – is there any further danger for the child/young person, you or others? Is it safe to approach?

Prioritise – examine casualty/casualties, then treat the most serious injuries first. Those who are unconscious, not breathing, severely bleeding or in shock will need urgent help.

Shout for help. Dial 999 or send someone to call. Ask for an ambulance, then answer the questions you are asked calmly and fully. You will need to know the exact location of the setting, the telephone number you are using, and the details of the incident.

Responding to a first aid emergency.

Managing an unconscious child who is not breathing

If a child is unconscious and not breathing, the heartbeat will slow down and eventually stop. You will need to breathe for them. **You will need to have done a registered first aid course to be able to do this.** If you are not trained to do this, you must get help as quickly as possible. If you are trained, send someone to dial 999 for an ambulance while you begin CPR.

You will learn how to recognise and deal with various illnesses and accidents on a first aid course, but a brief overview of key conditions is given here:

Table CYP 3.4.5: How to recognise and deal with emergencies

Type of emergency	Response required
Anaphylactic shock A severe allergic reaction that can be fatal. Blood pressure falls and breathing is impaired. Tongue and throat may swell.	Dial 999 – the casualty needs to be given an adrenaline injection. A child or young person with a known allergy may need to have their own adrenaline to be administered. A sitting position helps breathing. Watch for shock; lie casualty down and raise legs if you suspect it. The casualty may need to be resuscitated if they become unconscious.
Asthma The airways go into spasm making breathing difficult. This may occur after contact with allergens such as dust, pollen or pet hair. Severity of attacks vary, but they can be serious. Severe attacks are frightening for the casualty concerned and can also frighten those witnessing the attack. The casualty wheezes and becomes breathless. Prompt action is needed.	Reassure. Give bronchodilator inhaler as instructed if child is a known asthmatic. These inhalers should always be immediately available – they deliver medication to the lungs to relieve affected airways. Children and young people may also have another type of inhaler used to prevent attacks. Make sure that you know which to use in an emergency, particularly if older children or young people generally use their inhalers themselves. Sit casualty upright and leaning forwards in comfortable position. Stay with them. If this is the first attack or condition persists or worsens, call for an ambulance.
Electric shock	Do not touch casualty while he/she is in contact with an electrical current as he/she will be 'live' and you may be electrocuted. Break the electrical contact by turning off the power supply if possible or pulling out the plug or wrenching the cable free. If you cannot reach these, stand on dry insulating material (such as a telephone directory) and use something made of wood (such as a broom handle) to push the appliance aside. You can then check the casualty. They may need to be resuscitated. Dial 999.
Bleeding: 1. Minor cuts and grazes 2. Severe 3. Severe with an object embedded in wound (i.e. glass)	1. Clean with water and apply a clean dressing. 2. Lay casualty down and cover the wound with a dressing. Apply direct pressure with your hand. If a limb is bleeding, raise and support it. Raise and support legs if you suspect that shock may develop. Dial 999. 3. As before, but apply direct pressure to either side of the wound. Build padding up around the object, then bandage over the top of it, without pressing on the object.
Burns and scalds	Cool immediately with cold water. Place body part under running tap if possible, for at least 10 minutes. Otherwise, lie casualty down and douse the injury, through any clothes, by pouring on cold water if possible, or applying wet cloths. Remove any restricting clothes or jewellery, as long as clothes are not stuck to the burn. Cover with a clean, non-fluffy dressing. Watch for shock, and raise and support legs if you suspect it. Dial 999, take or send to hospital, depending on severity. Do not cover burns to the face – you could block an airway or cause distress. Do not over-cool or the body temperature may lower dangerously – this particularly applies to babies.

Suspected fractures	Keep casualty as still as possible. Immobilise the affected part of the body and support it. If possible, bandage it to an unaffected part of the body (e.g. bandage a fractured leg to the unaffected leg for support). Depending on the circumstances, take or remove to hospital, or dial 999.
Neck and back injuries	Steady and support the head, and tell casualty to keep still, with head, neck and back in alignment. Keep holding the head, but get a helper to place rolled up towels or other padding either side of the neck and shoulders. Send the helper to dial 999, and remain holding the head until help arrives.
Poisoning Swallowed poisons (e.g. tablets, chemicals, berries)	Dial 999. Take a sample of poison to hospital for analysis if possible. If casualty is sick, keep a sample, but never try to make a child or young person sick intentionally. Watch for signs of unconsciousness.
Bites and stings – minor 1. General, insect (For allergic reactions to bites and stings, see anaphylactic shock.) 2. To mouth and throat	1. Brush sting away with fingernail if it is visible. Do not use tweezers (if tweezers do need to be used, it is a job for a health professional and medical help should be sought). Raise the affected part and apply an ice-pack or cold-compress. Casualty should see a doctor if the pain and swelling persist. 2. Give casualty an ice-cube to suck or a cold drink. If swelling starts, dial 999.
Effects of extreme heat and cold **Heatstroke:** Body becomes dangerously overheated, generally due to high fever or overexposure to heat. There may be dizziness, headache, restlessness, hot flushed skin and rapid deterioration in casualty's level of response. Can cause unconsciousness. **Hypothermia in infants:** May develop over several days in poorly heated homes, or be due to prolonged exposure to the cold out of doors. Babies are particularly vulnerable. Signs are shivering, cold, pale skin, body may feel limp or there may be impaired consciousness, slow, shallow breathing, slow, weak pulse, refusal to feed, unusually quiet.	1. Remove casualty to a cool place, and remove as much clothing as possible. Dial 999. Wrap the casualty in a cold wet sheet until temperature falls to below 38°C. Then replace the sheet with a dry one. Watch for signs of unconsciousness. 2. Re-warm the baby gradually, by warming the room and wrapping the infant in blankets. You should call a doctor, or take or send a baby to hospital if you suspect hypothermia.
Meningitis **In children/young people:** There may be high temperature or fever, vomiting, severe headache, stiff neck, drowsiness, confusion, dislike of bright light, seizures, skin rash of red/purple 'pin prick' spots. If the spots spread, they can resemble fresh bruising, but this is difficult to see on black skin. The rash does not fade when the side of a glass is pressed against it. **In babies:** There may also be restlessness and a high pitched crying or screaming, a limp or floppy body, swelling of the soft fontanel area of the skull, and refusal to feed.	**For children, young people and babies:** If a doctor cannot be contacted or will be delayed, dial 999. Do not wait for all of the signs and symptoms to appear. If a casualty has already seen a doctor but is becoming worse, seek urgent medical attention again. Reassure the casualty and keep them cool until help arrives. **See also meningitis card on page 234.**

Foreign bodies stuck (not penetrating) in the: 1. eyes 2. ears 3. nose This may cause swelling and breathing difficulties.	1. Sit casualty down, facing the light, and tip the head back. Stand behind them, and open the eye with your finger and thumb. Pour clean water from a glass gently into the inner corner of the eye. The water will run out of the outer corner of the eye, hopefully flushing the eye clean. If this doesn't work, take or send casualty to the doctor/hospital. 2. If there is an insect in the ear, sit casualty down and tip their head to the side. Pour clean water into the ear gently, hopefully flushing the ear clean. If this doesn't work, take or send casualty to the doctor/hospital. For all other objects, do not try to remove the object yourself. Take or send to hospital. 3. Do not try to remove the object, even if you can see it. Take or send to hospital. Watch for breathing difficulties.
Choking: 1. Children and young people 2. Babies	1. If casualty is conscious, encourage them to cough. If this doesn't work, bend them forwards and give up to five back slaps between the shoulder blades with the heel of your hand. Check the mouth. If this has failed, try five chest thrusts, one every three seconds – stand behind the casualty and make a fist against the lower breastbone. Grasp the fist with your other hand. Pull sharply inwards and upwards. If this does not work, dial 999. Continue alternating between back slaps and thrusts until help arrives, or the casualty becomes unconscious. 2. Lay the baby along your forearm, with the head low, supporting the head and back. Give five back slaps with the heel of your hand. If this fails, do chest thrusts. Turn the baby on their back. Using two fingers push upwards and inwards towards the baby's breastbone (towards the head). This is one finger's width below the nipple line. Dial 999 and continue until help arrives or the infant becomes unconscious.
Febrile convulsions May be due to epilepsy or a high temperature. Violent muscle twitching, clenched fists, arched back. May lead to unconsciousness.	Do not try to restrain the casualty. Instead, clear the immediate area and surround the casualty with pillows or padding for protection. Cool the environment and the casualty gradually (as for a temperature), sponging skin if necessary. When seizures stop, place the casualty in the recovery position. Dial 999.
Head injuries There may be dizziness, disorientation, headache, vomiting. May lead to unconsciousness.	Give casualty a cold compress to hold against the head. Treat any bleeding, by covering with a dressing and applying direct pressure. Watch for unconsciousness. Take or send to hospital. If injury is severe, dial 999.

Dealing with bleeding.

Young children often take an inhaler via a spacer device that fits over their mouth and nose.

Meningitis signs and symptoms card from the Meningitis Trust.

Have a go!

You can get your own signs and symptoms card free of charge from the Meningitis Trust; this is handy to keep with you in your purse or wallet. You can request a card by calling 01453 768000 or emailing info@meningitis-trust.org

Link Up!

For information about preventing cross-infection, see Learning Outcome 4, Unit EYMP 3 Promote children's welfare and well-being in the early years

Emergencies involving adults

It's important to be aware that practitioners may also need to respond to an emergency involving an adult – for example, if a colleague or parent were to have an accident or to become ill.

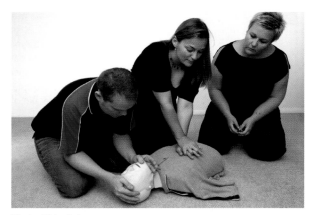

First aid training.

Good practice

It's good practice to enrol on a first aid training course that covers emergency first aid for adults as well as babies, children and young people. You will then learn to respond to conditions more common to adults, including heart attacks and strokes.

How are things going?

▶ Progress Check

1. Describe three factors to take into account when planning healthy and safe environments and services. (1.1)

2. Name four key issues likely to be covered in a setting's health and safety policy. (1.2)

3. What are the six steps of risk assessment? (2.3)

4. What is the purpose of monitoring and reviewing risk assessments? (2.4)

5. Why should you take a balanced approach to risk management? (3.1)

6. What action would you take to lower a child's temperature? (4.1)

7. Who should sign a medication record and accident record? (4.2)

Are you ready for assessment?

CACHE

Set task:

■ You must provide a resource to inform staff in your setting about a number of health and safety issues. This includes giving an example from your own practice.

You can prepare by reflecting on an instance when you have supported a child or young person to assess and manage risk. Make notes in your reflective journal.

Edexel

In preparation for assessment of this Unit, you may like to collect together risk assessment documents that you have completed in the workplace, to use as evidence.

City & Guilds

You must complete the mandatory Assignment 031. This has four tasks, each one relating to one of the four Learning Outcomes. It entails completing the tables provided, preparing reports/a presentation, and writing an ideal policy promoting equality, diversity and inclusion. You can prepare by accessing the equality, diversity and inclusion policy of your own setting. You will also need to research at least one other policy, so with the permission of your settings, you may like to arrange to exchange a copy of your setting's policy with that of a classmate.

Learning Outcome 2 must be assessed in real work environments.

UNIT 3.5

Develop positive relationships with children, young people and others involved in their care

LEARNING OUTCOMES

The learning outcomes you will meet in this unit are:

1 Be able to develop positive relationships with children and young people

2 Be able to build positive relationships with people involved in the care of children and young people

INTRODUCTION

The ability to foster good relationships with others is one of the foundation stones of being a good practitioner. It is essential to master the skills of developing and promoting positive relationships with children and adults; this includes family members, colleagues and other professionals.

LEARNING OUTCOME 1

...being able to develop positive relationships with children and young people

In this section you'll learn why positive relationships with children and young people are important. You'll also learn how to build them effectively, and how to evaluate your own effectiveness in doing so. This links with Assessment Criteria **1.1, 1.2, 1.3.**

Why positive relationships with children and young people are important

It's impossible for you to work effectively with children and young people unless you can form positive relationships with them. This is because positive relationships enable children and young people to feel happy and relaxed in your company, and to feel that they are being cared for. If children and young people don't feel comfortable with you and able to trust you to take care of them, any relationship established will be uneasy, and this will have an adverse effect on their well-being.

When you've established positive relationships, it's more likely that the children or young people that you work with will:

- feel settled in the setting and as a result more inclined to separate from their parents without upset

- want to spend time talking with you, which enhances their language and social skills and presents opportunities for spontaneous learning

- be keen to join in with play and learning activities alongside you

- feel confident to play and learn independently

- feel confident to make friends and interact with peers – your own relationship will also serve as a model for this

- feel content and therefore less likely to become stressed or frustrated, which in turn leads to less inappropriate behaviour

- be able to concentrate and learn effectively.

In addition, you will be able to get to know the child or young person better, and therefore do a better job of:

- understanding them

- assessing their progress

- supporting them

- motivating them

- interesting them.

Children are keen to join in when positive relationships exist.

Practical example

Interesting Tyler

Tyler is 3½. He's an active little boy who loves to play outside when he attends his local Sure Start centre. Practitioner Ellie makes good use of snack time to promote counting skills – the group count how many children there are and then count out the number of cups needed. Ellie then chooses someone to hand the cups out – there is never any shortage of volunteers! But Ellie has noticed that Tyler rarely joins in with the counting, and that he never shows interest in handing out the cups. Ellie thinks about another way to engage Tyler. After snack time, she asks him whether he could help her to set up some toys outside – she needs to get out five big balls, six small balls and seven beanbags. Tyler is keen! He finds the items himself, and counts them out with Ellie.

Question:
Why was Ellie's knowledge of Tyler's interests useful to her in this situation?

Building and maintaining positive relationships

Good relationships are built and maintained over time. Practitioners who are skilled in building and maintaining relationships use 'building blocks' in their practice as shown on the diagram below.

Communicating effectively

The way in which we communicate with children – what we say, our tone of voice, our body language, gestures and so on, is perhaps the most important building block of all when establishing and maintaining relationships. We communicate constantly, and if this is not done well, the negative effect will be significant. Good communication skills underpin many of the other building blocks. You can read more about how to communicate well in Unit SHC 31.

Link Up!

Unit SHC 31 Promote communication in health, social care or children's and young people's settings

The building blocks of building and maintaining positive relationships.

Showing courtesy and respect

You should always aim to make your relationships with children and young people warm and friendly, and this is achieved by showing them the same courtesy and respect as you would adults. Acknowledging them, talking to them politely and using good manners (in particular saying 'please' and 'thank you') will all demonstrate respect. Role modelling this behaviour will also encourage children to be courteous and respectful in their own interactions with others.

Related information about this can be found in Unit SHC 31 Promote communication in health, social care or children's and young people's settings

Being fair and consistent

If consistency is lacking, children will become confused. For instance, if some practitioners let children have extra turns during a board game to keep the peace, a child will learn that it is worth trying to get an extra turn rather than waiting for theirs because sometimes they are rewarded. The same applies if one practitioner varies their approach, sometimes allowing certain behaviour and sometimes not allowing it. This can make children feel insecure – they are not sure what is required of them, and they never know what reaction their behaviour will get. If a practitioner unfairly favours particular children or young people, it's likely to cause resentment and jealousy, and to negatively impact on well-being. However, when fairness and consistency is promoted trust is achieved, and children and young people learn to recognise and accept the behaviour boundaries.

Valuing and respecting individuality

In Unit SHC 33, you learned about the importance of valuing and respecting the individuality of children and young people. We cannot get to know someone in any real sense unless we do embrace their individuality – there will always be barriers,

Fairness and consistency are very important.

and relationships will be superficial. Children and young people need to sense that the people who care for them value and respect them to their very core. Anything less is likely to have an adverse affect not only on the relationship, but on the child or young person's self-esteem, self-image and self-respect.

Unit SHC 33 Promote equality and inclusion in health, social care or children's and young people's settings

Identifying and resolving conflicts and disagreements

All children and young people will have conflicts and disagreements with the adults in their lives. It's part of growing up. Your job is to identify and resolve any issues arising between you and a child or young person calmly and positively. Role modelling good conflict resolution techniques will also help them to resolve conflict with others in a positive manner in their own lives. There's more information about this on page 158.

Keeping promises and honouring commitments

Doing what we say we will do is one of the key ways in which children and young people come to trust and rely on us. Things that may seem trivial to an adult can be extremely important to young children, who can have surprisingly long memories! For instance, if you promise a 3-year-old that they can hand out the cups at snack time tomorrow and then fail to deliver, they may feel extremely let down and less inclined to take you at your word in the future. Even in the busiest of settings, keep track of what you are saying – if you promise someone the next turn on the swing, make sure they get it. If you say you'll set up the karaoke machine before you finish your shift, do it. Don't make promises you can't keep. Off-hand comments or answers such as, 'Yes, I'm sure if you're good Santa will bring you that mobile phone you want' can get you into all sorts of trouble! Also see 'Keeping confidentiality' below.

Make sure you keep promises and honour commitments.

Monitoring impact of own behaviour on others

This skill helps us to tailor our natural way of interacting to suit the needs of individual children and young people. For instance, you may unexpectedly notice a child become self-conscious and reluctant when you call on her to speak in the group, and so you modify your tone and behaviour to support her. A young person who likes his own space may take a step back if you stand too close when talking to him, so you modify your proximity next time. Children may become overly upset when you point out that they have not done something that was expected of them, such as helping to tidy up. In this case, you would

reassure them that while their help is expected next time, it isn't the end of the world. Teenagers often like to engage in banter, but they can also be very sensitive, even if they seem emotionally robust on the surface. Monitoring reactions closely is extremely helpful.

Keeping confidentiality as appropriate

In Unit SHC 31 you learned about the importance of keeping information about families confidential. Failing to do this can lead to a breakdown of trust and ultimately relationships. (You may like to turn to page 29 to refresh your memory). However, as practitioners will have reason to break confidentiality in order to report concerns if abuse is suspected or disclosed to you by a child or young person, you must never promise children or young people that you will keep what they tell you a secret.

Unit SHC 31 Promote communication in health, social care or children's and young people's settings

Recognising and responding to the underpinning power base

'Power base' refers to where the power lies in a relationship. Most relationships are not equal. This can be due to a number of reasons including differing levels of resources, experience, knowledge, skills and social and business contacts. In some relationships, the power shifts depending on the circumstances – if one person has something the other person wants, for instance. Sometimes the power base is formally recognised because of people's work roles – as in the case of a practitioner and their manager. In terms of your relationships with children and young people, you should be aware of the power that you have, and you should use it with great sensitivity. Remember that the point of this power is to enable you to protect and care for the children and young people you work with. You should aim to nurture them and to help them to flourish, not to exercise your power by bossing them around and getting them to do things for you! (For information on professional behaviour management, see Unit CYP 3.2, LO 5.)

Be aware of the power that you have.

Building relationships with children and young people

To ensure that each child within the setting has the opportunity to make a deeper relationship with an adult on a one-to-one basis, many settings operate a **key worker** system. This means that a member of staff is appointed to take a special interest in the welfare of a particular child, and to get to know them well. Most key workers will look after the interests of several children within a setting. They will also take the main responsibility for observing and assessing the development of their key children, and for liaising with their key children's parents and carers.

key term

Key worker a person appointed to take a special interest in the welfare of a particular child.

Building relationships with babies

It's particularly important for babies to have the opportunity to form key attachments within the setting. Consistency is an important aspect of this, so it's good practice for key workers to spend plenty of time with their babies, and to personally meet their care needs regularly (feeding, changing nappies, dressing, etc.), as these are ideal bonding opportunities. They give you a one-to-one opportunity to engage in eye contact, to talk to the baby, to touch

them and to be close to them. Relationships with other staff should still also be encouraged to avoid upset if the key worker is absent. Ideally, however, a small number of regular staff will work with babies and younger children. It is not good practice to pass a baby around between too many people.

Physical contact is extremely important, and along with the use of the voice (see below), it's the main way in which you can reassure babies and let them know that they are valued and cared for. The way in which you touch, hold and cuddle a baby will have a huge impact on the quality of the relationship you develop with them. Babies must always be touched respectfully during the meeting of care needs, and these tasks should always feel unrushed.

When interacting with young babies the following are crucial:

- the pitch and tone of your voice

- eye contact

- facial expression.

The actual words you say will not be understood, but the message you convey will be received – think how easy it is to distinguish anger, playfulness and empathy just from the above. You should always pay attention and respond to any interactions that a baby initiates with you – such as babbling, smiling, crying and making eye contact. To learn more about communicating with babies, turn to page 445. To learn more about the key attachment theory, turn to page 442.

An age appropriate approach to developing relationships

As you've learned, to develop good relationships with children and young people you must respond and relate to them as individuals. However, a good knowledge of children's and young people's development patterns will help you in your approach – the following table gives an example of this. For more detailed information, you are advised to also refer to the development tables on pages 83–101 – also see 'Have a go!' on page 243.

Table CYP 3.5.1: Children's development patterns

Age	Approach	Links to other units
0–1 years	Babies are entirely dependent and need to form key attachments. Consistency in terms of staff should be promoted. Give babies sensitive physical contact to reassure them and meet their care needs. Make eye contact with and talk with babies frequently, and value and respond to the interactions they make with you.	Unit CYPOP 1 Learning Outcome 2. Key attachments – pages 442–445. Communicating with babies
1–2 years	Key relationships continue to be extremely important. Children beginning a setting at this age may have difficulties settling and will need close support. They can be changeable emotionally, alternating between wanting to do things alone (which causes frustration if tasks cannot be managed) and being dependent, so an emotionally responsive approach is important to achieve a relationship that is supportive but not stifling. Children want to play and explore the world as long as carers are close by, providing security to which they can frequently return, so it's important to remain available to them, both emotionally and physically. Children begin to understand much of what is said to them and will develop an expanding vocabulary of single words, so talk with children often and encourage the learning of words as labels.	Unit CYPOP 1 Learning Outcome 2 See 'Helping new children to feel welcome and valued' section on page 243.
2–3 years	Children begin to be more responsive to the feelings of others and often relate to carers lovingly (e.g. initiating a cuddle). This paves the way for a deepening of relationships, as the child takes increasing notice of how the carer is responding to them – ensure that you demonstrate your approval of children and give plenty of praise and encouragement. Vocabulary increases and words are joined together. Children begin to understand their own feelings. Acknowledge feelings and give children words to express them – e.g. 'sad', 'happy'.	Unit CYPOP 1 Learning Outcome 2
3–4 years	Children understand more about their own role in relationships. They can talk about their feelings and tell carers what they want, so it's important to take the time to listen. They can empathise with the feelings of others, and they enjoy the company of peers and friends as they become increasingly confident socially. Children need carers to support them in these friendships, helping to smooth things out when there are conflicts or disagreements. Children want adult approval and they are affected by the mood of carers. Providing consistency and stability is therefore extremely important.	See below.
5–8 years	Children will have started school, and will need support during the transition. Children have an increasing sense of their own personality and they are keen to 'fit in' with others. Approval from adults and peers is desired. Show that you value and respect the child's individuality, and support the development of positive self-image and self-esteem. Adjust your level of physical support as children become increasingly able to meet most of their own care needs for themselves. Talk with children about the things they do independently when away from you – what they did at playtime or at a friend's house for instance. This will help to keep you connected to the child's world while allowing them to grow in independence and confidence.	See 'Helping new children to feel welcome and valued' section on page 243.
8–12 years	Children may feel unsettled when making the transition to secondary school, and as puberty approaches. A sensitive, responsive approach is needed, especially as this may result in some unsettled behaviour and reluctance. Stable friendships are relied upon, and children may develop stronger personal interests, some of which may result in a desire to learn out of school (e.g. dance class). Be sure to show an interest in things that matter to individual children, and informally check in with them about how the big things in their life are going – school, learning, relationships with friends, etc.	Unit CYP 3.1, LO 5.

| Young people | Young people develop a desire to express their individuality and yet also have a strong need to fit in with peers. They may worry about aspects of their appearance and experiment with their identity through appearance. Carers should aim to respect this process and the young person's choices as long as this is not inappropriate (e.g. you would not support someone under age in getting a tattoo, or doing something against the wishes of their parents). Young people are developing their own morals, beliefs and values, and these should be shown respect. They become interested in their own sexuality and feel attraction to others, and carers will need to establish boundaries around the development of such personal relationships. Young people may feel overwhelmed and anxious, particularly as exams loom. However, as they are now more likely to communicate their innermost thoughts and feelings to friends than to adults, you will need to remain vigilant in order to offer the emotional support that may be needed, while respecting that the young person may want to spend more time with friends than family and carers, and more time when at home on their own in their room. | |

Have a go!

The table above gives some pointers on the approach you may take in your relationships with children and young people of varying ages, based on children's and young people's development patterns. Now turn to the development tables which begin on page 83. Read through each of the sections on social and emotional development and communication and intellectual development. Consider and make notes on how the information can further inform your approach to developing and maintaining relationships with children and young people of all ages.

Eye contact is crucial.

Helping new children to feel welcome and valued

Starting at a new setting can be daunting for any child. It can be particularly hard for young children who are not used to being away from their parents or carers. Learning how to interact with children in a way that makes them feel welcomed and valued can make all the difference. We have all been in the position of being 'new' at some time. Even as adults

we are likely to feel anxious when we start work at a new setting. We feel relieved when we are made to feel welcome. We start to settle as we get to know people and the new environment. The same is true for children. However, the situation can be made even more difficult for children who are learning English as an additional language, or for those who have a communication difficulty. They may not be able to understand instructions, or be able to ask questions. Such a child could feel excluded without adult support.

The process of introducing new children to a setting is most successful when it is gradual. Ideally, children should accompany parents or carers on their first visit to view the setting. The child's initial response to the setting can then be considered when deciding to register the child. This can be very important for older children, who may ultimately settle more easily if they have been involved in the decision-making process. If a child's family is also learning English as an additional language, the setting can look for an interpreter to help them to communicate with the family at the important initial stage when crucial information is exchanged and people need to get to know each other.

Depending on a child's age, abilities and levels of confidence, children will usually be accompanied by their parent or carer on a second, longer visit. This time, the child should be invited to participate in the activities available. The child's key worker should join in sensitively.

A friendly welcome is always a relief.

Depending on the child, the practitioner may interact directly, or simply play close by to give the child the sense of sharing an experience with the key worker. This may also entice the child to interact with the key worker directly through play. This is a good opportunity for the key worker to get to know parents and carers too. It is reassuring for the child to feel that their primary carer is comfortable with their key worker.

On subsequent visits, the parent or carer should leave the child in the care of the key worker. At first, this can be done for just a few minutes. The length of time can then be gradually increased until the child attends a whole session alone. Children will be ready for this at different rates. It is important that parents and carers say goodbye, and it can be helpful to establish a routine. Perhaps a parent will go and hang up their child's coat with them every day, and then say goodbye, waving through the window as they leave. Routines help many children to feel secure.

All children need to feel welcomed and valued every day, even if have they have been attending a setting for some time. The following strategies help:

- verbally greeting each child by name, with a smile

- not asking questions if a child prefers not to talk on their arrival (You can still chat to them using statements, e.g. telling them about the activities planned for the session.)

- sensitively taking care of children who may become upset on arrival

- designing the layout of the environment so there is an easy, welcoming passage in

- encouraging children to play together or with you, while remembering that some children may want to watch on the fringes of the group until they settle

- telling older children which of their friends are expected

- having familiar/favourite activities or resources easily visible or displayed

- enticingly

- having comfortable, quiet areas as well as areas for being busy

- displaying welcoming signs and/or symbols (pictures of smiling faces near the entrance for example)

- making families feel welcome too.

Encourage children to play together or with you.

Have a go!

Think of the ways people interact with you – what makes you feel valued, or otherwise?

Children will unknowingly pick up and absorb numerous subtle signals from the way in which practitioners interact with them. These signals add up, influencing a child's overall sense of whether they are valued within the setting. In turn, this affects children's self-esteem and confidence, as well as how comfortable they feel. Factors that affect a child's sense of being valued include the way in which you:

- look at children

- talk and listen with children

- respond to children

- show your respect for children

- meet children's needs

- use facial expressions

- use body language.

Listening to children

See Unit SHC 31 Learning Outcome 2 for information on actively listening to children and young people.

Link Up!

Unit SHC 31 Promote communication in health, social care or children's and young people's settings

Evaluate your effectiveness in building relationships with children and young people

How effective you are in building relationships is indicated in the feelings of both yourself and the children and young people. In the case of the children and young people, this will usually be revealed through their behaviour. Behaviour indicators include:

- how well they separate from parents and carers on arrival

- if they approach you regularly to tell you things

- if they come to play with or near you, or involve you in their activities

- if they want you to share their accomplishments, e.g. they want you to look at their artwork or watch them climb up the climbing frame

- if they ask you for help

- if they come to you when they're tired, hurt, upset, unwell

- if they make good eye contact with you and smile

- if they're keen to tell their parents and carers about activities you've done together.

You'll find more information on self-evaluation in Unit SHC 32, Learning Outcome 3.

LEARNING OUTCOME 2

FOCUS ON

...being able to build positive relationships with people involved in the care of children and young people

In this section you'll learn why positive relationships with people involved in the care of children and young people are important. You'll also learn how to build these relationships effectively. This links with Assessment Criteria **2.1, 2.2.**

The people involved in the care of children and young people

In Unit SHC 31, you learned about effective communication, which is at the heart of forming positive relationships with the people involved in the care of children and young people.

The people involved in the care of children and young people may include the following:

Link Up!

You may find it helpful, as part of your study towards this unit, to refer back to Unit SHC 31 Promote communication in health, social care or children's and young people's settings

Positive relationships with parents, carers and other family members

We know that children are generally regarded as very precious by their parents, carers and other family members. It is normal for parents to feel anxious about sharing the care, learning and development of their child with practitioners. But as a positive relationship is established between parents and practitioners over time, trust is built, and parents generally begin to gain confidence in both the practitioner and the setting. Good practitioners work in partnership with parents and carers – but this can only be achieved when a positive relationship has been established.

The relationship between a child's key worker and his or her parents is therefore particularly important, as the key worker will normally be the parent's chief point of contact with the setting. Parents and

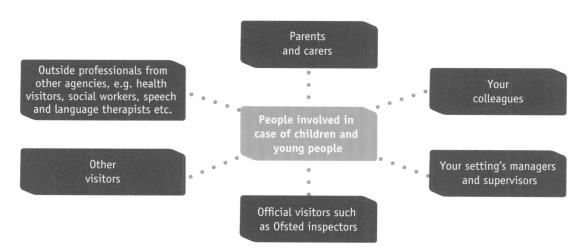

People involved in the care of children and young people.

practitioners are much more likely to share important information and concerns when a positive relationship exists.

Outside professionals, official visitors and other visitors

In your relationships with outside professionals and official visitors, remember that everyone has the same aim – to nurture children's development and well-being, and to protect and promote their rights. Positive relationships are necessary in order to coordinate the range of services working together for the benefit of a child. Coordinated services enable us to ensure a joined up, cohesive approach to meeting a family's needs. You'll learn about this in Unit CYP 3.6.

Other visitors will also come to the setting on occasion. These are likely to include families who are considering using the setting, those working with students on placement – tutors and assessors for instance – as well prospective employees and colleagues from other settings who are there for professional development reasons (as described in Unit SHC 32).

Unit CYP 3.6 Working together for the benefit of children and young people
Unit SHC 32 Engage in personal development in health, social care or children's and young people's settings

Relationships with colleagues

Most communication between colleagues (including managers and supervisors) takes place in conversation. But when practitioners are with the children, it is their duty to focus their attention on the children's care, learning and development. Remember this when you need to talk with other practitioners. Unless there is a reason for urgency, avoid interrupting colleagues when they are working closely with children, or when they need to concentrate fully on the task in hand. If you

Ask Miranda!

Q What should I do if a visitor enters when I'm working with the children?

A **Senior staff will generally let you know in advance if you are required to do anything during visits – such as talking to a parent about today's activities for instance. If nothing is specifically required, greet visitors politely and carry on as normal with your work. Most visitors will want to see things happening as they usually would – you are not required to put on a performance! If visitors should ask you questions, respond politely and give information as succinctly as possible.**

are unsure about this, you can always ask a colleague if it is a good time to talk. Detailed discussions are best scheduled for non-contact time, when practitioners are not responsible for children's care.

It is important to behave professionally within the setting – practitioners should only have appropriate discussions within earshot of children. Friendly chats about subjects unrelated to the setting should be kept for free time, spent away from the children. Children should not be aware of any conflict between practitioners.

There may be guidelines at your setting about how you should communicate formally, and you should familiarise yourself with these. For instance, there could be set procedures for passing information to practitioners working on a different shift. These procedures may include handing over written reports, or verbally running through a checklist. You may also find that there are systems for leaving messages for staff you will not see, and for making appointments to talk to senior staff. These systems are part of maintaining professional working relationships.

Did you know?

Lots of settings like to arrange out-of-hours 'socials' – time for the whole team to do something fun together outside of work. This can help a team to bond, and this in turn helps colleagues, supervisors and managers to communicate well with one another and to ask for support when it is needed.

Out-of-hours 'socials' can help a team to bond.

Conflicts and disagreements

In all settings, there are times when conflicts and disagreement arise between adults. These are typical situations that cause this:

- Practitioners feeling that others are not sharing responsibilities or tasks. They may express this by saying that a colleague is not pulling their weight.

- People have different ways of doing things, and adults may feel that their way is the right way, or the best way. Consequently, they may be unwilling to compromise.

- Change is challenging for many people. Adults may find changes of plan and staff changes unsettling, and they may be reluctant to accept new circumstances.

- People making comments that are insensitive, or inappropriate, to or about another person. This can lead to hurt feelings and resentment.

Resolving conflicts and disagreements

There are various techniques for resolving conflict. Some settings have set guidelines and procedures to help staff. It can be helpful to review such procedures at times of conflict. Resolution techniques centre on discussion, and will vary according to the situation. They include the following steps, which can be helpful in most circumstances:

- Approaching the resolution process positively – there may be an issue, but you are going to sort it out calmly. Think positively.

- Understanding an issue fully – identifying what exactly an issue is. If you have an issue, you should think it through carefully before you raise it with someone else. If someone raises an issue with you, make sure that you fully understand their source of conflict – repeat it back to them. Check you have understood correctly.

- Noticing and identifying feelings – take time to notice how you, and other people, are feeling about an issue. Does everyone feel the same? Sometimes simply understanding each other's feelings is enough to resolve conflict.

- Looking for solutions – there may be an outright solution that will work for everyone, or a good compromise. However, compromises may not be possible, not only because they can be difficult to reach, but also because it may breach regulations to compromise on certain issues, for instance, safety or confidentiality.

- Referring to superiors if you need support – you may want the advice of superiors before dealing with conflict. You may also want to refer to a superior if a solution cannot be agreed upon. Sometimes a superior may act as a mediator between adults.

- Reviewing – set a time to review the situation. Has the solution worked, or do you need to think again?

Good practice

It is important to act professionally and deal with conflict effectively. Conflict should normally be worked through in a discussion between the people involved. This should be done at an appropriate time, away from the children. Children should not be aware of conflict between practitioners. However, there may be exceptional circumstances when you have to speak up right away on a matter of conflict because not to do so might harm a child's safety or welfare, for instance if a colleague was about to do something you considered unsafe.

Practitioners should know that if disagreements arise when they are with the children, they can be raised and resolved later on. Generally, they then feel prepared to overcome any negative feelings, and to get on with working professionally. However, you should make sure that you do not leave matters longer than necessary. It is often better to catch conflict early and deal with it before resentment builds up.

Discussions should ideally occur away from the children.

How are things going?

▶ Progress Check

1. Why are positive relationships with children important? (1.1)

2. What are the 'building blocks' to building good relationships? (1.2)

3. How might you evaluate your own effectiveness in building relationships with children and young people? (1.3)

4. What are the advantages of good relationships with:

   ■ parents and carers?

   ■ colleagues?

   ■ outside professionals? (2.1)

5. What aims do you share with the outside professionals with whom you may work? (2.1, 2.2)

6. Explain two ways of working that will help you to build positive relationships with people involved in the care of children and young people. (2.1)

Are you ready for assessment?

CACHE

In preparation for assessment of this Unit, you may like to make notes in your reflective journal relating to your own effectiveness in building relationships with children or young people.

Edexel

In preparation for assessment of this Unit, you may like to make notes in your reflective journal relating to your own effectiveness in building relationships with children or young people.

City & Guilds

In preparation for assessment of this Unit, you may like to make notes in your reflective journal relating to your own effectiveness in building relationships with children or young people.

UNIT 3.6

Working together for the benefit of children and young people

The learning outcomes you will meet in this unit are:

1 Understand integrated and multi-agency working

2 Be able to communicate with others for professional purposes

3 Be able to support organisational processes and procedures for recording, storing and sharing information

INTRODUCTION

There are a range of statutory, voluntary and private agencies and services both locally and nationally, which provide support for children, young people and their families. These agencies and services work together to ensure that the needs of children, young people and their families are met in a holistic, coordinated way. Practitioners need to understand how these partnerships work, and how to communicate effectively with others for professional purposes.

LEARNING OUTCOME 1

FOCUS ON

...understanding integrated and multi-agency working

In this section you'll learn about the importance of multi-agency and integrated working, and how this can deliver better outcomes for children and young people. You'll learn about the barriers to working in this way and how they can be overcome. You'll also learn about assessment frameworks, and how and why referrals are made between agencies. This links with Assessment Criteria **1.1, 1.2, 1.3, 1.4, 1.5, 1.6.**

The following diagram shows the range of professionals who may work together to meet the needs of children, young people and their families:

Multi-agency and integrated working

'Multi-agency working' is the term we use to describe what happens when a range of practitioners and professionals from different agencies, services and teams work together to meet the needs of children, young people and/or their families. Workers from health, education, childcareand social care services will liaise with one another to enable them to meet a family's needs in a coordinated way.

'Integrated working' is the term we use when different services are offered in the same building. Sure Start centres are a good example of this, as under one roof there might be a health visitor running in-house baby clinics and an outreach service, a nursery providing early years education, an out-of-school club providing childcare and a speech and language therapist working with children and

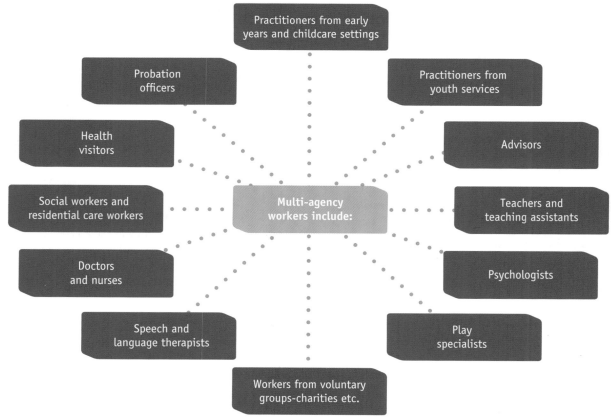

Professionals who may work together to meet the needs of families.

young people. There may even be career support and adult education classes with crèche facilities running alongside. For more information on Sure Starts, see page 397.

Did you know?

Traditionally services were organised separately, through strictly separate health, education and social care services. But multi-agency and integrated working meets families' needs far more effectively.

The importance of multi-agency and integrated working

Every Child Matters (ECM) is a government framework that aims to improve the following five major outcomes for all children and young people:

- be healthy

- stay safe

- enjoy and achieve

- make a positive contribution

- achieve economic well-being.

ECM is supported by a number of government policies and strategies that should work together to improve outcomes for children, young people and their families, and practitioners must work in accordance with these. This includes the Early Years Foundation Stage (EYFS), the overarching aim of which is to help young children achieve the five ECM outcomes. (See page 321 for further details.)

Learning Outcome 1, Unit EYMP 2 Promote learning and development in the early years

You can find out more about Every Child Matters at **www.education.gov.uk/childrenandyoungpeople/sen/earlysupport/esinpractice/a0067409/every-child-matters**

Three of the ways in which the EYFS aims to meet the ECM outcomes are as follows:

- **By creating a framework for partnership working between parents and professionals, and between all the settings that the child attends.**
  Multi-agency and integrated working result in established partnerships between professionals and settings.

- **By laying a secure foundation for future learning through learning and development that is planned around the individual needs and interests of the child.**
  Working together to meet the needs and interests of individual children is at the heart of multi-agency and integrated working.

- **By providing equality of opportunity and anti-discriminatory practice. Ensuring that every child is included and not disadvantaged because of ethnicity, culture, religion, home language, family background, learning difficulties or disabilities, gender or ability.**
  Multi-agency and integrated learning also provides strong benefits in terms of inclusion and equal opportunities. This is because families who, for instance, experience disability (including learning difficulties), English as an additional language, or a difficult family background (including poverty), are likely to need support from several different practitioners/professionals. In the past, these people each took a separate approach to meeting a family's needs, but with multi-agency and integrated working, these needs can be met in a coordinated, holistic way, which is much more effective in terms of providing equality of opportunity.

Also see the Practical examples below.

The impact on outcomes for children and young people

The following Practical examples demonstrate how multi-agency and integrated working enable the ECM outcomes to be promoted for children, young people and their families.

Professionals at a formal meeting.

Practical example

Meeting Erin's needs

There have been some concerns about the physical development of 2-year-old Erin. Her nursery key worker has been observing her regularly and completing developmental assessments. Erin's health visitor is also now due to see her. The health visitor arranges to come to the nursery to do this, so that she and the key worker can discuss and compare their findings, and agree a future coordinated approach to monitoring Erin's on-going development between them. They will also meet jointly with Erin's father.

Question
How does this benefit Erin and her father? Which ECM outcomes are promoted by this?

Practical example

Meeting Edward's needs

Four-year-old Edward has learning difficulties. He attends pre-school on a Monday and Tuesday, and goes to a childminder on Wednesday and Friday. The childminder contacts the pre-school, and arranges to meet with his key worker and the pre-school SENCO. They discuss learning targets for Edward, and how to plan to meet them. They decide to call a local advisory teacher for support, who makes an appointment to come to the pre-school to meet them all, to discuss effective teaching and learning methods that the practitioners can employ.

Question
How does this benefit Edward and the practitioners? Which ECM outcomes are promoted by this?

Practical example

Meeting Raya's needs

Raya is a refugee. Her family has not been in the UK for long and are just beginning to learn English. Raya's due to start at the local school. Her social worker Simon gets in touch to let the school know that he's available to provide information about the family's situation, background and culture, and to coordinate services to support Raya and her family. (This will include input from voluntary organisations as well as housing, employment and health services.) Simon arranges to accompany the family when they make their first visit to the school. He books an interpreter to ensure that all important information is understood and to assist the family and school in a) getting to know one another, and b) establishing how communication needs will be met on an on-going basis.

Question

How does this benefit Raya and her family, and the school? Which ECM outcomes are promoted by this?

Practical example

Meeting Jayden's needs

Three-year-old Jayden was taken to his GP by his parents, who were concerned that there may be something wrong with his mouth. The GP picks up a difficulty with speech/language, and refers Jayden to a speech and language therapist, who is based in the local Sure Start centre. Jayden's parents say they haven't been to the centre before; Jayden does not currently access any early years care or education, as his parents prefer to have him at home with them.

When they meet the therapist, she recommends a number of strategies to help Jayden with his speech and language, including weaning him off his dummy, talking to him more and providing opportunities for him to socialise. She suggests that Jayden and his family could benefit from the support and social opportunities available within the building, including drop-in family play sessions and a pre-school. She says if they decide to use the other services, she will be happy to speak to the practitioners there about the strategies they are using to promote Jayden's speech and language development, so that everyone works with Jayden in a consistent way.

Question

How does this benefit Jayden and his family, as well as the speech and language therapist and the Sure Start centre practitioners? Which ECM outcomes are promoted by this?

Functions of external agencies

As included in the diagram on page 252, a number of external agencies may work with your own setting or service. They may provide an integrated service, meaning that they are all based under one roof, or they may use the multi-agency approach, meaning that they are based in separated places but work together to meet the needs of children, young people and their families.

Agencies may be statutory and therefore part of the Local Authority (LA), employed by a local Primary Health Trust (PHT) or Social Services, or they may be voluntary. Some agencies may be private (if a family pays for private health care for example). The functions of key professionals are outlined below:

■ **Health care professionals such as health visitors and speech and language therapists**

These professionals are usually employed by the PHT. They work closely with families to support children and young people. In the early years of a child's life, health visitors will be instrumental in supporting and educating parents on preventative services such as immunisation, the nutritional needs of infants, children and themselves, coping with minor illnesses, behavioural issues (e.g. establishing good sleep patterns) and a child's developmental milestones. They also ensure that children receive standard physical examinations, and retain an overview of the health and well-being of children and families in their area. Speech and language therapists usually work with children and young people following a referral, which

A health visitor at work.

may have originated from concerns raised by a GP or a setting. Their role is to assess and treat speech, language and communication problems in people of all ages to enable them to communicate to the best of their ability. They assist children and young people who have difficulty producing and using speech, understanding language, using language, difficulty with feeding, chewing or swallowing, and those who have a stammer or a voice problem.

■ **Behaviour Support Service (BEST)**

BEST is part of the LA. Its workers or partnership practitioners may include specialist teachers and teaching assistants, educational welfare officers, children and young people's counsellors and educational psychologists (see page 257). The Department for Children, Schools and Families (DCSF) told us that the role of BEST is to 'work in partnership with schools, within a framework of inclusion, to help them promote positive behaviour, and to provide effective support to children, parents and schools where behaviour is a concern and may have an effect on achievement. Parents and schools have the main responsibility for promoting good behaviour. But LAs play an important supporting role, providing schools with some form of behaviour support service. Most behaviour support services will at least provide advice to schools on developing and reviewing school behaviour policies, advice and training on strategies for preventing and dealing with problem behaviour, individual support work with children, group work with children for example Circle Time, peer mediation schemes, anger management, problem solving, conflict resolution, support for special educational needs coordinators (for example, through networks).' (The DCSF is now the Department for Education.)

■ **Social workers**

Social Services employ social workers to assess the needs of service users and plan the individual packages of care and support to best help them. There is currently a recruitment campaign for social workers, in which the role of the social worker in children and young people's services is described as including these functions: providing assistance and advice to keep families together; working in children's homes; managing adoption and foster care processes; providing support to younger people leaving care or who are at risk or in trouble with the law; or helping children who have problems at school or are facing difficulties brought on by illness in the family.

A social worker at work.

Educational psychologists
Educational psychologists are employed by LA. The British Psychological Association describes the role of educational psychologists as tackling 'the problems encountered by young people in education, which may involve learning difficulties and social or emotional problems. They carry out a wide range of tasks with the aim of enhancing children's learning and enabling teachers to become more aware of the social factors affecting teaching and learning. Reports may be written about children for allocation of special educational places, or as part of court proceedings or children's panels. The work of an educational psychologist can either be directly with a child (assessing progress, giving counselling) or indirectly (through their work with parents, teachers and other professionals).'

Play specialists
These may be employed by PHT or social services,

working in hospitals or supporting families receiving support from social services. The NHS describe the role of the hospital play specialist (HPS) as 'playing a significant part within the child's stay in hospital. An HPS is trained to identify the needs and fears of children and young people in hospital through play-based observations and assessments. They work alongside doctors, nurses and other healthcare professionals. The HPS uses play to help children and young people in hospital to adjust to a strange environment, involve themselves in activities they enjoy and which are important for continued learning and development, express their concerns about being in hospital, familiarise them with hospital staff and roles, cope with hospital tests and treatments, learn about illness, meet and get to know other children and young people. Play specialists can be found in both outpatients' departments and on the wards of child and adolescent hospitals.'

A play specialist at work.

Voluntary agencies and services
These include both national and local services, such as the NSPCC, which supports children, young people and families who experience threatening situations such as abuse, and runs a 24-hour referral and counselling phone line; the National Deaf Children's Society (NDCS), which gives advice and support directly to families with deaf children; Women's Refuges, which provide 'halfway houses' for women and children who are victims of violent

partners until they can be re-accommodated; and the National Association of Toy and Leisure Libraries, which aims to make toys accessible to every child. There are many more. (See also the 'Have a go!' section below.)

- **Advisors**

  In addition, a range of advisors are also available to provide advice and support for children, young people and families on aspects of family life including matters such as housing, careers, employment, childcare options and benefits.

Your Local Authority will have a directory of voluntary services for children, young people and families in your area. There will be a copy at your local library, which is likely also to be available online. Make a point of looking through the local directory, and then continue to do so periodically to ensure that you stay up to date. This is part of your continued professional development (CPD).

Barriers to integrated and multi-agency working

There are some common barriers that exist in terms of integrated and multi-agency working. These include:

- professionals from different backgrounds using specific terms or jargon that are not familiar to or understood by other professionals or practitioners

- professionals trained to work in very different ways finding it difficult to agree the best way to work together

- professionals from different backgrounds having differing priorities

- professionals not accustomed to sharing their expertise, views or findings and having them questioned by other professionals

- professionals not accustomed to taking the expertise, views or findings of others into consideration

- professionals having different ways of interacting with colleagues and other adults (such as parents)

- professionals having different ways of interacting with children and young people

- professionals having different responsibilities in terms of documentation (e.g. the format of reports).

On-going, open communication is the best way to overcome these barriers, along with a willingness to embrace new ways of working. If difficulties are expressed, the parties can work together to address them. For instance, an educational psychologist will not know to explain his or her use of terms unless other practitioners express the fact that they do not follow what he or she is saying.

Good organisation also helps immensely, and there should always be a lead professional who takes responsibility for the coordination of services for a family. This person should also act as the point of contact for families when joint communication needs to take place. In the case of integrated working, it helps to ensure that professionals working under one roof have their own desk space, storage space, computer and telephone line.

Although there should be a lead professional, everyone involved has a part to play in making the organisational aspects of the partnership work in practice. It should not be underestimated how much attending to practicalities such as booking a room for a meeting at your setting when you have promised to do so, ensuring that you forward required documents and making requests for information in plenty of time can help professionals to work together effectively.

Did you know?

As multi-agency and integrated working continues, the processes and procedures will become more familiar to everyone involved. This way of working should eventually be so embedded in the sector that it becomes second nature.

Referrals between agencies

Generally speaking, each local borough will have set up their own multi-agency referral panel. Referrals will be made to the panel when a practitioner or professional feels that additional support is needed by a child, young person or family. The panel will then consider the information that has been made available to them, which will include common assessment (see below), and decide what support will be offered and how this will be coordinated.

The Common Assessment Framework

The purpose of the Common Assessment Framework (CAF) is to:

■ identify additional needs of children and young people

■ ensure that additional needs of children and young people are met through multi-agency working.

Practitioners working for children's services use CAF as a holistic assessment and planning tool. Having a common tool like this helps a range of practitioners to work together in the same way. Here's what the Department for Children and Families (now the Department of Education) told us:

The diagram below shows the range of professionals likely to access CAF:

About CAF

The CAF is a key part of delivering frontline services that are integrated, and are focused around the needs of children and young people. The CAF is a standardised approach to conducting assessments of children's additional needs and deciding how these should be met. It can be used by practitioners across children's services in England.

The CAF aims to help early identification of need, promote coordinated service provision and reduce the number of assessments that some children and young people go through.

Why the CAF has been introduced

We all want better lives for children and young people. We have high aspirations for this to be the best place in the world for children and young people to grow up. Most children and young people do well. Most move in and out of difficulties through their lives, and some have important disadvantages that currently are only addressed when they become serious. Sometimes their parents know there is a problem but struggle to know how to get help. We want to identify these children and young people earlier and help them before things reach crisis point. The most important way of doing this is for everyone in the children and young people's workforce to pay attention to their progress and well-being, and be prepared to help if something is going wrong.

CAF.

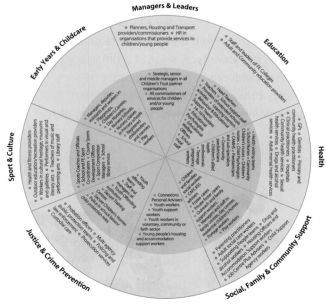

The range of professionals likely to access CAF.

The CAF consists of:

- a pre-assessment checklist to help decide who would benefit from a common assessment (There is no need to do a common assessment for every child or young person. Children and young people who are progressing well, or have needs that have already been identified do not need one.)

- a process to enable practitioners in the children and young people's workforce

- to undertake a common assessment and then act on the result

- a standard form to record the assessment

- a delivery plan and review form

- a standalone consent statement.

Although only trained practitioners can carry out common assessment, it's important that all practitioners recognise when it may be needed, so that they can arrange for a trained person to do the assessment. To enable this, any practitioner can use the short CAF pre-assessment checklist to help decide whether a common assessment should be undertaken. This guides practitioners in looking at the five ECM outcome areas and considering whether the child or young person is healthy, safe from harm, learning and developing, having a positive impact on others and is free from the negative impact of poverty. If the answer to any of these is no, and additional services might be required, this suggests that a common assessment would be an appropriate next step. The practitioner would then refer this to the person in their setting trained to complete common assessments.

Did you know?

The assessment covers three domains: development of the child or young person; parents and carers; and family and environment.

Undertaking common assessment

Practitioners must undertake a locally approved CAF training course before they are able to undertake common assessments. A range of training materials has been produced as part of a broader training strategy to support integrated working. You'll find further information at **www.cwdcouncil.org.uk/caf**

Practitioners must undertake a CAF training course before they can undertake common assessments.

 **Have a go!**

It's a good idea to complete a mock pre-assessment as a trial run. To access the pre-assessment form and for further information on completing it, visit **www.cwdcouncil.org.uk/caf**

Did you know?

The CAF is often the first assessment made of children and young people with special educational needs (SEN). They will then go on to further assessment in accordance with the SEN Code of Practice.

 **Link Up!**

For further details of the SEN Code of Practice see Unit CYPOP 6 Support disabled children and young people and those with specific requirements

LEARNING OUTCOME 2

FOCUS ON

...being able to communicate with others for professional purposes

In this section you'll learn about selecting and using appropriate communication methods for different services. You'll also learn about preparing reports. This links with Assessment Criteria **2.1, 2.2, 2.3.**

Selecting an appropriate communication method for the circumstances

In Unit SHC 31 Learning Outcome 2, you learned about the range of verbal and non-verbal communication methods, and you were introduced to the importance of selecting the appropriate communication method for the circumstance. The advantages and disadvantages of key communication methods are shown below:

Face-to-face conversation

Advantages: For many people this proves the quickest, easiest and most effective way to communicate on a day-to-day basis with children, young people, colleagues, parents and carers. It is effective for social interaction, discussion, giving and receiving information and feedback, asking questions and meetings of all sizes.

Disadvantages: Can be difficult to arrange a) a time to talk, and/or b) a place to talk in private when necessary. Detailed information may not be remembered. Barriers are common for people with communication difficulties, and for people who do not have English as their first language.

Good practice

Face-to-face: Make arrangements to overcome barriers that occur. Take notes when appropriate to ensure that you remember the details given to you – it's easy to make mistakes with times, dates and so on. If you have specific information to give verbally, make notes and refer to them to make sure that you cover everything, and consider providing a summary on paper for listeners too. Speak clearly and concisely, and listen actively (see page 19). Check that you have understood correctly, or if appropriate, that others have understood you.

Sign language/Makaton

Advantages: Sign language is the primary and most effective way for many deaf people to communicate on a day-to-day basis – providing that those they wish to communicate with also know sign language. Makaton may be used by children and/or those with learning difficulties.

Disadvantages: The majority of people do not know sign language or Makaton. Different sign languages are used in different countries, so there can still be barriers for those who do not have British Sign

Good practice

Sign language/makaton: Make arrangements to overcome barriers that occur (see page 26 for information on interpreters). If sign language or Makaton is used in your setting, make a point of learning some key signs – this is good practice in any case. An introduction course to sign language or Makaton is recommended. Speech and language therapists can sometimes arrange training for settings.

Language (BSL) as their first language. You also need to be able to see one another.

Telephone

Advantages:

Telephone is ideal for contacting people in an emergency (e.g. a parent when a child is taken ill, or the emergency services). It's also an effective way of arranging/confirming

If sign language or Makaton is used in your setting, make a point of learning some key signs.

appointments and meetings, and of giving, receiving and requesting information from parents, outside professionals and so on. It can be a popular way to order supplies and resources and a good way to overcome barriers that make a face-to-face meeting difficult. Conference calls can be arranged if a group of people need to contribute to a discussion. Messages can be left on answerphones when people are unavailable, and they can then call back at a convenient time. Mobile phones have made people more contactable than ever before.

Disadvantages: Not everyone has access to either a landline and/or a mobile phone. People with communication difficulties may find that phones present a barrier to clear communication. People with English as an additional language may also experience difficulty. In some settings, it's difficult to find somewhere quiet and/or private to call from. People may also call back at an inconvenient time – it is easy for busy people to keep missing each other and so the message is delayed.

Letter

Advantages: Letters are an excellent way of communicating both formally and confidentially, and of putting important details in writing, for example a letter may be sent to confirm that a place has been

Telephone: Think about what you want to say before you call. Speak clearly, give your message concisely and ensure that it has been understood. Make sure you call from an appropriately quiet room, and in private if your message is confidential. If you leave a message on an answerphone, check that it has been received. Avoid leaving confidential information in messages as they may be overheard when recorded or played. Make arrangements to overcome barriers that occur, for example an interpreter could be booked for a conference call to someone for whom English is an additional language. People with communication difficulties may use amplifying phones, text phones or the newer captioned phones (which use voice recognition to produce text).

booked at the setting for a new child, or a supervisor may write a letter of reference for a student who has worked with them on placement and is now applying for jobs.

Disadvantages: The written text may not be accessible to people who have difficulties with literacy, those with visual impairments and those with English as an additional language.

Letters are a good way of communicating formally and confidentially.

Letter: Provide information in different formats as necessary to meet the needs of those you are communicating with, for example, you may have a letter translated into another language or into Braille, or you may also give the information verbally. Write your message clearly and concisely, and check for spelling and grammatical errors. Always be sure to address people appropriately (e.g. 'Dear Mrs Foreman'). Mark envelopes 'Private and confidential' if this applies. Use the setting's letterhead if appropriate.

Text message

Advantages: Texts can be a useful way to send round-robin reminders a) to colleagues (e.g. 'Reminder: Staff meeting starts at 6pm this evening'), b) to young people to let them know what's happening at a setting (e.g. 'Youth club karaoke this Fri and disco on Sat!'), c) to parents/carers (e.g. 'Reminder: Pre-school fete from 3-5pm this Saturday!').

Disadvantages: They are not suitable for anything but very informal, short messages, and best used for reminders rather than messages that must be received by a certain time. Not everyone has a mobile phone, and those who do may not check messages regularly. The issues with written text (as described in 'Disadvantages' in the 'Letter' section above) also apply.

Internet

Advantages: This is a popular way to order supplies and resources. A website is also a useful way for a setting to communicate about its services and provision, particularly to new families interested in using the setting. Blogs can be used to give information about the setting's events and activities.

Text message: Do not use text abbreviations (e.g. '2' instead of 'to' or 'u' instead of 'you') unless they are accepted by your setting – this is not the norm, but may be permitted when texting colleagues or young people. Be wary of how you address people – 'Hi Sarah' would not be considered appropriate for a parent by many settings. You must have permission from the setting and parents before texting children or young people. Only ever text from a work mobile phone, not your personal number. Provide information in different formats as necessary to meet communication needs (as described in the 'Letter' section above).

Disadvantages: Information on the internet is in the public domain and can be accessed by anyone, including those with negative intentions for its use. Not everyone has access to the internet, and not everyone is familiar with the technology. The issues with written text (as described in 'Disadvantages' in the 'Letter' section above) also apply.

Internet: Be very careful about the information that you place on the internet, including the use of photographs of children and young people. Most settings will have very strict guidelines about this, which must be followed very carefully. Provide information in different formats as necessary to meet communication needs (as described in the 'Letter' section above). If ordering online, make sure that websites have secure payment systems.

Blogs can be used to give information about the setting's events and activities.

Email

Advantages: Using email, you can create groups of people to whom you send out the same message – for example, a group of parents, a group of committee members or a group of colleagues, which makes it a great way to distribute a range of information such as newsletters or minutes from the staff meeting. You can attach additional documents easily and provide web links. Your messages will be received by someone's inbox instantly, unlike the post. You have an electronic copy of all the messages you send and receive and you can also forward messages on easily when appropriate. You can have one-to-one correspondence with someone at a time that suits you both as people can read and respond to messages when convenient.

Disadvantages: Not everyone has access to the internet or an email account, and not everyone is familiar with the technology. Those who do email may not check messages regularly. As emails can be very quick to dash off, there's a danger of a) sending messages that have not been thought through (particularly if you are feeling annoyed), b) failing to send writing of a professional standard and c) sending too many emails.

Memos

Advantages: These are a useful way to leave brief messages and updates for colleagues. Can be typed

Email: Provide information in different formats as necessary to meet communication needs (as described in the 'Letter' section above). Make sure that the email account is set up so that when you send an email, your name or the setting's name is displayed as the 'sender' in the other person's inbox – this will help prevent your messages from being mistaken for spam and deleted. Don't send too many emails, and make sure that the ones you send are clear and concise. Be wary of how you address people as, for example, 'Hi Sarah' would not be considered appropriate for a parent by many settings. You must have permission from the setting and parents before emailing children or young people. Only ever email from a work email address, not your personal account. Think about confidentiality, especially when copying other people in. Take the same care as you would with a letter and check for spelling and grammatical mistakes. Avoid replying to emails when you are annoyed or you may send a message that you later regret. The issues with written text (as described in the 'Letter' section above) also apply.

or handwritten, making them easy to write when you don't have access to a computer.

Disadvantages: Memos are only used within an organisation – they would not generally be sent to anyone outside of the setting. Memos are not normally put in an envelope, so they are not appropriate for conveying confidential information. Only suitable for straightforward, brief messages.

See also Unit SHC 31 Promote communication in health, social care or children's and young people's settings

Good practice

Memos: Follow your setting procedures and leave memos in the designated place – such as in someone's pigeon hole, or on a supervisor's desk. Avoid writing too many memos. If you need a reply, be sure to make this clear.

Have a go!

Think of the last time you needed to communicate with your supervisor about your study towards this qualification. What communication method did you use? In hindsight, was the method you chose the most appropriate? Why is this?

Responding to requests for written information

At times, all practitioners are asked to supply other adults with information, so it's important that you learn how to respond professionally. For instance, practitioners often share information about children with teachers at **times of transition**, or they may share a child's assessment information with an outside professional such as a speech and language therapist.

Whatever the request, check that you are clear about:

- what is being asked for
- what format the information should be in (e.g. a report)
- when the information is needed by.

You must then be careful to give accurate information within the agreed timescales, as long as doing so will not compromise confidentiality.

key term

Times of transition times when children are moving onto a new stage in their lives or development (e.g. when children leave the baby room or start school).

Preparing reports

A report is a document that presents information, usually for a defined purpose and a defined readership. The information will generally be facts or findings – sometimes both. The information contained in reports is often collected as a record, and can often lead to recommendations or instructions. Reports can be paper-based or electronic.

Different types of reports are prepared within settings.

A number of different types of reports are prepared within any setting, such as the following:

- **Accident reports**

  Accident reports are completed as a factual record of how an accident occurred, any injuries, how injuries were dealt with and by whom. They are signed by a parent/carer as proof that they were informed. Over time, the record of accidents may be the catalyst for safety recommendations – if injuries are common when children or young people play with a certain piece of equipment, for instance.

■ **Assessment reports**

These will be completed at regular intervals, usually by key workers. They are kept as a record of children and young people's development and achievement and used to inform future plans, for example, what children should learn next and the opportunities, activities and experiences that should be made available to them. The readership is professional practitioners and the parents/carers of the child or young person concerned.

■ **Project reports**

These report on the findings of a particular project, giving opinions and recommendations. For instance, a practitioner may be asked to look into how well children's creativity is fostered within the setting, as outlined in the Practical example below. The readership is generally other practitioners and committee members, although families may also be consulted. Project reports are sometimes called 'leading reports'.

■ **Official reports**

Official reports are documents required by outside organisations, such as facts and figures about how many children and young people attend the setting, or evaluation forms about the service provided by the setting. There is often a tightly prescribed way of completing this type of report, and the information may be required by the outside organisation by law.

Practical example

Lexy's report

Lexy has been asked by her manager to look into how well their setting fosters and promotes children's creativity through planned activities, and to report her findings. After a period of planning, Lexy compiles some facts and figures as she examines existing documents within the setting. She looks at activity plans to consider the range and frequency of creative activities available, and she looks at a selection of children's assessment reports to see how their creativity is developing. She also looks at the training records for staff. Next, Lexy observes some planned creative activities taking place, and considers their quality.

Now she's ready to write her report. Lexy makes a title page, which includes the project title (she calls it 'The effectiveness of planned creative activities'), her own name and job title, and the date. She then writes an introduction explaining what she has been asked to do and why.

Lexy writes up her findings under the heading 'Evidence of current planned creative activities'. Next, she moves on to a section to which she gives the heading 'Conclusion.' Here, she states that she feels that the same activities are offered too frequently, and that, in particular, music is overlooked. Finally, she writes a section headed 'Recommendations,' in which she suggests a) some staff attend creative development workshops and feedback new ideas to their colleagues, b) the staff get together to plan some new creative activities in a staff meeting, c) some new resources to support musical activities are purchased.

Question

Lexy is taking an organised approach to her report. What methods might she have used to plan her work?

Key features of reports

Formal reports must always:

- be accurate

- be legible (clear to read)

- be concise

- meet legal requirements where applicable (e.g. learning in each area of the curriculum is reported on in an assessment record)

- meet the setting's organisational requirements, which may exceed legal requirements.

Whether or not you are required to personally complete formal reports will depend largely on the setting in which you work. For instance, in many schools the teachers and management team will be required to complete reports, but this will not be expected from other practitioners. Or, in a day nursery, it may be the team leaders, supervisors/managers who take the lead responsibility for compiling reports. However, all practitioners may be consulted as part of the reporting process and be asked to contribute thoughts and opinions.

Ask senior staff to check your reports until you have enough experience to write completely independently.

As you've learned, different reports are required in formats. In our Practical example on page 266, Lexy's report has five sections. There's a title page and an introduction, which are followed by the body of the report, which she divides into sections headed 'Evidence', 'Conclusion' and 'Recommendations'. This is all Lexy needs to include to meet the needs of her setting in this instance. However, the reports you are required to read and write may also include these:

- **A contents list**
  Often only included in longer reports, this is a list of sections of the report with the corresponding page numbers.

- **Appendix**
  Extra or supporting information is contained in the appendix (e.g. if a team leader was compiling a report on the skills of the current team of staff, he or she may include their CVs in the appendix).

- **References**
  There are two types of references a) a list of articles, books and web links that were consulted and/or referred to in the report, and b) a list of articles, books and web links that are recommended as further reading or background reading to the report. One or both types of reference may be included.

Ask Miranda!

Q Help! I've been asked to write my first report and I'm worried.

A It's not unusual for new practitioners to feel a bit apprehensive about the prospect of compiling reports for the first time. The best way to learn what is required of you is to read some reports that have already been compiled by experienced practitioners at your setting. Once you see what is expected and you are familiar with the style and language used, you will be able to produce your report with increased confidence. It's a good idea to ask senior staff to check your first reports until you are sure you have mastered everything.

■ **Glossary of terms**

This explains terms used and any abbreviations. This is helpful if a report introduces new information, or if it will be read by non-practitioners. For instance, parents may not be familiar with the term 'multi-agency working' and this might be a barrier for them in understanding a report about how children should be supported by adults within the setting.

The ladder diagram shows the order in which the key features of reports are presented.

With due respect to confidentiality, ask your supervisor if you can look at a range of reports compiled within your setting. Do you understand both their content and their purpose? If not, ask for clarification.

Presentations

Sometimes practitioners are asked to give the findings of their reports in a presentation. If you are asked to give a presentation by your setting, the first thing to do is to make sure that you understand what sort of presentation is required. What is the purpose of the presentation? Will it be informal, in which case you may talk through the key aspects of the report in a casual way, or will it be formal, in which case you may need to use visual/electronic aids, such as Microsoft PowerPoint? Who is the presentation for?

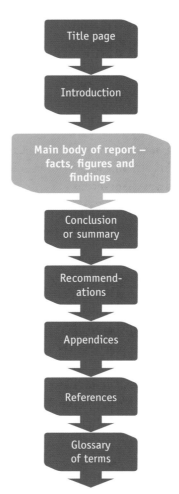

The key features of reports.

Is it for other practitioners, in which case you can use professional language, or for non-experts such as parents, in which case you will need to define terms or use alternative words? Also clarify how long your presentation should be, as this will guide you in terms of the required depth of information.

LEARNING OUTCOME 3

...being able to support organisational processes and procedures for recording, storing and sharing information

In this section you'll learn about the processes and procedures for recording, storing and sharing information. You'll learn how to maintain secure recording and storage systems for paper-based and electronic information. You'll also learn about potential tension between confidentiality and need to disclose information. This links with Assessment Criteria **3.1, 3.2, 3.3.**

Processes and procedures for recording, storing and sharing information

In Unit SHC 31 Learning Outcome 4, you learned about the principles and practices relating to confidentiality. These apply to information that is both paper-based and electronic. You may want to read that section again to refresh your memory as part of your study towards this unit.

Maintaining secure recording, sharing and storage systems for information

The following checklist will help you to ensure that you are acting professionally when recording and storing information:

- Have you read and understood your setting's organisational procedures for recording, sharing and storing information?

- Have you followed those organisational procedures to the letter?

- Have you met the requirements of the Data Protection Act 1998 (see page 30)?

- Have you made sure that confidentiality is maintained while you are using information (e.g. checking that no one else can see your computer screen or paper document, and closing and securing files as soon as the information has been used)?

- Have you made back-ups of electronic files and also stored them safely?

- Are computer security systems working properly, and are regular virus checks carried out to protect information?

- Have you made sure that you won't be overheard if confidential information needs to be discussed?

Unit SHC 31 Promote communication in health, social care or children's and young people's settings

Unit SHC 31 Promote communication in health, social care or children's and young people's settings

Practical example

Nigel reports a problem

Nigel works for a childcare company that owns a day nursery and an out-of-school club. He works at the out-of-school club, which meets within the premises of a primary school.

The main office is at the nursery, and so Nigel has a laptop, which he keeps locked away in a filing cabinet at the club.

Today, Nigel has received an onscreen message to say there is an error and that the scheduled virus check cannot be completed. He tries to run the check again, but it still won't work. He calls the manager at the nursery to let her know. She asks him not to use the laptop today, and arranges to come up to have a look. She says that if she can't resolve the problem herself, she'll get the 'tech support' person the setting uses to visit and sort things out.

Question
Why shouldn't Nigel use the laptop until the problem is resolved?

Did you know?

Some settings may ask you not to use children and young people's real names in some circumstances – when writing a report, for instance, or when writing up the minutes (notes) of a staff meeting.

 **Link Up!**

Unit SHC 31 Promote communication in health, social care or children's and young people's settings

Potential tension between confidentiality and need to disclose information

You learned about confidentiality in Unit SHC 31, Learning Outcome 4. As we discussed there, practitioners must disclose information if it is suspected that abuse is taking place or that a crime has been committed. This can be uncomfortable, but support is available to you. (You may like to turn to page 31 and refresh your memory.)

 **Have a go!**

Ask your supervisor what support would be available to you within the setting if you were duty bound to pass on information about a crime that may have been committed by a member of a family with which you work.

How are things going?

▶ Progress Check

1. Describe what is meant by a) multi-agency working and b) integrated working. (1.1)

2. How does multi-agency and integrated working deliver better outcomes for children and young people? (1.2)

3. Explain a) three common barriers to multi-agency and integrated working, and b) strategies for overcoming them. (1.4)

4. What is 'common assessment'? (1.6)

5. Give two advantages of communicating professionally via letter. (2.1, 2.2)

6. Give two disadvantages of communicating professionally via email. (2.1, 2.2)

7. What eight key features may be included in a professional report? (2.3)

8. Give examples of actions you would take to maintain secure recording and storage symptoms for a) paper based documents and b) electronic documents. (3.2)

Are you ready for assessment?

CACHE

Set task:

■ You've been asked to handle a new staff member's induction into multi-agency and integrated learning, and you must prepare handouts for them.

You can prepare by re-reading Learning Outcome 1, and making notes on the key points.

Edexel

In preparation for assessment of this Unit, you may like to collect together documents that demonstrate your use of a range of communication methods, to use as evidence, e.g. a written report, a letter, a printout of an email, etc.

City & Guilds

In preparation for assessment of this Unit, you may like to collect together documents that demonstrate your use of a range of communication methods, to use as evidence, e.g. a written report, a letter, a printout of an email, etc.

Learning Outcomes 2 and 3 must be assessed in real work environments.

UNIT 3.7

Understand how to support positive outcomes for children and young people

LEARNING OUTCOMES

The learning outcomes you will meet in this unit are:

1 Understand how the social, economic and cultural environment can impact on the outcomes and life chances of children and young people

2 Understand how practitioners can make a positive difference in outcomes for children and young people

3 Understand the possible impact of disability, special requirements (additional needs) and attitudes on positive outcomes for children and young people

4 Understand the importance of equality, diversity and inclusion in promoting positive outcomes for children and young people

INTRODUCTION

Social, economic and cultural factors can impact greatly on the outcomes and life chances of children and young people. So it's essential for you to learn about these factors and their affects. Once you understand them, you will be able to work in ways aimed at limiting the negative affects of factors such as poverty and disability.

LEARNING OUTCOME 1

FOCUS ON

...understanding how the social, economic and cultural environment can impact on the outcomes and life chances of children and young people

In this section you'll learn about how the social, economic and cultural environment can impact on the outcomes and life chances of children and young people. You'll also learn about the impact of poverty on children and young people, and the role of their personal choices and experiences on their outcomes and life chances. This links with Assessment Criteria **1.1, 1.2, 1.3**.

Social, economic and cultural factors that impact on children and young people

A range of social, economic and cultural factors impact on the lives of children and young people. During your career, you're likely to work with a number of families living with the negative effects of these factors. For instance, you may work with a child struggling to cope with the death of a parent (a social factor). Or you may have regular contact with a family living in poverty due to unemployment, who don't earn enough money to cover the bills, let alone money for toys, treats or days out (an economic factor). Or you may work with a young person of ethnic minority origin who's coping with discrimination on a regular basis (a cultural factor).

It's the job of practitioners to be aware of the factors which can impact negatively on the outcomes of children's lives, and to do everything possible to counteract them. Positive ways of working can help set children and young people on the way to achieving positive outcomes. You'll learn more about this in Learning Outcome 2.

The table on page 274 explains common social, economic and cultural factors that can negatively impact on young lives.

The importance and impact of poverty on outcomes and life chances

One of the five *Every Child Matters* outcomes is for families to **achieve economic well-being**.

This outcome is included because the Government recognises that living in poverty can have a significant impact on the outcomes and life chances of children and young people. This means that those living in poverty are disadvantaged in comparison to their peers who do not live in poverty (see page 321). Under the Children's Plan, each local authority has responsibilities to provide services to support these families.

The Child Poverty Act
The Child Poverty Act became law in March 2010. It makes tackling child poverty a priority for the current and all future governments. It makes them accountable for taking action to eradicate child poverty by 2020. A Child Poverty Commission provides expert advice to the Government, who are responsible for producing child poverty strategies.

The Campaign to End Child Poverty
The Campaign to End Child Poverty is made up of more than 150 organisations from civic society including children's charities, child welfare organisations, social justice groups, faith groups, trade unions and others, who are united in their vision of a UK free of child poverty. They campaign to ensure the voices of families facing economic disadvantage are heard, to increase understanding of the causes and impacts of child poverty and to hold politicians and the

Table CYP 3.7.1: Possible impact of social, economic and cultural factors on children and young people's lives

Social, economic and cultural factors	Possible impact on children and young people's lives
Personal choice	Some choices made by families have an impact, e.g. if young people live in a rural location, they may have limited opportunities to socialise. If the family lives a nomadic (or travelling) lifestyle, children's education may consist of time divided between several schools. Some children and young people go to boarding school and do not see their families for several weeks.
Being in the care system	Children and young people may not live in a stable family home. They may frequently move from one foster home or residential home to another, and have several different key workers during their life. They may have no contact at all with family members, or may see them infrequently. Lack of loving, lifelong relationships may lead to low self-esteem, and lack of consistency at home may lead to unsettled and challenging behaviour. This may lead to difficulties at school and being in trouble with the police. Education may also be disrupted by the necessity to change schools when moving on to a new home.
Poverty	Living in poverty is extremely stressful for families. There may be constant worries about having enough food to eat, clothes to wear, heat in the winter, etc. This can have an effect on everyone's mental health, as well as an impact on physical health. Children and young people may also experience the stigma of poverty, impacting on their self-esteem and self-respect. You'll learn more about this on pages 275–276.
Housing and community	Development and physical health can be adversely affected by living in overcrowded or poor-quality housing – damp can trigger asthma attacks for instance. There can also be physical danger in buildings that are not in a fit state of repair. Communities with high incidences of anti-social behaviour can be frightening and intimidating to live in, and it may not be safe for children to play outside.
Educational environment	Some children and young people do not have a good overall experience at school. Being bullied, not coping with the work or with the pressure of exams can affect them significantly, over a short or on-going period. Whenever children and young people are stressed, worried or anxious, they will not be learning to their optimum level.
Offending or anti-social behaviour	If parents or siblings are behaving in these ways, the family may be moved out of the area, disrupting schooling and stability, or a child or young person may be taken into care. It could be the case that the child or young person is behaving anti-socially, in which case negative outcomes related to crime are a very real concern.
Health status of self or family member	Education, home life and well-being can be significantly affected if a child or young person has a chronic medical condition. If a family member has the condition, a child or young person may be acting as a carer, which can significantly impact on opportunities for play, leisure activities and homework. They may have many responsibilities on their shoulders, and may worry about the family member when they are at school, affecting concentration and learning.
Disability	Being disabled can impact on outcomes for children and young people's lives in several ways. For example, there may be limited access to play and learning opportunities, and they may experience the negative effects of stereotyping. You'll learn more about this in Learning Outcome 3.
Health support	Receiving health support may mean time away from school. It may also mean time away from home for children and parent/s, if hospital stays are needed. This can impact on learning and development, and cause emotional upheaval and worry. There are also financial considerations that may have a negative impact on the family.
Addictions in family or self	Children and young people living with a parent addicted to alcohol or drugs may experience abuse in the form of neglect. Addicts may not be able to control mood swings, making life unpredictable and filled with anxiety. Those experiencing addiction themselves will be putting their health in danger, and will also be vulnerable when under the influence of alcohol or drugs. Other things in their lives (e.g. school, friends), may cease to seem important if the addiction becomes the central motivation in their lives.

Bereavement and loss	Losing a close loved one (such as a parent or sibling) can leave a gaping hole in a child or young person's world. Grief can impact on emotional and physical health, and well-being can be affected for a significant period. Children may also be afraid that others who are close to them will die too. Children will also be affected by how other family members are coping with their own grief.
Family expectations and encouragement	Different families have different parenting styles. Some children and young people may only get feedback on their behaviour when it is inappropriate – they may not receive much praise or encouragement. This will affect their self-esteem, self-confidence and behaviour – e.g. they may think misbehaving is the only way to get attention. Some parents may have inconsistent rules, which lead to a lack of security. At the other end of the scale, some parents have such high expectations that young people feel extreme pressure to perform well in exams, etc. This can affect emotional and physical health as well as their ability to perform in stressful situations.
Religious beliefs and customs	Children and young people may undertake religious activity during school or setting hours. They may also need to avoid particular settings, activities or events. They may experience discrimination because of this and a lack of equality could affect their opportunities in life.
Ethnic/cultural beliefs and customs	This can affect many aspects of children and young people's lives, including how they dress, socialise and their dietary requirements. They may experience discrimination and a lack of equality could affect their opportunities in life.
Marginalisation and exclusion	This can happen for a wide range of reasons, including those listed above. Being marginalised has a detrimental effect on self-esteem and self-confidence, and exclusion can mean being deprived of a number of opportunities, including those to play, learn and to socialise.

Government to account on the requirements of the Child Poverty Act, in an effort to ensure that child poverty is eradicated by 2020.

The Campaign to End Child Poverty reports the following effects of poverty on life chances:

- Poverty shortens lives. A boy in Manchester (which has a high incidence of poverty) can expect to live seven years less than a boy in Barnet. A girl in Manchester can expect to live six years less than a girl in Kensington, Chelsea and Westminster.

- Poor children are born too small; birth weight is on average 130 grams lower in children from social classes IV and V. Low birth weight is closely associated with infant death and chronic diseases in later life.

- Poverty shapes children's development. Before reaching his or her second birthday, a child from a poorer family is already more likely to show a lower level of attainment than a child from a better-off family. By the age of 6, a less-able child from a rich family is likely to have overtaken an able child born into a poor family.

- Children aged up to 14 from unskilled families are five times more likely to die in an accident than children from professional families, and 15 times more likely to die in a fire at home.

- Children growing up in poverty are more likely to leave school at 16 with fewer qualifications.

- Two per cent of couples and 8 per cent of lone parents cannot afford two pairs of shoes for each child.

- Twelve per cent of lone parents cannot afford celebrations with presents at special occasions. (Figures from the Mark Family and Children Study, 2004)

The Campaign to End Child Poverty is the source for the following statistics:

- Nearly 4 million children – 1 in 3 – are currently living in poverty in the UK (after housing costs), one of the highest rates in the industrialised world.

■ The proportion of children living in poverty grew from 1 in 10 in 1979 to 1 in 3 in 1998. Today, 30 per cent of children in Britain are living in poverty.

■ The UK has one of the worst rates of child poverty in the industrialised world.

■ The majority (59 per cent) of poor children live in a household where at least one adult works.

■ Forty per cent of poor children live in a household headed by a lone parent. The majority of poor children (57 per cent) live in a household headed by a couple.

■ Thiry-eight per cent of children in poverty are from families with three or more children.

■ Since 1999, when the previous Government pledged to end child poverty, 550,000 children have been lifted out of poverty.

You can research the child poverty statistics in your own region at **www.endchildpoverty.org.uk**

Reasons for poverty

There are a number of reasons why families live in poverty. However, the biggest common thread is unemployment. Statistics show that children and young people are most likely to live in poverty if one or more of the following reasons applies:

■ **Their parent/parents are unemployed**
At most, one wage is coming in.

■ **Their parent is a lone parent**
At most, one wage is coming in.

■ **Their parent/parents are in their teens**
They are unlikely to have had any financial security

Children from some inner city areas are expected to have a shorter life span.

before starting a family, and may still be in education and therefore not working.

■ **They are disabled**
A parent may care for them full- or part-time, reducing availability to work.

■ **Their parent/parents are disabled or have mental health problems**
This may mean they are unable to seek work.

■ **They are from an ethnic minority group.**

Comparison with those not living in poverty

Children and young people from more affluent families have better chances and prospects in life because they avoid many of these negative outcomes. They would generally be expected to:

■ live in better quality, safe homes

■ live in areas outside of the inner cities

■ eat healthier, better-quality food

■ experience better health care

■ have a range of toys, games and so on to play with

■ have access to somewhere safe to play outside

■ access a range of regular leisure experiences (e.g. outings, swimming)

■ have somewhere quiet to do homework

■ have holidays.

The role of children and young people's personal choices and experiences

Children and young people need to be empowered to make personal choices about the things that they experience in their lives. This enables them to influence their own outcomes and life chances. So it's important for us to give children and young people a voice, and to listen to what they tell us. This is a key part of providing services that are child-/young person-centred.

Did you know?

Children and young people need to understand how poor choices can affect their outcomes, for example the effect of choosing to break the law, take drugs, play on a building site, or have unprotected sex. This starts at a young age when explaining to children **why** they mustn't behave in certain ways, and what the **consequences** are if they do. This discussion must be age appropriate.

Children and young people have had rights to have their voice heard since the UN Convention on the Rights of the Child was ratified in 1989. Article 13 states that children must be consulted about matters and decisions that are important to them. You learned about how this can be achieved through advocacy, in Unit SHC 31, Learning Outcome 3. For information on advocacy in regards to disabled children and young people, see Unit CYPOP 6, Learning Outcome 1. Children and young people's voices also need to be sought and listened to on a day-to-day basis. This can be done effectively in settings through consultation.

Unit SHC 31 Promote communication in health, social care or children's and young people's settings

Unit CYPOP 6 Support disabled children and young people and those with specific requirements

Interacting and consulting with children and young people

Practitioners should consult with children and young people about their ideas, opinions and preferences, and involve them in decision-making. This becomes increasingly important as children grow up. Through consultation practices, you can interact with children and young people, finding out what they want and need. This enables practitioners to provide play activities and experiences that children and young people will enjoy participating in. But consultation has other advantages too. It can help children and young people to feel the following:

- **Listened to**
  Children and young people spend a lot of time listening to adults at school and perhaps in the home. Some children naturally initiate conversations with practitioners more frequently than others. When practitioners are consulting and actively looking to seek out everyone's opinion, they have the opportunity to encourage everyone to have their say, including those children/young people less likely to put forward their opinion without it being asked for, and those children who do not routinely approach adults and/or gain their attention easily.

- **Valued and worthwhile**
  We know as adults how good we feel if our employers ask for our opinions and ideas. It is good to feel that your thoughts are worthwhile

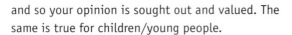

and so your opinion is sought out and valued. The same is true for children/young people.

■ **Included**
This is especially important for children belonging to groups that may be at risk of discrimination. It also gives children and young people the opportunity to make a positive contribution, which is one of the five Every Child Matters outcomes.

Asking for a young person's opinion makes them feel valued.

Consultation enhances participation. If children/young people are involved in devising play opportunities or play spaces, they will be keener to participate.

All of the above can lead to increased self-esteem and confidence and help to encourage the development of feelings of empowerment and ownership. Children and young people can also learn and practise skills during consultation. They will have opportunities to:

■ form and explain ideas and opinions

■ listen to and respect each other

■ discuss and debate

■ adapt and negotiate

■ plan

■ take responsibility

■ evaluate

■ give feedback

■ record information.

Did you know?

Listening to children and young people and encouraging them to express themselves contributes to keeping them safe from harm and abuse.

Consultation can take place during casual conversation as practitioners interact with children and young people. But planned consultation activities can also take place during:

■ meetings

■ Circle Time

■ planning sessions

■ evaluations and reviews.

Older children and young people may also take part in committees or 'children's parliaments' in settings and schools. It's important to tailor the methods of consultation utilised to the ages and abilities of the children in the group. Many methods can be used to consult, including the following:

■ **Discussion**
Practitioners can talk with children and young people individually or in groups about their ideas, opinions and preferences about experiences and play spaces.

■ **Questionnaires**
These can be written or pictorial, depending on the ages and abilities of the children.

■ **Interviews**
An alternative to questionnaires – an 'interviewer' can verbally ask children/young people questions and record their answers.

■ **Suggestion boxes**

Children/young people can write and draw their ideas, thoughts and feelings and put them into a box anonymously. Suggestion video tapes/audio tapes can also work well, although the element of anonymity is lost.

■ **Voting**

This is a good, quick way of consulting with children/young people – children can vote on the layout of the play space at the start of the session, for example. This can be as simple as a show of hands or can involve a ballot (anonymous paper vote).

■ **Evaluation**

Involving children/young people in the evaluation of play sessions reveals what they have enjoyed – this can inform future planning. There are several visual ways of recording evaluations. It is common to ask children to rank, in order of preference, the activities they have participated in. See 'Have a go!' on this page for examples.

A suggestion box allows ideas, thoughts and feelings to be contributed anonymously.

Have a go!

Why not try one of the following evaluation examples with a group of older children?

Evaluation techniques

■ Drawing out a large bull's-eye target and asking each child to place a cross on it to indicate how they felt about a particular experience. The nearer to the bull's-eye the cross is, the better they enjoyed the experience. See the diagram below.

■ Drawing up a list of play experiences. Children are given a gold, silver and bronze sticker. They are asked to place the stickers next to the experiences on the list awarding them first, second or third in terms of their favourites.

■ Drawing a list of numbers, perhaps one to five. Next to the relevant numbers, the children write or draw on their top five play experiences of the session.

■ Four corners of the play space are identified as 'really liked it', 'liked it', 'didn't like it', and 'really didn't like it'. Practitioners call out play experiences, and children run to the relevant corner depending how they felt about the experience.

■ Thought-storming (see the Practical example on page 280).

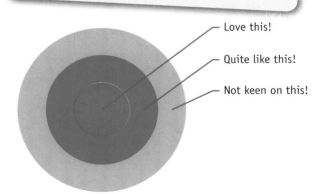

Love this!

Quite like this!

Not keen on this!

Evaluation target.

Practical example

Ravi gets the ideas flowing

Ravi is a playworker at an out-of-school club. He has been asked to plan activities for the coming non-pupil day. The children have voted for a beach theme. Ravi gathers the group in a circle. He sticks a big sheet of paper to the wall. He asks the children for their beach activity ideas, making a couple of suggestions himself to get the ball rolling. He lets the children know that they need lots of ideas to choose from later. Soon the children are calling out suggestions, and Ravi writes them all down, thanking each contributor. At this stage, the group is not worrying about how they would carry out the activities, or if the ideas have merit – they are simply getting them all out in the open. Consequently, the suggestions come thick and fast. At the end of the activity, the group have plenty of ideas to choose from.

Question

How does Ravi's activity support children effectively?

To encourage children/young people to participate in consultation, practitioners can:

■ be motivational in their approach by making the process fun

■ communicate the purpose of the consultation to the children – let them know that what they have to say influences future play experiences

■ ensure that everyone gets their say

■ choose methods to suit the children

■ ring the changes with regard to the consultation methods used

■ acknowledge and accept everyone's contribution

■ ensure all contributions are respected.

Ask Miranda!

Q My setting follows the Early Years Foundation Stage. Should I be doing anything to give children a say?

A **Your overall practice should be child-centred. In addition, you're required to provide a balance of adult-led and child-initiated activities and experiences. Young children can also be involved in thinking about their own learning and development, through participation in observations and assessment, and particularly through setting goals for learning and behaviour. This will help them to take ownership of their experiences, rather than being passive recipients of what's going on.**

Good practice

Hear by Right from the National Youth Agency consists of a voluntary framework and award scheme, which helps practitioners to follow best practice on the safe, sound and sustainable participation of children and young people in the services and activities they take part in. It helps settings to provide evidence of the participation that is already happening, and to plan for improvement where there are gaps. It involves children, young people and adults working together to plan for change.

Did you know?

As young people mature, having their voice heard helps them to understand that they can choose to take responsibility for the outcomes in their life, and that they can take positive action to look for and to seize chances and opportunities in life.

Have a go!

You can learn more about Hear by Right online at **www.nya.org.uk/quality/hear-by-right**

LEARNING OUTCOME 2

FOCUS ON

...understanding how practitioners can make a positive difference in outcomes for children and young people

In this section you'll learn about the positive outcomes for children and young people that practitioners should strive to achieve, and the importance of designing services around the needs of children and young people. You'll also learn about the importance of active participation, and how to support children and young people to make personal choices and experiences that have a positive impact on their lives. This links with Assessment Criteria 2.1, 2.2, 2.3, 2.4.

The positive outcomes that practitioners should strive to achieve

As you've already learned, Every Child Matters (ECM) sets out the following five positive outcomes for children and young people:

- be healthy

- stay safe

- enjoy and achieve

- make a positive contribution

- achieve economic well-being.

All practitioners have a duty to promote the ECM outcomes and to support children, young people

The impact of ECM on outcomes for children and young people is explored in Learning Outcome 1 Unit CYP 3.6 Working together for the benefit of children and young people, where several practical examples are given. It's a good idea to reread this as part of your study towards this unit

and families to achieve them. Much of your learning towards your qualification links to promoting the ECM outcomes. The primary links are given below. You can to refer to the linked units in this book for further relevant information:

'Being healthy' and 'staying safe' links with Unit SHC 34, Unit CYP 3.3 and Unit CYP 3.4.

Unit SHC 34 Principles for implementing duty of care in health, social care or children's and young people's settings
Unit CYP 3.3 Understand how to safeguard the well-being of children and young people
Unit CYP 3.4 Support children and young people's health and safety

Positive outcomes relating to 'enjoying and achieving' are specified in the goals or targets expressed in the learning and development frameworks that apply in each home country. In England, for example, this is the Early Years Foundation Stage (EYFS) and the National Curriculum. In the EYFS, each Principle into Practice resource card highlights a link to one of the five Every Child Matters outcomes. Using the EYFS effectively will enable settings to support children in meeting the outcomes. This links with Unit EYMP 1, Unit EYMP 2 and Unit CYPOP 1.

Unit EYMP 1 Context and principles for early years provision
Unit EYMP 2 Promote learning and development in the early years
Unit CYPOP 1 Work with babies and young children to promote their development and learning

'Making a positive contribution' links with Learning Outcome 2 in this unit, and Unit SHC 33, Unit CYP 3.5 and Unit CYPOP 6.

Unit SHC 33 Promote equality and inclusion in health, social care or children's and young people's settings
Unit CYP 3.5 Develop positive relationships with children and young people and others involved in their care
Unit CYPOP 6 Support disabled children and young people and those with specific requirements

'Achieving economic well-being' links with Learning Outcome 1 in this Unit.

Can you identify legislation that supports each of the ECM outcomes? For instance, the Children Act 2004 supports the 'stay safe' outcome.

Designing services around the needs of children and young people

To meet the outcomes of ECM, it's important that services for children and young people are child-/young people-

centred – this requires the services to be designed around the needs of children, young people and their families. This applies to individual settings and services (such as a childminding service) as well as statutory services.

In Unit CYP 3.6, you learned about relatively new requirements for agencies, professionals and organisations to work together to meet the needs of their users in an effective, coordinated and integrated way. This represented a significant nationwide shift in the design of services.

In the not too distant past, the Disability Discrimination Act marked a similar change to the design of services as it became law for services to be fully accessible to disabled children, young people and adults.

It's important that the delivery of services meets the needs of all families. This can be achieved in a number of ways. Some services are offered on an outreach basis. For example, rural, isolated communities may be visited by a mobile play bus and toy library. Workers from other services home visit, including health visitors, community nurses and Portage workers (see page 531). Many services are provided all under one roof in 'one-stop-shop' children's centres.

Encouraging children and young people to make positive choices

In Learning Outcome 1, you learned that children and young people need to understand how poor choices

Some services are offered on an outreach basis.

can affect their outcomes, for example, the effect of choosing to break the law, take drugs, play on a building site, have unprotected sex. They also need to know how making positive choices can empower them to have positive outcomes throughout their lives. For instance, choosing to apply themselves to school work, choosing to do positive activities in their leisure time, choosing to stay physically fit and healthy.

Active participation of children and young people in decisions affecting their lives

It's extremely important for practitioners to promote the active participation of children, young people and families in decisions affecting their lives, because:

■ When local authorities understand what families feel, want and need, they can adapt their services accordingly. This is in contrast to the traditional model in which authorities assumed they knew what was required by or what was best for families.

■ When practitioners understand what children, young people and families feel, want and need, we can adapt our practice and services accordingly. This includes the provision of play and learning activities and experiences, which impact on children's enjoyment and achievement.

■ Partnership working between practitioners and families has many benefits for children and young people, including a positive impact on learning and development. The EYFS states that 'Parents and practitioners have a lot to learn from each other.'

■ Consulting children and young people has many benefits, including increased confidence and increased self-esteem, as you learned in Learning Outcome 2.

■ Children and young people have a right to have

their say and have their opinions listened to when decisions on matters which are important to them are being made. (UN Conventions on the Rights of the Child, Article 13.)

See the information on advocacy in Learning Outcome 3 Unit SHC 31 Promote communication in health, social care or children's and young people's settings
For information on advocacy in regards to disabled children and young people, see Learning Outcome 1 Unit CYPOP 6 Support disabled children and young people and those with specific requirements

Parents and practitioners have a lot to learn from each other.

Ways of encouraging active participation in decisions

For information on working in partnership with parents and carers to engage them in active participation, see Unit EYMP 1, Learning Outcome 3. For information on consultation with children and young people, see Learning Outcome 2 in this unit.

Unit EYMP 1 Context and principles for early years provision

Supporting children and young people according to their age, needs and abilities

It's the role of practitioners to support children and young people to make personal choices and experiences that have a positive impact on their lives. This support needs to be appropriate to each individual's age, needs and abilities. To do this effectively, you must:

- provide a child/young person centred environment

- provide play-based environments for young children

- plan for and implement a balance of adult-led and child-initiated experiences appropriate to the ages and abilities of individuals

- know individual children well, enabling you to understand their needs, abilities and preferences (this entails interaction, observation, assessment and the planning of learning and development goals)

- plan for and implement adaptations and/or support to meet children's individual needs, fully enabling participation

- listen to children and young people, and actively consult them

- ensure effective key working, so children feel they have someone close to express themselves to

- plan for and implement activities that promote self-confidence and self-esteem.

Below there is an example of how you might support children and young people to achieve each of the five ECM Learning Outcomes:

- **Be healthy**
  Provide opportunities for exercise and physical activity.

- **Stay safe**
  Provide information about what to do if they are bullied.

- **Enjoy and achieve**
Provide enjoyable, open-ended activities that promote cross-curriculum learning.

- **Make a positive contribution**
Consult them on their ideas for future activities.

- **Achieve economic well-being**
Provid access to activities that build self-esteem and self-confidence, such as team games which give everyone the chance to be the leader.

Have a go!

Think of three more ways in which you can support children and young people to achieve each of the five ECM Learning Outcomes.

LEARNING OUTCOME 3

FOCUS ON

...understanding the possible impact of disability, special requirements (additional needs) and attitudes on positive outcomes for children and young people

In this section you'll learn about the impact of disability on outcomes and life chances, and about the importance of positive attitudes towards disability. You'll also learn about the social and medical models of disability and the different types of support available for disabled children and young people. This links with Assessment Criteria **3.1, 3.2, 3.3, 3.4**.

The impact of disability

Disabled children and young people may experience a wide range of **impairments**, such as:

- physical impairments
- visual impairments
- hearing impairments
- communication/speech difficulties

- emotional/behavioural difficulties
- general learning difficulties or developmental delay
- specific learning difficulties (such as dyslexia)
- chronic medical conditions.

key term

Impairment a condition that is not usually experienced by a child or young person at the current age or stage of development.

Practitioners should develop a good knowledge of particular impairments *as they affect the children and young people in their care*. It's important to know that the same impairment can be experienced by different individuals in very different ways – you need to understand how the children you are working with are affected so that you can meet their needs appropriately.

On page 286, you'll learn more about the 'social model of disability', which explains the modern view taken of disability in the UK today. The social model tells us that impairments give rise to disability, because society is not set up to meet the needs of people who experience them. The society 'dis-ables' them, rather than enabling them. This means that by ensuring the environment is adapted appropriately and taking any other necessary action (such as providing additional support or specialised equipment), we can limit the impact of the impairment on a child or young person's life outcomes.

These are the potential impacts of disability on the outcomes and life chances of children and young people:

■ Those with learning difficulties and those with impairments that affect their social and emotional development may find it difficult to relate to others and therefore lack friends and positive relationships. All round development and learning will also be affected.

■ Those with chronic medical conditions or physical disabilities may miss educational opportunities due to the effects on their health, medical appointments, hospital stays and so on.

■ Discrimination may limit the experiences and opportunities that are available to disabled children and young people (including the chance to learn, play and work).

■ The effects of stereotyping and discrimination can lead to low self-confidence and self-esteem.

■ If family members find it difficult to cope, disabled children and young people may feel they are a burden, again leading to low self-confidence and self-esteem.

■ Negative family attitudes can also have the same effect, for example, if a parent's focus is on what's 'wrong' with the child and what they can't do, rather than focusing on what they can do and achieve, or if they see them as a 'tragic victim' of disability. (The media often portray this unhelpful image.)

■ Meeting the needs of a disabled child can be expensive, and funded services vary from one local area to the next. In some families, a lack of money and resources may significantly limit the experiences of disabled children and young people.

Practitioners should also be aware of the expected pattern of development of the children and young people they're responsible for. Children generally (but not always) master skills or achieve learning in a similar sequence, even though they may not do so at the same rate as peers of the same age. However, some children may not be expected to achieve certain milestones 'in order', or to achieve them at all. For instance, some children will not be expected to carry out motor skills such as walking, jumping or running. But it may be appropriate to work with such a child on other ways of travelling, such as rolling across the floor or floating in water.

Understanding the needs of the individual children in your care will enable you to feel confident within your roles and responsibilities, empowering you to deliver a high-quality service to children, young people and their families.

It may be appropriate to work on differentiated ways of moving.

The importance of positive attitudes towards disability and specific requirements

A positive attitude couldn't be more important. There are numerous benefits for disabled children who grow up within positive families, and who experience care, education and leisure settings where a 'can do' attitude is taken towards both meeting disabled people's needs, and what disabled people can achieve. Perhaps most importantly, it helps the child to develop a positive attitude themselves, and to have high expectations for their life. Compared to the negative attitude we explored previously, this is likely to drastically increase children and young people's sense of self-esteem, self-confidence, independence and life purpose.

Positivity can also help children and young people to develop resilience to counteract some of the negative attitudes that they will no doubt experience from others during their lives – stereotyping and discrimination are prime examples.

The impact of the social and medical models of disability

The social and medical models of disability are explained in full in Unit CYPOP 6, Learning Outcome 1. You should read pages 514–517 now.

How the medical model impacts on practice

In the medical model of disability, non-disabled people focus on a disabled person's impairment as a 'problem' to be solved or cured (despite the fact that many impairments have no cure). This can often be revealed in their use of language. You may, for example, hear people referring to a 'Down's boy', rather than 'a boy who has Down's syndrome', or preferably, Joseph (or whatever his name is!). This particular example is all too commonly heard.

He is a boy who has Down's syndrome, not 'a Down's boy'.

Good practice

The impairment should not be used to define the child or young person. So you would say 'Sophie has epilepsy' rather than 'Sophie is epileptic', or 'Ollie has chronic asthma' rather than 'Ollie is a chronic asthmatic'. Children and young people should not be made to feel that their impairments are a label. **An impairment is not who they are**.

A practitioner whose thinking reflects the social model of disability might want to help disabled children and young people to 'fit into' the non-disabled world. This traditional view is no longer appropriate to modern practice. It is up to settings and practitioners to make sure that the environment, the activities/experiences and their own practice are adapted to meet the needs of disabled children and young people – it is not up to them to fit in the best they can.

How the social model impacts on practice

The social model of disability impacts on practice by favouring a child-/young person-centred approach. The emphasis is on how society should change to meet the needs of the child or young person, to ensure that they are empowered to achieve positive outcomes in their lives. This means that their needs, interests, strengths and participation are the priority, rather than the organisation's own needs. Disabled children and young people are encouraged to express their views and to

Did you know?

Not only does the medical model limit children and young people's opportunities and therefore their learning and development, it undermines their self-esteem, self-confidence and self-reliance. This will seriously affect the likelihood of them achieving positive outcomes.

make decisions about the way in which they experience the service, and how their needs are met. This fosters self-esteem, self-confidence and self-reliance.

Unit CYPOP 6 Support disabled children and young people and those with specific requirements

Support for disabled children and young people and those with specific requirements

Disabled children and young people may receive additional support. But this will depend not only on the type of impairment, but on the extent to which it affects them. For instance, some young people with cerebral palsy may have a personal assistant (PA), while others may not. Here are examples of other additional support:

- A child with cerebral palsy who has difficulty using speech may access support from a speech and language therapist.

- A young person who has cystic fibrosis will access support from health professionals.

- A child with autism may receive additional learning support at school.

- A young child with learning difficulties may receive support from a Portage worker (this is a specialised service – see page 531 CYPOP 6 for details).

AT enables disabled people to perform functions that might otherwise be difficult or impossible, such as mobility.

- A young person who has difficulty with fine movements may use a voice recognition package on their computer. This is the use of assistive technology.

Assistive technology (AT) is technology used by disabled people to perform functions that might otherwise be difficult or impossible. AT can include computer hardware and software, mobility devices (such as wheelchairs) and communication technology.

key term

Assistive technology (AT) technology used by disabled people to perform functions that might otherwise be difficult or impossible.

LEARNING OUTCOME 4

Link Up!

Unit SHC 33 Promote equality and inclusion in health, social care or children's and young people's settings

FOCUS ON

...understanding the importance of equality, diversity and inclusion in promoting positive outcomes for children and young people

In this section you'll learn about equality, diversity and inclusion in the context of positive life outcomes. You'll also learn about ways in which services take account of equality, diversity and inclusion to promote positive outcomes. This links with Assessment Criteria 4.1, 4.2.

Equality, inclusion and diversity

You learned about the meaning of equality, inclusion and diversity in Unit SHC 33, Learning Outcome 1, so you know how important it is that children and young people's rights in these areas are promoted. This means that they should:

■ have equal opportunities in terms of learning, development, safeguarding and well-being (equality)

■ be given full access to settings, services and the opportunities they provide (inclusion)

■ have their individual identity valued and respected (diversity).

You also learned about the effects of discrimination, which would clearly have a negative impact on children's outcomes in life.

Did you know?

Inclusive practice promotes equality and supports diversity.

Inclusive practice promotes equality and supports diversity.

Taking account of and promoting equality, diversity and inclusion

Taking account of and promoting equality, diversity and inclusion is part of a practitioner's overall work towards promoting positive outcomes for children and young people. We'll look at equality and diversity first.

In Unit SHC 33, you learned how to promote positive images of people, and that when doing so, it's particularly important to present strong images of those people who may be discriminated against in society.

This helps to challenge and overcome stereotypes. It also gives children diversity in terms of role models, which influences their expectations for their own future. For instance, if young people see images of disabled people playing sports at a competitive level, it will help to combat the stereotype that disabled people are dependent and passive. It may also help to shape a young disabled child's expectations of what they will be able to do when they're older. Other examples include showing people from ethnic minorities working in high status positions (such as the police force), or males taking a caring role and females taking a leadership or adventurous role.

Unit SHC 33 Promote equality and inclusion in health, social care or children's and young people's settings

A good indicator of whether children and young people have picked up stereotypes is how they assign roles in their imaginary play. Monitor this in your setting. Can you spot gender stereotypes being played out in the home corner for instance? (See also the Reflective Practice section at the end of this unit.)

Diversity is also promoted when settings demonstrate that they accept, value and welcome all children,

young people and families. This means acknowledging and respecting cultures, beliefs and preferences. As you learned in Unit SHC 33, this can be partly achieved through cultural activities such as celebrating festivals, and through representing children's identity's in the resources and materials

Strong images can help to challenge and overcome stereotypes.

within the setting (e.g. multicultural items to dress up in, food from around the world in the shop or home corner). However, the most important thing is the attitude of practitioners, and whether they demonstrate respect for children, young people and families in their manner and behaviour. It is here that the biggest gains or losses could be made in terms of children and young people's self-esteem, which will in turn affect their potential outcomes in life.

Cultural identity is expressed in many ways, as shown on the diagram below:

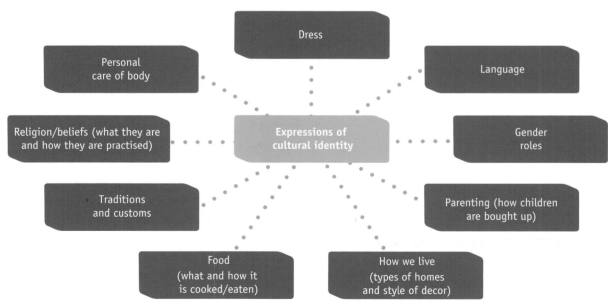

Expressions of cultural identity.

Good practice

We can all continually improve our practice, and part of this is to challenge any stereotypes you find yourself promoting, albeit accidently. Reflective practice is the key to this. Take time to think about the assumptions you make about individuals and groups of children and young people, and think carefully about what you are basing the assumption on.

Inclusive working promotes positive outcomes for children and young people.

For instance, are you more tolerant of boisterous behaviour from boys than you are from girls? (The saying, 'Boys will be boys', is based on the stereotype that boys should not be expected to behave as calmly as girls.) If you work with older children and you're looking for someone to buddy up with a new child to help them to settle in, would you be more inclined to choose a girl to take on the caring role?

Inclusion

You were introduced to inclusion in Unit SHC 33, and it is explored in detail in Unit CYPOP 6. You are advised to read Unit CYPOP 6, Learning Outcome 1 as part of your study towards this Unit. You'll learn about promoting the 'social model of disability', the principles of inclusive working and how to adopt a child-/young person-centred approach. All of these contribute towards the achievement of positive outcomes for disabled children and young people.

Unit SHC 33 Promote equality and inclusion in health, social care or children's and young people's settings
Unit CYPOP 6 Support disabled children and young people and those with specific requirements

Ask Miranda!

Q Do I need to promote positive images of people who don't come to our setting? For instance, we haven't got any disabled children, and at the moment, all of our families are white.

A **Yes, you absolutely do need to promote positive images of everyone. But remember that the purpose is to represent society's diversity overall. It would be unrealistic to attempt to cover every eventuality in each collection of resources. It might be a good idea to evaluate your setting's other practices too. Is equality, inclusion and diversity consistently promoted? Also think about the way your setting is perceived – does everyone in the community feel welcome? Does the setting need to advertise in a new way to ensure that all members of the community are reached?**

How are things going?

▶ Progress Check

1. Give six examples of social, economic and cultural factors that impact on the lives of children and young people. (1.1)

2. Describe the impact of poverty on outcomes and life chances. (1.2)

3. What are the positive outcomes for children and young people that practitioners should strive to achieve? (2.1)

4. Why is it important that children and young people know how making positive choices can impact on their life outcomes? (2.4)

5. Describe the potential impact of disability on the outcomes and chances of children and young people. (3.1)

6. Why are positive attitudes to disability important? (3.2)

7. Give examples of available support for disabled children and young people. (3.4)

8. Give an example of a way in which a service for children, young people and families might take account of and promote:

■ equality   ■ diversity and   ■ inclusion. (4.2)

Are you ready for assessment?

CACHE

Set task:

■ You've been asked to give a talk to parents and carers about the diverse factors which can affect children and young people in a multi-faceted society – you must prepare handouts for this.

In the task, you are given a series of bullet points to cover. Reread the Unit, making notes on the text that relates to each of the bullet points.

Edexel

In preparation for assessment of this Unit, you may like to make notes in your reflective journal about an instance when you have supported a child or young person to make a personal choice likely to have a positive impact on their life.

City & Guilds

In preparation for assessment of this Unit, you may like to make notes in your reflective journal about an instance when you have supported a child or young person to make a personal choice likely to have a positive impact on their life.

UNIT 1
Context and principles for early years provision

LEARNING OUTCOMES

The learning outcomes you will meet in this unit are:

1 Understand the purposes and principles of early years frameworks

2 Be able to provide environments within the work setting that support and extend children's development and learning in the early years

3 Understand how to work in partnership with carers

INTRODUCTION

When working with children in the early years, practitioners must meet the requirements of the curriculum framework that applies in their home country. Frameworks set out information about the learning and development opportunities that should be provided for children.

At first glance, there is a lot to take in. However, settings will have designed their programmes to meet the requirements of frameworks. So you may be surprised to find that you are already familiar with working in many ways that promote the framework that applies to you. While the theory may be new, you are likely to have many existing practical skills to draw upon.

This unit is closely linked to Unit EYMP 2. It will be helpful for you to read Unit EYMP 2 as part of your study towards this unit.

LEARNING OUTCOME 1

FOCUS ON ...understanding the purposes and principles of the early years framework

In this section you'll learn about the legal status and principles of early years frameworks, and about how national and local guidance materials are used in settings. You'll also learn how different approaches to work in the early years have influenced current provision, and why early years frameworks emphasise a personal and individual approach to learning and development. This links with Assessment Criteria **1.1, 1.2, 1.3.**

Early years frameworks

Most settings will plan how they will promote learning and development through the activities and care that they offer. Planning and the implementation of plans must be carried out in accordance with the statutory early years framework that applies to the setting. This is a legal requirement of the setting's registration. Frameworks vary across the four home countries, although there are many similarities, including a focus on learning through play. Each country has its own inspectorate:

- in England, this is Ofsted (**www.ofsted.gov.uk**)

- in Scotland, this is Her Majesty's Inspectorate of Education (**www.hmie.gov.uk**)

- in Wales, this is the Care and Social Services Inspectorate Wales (CSSIW) (**www.wales.gov.uk/ cssiwsubsite/newcssiw**)

- in Northern Ireland, this is the Education and Training Inspectorate (**www.deni.gov.uk**).

Inspectors working for the Government visit settings to inspect, judge and report on the quality of their provision.

Early years frameworks in the home countries

The early years framework in England is *The Early Years Foundation Stage (EYFS)*.

▶▶Link Up!◀◀

You'll find full information about the structure of the EYFS in Unit EYMP 2 Promote learning and development in the early years

Scotland

In Scotland the *Curriculum for Excellence* framework applies to children and young people aged 3–18 years, and is currently being developed and introduced. You can find full, up-to-date information at **www.ltscotland.org.uk**. Follow the links for Understanding the Curriculum and Curriculum for Excellence.

Did you know?

Another key Scottish document is *Birth to Three: Supporting Relationships, Responsive Care and Respect*. To read a guide to the document, visit **www.ltscotland.org.uk**, search for 'Birth to three'.

As an overview of the framework, Teaching and Learning Scotland tell us that:

Understanding the curriculum as a whole

The 3–18 curriculum aims to ensure that all children and young people in Scotland develop the attributes, knowledge and skills they will need to flourish in life, learning and work.

The knowledge, skills and attributes learners will develop will allow them to demonstrate four key capacities – to be successful learners, confident individuals, responsible citizens and effective contributors.

Developing skills and attributes

It aims to develop four capacities, helping children to become:

- successful learners
- confident individuals
- responsible citizens
- effective contributors.

The totality of experiences

The curriculum includes all of the experiences which are planned for children and young people through their education, wherever they are being educated. These experiences are grouped into four categories.

- **Curriculum areas and subjects**
  The curriculum areas are the organisers for setting out the experiences and outcomes. Each area contributes to the four capacities.
- **Interdisciplinary learning**
  How the curriculum should include space for learning beyond subject boundaries.
- **Ethos and life of the school**
  The starting point for learning is a positive ethos and climate of respect and trust based upon shared values across the school community.
- **Opportunities for personal achievement**
  Pupils need opportunities for achievements both in the classroom and beyond, giving them a sense of satisfaction and building motivation, resilience and confidence.

Added to this, because children learn through all of their experiences – in the family and community, pre-school centre, nursery and school – the curriculum aims to recognise and complement the contributions that these experiences can make. Find out more about the structure of the curriculum.

Planning learning experiences and positive outcomes

The experiences and outcomes are an essential component of Scotland's new curriculum and apply wherever learning is planned. They signpost progression in learning and set challenging standards that will equip young people to meet the challenges of the 21st century.

The title 'experiences and outcomes' recognises the importance of the quality and nature of the learning **experience** in developing attributes and capabilities and in achieving active engagement, motivation and depth of learning. An **outcome** represents what is to be achieved.

The experiences and outcomes are used both to assess progress in learning and to plan next steps.

Scotland's *Curriculum for Excellence*.

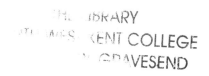

Wales

In Wales, children may be instructed in Welsh or English. There is a ten-year strategy in place, known as *Learning Country*. A new curriculum, *The Framework for Children's Learning*, is being introduced following a trial in some schools. There is a Foundation Phase for children aged 3–7 years, which is currently being phased. You can find full, up-to-date information about this at **www.wales.gov.uk** and search for 'Foundation Phase'.

The Welsh Assembly Government tell us that:

> The Foundation Phase is based on the principle that early years' provision should offer a sound foundation for future learning through a developmentally appropriate curriculum.
>
> The Foundation Phase places great emphasis on children learning by doing. Young children will be given more opportunities to gain first-hand experiences through play and active involvement rather than by completing exercises in books. They will be given time to develop their speaking and listening skills and to become confident in their reading and writing abilities.
>
> Mathematics will be more practical so that children can see how problems are solved and how important mathematics is in their everyday lives. There will be more emphasis on children understanding how things work and on finding different ways to solve problems.
>
> The curriculum will focus on experiential learning, active involvement and developing each child's:
>
> - skills and understanding
> - personal, social, emotional, physical and intellectual well-being so as to develop the whole child
> - positive attitudes to learning so that they enjoy it and want to continue
> - self-esteem and self-confidence to experiment, investigate, learn new things and form new relationships
> - creative, expressive and observational skills to encourage their development as individuals with different ways of responding to experiences
> - activities in the outdoors where they have first-hand experience of solving real-life problems and learn about conservation and sustainability.
>
> This framework sets out the curriculum and outcomes under seven Areas of Learning. For each Area of Learning, the educational programme sets out what children should be taught and the outcomes set out expected standards of children's performance.

Wales's *Framework for Children's Learning*.

Northern Ireland

In Northern Ireland, there isn't a statutory framework for children to follow before they are of statutory school age – at this point they will follow the *Foundation Stage*. There is, however, *Curricular Guidance for Pre-School Education*. You can view this at **www.deni.gov.uk/preschool_curricular-2.pdf.** The Department for Education says:

> **Curricular guidance**
>
> The purpose of this is to provide curricular guidance for those working with children in the year prior to compulsory education.
>
> The guidance is appropriate for use in a range of settings and should be used by staff to review, develop and promote good practice.
>
> The guidance outlines the range of learning opportunities, which children of this age should have through play and other relevant experiences.

Curricular Guidance for Pre-School Education.

Different approaches that have influenced current provision

As you learned in Unit CYP 3.1, psychologists and other theorists have developed different theories about how and why children play, learn and develop for hundreds of years. Some of the approaches to working with children that were developed as a result of these theories are still very much evident in provision in the UK today, as briefly outlined on page 297.

Have a go!

There are many books dedicated to the subject of play and education theories. You may find it interesting to learn about additional theories and the research and experiments that underpin them.

Unit CYP 3.1 Understand child and young person development

Friedrich Froebel (1782–1852)

The work of Froebel has been the most influential of the 20th century. He opened the very first kindergarten in 1837 (although he didn't use the term 'kindergarten' until 1840), and is often referred to as the 'father of kindergarten'. Thirty-one kindergartens had been opened in German cities by the time Froebel died 12 years later.

Froebel had studied in a training institute under Johann Pestalozzi. His teacher's basic ideals promoted a permissive school atmosphere and a focus on nature. Froebel accepted these, but felt a 'spiritual mechanism' was missing. He developed a philosophy of education centring on these four principles:

- **Free self-expression**
  Alongside maths and science, Froebel encouraged children to explore expressive arts (e.g. drawing, painting, model-making) and literature (listening to, reading and writing stories). He promoted exposing children to nature and beautiful objects. He taught his students to value children's ideas and feelings.

- **Creativity**
  Froebel encouraged imaginary play for children of all ages. He gave us the idea that children think at their highest level when they are at play, and particularly when they play imaginatively. Froebel said this was shown in children's symbolic play – this occurs when a child uses one object to stand in for another object. For instance, a child may pretend that a piece of string is a snake, or that a twig is a pen.

- **Social participation**
  Froebel emphasised the importance of children learning to have good relationships with adults, but he thought that children's relationships with each other were equally important. He recognised that parents were a child's primary educators and so he welcomed them into his centres, as he believed all schools should do.

- **Motor expression**
  Froebel believed that children learn as well outside in the garden as they do inside the classroom, and he promoted plenty of time to move around freely outside. He encouraged children to dance and do movements that he created. Children at his centres dressed in comfortable clothing that allowed them to move about freely. He did not like the idea of children being restricted.

Froebel developed two key principles as follows:

- **The principle of unity**
  This says that everything in the world is connected and linked in some way.

- **The principle of opposition**
  This says that while everything is linked to everything else, there are still comparisons and contrasts. Froebel believed that experiencing these first-hand helped children to think.

As you'll have recognised, many of Froebel's philosophies are still at the heart of integrated play and learning today. Unusually for that time, Froebel's institutes welcomed families from all religions (most commonly Jewish and Christian) and of all social classes. Froebel invented toys (which he called 'Gifts') and made up his own activities (which he called 'Occupations') to promote his principles. You'll be familiar with the use of these today. They include:

- beautiful sets of wooden blocks

- wooden rods in different colours

Children still play with blocks in early years settings today.

and shapes for mathematical discovery (e.g. each brown rod is the same length as two purples)

- songs and rhymes with actions and finger play
- activities with materials that could be manipulated, including paper, clay, sand and string
- movement and dance to music
- observing and caring for plants in the garden
- physical and intellectual games.

Froebel's children did not have to do formal activities given to them by adults, which was unusual in his day. Instead, children were encouraged to play and explore the Gifts and Occupations in their own way. This was the introduction of what we now know as 'free-play' (or free-form play).

Have a go!

Have a look at Froebel's Gifts online at **www.friedrichfroebel.com** – a website created by the Froebel family.

Did you know?

Froebel invented the word 'kindergarten' to describe the learning environments he created. He said, 'Children are like tiny flowers; they are varied and need care, but each is beautiful alone and glorious when seen in the community of peers.'

Rudolf Steiner (1861–1925)

Steiner developed his ideas when working as a private tutor. He went on to open schools in Germany, where he also trained teachers. Steiner believed that all children deserve to fulfil their full learning potential. But he did not believe that children should be forced into learning things before they are ready. In particular,

he thought it was wrong to push children towards goals that adults think are desirable, but a child may not. He encouraged his students to learn for the pleasure of learning, rather than for tests or exams. He believed that children passed through these three phases:

- **The Will (aged 0–7 years)**
  A deeply spiritual person himself, Steiner said children's spirits and their bodies became one in this phase.

- **The Heart (aged 7–14 years)**
  Steiner said feelings and relationships were paramount in this phase.

- **The Head (from age 14 years)**
  This was identified as the 'time for thinking'.

Steiner's promoted these ideals:

- In the first phase, children should play and spend plenty of time at home. Drawing and storytelling are important. Children should be exposed to nature and natural objects. One teacher should remain with a class throughout the first phase.

- Children shouldn't be taught to write until the second phase. They should learn writing before they learn reading.

- Children should be engaged, so they think enthusiastically about the information taught. Links between art and science are important.

- In the third phase, children should concentrate on one subject at a time. For example, Steiner might have taught literature every morning for a few weeks and then moved on to teach history in the same slot. This allowed children to become immersed in the subjects they studied.

There are private Steiner schools in the UK today, but Steiner's philosophies have not become embedded in the maintained sector.

Did you know?

The last original German Steiner school was closed when the Nazis came to power, not long after Steiner's death. Sadly, all of the original records were destroyed.

Did you know?

McMillan opened the very first open-air nursery with her sister Rachel. In 1917, she said that disadvantaged children could come and enjoy, 'Light, air and all that is good'.

Margaret McMillan (1860–1931)

An American-born educationalist, McMillan grew up in Scotland and first worked in Bradford. She was a member of the Froebel Society, and promoted many of his ideals. She agreed that children learned through doing and experiencing things first hand. She felt that their play was crucial to their learning, and thought children could not be 'whole' without opportunities for play. She believed free-play gave the best opportunities of all for learning and achievement.

McMillan agreed with Froebel's philosophy of welcoming parents into places of education. She liked the idea of both parents and children learning, and promoted sessions for adults where they could learn things such as foreign languages and crafts.

McMillan worked in the inner-city areas of northern Britain at a time when there was widespread poverty. She campaigned tirelessly for children, both for improved health care and nursery education. She made it known that children who were undernourished and those who were in poor health (suffering rickets, or problems with their ears and eyes for instance), could not possibly be expected to learn well. She also campaigned for school dinners.

The traditional British nursery school was modelled by McMillan. Many believe that we have her to thank for many aspects of the nursery provision we have here today – play-based environments with gardens and outside play spaces, which welcome and value parents. She also pushed for high-quality training for staff, recognising the difference this makes to the experience children have in nurseries.

Many modern settings are play-based environments with gardens and outside play spaces.

Maria Montessori (1870–1952)

As a doctor (and the first woman in Italy to qualify as a physician), Montessori worked with children who had learning difficulties. She observed the children over long periods, and developed her own method of educating them. Montessori first introduced the idea that there are naturally occurring periods of time during children's lives when they are most open and receptive to learning particular skills and understanding certain things. Montessori observed that it was harder for children to acquire these skills once this sensitive period had passed.

Modern research agrees with this, yet finding that while it may be more difficult for children who have missed sensitive times to learn the things they've missed, it is possible for them to fully catch up. For instance, if a baby has been seriously ill in hospital for several months, he or she may have missed the sensitive times to learn to crawl, stand and walk.

Once the baby is well, it may take longer than usual to master these skills, but he or she should catch up with other children of the same age eventually, and should not be at a long-term disadvantage in their large motor skills.

Montessori went on to work with a group of 50 non-disabled children who were living in poverty in Rome, where she developed the Montessori Teaching Programme. Many of Montessori's ideas are opposed to Froebel's, although she did take some of his work as the inspiration for her own. Montessori's programme was structured, featuring graded learning activities, including many for children to do with their hands. Teachers were seen as the 'keepers of the environment'. This meant that they set up the activities as required by the programme, then let children get on with the activities while they observed, only intervening from the 'edges'. Montessori did not place much value on play. Her programme didn't encourage children to express creativity through art, craft or ideas until they'd passed through all of her graded learning activities. She famously said, 'First education of the senses, then education of the intellect.'

Montessori thought working alone encouraged children to become independent learners, although she did think it was good for them to be in a social group with children of different ages. She believed that a child was thinking and learning at their highest level when they were silently working alone, completely engaged in their task. She called this the 'polarisation of the attention'.

Did you know?

There are private Montessori classes and schools in the UK today, but Montessori's work has not influenced the majority of private settings or maintained settings in the same way as Froebel's did.

Susan Isaacs (1885–1948)

Isaacs is best known for the work she did in her nursery school in Cambridge. She extensively observed the children, not only when they attended her setting, but after they had left and started infant school. Influenced by Froebel, Isaacs valued play highly, and this was the bedrock of her nursery provision. She was interested in what effect leaving this provision and starting formal schooling had on the children she worked with. Her research showed that many children didn't fare well when they moved on, and even **regressed**.

It may be more difficult for children who have missed sensitive times to learn the things they missed.

Isaacs concluded that young children physically need to be able to move around freely. She thought that it was wrong to put children under the age of 7 in classrooms where they are expected to sit and work at a table for much of the day. She thought children should remain in provision modelled on nurseries until this age. Isaacs also did some interesting work on feelings, particularly fear and anger. She stressed that bottling up these feelings could be damaging. She promoted the expression of all types of feelings through play, and this is of course still highly valued today.

key term

Regressed moved backwards.

Reggio Emilia

'Reggio Emilia' is a town in the hills of northern Italy, where a programme of early childhood education was developed. The programme is named after the town. It is based on 'socio-constructivist' theories, including those of Vygotsky, Piaget and Bruner (see Unit CYP 3.1). A group of parents originally founded the schools in 1945 (after the Second World War) because they didn't want to send their children to the existing ones run strictly by the church. By the end of the 1970s, the Reggio Emilia approach had taken over governing the schools in the area, which is largely credited to a man named Loris Malaguzzi. He believed that after years of Italy being ruled by the dictator Mussolini, this approach to education would help the region to start afresh, and work towards a better future. The approach has been given many international awards, and educators from all over the world visit Reggio Emilio to learn about the methods and see them in action.

Did you know?

The Reggio Emilio approach considers children to be strong and capable learners. The infant-toddler centres and schools treat children's ideas and thinking with great respect.

The Reggio Emilio programme has these features:

- Teachers work in pairs. This is known as 'co-teaching'. There isn't a staff structure, that is, for example there is no head teacher. Staff such as cooks and assistants are regarded as equal with teachers.

- To promote a feeling of community, teachers stay with the same class of children for three years.

- The majority of educational activities are done in the mornings when children are freshest.

- There is a sleep time after lunch.

- Teachers are encouraged to listen to children on a deep level. This is seen as a teacher's way of really getting to know a child's learning processes and how they think and understand.

- Infancy is regarded as a period of curiosity in its own right, not as the preparation or foundation for learning in later childhood.

- Topics and themes are used, sometimes at the children's suggestion.

- Teachers do plan and make preparations, but there is not a strict curriculum or timetable. Teaching and learning is allowed to evolve and unfold at the pace of the children, and follows the interests that they develop along the way.

- The programme believes that approaching things creatively can encourage children to look at the world from a new viewpoint.

- Expressive arts are valued as an excellent way to teach children about themes and the world in general.

- There are many opportunities to participate in music, painting, model making, sculpture, dance, writing and so on. Children draw every day.

Did you know?

Pioneer Loris Malaguzzi famously said that there are 'a hundred languages of children'. He saw the different ways in which children express themselves – through music, dance, art, writing and so on – as different languages used in childhood.

High/Scope

'High/Scope' is an educational approach founded in the USA by David Weikart. It grew from a programme originally for students who were considered talented. The name came from this – 'high' represents the high aspirations of those involved and 'scope' represents the broadness of the vision the founder hoped to achieve.

The approach is based on a philosophy of 'active participatory learning'. The High/Scope Education Research Foundation (High/Scope ERF) explain this as students having 'direct, hands-on experiences with people, objects, events, and ideas'. Again the 'active learners' theories of Piaget and Vygotsky can be recognised in this. Children are encouraged to 'construct knowledge' through direct interaction with people and the world in general. Like the Reggio Emilio approach, children make decisions and choices about their learning, and their interests inform the curriculum.

But uniquely, a 'plan, do, review' sequence is at the heart of the programme, and time is dedicated to this each day. Children are encouraged to make plans, and to follow them through. Adults involved in the child's life (including parents and carers) are there to give the child support and access to the materials and interactions that will help them. It's believed that children learn best when they plan their own activities, take part in them and then review them.

The High/Scope goals for young children are:

- to learn through active involvement with people, materials, events and ideas

- to become independent, responsible and confident – ready for school and ready for life

- to learn to plan many of their own activities, carry them out, and talk with others about what they have done and what they have learned

- to gain knowledge and skills in important academic, social and physical areas.

Teachers see themselves as partners in children's activities rather than their superiors, and they seek to share control with the children. They aim to encourage initiative, independence and creativity. They help

Did you know?

The High/Scope Education Research Foundation mission is to 'Lift lives through education. We envision a world in which all educational settings use active participatory learning so everyone has a chance to succeed in life and contribute to society'.

children to resolve conflicts for themselves, and focus on children's strengths.

In addition to the centres in the US, there are High/Scope Institutes in the UK. There are also institutes in other countries including Holland, South Africa, Singapore and Korea.

Common core of skills and knowledge for the children and young people's workforce

The Common core describes the skills and knowledge that the Government expects everyone who works with children and young people to have. These have been divided into six key areas:

- effective communication and engagement with children, young people and families

- child and young person development

- safeguarding and promoting the welfare of the child or young person

- supporting transitions

- multi-agency and integrated working

- information sharing.

The Common core underpins multi-agency and integrated working, professional standards, training and qualifications across the children and young people's workforce, including the qualification you are currently studying for with this book.

There are High/Scope Institutes in many countries, including the UK.

Did you know?

The Common core was introduced as a result of an inquiry into the handling of the Victoria Climbié case. Victoria died at the age of 8 at the hands of her carers. This has been considered preventable. In particular, the multi-agency working aspect of the Common core is altering the way in which professionals work together on cases of actual and suspected abuse.

Have a go!

You can find out more about the Common core at **www.cwdcouncil.org.uk/common-core**

A personal and individual approach to learning and development

Every child comes to a setting with their own unique learning and development pattern. No two children learn and develop in exactly the same way or at exactly the same rate. Their backgrounds, needs, interest and their previous life and learning experiences can differ hugely. So taking a personal and individual approach to learning and development is important to ensure that everyone receives the opportunities that they need. This approach impacts on the quality of learning for each child, it also recognises, respects and responds to children's individualism.

LEARNING OUTCOME 2

FOCUS ON

...being able to provide environments within the work setting that support and extend children's development and learning in the early years

In this section you'll learn about preparing areas within the setting that support and extend children's learning. You'll also learn about monitoring and evaluating the use and effectiveness of these areas, and about how the environment should meet children's individual needs. This links with Assessment Criteria **2.1, 2.2, 2.3.**

Providing areas that support learning and development

In line with early years frameworks, children should be provided with an environment that will support their learning and development through child-initiated play and adult-initiated planned activities and opportunities. The organisation and use of space has a huge impact on the quality of the overall experience that children receive while at the setting, and this in turn impacts on the quality of their learning and development. In Unit EYMP 2 Learning Outcome 3, you will learn about the types of experiences and activities that support and extend children's learning in each of the learning areas of the Early Years Foundation Stage (EYFS).

There are so many possibilities for wonderful play and learning activities. But because settings only have a limited amount of space, most will vary the use of their premises throughout each session. For instance, at the start of the day there may be an area dedicated to construction during free play, which is set up with wooden blocks. But this area may later be tidied away and used for Circle Time, when children will come together as a group to talk about their news. By the afternoon, the same area may be set up with musical instruments.

Unit EYMP 2 Promote learning and development in the early years

Most settings vary the use of their premises throughout each session.

A balanced approach

When deciding on the layout of the environment – or in other words, when deciding what areas for play and learning will be provided and where they will be located – the key word is BALANCE.

Taking a balanced approach to providing play and learning areas is about findings ways to meet the diverse range of children's environmental needs. This includes areas for the following:

- **Child-initiated free play of different types**
  For example, a range of free play areas may be set up in advance of each session. There could be a home corner for imaginary play, a messy play area with sand and water trays, a table-top area of board games and so on.

- **Taking part in a range of adult-initiated planned activities and experiences of different types**
  This might include story time, planting seeds, circle games and so on.

- **Playing and learning alone, with peers and with adults**
  Including opportunities to engage in all stages of play (see page 112).

- **Taking part in play and activities that are appropriate to the age and stage of development of the children in the group**
  This can vary greatly. For example, when considering physical play in a room for under 3s, practitioners must ensure that the areas provided meet the needs of babies who are not yet mobile, babies who crawl, those who are beginning to walk and those confident walkers who move around quickly.

- **Taking part in play and activities that are personalised**
  This means that individual children's abilities, needs, preferences and interests should be considered and reflected in the provision of areas.

- **Rest and quieter activities**
  This may be achieved through the provision of large floor cushions/children's beanbags/ upholstered children's furniture such as sofas. (In the case of settings caring for young children, these areas will be in addition to the sleeping area, which will feature cots/beds.)

- **Physical activity and exercise**
  Enough clear space for this is important. While it is preferable to have an outdoor area of a good size, opportunities for physical activity and exercise can also be successfully offered inside. In practice, most

settings will use a combination of approaches, e.g. playground games and riding tricycles and bikes may take place outside, while dancing and music and movement may take place inside.

- **Time both indoors and outdoors**

  However ... outdoors should not be regarded as simply for physical activities. The majority of activities that may have been traditionally thought of as 'indoor' pursuits can also take place effectively outside. There are also many unique experiences and opportunities that can only be had outside – collecting and measuring rainfall, for instance.

Areas for rest are important in the early years.

A cross-curricular balance

All early years curriculum frameworks are divided up into categories. In England, Wales and Northern Ireland, these are referred to as 'areas of learning'. In Scotland, the term 'areas of experience' is used. For clarity in this section, we will use the term 'areas of learning'.

In England, the areas of learning are:

- personal, social and emotional development

- communication, language and literacy

- problem solving, reasoning and numeracy

- knowledge and understanding of the world

- physical development

- creative development.

In Wales, the areas of learning are:

- personal and social development, well-being and cultural diversity

- language, literacy and communication skills

- mathematical development

- Welsh language development

- knowledge and understanding of the world

- physical development

- creative development.

In Northern Ireland, the areas of learning are:

- physical development and movement

- language and literacy

- the world around us

- mathematics and numeracy

- the arts.

In Scotland, the areas of experience are:

- expressive arts

- health and well-being

- languages

- mathematics

- religious and moral education

- sciences

- social studies

- technologies.

When planning the provision of areas for both child-initiated and adult-initiated opportunities within the setting, practitioners must make sure that there is a balance across all the areas of learning included in the curriculum framework of their home country. We refer to this as a '**cross-curricular balance**'.

key term

Cross-curricular balance the provision of opportunities across each area of learning included in the early years framework of the relevant home country.

You'll learn more about areas of learning and how to promote them through play and learning activities in Unit EYMP 2 Promote learning and development in the early years. You'll also learn about supporting and extending children's learning and development.

Considering the overall layout

Once practitioners have decided on the areas they will provide for play and learning activities within a session, they must give thought to where these should be located. The following guidelines are helpful:

- **Hygiene and cleanliness**

  Set up messy activities in areas that have furniture and flooring that can be cleaned easily. Make sure that there is easy access to sinks for hand washing too – you do not want children trailing paint over carpeted areas on their way to the bathroom!

- **Restful, quiet activities and noisy, busy activities**

  Locate quiet pursuits away from noisy or busy ones. This ensures that children neither disturb each other nor have to be told to keep the noise down needlessly.

- **Sufficient space**

  Give activities the space they need. Overcrowded areas or equipment can not only affect the quality of the experience, they can also be dangerous and/or difficult to supervise – restrict the number of children permitted in an area/at equipment at one time if necessary. Ensure that equipment is located safely, for example that a slide is placed on level ground, and that resources do not

obstruct fire exits at any time. Considering the needs of all the children, leave sufficient room for children to move around the play space between the activities, furniture and equipment. Also ensure that activities, furniture and equipment are accessible.

To enable flexible use of the space, practitioners need to think carefully about practicalities when they are selecting larger pieces of furniture and equipment. Key points to consider include these:

- **What size is the furniture/equipment?**

  It is best to measure accurately to be sure that equipment/furniture is the right size for the setting.

- **How will the furniture/equipment be used?**

  Because both space and money is limited, many settings try to purchase furniture/equipment that can be used in various different ways or for a number of different activities. For instance, a storage unit may have a work surface. A bookcase may have a cork board attached.

- **Where will equipment/furniture be stored?**

  If it will not be in use all the time, you will need somewhere suitable to store the furniture/equipment. Depending on your setting, you may need to think about transporting equipment too. This is sometimes the case for after-school clubs in particular, which may hire a room in a local school but have little, if any, on-site storage.

- **Is the furniture/equipment durable and easy to clean?**

  Choosing equipment that does not withstand group use, frequent assembly/packing away and frequent cleaning is rarely good value for money in the long run.

- **Is the furniture/equipment appropriate for all of the children's ages and stages of development?**

  If not, it could be unsafe. Look for the manufacturer's guidance and the safety marks. Chairs and tables should be of the correct height

Set up messy activities in areas that can be cleaned easily.

for the children. Weight restrictions may be given for furniture such as high chairs or babies' floor seats. Sometimes, settings may need to consult specialists, parents and carers if a piece of equipment/furniture must meet the needs of a disabled child.

Room layout can affect:

■ atmosphere

■ mood of children and adults

■ how children participate in activities

■ how children play

■ what children learn

■ whether children rest

■ whether children play indoors and/or outdoors.

As you've learned, most settings change the layout of the environment as the day progresses. However, it can also be valuable to periodically change the layout of the room in terms of large pieces of furniture, such as bookcases, and established areas such as the book corner or imaginary area. This can be refreshing and exciting for children. It encourages them to interact with resources in different ways, and to explore areas that they may not have visited in their play for a while. Thoughtful wall displays and interest tables can be stimulating too. They should also be changed regularly.

When presenting resources and activities, try to vary things. It is easy to always put the same things out in the same way without thinking about it, so you may find it helpful to record how an activity will be presented on your plans. Think about the following:

■ Use the outside area as an additional 'room'. Outside should not be just for letting off steam or large physical play, although they are important. Lots of activities that can be set up inside can also go outside. This may give children a fresh experience. For instance, when the tea set goes out, children may role play having a picnic. When magnifying glasses go out, children may spontaneously look closely at plants. Some children seem drawn to activities outside that do not hold so much appeal for them inside – mark-making for instance.

■ If extreme weather prevents you from taking children out (e.g. if the playground is icy), move furniture back and give children plenty of space to be physically active inside. Exercise is good for children.

■ Combine resources that do not usually go out together. Put interlocking bricks out with cars, and children may create garages; put cars out with long lengths of paper and they may draw roads.

■ Change the position of items. Try a train set on the table and move the chairs away instead of setting it up on the floor. Take craft resources such as paper, cellophane, fabric, tissue and so on and put them on the floor instead of the table.

■ Set activities up attractively, so they look welcoming, interesting and inviting. When setting up the home corner, set the table and sit a teddy there ready for play, for instance. Start off an activity as a play cue for children – for example, set out the blocks with a partially built tower, or begin a puzzle. Do activities look flat? When resources are just placed on a table, they often look static and uninspiring. A table of pipe cleaners that has two or three bright pipe-cleaner structures standing upright is far more interesting than just the raw materials lying flat.

Further guidelines on setting out areas and activities are given in Unit EYMP 2, Learning Outcome 3.

Unit EYMP 2 Promote learning and development in the early years

The use of safety equipment

There are various pieces of safety equipment available. Using such equipment can effectively minimise the risk of accident or injury to children. You must always ensure that equipment is in good working order, and that it is used according to the manufacturer's instructions. Always check for a safety mark when purchasing safety equipment. See Unit CYP 3.4 for further information.

Safety outdoors

While many of the safety requirements of the indoor play space also apply to outdoors (such as the safe positioning of equipment), there are also some particular considerations. It is important to address safety in respect of:

- external security
- weather
- animals
- plants
- sand pits
- water.

Common dedicated areas

Settings often have a number of dedicated broad areas within the setting that stay the same, although the individual play and learning activities offered in those areas are rotated. Here are common examples of dedicated areas that feature in settings:

- **The imaginary area**
  Over time this may be a home corner, a shop, a hospital and so on. Imaginary areas may sometimes be linked to a theme (e.g. if the theme is animals, the imaginary area may be turned into a vet's surgery for a week).

- **Construction area**
  Rotated resources may include wooden blocks in various shapes and sizes (e.g. Lego Duplo® bricks, Stickle Bricks®, natural objects such as small logs).

- **Messy play area**
  This can include sand and water trays, with their own sets of resources that are also rotated (e.g. water wheels, different-sized bottles and vessels, floating and sinking objects, sponges, buckets and spades, moulds, rakes, sieves). Malleable materials such as play dough, cornflour paste, earth and Plasticine® (with rotated equipment such as modelling tools, cutters, rolling pins, presses).

- **Interest area**
  This is often a table and may be theme related.

- **Arts and crafts area**
  This is equipped with resources such as paint, glue, card, paper, pipe cleaners, decorative items such as glitter, collage materials such as pasta, mark-making resources such as crayons, chalk and so on.

- **Book corner**
  This corner is a comfortable area with bean bags/cushions/child-sized soft furnishings, and stocked with books for children to handle and share.

Sensory experiences

Sensory experiences are those that stimulate children's senses (i.e. their sight, hearing, touch, smell and taste). Sensory experiences are valuable

Over time imaginary areas may be a home corner, a shop, a hospital and so on.

for all children as part of the general learning and play that is offered within a setting. They may also be used in specific ways to stimulate the senses of some disabled children. Practitioners must consider the needs of all children in their care when planning sensory experiences, making adaptations where necessary. Here are examples of sensory experiences:

- **Feely bags**
  Practitioners hide items of different textures inside a drawstring bag. Without looking inside, children take turns to delve their hands in. They describe the item they can feel. Older children may enjoy playing this game in teams, scoring points when they can guess the identity of an item.

- **Tasting fruit**
  Children have the opportunity to taste a range of different fruits, from sour lemon to sweet pineapple. They can compare

Sensory experiences are valuable for all children.

the different tastes, textures and the visual appearance of the fruit.

- **Sound lotto**
  This game is played similarly to ordinary lotto, but instead of matching picture cards to their playing boards, children listen to familiar sounds on a compact disc or audio tape, matching the sounds to the pictures on their boards.

- **Many everyday toys that have sensory features**
  These include rattles, teething rings, battery operated toys such as cars with lights and sirens, play telephones, textured play mats and so on.

Displays

Displays are also a good way of providing children with sensory experiences. Displays tend to fall into three categories:

- **Paper-based artwork or writing that is displayed on the wall**
  (e.g. individual pictures showing various methods of painting that children have used, a large group picture that may be related to a theme such as a seasonal scene with autumn trees)

- **Craftwork displayed on shelves or tables or other suitable areas**
  (e.g. models made from recycled materials, mobiles hung from the ceiling)

- **Interest tables displaying three-dimensional objects, linked together by type or a common theme**
  (e.g. an autumn table, featuring leaves of different colours, conkers and acorns; a shape table, featuring solid objects of different shapes, including a ball, a dice and a brick).

Displays can have features that are:

- visual

- tactile

- auditory.

Using a combination of features can stimulate more

than one sense. It also helps practitioners to appeal to different styles of learners through their displays. You should ensure that the range of displays available meets the sensory needs and abilities of all the children that attend the setting. There are many ways to include visual, tactile and auditory features in displays. For example, you can:

- use fabrics and materials of various textures – smooth, rough, hard and soft

- use bold or contrasting colours – canary yellow, burnt orange, black and white

- use bells (e.g. tied onto mobiles), or materials that crunch, rustle or hiss.

With a bit of creativity, practitioners and children can come up with many alternatives. It is important to remember that displays should attract children and stimulate their curiosity, so that they are drawn to explore them. Involving children in the design and construction of displays gives them the chance to be creative while interacting with the materials. Older children may enjoy labelling parts of their display, and devising questions to encourage others to come and explore it. For instance, a label may read 'What noise do the leaves make when you touch them?' or 'How many different shapes can you find on the table?'

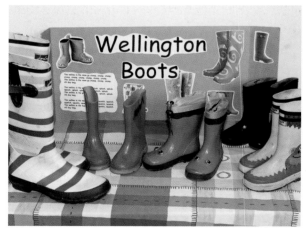

There are many ways to include visual, tactile and auditory features in displays.

Displaying children's work

When children's work is displayed within settings, it can:

- add colour, vibrancy and texture to the environment

- help give children a sense of ownership of the setting

- give families and visitors a flavour of the activities that children undertake at the setting

- remind children of past experiences and learning

- encourage children to feel pride for their work, fuelling self-esteem.

In order to promote children's self-esteem, practitioners need to monitor the work that is chosen for display. It is important to value the PROCESS of being creative, rather than the end PRODUCT. Practitioners should not display just the neatest artwork or the tidiest handwriting. Over time, all children should experience having their work on display, because it is the PROCESS of producing it that should be recognised, not just the quality of the end PRODUCT.

Displaying work encourages children to feel pride for their work, fuelling self-esteem.

Monitoring children's use of prepared areas

Monitoring children's participation and use of areas is a good way of keeping track of individual children's learning experiences. It also gives feedback about how interested and engaged children are in the various activities and experiences that are provided for them. Monitoring can be effectively achieved in a number of ways. Some settings keep a checklist of activities and indicate via initials which children have participated that day. Other settings make a note of participants directly on the plan as it is implemented.

Also see Unit EYMP 2. In Learning Outcome 1, you'll learn about the assessments practitioners make of children's learning and development. In Learning Outcome 5, you'll learn how these assessment findings can inform reflection on how effectively the setting supports and extends children's learning through the provision of areas, activities and experiences.

Unit EYMP 2 Promote learning and development in the early years

Expectations of children

You should have high expectations of children, and commitment to raising their achievement. Practitioners' attitudes are believed by many to be an important part of how well children actually achieve. An old saying goes, 'If you think you can or if you think you can't, you're probably right' – it is important to think you can help children to do well. However, you should base your expectations on a realistic appraisal of what children's current capabilities are, and what they might achieve within a given timescale in the light of this.

Meeting the needs of individual children

The environment and the activities and experiences offered within must meet the individual needs of children. Depending on these needs, you may need to consider some of the following:

- using bright lighting/diffused lighting in some areas

- using colour to indicate certain areas

- using scents to indicate areas or activities

- having tactile wall borders or floor runners

- changing the height of tables

- increasing the space between activities

- taking some activities to children instead of children going to them (e.g. having individual trays of sand or bowls of water to play with)

- installing hearing loops

- making the environment quieter by having carpet and rubber cushioning under furniture

- having non-slip rubber matting on meal tables so that plates and bowls do not move around.

You can read more about this in Unit SHC 33 and Unit CYPOP 6.

Unit SHC 33 Promote equality and inclusion in health, social care or children's and young people's settings
Unit CYPOP 6 Support disabled children and young people and those with specific requirements

LEARNING OUTCOME 3

FOCUS ON

...understanding how to work in partnership with carers

In this section you'll learn about the partnership model of working with parents and carers, and how to overcome barriers to parents' and carers' participation. You'll also learn about strategies to support parents and carers when they respond to partnership opportunities, and about the benefits of multi-agency working. This links with Assessment Criteria 3.1, 3.2, 3.3, 3.4.

The partnership model of working with parents and carers

You must always respect and value the important role of family members in their children's lives. Although we may share the care of children, parents are usually the primary carers. They usually know their children best, and have a closer bond with them than anyone. It's your role as a practitioner to form partnerships

with families based on this fact. Children generally feel a deep sense of love and connection with their parents and carers. They are usually the most consistent people in a child's life to provide them with love, affection and care. Children share experiences with family members that they will remember for the rest of their lives. Good relationships and sharing information is the key to effective shared care.

Link Up!

You can read more about establishing positive relationships and communication effectively and with respect in Unit SHC 31 and Unit CYP 3.5

Unit SHC 31 Promote communication in health, social care or children's and young people's settings

Unit CYP 3.5 Develop positive relationships with children, young people and others involved in their care

The benefit of working in partnership with parents and carers

The diagram below shows the benefits of good relationships between families and practitioners:

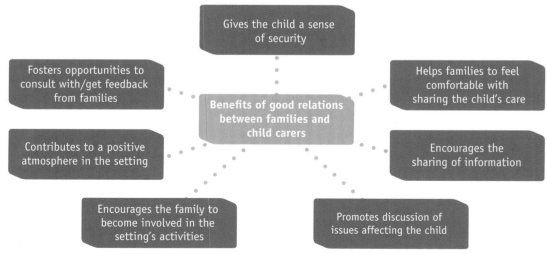

Benefits of good relationships between families and practitioners.

Good practice

The relationship between a child's key worker and their parents is particularly important, as the key worker will normally be the parent's main point of contact with the setting.

Link Up!

You can read more about this in Unit CYP 3.7 Understand how to support positive outcomes for children and young people

Valuing diverse family backgrounds

A wide range of types of families love and care successfully for children. Backgrounds will reflect different cultures, religions, beliefs and relationships between adults. Some children will live with family members other than their parents, while some children will live with carers they are not related to by blood. Some children may divide their time between more than one home (if parents have separated for instance), and some children may live within social care facilities rather than a family home. You should value and accept the diverse family backgrounds of all children, and the homes in which they live, and work to form positive relationships with their primary carers.

Encouraging families to participate within the setting

The act of encouraging families to participate within a setting is another way to demonstrate that families are valued and respected. It also strengthens the partnership between practitioners, parents and carers, which is good for everyone concerned. There are many ways to encourage families to participate, including:

- invitations to social activities, such as fundraising events or coffee mornings

- invitations to make a one-to-one appointment with the key worker to discuss their child's progress

- written reports on child's progress

- home to setting link diaries or books

- invitations to join the setting's committee

- invitations to annual general meetings (AGMs)

- collection of feedback via suggestion boxes and evaluations

- running family sessions, where adults can attend with their child and the child's siblings

- having training or information evenings on topics of interest, such as first aid, or baby massage

- organising family trips out

- organising family festival celebrations, e.g. a Christmas party

- inviting family members to volunteer during sessions, or to help by using their skills, e.g. making dressing-up clothes or story sacks, or demonstrating to the children how to cook a particular dish, or how to do woodwork

- holding exhibitions of children's art and craft work

- holding open days and/or evenings

A parent meets with a key worker to discuss their child's progress.

- organising children's concerts or plays

- holding a toy library or book exchange.

Some settings may also offer a parents' group, which may organise their own events, including some of those mentioned above. A parents' room may also be provided within the setting. Newsletters, blogs and noticeboards help families to feel involved and up to date with activities within the setting.

Imagine that your setting has put you in charge of organising an event to encourage families to participate within the setting. Choose an event that appeals to you from the list above, or think of one of your own. Now write the invitation you would send to families. Explain what the event is, and what will happen. Include the reasons why you'd like them to come. You could design a poster instead if you prefer.

Barriers to participation

As you learned in Unit SHC 33 Learning Outcome 3, barriers can prevent parents and carers from participating fully in a setting's activities, or from accessing their services, in the same way as barriers can affect children and young people's rights to inclusion and equal opportunities. To identify barriers, a setting must get to know parents and carers, as explained in Unit CYP 3.5. The key worker has a very important part to play in this. This is illustrated in the Practical examples on page 315.

Unit SHC 33 Promote equality and inclusion in health, social care or children's and young people's settings
Unit CYP 3.5 Develop positive relationships with children, young people and others involved in their care

Overcoming barriers to participation

It's up to practitioners to put their setting's equal opportunities policy into practice by overcoming any barriers that are identified for individual parents and carers. You were introduced to this in Unit SHC 33. Further information on supporting diversity, inclusion and participation is included within Unit EYMP 4 Learning Outcome 3. You should read this as part of your study towards this unit.

Unit EYMP 4 Professional practice in early years settings
Unit SHC 33 Promote equality and inclusion in health, social care or children's and young people's settings

Example of barriers that may be identified and strategies that may be developed to overcome them are given in the series of Practical examples on page 315.

Practical example

Breaking down a language barrier

A Polish couple have booked a place in a setting for their new baby. They have just started to learn English as an additional language, and so there is a language barrier between the staff and the parents.

Using the computer, the setting's manager translates the setting's 'Welcome Pack' into Polish. This contains the information given to all new parents. She arranges for a Polish-speaking interpreter to come to a meeting with the family and the key worker. They talk about on-going strategies to meet the family's needs. At the meeting, the practitioners find out that the baby's uncle will soon be living locally. He speaks English, and will be staying with the family. It's agreed that the uncle will act as an interpreter when necessary. The manager will carry on translating written material for as long as necessary.

Question

What other strategies might support the parents to fully participate within the setting?

Practical example

Literacy support

A father meets his daughter's key worker on her first visit to a holiday club. He tells the key worker he has difficulties with literacy. He struggles to read and write without support. He's worried this will be a problem because there are registration forms to fill out, and information to read.

The key worker tells him there's no need to worry; she can talk him through the written information. She suggests that she takes responsibility for verbally telling him about new information contained in newsletters and so on. They agree she should also give a copy to the child to take home as usual. When forms need to be completed, the key worker invites the father into the office. She asks him questions verbally and records the answers on the form.

Question

What other strategies might support the father to fully participate within the setting?

Practical example

Staying in touch

The mother of Liam, a child at nursery, has become seriously ill. She doesn't leave her home very often, but she still wants to feel involved in her son's life at nursery. His grandmother will be bringing him in and collecting him from now on.

The setting makes really good use of a home-to-nursery diary, recording details of Liam's experiences. They take digital photos of nursery activities and displays, and email them to Liam's mother often. If she isn't well enough to visit the setting to discuss Liam's development from time to time, Liam's mother knows the setting will arrange for Liam's key worker to visit her at home or talk to her on the phone. She also knows that she can call the key worker at any time.

Question

What other strategies might support Liam's mother to work in partnership with the setting?

See also the Practical example 'Teresa's nativity play tickets' on page 401 of Unit EYMP 4 Professional practice in early years settings

Responses to partnership opportunities

Settings generally come across a range of responses from parents and carers to the partnership opportunities that they make available. Some of these are positive, and some are negative. However, the job of practitioners is to handle all responses positively.

The diagram on page 317 shows the factors that may lead to a negative response.

Strategies to overcome a negative response

If a parent responds negatively to opportunities for partnership working, it's good practice for practitioners to find out why, and to offer strategies to overcome a negative response. Reasons may include the following:

- **Time**

  People's lives are increasingly busy, and with employees in the UK typically working longer hours than anywhere else in Europe, working parents can be particularly pushed for time. But there are many other demands on time too, which may include running a family home, caring for a number of children, supporting extended family members and so on. It can help to be as flexible as possible in the timing of partnership opportunities, for example, by allowing appointments to discuss children's progress to be made in the evening as well as in the day. If parents don't have the time to attend group meetings and so on, you can distribute information afterwards via newsletters or emails, which parents can read at a time that suits them.

- **Lack of confidence**

  Levels of confidence differ greatly. Some people may not feel confident about participating in a group of people – for instance, the thought of running a game stall at the summer fair may make some parents feel anxious. Other parents, particularly new, first-time parents, may not yet feel confident about their own skills and knowledge, and may need encouragement to share

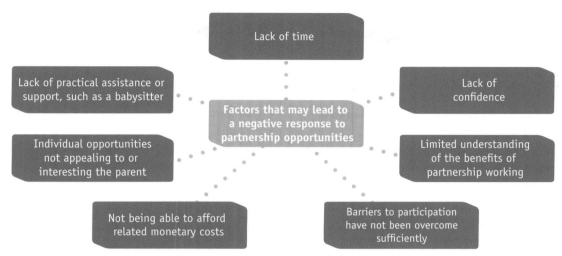

Factors that may lead to a negative response to partnership opportunities.

their preferences for their child's care with the key worker, particularly if they think they should go along with what the 'expert' practitioner says. They may not feel able to contribute to events such as committee meetings, which require expressing an opinion. It's important not to push anyone who is feeling insecure about participating in a certain way. A better strategy is to find a way of engaging the parents that is within their comfort zone, and steadily, confidence can grow. For instance, the parent reluctant to run a stall at the summer fair may be very happy to sell raffle tickets.

■ **Limited understanding of the benefits of partnership working**
All parents should be made aware of the advantages of working in partnership with practitioners. Not only is it good practice to share this information, it also increases levels of participation. Most settings have a policy on partnerships with parents and carers, which explains the advantages. However, there is a lot for parents new to a setting to take in, so if a family responds negatively to opportunities for participation at first, it can be helpful for the key worker to discuss this with them again.

■ **Barriers to participation have not been overcome properly**
Check in with families to see whether there are any barriers that have not already been identified, and to see whether further action is necessary to overcome barriers that have been previously identified. It may be that previous strategies weren't adequate, or that they are no longer effective.

■ **Not being able to afford monetary costs**
The majority of partnership opportunities should not incur any expense. However, some events, such as a family day out, may incur a charge. It's good practice to keep charges as low as possible, and if a number of trips are available, to include some that are free or require a nominal fee only. For instance, a play day in the local park may be free, while a trip to the zoo will entail admission fees, which can be pricey for families. Financial support may be found in some settings for families on low incomes.

■ **Lack of practical assistance or support**
Find out what support is needed and see whether you can offer a solution. Two common problems are a lack of transport or a babysitter – these can make attending events difficult. Settings

may be able to help by providing a crèche service alongside key events such as the annual general meeting (AGM) of the setting's committee, or by letting everyone know that any offers to share transport would be much appreciated.

■ **Individual opportunities not appealing to or interesting the parent**

It would be unrealistic to expect all the partnership working opportunities to appeal to and interest of all parents and carers at the setting, and you must respect people's preferences for involvement. A good range of types of opportunity will help you to appeal to the widest range of parents – for instance, special events that require attendance as well as ways to communicate remotely – perhaps via suggestion boxes and

evaluations. It's good practice to collect feedback on the opportunities that are offered, so that they can be developed and improved.

Multi-agency working

As you learned in Learning Outcome 1, multi-agency working has become an increasingly important aspect of early years provision, thanks to the Common Core.

For information on how multi-agency working operates and benefits that it brings, see Unit CYP 3.6 Working together for the benefit of children and young people

How are things going?

▶ Progress Check

1. What is an early years framework? (1.1)

2. Give examples of how two different approaches to working with children in the early years has influenced current UK provision. (1.2)

3. What is the advantage of emphasising a personal and individual approach to learning and development? (1.3)

4. Give examples of how two common areas found in children's settings support children's learning (e.g. an imaginary area and a construction area). (2.1)

5. What is the partnership model of working with parents and carers? (3.1)

6. Give examples of strategies to support carers who respond negatively to opportunities for partnership working. (3.3)

7. What are the key advantages of multi-agency working for families? (3.4)

Are you ready for assessment?

CACHE

Set task:

■ A setting is preparing to do their annual self-evaluation to ensure they comply with the Early Years Framework requirements. You must prepare some evidence for the manager.

The evidence you must gather includes how local guidance materials are used in settings. You can prepare by asking questions at your setting to ensure you understand this.

Edexel

In preparation for assessment of this Unit, you may like to take responsibility for a specific area within the setting. You can then practice telling a colleague about how the area supports and extends children's learning and development.

City & Guilds

In preparation for assessment of this Unit, you may like to take responsibility for a specific area within the setting. You can then practice telling a colleague about how the area supports and extends children's learning and development.

Learning Outcome 2 must be assessed in real work environments.

UNIT 2

Promote learning and development in the early years

LEARNING OUTCOMES

The learning outcomes you will meet in this unit are:

1 Understand the purpose and requirements of the areas of learning and development of the relevant early years framework

2 Be able to plan work with children and support children's participation in planning

3 Be able to promote children's learning and development according to the requirements of the relevant early years framework

4 Be able to engage with children in activities and experience that support their learning and development

5 Be able to review own practice in supporting the learning and development of children in their early years

INTRODUCTION

This unit is closely linked to Unit EYMP 1. It will be helpful for you to read Unit EYMP 1 as part of your study towards this unit.

LEARNING OUTCOME 1

...understanding the purpose and requirements of the areas of learning and development of the relevant early years framework

In this section you'll learn about the areas of learning and how these are interdependent. You'll also learn about the documented outcomes for children, and how these are assessed and recorded. This links with Assessment Criteria **1.1, 1.2, 1.3.**

Early education curriculum requirements

As you learned in Unit EYMP 1, each home country has their own early years curriculum framework. In England, Wales and Scotland these are statutory, and in Northern Ireland settings may follow the non-statutory framework. Although the frameworks vary across the four home countries, there are many similarities, including a focus on learning through play in the early years.

For our example in this unit, we will take the Early Years Foundation Stage (EYFS) curriculum framework and the requirements of Ofsted (the Office for Standards in Education), which apply to settings in England. However, you will be required to learn about the specifics of the framework that applies to your own home country. Web links to this information are provided on page 294. We'll begin with an overview of the EYFS.

The Early Years Foundation Stage

Since September 2008 *The Early Years Foundation Stage* (EYFS) has been mandatory for:

- all schools
- all early years providers in Ofsted registered settings.

It applies to children from birth to the end of the academic year in which the child has their fifth birthday.

In the Statutory Framework for the Early Years Foundation Stage, we are told that:

> 'Every child deserves the best possible start in life and support to fulfil their potential. A child's experience in the early years has a major impact on their future life chances. A secure, safe and happy childhood is important in its own right, and it provides the foundation for children to make the most of their abilities and talents as they grow up. When parents choose to use early years services they want to know that provision will keep their children safe and help them to thrive. The Early Years Foundation Stage (EYFS) is the framework that provides that assurance. The overarching aim of the EYFS is to help young children achieve the five *Every Child Matters* outcomes...'

Every Child Matters is the Government agenda that focuses on bringing together services to support children and families. It sets out five major outcomes for children:

- being healthy
- staying safe
- enjoying and achieving
- making a positive contribution
- economic well-being.

The EYFS aims to meet the *Every Child Matters* outcomes in the following ways:

- **Setting standards** for the learning, development and care young children should experience when they attend a setting outside their family home. Every child should make progress, with no children left behind.

- **Providing equality of opportunity and anti-discriminatory practice.** Ensuring that every child is included and not disadvantaged because of ethnicity, culture, religion, home language, family background, learning difficulties or disabilities, gender or ability.

- **Creating a framework for partnership working between parents and professionals**, and between all the settings that the child attends.

- **Improving quality and consistency in the early years** through standards that apply to all settings. This provides the basis for the inspection and regulation regime carried out by Ofsted.

- **Laying a secure foundation for future learning** through learning and development that is planned around the individual needs and interests of the child. This is informed by the use of on-going observational assessment.

Note: The EYFS replaces The Curriculum Guidance for the Foundation Stage, the Birth to Three Matters Framework and The National Standards for Under 8s Daycare and Childminding, which are now defunct.

Themes, Principles and Commitments

The EYFS is based around four **Themes.** Each Theme is linked to a **Principle**. Each Principle is supported by four **Commitments**. The Commitments describe how the Principles can be put into action. The Themes, Principles and Commitments are shown in the table below.

Additional statements are provided within the EYFS to explain each Commitment in more detail. You can see these on the Department for Education 'EYFS overview' poster, which is reproduced on page 323.

Areas of Learning and Development

Theme 4, Learning and Development, also contains six Areas of Learning and Development. These are shown on the diagram on page 323.

Each Area of Learning and Development is divided up into Aspects. You can see these on the Department for Education's Learning and Development card, reproduced on page 324, and you'll also learn more about them in Learning Outcome 3. Together, the six areas of Learning and Development make up the skills, knowledge and experiences appropriate for babies and children as they grow, learn and develop. Although these are presented as separate areas, it's important to remember that for children everything links and nothing is compartmentalised. All areas of Learning and Development are connected to one another and are equally important. They are underpinned by the principles of the EYFS. You'll learn more about this in the 'Integrated approach to planning' section of Learning Outcome 2.

Table EYMP 2.1: Themes, Principles and Commitments

Theme	Principle	Commitments
A Unique Child	Every child is a competent learner from birth who can be resilient, capable, confident and self-assured.	1.1 Child development 1.2 Inclusive practice 1.3 Keeping safe 1.4 Health and well-being
Positive Relationships	Children learn to be strong and independent from a base of loving and secure relationships with parents and/or a key person.	2.1 Respecting each other 2.2 Parents as partners 2.3 Supporting learning 2.1 Key person
Enabling Environments	The environment plays a key role in supporting and extending children's development and learning.	3.1 Observation, assessment and planning 3.2 Supporting every child 3.3 The learning environment 3.4 The wider context
Learning and Development	Children develop and learn in different ways and at different rates. All areas of learning and development are equally important and interconnected.	4.1 Play and exploration 4.2 Active learning 4.3 Creativity and critical thinking 4.4 Areas of learning and development

The Early Years Foundation Stage: Themes and Commitments

A Unique Child	Positive Relationships	Enabling Environments	Learning and Development
1.1 Child Development Babies and children develop in individual ways and at varying rates. Every area of development – physical, cognitive, linguistic, spiritual, social and emotional – is equally important.	**2.1 Respecting Each Other** Every interaction is based on caring professional relationships and respectful acknowledgement of the feelings of children and their families.	**3.1 Observation, Assessment and Planning** Babies and young children are individuals first, each with a unique profile of abilities. Schedules and routines should flow with the child's needs. All planning starts with observing children in order to understand and consider their current interests, development and learning.	**4.1 Play and Exploration** Children's play reflects their wide ranging and varied interests and preoccupations. In their play children learn at their highest level. Play with peers is important for children's development.
1.2 Inclusive Practice The diversity of individuals and communities is valued and respected. No child or family is discriminated against.	**2.2 Parents as Partners** Parents are children's first and most enduring educators. When parents and practitioners work together in early years settings, the results have a positive impact on children's development and learning.	**3.2 Supporting Every Child** The environment supports every child's learning through planned experiences and activities that are challenging but achievable.	**4.2 Active Learning** Children learn best through physical and mental challenges. Active learning involves other people, objects, ideas and events that engage and involve children for sustained periods.
1.3 Keeping Safe Young children are vulnerable. They develop resilience when their physical and psychological well-being is protected by adults.	**2.3 Supporting Learning** Warm, trusting relationships with knowledgeable adults support children's learning more effectively than any amount of resources.	**3.3 The Learning Environment** A rich and varied environment supports children's learning and development. It gives them the confidence to explore and learn in secure and safe, yet challenging, indoor and outdoor spaces.	**4.3 Creativity and Critical Thinking** When children have opportunities to play with ideas in different situations and with a variety of resources, they discover connections and come to new and better understandings and ways of doing things. Adult support in this process enhances their ability to think critically and ask questions.
1.4 Health and Well-being Children's health is an integral part of their emotional, mental, social, environmental and spiritual well-being and is supported by attention to these aspects.	**2.4 Key Person** A key person has special responsibilities for working with a small number of children, giving them the reassurance to feel safe and cared for and building relationships with their parents.	**3.4 The Wider Context** Working in partnership with other settings, other professionals and with individuals and groups in the community supports children's development and progress towards the outcomes of *Every Child Matters*: being healthy, staying safe, enjoying and achieving, making a positive contribution and economic well-being.	**4.4 Areas of Learning and Development** The Early Years Foundation Stage (EYFS) is made up of six areas of Learning and Development. All areas of Learning and Development are connected to one another and are equally important. All areas of Learning and Development are underpinned by the Principles of the EYFS.

department for **education and skills**   ISBN 978-1-84478-886-6   00012-2007DOM-EN © Crown copyright 2007

ST IVES DIRECT 02-2007

♻ recycle   When you have finished with these cards please recycle them   **80% recycled** These cards are printed on 80% recycled paper

Principles into practice.

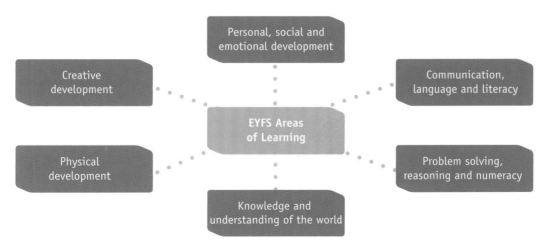

Areas of Learning and Development.

As you'll read below, there are a set of EYFS resource cards for practitioners. This includes a card for each Area of Learning, which provides guidance on what practitioners must do to promote children's development, and outlines what this means to children.

Documented outcomes

In the EYFS, there is a series of outcomes for each Area of Learning. These are known as the Early Learning Goals (ELGs). They are linked to children's development, and give an indication of what most children are expected to have learned by the end of their reception year. The existence of the ELGs also allows children's progress to be measured.

Good practice

Children are **not expected** to achieve the ELGs while still at nursery or pre-school, and the ELGs are **not intended** as outcomes for these settings. Practitioners should assess children's progress **towards** the ELGs throughout the EYFS. At the end of the EYFS (the end of the reception year), there is a statutory requirement for progress to be assessed in a record known as the Early Years Profile. This documents children's final attainment. You'll learn more about this on page 331.

Learning and Development

4.4 Areas of Learning and Development

The Early Years Foundation Stage

Every Child Matters
Change For Children

The EYFS is made up of **six areas of Learning and Development**. All areas of Learning and Development are connected to one another and are **equally important**. All areas of Learning and Development are underpinned by the Principles of the EYFS.

The areas of Learning and Development are:

- Personal, Social and Emotional Development
- Communication, Language and Literacy
- Problem Solving, Reasoning and Numeracy
- Knowledge and Understanding of the World
- Physical Development
- Creative Development

The aspects of Learning and Development

Each area of Learning and Development is divided into aspects. The aspects for each area are:

Personal, Social and Emotional Development
- Dispositions and Attitudes
- Self-confidence and Self-esteem
- Making Relationships
- Behaviour and Self-control
- Self-care
- Sense of Community

Communication, Language and Literacy
- Language for Communication
- Language for Thinking
- Linking Sounds and Letters
- Reading
- Writing
- Handwriting

Problem Solving, Reasoning and Numeracy
- Numbers as Labels and for Counting
- Calculating
- Shape, Space and Measures

Knowledge and Understanding of the World
- Exploration and Investigation
- Designing and Making
- ICT
- Time
- Place
- Communities

Physical Development
- Movement and Space
- Health and Bodily Awareness
- Using Equipment and Materials

Creative Development
- Being Creative – Responding to Experiences, Expressing and Communicating Ideas
- Exploring Media and Materials
- Creating Music and Dance
- Developing Imagination and Imaginative Play

The DfE's Learning and Development card.

Ask Miranda!

Q Does this mean that all children will achieve the ELGs by the end of the Reception year if their setting delivers the EYFS properly?

A It would be unrealistic to expect all children to achieve all of the ELGs by the end of the Reception year, as children learn and develop at different rates. This may be due to individual needs or a health issue, and these can mean that some children may never attain some of the ELGs. We should also take children's age into account when thinking about their achievement of the ELGs. Depending on when they are born, there can be several months' difference in age between the youngest and the oldest children in the Reception class. A lot of learning and development takes place in those few months.

The Early Learning Goals in detail

The ELGs for each Area of Learning and Development follow. A brief overview of the educational programme requirements for each area is also given:

Personal, Social and Emotional Development

Educational programme

Children must be provided with experiences and support that will help them to develop a positive sense of themselves and of others; respect for others; social skills; and a positive disposition to learn. Providers must ensure support for children's emotional well-being to help them to know themselves and what they can do.

Early learning goals

- Continue to be interested, excited and motivated to learn.

- Be confident to try new activities, initiate ideas and speak in a familiar group.

- Maintain attention, concentrate and sit quietly when appropriate.

- Respond to significant experiences, showing a range of feelings when appropriate.

- Have a developing awareness of their own needs, views and feelings, and be sensitive to the needs, views and feelings of others.

- Have a developing respect for their own cultures and beliefs and those of other people.

- Form good relationships with adults and peers.

- Work as part of a group or class, taking turns and sharing fairly, understanding that there need to be agreed values and codes of behaviour for groups of people, including adults and children, to work together harmoniously.

- Understand what is right, what is wrong and why.

- Consider the consequences of their words and actions for themselves and others.

- Dress and undress independently and manage their own personal hygiene.

- Select and use activities and resources independently.

- Understand that people have different needs, views, cultures and beliefs that need to be treated with respect.

- Understand that they can expect others to treat their needs, views, cultures and beliefs with respect.

By the end of the EYFS, most children will dress and undress independently.

Communication, Language and Literacy
Educational programme

Children's learning and competence in communicating, speaking and listening, being read to and beginning to read and write must be supported and extended. They must be provided with opportunity and encouragement to use their skills in a range of situations and for a range of purposes, and be supported in developing the confidence and disposition to do so.

Early learning goals

- Interact with others, negotiating plans and activities and taking turns in conversation.

- Enjoy listening to and using spoken and written language, and readily turn to it in their play and learning.

- Sustain attentive listening, responding to what they have heard with relevant comments, questions or actions.

- Listen with enjoyment, and respond to stories, songs and other music, rhymes and poems and make up their own stories, songs, rhymes and poems.

- Extend their vocabulary, exploring the meanings and sounds of new words.

- Speak clearly and audibly with confidence and control and show awareness of the listener.

- Use language to imagine and recreate roles and experiences.

- Use talk to organise, sequence and clarify thinking, ideas, feelings and events.

- Hear and say sounds in words in the order in which they occur.

- Link sounds to letters, naming and sounding the letters of the alphabet.

- Use their phonic knowledge to write simple regular words and make phonetically plausible attempts at more complex words.

- Explore and experiment with sounds, words and texts.

- Retell narratives in the correct sequence, drawing on language patterns of stories.

- Read a range of familiar and common words and simple sentences independently.

By the end of the EYFS, most children will write simple regular words.

- Know that print carries meaning and, in English, is read from left to right and top to bottom.

- Show an understanding of the elements of stories, such as main character, sequence of events and openings, and how information can be found in non-fiction texts to answer questions about where, who, why and how.

- Attempt writing for different purposes, using features of different forms such as lists, stories and instructions.

- Write their own names and other things such as labels and captions, and begin to form simple sentences, sometimes using punctuation.

- Use a pencil and hold it effectively to form recognisable letters, most of which are correctly formed.

Problem Solving, Reasoning and Numeracy
Educational programme

Children must be supported in developing their understanding of Problem Solving, Reasoning and Numeracy in a broad range of contexts in which they can explore, enjoy, learn, practise and talk about their developing understanding. They must be provided with opportunities to practise and extend their skills in these areas and to gain confidence and competence in their use.

Early learning goals

- Say and use number names in order in familiar contexts.

- Count reliably up to 10 everyday objects.

- Recognise numerals 1 to 9.

- Use developing mathematical ideas and methods to solve practical problems.

- In practical activities and discussion, begin to use the vocabulary involved in adding and subtracting.

- Use language such as 'more' or 'less' to compare two numbers.

- Find one more or one less than a number from 1 to 10.

- Begin to relate addition to combining two groups of objects and subtraction to 'taking away'.

- Use language such as 'greater', 'smaller', 'heavier' or 'lighter' to compare quantities.

- Talk about, recognise and recreate simple patterns.

By the end of the EYFS, most children will count reliably up to ten everyday objects.

- Use language such as 'circle' or 'bigger' to describe the shape and size of solids and flat shapes.

Use everyday words to describe position.

Knowledge and Understanding of the World
Educational programme

Children must be supported in developing the knowledge, skills and understanding that help them to make sense of the world. Their learning must be supported through offering opportunities for them to use a range of tools safely; encounter creatures, people, plants and objects in their natural environments and in real-life situations; undertake practical 'experiments'; and work with a range of materials.

Early learning goals

- Investigate objects and materials by using all of their senses as appropriate.

- Find out about, and identify, some features of living things, objects and events they observe.

- Look closely at similarities, differences, patterns and change.

- Ask questions about why things happen and how things work.

- Build and construct with a wide range of objects, selecting appropriate resources and adapting their work where necessary.

- Select the tools and techniques they need to shape, assemble and join materials they are using.

- Find out about and identify the uses of everyday technology and use information and communication technology and programmable toys to support their learning.

- Find out about past and present events in their own lives, and in those of their families and other people they know.

- Observe, find out about and identify features in the place they live and the natural world.

By the end of the EYFS, most children will use information technology to support their learning.

- Find out about their environment, and talk about those features they like and dislike.

- Begin to know about their own cultures and beliefs and those of other people.

Physical Development
Educational programme

The physical development of babies and young children must be encouraged through the provision of opportunities for them to be active and interactive and to improve their skills of coordination, control, manipulation and movement. They must be supported in using all of their senses to learn about the world around them and to make connections between new information and what they already know. They must be supported in developing an understanding of the importance of physical activity and making healthy choices in relation to food.

Early learning goals

- Move with confidence, imagination and in safety.

- Move with control and coordination.

- Travel around, under, over and through balancing and climbing equipment.

- Show awareness of space, of themselves and of others.

- Recognise the importance of keeping healthy, and those things which contribute to this.

- Recognise the changes that happen to their bodies when they are active.

- Use a range of small and large equipment.

- Handle tools, objects, construction and malleable materials safely and with increasing control.

By the end of the EYFS, most children will travel around, under, over and through balancing and climbing equipment.

Creative Development
Educational programme

Children's creativity must be extended by the provision of support for their curiosity, exploration and play. They must be provided with opportunities to explore and share their thoughts, ideas and feelings, for example, through a variety of art, music, movement, dance, imaginative and role-play activities, mathematics, and design and technology.

Early learning goals

- Respond in a variety of ways to what they see, hear, smell, touch and feel.

- Express and communicate their ideas, thoughts and feelings by using a widening range of materials, suitable tools, imaginative and role play, movement, designing and making, and a variety of songs and musical instruments.

- Explore colour, texture, shape, form and space in two or three dimensions.

- Recognise and explore how sounds can be changed, sing simple songs from memory, recognise repeated sounds and sound patterns and match movements to music.

- Use their imagination in art and design, music, dance, imaginative and role play and stories.

Welfare requirements

Settings must also meet the EYFS Welfare requirements, which fall into the following categories:

By the end of the EYFS, most children will use their imagination in art and design, music, dance, imaginative and role play and stories.

- Safeguarding and promoting children's welfare

- Suitable people

- Suitable premises, environment and equipment

- Organisation

- Documentation.

This is in addition to the Learning and Development requirements.

So what does all this mean?

Child carers working in settings following the EYFS need to meet the standards for learning, development and care. Their responsibilities include:

- planning a range of play and learning experiences that promote all of the Aspects within all of the Areas of Learning and Development

- assessing and monitoring individual children's progress through observational assessments

- using the findings of observational assessments to inform the planning of play and learning experiences

- ensuring that children's individual interests and abilities are promoted within the play and learning experiences.

EYFS resources for child carers

The EYFS pack of resources for providers includes the following:

The Statutory Framework for the Early Years Foundation Stage

This booklet includes:

- **The welfare requirements**
  These set out providers' duties to ensure children's welfare and well-being within the setting.

- **The learning and development requirements**
  These set out providers' duties under each of the six areas of Learning and Development.

Practice Guidance for the Early Years Foundation Stage

This booklet provides further guidance on:

- legal requirements

- the areas of Learning and Development

- the EYFS principles

- assessment.

A set of resource cards

These give the Principles and Commitments at a glance, with guidance on putting the principles into practice. They include an overview of child development.

A CD-ROM

This contains all the information from the booklets and cards. It includes information on effective practice, research and resources. This can also be accessed via the EYFS website (**http://nationalstrategies.standards.dcsf.gov.uk/earlyyears**).

The EYFS review

At the time of writing, a review of the EYFS has been completed. The Department for Education tells us that, 'The Minister of State for Children and Families, Sarah Teather, has asked Dame Clare Tickell to lead a review of the EYFS. The review began in September 2010, and interim findings were reported on in

Have a go!

Many practitioners find it helpful to refer to a toolkit called 'Learning, Playing and Interacting: Good practice in the Early Years Foundation Stage'. This supports practitioners' work with advice on pedagogy, practice and assessment. You can access it online at **http://nationalstrategies.standards.dcsf.gov.uk** You can also register online to receive free access to further EYFS updates and materials, practical advice and discussion groups by visiting **http://nationalstrategies.standards.dcsf.gov.uk** and click on 'Register'.

Good practice

Effective practitioners plan assessment in accordance with the requirements of the curriculum framework they are following. They make and record their assessments with care, and use them to inform their planning. With regard to confidentiality, they share their findings with those who need the information.

key terms

Formative assessment initial and on-going assessment. *(National Occupational Standards)*

Summative assessment assessment that summarises findings and may draw overall conclusions. *(National Occupational Standards)*

December 2010. The final report was published on 31st March 2011. The Government will now consult on any planned changes before they take effect from September 2012. Registering for updates at the address given above should help you to stay informed about the progress and outcomes of the review.

You can also access Nelson Thornes' Childcare portal for up-to-date information as soon as it becomes available **www.nelsonthornes.com/childcare**

The assessment process

Through initial and on-going assessment (**formative assessment**) of children's learning and development, practitioners can monitor children's progress towards the documented outcomes – in the case of the EYFS, this means assessing progress towards the ELGs. By summarising findings and drawing overall conclusions (**summative assessment**), practitioners can see what children should be learning next, and they can then provide the appropriate learning opportunities. Assessment also helps practitioners to identify areas where children need specific support.

There are various methods of assessment, which we

will go into below, but essentially, practitioners make observations of the children they work with, noticing the things they can do. Some of the observations:

- will be mental notes, part of what the practitioner knows about individual children

- are likely to be written down because they have been made at a planned time that the practitioner dedicated to observing that child's behaviour.

In addition, some knowledge may have been gained from seeing children's work, or through conversation with parents, carers, colleagues or other professionals. All of these things provide evidence of a child's achievements, and knowledge of them is collected over time.

When practitioners carry out assessment in relation to a curriculum framework, they generally use an assessment form that prompts them to make judgements about children's achievements. Then, all the accumulated knowledge is used formally, and the judgements based on it are recorded.

Assessment forms are helpful because they ensure that practitioners remember to consider every aspect of development. The forms also ensure that over time the picture of progress built is based on assessment in the same areas – otherwise progress could not be accurately tracked. Formats used for assessment purposes differ from setting to setting.

Practitioners make observations of the children they work with.

It is important to remember that each assessment is only a snapshot of the child's learning and development at that time because young children are constantly mastering new skills, learning new concepts and making new discoveries. The initial formative assessment gives practitioners information about the child's current abilities. After that, on-going assessments will track the progress that children are making. The findings will be summarised and conclusions will be drawn from them during summative assessment. Staff will share the information with parents, carers, colleagues and possibly outside professionals.

Assessment at the end of the EYFS

The 'EYFS Profile' is an assessment document. All registered early years providers are required to complete an EYFS Profile for each child at the end of the reception year – the academic year in which they reach the age of 5.

Link Up!

There is further information on observation and assessment in:
Unit CYP 3.1 Understand child and young person development
Unit CYP 3.2 Promote child and young person development

The Department for Education tells us:

> 'The primary purpose of the EYFS profile is to provide Year 1 teachers and parents with reliable and accurate information about each child's level of development as they reach the end of the EYFS. This will enable the teacher to plan an effective, responsive and appropriate curriculum that will meet all children's needs, to support their continued achievement more fully.'

The EYFS profile.

A practitioner will use their observations to make judgements and to record each child's development against the profile's 13 assessment scales. These are based on the ELGs and divided between the six Areas of Learning and Development.

Where practitioners feel they need further information to support judgements, they can carry out additional observations of the child's behaviour in different contexts – these should be planned for but integrated into the normal curriculum provision. Special assessment activities do not have to be provided. If a practitioner did not know about a child's singing and rhyming activity, they could plan to observe the child during some appropriate everyday activities. In addition, practitioners may, when appropriate, consider records from previous settings that a child has attended. The practitioner may be able to gain some insight into singing and rhyming capacity from previous records completed at another setting – but these will only be a snapshot of the child's ability at the time the records were made. The practitioner may be able to gather contributions from the following:

Scale points 1–3	describe the attainment of a child who is still progressing towards the early learning goals.
Scale points 4–8	describe the attainment of a child in the context of the early learning goals. They are not hierarchical or linear, indeed some scale points require ongoing assessment over time and a child may achieve them in any order.
Scale point 9	describes the attainment of a child who has achieved scale points 1–8 and developed further, working consistently beyond early learning goals. This will be attained by children who have significant abilities in an area of learning. Its purpose is to identify these abilities to year 1 teachers and ensure that these children's specific development and learning needs will be met.

Using the assessment scales.

Have a go!

By following links on the National Assessment Agency website (**naa.org.uk/eyfsp**) you can view the EYFS profile, the EYFS profile handbook, the Assessment Scales Guidance sheet and other support materials. You can also turn to page 561 for an extract of the EYFS profile document for Communication, language and literacy. You can also watch video clips that show children displaying behaviours that link with the assessment scales.

- **The child**
  The practitioner could ask the child whether they like to sing and join in with rhymes.

- **Parents and carers**
  Parents and carers can tell the practitioner whether their child enjoys singing or rhyming – some children are reluctant to sing in a group but are comfortable to do so at home.

- **Colleagues**
  The practitioner's colleagues may have had experience of singing or rhyming with the child.

- **Other professionals**
  For example, a speech therapist may already have made observations about a child's singing, rhyming and general use of language, which could inform the assessment.

Observations

There are many different ways of carrying out observations, as you learned in Unit CYP 3.1 and Unit CYP 3.2. You should always work in line with the guidelines of your setting and the requirements of the inspectorates within your home country. However, many settings have decided to record ongoing observations and formative assessments in a narrative that reflects the style shown in the example of 'Linking sounds and letters' (reproduced above).

Sharing assessment findings

Practitioners should share the findings of their assessments with parents and carers. Informing them about their child's progress is a crucial part of working in partnership. Many settings do this effectively by arranging a time for parents and carers to meet privately with their child's key worker. At the meeting, the key worker talks about the assessment methods that were used and the outcome of the assessment. They will summarise the progress that has been made and establish what children are expected to learn next, drawing attention to any areas that may need

Unit CYP 3.1 Understand child and young person development

Unit CYP 3.2 Promote child and young person development

particular attention. Parents and carers are often keen to know how they can support their child's learning at home, so practitioners are advised to think this through before the meeting. If a child has not been progressing as expected, this will of course need to be discussed. The matter should be handled openly but sensitively. The practitioner should ensure that they focus on what children *can* do and the achievements they *have* made too, as this will give parents and carers a balanced report. Practitioners will want to work in partnership with parents and carers with regard to what should happen next, and to decide whether outside support is needed.

Practitioners should also share their assessment findings with appropriate colleagues and outside professionals. This ensures that everyone working with a group of children understands how individual children are progressing, what the child is expected to learn next, and how this will be achieved. This informs practitioners' practical work with the children – they know how to support them effectively to encourage and extend their learning and developmental progress. You'll learn more about this in Learning Outcome 2.

Did you know?

Representatives of visiting local or national inspectorates (Ofsted, for example) will also require access to assessments.

LEARNING OUTCOME 2

FOCUS ON

...being able to plan work with children and support children's participation in planning

In this section you'll learn about the different sources to plan work for individuals and groups of children. You'll also learn how to engage effectively with children to promote their involvement with planning, and how to support the planning cycle. This links with Assessment Criteria **2.1, 2.2, 2.3.**

The planning cycle

The **planning cycle** has three parts:

■ planning for learning and development

■ implementing opportunities for learning and development, and

■ reviewing/evaluating learning and development.

The process of reviewing/evaluation informs the next lot of planning, and so the cycle begins again.

Did you know?

Many practitioners call this the 'plan, do, review cycle', as this is easy to remember.

key term

Planning cycle constant cycle of planning, implementing, reviewing/evaluating. *(National Occupational Standards)*

Assessment of children's learning and development (see Learning Outcome 1) is a key part of reviewing and evaluating. Once assessments have been made, practitioners use the information they have gathered about a child's progress to inform their planning. This is achieved by analysing the summative assessment. Practitioners should ask themselves, 'In light of the conclusions drawn, what should I plan to do to support this child's future progress and learning?'

Here are a few examples:

- **If children are having difficulties learning a particular skill and/or understanding a certain concept, extra support or learning opportunities may be planned to help them.**
  For example, a child may need more opportunities to use scissors because he or she is having difficulties mastering this skill. Or a child may find it difficult to follow stories and have little idea of how to handle books – and would benefit from opportunities to share books on a one-to-one basis with an adult.

- **If children have particular, persistent difficulties in one or more areas of their learning or development, further consideration is needed to plan the next step.**
  Sometimes difficulties are expected, for example when a child has a special educational need, when they have missed learning opportunities due to a period of illness, or because they are bilingual or multilingual and learning the home language of the setting. In these cases, practitioners may already be receiving support from outside professionals and agencies, and an Individual Education Plan (IEP) may already be in place. If so, practitioners should consider the child's progress towards curriculum requirements and their IEP since the last assessment. If progress is being made, practitioners should consider what children should learn next in light of their current development. If sufficient progress is not being made, practitioners can, in consultation with families, refer back to outside professionals and agencies for advice and support. If those difficulties are unexpected, practitioners should work in consultation with colleagues, families and, where appropriate, children to try to identify the cause. Then children can be given the right support. Outside professionals and external agencies should be contacted if necessary (again in consultation) if practitioners suspect that a child has an impairment or special educational need. There's further information about this below.

- **Where children are progressing well, practitioners should plan for continued progress.**
  Practitioners should consider what children should learn next. What is the next step of their development? What opportunities should be provided for them? What support may they need to continue their progress? You should refer to curriculum guidance to assist you.

A child may need more opportunities to use scissors because he or she is having difficulties mastering this skill.

Curriculum planning

Practitioners must plan how they will provide activities and experiences that will promote children's learning and development and help them to progress, in line with the framework that applies to the setting. Planning allows practitioners to ensure that the learning environment is as follows:

■ **Purposeful**
Play and activities should benefit children in terms of learning and experience. (Don't forget that having fun is an experience!)

■ **Supportive**
Activities and play are planned with regard to the support that individual children may need. They are also devised with children's sense of confidence, self-esteem and general well-being in mind.

■ **Challenging**
Opportunities that challenge children are offered as well as those that consolidate learning. This encourages motivation and progression in terms of learning.

■ **Varied**
There should be both planned adult-led activities as well as free-play and child-initiated activities. Learning should take place both indoors and outside. A range of physically active pursuits should be offered as well as those that require quiet concentration.

■ **Balanced**
Opportunities should be provided to stimulate children's learning in all areas of their development and learning, and should appeal to different styles of learner (see pages 304 and 338).

■ **Vibrant and exciting**
Interesting, exciting activities motivate children, helping to foster a love of learning and discovery.

Practitioners make plans to show how learning will take place in the short term, medium term and long term.

Most practitioners approach this by planning for the long term first, then the medium term and lastly the short term.

Making and recording plans

There are many good ways to make and record plans. Examples are given here, but it's important that you

Table EYMP 2.2: Long-term planning

	SEP	OCT	NOV	DEC	JAN	FEB	MAR	APR	MAY	JUN	JUL	AUG
Theme	Autumn	Animals	Light	Patterns	Winter	Storytime	Health	Spring in the garden	Carnival	Summer holidays	Sport	Our home
Special events and activities	Trip to country park	Visits to children's farm	Diwali visit to Hindu temple	Visit by artist Christmas	Parents' evening	Visit from an African storyteller	Visits from a dentist and a doctor	Trip to garden centre	Fancy dress party	Picnic by the sea	Sports open day	Family barbecue
PSED												
CLL												
PRN												
KUW												
PD												
CD												

The aspects of Learning and Development to be promoted are entered here. Settings often number the bullet points of the aspects so that they can be identified easily on the plans, e.g. if ICT is being promoted, practitioners may enter 'KUW 3'.

Table EYMP 2.3: Short-term planning

Theme: 'All About Me'	Date: 10–14 September				
	What do we want the children to learn?		**How will we enable this learning to take place?**	**How will we know who has learned what?**	**What next?**
	Learning intentions based on the aspects of learning and development	**Vocabulary**	**Activities/ routines**	**Assessment**	**Notes on how assessments made will inform future plans**
Personal, social and emotional development	Separate from family with support.	Greetings in various languages	Self-registration. Selecting activities. Changing books.	Note which children are finding it hard to separate.	[This column will be filled as assessments are made.]
Communication language and literacy	Talk about home/ community. Listen to others. Enjoy rhymes. Show awareness of rhymes. Use talk to connect ideas. Listen with enjoyment and respond to stories, songs and other music, rhymes and poems and make up their own stories, rhymes and poems.	Names of body parts Name for family Alliteration in rhymes	Circle time focus. Make a class book about the children. Sing and recite favourite nursery rhymes.	Collect examples of stages in drawing and mark making. Record significant comments made by children.	
Problem solving, reasoning and numeracy	Numbers connected with home. Numbers in games. Show an interest in counting. Use number names. Begin to understand and use numbers.	Counting numbers more/ less	Workshop – make house fronts. Count games in garden.	List children who know and can use numbers 1–5. List children who are aware of larger numbers.	
Knowledge and understanding of the world	The 'Now' and 'Me' in the past. Show interest in the lives of people familiar to them. Begin to understand past.	Family name Home Work Body parts	Circle time focus. Collect baby photos. Take photos. Class book (graphic).	Checklist of the names of the parts of the body.	
Physical development	Use space safely. Show increasing control in using equipment. Use tools appropriately. Understand that equipment and tools have to be used safely.	Climb, jump, scramble swing Cut, stick	Garden – climbing equipment, etc. Workshop and graphics.	Record children who use/do not use equipment. Note on their ability to cut with scissors. Record right- and left-handed children.	
Creative development	Use bodies to investigate colours and textures.	Feel hard, soft, rough food	Creative area. Finger painting. Materials for collages.	Keep selection of items for 'me' booklet.	

follow your setting's requirements when drawing up your own plans.

The short-term planning example shows that a theme has been selected. While it's generally agreed that themes are not beneficial for younger children under 2½ years, many settings do find them effective for older children. They can be a good way to link activities and play experiences, making them purposeful and progressive. The table before shows how a group of practitioners may plan a theme together for a setting following the EYFS. Other settings might plan by selecting some ELGs, or themes of the EYFS, or some of the Development Matters statements. Some groups start by choosing calendar events that they want to focus on at key times of the year. There are no right or wrong methods – it's up to settings to develop a system that's effective for them.

An integrated approach to planning

It's important to develop an integrated approach to planning. To do this, you must recognise that the activities and experiences you provide for children will generally promote more than one area of their development, because children's learning is not compartmentalised. For instance, children playing with ride-on toys in the playground could be simultaneously learning and consolidating in many ways. They could be:

■ co-operating and taking turns (Personal, Social and Emotional Development)

■ using pedals, steering, changing direction (Physical Development)

■ pretending they are going to the garage for petrol (Creative Development).

Table EYMP 2.4: Theme planning process

Step one
Take a theme and set a timescale, e.g. gardening, two weeks (This may be informed by the long-term plan). Let parents and carers know the theme and encourage them to become involved – with planning ideas, or collecting resources perhaps.
Step two
Divide the theme into subcategories, identifying a logical order for progressive learning, e.g. planting, growing, etc.
Step three
Referring to the Aspects within the Areas of learning, plan activities and play for children's learning, related to the theme. Take account of individual children's needs, play plans and individual learning styles. Plan a balance of activities and play across the curriculum, for all areas of learning.
Step four
Take the activities and play opportunities identified, and fit them into a timetable for each week, around the normal routines such as circle time and snack time. Ensure variation between the types of activities to keep children interested and to give time for being active as well as time for them to rest and recharge their batteries, taking children's attendance patterns into consideration.
Step five
Identify the roles of adults. Who will do what, and how should children be generally supported? What resources/equipment are needed, and who will organise them?
Step six
Identify opportunities for assessment/observation and plan for them.
Step seven
Identify how the plan will be monitored/evaluated.
It is important to note that everything does not need to be themed, and that a theme need not cover all aspects of learning – in fact, this could be rather overwhelming. Routine activities such as news time or pouring out drinks should still be recognised as learning opportunities although they are not theme related. Free-play and child-initiated activities should not be replaced with themed activities.

By pulling together different areas of learning into activities and experiences when you are planning, you can maximise the potential learning opportunity for children. It's not necessary to mould every activity to fit every area – this would probably make your activity so broad that it would lack purpose – but it is effective to integrate those that are a natural fit.

For example, if you were planning to plant sunflower seeds with the children, you could cover the following:

- reading about seeds and how they grow, and discussing things already growing in the environment (Communication, Language and Literacy)

- handling seeds, looking at them closely (Knowledge and Understanding of the World)

- counting the seeds and sharing them out (Problem-solving, Reasoning and Numeracy)

- planting the seeds gently, thinking about how to care for them (Physical Development, Knowledge and Understanding of the World)

- pretending to be seeds unfurling and growing to music (Creative Development).

Consider the best way to group children for activities,

Children playing with ride-on toys in the playground could be simultaneously learning and consolidating in many ways.

and what the role of adults will be in terms of supporting children's learning. For instance, through effective deployment of adults and thoughtful grouping of children, it's possible to plan activities that operate on more than one level. This meets the needs of different children working on the same activity.

Learning styles

People (adults and children) have different preferred **styles of learning**, that is, ways of learning that are particularly effective for them. The styles are known as visual, auditory and kinaesthetic. There are some differing theories about these, but essentially styles of learning are about the way people:

- **perceive information** – the way they learn information

- **process information** – the way they think and interpret

- **organise and present information** – how they retain and pass on information.

People generally employ all of their senses to perceive, process, organise and present information, but they tend to employ one of the senses more than the others.

Visual learners prefer to learn by seeing. They may:

- often prefer an orderly environment

- become distracted by untidiness or movement

- be good at imagining

- be good at reading (may have good early literacy skills, such as letter recognition)

- particularly enjoy looking at pictures.

Auditory learners prefer to learn by hearing. They may:

- learn things well through discussion

- think things through well when asked questions

- enjoy listening to stories

- like reciting information

■ be good at remembering what they are told.

Kinaesthetic learners learn through doing, movement and action. They may:

■ learn well when they are moving around

■ learn best when they have the opportunity to do a task rather than listen to theory

■ be good at constructing things

■ use expressive movements

■ become distracted by activities around them

■ prefer to jump right in rather than being shown what to do

■ prefer action stories.

When you are planning, you should take the different learning styles into consideration so that you provide a balance of activities that are likely to be beneficial for the different styles of learner. However, you should remember that young children are only just establishing their styles, and you should be wary of labelling them as solely a particular type of learner. Even if you recognise yourself as a particular type of learner, you probably have several traits that will fit into the other styles.

key term

Learning styles styles people prefer to use when learning and that help them to learn best, such as seeing, hearing or doing. *(National Occupational Standards)*

Starting points

When establishing group plans, you also need to consider the starting point of all the children. What do they already know and understand? What do they have experience of? This allows you to pitch the activity to the right level for the children. The starting points will differ within any group of children, even those of the same age, so this will require knowledge of the children and some careful thinking. Consider the best way to group children for activities, and what the role of adults will be in terms of supporting children's learning. For instance, through effective deployment of adults and thoughtful grouping of children, practitioners can plan activities that operate on more than one level, meeting the needs of different children working on the same activity.

Using different sources to plan work

As we've discussed, your own assessment of children's learning and development is a key source that informs future plans. But when planning work for an individual child or group of children, it is good practice to use a range of additional sources, including the following:

Observations

Observations will of course have informed your assessments of children's learning and development, as you learned in Learning Outcome 1. They are mentioned again here because you will carry on observing children in between formal assessments, and you can use this knowledge right away when making plans.

Children's interests and preferences

Practitioners should plan learning activities and opportunities that children find both challenging and enjoyable. Taking note of children's interests and preferences will help you to meet the statutory requirement to provide children with enjoyment. When planning, you might consider where and how children like to play, the resources or toys that they like to play with, or topics or ideas they are interested in. A balanced approach to this is the key, as children also need access to new opportunities and experiences. It's also important to consult children when supporting their learning, as appropriate to their abilities. This helps you to plan activities that meet children's needs, and to work with children in the ways that suit them best. Babies and very young children won't be able to tell you what they want verbally. But by being a responsive carer, you can notice what they want and how they want to do things. Think of it as a kind of 'silent consultation'. Also, see the Practical example on page 342.

Practical example

Lisa's planning

Practitioner Lisa is planning some table-top games for her group. She decides to split the group into three sub-groups for the activity. One group of mainly 4-years-olds will play a game of sound lotto. An adult will be on hand, but they will be encouraged to manage the game themselves, and to operate the tape recorder. A group of mainly 3-year-olds are going to play a sequencing lotto game. An adult will work with them, encouraging them to talk about what is happening in the pictures, and the order the pictures should go in. A third group of mainly 2½-year-olds will play a game of picture lotto with two adults. They will focus on sharing out the cards, taking turns, naming the pictures and matching.

Question

Why is the focus of the game different for each group, despite the fact they are all playing lotto games?

Parents and carers

The EYFS emphasises the importance of working in partnership with parents and carers, and familiarity with the setting's plans can help parents and carers to understand how the EYFS works and how their children are learning. As the primary carers of their children, parents usually know them better than anyone, so they are well placed to provide a lot of helpful information, which will inform planning. This will include details of interests and preferences outside of the setting (perhaps the child is fascinated by people's pets for instance), as well as learning opportunities and experiences that children engage in with their parents (such as going swimming) and the progress parents have observed them making. You may have parents and carers who would like to join in and suggest ideas, which is to be encouraged. However, many parents and carers may be willing to participate in other ways. For instance, they can help to collect resources (such as yoghurt pots to plant seeds in), or they might like to volunteer practical help during a session. Also see Unit EYMP 1 Learning Outcome 3.

Link Up!

Unit EYMP 1 Context and principles for early years provision

Colleagues

Although the key person will take the lead in the assessment of their key children, in group settings no one works in isolation with children, and it is considered good practice for other practitioners to conduct observations periodically. These will inform planning. In addition it is important that colleagues plan together where possible, or make another arrangement for consultation on planning matters. This allows for a melting pot of ideas, and it also shares the workload. It is an effective way to make sure that everyone understands their roles and responsibilities during a session (that includes volunteer helpers and students) so that the children can be supported effectively, and the activities led as intended. If a child has special educational needs, the setting's SENCO will also be a source of input.

Other professionals

In consultation with parents, carers and children (where appropriate), specialist support and advice can be sought from many professionals who focus on particular areas including:

- educational psychologists – focusing on behaviour and learning

- child psychiatrists – focusing on thoughts and emotions

- play therapists – focusing on dealing with emotions through play

- paediatricians – focusing on health and development

- health visitors – focusing on development of under-5s

- physiotherapists – focusing on the function of the body

- speech therapists – focusing on speech and language

- advisory teachers – focusing on learning and progress towards national or local curriculum

- SENCO adviser – focusing on supporting SENCOs in settings.

The support available from professionals can vary between regions. Also see Unit CYPOP 6.

Unit CYPOP 6 Support disabled children and young people and those with specific requirements

Children's participation and involvement

As practitioners, it's up to us to encourage children's participation and involvement in planning their own learning and development activities. It is a statutory requirement of the EYFS that settings include child-initiated activities and experiences alongside those which are initiated by adults. There are several ways of achieving this, including the following.

Making sure that children have the opportunity to select their own toys and resources

Settings will have far more resources and equipment than it is practical to make available during a session, so even at 'free play' times, adults influence children's selection by setting out certain resources, usually on a rota system. However, there are ways to overcome this. You can let children know that they can choose from the 'put away' toys too. To facilitate this, many settings make sure that resources are accessible to children (they could be stored in a low floor unit for instance, as shown in the picture on page 342). Labelling the boxes with pictures of the equipment inside assists children in making independent selections. You may also schedule 'off rota' times when the children can select all of the activities entirely for themselves. Or, you could routinely leave one area of the setting free for children to set up themselves at every free play session.

Noticing children's reactions to the opportunities already available to them, and talking about what they'd like to do in the future

This links with taking children's interests into account. For instance, if some theme work really engages children, you may decide to spend longer on it, perhaps repeating activities that were originally intended to be one-offs. This is illustrated by the Practical example of Marlon on page 342. Older children will be able to answer your questions about future activities, while younger children need you to be entirely perceptive.

Providing choice whenever possible

Opportunities to choose can be offered frequently throughout activities, including those that are adult-initiated. For instance, if children are making Christmas cards, they can choose the colour of their card and which craft materials to use as decoration.

They can also decide who their card will be for, what colour pen they would like for the writing inside and so on. Children may take turns to make some decisions in group settings, such as choosing a song at music time, or a book at story time. The layout of some settings facilitates giving children the freedom to move between the indoor and outdoor play areas at will during free play time.

A child selecting resources independently.

Good practice

It's good practice to note on your plans any special support, adaptation, resources or equipment that may be required to facilitate a child's participation. You must make the necessary arrangements as part of your preparation. Where children have individual education plans (IEPs) or play plans, you should incorporate the goals contained within them into the overall planning, indicating them on your plan. For instance, a child who lacks confidence when speaking within the group may be identified within the plan as in need of support during circle time, when they may feel under pressure. See Unit CYPOP 6 for more information about IEPs.

Practical example

Marlon's sea bed activity

Marlon's nursery is having a beach theme. He read the children a story about sea creatures today, and he's following it up with a linked learning activity.

Marlon has lined the water tray with sand, added some real sea shells and some new play sea creatures (starfish, sea-horses etc.) and topped it up with water to create a 'sea bed'. He notices that several of the 4-year-olds he's working with play for an extended period, and show signs of fascination and wonder. At the end of the day, Marlon asks the children whether they'd like the opportunity to play with the 'sea bed' again. The children are keen, and so Marlon decides to add this way of presenting sand and water to the usual rotation of sand and water opportunities that are routinely offered during free play.

Question
How do children benefit when practitioners such as Marlon notice and respond to their reactions to planned learning and development activities?

Practical example

Sam plans resources

Practitioner Sam is planning to show photographs of different trees to the children in her group during a gardening theme. She is aware that she will need to enlarge them so that Nathan, who has a visual impairment, can see them clearly. She makes a note on her resource list to organise this. She adds a note on the daily plan to remind her to use the enlargements for the activity.

Question
What has Sam done that will ensure that Nathan's needs would still met during the activity, even if she is off sick and someone else leads the group in her place?

It is important to remember that plans should be regarded as guidance. They should be flexible, a work in progress. You should be prepared to adapt them when appropriate – some practitioners find this difficult to accept after they have spent time on the planning stage. However, it is necessary to remain flexible so that your plan fits changing circumstances, meets the needs of the children and makes the most of opportunities that arise unexpectedly.

Unit CYPOP 6 Support disabled children and young people and those with specific requirements

Communicating plans

Once your planning is complete, you must communicate your plans to all relevant people within the setting. Make sure that you discuss the roles and responsibilities of other adults – the plan cannot be implemented well if people are unsure what is required of them. Some settings display a copy of the plan in a communal area for all to see, while others distribute a copy of plans to those concerned – this is handy for practitioners to refer to when they may be bringing in resources from home or perhaps working from home during non-contact time. However, it is still advisable to verbally check that everyone has looked at, and is happy with, the plan and their role within it.

Underpinning children's future learning

What children learn during their early years underpins all of their future learning. Children should be encouraged to develop positive attitudes and dispositions towards their learning. They should *enjoy* their learning so that they become *motivated* to learn. Activities should be playful, and learning and achievements should be celebrated. If children come to dislike learning at an early age, they may well be unhappy in school – and there are many school years ahead of young children.

Young children often become disillusioned with activities if they are too formal, because they have not yet reached the stage of development when formal teaching experiences are appropriate for them. For instance, worksheets are now widely regarded as inappropriate for children aged 4 and under because they are too formal. Children will become frustrated by activities that are inappropriate for them in terms of their age, needs or abilities. In addition, they are unlikely to learn much – they certainly will not learn effectively.

Learning through play

Play is an effective vehicle for children's learning because:

- children enjoy playing
- children are intrinsically motivated to play (they are internally driven)
- children can make their own discoveries through play

- children can initiate their own activities and explore their own thoughts and ideas through play
- children can actively learn through play – the learning is a real, vivid experience
- play is necessary for children's well-being – under the UN Convention on the Rights of the Child, children have a right to play.

For more on the UN Convention on the Rights of the Child, see Unit SHC 31 Promote communication in health, social care or children's and young people's settings

LEARNING OUTCOME 3

FOCUS ON

...being able to promote children's learning and development according to the requirements of the relevant early years framework

In this section you'll learn about how practitioners promote children's learning within the relevant early years framework. You'll also learn about setting out and supporting activities and experiences that encourage and develop each area of learning frameworks. This links with Assessment Criteria 3.1, 3.2.

Activities and experiences to promote each area of learning

In order to promote learning and development across all of the areas, practitioners need to provide a diverse range of activities and experiences, facilitated through access to a wide range of equipment and materials. The list is extensive, and there are a few examples for each area of learning and development in the EYFS on page 346.

Using ICT to support children's learning and development

You should ensure that you make effective use of ICT (information and communication technology) to support children's learning and development. In the area of Knowledge and understanding of the world, there's an ELG (early learning goal) that directly refers to the use of ICT. It's important to note that this refers to its use across the curriculum, within the

integrated approach. ICT resources may include the following:

- **Computers**
  These may be used to find out information, or with CD-ROMs that may support particular areas of learning via activities included (e.g. counting programmes).

- **Talking books**
  Talking books can develop communication, language and literacy skills, and personal, social and emotional development when shared.

- **Programmable toys such as floor robots, roamers, painters**
  These can help with understanding why things happen and how things work, and learning about direction.

- **Audio recorders/CD players/MP3 players**
  These are for recording voices, sound games and playing music and story tapes.

- **Video, DVD and television**
  These can be used for finding things out and recording.

In addition, children can be encouraged to notice ICT and its use in the environment, for instance traffic lights, telephones, cash register scanners and bar-codes, remote controls, street lights, walkie-talkies, satellite navigation systems. You can also use appropriate ICT language such as on, off, switch, rewind, fast forward, record, eject, play, stop, pause, mouse, screen, keyboard, cursor, cassette, CD, CD-ROM and so on.

Effective organisation and management

To promote children's learning effectively, practitioners must take an organised approach to the management of the setting. This includes the organisation of:

- the key worker system (see pages 111 (Bowlby) and 442–445 (attachment)

- planning systems and documentation, including the provision of both child-initiated and adult-initiated activities (see Learning Outcome 2)

- the implementation of plans, including how practitioners will promote children's learning through the use of a range of practical techniques (see below)

- observation and assessment systems and documentation (see Learning Outcome 1)

- reflection and monitoring of the provision offered (see Learning Outcome 5).

Practical techniques for promoting children's learning

While working with children, effective practitioners employ a range of practical techniques to promote and enhance learning. These include:

- sensitive intervention

- following a child's interest and stage of development

- supporting, facilitating and extending

- coaching

- modelling.

Sensitive intervention

Sensitive intervention is at the heart of all of the techniques to support children's learning. It's important that children feel that they have ownership of their play and learning, so taking a moment to think your approach through can make all the difference. Consider the point of your intervention, and the effect it may have. For instance, are you picking up signals that children want or need you to intervene? Will your intervention enhance learning and play, or are children learning and playing effectively as it is? How can you intervene without taking over the children's play (e.g. by changing its direction)?

Table EYMP 2.5: Resources

Area of learning	Resources/equipment	Activities
Personal, social and emotional development	Puppets, dolls and soft toys (with expressions for exploring feelings), table-top games, dressing-up clothes, cultural artefacts, a range of dolls showing a representation of people in the world (in terms of ethnicity, age, gender, ability), well-resourced imaginary areas including a home corner, comfortable quiet areas for resting and talking	New activities to build confidence, excitement, motivation to learn: leaves in the water tray, or earth to dig instead of sand, games for rules and turn-taking, celebrating festivals for awareness and respect of the wider world, handling living things for sensitivity, pouring drinks for independence, circle time for talking about home
Communication, language and literacy	Varied range of mark-making materials and paper, letter frieze, letter cards/tiles/magnetic letters, comfortable book area/corner, books, pictures, poetry, fiction and non-fiction, story tapes, talking books, word processor, musical recordings, communication boards, signs, notices, labels, lists, sequencing cards/pictures	Story time, children retelling stories with props for understanding elements of stories, feely bags to promote descriptive language, role play for negotiation, mark-making opportunities in role-play area for writing with purpose, participating in and making up stories, rhymes, songs and poems, opportunities to write alongside adults
Problem solving, reasoning and numeracy	Counting beads, sorting trays, diverse objects to sort, scales, weights, rulers, measures, height chart, number cards/tiles/magnetic numbers, number and shape friezes/posters, number line, numbers signs/notices/symbols and labels, shape sorters, shape puzzles, different-shaped construction resources, clocks, cash till, money	Counting how many they need (cups, for example), sharing out for calculating, singing number songs/rhymes for number operations (e.g. 'How many speckled frogs are left now?'), tidying up for sorting objects/positioning (e.g. 'That goes on the shelf'), finding numbers we see on our own front doors for number recognition, weighing cooking ingredients
Knowledge and understanding of the world	ICT resources (e.g. computers, programmable toys, tape recorders), magnifying glasses, binoculars, money, books and CD-ROMs, water and sand tray/water and sand resources (e.g. funnels, wheels, rakes) living plants, manufactured construction materials (e.g. interlocking bricks), natural resources (e.g. fir cones, wooden logs)	Bark rubbings for observing closely, looking up information for asking questions and investigation, growing plants from seeds for observing change, patterns, similarities and differences, going for a walk and discussing ICT (e.g. traffic lights to identify technology, making recycled models from junk for building and joining)
Physical development	Tools – scissors, brushes, rolling pins, cutters, computer mouse, etc. – threading beads, modelling clay/cornflour paste/jelly, different-sized balls, hoops and quoits, large-wheeled toys (ride-on toys), tunnels, carts to push and pull, low stilts, skittles, hoopla, bats, parachutes, slide, climbing frame, balance beam, swing, stepping stones	Playground games (e.g. 'What's the time Mr Wolf?') for movement – creeping, running etc., negotiating a chalk-drawn 'road' on wheeled toys for awareness of space (themselves and others), obstacle courses for travelling around, under, over and through, pretending to go 'on a bear hunt' for moving with confidence/imagination
Creative development	Diverse range of art and craft resources including different colours and textures (e.g. paper, card, tissue, cellophane, paint, glue, felt tips, crayons, craft feathers, lollipop sticks, sequins, buttons, pipe cleaners, etc.), musical recordings, musical instruments, equipped role-play areas, dolls	Painting anywhere outside with water and large brushers for expression and imagination, making tactile collages for responding to what they see, touch and feel, music and movement for using imagination in movement and dance, singing time with musical instruments for play with expression

Remember: children's learning is not compartmentalised – all of these activities and resources can be used in many ways to promote different aspects/areas of learning, even at the same time

ICT resources include audio recorders/CD players for recording voices, sound games and playing music and story tapes.

Have a go!

While intervening, take notice of the way children are responding. Do you need to adjust your technique? Children's play shifts and changes over time, and becoming attuned to this will help you to see when it is appropriate to end an intervention and withdraw.

Following a child's interest and stage of development

One of the key factors that affects individual children's learning is the development of their concentration span – that is the period of time that they are able to focus completely on one activity or task.

Children's **concentration span** (or attention span) typically lengthens as they get older and develop. Three-year-olds can generally concentrate for a short period. By the time they are 5, this period has generally lengthened considerably. However, children's concentration spans vary considerably from child to child and even from activity to activity. It is the

job of practitioners to provide interesting, engaging activities for children that will capture their attention and encourage them to concentrate. It also helps to minimise distractions – for instance, ensuring that adults cannot be heard talking at story time when you want children to listen, or keeping noisy and quiet activities separate as far as possible. However, practitioners should have realistic expectations of children's concentration. For information about following children's interests, see page 339.

key term

Concentration span the period of time that an individual child is able to focus completely on one activity or task.

Supporting, facilitating and extending learning

It is generally accepted that children need a variety of activities and experiences appropriate to their stage of development that will allow them to do the following:

■ **Consolidate**

Consolidation is when children have opportunities to repeat activities and experiences, confirming their previous learning, practising skills and perhaps developing a deeper understanding. Children are naturally drawn to consolidating in their play, e.g. a child may frequently build the same house or aeroplane from small interlocking bricks. Practitioners facilitate this by providing children with the opportunity to revisit favourite resources and activities.

■ **Extend**

Extension occurs when children's existing learning is moved forward in a new way, perhaps by applying consolidated learning and skills to a new situation. For example, a child who has learned to thread cotton reels learns to do the same with threading buttons. Practitioners can facilitate this by linking activities to encourage such learning (see the Practical example on page 348). Extension

Practical example

Antonio's extension activity

Practitioner Antonio has planned to read a story about a bird that drops pebbles into a bottle of water to make the water level rise. Afterwards, one group of children goes outside with another practitioner to play with pebbles in the water tray. Antonio stays with a group of children who are ready for an extension activity he has planned. The children retell the story themselves using props – a bird puppet, pebbles, water and a bottle. They measure the water level and record how much it rises.

Question

How did the extension activity extend the children's learning?

activities are particularly helpful when you are working with groups of children with different levels of development. For instance, you can plan a core activity for all of the children and follow this up with an extension activity for the children who are ready for it.

- **Challenge**

  Children are challenged when they are introduced to new activities and experiences that are just beyond their current competence, for example a child who has learned to jump is introduced to the skill of hopping on one leg. These strategies promote learning and development.

You should look out for spontaneous opportunities to support, extend and facilitate learning during the implementation of a session. It will be appropriate to offer your support if children:

- could be encouraged to think or discuss further if they were asked a question

- need a suggestion to initiate an activity or experience

- show signs that their play is flagging, and new input is needed

- are becoming frustrated or struggling

- seem nervous, reluctant or unsure

- directly ask you to help them or play with them

- need a demonstration of a skill (e.g. how to hold scissors)

- are not understanding something – a story perhaps

- are beginning to behave inappropriately.

Coaching

Coaching is a way of interacting with children to help them build confidence. This is a gentle way of encouraging children, without putting pressure on them to achieve or to participate if they do not feel ready.

Low self-esteem and confidence can have a considerable effect on learning. If a child has low self-esteem, they may feel that they are incapable of doing all sorts of things well. They may expect to fail, or expect adults and their peers to disapprove of them. When a child feels that way, they may stop trying to achieve, or only attempt tasks half-heartedly. They may withdraw from activities and/or the group. This is a self-fulfilling prophecy: the less a child tries, the more likely they are to fail; this reinforces their belief that they will fail, and they may try even less as a result.

All children lack confidence sometimes, particularly when they find themselves in a new situation.

However, some children experience an intense lack of confidence that may persist for long periods or occur in many different situations. This can stop children from participating in activities altogether, limiting their experience and therefore their learning; or they may only partially join in. Children cannot become fully absorbed and engaged in an activity if they are unable to relax. Children who feel tense and unsure are therefore less likely to learn as much as their peers.

It is important that practitioners identify children who appear to have low self-esteem and/or a lack of confidence. The two often go hand in hand. Look out for children who:

- are frequently reluctant to try activities or experiences

- frequently show little enthusiasm

- are often reluctant to join in, or only partially join in, hanging around the edges of activities or withdrawing altogether

- seem tense or worried

- often say phrases like 'I can't' or 'I don't know how to' or 'I won't be able to'.

Children with low self-esteem and/or confidence need:

- to have their problem identified

- to have practitioners who understand the implications on their learning

- to have activities and experiences planned sensitively to help them develop their self-esteem

Give children with low self-confidence lots of praise when they do try or participate.

and confidence – a practitioner may participate alongside them for instance

- gentle encouragement – but they should not be pushed into things

- lots of praise when they do try or participate.

Modelling

Modelling is a simple and effective technique that is particularly good for encouraging participation. This is something that is often overlooked as practitioners sometimes make the mistake of thinking that children have experienced or learned all of the things that they were offered that day, or that week or month. However, children may have benefited little or not at all if they have not actually participated actively themselves. By modelling a way of playing or the use of a skill (such as cutting) practitioners can effectively influence children to try the same things themselves.

Did you know?

Practitioners are constantly role-modelling their behaviour, attitude and language.

Have a go!

During a free play session, go into the dressing-up area alone and begin to try on hats. You are likely to have company very soon, and before long several children will probably be doing the same.

Preparing and setting out activities and experiences

If you plan activities well and ensure that the resources you need will be available, preparation and setting out should not be a difficult task. The following guidelines will help you:

■ Refer to your plan – it's easy to forget something like a special piece of equipment to support a particular child.

■ Ensure that you've provided any safety equipment or protective coverings (such as a mat beneath the slide or aprons and table coverings for messy play).

■ Think carefully about the best position for the activity or experience within the overall layout of the setting.

■ Consider how you can provide the children with choice (e.g. by setting out a range of painting implements to choose from – brushes, rollers, stampers, etc.).

■ Consider how the children can contribute to preparation and setting up – this can often extend the learning opportunities provided by the activity (e.g. children could help to mix the paint).

■ Consider what might encourage children to interact with the activity or experience – starting something often draws children in (e.g. rather than leaving all the wooden blocks flat on the floor, you could build a tower to add interest, or divide them up into small piles according to their colour. Or in the home corner you might set the table, or put some food in the oven, etc.).

■ When setting up free play, occasionally combining resources that don't normally get put together can be a great way to ring the changes and inspire children to play in new ways. Try putting the small-world animals out with the modelling clay, for example, or put the vehicles out with the interlocking bricks.

You'll learn more about supporting activities in Learning Outcome 4.

Ask Miranda!

Q I want to set up activities and experiences as attractively as possible. At the end of each day, I have plenty of time to do this ready for the next morning. But when we change over activities during the session, I only get a few minutes and it's not long enough to present everything the way I'd like.

A **It's good practice to set out activities and experiences in a way that's attractive and interesting to children. However, this shouldn't take you too long. Do remember that activities are there to be used and interacted with – you are not creating a work of art! How about involving the children in setting out some of the play opportunities now and then – this will enable you to ensure that they are presented in a way that children like. Looking at the scheduling can also help. You might be able to re-jig things to give you an extra few minutes. It could also be worth taking another look at your activities – are they overly complex for young children?**

Ensure you've provided any safety equipment or protective coverings.

LEARNING OUTCOME 4

FOCUS ON

...being able to engage with children in activities and experience that support their learning and development

In this section you'll learn about engaging with children to support their learning and development, and the importance of supporting sustained shared thinking. You'll also learn how to use accurate and appropriate language to support and extend learning. This links with Assessment Criteria 4.1, 4.2, 4.3.

Engaging with children to support their learning and development

Engaging with children and working alongside them enables practitioners to enhance learning and development. It also shows that you're interested in individual children, and that you value their activities and experiences. As you learned in Learning Outcome 3, it's important to intervene sensitively when engaging with children.

Supporting future learning

What children learn during their early years underpins all of their future learning. Always aim to let children know that you believe they are good at learning, and remember to praise them for both achieving and trying their best. Key skills that help children to become effective learners throughout their lives are shown on the diagram below.

By engaging with children you can encourage these skills in a range of ways, including the following:

Determination and motivation

Encourage children to persevere when they can't get something right at first. Motivation and determination are linked, because a child who is motivated to achieve a goal grows in determination. You can motivate children by celebrating their achievements and praising them for trying. But the best motivation of all is the desire to learn. That's why it's so important to foster a love of learning and an interest and curiosity about the world when children are young.

Confidence

Children who feel nurtured (cared for) and respected for who they are as an individual are likely to develop

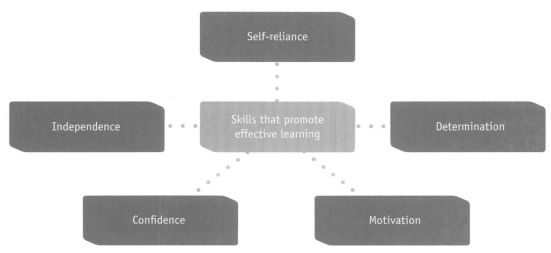

Key skills that promote effective learning.

confidence. Children also develop confidence when they take emotional risks successfully (see page 221). Experiencing physical risk and taking on challenges in a supporting environment also helps (see page 223).

Independence

Confidence breeds independence. Children experience a desire to do things for themselves and in their own way from an early age. Most of us will have experienced a frustrated 2-year-old who can't quite manage a task such as putting on shoes themselves, but definitely doesn't want our help! It's important to encourage independence as appropriate to children's age and abilities from early on. This helps children to become increasingly independent as they grow up.

Self-reliance

Independence breeds self-reliance. Self-reliant learners trust themselves to pick up the knowledge and skills they need. This helps children to feel relaxed, which makes it easier for them to concentrate and participate in activities and experiences. In turn, this helps them to learn. It can help to remind children of their past learning successes.

Children's achievements

When children have made achievements you should sensitively acknowledge, praise and celebrate them. If you involve children in the assessment of their progress, milestones can be recorded together. It is important to look out for such achievements not only in order to mark them, but in order to recognise when children are ready to move on in terms of what they are ready to learn and experience next. When you decide what children should learn from activities, consider how you will know when they have learned it – this will help you to notice new learning.

Supporting sustained shared thinking

Sustained shared thinking occurs when a child has a strong interest in something that is happening or something they are doing, and talks about this in a focused way – in this case, with a practitioner. Talking helps children to process information more effectively, and to sustain their engagement. A deep engagement enables children to explore related concepts and

Acknowledge, praise and celebrate achievements.

ideas at a deeper level, and to draw conclusions. This develops thinking, problem solving and reasoning skills, and it helps children to link together past learning and experiences with new learning and experiences. This type of 'joined-up learning' is extremely valuable. When we think in this way, new neuro-pathways (connections) can actually be formed in the brain.

Practitioners can support **sustained shared thinking** by noticing when a strong interest occurs, and initiating focused conversation about the event or activity. Asking open questions is the key to prompting children to think about concepts and ideas. You should also routinely encourage children to ask questions themselves, as this promotes curiosity and encourages children to initiate sustained shared thinking themselves. You'll learn more about this on page 353.

key term

Sustained shared thinking occurs when a practitioner uses language to encourage children to explore an activity, event, idea or concept on a deeper level.

Using language accurately and appropriately

Whenever we talk to or in front of children, we are modelling the use of language. Children learn not only from what we say, but from how we say it.

Because of this, it's important that practitioners model language that is accurate and appropriate. For instance, if we are using mathematical language, the correct terms must be used or children's learning will be flawed.

The same applies to the way we speak. If our grammar is incorrect, children are also likely to speak in ungrammatical ways. There is of course variation in the way people from different regions talk and structure sentences (dialect), and this diversity should be respected. However, children do need experience of the standard way in which language is used, or they are likely to have difficulties with writing later on. This is because when writing formally, grammar is expected to be correct, but a child's writing will reflect their experience of spoken language. Some examples of correct and incorrect conversational grammar are given below.

The same applies to pronunciation, as children will sound out words and then write them in the way in which they say them. For instance, if a child is used to 'h' sounds being dropped, they may write 'ot' instead of 'hot'. Another common sound to be dropped is the 't' sound in the middle of word, which can lead to misspelling words such as 'later'.

We can also increase children's vocabulary by introducing them to a wide range of words. We all know many more words than we use on a daily basis, so it's just a case of getting into the habit of extending our use of vocabulary when we are with children. For instance, instead of saying that you are 'pleased,' you could say that you are 'delighted' or 'thrilled'.

Examples of grammar

Incorrect: Well done! You was really trying hard then, wasn't you?

Correct: Well done! You were really trying hard then, weren't you?

Incorrect: It's sunny today, innit?

Correct: It's sunny today, isn't it?

Incorrect: We need to tidy up cos it's almost lunch time.

Correct: We need to tidy up because it's almost lunch time.

Increase vocabulary by introducing children to a wide range of words.

Open questions

Open questions are those that can be answered in a number of ways, while the possible answers to closed questions will be limited. For instance, if you were to ask a child 'What would you like to do?', the possible answers are endless. But if you were to ask, 'Would you like to play inside or outside?' you will get one of two responses. Closed questions have their purposes, but when we want to promote thinking, curiosity, problem solving and investigation, open questions are most effective.

Open questions open up discussions, often about thoughts and ideas. For questions to be used effectively in this context, it is important that children feel comfortable, and that they are not concerned about right or wrong answers. This is best achieved when a practitioner has already been playing alongside a child for a while, and they are relaxed in each other's company. If you approach a child and ask them lots of questions right away, you will not be intervening sensitively, and the child may feel under pressure. The following types of open questions are commonly used by skilled practitioners:

'I wonder what would happen if...'

'I wonder what will happen next...'

'I wonder why...'

'What could we do to...'

'How can we find out...'

Did you know?

Open questions can effectively lead to children suggesting ideas and then testing them. This promotes the skills of investigation. Perhaps children have suggested ways of sinking a toy boat in the water tray – they can then try out their ideas and find out what actually sinks the boat.

Encouraging children to ask questions

It's also good practice to encourage children to ask their own questions. This promotes curiosity and inquisitiveness, which enhances children's thirst for learning. Asking questions is a key way for children to check their understanding and expand their knowledge. It also encourages them to communicate, and in particular to practise active listening. You can encourage children to ask questions and to share their ideas and suggestions by doing the following:

- **Inviting them to contribute**
  'Has anyone got a question they'd like to ask?' or, 'Can you suggest some places we could visit on our summer trips?'

- **Role modelling**
  Let children hear you put forward your own ideas and questions.

- **Planning questions with children**
  For instance, if a visitor is coming to the setting, you can plan questions to ask them beforehand. What do the children want to find out?

- **Responding positively when children ask questions or make suggestions**
  Answer questions fully. Praise children's efforts, and thank children for their contributions. 'I'm glad you asked me that' or 'What a good idea!'

- **Giving opportunities for children to listen to one another**
  Children may be inspired by each other's ideas.

Mathematical language

Using mathematical language enhances children's mathematical learning and development. In the EYFS, the area of Problem Solving, Reasoning and Numeracy is made up of three Aspects. Examples of mathematical language associated with the aspects are given in the table on page 355. Look for spontaneous, everyday opportunities to use this language as you work alongside children. Don't save it just for when there's a planned activity designed to specifically promote Problem Solving, Reasoning and Numeracy. The more familiar children are with this language, the more they will understand and feel comfortable with not only the mathematical terms, but with the concepts they are related to.

Have a go!

You can go online to view the full requirements of Problem Solving, Reasoning and Numeracy at **http://nationalstrategies.standards.dcsf.gov.uk/earlyyears**

Table EYMP 2.6: Examples of mathematical language associated with the aspects

Aspects	Numbers as labels and for counting	Calculating	Shape, space and measures
Language	Counting out objects, naming numbers on sight (e.g. when seen on someone's front door), age, how old	Add, increase, take away, subtract, decrease, equals, same as, how many, how much, altogether, nothing left, zero, more than, less than, fewer than, most, least	Names of shapes, narrow, wide, sides, corners, points, where, behind, in front, next to, beside, under, over, above, below, opposite, parallel, inside, outside, furthest, far away, nearest, closest, distance, long, longer than, longest, short, shorter than, shortest, medium, small, smaller than, smallest, large, larger than, largest, high, higher than, highest, low, lower than, lowest, heavy, heavier than, heaviest, light, lighter than, lightest, difference

LEARNING OUTCOME 5

FOCUS ON

...being able to review own practice in supporting the learning and development of children in their early years

In this section you'll learn about reflecting on your own practice in supporting learning and development of children in their early years. You'll also learn about using reflection to make changes in your own practice. This links with Assessment Criteria 5.1, 5.2.

Reflect on your own practice in supporting children's learning and development

Reflecting on what you do, how you do things and what you achieve, helps you to see how well you are supporting children's learning and development in practice. To reflect on your planning and implementation of curriculum frameworks consider the following points:

■ **How effectively do you plan?**
Is it clear what children should learn and how? Are all children's needs met? Are activities varied and balanced appropriately? Do adults know their roles?

■ **Are you sufficiently organised?**
Are the resources and equipment available when you need them? Are activities set up and ready at the right time? Is the environment set out attractively?

■ **Analyse your actions in implementing**
Do you support children effectively when support is planned for, and when it is needed spontaneously? Do you group children effectively to maximise their learning and experiences? Do you look out for children's achievements and signs indicating they are ready to move on? Do you follow plans flexibly? Do you gently encourage children to participate?

It is helpful for practitioners to:

■ record their reflections, perhaps in a journal

■ discuss their reflections with others

■ use feedback from others to improve their own evaluations.

Make sure that you actively use your reflections to inform your future practice. It is only then that they are worthwhile and your practice will develop and evolve. This is illustrated in the Practical example on page 357. Full information on reflection is given in Unit SHC 32.

Link Up!

Unit SHC 32 Engage in personal development in health, social care or children's and young people's settings

Improvement of provision and staff development

Summative assessments can reveal not just how well an individual child is learning and progressing, but also how well the provision is meeting children's learning and development needs.

Looking at a number of summative assessments allows practitioners to evaluate the bigger picture. If children are generally not progressing well in one or more particular areas, it may be necessary to improve the way the setting works in that area. Practitioners should discuss this to pinpoint what action can be taken. In some regions, an Advisory Teacher may be able to offer support. For instance, it may be that more activities are needed to promote the learning

If children are not progressing well in a particular area, practitioners should discuss this to pinpoint what action can be taken.

of certain concepts that have not been given due attention. Or perhaps there is a lack of equipment to support specific types of play and learning.

Sometimes staff lack confidence in a certain area or have gaps in their knowledge, which impacts on children's progress. In this case, staff development or training is needed. Identifying these issues is a positive step – once the issues are identified, they can be addressed and rectified.

Monitoring strategies and documentation

It is good practice for settings to regularly monitor how well they are delivering their relevant curriculum. You will need to do this and record your findings in line with your organisational procedures and the requirements of your relevant home inspectorate. To monitor effectively, you will need to work in partnership with families, colleagues and outside professionals to consider evidence including these points:

■ **The formative and summative assessments of children's progress**
The amount of progress that children make reveals how good the planning and implementation is.

■ **Colleagues'/outside professionals' comments, opinions, evaluations and reflective practice notes**
Do they feel plans are specific enough? Do they generally understand their roles and responsibilities in the delivery of the curriculum? Do they feel organised and well prepared? Do they feel children are engaged and interested?

■ **Your own evaluations and reflective practice notes**
See 'Reflective Practice' on page 37.

■ **Families' comments, opinions, evaluations (including children)**
Do children enjoy activities? Are they motivated, keen to attend and to participate? Do they talk about things they like/dislike about the setting?

Practical example

Justine uses reflection to make changes to practice

Justine has been reviewing summative assessments at her setting. She has noticed that several 3- and 4-year-olds are not making good progress with their mark-making and early (or emergent) writing skills. She raises this in a staff meeting so that she can discuss the possible implications with her colleagues. The practitioners conclude that while they have mark-making activities available on the table tops at every session, not all of the children choose to participate in them. So some children actually have very little experience of making marks and practising early writing. The practitioners decide to provide children with opportunities to write and mark-make in many different areas of the setting. They introduce several new strategies, including the provision of paper and pencils to the role-play area – children can now make shopping lists and so on. They also take chalk outside so that children can make marks on the ground. They plan to purchase some new and interesting mark-making materials, as supplies are old and have started to dwindle.

Question

How can Justine and her colleagues monitor the impact of their new strategies over time?

Do the families feel that the children's needs are met? Have they noticed the children's progression? Are they aware of opportunities to work in partnership with the setting?

■ **Inspectorate findings and reports (e.g. Ofsted report)**
Written reports and verbal feedback.

■ **Quality Assurance scheme findings and reports**
Written reports and verbal feedback.

You must ensure that all areas of the curriculum are monitored. You should check that all areas are implemented to a consistently high quality. For example, personal, social and emotional development may be delivered very well when the theme is 'All about me', but is it still promoted to a high standard when the theme is 'Shapes'?

There are various methods of recording monitoring. For instance, some settings may hold monitoring meetings, recorded in the style of minutes. Others may complete forms they have designed for the purpose. Whatever method is used, it is important that records are dated and stored appropriately.

Also see 'Monitoring children's use of prepared areas' in Unit EYMP 1, Learning Outcome 2.

Link Up!

Unit EYMP 1 Context and principles for early years provision

How are things going?

▶ Progress Check

1. What are the Areas of Learning and Development in the EYFS? (1.1)

2. What are early learning goals? (1.2)

3. Give three sources to draw from when planning work for children. (2.1)

4. What are the three stages of the planning cycle? (2.3)

5. Give three factors you would consider when setting out activities and experiences in a group setting. (3.3)

6. How do practitioners engage a child in sustained shared thinking? (4.2)

7. Why is it important to model accurate and grammatically correct language? (4.3)

8. Describe how you can use reflection to make changes to your own practice. (5.2)

Are you ready for assessment?

CACHE

Set task:

■ This is an extension to the set task for Unit EYMP 1. It relates to the monitoring, evaluating and reviewing of children's learning.

Prepare by rereading Learning Outcome 1, and making notes on the key points.

Edexel

In preparation for assessment of this Unit, you may like to collect together documents that you have completed when assessing children's progress against the documented outcomes of the early years framework that applies, to use as evidence.

City & Guilds

In preparation for assessment of this Unit, you may like to collect together documents that you have completed when assessing children's progress against the documented outcomes of the early years framework that applies, to use as evidence.

Learning Outcomes 2, 3, 4 and 5 must be assessed in real work environments.

UNIT 3

Promote children's welfare and well-being in the early years

LEARNING OUTCOMES

The learning outcomes you will meet in this unit are:

1 Understand the welfare requirements of the relevant early years framework

2 Be able to keep early years children safe in the work setting

3 Understand the importance of promoting positive health and well-being for early years children

4 Be able to support hygiene and prevention of cross-infection in the early years setting

5 Understand how to ensure that children in their early years receive high-quality, balanced nutrition to meet their growth and development needs

6 Be able to provide physical care for children

INTRODUCTION

Children in the early years have specific physical and nutritional care requirements. Practitioners must meet them sensitively and with confidence, so children can thrive in terms of their health and development. The welfare requirements and guidance of early years frameworks set out the minimum standards that must be met in each home country. However, practitioners should always strive to achieve the very best practice in this important area.

LEARNING OUTCOME 1

FOCUS ON

...understanding the welfare requirements of the relevant early years framework

In this section you'll learn about the welfare requirements of early years frameworks. You'll also learn about the lines of reporting and responsibility within the work setting. This links with Assessment Criteria **1.1, 1.2.**

Welfare requirements

Each home country in the UK has set out welfare requirements or standards. These are the minimum standards that settings must meet in order to ensure children's health, safety and well-being. It's important that you know and understand the welfare requirements for your own home country. In England, the welfare requirements are part of the Early Years Foundation Stage, which is linked to *Every Child Matters*.

Link Up!

You'll find further details on pages 209–210 of Unit CYP 3.4 Support children and young people's health and safety

Have a go!

Visit **http://nationalstrategies.standards. dcsf.gov.uk/node/83954** to see the welfare requirements for England in full.

Lines of responsibility and accountability

To ensure that no important jobs are left undone, it's crucial for practitioners in all settings and services to be clear about their own responsibilities relating to health and safety. Practitioners should also have a firm understanding of their accountability in these matters. To put it another way, they should know who within the setting or service they are answerable to in regards to their responsibilities.

Good practice

All settings and services will have established lines of responsibility and accountability. It's good practice to be familiar with the responsibilities and accountability of your colleagues as well as yourself. You'll then be clear who to go to should you have a health and safety issue to resolve.

Being clear about responsibilities ensures that no important jobs are left undone.

Practical example

Lara's concern

Lara recently started work at an out-of-school club, which meets in the hall of a primary school. The club is owned by a local company that manages a small chain of clubs.

When one of the children falls down in the playground and grazes his knee, Lara fetches the first aid box so she can attend to the minor injury. She notices that supplies seem to be running low, and she also uses the last of the first aids wipes to clean the child's knee. Lara realises that she doesn't know who to tell. She asks the play leader who's responsible for the first aid box. The play leader says that the club doesn't have an allocated person, it's something everyone shares responsibility for – anyone can ring the main office and request further supplies.

Question
What could be changed to ensure that the first aid box is always well stocked in the future?

Safeguarding children

There will also be clear lines of reporting to follow in your setting should you suspect child abuse.

Link Up!

You can read more about this in Unit CYP 3.3 Understand how to safeguard the well-being of children and young people

LEARNING OUTCOME 2

FOCUS ON

...being able to keep early years children safe in the work setting

Safe supervision while allowing exploration, risk and challenge

As you learned in Unit CYP 3.4, it's essential that you supervise children safely without preventing them from exploring or experiencing challenge. The key to this is to manage risk effectively. Refer to Learning Outcomes 2, 3 and 4 of Unit CYP 3.4 for full information on:

■ risk assessment

In this section you'll learn about the safe supervision of children while allowing exploration and managing risk and challenge. You'll also learn about systems for supporting children's safety on off-site visits and when arriving and departing from the setting. You'll learn about evaluating and checking that equipment and materials are safe, and about the minimum requirements for space and staff ratios. This links with Assessment Criteria **2.1, 2.2, 2.3, 2.4.**

- staff deployment

- levels of supervision.

Also see staff ratios on page 364.

Unit CYP 3.4 Support children and young
people's health and safety

Security

Settings must make suitable security arrangements in
the interests of the children's safety. There should be
clear procedures for children's arrival at the setting,
their departure from the setting, and their security
when on outings.

Arrivals and departures

All settings must keep a record of the children
and adults who are in attendance at each session.
This is known as keeping a register. In addition, a
record of when children arrive and leave must also
be kept. Some settings may keep a 'signing in/out

All settings must keep a record of the children and adults
who are in attendance at each session.

book' for this purpose, while others may include this
information on their register document. Whatever
the arrangement at your setting, it is essential that
children are signed in as soon as they arrive, and
signed out as soon as they leave.

If a child fails to arrive

For many settings, if a child does not arrive, then it
is generally no cause for concern. The child is not
the responsibility of the provider until their parent or
carer brings them along. However, this is different for
after-school clubs. If a child who has been booked in
does not turn up, practitioners must quickly find out
their whereabouts. It is helpful to bear in mind that a
club may be:

- based within a school; or

- based elsewhere, in which case club escorts will
  be collecting children from school and then taking
  them to the club premises. (The escorts will need
  to deal with the situation if children they are
  expecting to collect do not appear.)

Staff should contact the parent or carer to find out
whether other arrangements have been made for the
child's care. Frequently in these events, parents have
forgotten to cancel a place that they no longer need.
It often helps the situation if a practitioner can talk
with the child's teacher to find out whether the child
was absent from school or if they saw who collected

Try the following visualisation to see why this
is so important: Imagine that there is a fire.
You must evacuate. You take the register or
signing in/out book with you. After checking
these, you think all of the children have got
out safely. But one child was not marked in on
his arrival, and so you have not yet noticed
that he is missing.

There could be awful consequences, couldn't
there? **Do not forget to mark children in!** In
a similar scenario, if a child who has already
been collected has not been signed out,
firefighters could end up searching a burning
building for a child perceived to be missing.
Do not forget to sign children out!

the child. It may be the case that a parent has rung the school to let them know that their child is off sick, but forgotten to let the club know. If a child did not attend school and a parent has not called either the school or the club, it may mean that the child went missing early in the morning on their way to school, and so contacting parents is still a matter of urgency to confirm the child's whereabouts.

Written procedures for non-arrival are helpful for out-of-school club practitioners to refer to in these often complicated circumstances. It is also important that practitioners at all settings are aware of who is authorised to collect each child. This information must be held on the registration form.

Security during settings

During sessions, practitioners must ensure that children do not leave the setting unattended, and that visitors cannot gain entry without detection. The indoor and outdoor premises must be secure. The way in which this is achieved depends entirely on the building and the age and stage of development of the children. However, fire exits must always be unobstructed, and the method of opening the door to escape must be quick and easy. Many settings fit an alarm to fire doors so that practitioners are alerted immediately if a child should open an outside door.

Visitors should not be able to gain entry without detection.

Off-site visits

On 'off-site visits' (or in other words, outings) settings need to take extra care with regard to security. It is important to ensure that the staff-to-child ratio is sufficiently high to enable the increased supervision that is necessary. Take the children's ages, needs and abilities into consideration, as well as regulations. It is usual practice to split the children into small groups or pairs, with each assigned one or more adults to take care of them. This is particularly useful when children are walking around in a public place, from one location to another, even though the whole group may join in activities together on arrival. Whenever you change location, enter a building or get on or off transport, count the children TWICE, in case of a miscount. It is good practice for more than one practitioner to count, so that you have double-checked that everyone is present before you move off.

Ask Miranda!

Q What sort of things should I say to children before we leave the setting?

A **Remind children that they must stay in their small groups when asked to do so, and that they must not wander off at any time. Talk through your procedures for crossing roads too if this is applicable. If you will be using transport, remind children about the importance of wearing their seatbelts and not leaving the vehicle until instructed. Tell children what they should do if they do get separated from the group. This will depend largely on where you are going. Let them know that you expect them to pay attention quickly should you need to give the group further instruction while you are out. This is important in case of an emergency.**

Did you know?

Before embarking on a trip, it is wise to talk with children and staff about security. It is reassuring to know that the safety information they need is fresh in their minds.

Good practice

Children may be very excited when they arrive at their destination, so it is best to talk with them before leaving the setting. You do not want to dampen the children's good spirits, but do insist that they listen carefully to all you have to tell them. Reassure the children that the additional rules will help everyone to stay safe and enjoy the day.

Did you know?

You should plan frequent toilet stops throughout the trip. Staff should always enter public toilets with the children to keep them safe from harm.

Keeping equipment and materials safe and hygienic

You should carefully check and evaluate the condition of materials and equipment as you set it out and as it is tidied away. Worn or broken equipment or materials can pose a hazard to safety. When plastic breaks there may be sharp edges, or wood may splinter. Remove any worn or broken items from the play space, and report the condition to the appropriate person within your setting.

Some equipment or materials can be safely mended, such as a broken zip on an item of dressing-up clothes. But sometimes it is necessary to dispose of an item and replace it because it would not be safe to

attempt to mend the item. For instance, it is doubtful that a broken plastic fence from the farmyard could be mended safely, because glue strong enough to hold the fence together would not be safe to use on an object that children will play with.

You should also check that resources are in a hygienic condition. Settings will have established a schedule for washing or sterilising appropriate materials and equipment. However, you may notice that resources need cleaning in between times. (Feeding equipment, nappy-changing equipment and baby toys will need cleaning every time they are used.) The process of cleaning gives practitioners a further opportunity to check that equipment is in a safe condition.

Remember to check the condition of large pieces of equipment (which may stay in one place) and furniture too, such as chairs, tables, swings, slides, bookcases and cots.

Minimum requirements for space and staff ratios

Registered settings must meet the minimum requirements for space and staff as set out in their home country's welfare requirements or standards. In England, the welfare requirements tell us that in registered provision, providers must meet the following space requirements:

- children under 2 years: 3.5 square metres of space per child

- 2-year-olds: 2.5 square metres of space per child

- children aged 3 to 5 years: 2.3 square metres of space per child.

Worn or broken equipment or materials can pose a hazard to safety.

This ensures that settings do not become overcrowded, which would affect children's safety and well-being.

Link Up!

Unit CYP 3.4 Support children and young people's health and safety

Practical example

Stepping Stones becomes registered

Stepping Stones is a new day nursery in England, due to open in a few months' time. Today they are receiving a visit from a registration officer, who will inform them how many children they will be able to take.

She measures the floor space of the pre-school room, which will be for 3- to 5-year-olds. They will need a minimum of 2.3 square metres each. The room measures 37 metres squared, so she does the following sum: $37\,m^2 \div 2.3\,m^2 = 16.08\,m^2$. This means that the pre-school room can take up to 16 children. Next she measures the floor space in the toddler room, which will be for 2-year-olds. They will need a minimum of 2.5 square metres each. The room measures 41 metres squared, so the she does the following sum: $41\,m^2 \div 2.5\,m^2 = 16.40\,m^2$. This means that the toddler room can take up to 16 children. Lastly, she measures the baby room, which will be for children under 2 years old. They will need a minimum of 3.5 square metres each. The room measures 41 metres squared, so she does the following sum: $53\,m^2 \div 3.5\,m^2 = 15.14\,m^2$. This means the toddler room can take up to 15 children.

Question

According to the minimum staff ratios in England, how many staff will be required for a) the baby room, b) the toddler room and c) the pre-school room? (The nursery will not employ a nursery teacher.)

LEARNING OUTCOME 3

FOCUS ON

...understanding the importance of promoting positive health and well-being for early years children

Promoting children's health and well-being

There are many aspects contributing to the overall health and well-being of children, and if there are difficulties with any of these, there can be a detrimental effect.

In this section you'll learn how to promote children's health and well-being in an early years setting. You'll also learn about the roles of key health professionals and about the sources of professional advice in promoting health and well-being for early years children and their families and carers. This links with Assessment Criteria **3.1, 3.2.**

Diet

Children need a balanced diet that includes plenty of fruit and vegetables in order to be healthy and to grow and develop. You'll learn more about this in Learning Outcome 5.

Rest and sleep

Rest and sleep is extremely important for all humans, whatever their age. A good balance of restful, quiet activities and adequate stimulation (see below) is needed throughout the day, alongside sufficient night-time sleep and if required, daytime naps. Not getting enough sleep – known as 'sleep deprivation' – can have a far reaching effect. This is because sleep fulfils so many functions when the right amount is received.

Neural connections are being made in the brain while children sleep. Sleep aids the brain to process information, and also aids concentration and memory function, all of which is important to learning and development. It also seems to contribute to the formation of memories. Sleep supports a healthy immune system and the repair of damage to the body's cells – tissue damage to skin caused by UV light can also be supported via sleep. In children, human growth hormone is released during a deep sleep, and a chronic lack of sleep can affect this hormone release and disrupt growth patterns.

Lack of sleep can lead to lethargy, irritability and emotional outbursts, affecting behaviour – children who are suffering from lack of sleep are less able to control their behaviour and their impulses. Reduced immunity can lead to frequent colds and infections, and there can be an increased risk of becoming overweight. Concentration and memory are affected, and creativity and problem solving skills can be reduced, which has a further detrimental effect on learning and development.

How much sleep is enough?

Sleep patterns can vary from child to child by a matter of hours. From birth, some babies need more sleep or less sleep than others. The following list from the NHS shows the average amount of sleep that babies and children need during a 24-hour period, including daytime naps:

- 0–3 months: most newborn babies are asleep more than they are awake. Their total daily sleep varies, but can be from 8 hours, up to 16–18 hours. Babies will wake during the night because they need to be fed. Being too hot or too cold can also disturb their sleep.

- 3–6 months: as babies grow, they need fewer night feeds and are able to sleep for longer. Some babies will sleep for 8 hours or longer at night. By 4 months, they could be spending around twice as long sleeping at night as they do during the day.

- 6 months to 1 year: at this age, night feeds should no longer be necessary, and some babies will sleep for up to 12 hours at night. Teething discomfort or hunger may wake some babies during the night.

- 1 year: babies will sleep for around 12–15 hours in total.

- 2 years: most 2-year-olds will sleep for 11–12 hours at night, with one or two naps in the daytime.

- 3–5 years: most children of this age will need about 12 hours' sleep, but this can range from 8 hours up to 14. Some young children will still need a nap during the day.

Sleep fulfils many important functions.

A good sleep routine

A regular bedtime routine can really make a difference to how well children settle down for a nap or for the night. Going to bed and getting up at the same time each day programmes the brain and the internal body clock to settle into the pattern naturally. Winding down before bed in the same way each night is also helpful. Relaxing warm baths help to get the body to the optimum temperature for sleep, and cosy bedtime stories and a cuddle help children to feel safe and emotionally ready for going to sleep. Visual distractions and noise should be minimised. A dark room is preferable – black-out blinds can be used. A comfortable bed with clean bedding is also a necessity. The sleep area should also be free of hazards – a risk assessment of the area used for sleep in the setting should have been carried out to ensure there are no choking, suffocation or other safety

Winding down before bed helps children to settle down ready for sleep.

hazards. The room should be well ventilated, and kept at an appropriate temperature. Sleeping children should be checked on regularly, and precautions to prevent Sudden Infant Death Syndrome should be taken – see pages 474 and 475.

Stimulation

Children need stimulation in order for their brains to develop and for learning to take place. Free play, activities, experiences and interactions with adults and with other children all provide stimulation.

There's more about this in:
Unit EYMP 2 Promote learning and development in the early years
Unit EYMP 5 Support children's speech, language and communication

Physical activity and exercise

Physical activity and exercise is essential for all humans. It helps to keep the heart healthy, and strengthens the lungs, muscles and bones, while simultaneously helping children to learn and consolidate physical skills.

You'll learn more about this in Unit EYMP 2 Promote learning and development in the early years and Unit CYPOP 2 Care for the physical and nutritional needs of babies and young children

Ask Miranda!

Q What do I do if a child is very tired, but his parent has asked me not to put him down for a nap, or he won't sleep through the night?

A Situations like this can be difficult to handle, and it's extremely helpful if a setting has guidelines in place to clarify what should be done. The effects of sleep deprivation are real and unpleasant for children, and it can be argued that not allowing a tired child to go to sleep is abusive. It certainly goes against the grain for many practitioners and experts, who feel that in this position it is up to them to exercise their duty of care and put the child down for a nap if it is in the child's best interests at the time. The situation would then be explained later to the parent. Many hope that Ofsted may eventually clarify that children's right to sleep should be given priority over a parent's wish for them to remain awake.

A safe environment

All children need a safe, hygienic and secure environment. Children who grow up in homes where this is not provided will be at an increased risk of illness and accident. As you learnt in Learning Outcome 1, the welfare requirements of your home country exist to ensure that settings provide an environment that supports children's health, safety and well-being. This includes the provision of adequate space, ventilation and temperature. (Temperature indoors should be kept at 18–21°C. Sleep rooms for babies should be kept at 16–20°C, as becoming too hot, especially when sleeping, is a risk factor for Sudden Infant Death Syndrome. Ventilation is important because it helps to prevent the spread of airborne infections.)

This subject links with your learning in Unit CYP 3.4 Support children and young people's health and safety

Natural light and fresh air

Although children should be protected from the sun during the summer (see Learning Outcome 6), sunlight on the skin is an important source of vitamin D for children, and it's good for them to play outside in the weaker sunshine of the cooler months. Light also influences the way in which our bodies regulate hormones, and this has an impact on our sleeping patterns and mood. Also, the air outside is more oxygenated. It's healthy for children to have opportunities to play outside and

Sunlight on the skin is an important source of vitamin D for children.

to breathe fresh air, ideally on a daily basis. Fresh air seems to help children to eat and sleep well – this is often said to be true even of babies who have been taken out for a walk in their pram.

Think about how your own moods may be affected by light. How often have you felt a spring in your step when you wake up to a sunny winter morning after a string of grey days?

Health surveillance

The term 'health surveillance' can be explained as close supervision or observations that are primarily carried out to detect any problems with a child or young person's development, with the aim of getting them the appropriate support and/or treatment early on. Health visitors and the primary health care team have local responsibilities to manage limited resources, including the caseloads of workers. To help them, they may identify target groups of people who are likely to benefit most from health surveillance. These may include:

- families living in bed and breakfast accommodation
- families living in poor housing
- families living in poverty
- families dealing with a bereavement
- families within which a previous child died from Sudden Infant Death Syndrome (SIDS)
- very young parents
- parents who are isolated – they may have little or no support from other adults, have emotional difficulties (mental health difficulties), or experience cultural, linguistic or environmental barriers (if they are disabled)
- parents having difficulty relating to their child or

understanding their needs, particularly with their first child

■ parents with low self-esteem and/or confidence, particularly with their first child

■ where there are concerns that abuse may take place within a family.

Unit EYMP 2 Promote learning and development in the early years
Unit EYMP 5 Support children's speech, language and communication

Personal hygiene

Good personal hygiene is necessary to prevent disease and the spread of infection, and to prevent sore areas developing on the skin and scalp. A lack of personal hygiene also leads to an unpleasant smell. You'll learn more about meeting children's personal care needs in Learning Outcome 6.

Love, attention and stability

Being loved and shown attention impacts on children's emotional well-being and sense of security, just as it does on your own. It is also linked to children's levels of self-esteem and their own self-image. When they are missing the love and attention shown to them by the key people in their lives, children can become unhappy, and even depressed. Children who are not shown love and attention and who are suffering neglect will 'fail to thrive'. There's more about this in Unit CYP 3.3. As you learned in Unit CYP 3.7, the key worker system enables settings to meet the attachment needs of young children when they are away from their families. You may like to recap this information as part of your study towards this unit.

Unit CYP 3.3 Understand how to safeguard the well-being of children and young people
Unit CYP 3.7 Understand how to support positive outcomes for children and young people

Key aspects of health and well-being are summarised on the diagram on page 370.

Roles of key health professionals

A number of health professionals support and promote the health and well-being of children:

■ **Doctors: general practitioners (GPs) and paediatricians**
A GP surgery provides a range of health care, and the GP is often the first port of call for parents when their child has a health problem. GPs are trained to see the scope of a patient's symptoms, then to pinpoint a cause. They will treat the problem if possible, or refer patients to a specialist who has trained intensively in the area of the problem. Doctors based in hospitals who specialise in treating children with health problems are called paediatricians.

■ **Health visitor**
A health visitor supports and educates parents on preventative services such as immunisation, child nutrition, minor illness, behaviour issues and child development. Also see pages 177 and 256.

■ **School nurse**
School nurses work in partnership with a school, monitoring health and promoting healthy living to school-aged children. They also respond to the needs of individual children.

■ **Dentist**
Dentists provide preventive and restorative treatments for problems that affect the mouth and teeth.

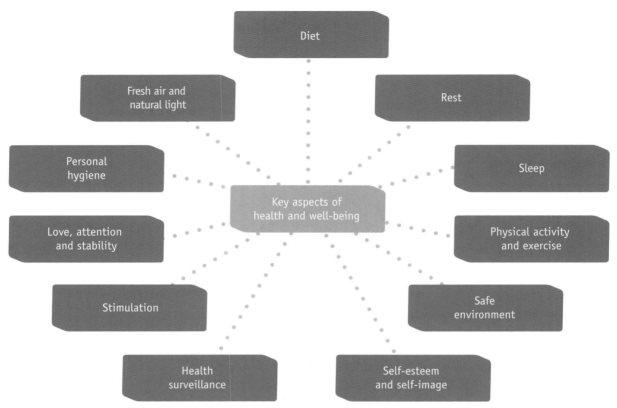

Key aspects of health and well-being.

- **Optometrist**
  Optometrists examine eyes, test sight, advise on visual problems and prescribe and fit glasses or contact lenses when needed.

- **Orthoptist**
  An orthoptist investigates, diagnoses and treats sight-related problems and abnormalities of eye movement and eye position, including lazy eye and squints.

- **Physiotherapist**
  Physiotherapists help children with physical problems caused by illness, injury or medical conditions to achieve increased movement and coordination.

- **Speech and language therapists**
  Speech and language therapists assess and treat speech, language and communication problems to enable children to communicate to the best of their ability. Also see page 256.

Good practice

Experienced practitioners can be a valuable source of general advice for parents and carers, particularly about practicalities such as effective night-time routines. However, it is important that all practitioners are aware of the limitations of the role. If there are problems with health or well-being, practitioners must refer parents to the appropriate professional, just as a GP would do. Always remember that your role is NOT to diagnose medical problems. In the early years, it's probably most common to recommend that families visit their GP or consult their health visitor.

- **Audiologist**

  Audiologists measure children's hearing levels. They also assess, diagnose and rehabilitate patients with hearing, balance and tinnitus problems.

- **Dieticians**

  Dieticians provide nutritional advice to enable families to make informed and practical choices about food and lifestyle, in both health and disease.

- **Psychologists**

  Child psychologists have a special interest in the issues and problems faced by children. They frequently work with children who have learning difficulties and/or behavioural difficulties. Educational psychologists work with children of school age, mainly children who experience problems brought about by events or stresses related to or affecting schooling. Also see page 256.

Sources of professional advice

All of the key professionals described above are a source of advice and health support for children and families. But as mentioned above, the first port of call will often be the GP, who will refer families on as necessary.

Practical example

Immunisation advice

You are working as a childminder in your own home. One of the parents wants to talk to you about the MMR vaccination (measles, mumps and rubella). She's unsure whether or not she should take her daughter to her upcoming appointment for immunisation because she's concerned about the possible adverse effects on health. She's done some reading, but opinion seems to be divided. She asks what you think – should her child get the injection?

Questions

Would it be appropriate for you to give your opinion in these circumstances? Which health professional/s would it be appropriate to refer the parent on to?

LEARNING OUTCOME 4

FOCUS ON

...being able to support hygiene and prevention of cross-infection in the early years setting

Keeping settings clean and hygienic

All areas of settings must be kept clean and hygienic at all times. Jobs such as hoovering, sweeping and mopping floors should be carried out at the end of each day, before the setting up of activities and resources for the following day. It's also important to dust regularly – this is often done with a damp

In this section you'll learn how to keep equipment and each area of the setting clean and hygienic. You'll also learn about preventing cross-infection and how to prepare and store food, formula and breast milk safely. This links with Assessment Criteria **4.1**, **4.2**, **4.3**.

cloth to prevent dust flying around as it is a common allergen for those with asthma. Attention should be played to skirting boards, which can be dust traps and are in the reach of children.

You should follow your setting's full procedures for keeping the environment clean and hygienic. However, some special considerations for key areas are outlined on the table on page 373. Also see 'Keeping equipment and materials safe and hygienic' in Learning Outcome 2.

Preventing cross-infection

Good standards of hygiene are the key to preventing disease and the spread of infection. Cross-infection occurs when germs are passed from one affected person or material, to another, previously unaffected person or material. Settings should have written guidelines covering the prevention of cross-infection through the safe handling of body fluids (blood, urine, faeces and saliva), and other waste. This is necessary because waste products are a source of germs. An example of this is the risk of infection from blood-borne viruses. This includes hepatitis B, hepatitis C and HIV (Human Immunodeficiency Virus).

Hand-washing guide from the NHS 'Clean your hands' campaign.

Did you know?

We wash our hands regularly as part of cross-infection control. One of the most effective measures you can take is to ensure that you wash them thoroughly each time, and teach children and young people to do the same. The following diagram is from the NHS 'Clean your hands' campaign.

Good practice

It is recommended that all practitioners become immunised against hepatitis B. This entails three injections given in the arm. There is currently no vaccine against HIV or hepatitis C. However, the viruses can only be transmitted through an exchange of body fluids. Such an exchange could happen within a setting – if an affected person's blood made contact with a practitioner's blood, through a cut or graze on the practitioner's hand, for example. But if you follow good practice guidelines and take sensible precautions, you will not need to be overly anxious. Also see the 'Reflective Practice' activity on page 557, which focuses on evaluating your practice in regards to preventing cross-infection.

Table EYMP 3.1: Special considerations for how to keep key areas clean and hygienic

Area	Special considerations
Kitchen	Food storage, preparation and cooking facilities, equipment and utensils must be kept scrupulously clean – this includes cookers, microwaves and fridges. Work surfaces to be wiped with a disinfectant spray before and after each use. Cloths to be kept scrupulously clean and to be replaced as necessary. Separate equipment and utensils to be used for raw meat (e.g. dedicated chopping board and knife). See also 'handling waste' below.
Toilet/bathroom areas	To be cleaned daily with a disinfectant agent, which should be rinsed/wiped off after use in areas accessible to children. In between times, areas should be cleaned as necessary – toilets and sinks may both need attention during the day. Also see 'handling waste' below.
Play rooms	A cover should be used for floors and tables to protect them during messy play and activities, and to make cleaning up afterwards easier. All traces of paint, modelling clay, cooking ingredients, etc. should be cleaned away without delay when play/activities are finished. Tables, etc. should be wiped daily at the end of the session before resources are set up again for the next play session. Also see 'handling waste' below.
Eating areas	Tables should be wiped with a disinfectant spray before and after each use. The floor should be cleaned as appropriate after each meal/snack, to remove food remains.
Sleep rooms	Cots, beds, mattresses and bedding should be kept clean and hygienic at all times, with bedding changed in between each child. If a child wets or soils a cot or bed, it must be fully cleaned with disinfectant, which should then be wiped/rinsed off.
Outside areas	Playgrounds and paths should be swept regularly, and hosed down as necessary. Lawns should be well cared for. Following a daily visual check, any inappropriate matter (e.g. animal faeces, berries dropped by birds, litter) must be disposed of safely and the area cleaned with disinfectant if appropriate.

If taps cannot be turned off with the arm as shown in the Handwashing guide on page 372, it's advised that if possible you cover your hand with a paper towel when turning them off, to avoid recontamination from germs.

Handling waste

When dealing with waste you should ensure that:

- there are designated areas for covered bins

- there are covered bins kept specifically for different types of waste, including waste items containing body fluids and domestic waste

- items containing body waste, such as nappies, dressings and used gloves are disposed of in a sealed bag, which is placed into a sealed bin for disposal

- bins are emptied daily

- you always put on disposable latex gloves before dealing with any body fluids, and before you begin first aid treatment. You may also wear a disposable apron. Wash your hands well with antiseptic soap afterwards (and before you approach a first aid casualty if possible)

- you cover any cuts or grazes on your hands with a waterproof dressing

- you cover blood with a 1 per cent hypochlorite solution before wiping it up

- teach children and young people good hygiene procedures – make sure that they wash hands after going to the toilet and before eating or preparing food. Teach them to cover their mouths and noses when they cough and sneeze, and make sure they dispose of tissues in the bin. Adults must do these things too! Make sure that you wash your hands with antiseptic soap after wiping a child's nose.

Babies and young children

Information about maintaining cleanliness and hygiene for babies and young children is given in Unit CYPOP 2.

Unit CYPOP 2 Care for the physical and nutritional needs of babies and young children

Food hygiene

Food hygiene is essential for the prevention of food poisoning. Those handling or preparing food should attend a course about food hygiene, gaining a Basic Food Hygiene certificate. Essentially, you should ensure that food is stored safely, prepared and cooked safely, and that food areas are kept hygienically. You should wash your hands with antiseptic soap before and after handling food. Food storage guidelines are as follows:

- Keep the fridge and freezer cold enough. Use a thermometer to check. Fridges should be below 4°C, and freezers −18°C maximum. They must be cleaned/defrosted regularly.

- Cool food quickly before placing in the fridge.

- Cover food stored, or wrap with cling-film.

- Label items with a correct use-by date if necessary.

- Separate raw and cooked food – store raw food at the bottom of the fridge, and cooked food higher up, so that raw juices (should they spill) will not contaminate cooked food.

- If food has started to thaw, never refreeze it.

- Ensure that food is fully thawed before cooking.

Food preparation guidelines are as follows:

- use waterproof dressings to cover any cuts or grazes on hands

- do not cough or sneeze over food

- wear protective clothing (such as an apron) that is only used for food preparation

Cover food stored, or wrap with cling-film.

- cook food thoroughly – cook eggs until firm and cook meat all the way through

- test chicken to check that it is cooked properly

- do not reheat food.

Food preparation area guidelines are as follows:

- Keep all areas of the kitchen scrupulously clean. Use a bin with a lid and empty it daily. Keep bins away from food. Disinfect them regularly.

- Keep all kitchen appliances and utensils scrupulously clean, including ovens and microwaves.

- Keep kitchen cloths and other cloths separate, and keep them scrupulously clean.

- Tea towels, cloths and oven gloves must be washed/boiled frequently.

- Disposable towels should be used to clear up spills and to dry hands.

- Keep insects and pets out of the kitchen.

- Do not allow anyone who is unwell to prepare food or enter food preparation areas. This is particularly hazardous when someone has had diarrhoea or vomiting.

Babies and young children

Information about preparing and storing food and milk for babies and young children is given in Unit CYPOP 2, Learning Outcome 5.

▶▶▶**Link Up!**◀◀◀

Unit CYPOP 2 Care for the physical and nutritional needs of babies and young children

LEARNING OUTCOME 5

FOCUS ON

...understanding how to ensure that children in their early years receive high-quality, balanced nutrition to meet their growth and development needs

In this section you'll learn how to identify and plan balanced meals, snacks and drinks for children in their early years and why it is important to follow carers' instructions in respect of their child's food allergies or intolerances. You'll also learn about methods of educating children and adults in food management. This links with Assessment Criteria **5.1, 5.2, 5.3, 5.4.**

Healthy eating and nutrition guidelines

Food and water is the body's fuel. Without it, humans literally cannot keep going – they die. The body must have a combination of different nutrients to be healthy. This is especially important during childhood when the body is growing and developing. Large quantities of the protein, fat, carbohydrates and water (see the diagrams on the following pages) are found in our food and drink.

However, only small quantities of vitamins, minerals and fibre are present.

Consequently, it is most common for vitamins, minerals and fibre to be missing from children's diets. Vitamins and minerals are needed for healthy growth, development and normal functioning of the body. Water

Proteins provide material for:
• growth of the body
• repair of the body.

Types of proteins:
• **Animal** – first-class or complete proteins, supply all ten of the essential amino acids
• **Vegetable** – second-class or incomplete proteins, supply some of the ten essential amino acids.

FOODS CONTAINING PROTEINS

Examples of protein foods include:
• **Animal proteins** – meat, fish, chicken, eggs, dairy foods
• **Vegetable proteins** – nuts, seeds pulses, cereals.

Protein foods are made up of amino acids. There are ten essential amino acids.

Foods containing proteins.

Carbohydrates provide:

- energy
- warmth.

Types of carbohydrates:

- sugars
- starches.

**FOODS CONTAINING
CARBOHYDRATES**

Examples of carbohydrate foods include:

- **Sugars** – fruit, honey, sweets, beet sugar, cane sugar
- **Starches** – potatoes, cereals, beans, pasta.

Foods containing carbohydrates.

Carbohydrates are broken down into glucose before the body can use them. **Sugars** are quickly converted and are a quick source of energy. **Starches** take longer to convert so they provide a longer-lasting supply of energy.

Fats:

- provide energy and warmth
- store fat-soluble vitamins
- make food pleasant to eat.

Types of fats:

- saturated
- unsaturated
- polyunsaturates.

**FOODS
CONTAINING FAT**

Examples of foods containing fat include:

- **Saturated fat** – butter, cheese, meat, palm oil
- **Unsaturated** – olive oil, peanut oil
- **Polyunsaturated** – oily fish, corn oil, sunflower oil.

Foods containing fat.

Saturated fats are solid at room temperature and come mainly from animal fats.
Unsaturated and polyunsaturated fats are liquid at room temperature and come mainly from vegetable and fish oils.

contains some minerals, but primarily it maintains fluid in the cells of the body and in the bloodstream. Fibre adds roughage to food. This encourages the body to pass out the waste products of food after it has been digested, by stimulating the bowel muscles.

The charts and tables on pages 377–8 explain the sources and functions of nutrients.

A regular supply of water-soluble vitamins is needed as these cannot be stored in the body. Fat-soluble vitamins can be stored in the body, but intake should still be regular.

Too much salt can be bad for children. The **maximum** amount children should be having depends on their age:

- 1–3 years – 2 g a day (0.8 g sodium)
- 4–6 years – 3 g a day (1.2 g sodium)
- 7–10 years – 5 g a day (2 g sodium)
- 11 years upwards – 6 g a day (2.4 g sodium).

You should never add salt to children's food during or after preparation, and if buying processed foods, check the salt information on the labels (see below) and choose those with less salt content. Nuts are considered a choking hazard for young children, and they are a common cause of food allergy. Consequently, many settings have introduced a 'no nut policy'. They do not use nuts or nut products, and children may not bring them in even for their own consumption.

Traffic lights labelling system

The Food Standards Agency traffic lights system allows us to see the nutritional content of commercially produced foods. The aim is to help us to make more healthy choices easily and quickly, for ourselves and for children. The amount of fat, sugar, saturates and salt per serving is shown in grams, and a corresponding traffic light colour lets us know whether this amount is considered high (red), medium (amber) or low (green). The amount of calories will also be shown. The estimated average of calories required each day is shown in the table on page 379.

Table EYMP 3.2: The main vitamins

Vitamin	Purpose	Foods
A Fat-soluble. Pregnant women must avoid too much vitamin A	Maintenance of good vision and healthy skin. Promotes normal growth and development. Deficiency may lead to skin and vision problems.	Carrots, tomatoes, eggs, butter, cheese
B Water-soluble. Very regular intake required	Promotes healthy functioning of the nerves and the muscles. Deficiency may lead to anaemia and wasting of the muscles.	Meat, fish, green vegetables. Some breakfast cereals are fortified with vitamin B (it is added to them)
C Water-soluble. Daily intake required	Maintenance of healthy tissue and skin. Deficiency leads to a decreased resistance to infection, and can result in scurvy.	Fruit. Oranges and blackcurrants have a high vitamin C content
D Fat-soluble	Maintenance of bones and teeth. Assists body growth. Deficiency in children may lead to bones that do not harden sufficiently (skeletal condition known as rickets). Also leads to tooth decay.	Oily fish and fish oil, egg yolk Milk and margarines are fortified with vitamin D. Sunlight on the skin can cause the body to produce vitamin D
E Fat-soluble	Promotes blood clotting, healing and metabolism. Deficiency may result in delayed blood clotting.	Cereals, egg yolk, seeds, nuts, vegetable oils
K Fat-soluble	Promotes healing. Necessary for blood clotting. Deficiency may lead to excessive bleeding due to delayed blood clotting. Vitamin K is normally given to babies after birth as deficiency is sometimes seen in newborns, although rare in adults.	Whole grains, green vegetables, liver

Table EYMP 3.3: The main minerals

Mineral	Purpose	Foods
Calcium	Required for growth of teeth and bones. Also necessary for nerve and muscle function. Works with vitamin D. Deficiency may lead to rickets and tooth decay.	Milk, cheese, eggs, fish, pulses, whole grain cereals. White and brown flour are fortified with calcium
Fluoride	Maintenance of healthy bones and protection from tooth decay.	Present in water in varying quantities. May be added to water. Many toothpastes contain fluoride
Iodine	Used to make the thyroid hormone. Also required for normal neurological development. Deficiency may lead to thyroid problems.	Dairy products, sea foods, vegetables, water. Salt is fortified with iodine
Iron	Essential for the formation of haemoglobin in the red blood cells, which transport oxygen around the body. Deficiency may lead to anaemia. Vitamin C helps the absorption of iron.	Meat, eggs, green vegetables, dried fruits
Phosphorus Babies must not have a high intake as can be harmful.	Promotes the formation of teeth and bones.	Meat, fish, vegetables, eggs, fruit
Potassium	Essential for water balance in the body. Also promotes functioning of cells, including the nerves.	A wide range of foods
Sodium chloride Salt must not be added to food for babies or young children during food preparation or at the table.	Essential for water balance in the body. Involved in energy utilisation and nerve function.	Salt, meat, fish, bread, processed food

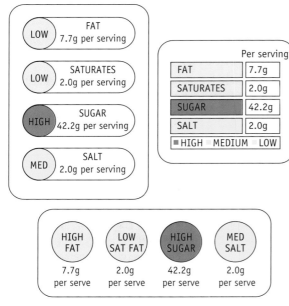

Examples of traffic lights labelling from www.eatwell.gov.uk/foodlabels/trafficlights.

Specific dietary requirements

When a child is registered with a setting, it is important for practitioners to find out whether the child has any specific dietary requirements so that they can meet the child's needs while still promoting a healthy diet.

Food has a spiritual significance within some cultures, religions and ethnic groups, which may mean that certain foods cannot be eaten or that food should be prepared in a particular way. Others make decisions about food based on personal beliefs. It is important that practitioners respect and comply with parental wishes. Individual people vary in terms of the dietary codes or restrictions that they follow. You should never assume that you will be able to tell what a child may or may not eat from their religion – always find out directly from the family. However, in general terms, the table on page 379 gives some helpful guidance.

Table EYMP 3.4: The estimated average of calories required each day

Age	Daily calorie intake for males	Daily calorie intake for females
1–3	1,230	1,165
4–6	1,715	1,545
7–10	1,970	1,740
11–14	2,220	1,845
15–18	2,755	2,110
Adults	2,550	1,940

Vegetarian diets

The lacto-ovo-vegetarian diet excludes meat but includes milk, milk products and eggs. The lacto-vegetarian diet also excludes eggs. The semi-vegetarian diet eliminates some meat, often red meat, but may include poultry and fish.

Did you know?

Some families follow ethical or environmentally aware diets. This means that they consider where food has come from and the conditions from which it has come. For example, a parent may buy local food because of the lower carbon footprint, or Fairtrade foods to support those in poorer nations; or, as is increasingly common, organic produce may be used whenever possible.

Vegan diets

These generally exclude all foods of animal origin including meat, milk and milk products, honey, and additives made from animal products, such as gelatine.

Food allergies and intolerances

Some children have food allergies, intolerances or medical conditions that mean their diets have to be restricted. This can be caused by an allergic response, diabetes or an enzyme deficiency. Common allergens include nuts and milk. Some children may need to

Table EYMP 3.5: Cultural food

Group	Principles
Christians	May give up certain foods for Lent.
Jews	May not eat pork or shellfish. May not cook or eat milk and meat products together. May use different sets of crockery and cutlery for milk products and meat products. May only eat meat and poultry prepared by a kosher butcher. May fast for Yom Kippur (Day of Atonement).
Rastafarians	May be vegetarian. May not eat food from the vine. May only eat 'Ital' foods – those in a whole and natural state. May not eat processed or preserved foods.
Muslims	May not eat pork or pork products. Children may be breast-fed until the age of two years. Families may fast between sunrise and sunset during Ramadan, so they may rise early to eat at these times. Children under 12 do not generally fast. May drink no alcohol.
Sikhs	May be vegetarian or eat only chicken, lamb and fish. May fast regularly or just on the first day of Punjabi month.
Hindus	May eat no beef or be vegetarian. During festivals may eat only pure foods such as fruit and yoghurt. May drink no alcohol.

eat at certain times of the day. They might take medication daily or they may have medication to take if they show symptoms of their condition or if you become aware that they have eaten, or in the case of some children even touched, a food they should not have. (The issues relating to this and your setting's policy for administering medication should have been discussed at the time of the child's enrolment.) Often, time is of the essence in these situations. Practitioners must ensure that they are absolutely clear about what to do for the individual child, and they must know how to recognise their symptoms. The following guidance in this section applies to all dietary requirements, but in the case of children with allergies and illnesses it can save a life.

It is *very important* to ensure that you fully understand children's dietary requirements so that you efficiently meet their needs without

Diabetes UK provides support for parents and practitioners caring for children with diabetes. They have produced resources to help children in the early years to learn about the condition. Have a look online and learn more yourself too at **www.diabetes.org.uk**

Coeliac disease is triggered by gluten, which is contained in wheat, rye and barley. Children with coelic disease must follow a gluten-free diet. You can learn more about the condition and access gluten-free recipes at **www.coeliac.org.uk**

error. Practitioners should ensure that full details are recorded on the registration form. They must communicate children's requirements to everyone involved in caring for the child. A list of requirements should be displayed in the kitchen and eating area to remind all staff. These lists must be updated regularly so that they can be safely relied upon. *Never give a child food or drink without checking*. This also applies to raw cooking ingredients or food used in play that is not intended for consumption.

Encouraging healthy eating

It is good practice to make children aware of healthy foods and how good these are for their bodies. This establishes the link between food and health. It is generally considered appropriate to make children aware that no foods are completely unacceptable, but that sugary foods (such as sweets and many drinks)

and those that are high in saturated fats (such as cakes) should be regarded as occasional treats. The diagram on page 381 shows how you can encourage children of various ages to eat healthily.

Planning menus

When planning menus, including snacks and drinks, it is important to consider:

- the nutritional balance needed by children for a healthy diet, including the required calorie intake (What have children eaten for their previous meal/snack, and what will they have next? Always consider this across the day, and ideally across the week.)

- the current Government guidelines, including five servings of fruit/vegetables a day

- the time of day the food will be consumed

- children's individual dietary requirements and allergies

- children's preferences

- variety

- offering children new and interesting foods to try

- involving children (page 381)

- how food will be presented to add interest (page 381)

- how families can be consulted.

If children are reluctant to try something new, or they do not like new food, practitioners are advised to simply remove it and offer an alternative. However, do present the food again on another occasion – some children change their minds once a food is familiar to them. If not, once again, do not make a fuss. Our tastes for food change throughout our lives – we go off things, or suddenly start to enjoy a taste. The child may enjoy the food at some point in the future. Not making a fuss about food is a good general rule – battling with children over food is unproductive, and

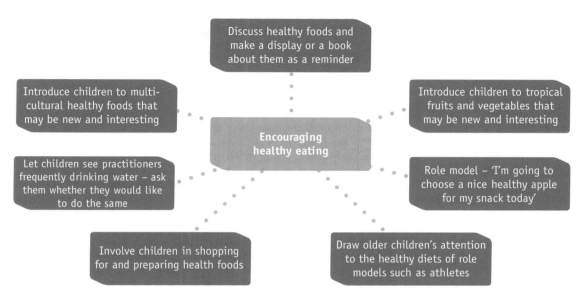

Encouraging healthy eating.

the child may come to dread mealtimes, which is not a very positive sign. If children regularly refuse food, not offering food outside of mealtimes can be the solution. If you are concerned about a child's eating habits, talk to their parents or carers to agree a way forward. Dieticians will advise if necessary. Also see 'Food management' and the advice given by the Food Standards Agency shown on page 382.

Presenting food attractively

In group settings, mealtimes can feel hectic unless practitioners plan well. It is good practice to present food attractively to children and this can be achieved by setting the table pleasantly, having all the right utensils in place, and a creating a calm atmosphere – quiet, gentle music playing in the background can help to settle children at lunchtime after a busy morning. Consider how much food you put on children's plates. You do not want children to go hungry, but too much food can be overwhelming and put a child off. Consider how the food looks. Sometimes reluctant eaters can be intrigued if you present their food in a new creative way. For instance, there is nothing wrong with standing carrot batons up in mashed potato or making a tower out of sliced carrot – especially if it means the carrots are eaten!

Involving children in the planning and preparation of food

Involving children in the planning and preparation of food is a good way to ensure that you are providing things they like and it is a good opportunity to discuss healthy foods. Children are often much keener to eat food they have helped to prepare. Children are even more eager when they have grown vegetables themselves. Even settings without access to a garden can grow herbs and cress in pots. Children can help in many ways depending on their age, including by:

- washing fruit

- scrubbing vegetables

- cutting fruit (soft fruits such as bananas can be easily cut or mashed with children's knives)

- putting spread on bread or toast

- making sandwiches

- preparing salad

- growing vegetables

- harvesting vegetables

- mixing drinks

Children need a healthy, balanced diet, which is rich in fruit, vegetables and starchy foods.

Encourage your child to choose a variety of foods to help ensure that they obtain the wide range of nutrients they need to stay healthy.

Remember to include these sorts of foods:

- Milk, cheese, yoghurt, soya beans, tofu and nuts are rich in calcium, which is needed for healthy bones and teeth.
- Fortified breakfast cereals, margarine and oily fish are good sources of dietary vitamin D, which helps ensure a good supply of calcium in the blood and therefore healthy bones. The main source of vitamin D is from the action of sunlight on skin, but avoid strong sun especially around midday when there is a risk of burning.
- Meat, particularly red meat, and fish are rich sources of iron. Pulses (beans and lentils), green vegetables and fortified breakfast cereals are also good sources of iron. Iron is needed for healthy blood and research has shown that some children have low intakes of iron, particularly older girls.
- At least two portions of fish a week, because fish are a good source of protein, vitamins and minerals and they are low in saturated fat. Oily fish, such as mackerel, salmon and sardines, also contain omega 3 fatty acids. You can give boys up to four portions of oily fish a week, but it's best to give girls no more than two portions of oily fish a week.
- Citrus fruit (such as oranges and lemons), tomatoes and potatoes, are all good sources of vitamin C, which is essential for health. Vitamin C may help the absorption of iron, so having fruit juice with an iron-rich meal could increase iron absorption.
- Milk, margarine with added vitamins, green vegetables and carrots are all good sources of vitamin A, which is important for good vision and healthy skin.

Avoid giving children shark, swordfish and marlin. This is because these fish contain relatively high levels of mercury, which might affect a child's developing nervous system.

Drinks

- Cartons of fruit juice are extremely convenient, but like dried fruit, are high in sugar and should be eaten at mealtimes.
- Sweet drinks also damage the teeth, especially if drunk frequently or sipped from a bottle over long periods between meals.
- So, keep drinks such as fruit juices or squashes to mealtimes, and try to encourage your child to drink water or milk in between.

Foods to limit
Sweets and snacks

Eating sweet and sticky foods frequently between meals causes dental decay. Snack foods such as cakes, biscuits, chocolate and sweets can be high in sugar and saturated fat, and low in certain vitamins and minerals. So if your child does eat these sorts of foods:

- try to make sure they eat them only occasionally or in small amounts, so they only make up a relatively small part of the overall diet
- help and encourage your child to clean their teeth every day
- try picking a weekly sweet day, or choose the weekends as a time when your child is allowed to eat sweets
- check the label and choose those options lower in fat, saturated fat, sugars and salt.

Advice from the Food Standards Agency.

- pouring out drinks

- sharing out food

- setting the table

- washing the dishes.

Food management

It's important for both practitioners and parents and carers to think about food management for the children in their care.

It's not just what children eat that matters, it's the portions that they have. Portion control is important because if children eat too much food they will become overweight, even if the food they are eating is generally healthy, and this has health implications. However, if children don't eat large enough portions, they won't get sufficient nutrients from their food, and they will become undernourished. It can be easy to forget about the calories that are contained in healthy drinks – juices and smoothies in particular – so remember to factor these in.

If there's concern that a child is eating too much or too little, it can help to keep a food journal for a few days. Feeding a child as usual, parents and practitioners keep track of the food and portion sizes given to them (you can weigh food if necessary) on a meal-by-meal, snack-by-snack basis. The calorific content can then be worked out by referring to food labels and calorie tables. If food portions are too large or small, this can then be tackled (see below). Adults may need to weigh food out once or twice, so they can see exactly what size a portion should be.

Tackling underweight and overweight children

Parents often find it difficult to recognise when their child's weight is not how it should be in the early years, particularly if children are overweight. This could be because the physique of a healthy toddler is generally thicker set than that of children aged 3 years and over. By the age of 4, a healthy weight for a child will usually be a slim build. If a practitioner is concerned about a child's weight in proportion to their height, this can be sensitively raised with parents, so that professional advice can be sought.

Food phobias

You've learned how important it is to take a low-key approach to food and to stay relaxed about mealtimes to avoid turning them into a battleground. However, while many children will have strong preferences and be determined about what they will and will not eat (or even try), others may take this a step further and become worried or distressed about food and/or mealtimes.

Involve children in the preparation of food.

Good practice

If there are concerns about weight in the early years, children should not be made aware of them. If children become stressed, anxious or feel guilty about what they do or do not eat, psychological issues with food can develop or become apparent later. In a worst-case scenario, they may last throughout life.

There can be several reasons for this, but experts have been reporting increasing concerns that even very young children may be picking up and reacting to adult anxieties about becoming or being overweight themselves. This demonstrates that it is important for parents and carers to role model positive attitudes to food and weight.

Did you know?

If there is a concern about a child developing a phobia, a visit to the doctor will be the first step to accessing help.

LEARNING OUTCOME 6

FOCUS ON

...being able to provide physical care for children

In this section you'll learn how to care for skin, hair, teeth and the nappy area in a respectful manner tailored to individual needs. You'll also learn how to meet the preferences of parents and carers, and about procedures that protect babies, children and practitioners when providing personal care needs. This links with Assessment Criteria **6.1, 6.2, 6.3.**

Skin and hair care

The skin and hair need to be kept clean to prevent disease and the spread of infection. If they are not washed regularly, dead skin cells and bacteria on sweat cause an unpleasant smell, and sore areas develop on the skin and scalp. Good hygiene practices include:

- Children should have a daily bath or shower. If this is not possible, a thorough wash should be given instead. Care should be taken to ensure that children are properly washed and dried in their skin creases and between their toes (to prevent dryness and skin cracks). Children must learn to wash their bottoms last for hygiene reasons. For younger children, these showers/baths/washes should ideally be taken at the end of the day, as children become dirty during play. The skin should be observed for soreness/rashes.

- Hair should be washed three times a week or more frequently if families prefer. Shampoo should be thoroughly rinsed out with clean water, until the water runs clear. Wet hair should be combed not brushed, to prevent hair shafts from breaking.

- Hands and face should be washed each morning.

- Hands should be washed after toileting, after

messy play and before eating, drinking or touching food.

- Nails should be kept short by cutting straight across. This should be done as necessary to stop dirt from accumulating beneath the nails.

For information on bathing and topping and tailing babies, see Unit CYPOP 2, Learning Outcome 1.

Unit CYPOP 2 Care for the physical and nutritional needs of babies and young children

Head lice

Most children get head lice at some time during childhood. They are most common in children between 4 to 11 years old, although anyone can catch them, including practitioners! Head lice are tiny wingless insects of a grey-brown colour. They are only 3mm long when fully grown, and are spread by head-to-head contact when they climb from the hair of an infected person to the hair of someone else.

The life cycle of head lice

A female lays eggs, so tiny they are hard to see, by cementing them to hairs usually near the root. Around 7 to 10 days later, baby lice hatch. The eggshells – called nits – remain in place. Nits will glisten white and become more noticeable.

Head lice bite the scalp and feed by sucking blood. After 6 to 10 days, a louse is fully grown and can transfer from head to head. From 7 days old, females who have mated can start to lay eggs. So to stop head lice spreading, they must be removed from a child's head before the sixth day after hatching.

Getting rid of head lice

Various medicated lotions are available over the counter – pharmacists can provide advice. Lice can be removed by wet-combing, using a specially designed head lice comb, also available from pharmacies.

Differing care needs preferences

Families will have differing preferences about how their children's care needs are met, from the timings of the daily routine (e.g. whether a child bathes in the morning or the evening, or how often hair is washed) to which toiletries are selected. Sometimes these differences may be based on cultural or religious practices. Care needs should be met in a way that reflects the requirements of individual children, as long this does not compromise the welfare of children.

Differences based on culture

For example:

- Muslim children and some Hindu and Sikh children may to be taught to use the right hand for eating and the left hand for matters of personal hygiene. They may also learn to wash their hands before prayer.

- Some Jewish boys may wear a skull cap (known as a *kippah*).

- Muslim girls may be required to keep their heads, hair and legs covered.

- Rastafarian girls may wear a headscarf, and boys may wear a hat (a tam) over dreadlocks.

- Some Jewish and Christian groups require girls to wear headscarves.

- Sikh boys may not have their hair cut when they are young, but have it plaited around their head. Next they may put their hair in a *jura* (similar to a bun) covered by cloth. When they become teenagers, they may wear a turban.

Differences based on ethnicity

Children will also require different care depending on their skin colour or type and the type and texture of their hair. For instance:

- It is important to note that all skin types need to be protected from the sun. It is sometimes thought that black skin does not need protection – but this is *not* the case.

- Dry skin needs to be moisturised with lotions or oils. These may be massaged in or added to bath water. Black skin may have a tendency to be dry.

- Very curly hair or thick hair that is difficult to comb out may need to be treated with conditioners after shampooing. A wide-toothed comb with rounded ends should be used for combing out.

- Curly black hair may need to be treated daily with oil that is massaged in. This prevents dryness and reduces breakage of the hair shafts. A wide-toothed comb with rounded ends should be used for combing out. This type of hair can have a tendency to pull out from the root. Care must be taken when combing or when styling the hair into braids, bunches and so on.

Care of the nappy area

Full details on care of the nappy area, types of nappies and changing nappies can be found in Unit CYPOP 2, Learning Outcome 2.

Unit CYPOP 2 Care for the physical and nutritional needs of babies and young children

Sun protection

Sunblock or high-factor sunscreen should be applied to skin (according to the directions) when necessary. Children should also wear a hat – legionnaire-style caps or wide-brimmed sun hats cover the neck as well as the head. Children should also remain covered in the sun, so leave T-shirts on. Also see the sun protection guidance for babies and young children in Unit CYPOP 2, Learning Outcome 1.

Did you know?

It is strongly advised that, on hot days, children stay out of the sun during the hottest part of the day – between 11am–3pm. There's still plenty of fun to be had in the shade!

Sun damage can cause the skin to become painful, to peel and blister. It can also lead to heatstroke, which makes children feel extremely unwell – see the table in Unit CYP 3.4 Learning Outcome 4 for further details. These symptoms occur soon after the exposure to the sun. But long-term damage to health may also occur. Some skin cancers that develop in later life are believed to be caused by sun damage in childhood. In addition, sun damage can cause skin to age prematurely.

> Unit CYPOP 2 Care for the physical and nutritional needs of babies and young children
> Unit CYP 3.4 Support children and young people's health and safety

Sun damage can cause the skin to become painful, to peel and to blister.

Dressing and undressing

Clothing needs to the right size for the child and suitable for the both the weather conditions and the activity that children will be engaged in. Layers are generally better than one thick item of clothing as they can be removed as necessary.

Most settings try to encourage parents and carers to send children in play clothes rather than their best clothes, so that they can play freely without undue concern for their outfit. It's important for practitioners to provide protective clothing – aprons and so on – when children will engage in messy or water play, or arts and crafts involving things such as paint and glue.

Some children may wear particular clothing as part of their cultural identity, as mentioned on page 385.

Toileting

The toilet area should be kept clean and tidy at all times, and well-stocked with toilet paper, anti-bacterial soap, paper towels and so on. Children often need reminding to go to the toilet, so it's sensible to build regular opportunities to go into the daytime routine.

> There's more about this, and toilet training, in Learning Outcome 2, Unit CYPOP 2 Care for the physical and nutritional needs of babies and young children

Caring for teeth

A child's first set of teeth, known as milk teeth, usually start to appear during the first year. Cleaning the teeth should become a habit from the time a baby has their very first tooth – information about introducing tooth care habits to young children is provided in Unit CYPOP 2 Learning Outcome 1. Most children have all 20 of their milk teeth by the time they are 3. From the age of 5 or 6, children's milk teeth begin to fall out as their permanent teeth grow from inside the gum and eventually push them out. Thirty-two permanent teeth are expected in all. As the name suggests, these teeth should be kept as long as possible – hopefully a lifetime – so it is very important to look after them from the outset.

Children should be encouraged to do the following:

- Begin brushing their own teeth as soon as they are able.

- Brush at least twice a day: after breakfast and after the last time they eat or drink before bedtime.

■ Brush after all meals if possible. Some settings facilitate this and minimise cross-infection from toothbrushes by providing safe individual storage for each child's own brush.

■ Visit the dentist regularly. It is a good idea to read stories about going to the dentist to familiarise children with this process. Role play can also be helpful.

■ Families are generally encouraged to take a child along to an adult's appointment initially before they have an appointment of their own. Do your best to ensure children do not become aware of any adult fears of the dentist's surgery.

■ Eat a healthy diet that is high in calcium (which is good for teeth) and low in sugar (which encourages decay). Avoid giving children sugary snacks between meals. Sugary drinks should also be avoided. Never give sweet drinks from a bottle as this helps to coat the teeth with sugar. Sugar can even pass through the gums and cause decay in teeth that have yet to come through.

■ Eat foods that are hard and crunchy to chew as they are good for teeth and gums – apples, raw carrot and celery are good options.

Unit CYPOP 2 Care for the physical and nutritional needs of babies and young children

Modelling and encouraging good personal hygiene

Practitioners should both encourage and model good personal hygiene for children. They will learn from seeing you washing your hands, disposing of waste such as tissues appropriately, covering your mouth when you yawn or cough and so on. Early years children will often forget these things unless they are reminded.

Showing respect for children when meeting personal needs

You must always take the greatest care to touch children respectfully when carrying out physical

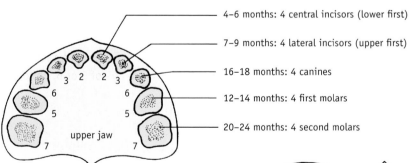

- 4–6 months: 4 central incisors (lower first)
- 7–9 months: 4 lateral incisors (upper first)
- 16–18 months: 4 canines
- 12–14 months: 4 first molars
- 20–24 months: 4 second molars

The first teeth normally come through in this order

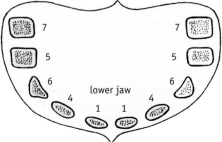

Tooth development.

care, and it's important to ensure that all children are allowed their dignity, and their privacy, when appropriate. You should remain professional and you should be sensitive to children's preferences, which will vary, partly in relation to their age and stage of development.

For instance, some children may prefer privacy when they are undressing to go swimming, while others may be happy to get changed alongside their peers in a communal room. Older children with disabilities and/ or special educational needs may require personal assistance for toileting, dressing or washing. They may still use nappies. Practitioners should attend to these needs in private to protect the child's dignity.

For children to have a positive experience, it is important that practitioners do not rush when attending to care needs. Every child must be and must feel respected and properly cared for. This is achieved through affectionate and appropriate touch, speech and gesture.

Link Up!

There's more about showing this respect in Learning Outcomes 1 and 2, Unit CYPOP 2 Care for the physical and nutritional needs of babies and young children

Supporting independence and self-care

Most children will eventually take care of their bodies independently. The skills required to do this are learned gradually. When attending to a child's care needs, practitioners can:

- show children how to carry out tasks such as washing, dressing and cleaning their teeth

- encourage children to help the adult as the child is washed, dressed and so on – the extent of help will depend on the child's age and ability

- encourage children to take care of the environment as they care for themselves by keeping areas tidy and safe (e.g. by avoiding or cleaning up spillages of water in the bathroom)

- praise children for their attempts at self-care

- have high expectations of what children can achieve, while ensuring that they are properly supported.

Good practice

Practitioners should appreciate which aspects of self-care children are comfortable with and respect their wishes when it comes to the level and type of assistance they require. However, sometimes practitioners may need to step in. For example, in preparation for lunch, a child may have washed their own hands after painting, but they may still be covered in paint. In this situation, the practitioner should gently point out the missed paint and direct the child back to the sink, offering help if it is needed. This must be done sensitively so that the child's confidence in hand washing is not undermined. It is part of having high expectations while ensuring that proper support is available.

Practical example

Gail adjusts her approach

Practitioner Gail adjusts her approach when washing the hands of different children. She knows that 1-year-old Daniel still needs lots of help from her, but he will hold out his hand ready for some liquid soap. Eighteen-month-old May will press the nozzle on the soap bottle herself, and rub her hands together – but she still needs Gail's help to rinse and dry her hands. Two-and-a-half-year-old Kayleigh can manage everything but turning the tap on and off. Gail assists her with this.

Question

Why is it important for Gail to adjust the level of help she offers to these children?

Routines that provide opportunities for learning and development

Everyday routines such as eating, drinking, personal hygiene, washing and dressing give opportunities for children to learn about independent self-care, as we have discussed. But there are also many opportunities for children to learn and develop in other areas. The list is extensive, but here are some examples of learning opportunities:

- When dressing, children can practise the fine motor skills required to fasten buttons, Velcro®, toggles and zips.

- Children can help each other with putting on outside clothes, developing their social skills.

- When eating, children can practise the hand/eye coordination needed to pick up food with cutlery.

- When pouring out their own drinks from a jug, children can learn about capacity and volume.

- While sitting at the table at mealtimes, children can learn about manners and social skills as they interact with one another.

- Children can count out the right number of cups or plates at snack time, learning about numbers.

- Children can communicate with their carers, practising their language skills. Adults and children may also share rhymes or songs, such as 'This is the way we wash our hands...'

Link Up!

There's more about what adults can do to engage with children during care routines in Learning Outcome 2, Unit CYPOP 2 Care for the physical and nutritional needs of babies and young children – see the bullet points on page 466

Management of medicines

Some children and young people may take medication regularly to treat conditions they have. For instance, a baby with asthma may take inhalers, and a child with ADHD may take tablets, or a young person with eczema may use creams. Other children and young people may need to take medication prescribed to treat an illness, which they have now recovered from. For instance, a child may have been ill for several days, and absent from the setting. But when there are well enough to return, they may still need to finish a course of antibiotics.

Parents need to give written consent for their child or young person's medication to be administered by the setting. The dosage, when medication should be given and by whom, should all be recorded. The medication should be clearly labelled with the child or young person's name, and it should be kept in a safe, appropriate place. (Some medicine needs to be kept in a refrigerator).

Settings will have strict, but differing policies about the way in which medicine is stored and administered, and these must be followed. You should be shown how to administer medication such as inhalers – make sure that you are confident in how to use the particular type, and rather than make an error, ask for help or clarification if you are in any doubt at all. In some settings, older children and young people may keep their own inhalers close at hand – this will depend on the policy of individual settings.

Did you know?

Often, one practitioner will administer medication under the supervision of a colleague – this ensures that two people check the dosage and so on.

Record keeping

In addition to keeping a medication log that includes written parental permission to administer medication, settings should log the details of when medication has been given, and the practitioner should sign the record. Parents and carers should also be asked to sign the log at the end of the session.

Settings must also keep a record of illness, accidents and incidents that occur.

Link Up!

For further information on keeping these records, see Unit CYP 3.4 Support children and young people's health and safety

Manual handling

There are some risks associated with lifting and carrying children and equipment. Manual-handling courses teach practitioners to employ the correct lifting methods to avoid injury, and you will be given demonstrations. It is recommended that you take such a course.

But essentially, you should:

- plant your feet firmly either side of the child/ equipment you will be lifting

- bend your knees and keep your back straight

- use your legs to power the lift to avoid straining your back or neck

- do not pick up or carry alone any child/equipment that you find too heavy for you – seek assistance

- check that equipment is safely positioned after putting it down.

It is often possible to help toddlers climb a specially designed slope up to a changing unit to save practitioners from frequently lifting them up and down when changing nappies.

How are things going?

▶ Progress Check

1. What are the welfare requirements? (1.1)

2. What document/s do practitioners complete to keep a record of which adults and children are present? (2.2)

3. When should you check that toys and equipment are in a safe condition? (2.3)

4. What are the minimum requirements of space for: a) under 2s? b) 2-year-olds? c) children aged 3-5? (2.4)

5. How does a good sleep routine benefit children's health and well-being? (3.1)

6. What key measures are taken in settings to prevent cross-infection? (4.2)

7. Why is it so important to follow a parent's instructions about their child's food allergies or intolerance? (5.2)

8. Explain the regulations relating to the management of medicines. (6.1)

Are you ready for assessment?

CACHE

Set task:

■ This is an extension to the set task for Unit EYMP 1 and Unit EYMP 2. It relates to taking a holistic approach to children's health and welfare.

You can prepare by ensuring that you are aware of the Government's most up-to-date guidance on children's nutritional needs, as this changes regularly. You can find this out online.

Edexel

In preparation for assessment of this Unit, you may like to access your setting's policy and procedures for off-site visits, and talk about them with a colleague.

City & Guilds

In preparation for assessment of this Unit, you may like to access your setting's policy and procedures for off-site visits, and talk about them with a colleague.

Learning Outcomes 2, 4 and 6 must be assessed in real work environments.

UNIT 4

Professional practice in early years settings

LEARNING OUTCOMES

The learning outcomes you will meet in this unit are:

1 Understand the scope and purposes of the early years sector

2 Understand current policies and influences on the early years sector

3 Understand how to support diversity, inclusion and participation in early years settings

4 Review own practice in promoting diversity, inclusion and participation in early years settings

INTRODUCTION

Over the years, early years care and education changes in response to current policies, frameworks and influences, including parental demand and current research. As a result, professional practice also evolves. The last two decades are particularly interesting to learn about as there has been huge development in terms of the scope and purpose of the early years sector. As this will always be subject to further change, staying up to date is an important part of a practitioner's role.

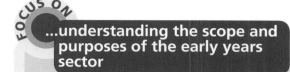

LEARNING OUTCOME 1

FOCUS ON

...understanding the scope and purposes of the early years sector

In this section you'll learn about the range of early years settings and the purpose of the sector. This links with Assessment Criteria **1.1**.

Services and facilities for children and families

There are many different services and facilities for children and their families in the UK. These can be divided into three categories:

- statutory

- voluntary

- private/independent sectors.

Statutory settings are provided by the state, and funded by either central government or local government. A statutory service is one that exists because Parliament has passed a law to say that the service either must or can be provided. Schools are an example of a statutory service. They exist because legally education must be provided free of charge by the Government for all children aged 5–16 years.

Private provision is owned by an individual person or a company, and aims to make a profit. Families pay fees for their children to attend. Some families may receive funding to help them pay. Private providers of childcare must still meet the requirements and standards laid down by Government. Examples of private provision include day nurseries, crèches and out-of-school clubs. Some schools run independently of the Government and do not receive government funding. These are called independent schools (although they're sometimes referred to as 'private schools').

Voluntary provision doesn't make a profit. Voluntary settings are run by organisations such as charities and committees. They may raise funds themselves and apply for grants. Users of the service may also pay a fee to attend (often a small amount). Examples of voluntary provision include parent and toddler groups, and some pre-schools and out-of-school clubs.

The table on page 394 shows a range of key provision – this includes provision for older children and young people, as this helps to put early years provision into context. Providers generally offer childcare (which allows parents to work or do other things), education for children, or a mixture of both. Some settings (such as children's centres) also offer additional services. The range of settings promotes the purpose of the early years sector – to meet the diverse needs of families and children while giving parents and carers a choice about the type of setting they use. Many families in fact use more than one setting for early years education and childcare, as the Practical example 394 shows.

Did you know?

In England, settings that provide the EYFS for children will receive some Government funding. In return, the setting must provide high-quality education. The provision will be regularly inspected by **Ofsted**.

A pre-school setting.

Table EYMP 4.1: The range of key provision

Setting/Provider	Provision offered*
Day nurseries	Provide childcare and early education throughout the day to suit the needs of working parents. Usually open from 8am–6pm, Monday to Friday, closing only during the Christmas period. Nurseries often care for babies and children from 12 weeks to 5 years. There will usually be a separate baby room. Some workplaces set up their own nursery for the children of their staff.
Pre-schools	Pre-schools can vary greatly in terms of opening times. Many open the same hours as schools, closing for holidays. Some have hours similar to day nurseries. Some open every weekday, others just on two or three days a week. Most cater for children aged 3–5 years, providing early education.
Childminders	Provide childcare and education in their own home, caring for children of any age.
Nannies	Provide childcare in the child's home, caring for children of any age. A nanny may live in or live out of the family home.
Crèches	Provide childcare for a period of time (often only up to 2 hours) while parents do another activity such as shopping, attending a short course or going to a leisure centre.
Children's centres	(Including Sure Start centres.) These are known as multi-agency settings because professionals from different sectors will work there. Provision may include a combination of childcare for children of all ages, early education, health services, family support services, drop-in sessions and special events.
Nursery schools	Provide early years education for children from age 2 years upwards during term time. Childcare may also be offered as an additional 'wraparound service' (before and/or after the nursery sessions. Holiday care may also be available).
Infant schools	Provide education for children aged 5–7 years during term time. Children follow the Early Years Foundation Stage (EYFS) and the National Curriculum. A nursery class for children aged 3 upwards may be attached to the school.
Primary schools	Provide mandatory education for children aged 5–11 years during term time. There may also be a nursery class. Children follow the EYFS and the National Curriculum.
Secondary schools	Provide mandatory education for children aged 11–16 years during term time. Children follow the National Curriculum. They may choose to stay on for an additional two years.
Out-of-school clubs	These may include before-school, after-school and school holiday provision. Childcare is combined with a safe place to play for children of school age. Breakfast clubs usually open at 8am. Staff look after children until it's time to escort them to school. After-school clubs collect children from school, usually staying open until 6pm. Holiday clubs often open all day from 8am–6pm. Clubs may be attached to another setting such as a school, day nursery or leisure centre.

*The provision of the Early Years Foundation Stage and the National Curriculum applies to settings in England.

Practical example

Benji's early years experience

When Benji was a baby, his parents decided that when his mother returned to work, they'd like him to continue to be cared for in a home setting, and so he began attending a childminder's house. He was settled and happy, and got along well with the another boy also looked after there on a full-time basis. His parents were very pleased with the childminder, but when Benji was 2½, they felt they'd like him to start socialising with more children. They arranged for him to stay with the childminder for three days a week, but to go to the local day nursery for the other two days.

key term

Ofsted The Office for Standards in Education, Children's Services and Skills, which inspects and regulates care and education for children and young people.

Local early years providers

To find out about early years providers in your local area you can do the following:

■ Contact your local authority, which will provide a Children's Information Service holding details of all the providers in your area. You will probably find a link to the Children's Information Service on your local authority's website.

■ Look in the local telephone directory.

■ Ask at the library. Most libraries keep a directory of local clubs and organisations.

■ Keep an eye on your local newspaper. New provision opening in the area is likely to be mentioned. Some settings may place adverts. Children's special events and open days may be listed in the 'What's on' pages.

The diagram below shows some of the additional provision that you may find for children and young people in your local area.

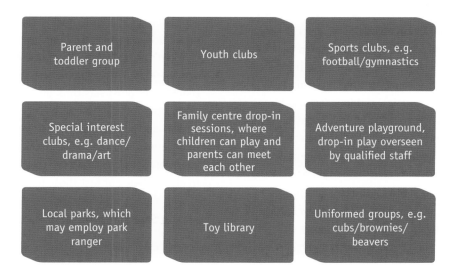

Parent and toddler group	Youth clubs	Sports clubs, e.g. football/gymnastics
Special interest clubs, e.g. dance/drama/art	Family centre drop-in sessions, where children can play and parents can meet each other	Adventure playground, drop-in play overseen by qualified staff
Local parks, which may employ park ranger	Toy library	Uniformed groups, e.g. cubs/brownies/beavers

Additional provision that you may find for children and young people in your local area.

LEARNING OUTCOME **2**

FOCUS ON

...understanding current policies and influences on the early years sector

Policies, frameworks and influences

Early years policies and frameworks emerge and change over time in response to current influences. In the last 15 years, there has been much more political focus on childcare and education than had previously been the case, resulting in a rapid expansion of early

In this section you'll learn about the current policies, frameworks and influences on the early years sector, and the impact that these have had. You'll also learn about evidence-based practice and how this has influenced work with children in the early years. This links with Assessment Criteria **2.1, 2.2, 2.3.**

years provision. Influences over the last 15 years have included two key factors:

- **A huge increase in the demand for childcare while parents work**

  This is in large part due to the fact that around 60 per cent of mothers now return to work outside of the home while their children are under the age of 5 years. This has been influenced by several factors. Gender equality has improved in schools and in the workplace, resulting in increased academic achievement, career aspirations and expectations for women. There has also been an increase in the number of lone parents bringing up children and also needing to work (the majority of lone parents are women). In the same period, government policies were introduced to cut down the numbers of people on benefits, and parents were encouraged back into training or work. The impact of all these things led to the increased demand for childcare. This was originally met by nannies, childminders and by steadily increasing numbers of private day nurseries, as public expenditure on childcare had been focused on the 'deficit model'. This provided support primarily for families in social need or who experienced other difficulties, through local authority nurseries/family centres, usually located in areas of social and economic disadvantage. You can compare this with the information on the Sure Start programmes of today (see the 'Sure Start' section on the next page) to see how much things have changed.

- **Research**

  Thanks to on-going research into the impact of early years education and services, we now know more than ever before about how children's experiences in the early years can impact on their future outcomes. In other words, we understand that good-quality care and education in the early years has a positive effect on children throughout the whole of their lives, and particularly within the areas of learning and development. In the 1990s, the Government studied work being done in other countries to improve the outcomes for children from low-income families. They saw

A drop-in session at a children's centre.

evidence that programmes promoting health, education and parental involvement resulted in raised achievement on a long-term basis, improving children's prospects for gaining better qualifications and therefore better jobs, which in turn would give them better prospects throughout their lives. This early years intervention also had a positive effect on anti-social behaviour. The Government went on to develop similar services. Thanks to recent 'social inclusion policies', these services are now available to all families, not just those families in social need or who experience other difficulties. (Once again, see the 'Sure Start' section on page 397.)

Early years frameworks

Frameworks set the standards that must be met by early years providers. These reflect current opinion of what constitutes good practice, and so frameworks also evolve and change over time as research continues to shape our understanding of how children learn and develop. Most recently, work by neurologists (brain scientists) has been revolutionary, as advances in technology have enabled them to look into living brains and observe what happens while someone is actually learning – see pages 111 and 434 for further details.

You may want to return to Unit EYMP 2 and reread the information on frameworks as part of your study towards this unit. Other relevant policies include the UN Convention on the Rights of the Child and equality legislation – see Unit SHC 33, Learning Outcome 2.

Sure Start

Sure Start is the Government's programme to deliver the best start in life for every child by bringing together early education, childcare, health and family support through Sure Start programmes and children's centres offering a range of services for children and families under one roof, giving staff the opportunity to work in a multi-disciplinary team. This may include early years practitioners and workers from the health and social care sectors, such as health visitors, speech and language therapists and social workers.

Some Sure Start initiatives apply universally, while others only apply in targeted local areas and/or to disadvantaged groups in England. Responsibility for Sure Start lies with the Department for Education. Sure Start tells us the following about their service:

Services

- Sure Start covers children from conception through to age 14, and up to age 16 for those with special educational needs and disabilities. It also aims to help parents and communities across the country.
- There are a wide range of services currently available, from children's centres and early support programmes to information and advice on health and financial matters. We are helping set and maintain childcare standards.
- Sure Start is the cornerstone of the Government's drive to tackle child poverty and social exclusion working with parents-to-be, parents/carers and children to promote the physical, intellectual and social development of babies and young children so that they can flourish at home and when they get to school.
- All Sure Start local programmes have become children's centres. Local authorities are responsible for Sure Start children's centres, and the services on offer may vary from area to area.

How do our services work?

Our services bring together universal, free, early education and more and better childcare. Sure Start does this with greater support where there is greater need through children's centres and Sure Start local programmes.

Integrated Early Years Services

For some time we have been encouraging the delivery of childcare alongside early education and other health and family services.

Sure Start children's centres

Sure Start children's centres are building on existing successful initiatives like Sure Start local programmes, neighbourhood nurseries and early-excellence centres, and bringing high-quality integrated Early Years services to the heart of communities.

By 2010, there will be 3500 children's centres, so that every family has easy access to high-quality integrated services in their community and the benefits of Sure Start can be felt nationwide.

Early education

All 3- and 4-year-olds are now guaranteed a free, part-time (12½ hours per week, 38 weeks per year), early-education place. There are over 37,000 settings delivering free, Government-funded, early education in the maintained, private, voluntary and independent sectors.

For more information on raising the quality of learning and development opportunities for children, and giving children the best possible start to their learning journey, see the Early Years Foundation Stage.

Childcare

At the end of March 2009, the stock of registered childcare places recorded by Ofsted stood at over 1.5 million (more than double the 1997 level).

There will be a childcare place for all children aged between 3 and 14, between 8am and 6pm each weekday by the end of 2010, when there will be over 2 million sustainable childcare places for children up to 14.

Sure Start services.

Link Up!

Unit EYMP 2 Promote learning and development in the early years
Unit SHC 33 Promote quality and inclusion in health, social care or children's and young people's settings

The impact of Sure Start Local Programmes

An evaluation has been done into the impact of Sure Start Local Programmes (SSLP) on 3-year-olds and their families. It investigated child and family functioning in over 9,000 families in 150 SSLP areas, making comparisons with children and families in similarly disadvantaged areas that do not have a SSLP.

The Department for Children, Schools and Families published the following key findings:

Did you know?

Sure Start is one of the key ways in which the Government aims to tackle 'social exclusion'. Social exclusion describes the experience of those who are not able to participate fully in society due to a range of reasons, for example a disability, discrimination, their low income or where they live.

Have a go!

You can read about the evidence collected in this study at **www.education.gov.uk/ rsgateway/DB/RRP/u015389/index.shtml** Reading this sort of information enables a practitioner to stay up to date with current influences on the early years sector, which is an important part of continued professional development.

Key findings

All findings of SSLP effects are reported after adjusting for a wide range of family and area background factors. Comparison between children and families living in SSLP areas and those in similar areas not having an SSLP revealed the following benefits associated with living in an SSLP area:

- Parents of 3-year-old children showed less negative parenting while providing their children with a better home learning environment.
- Three-year-old children in SSLP areas had better social development with higher levels of positive social behaviour and independence/self-regulation than children in similar areas not having a SSLP.
- The SSLP effects for positive social behaviour appeared to be a consequence of the SSLP benefits upon parenting (i.e., SSLP→Parenting→Child).
- Three-year-old children in SSLP areas had higher immunisation rates and fewer accidental injuries than children in similar areas not having a SSLP; it is possible that instead of reflecting positive effects of SSLPs these health-related benefits could have been a result of differences in when measurements were taken of children living in SSLP areas and those living elsewhere.
- Families living in SSLP areas used more child-and-family related services than those living elsewhere.

The effects associated with SSLPs appeared to apply to all of the resident population, rather than suggesting positive and negative effects for different subgroups as detected in the earlier (2005) report. The more consistent benefits associated with SSLPs in the current study compared with an earlier study may well reflect the greater exposure of children and families to better organised and more effective services, as SSLPs have matured over time, though it remains possible that differences in research design across the two studies could also be responsible.

DCSF key findings of Sure Start local programmes.

Evidence-based practice

With the expansion of early years provision, ensuring an appropriate balance between quality and quantity is a constant concern, and this has prompted a move towards evidence-based practice. This means that we work towards set outcomes, and then collect evidence that shows whether – or how well – the outcomes have been met. Evidence-based practice is at the heart of early years frameworks including the Early Years Foundation Stage, as you learned in Unit EYMP 2 – the job of practitioner is to promote the early learning goals (the outcome) and then to collect evidence about children's progress towards them via observation and assessment (the collection of evidence). This then informs the next cycle of planning and activity to promote the early learning goals. Evidence-based practice is also central to the way settings are inspected by Ofsted, and the way in which this qualification is assessed.

Unit EYMP2 Promote learning and development in the early years

LEARNING OUTCOME 3

FOCUS ON

...understanding how to support diversity, inclusion and participation in early years settings

In this section you'll learn about diversity, inclusion and participation. You'll also learn about the importance of anti-bias practice, and about how active participation of children in decisions affecting their lives promotes the achievements of positive outcomes. This links with Assessment Criteria **3.1, 3.2, 3.3.**

The meaning of diversity, inclusion and participation

As you learned in Unit SHC 33, diversity is the acknowledgement and respect of differences between individuals and within and between groups of people in society, which arise from social, cultural or religious background, ethnicity (ethnic origin), disability, gender, sexuality, appearance and family structure or background.

Inclusion occurs when a setting embraces diversity and ensures that all children, young people and families are able to fully participate in society – or in other words, the setting ensures that everyone is fully included. Inclusion and participation are therefore closely linked.

Unit SHC 33 Promote equality and inclusion in health, social care or children's and young people's settings

Anti-bias practice and the promotion of diversity, inclusion and participation

To recap on your previous learning, anti-bias practice (sometimes called anti-discriminatory practice) describes the ways in which settings and individual practitioners work and the steps they take in order to challenge and overcome prejudice and discrimination. The foundation stone of this is having a positive attitude towards the differences between people.

The ways of working outlined in Unit SHC 33 promote anti-bias practice, and enable you to promote diversity, inclusion and participation in your own work. These include:

- working in line with legal requirements and your setting's equal opportunities policy at all times

- getting to know all the children and not having favourites

- finding reasons to praise all children and resolving conflict between them fairly

- meeting the needs of all individual children to ensure participation, and noticing when children need your help

- respecting beliefs, culture, values and preferences

- developing a positive relationship with families

- identifying barriers to inclusion and working to overcome them – these may be physical, environmental or attitudinal

- assessing children's needs

- promoting diversity through positive images of people

- ensuring that activities reflect the wider multicultural world

- positively challenging discrimination when you encounter it from children or adults within the setting.

Link Up!

Unit SHC 33 Promote equality and inclusion in health, social care or children's and young people's settings

Further ways of promoting diversity, inclusion and participation are shown in the following Practical examples:

Practical example

Pre-school planning

Justin works at a pre-school. He's in charge of reviewing the setting's equal opportunities policy, and so he's reviewing the activity plans from the last few months to see how well the setting has enabled children to learn about cultures other than their own. He sees that the group have celebrated and learned about both Christmas and the Chinese New Year. They also focused on countries around the world coming together to participate in the Commonwealth Games, which was exciting and relevant for the group because a local athlete was competing. The group took a special interest in India, the host nation, and the Games also provided the opportunity to introduce positive images of disabled athletes. On a day-to-day basis, resources available during free play include baby dolls and adult figures of different ethnic origins, a number of skin-toned resources for mark-making (paints, crayons, etc.), a range of multicultural foods, cooking equipment and dressing-up clothes. A range of positive images are reflected in books, posters and puzzles. There's a huge poster at the entrance to the pre-school, which spells out 'Welcome' in several different languages. The setting also includes a range of multicultural foods in its snack menu.

Question

How effectively do you think the pre-school promotes and values diversity?

Practical example

Hattie's activity

Hattie is a student on placement at a drop-in crèche. She's planned to play a circle game with the children who turn up today – it will be the first time that Hattie has led her own activity at the crèche. She's planning to call out the names of certain foods, and all the children who have tried that food will run across the circle to swap places. Today, 4-year-old Jasmine, who is deaf, has come along to the crèche, just before the game is about to start. The supervisor greets her, and uses sign language to tell her about the rules of the game. Hattie doesn't know the signs for foods, so she thinks quickly, pops into the kitchen and returns with an armful of fruit and vegetables. She holds each item up as she calls out its name, and all the children join in with the game.

Question

How effectively did Hattie's action promote inclusion and participation?

Practical example

Teresa's nativity play tickets

It's November, and Teresa has got a new job in a nursery class at a primary school. Every year, the nursery class and the reception class put on a nativity play. As the school hall is not that big, traditionally only two adult tickets per child are allowed. Siblings sit in the front on the floor. Teresa is put in charge of the tickets – she's told that over the years there have been requests for extra tickets for extended family members (grandparents, etc.), but the policy must always be strictly observed as they can't say yes to everyone, so it just wouldn't be fair.

Teresa is soon being asked for extra tickets. However, a number of the requests are for tickets to enable step-parents to attend as well as a child's birth parents, and one child wants to invite his birth mother to see him as well as his foster parents. Teresa doesn't feel that it's right to exclude them from the event. She arranges to talk about it with the reception teacher. As a result, they get permission from the headteacher to hold the nativity in the local church instead, which is much bigger. They're now able to offer four tickets for every child.

Question

In terms of diversity, inclusion and participation, what are the benefits of Teresa's actions?

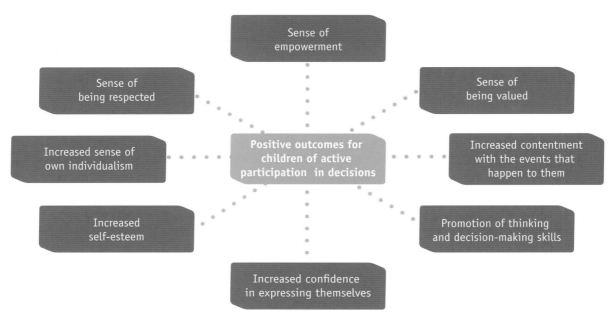

Positive outcomes for children of active participation in decisions.

Good practice

It's important that settings avoid tokenism in terms promoting diversity, inclusion and participation. For instance, you cannot celebrate a festival such as Diwali or the Chinese New Year and then think that you have 'done multiculturalism' with the children so you can tick it off your to do list! There's nothing wrong with celebrating festivals, as long as that is just regarded as one small way in which children within the setting will learn about other cultures. It's the everyday aspects of life that really enable us to learn about another culture, not what people eat and wear once a year on a special occasion. You should also ensure that you use everyday language to present other cultures in a realistic, everyday way. This means that you should avoid talking about people and countries in a way that makes them sound exotic or mysterious – it's real people's lives you're talking about, not a fairy tale, so there's definitely no room for talk of 'faraway lands' and the like! Avoid making the way other people live their lives sound strange or unusual. Differences should be regarded as commonplace, and you should never value one culture or belief system above another.

Did you know?

'Tokenism' (the practice of making only a symbolic effort at something, often just to meet the minimum requirements of laws or policies), is a word that's often used in connection with diversity, inclusion and participation. See the 'Good practice' section.

The everyday aspects of life, like getting dressed, enable learning about another culture.

Active participation of children in decisions affecting their lives

In Unit SHC 33 you learned that under the UN Convention on the Rights of the Child, children have the right to have their views heard. This means that practitioners should consult with children, particularly about decisions affecting them, and take notice of what they say. It's good practice to find out and to respect the views and preferences of children you work with. In the early years this may be achieved through conversation, 'All About Me' theme work, or even through artwork. As long as they're not overwhelmed with options, even younger children can be presented with choices and given the space to make decisions, for example by choosing which colour paper to make handprints on. Some children may talk to and be represented by an advocate on some very significant matters in their lives, such as where they will live following the separation of their parents. (See pages 27 and 517). Allowing the active participation of children in decisions that affect them promotes the achievement a range of positive outcomes, as shown on the diagram on page 402.

Unit SHC 33 Promote equality and inclusion in health, social care or children's and young people's settings

LEARNING OUTCOME 4

Reviewing own practice

The process of reviewing your own practice is an important part of your continued personal development, and in turn, an important part of being an effective practitioner. Review helps you to both notice and develop your strengths and to recognise and address your weaknesses. This may be through trying to do things more effectively with the use of a new method, strategy or tactic, or it may lead you to

FOCUS ON ...reviewing own practice in promoting diversity, inclusion and participation in early years settings

In this section you'll learn about the importance of reviewing your own practice. You'll also learn about reflective analysis of own practice and strategies to deal with areas of difficulty and challenge encountered within professional practice. This links with Assessment Criteria 4.1, 4.2, 4.3.

develop your understanding and skills in another way – via a training course or research perhaps.

Practitioners aim to review all aspects of their practice overtime. This should include your anti-bias practice as well as how effectively you promote diversity, inclusion and participation.

Reflective analysis

Reflective analysis is an effective tool for reviewing your practice.

For details of a range of reflective analysis techniques, refer to Learning Outcome 2, Unit SHC 32.

You can read more about this in Unit SHC 32 Engage in personal development in health, social care or children's and young people's settings

Strategies for dealing with areas of difficulty and challenge

Every practitioner has to deal with areas of difficulties and challenge during their career. If you feel you're experiencing problems with promoting diversity, inclusion and participation, reflective analysis will help you to pin down the issue and to see possible solutions. Your tutor and/or workplace supervisor is also there to offer support, and should action be necessary for improvement, they will be able to point you in the direction of further learning opportunities.

There are times when practitioners may come across discrimination within a setting. In this situation, the practitioner has a duty to challenge the discrimination in a positive way that is likely to bring about change. Although this is not always easy to do, it is an important responsibility.

There's more information about this in Learning Outcome 3, Unit SHC 33 Promote equality and inclusion in health, social care or children's and young people's settings
You may also like to review the conflict resolution guidelines in Learning Outcome 2, Unit CYP 3.5 Develop positive relationships with children, young people and others involved in their care

Practical example

Casey's plans

Casey is a newly qualified practitioner working in a day nursery. The setting already has some long-term plans in place – they have identified themes to explore over the next 3 months. Casey has been asked to produce a weekly plan for the 'holiday' theme. She has written in some activities connected to 'exotic places' that 'adventurous people' visit, and the 'quirky customs' that they experience there. She shows her plans to a colleague, who says she feels that Casey isn't taking a positive and realistic view of the differences between cultures. Casey realises that she needs to give this further thought.

Questions
In Casey's position, what would you do to review your practice?

How are things going?

▶ Progress Check

1. Explain three ways in which the Sure Start programme has responded to policies, frameworks and influences on the early years sector. (1.1)

2. Why is anti-bias practice so important? (1.2)

3. How does the active participation of children in the decisions that affect their lives promote the achievement of positive outcomes? (3.2, 3.3)

4. What are the benefits of reviewing your own practice? (4.1)

5. Give a strategy you may use to deal with an area of difficulty or challenge encountered in your professional practice. (4.3)

Are you ready for assessment?

CACHE

Set task:

■ This is an extension to the set task for Unit EYMP 1, Unit EYMP 2 and Unit EYMP 3. It relates to the day-to-day management of the care of a group of children.

You can prepare by following the relevant links in this Unit to ensure that you fully understand the meaning of diversity, inclusion and participation.

Edexel

In preparation for assessment of this Unit, you may like to make notes in your reflective journal about an instance when you have dealt effectively with a challenge encountered in your professional practice.

City & Guilds

In preparation for assessment of this Unit, you may like to make notes in your reflective journal about an instance when you have dealt effectively with a challenge encountered in your professional practice.

Learning Outcome 4 must be assessed in real work environments.

UNIT 5

Support children's speech, language and communication

EYMP

INTRODUCTION

Communication is a complex, two-way process. In order to communicate effectively, children need to develop a number of skills including listening, understanding and self-expression (both verbal and non-verbal). They also need to develop interaction skills. In this unit, we will consider this complex process and the many factors that underpin effective communication in practice.

LEARNING OUTCOME 1

FOCUS ON

...the importance of speech, language and communication for children's overall development

In this section you'll learn about the meaning of relevant terms. You'll also learn about how speech, language and communication skills support other areas of learning, and about the potential impact of speech, language and communication difficulties. This links with Assessment Criteria **1.1, 1.2.**

The terms relating to speech, language and communication

It's important that you understand the meaning of the key terms relating to speech, language and communication. These are as follows:

Speech

Speech is the process of vocalising language. It is produced by muscle actions that occur in the head, neck, chest and abdomen. When learning to speak, children are discovering how to regulate and coordinate muscles to produce a number of sounds, which when combined result in words that others can understand. There are more than 40 sounds to master in the English language.

Language

Language is a symbolic communication system. The symbols can be spoken aloud, written down or signed. There are conventions (rules) about the way these symbols are used, but once they are understood, the rules allow people to say anything they want within the limitations of their vocabulary. For example, we can say sentences that we have never heard said before. Each of the symbols in a language system have

meaning, but these are often abstract, which makes them complex to learn. For instance, the word for 'egg' in no way resembles an egg. The only way a child will learn the meaning of the word for egg is if they hear it used in context – when they are being offered a boiled egg, for instance. However, they will also need to learn that the term 'egg' applies to a raw egg, a scrambled egg, a fried egg and so on. Although lots of species of animals communicate, humans are unique in using a learned symbolic system, so it's often said that language is the 'essence of being human'.

Communication

This is an umbrella term that refers the way in which people send messages or signals to one another. Communication methods can be both verbal and non-verbal.

Link Up!

Full details on verbal and non-verbal communication are given in Learning Outcome 1, Unit SHC 1 Promote communication in health, social care or children's and young people's settings

Speech, language and communication needs (SLCN)

Children with SLCN have difficulties in communicating with others across one or more of the elements of speech, language and communication described above. This may mean that:

- they cannot express themselves

- they experience difficulty expressing themselves

- they have difficulties in understanding what people say to them

- other people have difficulties understanding the ways in which they communicate.

Children's SLCN may be minor, or they may be complex. They may be experienced temporarily over a short-term period, temporarily over a long-term period, or they may be life-long. In their leaflet *'Explaining Speech, Language and Communication Needs (SLCN)'*, the Communications Consortium tells us that, 'The term "needs" refers both to the needs of the individual and to what society can do to support their inclusion. It implicitly looks both at the individual and the environment in which children play, learn, communicate and live.'

This links with your learning in Unit SHC 1.

Link Up!

Unit SHC 1 Promote communication in health, social care or children's and young people's settings

Children's SLCN may be minor, or they may be complex.

Development patterns of speech, language and communication skills

Experts have identified two phases of language development, in which babies and children listen, watch, make sounds and talk:

- the pre-linguistic phase, occurring at the age of approximately 0–12 months

- the linguistic phase, occurring at the age of approximately 1–5 years.

The pre-linguistic phase can be divided into three typical age categories:

Age 0–3 months
Babies express their feelings (such as tiredness, hunger and emotional distress) by crying. They learn to recognise the sound of their parents' and carers' voices through listening. They can be soothed with gentle tones from a well-known adult. They will smile. They are interested in faces – they watch them and respond to them.

Age 3–6 months
Babies start to make a range of playful, short sounds – they babble and coo. They experiment with sounds, rhymes and volume. They enjoy vocal exchanges with adults in the style of conversation. They laugh and squeal to express delight, and cry to express distress.

Age 6–12 months
Babies learn to use sound deliberately – to imitate and to get attention. They may make sounds while gesturing to show adults what they want. Babbling begins to sound tuneful. Babies play around with sound, joining vowel sounds and consonant sounds together. Most of the sounds needed for language can now be made. By 12 months, most babies understand the meaning of around 15–20 words.

At 12 months, children make sounds and gesture to show adults what they want.

The linguistic phase can also be divided into three typical age categories:

Age 12–18 months

Babies begin to say single words at around 12 months, although these may only be understood by their parents/carers. The vocabulary expands to about 15 words within the next three months. Babies become more aware of other people's body language – for instance, they may follow someone else's gaze.

Age 18–24 months

Children start to use two words together first, and then begin to say simple phrases. Most children can communicate their meaning to parents/carers by two years or shortly after. They have a vocabulary of about 200 words – they are saying up to 20 new words each month.

Age 2–3 years

Children speak in simple sentences. They begin to ask simple questions (what/where). They pick up new words easily, and their vocabulary continues to expand. They make mistakes such as saying, 'I goed' rather than 'I went', or 'I sleeped' rather than 'I slept'. Children now use plurals and negatives, for example 'dolls' and 'No drink left'. Children may need time to stop and think during speech, which can be mistaken for stammering.

Language continues to develop – most children talk fluently by the age of 5. The diagrams here show

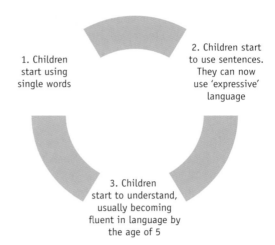

The linguistic phase.

the main characteristics of the phases of language development.

Listening

Listening is also a communication skill, which develops alongside speech and language. In this context, the term 'listening' refers to both hearing and understanding what is said. This is an important skill, because as you have learned, babies and young children increasingly begin to understand words when they hear them said in context. Listening is sometimes called 'receptive speech'.

Reading and writing

As we have identified, reading and writing are forms of communication. Information on the development of these communication skills is given in Learning Outcome 2.

Sign language

Other forms of non-verbal communication include sign language, as we have mentioned.

Sign language is generally used with children who have a hearing impairment. Makaton, a basic form of sign language, is frequently used with children who have learning difficulties that affect their ability to communicate through speech. There has recently been some interest in using signs with hearing babies. Some experts believe that teaching babies simple

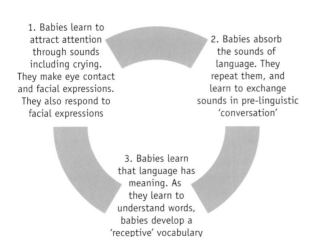

The pre-linguistic phase.

signs can help them to communicate before they have the ability to express themselves with words. They believe that this reduces frustration in babies, and that it does not delay verbal communication.

For further information about the development of communication, see the development tables in Unit CYP 3.1 Understand child and young person development, pages 83–101

How speech, language and communication skills support other areas of development

Speech, language and communication skills underpin much of children's development. This is because the ability to communicate – that is the ability to both understand what is said and to be understood – facilitates so much. If a child cannot understand and/or be understood, overall development will be affected. You'll learn more about this below. The following diagram shows the areas of development that are supported by children's speech, language and communication skills.

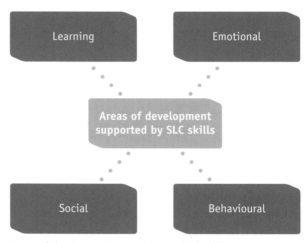

Areas of development supported by SLC skills.

We'll look at each area in turn:

Learning

Learning occurs when children receive information, process the information and then use the information. Information is received in various ways, some of them non-verbal. For instance, if a child touches a radiator that is on, they will receive information that it is hot when their hand feels uncomfortable. They may then process the information and make the connection that touching the radiator leads to discomfort. If they then use the information, they will avoid touching the radiator again. However, much of children's learning (receiving information, processing information and using information) is verbal. Children learn from what is said directly to them and what they hear, as the Practical example below shows.

Practical example

Alicia waters the plants

Alicia doesn't have a garden or houseplants at home, so her first experience of watering plants happens at pre-school. The practitioner explains to her that the plants will die without water. Two days later, Alicia visits her Gran, who has a houseplant on the kitchen window sill. Alicia says to her, 'Can I water your plant? Or it might die.'

Question

How do we know that Alicia had processed the information given to her by the pre-school practitioner?

Children can also use their communication skills to ask questions, a key way of learning throughout life. There's evidence that language also assists the processing of information – speaking aloud helps young children to think. You can learn more about 'language for thinking' and about the role of questioning in creative learning in Unit CYPOP 7. On page 338 of Unit EYMP 2, you were introduced to styles of learning. The 'auditory' style of learning is also relevant here.

Link Up!

CYPOP 7 Promote creativity and creative learning in young children
EYMP 2 Promote learning and development in the early years

Emotional

A key aspect of children's emotional development is the increasing ability to recognise, understand and express their own emotions. Through language development, children learn a label for the emotions they feel – 'upset', 'angry' and so on. They can then go on to talk about their feelings. Babies cannot control their emotions, and toddlers characteristically find this difficult, hence temper tantrums at this age. But young children generally tend to gain more control of their emotions as their language develops. The ability to communicate feelings through words seemingly relieves frustration at not understanding their emotions and not having them understood by others.

Behavioural

Behavioural development is strongly linked to language and communication. The word 'no' is generally learned while children are still babies. This is important because understanding the meaning of 'no' helps to keep children safe, as well as teaching them how to behave in socially acceptable ways. Language acquisition also enables young children to communicate their own likes, dislikes and preferences. This leads to a decline in the impulsive behaviour linked to frustration.

Good practice

The next developmental step is for children to understand the information they're given about the reasons for behaving in certain ways, to process the information and to use it. For instance, if a child is told not to touch a neighbour's dog, they are likely to learn just that. However, if a child receives an explanation as to *why* they shouldn't touch *any* dogs they come across without permission from the owner and their parent or carer, they have the opportunity to understand and to process. In the future, they may then use the information by refraining from touching a strange dog in the street. The process of talking about rules, behaviour and consequences will also help children to think about and understand them.

Language acquisition leads to a decline in the impulsive behaviour linked to frustration.

Social

You've learned how part of children's emotional development is to understand and express their own emotions. This is closely linked to social development, in which children will learn to recognise and understand the emotions and responses of other people, including whether or not they approve of the child's own behaviour. This enables children to learn about what it is socially acceptable to say and to do. The information children receive will be partly verbal, but they will also be learning to read people's body language and facial expressions. Toddlers will happily play in each other's company without conversing, but as they reach around 3 years of age, children typically begin interacting with one another on a new social level, and talking becomes increasingly important to peer relationships and play.

Speech, language and communication difficulties

Practitioners should learn to recognise when children have speech, language and communication difficulties. This is important because the earlier a difficulty can be detected, the earlier a child can get the specialist support that they need. Some children with minor or temporary difficulties progress quickly when they receive the appropriate help. Children may experience difficulties speaking, hearing or understanding, or they may lack a general interest in communicating.

Practitioners must be sensitive to the communication needs of children. It may be necessary to adapt communication methods to suit children's needs. It is helpful to find out what you can about specific difficulties, and for the setting to liaise with families and other professionals about communication strategies.

Did you know?

It's beneficial for all practitioners to learn some key signs in both British Sign Language (BSL) and Makaton. You can take introduction courses and workshops to learn these.

Link Up!

Unit CYP 3.1 Understand child and young person development

The impact of speech, language and communication difficulties on children's development

Speech, language and communication difficulties can impact negatively on children's development in a number of ways. But it's important to remember that all children are different, and much will depend on the degree of the difficulty.

There is often an impact on children's behaviour. Children with communication difficulties may have an Individual Education Plan (IEP) that has been drawn up as part of their special needs assessment. In this case, behaviour programmes must complement and fit in with the IEP. Speech, language and communication difficulties may impact on behaviour because:

- children may have difficulty understanding the meaning and structure of language and therefore understanding boundaries and instructions

- children may have difficulty expressing themselves, leading to frustration when other people do not understand their feelings.

Children who have difficulties communicating may have difficulties forming relationships with adults and peers as communication is the cornerstone of our relationships with other people. As a result, children may feel lonely, left out, frustrated, angry or experience a diminishing motivation to communicate – particularly if they find it hard to make themselves understood. Confidence and self-esteem may also be affected.

Children may experience difficulties listening (receiving and understanding) to the information they are given, which can be a considerable barrier to learning. Children use language to think as well as to speak, and so there may also be an impact on cognitive development.

In the long term, these effects may lead to children:

■ not fulfilling their potential

■ not becoming independent

■ becoming isolated

■ becoming withdrawn

■ becoming depressed

■ continuing to experience behaviour issues as they grow up. (These may become classed as anti-social behaviour.)

LEARNING OUTCOME 2

FOCUS ON

...understanding the importance and the benefits of adults supporting the speech, language and communication development of the children in own setting

In this section you'll learn about ways to support and extend speech, language and communication development, and the positive effects of this support. You'll also learn about how to take account of differing levels of speech, language and communication between children in group settings. This links with Assessment Criteria **2.1, 2.2, 2.3.**

Supporting and extending speech, language and communication development

The primary way to support and extend children's speech, language and communication is via the conversations and the interactions that you have with them. You should be talking with individual children frequently. It's important that you pitch the level of language and the words that you use in line with children's age and stage of development. Practitioners need to simplify the words they use and their sentence structure when working with babies and younger children. But by the time most children are 3, they are ready to hear more complex dialogue. They need this stimulus to increase their own vocabularies and achieve further language development. With experience, switching between levels like this becomes second nature.

In addition to the guidance below, you may find it helpful to refer to the development tables in Unit CYP 3.1 Understand child and young person development, pages 83–101

Age 0–3 months

Methods to support and extend: spend plenty of time talking to babies in a lively tone when they are content, and soothe them reassuringly with gentle tones when they are distressed. Ensure that babies can see your face – make eye contact with babies when communicating with them. An ideal time to communicate is when attending to babies' care needs. The baby and carer can look into each other's eyes during nappy changing and bottle feeding, for example.

There's more about communication with babies in Unit CYPOP 2 Care for the physical and nutritional needs of babies and young children

Make eye contact with babies when communicating with them.

Babies enjoy sharing first picture books with adults.

Age 3–6 months

Methods to support and extend: join in with babies' playful babbles, repeating sounds back to them. Continue to talk to babies frequently and engage them in 'conversation' – talk to them, then pause to allow the baby to 'reply', then 'answer' them once again. Respond with delight with your facial expressions, body language and your speech when babies communicate their delight to you. Show sympathy in your facial expressions, body language and your speech when babies communicate their distress to you. Remember to talk *with* babies, not *to* them.

Age 6–12 months

Methods to support and extend: continue talking with babies. Look out for signs that they are using sounds for deliberate communication – respond to this to encourage babies to repeat their efforts. Simple songs and rhymes are often appreciated – babies enjoy getting to know them and like to anticipate the fun endings to old favourites such as 'Round and Round the Garden' (that ends in a tickle), or 'Horsey, Horsey' (that ends with the child being softly bounced up and down on the carer's knee). As babies learn to clap, they can join in with 'pat-a-cake' rhymes.

Age 12–18 months

Methods to support and extend: make sure that you respond encouragingly to babies' first words, so that they will be motivated to keep talking to you. Babies

enjoy sharing first picture books with adults. They enjoy learning the names of objects they see in the pictures. They also enjoy learning the sounds that familiar animals make. As they become aware of body language, children enjoy simple songs with actions they can copy.

Age 18–24 months

Methods to engage and interest: show lots of interest in what children have to say. Ensure that you reply to children whenever they talk to you. Take what they say seriously, even if words are missing, or you are not sure what is meant. Take note of children's gestures – they often use them to fill in the gaps in their vocabularies. It is important that children feel that their efforts at communicating meaning are worthwhile. Give them plenty of opportunities to interact with their peers and slightly older children if possible. Read children short, simple stories, and sing familiar songs slowly so they can join in with words or phrases they know.

Age 2–3 years

Methods to support and extend: make sure that children are in an environment rich with exciting language – conversation, songs, rhymes and stories will be absorbed and used as inspiration for communication. Children's questions should be answered, even if they are repetitive. Introduce children to expressive words for feelings and describing, for example 'happy', 'sad', 'excited', 'angry', 'wet', 'dry', 'soft', 'hard'. Demonstrate language for thinking by using it aloud yourself: 'I wonder what will happen if I pour this water into the sand . . . oh look, it's all wet now!'

For further information about on-going ways of developing children's creative learning skills, which include language for thinking, see Unit CYPOP 7 Promote creativity and creative learning in young children

Questions

Questions are a very useful tool in supporting speech, language and communication development. You can read about open and closed questions on page 353. You can also read about the use of questioning to encourage thinking skills, and the value of children asking their own questions, in Unit CYPOP 3.7.

Unit EYMP 2 Promote learning and development in the early years
Unit CYPOP 3.7 Promote creativity and creative learning in young children

Reading and writing

As we have identified, reading and writing are forms of communication. Children are not expected to read and write in the under-3 age range. However, children under 3 can be encouraged to develop an interest in books – this will provide motivation to learn to read later on. Children under 3 can also be encouraged to make marks. In time children learn to make finer marks, and eventually they are able to write letters and words. It is never too early to read to babies and young children. Even the youngest infants will enjoy hearing the rise and fall of an expressive voice reading aloud, even if the words cannot yet be understood. Children will enjoy stories long before they can read words – but a desire to read is the first step, and a love of stories fuels the desire. Just as children learn that spoken words carry meaning, they will learn that the

words on the page are meaningful too. Children often learn this before the age of 3 – think how often a 2-year-old will bring you a book to read to them. Most children will learn to recognise letters and odd words that are familiar to them by the time they leave early years education, but most will not read until they start school.

Mark-making is the term we use to describe any activity in which children can deliberately make a mark. The obvious activities are art-based – children make marks when they draw, crayon, paint, print, stamp and so on. But there are also more subtle alternatives – children can draw with a twig in the sand, or trace patterns on the ground with water. Whenever children deliberately make such marks they are practising the skills they will need to write. They are learning the techniques for pencil control, and learning how to make their marks stop, start, flow and join. They are discovering how to move their arms and hands to make big shapes, small ones, thick ones and thin ones. They are feeling the satisfaction of leaving their mark, and feeling proud of their achievements.

Whenever children make marks, they are practising the skills they will need to write.

It is not until their third or fourth year that most children make the small symbols in a row that we recognise as 'emergent writing', which is often mingled with real letters children have learned from their own name. This emergent writing, which eventually evolves into writing, has its roots in those important early mark-making opportunities.

For information about creative mark-making opportunities, see Learning Outcome 3, Unit CYPOP 3.7 Promote creativity and creative learning in young children

Information and activities

A key part of supporting and extending young children's skills is providing them with engaging information and activities that motivate them to communicates and give them something to talk about. For example, interest tables are a fantastic way to get children talking about new information and the objects available for exploration, as the Practical example below illustrates. 'Feely bags' are a good example of an activity which promotes communication and use of descriptive language. (A practitioner will place an object in a drawstring bag, e.g. an apple. Without looking, a child puts their hand inside and describes what they can feel. The group try to guess what the object is – the practitioner can give clues. Once the object is revealed, a new one is placed in the bag and another child has a turn.) Also see the Communication, language and literacy section of the short-term planning table on page 336 of Unit EYMP 2.

Unit EYMP 2 Promote learning and development in the early years

Practical example

Iona's interest table

Iona works at a children's centre. It's her turn to organise the interest table this week. She's decided to have an autumn theme, and arranges for a small group of children to go for a walk with her and a colleague. They collect a range of fallen leaves and some conkers. When they get back, Iona arranges these on the table. She adds some magnifying glasses so that children can look closely at the items. She soon has some eager children exploring them. They ask Iona where the leaves and conkers came from, and why they fell off the trees. Iona gives them the information. She then asks the children some questions – what do the leaves and conkers feel like? What do they smell like? What similarities and differences are there in colour, shape and so on? Why do they think some of the leaves are brown and brittle?

Question

How might this activity help to expand children's vocabularies?

Working with parents and carers

As the primary carers of their children, parents and carers are generally in the strongest position to support and extend children's communication skills. Talking to children frequently in a running commentary style throughout the day – about what's going on around them or about what the child or parent is doing perhaps – will instantly provide rich, on-going communication experiences.

Making time for uninterrupted, one-to-one communication with parents every day is also important. A story, an activity or a conversation about the day's events are all ideal ways to spend this time. It can fit in with the general routine of the family –

bath time or bed time for instance, or a conversation over breakfast, when walking to pre-school and so on. Singing is a great way to pass time spent in the car and also promotes children's communication, language and literacy skills.

Uninterrupted, one-to-one communication time with parents is important.

Talking to young children needn't take a lot of special effort, but parents may be unaware of how important it is. This is especially true in the case of babies, as parents may think there is little point talking to them because they won't understand what is said. Practitioners and settings have a role to play in raising awareness about this. For example, some settings include tips on how to support children's development in their newsletters, some may have compiled a fact sheet on promoting communication, and some may run workshop sessions for parents in which they learn techniques for supporting their child.

Positive effects of adult support

When children, parents and carers receive support from practitioners, the positive effects for children include:

- increased speech, language and communication experience

- increased speech, language and communication skills

- increased support for the child's development from parents and carers

- increased levels of social interaction, impacting positively on relationships with peers and adults

- increased levels of self-confidence and self-esteem (emotional development)

- less challenging behaviour (caused by less frustration and attention seeking)

- increased creative learning skills.

Taking variations of speech and language levels into account

In group settings, practitioners must take variations of speech and language levels among the children they work with into account. As you know, children develop at different rates, and even within a group of the same age, children can be at quite different stages of speech, language and communication development. Practitioners should plan activities and experiences to support and extend the development all of the children. Many settings achieve this by grouping the children into smaller groups for some key activities. For an example of how a practitioner sensitively groups children for a listening activity, see page 422. Practitioners should also vary the support they give when working with individual children accordingly. (There's more about this in Learning Outcome 3.)

When children enter the provision

When a child first enters the provision, their key worker (see Unit CYPOP 1) should find out from parents or carers about the child's communication development and any speech, language and communication difficulties. As you learned in Unit CYP 3.5, communication is at the heart of developing relationships with children, so it's important that the key worker can support children in this area right from the start, as establishing relationships is crucial to a new child settling into the provision.

Link Up!

Unit CYPOP 1 Work with babies and young children to promote their development and learning
Unit CYP 3.5 Develop positive relationships with children, young people and others involved in their care

LEARNING OUTCOME 3

FOCUS ON

...being able to provide support for the speech, language and communication development of the children in own setting

In this section you'll learn about the methods of providing support for speech, language and communication development. You'll learn about the use of everyday activities and about working with children in groups and on a one-to-one basis. You'll also learn how to evaluate the support provided within your own setting. This links with Assessment Criteria 3.1, 3.2, 3.3, 3.4.

Key factors of supporting speech, language and communication development

As you learned in Learning Outcome 2, practitioners must support the speech, language and communication development of all the children they work with. To do this effectively, there are a number of factors you should take into account as shown on the diagram below.

We'll look at these in turn.

Age

Children develop at different rates, but it is important for practitioners to have a good understanding of the expected patterns of development of speech, language and communication – you learned about these in Unit CYP 3.1. This enables practitioners to pick up any difficulties and to provide the appropriate support. (This is also covered fully in Unit CYP 3.1.) It also enables the practitioner not only to support the current stage of communication development, but also to support the next stage, for example by providing appropriately challenging activities and scaffolding learning (see below).

▶▶▶ Link Up! ◀◀◀

Unit CYP 3.1 Understand child and young person development

Specific needs

Alternative and Augmentative Communication (AAC) describes any system or special method

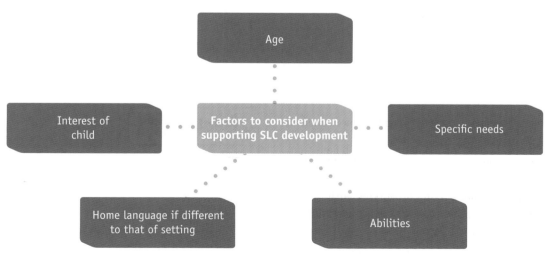

Factors to consider when supporting speech, language and communication development.

of communication that is used to overcome communication barriers. Using AAC can help children with communication difficulties to make the most of their available senses and experiences. Methods of AAC include the following:

■ **Symbols**

A child may carry a deck of symbol cards, using them to signify meaning. These can be personalised. For instance, children may have cards showing pictures of different resources. They may show staff the relevant card to indicate what they would like to play with. A commonly used system is the Picture Exchange Communication System (PECS).

■ **Communication boards**

These generally contain a number of symbols or words. Children express themselves by indicating to these symbols or words. Some boards are designed to fit onto wheelchairs.

■ **Voice output communication aids**

These may be connected to an electronic speaking communication board, or a laptop computer, that enables a child to 'talk'.

■ **Sign language**

Including Makaton – a basic version of British Sign Language, which may be taught to younger children or those with learning difficulties. Gestures may also be used.

■ **Facial expressions**

Useful for conveying emotion.

It is important to identify methods of breaking down communication barriers for individual children and to monitor their effectiveness. Sometimes very simple steps can make a real difference. For instance, if a child lip reads, adults and peers can be encouraged to face the child when speaking directly to them or to the group they are playing or working within. If a child has partial hearing, it may help to eliminate all unnecessary background noise when communicating with him or her. Slowing the pace of conversation and speaking clearly may also help. Children with

learning difficulties may find it easier to understand sentences that are short and simply structured.

See also Unit Learning Outcome 4, Unit CYP 3.1 Understand child and young person development

key term

Alternative and Augmentative Communication (AAC) this refers to any device, system or special method of communication that helps individuals who have communication difficulties to communicate more easily and effectively. *(National Occupational Standards)*

Abilities and adapting own language

As you've learned, children develop at different rates. It is the job of practitioners to be aware of the abilities of the individual children they're working with, and to adapt their own language accordingly, so that children can understand them. Common methods include talking more slowly, using sentences that are short and simply structured and making use of gesture/body language alongside speech. Also see the section on 'taking variations of speech and language levels into account' on page 417.

Making use of gesture alongside speech.

Home language

We live in a culturally diverse society, so it is important for practitioners to recognise that many children will learn more than one language.

- Children who are learning two or more languages at the same time sometimes show a delay in their communication. This is generally put down to the fact that they are absorbing two languages – or twice as much. However, with support, children's overall communication development need not be affected.

- Some experts believe that children pick up a second language more easily if it is introduced to them after they have mastered the basic use of one language.

- Someone who speaks two languages is bilingual. Someone who can use three or more languages is multilingual.

- Children tend to learn languages best by simply absorbing them naturally. This happens when people frequently interact and talk with children in a language.

- **Bilingual** and **multilingual** children may confuse languages at times, mixing up simple words, sentences or phrases. This might be because they have not yet learned the particular word they want in the language they are currently speaking. For instance, if a child usually eats their meals at home where they speak only Italian, they may not know 'mealtime' words in English, even though they speak English at their pre-school every morning. So when they play with a tea set at pre-school, they may introduce some Italian words into their spoken English. Word games and activities (such as picture lotto) can help fill children's vocabulary gaps.

- It is thought that children learn to separate different languages most easily when they clearly identify them with people and places. For instance, if grandparents only talk to their grandson in Chinese, he is likely to only communicate back in that language. If children only speak English at a setting, they are less likely to switch between English and their home language when they are there. Difficulties are more likely to occur when children hear adults switching in and out of languages frequently when they talk.

key terms

Bilingual someone who speaks two languages.
Multilingual someone who speaks three or more languages.

You may speak just one language with a bilingual or multilingual child, but it is important to recognise that they are developing their communication skills in other languages too. This achievement should be acknowledged. Bilingual and multilingual settings should ensure that all languages spoken are recognised and valued as part of children's culture. The languages we speak are part of our identity, and not to value a child's language is not to value part of that child. By broadly celebrating cultural diversity, settings show that they value different languages.

Assessments are helpful for pinpointing the support that individual multilingual and bilingual children may need. But practitioners must understand that language may impact on the assessment process and the findings. For instance, children may have difficulties carrying out instructions or following a game not because they do not have the ability to do so, but because they have not fully understood the language used to explain what to do. In this case, working closely with parents and carers will help practitioners to build up a true picture of a child's learning and development. It will be important to provide good opportunities for a range of speaking and listening activities with adults and peers. You should also adapt your own language as appropriate (see page 419), for example by simplifying the sentences you use.

Provide good opportunities for speaking and listening activities with adults and peers.

Interests

Young children need to be motivated to speak. A good example of this is the way in which toddlers point to what they want and make a general vocalisation before progressing on to saying the name of the object – it is the desire to have the object that motivates the interaction. So if we want to engage children in conversation, it helps to talk about things that they are interested in. Children are more likely to feel the motivation to both talk and listen when the topic engages them. For instance, a child who loves the setting's toy cars may respond well to a question about the cars he has at home.

Scaffolding the child's learning

Scaffolding is about verbally giving children the support and help they need to be able to complete a task that they can't manage alone. This should help them to move towards carrying out the task independently in the future. A good example of this is how practitioners encourage children to use the language of creative thinking. See the sections on 'Supporting language development', and 'Using creative thinking questions' in Unit CYPOP 7, Learning Outcome 2. Scaffolding the child's learning is a very natural part of a practitioner's role – just think about how often you prompt verbally. For instance, a conversation with a child may go like this:

Practitioner approaches a child.

Practitioner: It's raining today, so before we go outside we need to put on our...

Child: Shoes.

Practitioner: We do need our shoes on, yes. We always wear them outside, don't we? And what else do we wear when it's raining? We put it on and we zip it up...

Child: Coat!

Practitioner: That's right, we need our coats to keep us dry. And we can put our hoods up, can't we?

In the future, this type of scaffolding may lead to the following scenario:

Child approaches practitioner.

Child: I need to put my coat on because it's raining outside.

This shows that the child has gained both an understanding of the concept of needing to put their coat on, and the language, motivation and confidence needed to express this.

Unit CYPOP 7 Promote creativity and creative learning in young children

Giving children the time and opportunity to communicate

We've looked at the varied opportunities that children need to communicate. However, it's also important they are given time to communicate, as outlined in the section on 'Working with parents and carers' in Learning Outcome 2.

During conversation young children need time to think, which often results in a pause in their speech. When this happens, you should allow children to take the time they need. Some children start to stutter or stammer early on in their language development.

This is reasonably common. It can often be attributed to the fact that children cannot talk as fast as they are able to think, and this causes them to stumble over their words. Again, adults should give children the time they need to finish their words or sentences. Avoid interrupting children and finishing their sentences for them. It is counterproductive; it encourages children to rush what they say even more, because they expect not to be given adequate time to speak slowly *and* finish all they have to say. Childhood stutters and stammers often fade away, but they can progress into adulthood too, or develop later on.

Allow children to take the time they need to think during conversation.

Learning through play

For information on how play and activities are used to support the development of speech, language and communication, see Unit CYP 3.1, Learning Outcome 4.

Unit CYP 3.1 Understand child and young person development

Working with parents and cares

If children live in a home which provides rich, on-going communication opportunities, this will do much to support their learning and development. See Learning Outcome 2 for further details.

Using day-to-day activities to encourage development

Specific activities aimed at promoting speech, language and communications are extremely helpful, but don't forget just how important day-to-day activities are too. They provide so much opportunity for conversation and interaction, including time on a one-to-one basis – for example, when changing a nappy. Daily activities also present opportunities to repeat phrases and words, which is an effective way of scaffolding learning. For example, at circle time you might complete a 'today' chart every day, which involves talking about the weather and selecting an appropriate image (e.g. the sun, a cloud) to display. There are very few routine activities that cannot be turned into an opportunity to encourage communication development. One of the most basic and natural ways to do this is simply talking about an aspect of what you are doing or what is happening. For instance, at tidy-up time, you could ask a child which of the toys he played with today and how. When taking children to hang up coats on arrival, you could engage in a guessing game about how they got to the setting today – did they walk, ride in a car, catch the bus and so on?

For more information on interacting with children while attending to their care needs, see Unit CYPOP 2.

Unit CYPOP 2 Care for the physical and nutritional needs of babies and young children

Working with children individually and in groups

We've talked about the importance of working with children on a one-to-one basis to support their individual speech, language and communication development. Working with children in groups is also valuable. It gives children the opportunity to learn from one another, and it also facilitates communication between children. Being able to communicate with peers is at the heart of forming the relationships and friendships that have a key role to play in children's personal, social and emotional development. For further information on group and one-to-one activities that promote speech, language and communication, see Unit CYP 3.1, Learning Outcome 4.

Evaluating the effectiveness of the support provided for children

How effectively children are learning and developing in their speech, language and communication can be a good indicator of the quality of support they are receiving. To monitor and evaluate this, practitioners can analyse the observations they make of children's play, and the assessments they make of children's learning and development.

This can include target child observations, in which the observer tracks the child and records their interactions with their peers and adults, as well as what they say during their play (when they are talking to a doll in the home corner, for instance). This may be recorded on paper, but you can also use an audio recorder or a video camera to great benefit. Periodically using these to record children's speech during play is a good way to track their progress, as recordings can easily be compared. See Unit CYP 3.2 Learning Outcome 1 for further details about observation.

It can also be helpful to have someone record you or to record yourself as you work with children, either using a video camera or an audio recorder. You can then analyse the recordings at your leisure to see how well you are supporting children. It will be helpful to reflect on how well you:

- interact with children on a one-to-one basis

- interact with children in groups

- facilitate language between children

- meet children's speech, language and communication needs

- give children the time and opportunity they need to communicate

- use day-to-day activities to encourage development

- scaffold children's learning

- consider children's interests

- adapt your own language

- consider children's ages and abilities

- support children with a different home language

- work effectively with parents and carers.

It can also be helpful to ask colleagues to give you feedback on how well they feel you do these things.

Unit CYP 3.1 Understand child and young person development
Unit CYP 3.2 Promote child and young person development

Unit SHC 32 Engage in personal development in health, social care or children and young people's settings

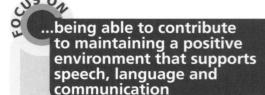

LEARNING OUTCOME 4

FOCUS ON

...being able to contribute to maintaining a positive environment that supports speech, language and communication

In this section you'll learn about the importance of the environment in supporting speech, language and communication, and the key factors involved in its provision. You'll also learn how settings use the environment to support speech, language and communication. This links with Assessment Criteria **4.1, 4.2, 4.3.**

The importance of the environment in supporting speech, language and communication

The physical environment we provide for children can contribute significantly to their speech, language and communication development. Likewise, a poor physical environment may present a barrier to speech, language and communication development. For instance, if music or the radio is playing in the background, children's ability to concentrate on what others are saying – and even to hear them – can be affected.

Key factors of providing a supportive environment

There are a number of factors that contribute to the provision of an environment that supports children's speech, language and communication development. These are shown on the diagram below.

We'll look at these in turn.

Physical environment

The physical environment not only contains the activities and opportunities within the setting, it dictates to a certain extent how children experience them. Sound travels, and so it's important that the layout of the environment is thought out carefully. Quieter activities, such as looking at a book in the book corner, need to be kept away from busier, more noisy activities, such as children building a den together. There's more about this on pages 306–308.

There should be a good range of resources and materials to support speech, language and

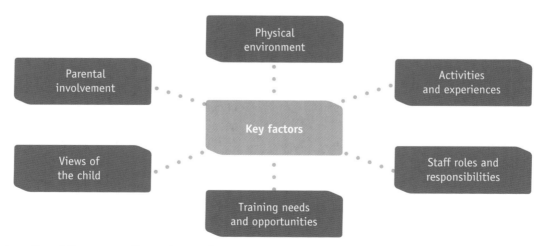

Key factors of providing a supportive environment.

communication development. Examples include small-world toys, imaginary resources and board games such as lotto. Puppets are also a great favourite, and there are many useful ITC resources including interactive books, walkie-talkies, telephones and gadgets that incorporate microphones (such as karaoke machines) and those that enable children to record their voices.

For children with speech, language and communication difficulties, any necessary specific resources to meet their needs should also be in place. Adequate light is also a consideration, as children need to be able to see facial expressions, gestures, signs and lip movements clearly.

Good practice

While recorded music can undoubtedly be valuable to listen to during certain activities and experiences, several experts believe that it becomes a distraction if it is constantly playing in the background. So it's good practice to think carefully about how music will enhance the activity or experience currently on offer before pressing the play button.

Activities and experiences

You learned about how play and activities are used to support the development of speech, language and communication in Unit CYP 3.1 Learning Outcome 4. In summary, it's important to provide a balance of activities that:

- are child-led

- are adult-led

- children can engage with in groups

- children can engage with individually

- meet the needs of all the children within the group.

Unit CYP 3.1 Understand child and young person development

There should be a good range of resources and materials to support speech, language and communication development.

Staff roles and responsibilities

It's important that practitioners ensure that all children are given the time and opportunity to communicate. Communication is at the heart of all our relationships, and children's overall experience within the setting depends largely on the relationships they form. As you know, the key worker system supports children in forming a key attachment with a practitioner. To nurture that relationship, key workers need to regularly talk with their key children on a one-to-one basis. The responsibility of key workers to do this can be embedded into the setting's overall systems for supporting children's speech, language and communication development and learning. Not only does this practice also assist the key worker in monitoring the child's progress, it also helps to ensure that quieter children do not fall between the cracks. It is all too easy for children who are a) confident communicators, or b) need communication support, to attract adult attention while those children in the middle are overlooked.

Training needs and opportunities

Practitioners have a responsibility to stay up to date in all areas of their practice, and this includes speech, language and communication. There is much to learn on the subject, and on-going training can help you to deepen and improve your knowledge and skills. In the future, you may even want to consider developing your work to support children's speech, language and communication as an area of specialism (see Unit SHC 32). You may also need to undertake training to enable you to support a specific child within the setting who has speech, language and communication needs – you may learn Makaton for example.

Unit SHC 32 Engage in personal development in health, social care or children's and young people's settings

Views of the child

You've learned that following children's interests is an effective way to motivate them to communicate. You can also consider children's views during conversations and activities. Is a child giving you a signal that they don't feel like talking? Perhaps they are avoiding eye contact or seem distracted. Or, is there a reluctance to speak aloud during group activities such as circle time? Perhaps a child wants to talk to you but it is an inappropriate time – you might be in the middle of reading a story to the whole group, for instance. If this happens, you can tell the child that you'll listen to them just as soon as you've finished the page, or the book – and make sure that you remember to do so! It may be that a child is desperate to tell you something so they interrupt someone else. In this case, it's best to acknowledge their desire to talk and then to ask them to wait. So you may say, 'Jack, I'm going to finish listening to Keisha, and then I'll listen to you.'

Parental involvement

For information about working effectively with parents and carers to support speech, language and communication, see Learning Outcome 2.

Using the environment to provide support for speech, language and communication

As you gain more experience, you will see first hand how a variety of settings use their environment effectively to support speech, language and communication. To reflect on these, you can use the key factors outlined above as a starting point.

Have a go!

If you are a student on placement, you can increase your knowledge of how a setting's environment is used to provide effective support by asking whether you can look at past session plans.

How are things going?

▶ Progress Check

1. Explain the meaning of the following terms:

   a) speech, b) language, c) communication, d) speech, language and communication needs. (1.1)

2. Describe the potential impact of speech, language and communication difficulties on the overall development of the child, in:

   a) the short term, and b) the long term. (1.3)

3. Explain the positive effects of adult support for children and their parents and carers. (2.2)

4. Explain how three day-to-day activities can be used to encourage speech, language and communication development. (3.2)

5. Explain the importance of the environment in supporting speech, language and communication development. (4.1)

6. Identify four key factors that contribute to a supportive speech, language and communication environment. (4.2)

Are you ready for assessment?

CACHE

■ This is an extension to the set task for Unit EYMP 1, Unit EYMP 2, Unit EYMP 3 and Unit EYMP 4. It relates to the support of children's speech, language and communication skills.

You can prepare by referring to Learning Outcome 1 to ensure that you fully understand the meaning of these terms: a) speech, b) language, c) communication, d) speech, language and communication needs.

Edexel

In preparation for assessment of this Unit, you may like to refer to Learning Outcome 1, to ensure that you fully understand the meaning of these terms: a) speech, b) language, c) communication, d) speech, language and communication needs.

City & Guilds

In preparation for assessment of this Unit, you may like to refer to Learning Outcome 1, to ensure that you fully understand the meaning of these terms: a) speech, b) language, c) communication, d) speech, language and communication needs.

Learning Outcomes 3 and 4 must be assessed in real work environments.

UNIT 1

Working with babies and young children to promote their development and learning

LEARNING OUTCOMES

The learning outcomes you will meet in this unit are:

1 Understand the development and learning of babies and young children

2 Be able to promote the development and learning of babies and young children

3 Understand the attachment needs of babies and young children

4 Be able to engage with babies and young children and be sensitive to their needs

5 Be able to work in partnership with carers in order to promote the learning and development of babies and young children

INTRODUCTION

Babies and children under the age of 3 are developing rapidly. They also have strong emotional needs. Practitioners must learn to recognise these and to meet them sensitively and with confidence, so that babies and young children can thrive in terms of their well-being, health and development.

LEARNING OUTCOME 1

FOCUS ON

...understanding the development and learning of babies and young children

In this section you'll learn about the development and learning of babies and young children, and how this takes place. You'll learn about the potential effects of pre-conceptual, pre-birth and birth experiences. You'll also learn about the impact of current research into the development and learning of babies and young children. This links with Assessment Criteria **1.1, 1.2, 1.3, 1.4.**

Patterns of development

Babies and young children develop rapidly in the first three years, and it's essential for you to have a sound knowledge and understanding of the expected patterns of development, and the skills typically acquired at each stage. This will enable you to assess the learning and development of the babies and young children you work with, and to provide appropriate activities and experiences to meet their learning and development needs.

Link Up!

For details of development patterns for the 0–3 age group, see Learning Outcome 1, Unit CYP 3.1 Understand child and young person development

The interconnection between development and learning

Development and learning are closely connected. Children need to develop certain skills before they are able to learn certain things, and vice versa. For example, when babies drop items and the items are returned to them, it helps them to learn that the

objects continue to exist when they can no longer see them. (This concept is called 'object permanence' – you'll learn more about it later in this chapter on page 438.) But a baby won't be able to drop things intentionally to explore this concept until they have developed the fine motor skills to deliberately release things from their grasp.

Another example is learning to walk, a significant milestone in babies' development, because it opens up a whole new range of possibilities in terms of exploration and learning about the world. Learning to walk is challenging because babies need to develop strength, balance and coordination. There will be lots of false starts and falls, so a child really needs to feel motivated to achieve the skill that will facilitate so much future learning. It will also facilitate the development of further physical skills, as it won't be long before new toddlers will progress to running around.

Development and learning are closely connected.

Variations in rate and sequence of development

Children develop at different rates and the sequence of development may vary. This can be due to a number of reasons including:

■ learning difficulties

- impairments

- giftedness (being gifted in certain areas)

- environment

- genetic factors

- varying opportunities and experiences.

This is covered in detail in Unit CYP 3.1, Learning Outcome 1. You're advised to re-read this section as part of your study towards this unit. Also see the section below on the effects of pre-conceptual, pre-birth and birth experiences on development.

Unit CYP 3.1 Understand child and young person development

Learning taking place in different ways

Learning takes place in a number of different ways, and the beauty of play-based activities and experiences is that they allow babies and young children to make discoveries for themselves, in their own unique ways. Most of young children's learning comes from what they do in their play rather than what they're told or shown, so they really do 'set their own curriculum' through their actions. Because of this, you can maximise children's learning by following their interests.

Did you know?

Even twins who spend all their time in the same environment, with the same people and the same access to activities and resources, will learn in different ways. They'll interact differently with people and materials, and make connections between their experiences in their own unique fashion.

The importance of play

Play is the primary way that babies and young children learn and develop, but they need adults to engage them from early on. Immobile young babies will have very little stimulus unless their primary and key carers interact with them playfully and frequently and provide them with toys and materials to explore.

You can learn much more about the importance of play on pages 112–116 Unit CYP 3.1 Understand child and young person development and page 140
Unit CYP 3.2 Promote child and young person development

Pre-conceptual considerations

Prospective parents are advised to think about their lifestyle and to make any necessary changes before they try to conceive, because pre-conceptual factors that damage sperm and eggs can affect both fertility and the babies that are conceived. Advice to couples includes the following:

- Give up smoking.

- Give up alcohol.

- Avoid recreational drugs.

- Avoid coffee.

- Take food supplements including folic acid (women).

- Visit the doctor to discuss any prescribed medication as it may not be suitable to take when pregnant.

- Get into good physical health (exercise, lose weight if necessary, take steps to reduce high blood pressure).

- Don't leave starting a family too late as over time a woman's eggs start to deteriorate. (Once menopause occurs, she will no longer be fertile).

Prospective parents are advised to think about their lifestyle.

Effects of pre-birth and birth experiences on development

There are several key pre-conceptual, pre-birth and birth stage factors that can impact on a babies' development. These are shown on the diagram below.

We'll look at these in turn.

Smoking

If a mother smokes during pregnancy, she restricts the amount of oxygen that should be reaching the baby. This has a negative effect on the baby's growth and development, and as a result, babies born to smokers are more likely to be premature, and more likely to be of a low birth weight. The on-going effects are of this are a concern. Babies are also at greater risk of cot death, and of developing asthma, a condition that may affect them throughout life and require lifelong medication. Asthma attacks can also be fatal.

Alcohol

Drinking during pregnancy is extremely dangerous for babies because the alcohol enters their bloodstream. The impact is most strongly felt in the early weeks of pregnancy, at which stage a woman may not know that she's pregnant – this is a key reason why women trying to conceive are advised to give up drinking. However, harm can still be caused via drinking during the later pregnancy. 'Alcohol foetal syndrome' is the name given to a condition caused by drinking during pregnancy. It describes a number of effects including learning difficulties.

Maternal ill health

Some women experience ill health during pregnancy due to complications, and it's possible for these to

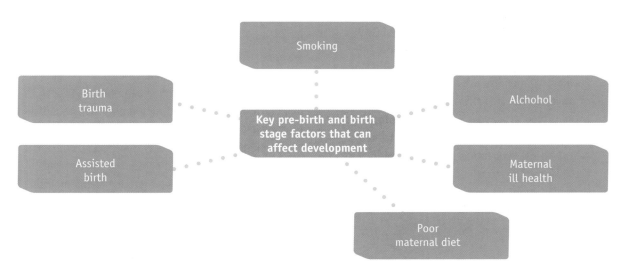

Key pre-birth and birth stage factors that can affect development.

also affect the baby. Throughout their pregnancy, women will attend antenatal appointments so that health professionals can check that their pregnancy is progressing healthily – this is the case for the majority of women. For the minority, serious conditions such as pre-eclampsia or diabetes will need to be treated without delay. Pre-eclampsia can occur when there's a problem with the placenta (which links the baby's blood supply to the mother's). The woman can develop high blood pressure, fluid retention and protein in the urine. This can affect the baby's growth. Ectopic pregnancy is a potentially life-threatening condition affecting 1 in 80 pregnancies. It occurs when the fertilised egg implants outside the cavity of the womb, usually in the fallopian tube (rather than inside the womb). As the pregnancy grows, the fallopian tube stretches, causing pain. If left untreated, an ectopic pregnancy can be fatal. In a tubal ectopic pregnancy, it isn't possible to save the baby, but the pregnancy can be safely ended without the woman experiencing further complications.

Ask Miranda!

Q Can infections unrelated to pregnancy harm unborn babies if a mother contracts them?

A Yes, such infections picked up by a mother which are unrelated to the pregnancy can affect the baby. Examples include rubella (pregnant mothers are advised to stay clear of anyone who has this) and some sexually transmitted diseases. Food poisoning is also a concern, so mothers are advised to avoid certain high-risk foods during pregnancy, including unpasteurised dairy products. However, most common infections such as coughs and colds are harmless to the baby.

Poor maternal diet

Women should have a healthy, balanced diet during pregnancy so that the baby receives all the necessary nutrients. Plenty of iron is recommended as some women become iron deficient during pregnancy. Women who are planning pregnancy are advised to take daily supplements of the mineral folic acid (400 mcg per day) until the twelfth week of pregnancy, as a lack of this early in pregnancy can result in the baby having spina bifida. Foods that present a high risk of food poisoning should be avoided. Some recommend an organic diet if possible. It is always good practice to wash fruit and vegetables well.

Substance abuse

Drugs taken by the mother can enter the bloodstream of the baby, and so women should not take any drugs – recreational *or* otherwise, unless prescribed by a doctor. The effects of recreational drugs depend on what has been taken, but can include miscarriage, growth and development problems, premature birth, low birth weight, limb deformities and learning difficulties. Babies are also at a greater risk of cot death if their mothers have taken drugs.

Assisted birth

A woman may give birth via a caesarean section. She is given an anaesthetic, and an incision of about 20 cm is made across her lower abdomen. The baby is delivered via the opening. A caesarean may be elective, which means that it's been planned in advance, or it may be an emergency that becomes necessary when difficulties occur during labour. Elective caesareans may have been planned for a number of reasons, including a pre-existing condition that means it's safer to avoid the stress of childbirth, a multiple birth (e.g. triplets), pre-eclampsia, or the placenta being positioned across the neck of the womb. It may also be the preference of the mother.

Birth trauma

Most babies are born without trauma. However, the most common trauma to occur is 'anoxia'. This is lack of oxygen that occurs when the baby's oxygen supply is interrupted. The longer this lasts, the more severe the effect. Effects can include brain damage and it can also be fatal. Lack of oxygen can be due to several reasons, including the umbilical cord becoming tangled around the baby's neck.

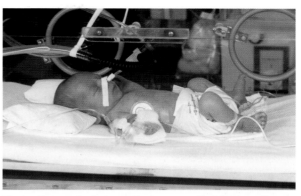

The earlier a baby is born, the more medical intervention they will need.

Ask Miranda!

Q Premature babies aren't as developed as full-term babies when they're born. Will there be on-going effects on their development?

A Not necessarily, although this will be the case for some. The earlier a baby is born, the more likely it is that they'll experience on-going effects. Babies born from 35 weeks onwards don't usually experience effects in the long term. They are generally sufficiently developed to breathe and feed independently from birth. However, babies born 10 weeks or so earlier than this may survive, thanks to advances in medical technology in recent years. They will be significantly smaller and less developed. The baby's immune system and organs would still have been developing during the last missed weeks of pregnancy, and so the baby is vulnerable and will need intensive medical intervention.

Did you know?

Around 10 per cent of babies are born before they are full term. Sometimes this happens naturally, but sometimes labour is induced early for medical reasons.

Current research into development and learning

The current focus of research into the learning and development of babies and young children is the physical development of the brain, and what happens to the brain when children learn. Thanks to breakthroughs in technology in recent years, we're discovering more about this all the time.

A baby's brain begins forming just three weeks after conception. When they are born, babies have around 100 billion neuron cells. These start to function when connections are made between them. Babies and young children are making connections all the time, even in their sleep when they are processing information they have taken in during the day, so plenty of rest is important. Connections are made in response to all sorts of stimulus that the baby receives. Early on, much of this is sensory. Evidence shows that good health and a healthy diet also influence the making of connections.

Did you know?

A brain growth spurt occurs over the first two years of life. At birth the brain is about 25 per cent of adult weight, but is 75 per cent of adult weight by two years of age.

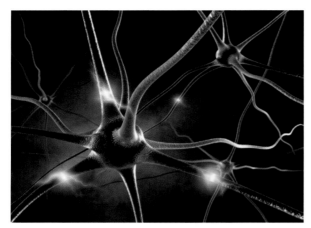

Babies' and young children's brains make connections in response to a wide range of stimuli.

Thanks to recent research, we know that brain development is something that happens throughout our lives. Even as adults, we make actual connections in our brains when we learn something new, such as a skill. Young children's brains make connections as they learn language, as yours would if you were to learn to speak a new language yourself.

But we know that children's brains are much more impressionable than adult brains. The upside of this is that babies and young children are very receptive to enriching learning activities and influences. They make connections in response to a wide range of stimuli – when loving carers cuddle and talk with them, sing to them, read stories and share playful exchanges, they are actually helping the children's

brains to physically develop, as more and more connections are made – the more the better in terms of learning and development. The downside is that babies and young children are more vulnerable to a lack of brain development if their early experiences do not nurture and stimulate them.

The impact of this research

The impact of this is that we know it's more important than ever that we reach babies and young children at risk of poor outcomes in their lives due to a lack of stimulation, a lack of loving relationships or a lack of good-quality physical care.

You can find out more about this in Unit CYP 3.7 Understand how to support positive outcomes for children and young people

Have a go!

Brain development research is moving quickly and it's hot news! Do a web search for current studies, and stay up to date with the latest developments.

LEARNING OUTCOME 2

The purpose of observing and assessing babies and young children

Observation is a tool used by practitioners to distance themselves from the babies and children they work

FOCUS ON

...being able to promote the development and learning of babies and young children

In this section you'll learn about assessment of development and learning needs. You'll learn how the indoor and outdoor environment is responsive to development and learning needs. You'll also learn about planning and provision of play-based activities. This links with Assessment Criteria **2.1, 2.2, 2.3, 2.4.**

with, so that they can be objective about their behaviour and development.

Through observation, practitioners can assess and track the progress and development made by babies and young children in all areas of their development. This information can then be used to inform planning for future learning and development.

For full details of observation and assessment, see Learning Outcome 1, Unit CYP 3.2 Promote child and young person development

The indoor and outdoor environment

Practitioners should ensure that both the indoor and outdoor environment is responsive to the development and learning needs of babies and young children as follows:

- **Be well equipped, clean and safe with age-appropriate equipment and materials**
  As you learned in Unit EYMP 3, environments must be kept clean and safe to safeguard highly vulnerable babies and young children. The equipment and materials selected for them must be suitable for the age group and safe for them to explore. However, it's important to avoid the setting and the equipment and materials on offer feeling 'sterile' and bland. Aim for safe and stimulating.

- **Provide appropriate challenge**
  Babies and children under 3 are developing rapidly, and the environment and opportunities available to them need to keep up with this. Otherwise, they won't be appropriately challenged and this could hold back learning and development. Make sure that you're aware of the current stage of development of the children you work with, and

that you know what they're likely to learn next. You can then plan an appropriately stimulating environment for them. This links with your learning in Unit CYP 3.2.

Provide quiet calming spaces for babies and young children.

- **Offer appropriate levels of sensory stimulation**
  Babies and young children use their senses to explore objects, and both enjoy and learn from sensory stimulation. You'll learn more about this on page 440.

- **Provide quiet calming spaces for babies and young children**
  Group settings can be busy places. So it's important for practitioners to focus on providing quieter, calm spots in which babies and young children can feel relaxed. Soft furnishing such as floor cushions and upholstered chairs or sofas are ideal for children and adults to cosy up together. Many young children also enjoy small, semi-enclosed spaces they can enter on their own, such as tunnels to crawl into, or tents or dens that give a feeling of separateness, while very much remaining under the supervision of adults. As you learned in Unit EYMP 3, babies and young children also need sufficient opportunities to rest and sleep during the day as well as at night.

- **Be planned and organised around individual needs of babies and young children**

In group settings, it takes a lot of equipment to care for babies and young children. Sleeping areas with beds and cots, eating areas with chairs and high chairs, changing areas and places to store belongings all have to be fitted in. There are also many physical care needs to fit into the daily routine – feeding, changing nappies, toileting, naps and so on. However, it's important that physical care routines and the equipment they necessitate don't dictate the way the environment is experienced by the children – they are not 'pieces' to be slotted into the 'jigsaw' of the setting's daily routine. Instead, a compromise should be reached so that the setting runs effectively but allows flexibility in terms of responding to individual needs and the way the physical environment is laid out. Examples of this are facilitating individual mealtimes so that children eat when it is best for them, and providing plenty of clear floor space that can be used in any number of ways alongside the necessary fixtures and fittings.

Link Up!

Unit EYMP 3 Promote children's welfare and well-being in the early years
Unit CYP 3.2 Promote child and young person development

Play-based activities tailored to support needs, learning and development

When planning activities for babies and young children, practitioners should:

- include a good range of activities to support all areas of children's learning and development

- provide activities that are sufficiently challenging

- consider the interests and needs of individual children (this will be informed by observations and assessments)

- plan to use the play space effectively

- plan with reference to relevant curriculum frameworks for the age range, in line with current best practice.

Provide activities that are sufficiently challenging.

Areas of babies' and young children's learning and development to plan for include:

- gross motor skills (GMS)

- fine motor skills (FMS)

- hand/eye coordination (H/EC)

- language and communication development; listening and responding (LCD)

- emotional expression and social competence (EESC)

- intellectual skills and understanding (ISU)

- imagination and creative skills (ICS).

For ease of reference, each of these areas has been given an abbreviation, which appears in brackets alongside. It's important to develop an integrated approach to planning. To do this, you must recognise that the activities you provide for babies and young children will generally promote more than one area of their learning development. Children's learning is not compartmentalised, even though we may talk about the different areas of learning and development separately. For instance, when a young child talks with an adult while they are watering the setting's houseplants together, the child could be simultaneously learning and developing in all of the following areas:

- fine motor skills (FMS)

- hand/eye coordination (H/EC)

- language and communication development; listening and responding (LCD)

- emotional expression and social competence (EESC)

- intellectual skills and understanding (ISU).

By pulling together different areas of learning into activities when you are planning, you can maximise the potential learning opportunity for babies and young children. It is not necessary to mould every activity to fit every area – this would probably make your activity so broad that it would lack purpose – but it is effective to integrate those that are a natural fit.

Activities will generally promote more than one area of learning development.

Here are some examples of activities for babies and children across the 0–3 age range.

The abbreviations are used to show which areas of learning and development are promoted by the activities:

0–6 months
- playing with rattles (FMS, H/EC)

- lying underneath a baby gym, reaching up to play with the resources suspended (FMS, GMS, H/EC)

- interacting with carer in early conversational style – the adult will talk, wait for the baby's response of a babble or coo, then talk again (LCD, EESC, ISU)

- game of 'Round and round the garden' with carer (LCD, EESC, ISU)

- splashing in the bath or a pool (GMS, EESC, ISU).

6–12 months
- sitting up at the table with peers at mealtimes, helping to feed oneself (FMS, H/EC, LCD, EESC, ISU)

- crawling or walking after pull-along toys (GMS, ISU)

- plenty of conversation with time to respond as first words are spoken and babbling becomes expressive (LCD, EESC, ISU)

- playing with stacking cups (FMS, H/EC)

- finger painting (FMS, H/EC, EESC, ICS).

1–2 years
- playing with sand and water (FMS, H/EC, ISU, ICS)

- pushing and pulling large wheeled toys, such as baby walkers and prams (GMS, ISU)

- sharing rhymes and baby songs with actions (FMS, GMS, LCD, EESC, ICS)

- colouring with chunky crayons (FMS, H/EC, EESC, ICS)

- playing with dolls, puppets and soft toys (LCD, EESC, ICS).

2–3 years
- using large wheeled ride-on toys (GMS, ISU)

- throwing and catching large soft balls (GMS, H/EC, EESC, ISU)

- learning and sharing songs, rhymes and stories (LCD, EESC, ISU, ICS)

- playing first lotto games (LCD, EESC, ISU)

- making simple collages with paste and brush (FMS, H/EC, EESC, ISU, ICS).

Core playful activities

The following playful activities are staples used frequently by practitioners to engage babies and young children. They are more concerned with the nature of the play than the resources or materials available:

Bee, bee, bee, bo!

Games of 'beebo' delight babies from around 8–12 months. Beebo is played by interesting a baby in either yourself or a toy such as a teddy. You then hide your face or the teddy from view for a moment – you can cover your face with your hands or a cushion, or hide the teddy behind your back. In a playful tone, you build up a little tension by saying 'bee, bee, bee... bo!' On 'bo!', your reveal your smiling face or bring the teddy back into view. There are numerous variations of this that you can then make up.

The game is loved at this age because babies usually develop 'object permanence' between 8–12 months. This means that they understand that an object continues to exist even when it's out of sight. Beforehand, babies won't look for an object that disappears or falls out of sight. (If a baby has developed object permanence, you can interest them in a toy, then hide it under the corner of the blanket the baby is sitting on, and they will attempt to retrieve it.) Now 'beebo' is fun, because babies can excitedly anticipate you or a toy popping back up in a playful way.

Bee, bee, bee, bo!

Dropping things

Dropping things and watching them fall is another enjoyable activity for babies who have developed object permanence. This activity helps babies to understand the concept of cause and effect – releasing the item causes it to drop satisfactorily to the ground. Babies like an adult partner to play this game with, whose job it is to retrieve the item and give it back to them, so they can enjoy dropping all over again! Once a baby is mobile, you can also encourage them to play this game with balls that they can then enjoy crawling after. Be aware that babies have no concept of which items are or are not suitable for dropping – for example, bowls of food may very well be dropped over the side of a highchair with glee!

Knocking things down

Babies and young children enjoy knocking down towers of objects such as bricks or beakers and so on long before they are able to build them up. You can encourage a baby to do this by building up a small tower in front of them, then knocking it down with a playful expression that you can repeat each time – something along the lines of 'All fall down!' is a favourite. If you build a tower in the middle of a group setting, it's unlikely to stay there for long! This activity also helps babies to understand the concept of cause and effect – pushing the blocks causes them to collapse. Enjoying the payoff of the collapse will also motivate them later to persist with working out how to stack objects for themselves.

Posting things

Babies and young children also enjoy posting things, or in other words, putting objects in and out of places. Provide all sorts of receptacles, such as containers, tubs and tins that they can drop items into, and then retrieve again. It's good to have a variety of materials, shapes and sizes, as these will look and feel different, and will result in different sounds, stimulating the child's senses.

Challenging activities

Lev Vygotsky developed a theory about how children learn from challenging activities, known as the 'zone

All fall down!

of proximal development'. You can read about this on page 107.

The theory still influences the activities we provide for babies and young children today.

Many experts now agree that providing babies and young children with challenging activities helps to:

■ encourage their developmental progress

■ stimulate their interest and curiosity

■ keep them motivated to participate

■ foster a love of learning.

It is important that you have a good understanding of the patterns of child development. This enables you to provide activities that are challenging enough to stretch the abilities of babies and young children, without causing the frustration that comes when activities are *too* challenging and difficult.

Routines provide opportunities for learning and development

Everyday routines such as eating, drinking, personal hygiene, washing and dressing give opportunities for children to learn about independent self-care, as we have already discussed. But there are also many opportunities for children to learn and develop in other areas. The list is extensive, but here are some examples of learning opportunities:

■ Babies and young children can communicate with their carers, practising their early language. Adults and children may also share rhymes or songs.

Practical example

Asher's activity plans

Asher works in a crèche. He is planning some art and craft activities for a group of 1- and 2-year-olds. He plans finger painting, a new experience for some of the youngest children.

He also plans painting with brushes of varying thickness, which will be a challenge for several children of 15 months and over who are learning how to manipulate tools. He plans a simple collage-sticking activity for the 2-year olds. This will be challenging and it will build on the children's existing ability to use a paintbrush. They will use similar skills in a new way to paste pictures onto paper.

Question

Why has Asher planned different activities for different age ranges?

- When dressing, children can practise the fine motor skills required to fasten buttons, Velcro®, toggles and zips.

- Children can help each other with putting on outside clothes, developing their social skills.

- When eating, children can practise the hand/eye coordination needed to pick up food with cutlery.

- When pouring out their own drinks from a jug, children can learn about capacity and volume.

- While sitting at the table at mealtimes, children can learn about manners and social skills as they interact with one another.

- Children can count out the right number of cups or plates at snack time, learning about numbers.

Sensory exploration

Babies use their senses to explore the world by:

- seeing

- hearing

- touching

- tasting

- smelling.

Babies rely on their senses to tell them about the world, so sensory exploration is an important part of a baby's development. Babies can use their senses to find out about the world long before they can crawl or walk to explore their physical environment.

Practitioners can promote sensory opportunities in many ways:

- **Introducing babies to a range of textures**
  There are many good textured toys on the market, such as baby mats or soft toys made from several different materials: some that are furry, others that are silky and so on. This allows the baby to make comparisons as they play.

- **Introducing babies to music and songs**

- **Having a good range of toys that make sounds**

- **Providing a range of coloured and contrasting resources to explore**

- **Providing interesting features in the environment to see and hear, such as mobiles and wind chimes**

- **Taking babies out**
  Babies can then experience the sights and sounds of the wider world.

- **Introducing babies to a range of safe food and drink when they are ready.**

Practical example

Ty stimulates babies' senses

Practitioner Ty works in the baby room of a day nursery. He has been looking for a way to stimulate babies' senses during care routines. He decides to hang a brightly coloured mobile that incorporates wind chimes above the changing mat.

Question

How will this help to stimulate babies' senses?

Using indoor and outdoor space effectively

All children need space to exercise their whole bodies and to develop their physical skills.

However, young children need more clear floor space than older children because of the way that they play and learn. This is because it is during the development phases of the first three years that children master key physical skills – rolling, sitting, crawling, standing, walking and running. Children become naturally very physically active from about 15–18 months, and they need plenty of opportunities to move and exercise their bodies, and to explore their environment safely.

In addition to providing appropriate space, practitioners can encourage babies and young children to exercise, develop mobility and explore their surroundings by:

- providing appropriate resources, equipment and experiences for the developmental stage of babies and children

- joining in play with babies and young children

- praising babies and young children when they exercise, explore or engage in activities that develop mobility

- helping babies yet to crawl to explore their environment by moving them periodically and changing the resources within their grasp.

Interests and needs

As human beings, what we are interested in and what like to do is part of our personality and identity. Personal interests are important and should be respected. All children, even babies, have their own interests. Practitioners can find out about these through:

- conversations with families

- own observations of babies and children

- discussions with colleagues.

Children become very physically active from about 15–18 months.

The interests of the children in your care can be incorporated into the activities that are offered. This fuels the motivation of individual children to participate and helps to foster a love of learning early on in childhood. The provision of activities should also take into account the individual development capabilities of babies and young children. This will be informed by discussions with families and observations made by key workers and colleagues. It may also be necessary to adapt some activities to meet individual children's needs.

Rewards

Babies and young children respond well when they are rewarded for something they have done. They are encouraged to repeat the rewarded behaviour. Praise is the most effective (and most practical) reward. Show that you are pleased when babies and young children make an effort during activities as well as when they achieve. It will motivate them to try again and it will build up their confidence to try something new. It also helps to foster a love of learning.

Did you know?

Basic but effective forms of praise appropriate for use with babies and young children include giving a big smile, saying 'well done' and clapping.

Changing and adapting activities or routines

Sometimes it is necessary to change or adapt activities that have been planned. For instance, babies who have had a poor night's sleep may refuse breakfast because they are over tired. They may need to go to sleep instead, and have their breakfast when they wake up. Consequently, the rest of the day's usual meal and sleep times will need to be adjusted.

Other circumstances that may affect a baby's or child's routine include illness, teething, weaning, adjusting to new environments and going on an outing. It is also necessary it change routines in response to children's development – as time goes on, babies and children will need less daytime sleep for example, and new routines will be introduced as toilet training begins. This is part of 'responsive care', which you'll learn more about in Learning Outcome 4.

LEARNING OUTCOME 3

FOCUS ON

...understanding the attachment needs of babies and young children

In this section you'll learn about the benefits of the key worker system and how babies and young children learn best from a basis of secure relationships with adults. You'll also learn about the possible effects of poor-quality attachments. This links with Assessment Criteria **3.1, 3.2, 3.3.**

attachment felt by the child is strengthened when a familiar adult attends to their care needs. A young child will come to trust and depend on the adult to support them, both emotionally and in a practical sense. Good care routines help children to feel cared for, as the Practical example on page 443 shows.

▶▶▶ Link Up! ◀◀◀

Unit CYP 3.1 Understand child and young person development

Key attachments

Babies begin to emotionally bond with their parents or primary carers soon after birth, and this gives them a sense of safety, security and love. In order for babies and young children to feel happy, settled and secure, they also need to make emotional attachments with other adults that care for them when their parents aren't there. (This links with your learning about Bowlby's attachment theory in Unit CYP 3.1.)

Key attachments are made when familiar adults spend extended periods of time with babies and children, interacting with them frequently and sensitively. The

Good practice

To allow such attachments to form and thrive between babies, young children and adults, it's good practice for group settings to appoint a key worker for each child. The role of a key worker is to take special interest in the well-being of their key children, and to spend time forming close attachments with them. They will also get to know the child's family well, and will be their primary contact at the setting.

Practical example

Clare feeds her key child

Clare works at a children's centre, where she's a key worker for 4-month-old Stephan. It's time for his feed, so she settles down with him in a quiet spot, so he can receive her undivided time and attention. Clare holds him securely against her body, and as she starts to feed him, Stephan gazes into her eyes. He holds on to Clare's fingers, which are wrapped around the warm bottle.

Question
What does Clare do to ensure a time of closeness that they can both enjoy?

Loving, secure relationships

Babies and young children learn and develop best when they feel emotionally settled and secure in the care of the people they are close to and with whom they share strong emotional bonds. When loving relationships have been formed and maintained with primary carers and their key worker, children have a sound base from which they can explore the world, interact with peers and engage with new experiences, secure in the knowledge that they can return to the safety of the relationship whenever they need reassurance, care, attention and support.

Possible effects of poor-quality attachments

Just as there are many advantages of strong, high-quality attachments, there are serious disadvantages associated with poor-quality attachments, as shown on the diagram on page 444.

We'll look at these in turn.

Effects on social and emotional development and security

If young children's attachments are poor quality (perhaps due to inconsistent parenting), or if attachments are regularly broken (perhaps a child in care is moved around, or a baby attending nursery full time has a series of frequently changing key workers), their emotional security will be affected because they will have issues relating to trust. Research has shown that young children who experience poor attachments are likely to show aggressive behaviour, which impacts on social interactions with peers and adults. This may continue as the child matures.

Effects on ability to settle, take risks and make the most of learning opportunities

Babies and young children who are feeling emotional distress are unlikely to display the desire, self-esteem or self-confidence necessary to take risks, and we know that those who are unhappy or anxious are unlikely to be fully engaged in learning opportunities.

A lack of ability to settle for an extended period can be seen in settings if the initial settling-in process has not been taken at the child's pace at the induction period. There's no substitute for giving children time to feel comfortable with their key worker before they are left for long periods by their parent or primary carer. It's also counterproductive for parents to try to 'sneak away' rather than saying goodbye, as it can damage trust and the associated sense of emotional security built up between the child and their parent. Children may also feel angry that they have been 'tricked', or become clingy at other times because they can't trust their parent not to disappear if they let him or her out of sight.

Babies and children who experience difficulty settling when they're young can be more likely to have difficulties with transitions such as starting school

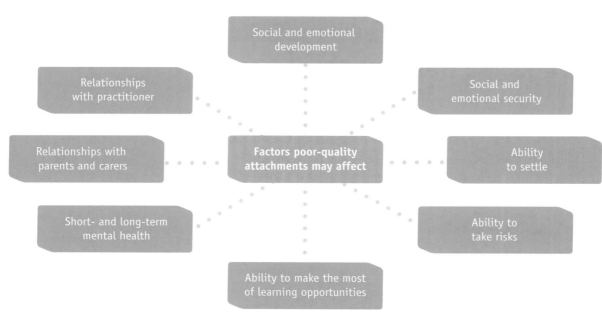

Possible effects of poor-quality attachments.

If attachments are poor quality, emotional security will be affected.

later on. It seems that later transitions may trigger earlier traumatic feelings, although memories of this time are unlikely to be conscious.

Possible effects on short- and long-term mental health

Effects of poor attachment on short-term mental health have been observed in studies when babies and young children have been left by their parent in the care of an adult they have not established a relationship with. Immediate emotional distress is predictably typically shown through crying, but this can be followed by withdrawn behaviour associated with depression. On-going distress caused by poor attachment can lead to long-term mental health problems, and can encompass worrying effects such as sleeping difficulties, self-harm, signs of bullying behaviour and regression behaviour (reverting to the behaviours of a younger child). You'll learn more about this in Learning Outcome 4.

Effects on relationships with parents, carers and practitioners

If a baby or young child doesn't form or isn't able to maintain good-quality attachments when they're young, there's evidence that they may have difficulties forming attachments and relationships in the future. This can lead to them feeling emotionally isolated or detached from parents and practitioners, who may in return find it difficult to make connections with them, and to reach them emotionally.

Ask Miranda!

Q I'm a key worker for several children. Should I always be the one who meets their care needs?

A It's good practice for you to spend plenty of one-to-one time with your key children, and meeting their care needs is an ideal way to do this. It also helps them to feel close to you and to trust you to take care of them. However, it's good practice for them to build relationships with other staff too. Otherwise, they're likely to be distressed if you're off sick or taking a holiday.

LEARNING OUTCOME 4

FOCUS ON ...being able to engage with babies and young children and be sensitive to their needs

In this section you'll learn about engaging sensitively and in playful activity with babies and young children. You'll learn how they express their emotions and needs, and how you can work as a responsive carer. You'll also learn about managing transitions and why babies and young children require periods of rest and sleep. This links with Assessment Criteria 4.1, 4.2, 4.3, 4.4, 4.5.

Engage sensitively with babies and young children

Babies and young children need adults to engage with them sensitively, in a way that respects their emotional needs, as well as their current stage of development. For instance, many very young babies enjoy being sung to, and perhaps the gentle sound of a maraca or shaker being played. However, sudden loud music will be overwhelming and likely to cause the baby to cry.

Empathy

An important method of engaging sensitively with babies and young children is to show empathy for the way they are feeling. If they're upset, use a sympathetic tone and show concern in your facial expressions and body language. If they're happy, smile and use upbeat tones. If they're bored, capture their interest with a new activity and lively, motivating language.

Giving time to respond

Babies and young children are learning the ways of the world, and they need time to process the information that they receive. You need to remember to give babies the time they need to respond when you are interacting with them. This is often a very intuitive part of a practitioner's role. It's natural to slow down, to pick up the baby or child's cues, and to interact at their pace. This is demonstrated in the Practical example on page 446.

Engage in playful activity with babies and young children

You learned about play-based activities for babies and young children in Learning Outcome 2. However, it's possible to take a playful approach to many of the routine interactions that you have with them throughout the day. The simple things that you do frequently on an everyday basis add up to form a significant part of the child's experience of being in the setting, and being with you. These will also be key learning experiences.

Running commentary

Talking to children in a running commentary style about what you're doing, what they're doing or what's going on around you, can be a wonderful way to both engage them and include them, and to expose them to new, rich language. This can often be observed when practitioners are meeting physical care needs. For instance, when changing clothes you may hear a practitioner say 'Here we go, I've found you a nice clean vest. That will keep you warm, won't it? Let's pop it on you, and then we'll put on some nice clean trousers...' Response will be limited, but this doesn't mean that the commentary isn't appreciated.

Engaging in playful activity.

Capturing interest

This complements the running commentary method, because you can point out what's going on around you to babies and young children, using an excited, engaging tone. A favourite activity is to look out of the window together and see what's going on in the world. For example, you might say 'Look, Ruby, the postman's coming! Do you think he's got a letter for us?' You can also draw their attention to an object and motivate them to explore it. A good way of doing this is to do something interesting with the object. So instead of just giving a rattle to a baby, you can

Refer to Learning Outcome 2, Unit EYMP 5 Support children's speech, language and communication, for playful methods to support and extend the language of babies and children throughout the 0–3 year age range, including talking together, singing songs and sharing stories.

Practical example

Nita gives time to respond

Nita is a childminder caring for 6-month-old Ellis. They both enjoy their lively 'conversations'. Nita sits with Ellis, and talks to him in light, playful tones. She then pauses, but maintains eye contact with Ellis, to let him know that she's still engaged with him. During the pause, Ellis has time to process what he has heard. He responds with a string of babbling sounds. Nita waits for him to finish, then she replies, and pauses once again.

Question
How is Nita respecting Ellis's emotional needs, and his current stage of development?

shake it – the motion and noise will help to capture their interest. Or if you hold a child up to look at a homemade mobile fashioned from old CDs, you can give it a nudge so that it moves and catches the light.

Good practice

Babies and young children will also start to show things to you. This is a wonderful time, because they're demonstrating that the experiences they share with you are meaningful to them, and they want to initiate shared experiences themselves. So it's very important that you show a great deal of interest in the things that they point to, or bring to you. This helps to build babies' and young children's self-esteem and self-confidence.

How babies express emotions, preferences and needs

Babies' and young children's feelings can be confusing, both for the children themselves and for adults. Practitioners must understand that while adults will moderate and control their feelings, most young children will not. That's why young children may be happy and laughing one minute and very upset moments later. Children can experience a range of feelings each day. The diagram on page 448 gives examples of this. Practitioners can help young children to understand their feelings and to express them in an emotionally safe and secure environment.

Did you know?

Children should be encouraged to express negative feelings as well as positive ones. This is important, as repressing feelings can lead to pent-up aggression, tension and anger.

Expressing emotional distress

Practitioners should respond to the feelings of babies and young children in a way that lets them know that their feelings are important. Babies and young children will have little or no language to express their feelings, and so it is up to the practitioner to identify signs that reveal how a child may be feeling. Children may demonstrate emotional distress in several ways including:

- crying
- having an emotional outburst/temper tantrum
- becoming quiet and/or withdrawn
- clinging to an adult
- comfort-seeking behaviour (e.g. thumb sucking, asking for a favourite soft toy/comforter or a bottle)
- reluctance to play or participate in activities.

Distress can be caused by a number of everyday events including:

- frustration at not being able to do something – either because of the limits of the child's own ability or because of limits set by adults
- jealousy over another child's toy
- uncertainty of a new place, situation or person
- sudden noises or movements that frighten them
- finding that they are alone – at an activity or at the table, for example, or on waking in the sleep area (young children should never be left unsupervised, but sometimes children can still *feel* alone).

Techniques for calming and comforting

There are various techniques for calming and comforting children. Practitioners must use techniques that suit individual babies and children, taking their age, needs, levels of understanding and preferences into account. Whatever technique is used, it is important to remember that sensitivity is at the

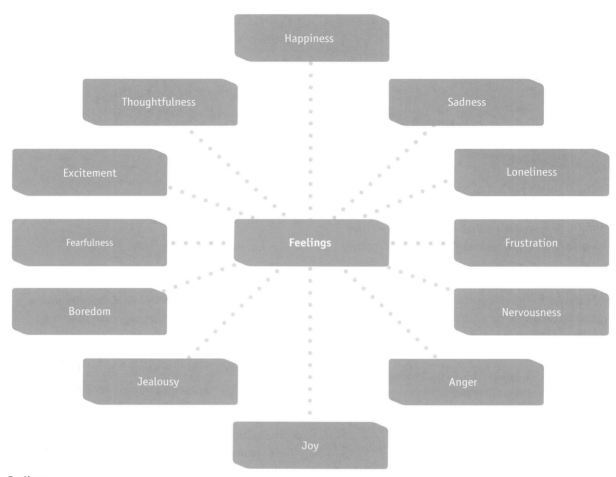

Feelings.

heart of helping children to deal with their feelings. Practitioners must remember the following:

- **Be respectful of children's feelings**
  Never belittle children's emotions or dismiss them. For instance, do not tell children they are 'being silly' or 'getting upset over nothing'.

- **Use only respectful and appropriate physical contact**
  Sometimes children need physical comfort or reassurance from well-known carers. This is particularly true of babies and young children because they have less understanding of the language we use to comfort and reassure (although a soft and gentle tone may still have some effect). Babies and children may gain comfort and/or reassurance from:

- being picked up and held

- having an adult's arm around their shoulders

- holding hands with an adult

- having an adult's hand on their back

- having a cuddle

- sitting with an adult or being close by.

These techniques should only be used when children want them, and always with respect. Carers must respect times when children would prefer their own space.

A cuddle from a well-known carer can comfort a baby or young child.

Acknowledging and talking about feelings

It is possible for practitioners to calm, comfort and reassure babies and children in ways that also encourage them to express their feelings. If you notice a child showing signs of unhappiness, you can begin by acknowledging the child's emotions, then talking about them. You can do this by using a soothing, gentle tone to enquire about a child's feelings. For instance, you may say 'Are you feeling a bit sad?' You can demonstrate empathy by showing your concern in your facial expression and your body language. It is helpful to get down to the child's level. This can be effective with babies and children of all ages – as an adult you will know that sometimes all you need is someone else to understand you. However, if the child has a suitable level of understanding, practitioners can also talk with the child about feelings. By doing this a practitioner can:

- show that the child's feelings are important

- show that the child is understood

- demonstrate language for expressing feelings

- encourage children to share their feelings in the future

- offer comfort where appropriate, and perhaps a solution to an upsetting situation.

Be aware that young children may use basic language to describe how they are feeling – the word 'sad' may cover a range of negative feelings such as frustration, jealousy and anger, for instance.

Play activities

Children can also learn to recognise, explore and deal with their feelings through play. The following activities can be helpful for young children:

- Imaginary play with dolls, puppets and so on – children can act out and work through their own feelings.

- Expressive art such as painting or crayoning – children can use colour, shapes and images to express their feelings.

- Gross motor activities such as running freely outside – children can experience physical release of emotion, including stress, which may be pent up.

- Playing with malleable materials such as dough – children can experience physical release of emotion through the pounding of the material (which is not generally permitted with other types of resources).

Distraction

Babies and young children should be given opportunities to express their feelings as we have discussed. However, it is in their interests to move on positively after they have experienced emotional distress. Once a child has been comforted, finding a way to distract them can help them to move on. Introducing favourite toys or a new activity, a look out of the window or an adult joining in with play can all be effective distraction techniques. A change of environment (such as going outside) can also be very helpful.

Responsive care

'Responsive care' is the term used to describe how practitioners identify and respond to the care needs of babies and young children. Responsive carers respond sensitively, consistently and promptly to the emotions, needs and preferences of babies and young children.

The techniques described above all promote responsive care. There's more information about this in Unit CYPOP 2 Learning Outcome 4. You should read this as part of your study towards this unit.

Children can use colour, shapes and images to express their feelings.

Managing transitions for babies and young children

It's important to manage transitions for babies and young children carefully to limit distress and prevent them from becoming overwhelmed. This is especially important if they will be leaving the safety of people with whom they have a key attachment, and entering an environment that isn't familiar to them. Within settings, this means planning how babies and young children will be gradually introduced to the key worker and the environment before attending full sessions, and how moving on up through the setting will be handled as children progress. If transitions are not effectively managed, they can be the cause of on-going emotional distress.

Link Up!

There's more about this in Learning Outcome 5, Unit CYP 3.1 Understand child and young person development

On-going emotional distress

If emotional distress is on-going over time, babies and children may respond to their feelings in additional ways:

- **Wetting or soiling**
  This may occur in the case of children who have previously been dry and clean during the night and/or day.

- **Changes to the appetite**
  Babies and children may be less or more hungry.

- **Sleeping difficulties**

- **Self-harm**
  This may be seen in children hurting themselves, for example biting their own hand or pulling their own hair.

- **Difficulties getting along with other children**
  Children may show signs of bullying behaviour.

- **Regression behaviour**
  Children may revert to behaviours of a younger child – for example, a 2½-year-old may want to be fed by a carer. This could be in response to many events, including:
  - a new sibling
  - moving house
  - change of carers
  - transitions within settings – starting a setting or moving groups (e.g. from the baby room to the toddler room)
  - a stay in hospital
  - bereavement (deep sadness after a death)
  - tension/illness within the family
  - harm or abuse.

In such cases, practitioners should speak with their supervisor to discuss the way forward. In line with the setting's policies, practitioners will also need to discuss the issue with parents and carers. Some children may need to be referred to outside professionals, such as social workers or psychologists, for assistance.

For more on harm or abuse, see Unit CYP 3.3 Understand how to safeguard the well-being of children and young people

Rest and sleep

Babies and young children need sufficient quiet time to rest and to sleep during the day as well as at night. Up to the age of 3 months, some babies can sleep for up to 16–18 hours in every 24-hour period.

Why and when babies and young children need to rest and sleep is explained in Learning Outcome 3, Unit EYMP 3 Promote children's welfare and well-being in the early years

LEARNING OUTCOME 5

FOCUS ON

...being able to work in partnership with carers in order to promote the learning and development of babies and young children

In this section you'll learn about the primary importance of carers in the lives of babies and young children. You'll also learn about ways of exchanging information with carers, and how to evaluate ways of working with them in partnership. This links with Assessment Criteria 5.1, 5.2, 5.3.

As you learned in Learning Outcome 3, babies and young children need key attachments in their lives. The strongest bonds of greatest importance are the bonds between the child and the parents or other primary carers, such as foster parents. Bonds with siblings and other close family members, including grandparents, are also extremely important. This is because these bonds and relationships are on-going throughout the child's life.

These strong, close, on-going bonds provide a safe base from which children can explore the world and interact with new people, and this impacts on their self-esteem and self-confidence. The love, support, encouragement and care they receive from those with whom they share key bonds, allows them the security of knowing that there are people who will protect them and defend them if necessary. The reason for this protection and defence is that the strong bond between a primary carer and a child is reciprocal.

These strong feelings and internal motivation to protect and defend must be understood by practitioners. It's the reason why parents can find it so difficult to leave their young baby in the care of practitioners. It's important that baby room staff don't get offended because they think that a parent doesn't trust them when he or she becomes upset, or calls during the session to see whether the child is OK.

Did you know?

All children need to feel loved and special to other people in their lives.

In group settings, all children should have their special key person.

Exchanging information with parents and carers

The Early Years Foundation Stage (EYFS) states that, 'Parents and practitioners have a lot to learn from each other.'

The relationship between a child's key worker and the child's parents is therefore particularly important, as the key worker will normally be the parent's chief point of contact with the setting. Parents and practitioners are much more likely to share important information and concerns when a positive relationship exists.

Practitioners must share information that can affect the care and well-being of young children. Details of day-to-day information to be shared when babies and young children are handed back to parents and carers are given in Unit CYPOP 2. Passing on this information allows parents and carers to continue the child's care appropriately. Parents and carers should also be informed periodically about the developmental progress of babies and young children, as you learned in Learning Outcome 2.

Unit CYPOP 2 Care for the physical and nutritional needs of babies and young children

Did you know?

Settings are increasingly making use of technology to stay in touch with parents and carers, and to pass on information to them about their child's time at the setting. Digital photos, video clips and audio clips may all be emailed home.

Benefits of encouraging families to share information

Practitioners should also encourage families to share information they have about their baby or child that may affect the child's care and well-being. This information may include details about and changes to:

Practical example

Barinder hands back

Barinder works in the baby room of a day nursery. It's nearly the end of the session, and her 5-month-old key child, George, will soon be going home. During the day, Barinder has been keeping notes on a 'daily routine sheet' designed by the setting. She's recorded when George was fed and how much milk he took, when he slept and how long for, when his nappy was changed and whether it was wet or soiled. She checks that the record is up to date. She then adds a short message about some experiences that George has enjoyed today. She pops it into his bag.

Question

What are the advantages of adding a message about experiences that George has had today?

Good practice

Establishing a good partnership with parents and carers helps families to feel confident in approaching staff to discuss issues at home that may affect their child's emotional well-being. This allows practitioners to be aware and understanding of children's feelings. It gives them the opportunity to plan how they can best offer appropriate support. This is important not only when big life events occur, but also on a day-to-day basis. For instance, a baby or young child may be in an irritable mood if they are tired following a night of disturbed sleep at home. Or they may feel cross because they have been told off by a parent before coming to the setting.

- medical conditions including allergies and details of any medication or treatment

- medical history

- dietary requirements

- likes and dislikes

- general routine – including details of eating and sleeping patterns

- events in the child's life that may impact on their emotions.

The information should be documented on the registration form, in line with the setting's organisational policies and procedures. Some information, about feeding or allergies, for example, will also be displayed in food preparation and eating areas.

Practitioners must pass on relevant information to colleagues – such as a child's sleeping pattern. However, information of a confidential nature must only be shared on a need-to-know basis.

Methods of encouraging families to share information

You can encourage families to share such information by:

- explaining the benefits of working in partnership when families first visit the setting

- making families aware of the setting's confidentiality policy

- making a private area available for confidential conversations

- ensuring that key workers are accessible to parents who wish to talk.

Evaluating ways of working in partnership

There are a number of ways of working in partnership with parents and carers, as the following paragraphs show:

Observations and assessments

As babies and young children are developing fast in their earliest years, many parents appreciate the opportunity to be involved in the observation and assessment of their learning and development. This process can really engage parents and carers, who will be able to contribute information about the children's learning and development away from the setting, and the skills that this is helping children to develop. For instance, you may learn that a child has started to walk down the stairs alone, holding on to a handrail. This is something you might not otherwise know if your setting is single storey.

Planning

After involving parents in the observation and assessment of their child's learning and development, it makes sense to progress onto involving them in planning future activities and experiences for the child. It's beneficial to consult parents about how they see the child's needs, and how they feel about how these needs are met. You may gain new insight into what the child might enjoy or be interested in based on popular activities at home, and parents may also have some great new ideas to try out.

Link Up!

For more ways to work in partnership with parents and carers, see Learning Outcome 3, Unit EYMP 1 Context and principles for early years provision

How are things going?

▶ Progress Check

1. Explain how development and learning are interconnected. (1.2)

2. What is the impact of current research on brain development of babies and young children? (1.4)

3. Why are assessments of the learning and development of babies and young children undertaken? (2.1)

4. Explain the benefits of a key worker system. (3.1)

5. Give two possible effects of poor-quality attachments. (3.3)

6. Give an example of how you might engage playfully with a 6-month-old baby. (4.2)

7. Why do babies and young children need periods of quiet to rest and sleep during the day? (4.5)

8. Explain the primary importance of carers in the lives of babies and young children. (5.1)

9. Give three examples of ways in which you might work in partnership with parents and carers. (5.5)

Are you ready for assessment?

CACHE

In preparation for assessment of this Unit, practice assessing and recording the development and learning of babies.

Edexel

In preparation for assessment of this Unit, practice assessing and recording the development and learning of babies.

City & Guilds

In preparation for assessment of this Unit, practice assessing and recording the development and learning of babies.

Learning Outcomes 2, 4 and 5 must be assessed in real work environments.

UNIT 2

Care for the physical and nutritional needs of babies and young children

LEARNING OUTCOMES

The learning outcomes you will meet in this unit are:

1 Be able to provide respectful physical care for babies and young children

2 Be able to provide routines for babies and young children that support their health and development

3 Be able to provide opportunities for exercise and physical activity

4 Be able to provide safe and protective environments for babies and young children

5 Be able to provide for the nutritional needs of babies under 18 months

6 Understand how to provide for the nutritional needs of young children from 18–36 months

INTRODUCTION

Babies and children under the age of 3 have specific physical and nutritional care requirements. Practitioners must learn to recognise these and to meet them sensitively and with confidence, so that babies and young children can thrive in terms of their health and development.

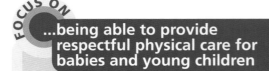

LEARNING OUTCOME 1

In this section you'll learn how to care for
skin, hair, teeth and the nappy area in a
respectful manner tailored to individual needs.
You'll also learn how to meet the preferences
of parents and carers, and about procedures
that protect babies, children and practitioners
when providing personal care needs. This links
with Assessment Criteria **1.1, 1.2, 1.3, 1.4**.

Preferences of parents and carers

Practitioners must always respect parents as the
primary carers of their children. As such, the views
and preferences of parents must also be respected.
Families will have preferences concerning all of the
care routines of their babies and young children – how
and when they are fed and put down for a sleep for
example, as well as how their personal care needs are
met.

It is good practice for practitioners to meet with
parents or carers to discuss their child's care routines
before the child starts attending the setting. The
meeting is usually conducted by the child's key
worker. At this meeting, the key worker should ensure
that they fully understand the child's needs and the
parent's preferences. These should be documented on
the registration form.

Where possible, practitioners should always
accommodate parental preferences if they are in
line with current best practice. It is best for babies
and young children to have similar routines at
home and in the setting. Consistency makes for
smooth transitions and continuity of care. Disturbed
routines can affect children's well-being, leaving

them unsettled and out of sorts. However, sometimes
the wishes of parents and carers do not reflect the
current accepted best practice. In this case, it is
important to discuss and resolve the issue in a
harmonious way, with the best interests of the child
in mind. Further information about this can be found
on page 372.

Did you know?

Care routines need to be monitored, adapted and
changed from time to time to ensure that they
meet the needs of babies and children. These
changes should be discussed and agreed with
parents and carers.

Cultural and ethnically appropriate care

Families' preferences about how the care needs of
their babies and young children are met may be
based on cultural or religious practices. Care needs
should be met in a way that reflects the requirements
of individual children, as long as this does not
compromise the welfare of children.

For more on cultural and ethnically appropriate
care, refer to Learning Outcome 6, Unit EYMP
3 Promote children's welfare and well-being in
the early years

Skin and hair care

The skin and hair of babies and young children needs
to be kept clean to prevent disease and the spread of
infection. If they are not washed regularly, dead skin
cells and bacteria on sweat cause an unpleasant smell,
and sore areas develop on the skin and scalp.

Good hygiene practices are outlined in Learning Outcome 4 Unit EYMP 3 Promote children's welfare and well-being in the early years

Sun protection

Sun protection should be applied to everyone's skin, whatever their age (according to the directions) when necessary. This is particularly important for babies and younger children who have highly vulnerable skin. It's also important to keep babies and young children cool to prevent them from becoming ill during spells of very hot weather. Their health can be seriously affected not only by sunburn but also by dehydration, heat exhaustion and heatstroke. Here's the current advice from the NHS on keeping your child safe in the sun and the heat:

There's further information about sun protection in Learning Outcome 6, Unit EYMP 3 Promote children's welfare and well-being in the early years

---

Sun safety

- Keep your baby out of the sun as much as possible, especially when the sun is at its strongest (between 11am to 3pm). If you do go out on a hot day, attach a parasol or sunshade to the pushchair to keep them out of direct sunlight.
- Remember to apply high factor sunscreen. Many brands are formulated specifically for babies and young children, offering a total sun protection factor (SPF) of 50 plus. Apply the suncream regularly, particularly if your child is in and out of the sea or a paddling pool.
- A sunhat, preferably one with a wide brim or a long flap at the back, will protect your child's head and neck from the sun.

Avoiding dehydration

Drink plenty of fluids so you and your baby don't get dehydrated.

- If you're breastfeeding your baby, you don't need to give them water as well as breast milk. However, they may want to breastfeed a little more than usual.
- If you're bottle-feeding, as well as their usual milk feeds, you can give your baby cooled boiled water throughout the day. If your baby wakes at night, they'll probably want milk but if they've had their usual milk feeds, try cooled boiled water as well.

Try being creative to keep your infant hydrated. If your baby is over 6-months old and they get bored with water, try giving them a combination of very diluted fruit juices, ice cubes and homemade fruit juice lollies throughout the day. For older toddlers and children, plenty of fruit and salad will also help to keep their fluid levels up.

Keeping cool

- Playing in a paddling pool will help to keep babies and children cool. Remember to keep the pool in the shade and supervise the children carefully at all times.
- A cool bath before bed is often beneficial.
- Keep bedrooms cool throughout the day by keeping blinds or curtains closed. You can also use a fan to circulate the air in the room.
- Keep nightwear and bedclothes to a minimum. If your child kicks or pushes off the covers in the night, consider putting them in just a nappy with a single layer (0.5 tog) baby sleeping bag or a well-secured sheet (that won't work loose and cover their face or get entangled during the night).
- A nursery thermometer will help you to monitor the room temperature. Your baby will sleep most comfortably when the room is between 16°C (61°F) and 20°C (68°F).

Sun safety advice from the NHS.

Bathing and washing babies

Parents and carers will have differing preferences about the way their babies are bathed. Some families will give their baby a bath each day. Others may bath their baby less often, but 'top and tail' the baby daily. This term describes the process of washing a baby's face, neck, hands and bottom without putting them in a bath of water. Some families make bath-time part of the getting ready for bed routine. Others prefer to wash babies in the morning so that they start the day feeling fresh.

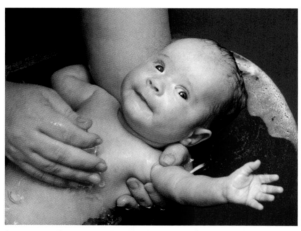

Parents and carers will have differing preferences about the way their babies are bathed.

There are also choices to be made about the type of bath. Some families or carers may use a baby bath that fits over a normal bath tub, a baby bath on a stand, a baby bath on the floor, or even a large sink. Older babies may go in a normal bath that has a safety mat fitted to the bottom of the tub and a rubber ring for them to sit in. Whatever bath is chosen, it is important that it is securely placed on a flat surface. The toiletries used must be suitable for the individual baby, and they must be selected in line with the parent and carer's wishes.

How to bath a baby

In a daycare setting, it is unlikely that you will be required to bath a baby. However, childminders and nannies working in the home may carry out this task more frequently.

Before bathing a baby alone, you should ideally watch an experienced practitioner so that you can see at first hand the correct way to securely hold a slippery baby. It is necessary to adjust the way you support babies according to their age. You must NEVER LEAVE A BABY UNATTENDED IN OR NEAR WATER, and you must NEVER LOOK AWAY, EVEN FOR A SECOND. If you do have to leave the bathing area YOU MUST TAKE THE BABY WITH YOU. Basic guidelines for bathing a baby of approximately 5 to 7 weeks of age are given below:

1 Make preparations – gather together all the equipment you will need – bath, changing mat, nappy changing equipment, clean clothes, baby toiletries, such as bathing lotion and other lotions/oils if necessary, cotton wool, a soft, warm towel and blunt-ended nail scissors. Close windows and doors to ensure that there isn't a draught, and ensure that the room is sufficiently warm, as babies loose heat quickly. Consider and remove any risks – taps that are hot to the touch can be covered by a cold, wet flannel for instance, and soap should be placed out of reach. Wash your hands thoroughly, and ensure that your nails are clean and not too long, or they may dig into the baby. It is advisable to remove jewellery on your hands and wrists and any jewellery that may dangle down, and tie long hair back if appropriate. Wear protective clothing such as an apron and latex gloves. You should also wear flat shoes as the floor may become slippery.

2 Using a bath thermometer, fill the bath with water of the correct temperature – approximately 38°C. Mix the water with your hand to ensure that there are no 'hot spots'. You should also prepare a small bowl of boiled, warm water to be used for the baby's face.

3 Undress the baby, but leave the nappy on for the time being. Wrap the baby securely in a warm towel (from below the neck) and lay him or her on the mat.

4 Wash the baby's face first, using cooled, boiled water to dampen cotton wool. Using a different piece of

cotton wool for each eye, gently wipe across each eye in one movement, beginning at the inside corner and moving to the outside edge (nose to ear). The cotton wool should only be used once for hygiene reasons. Use more dampened cotton wool to wipe around the rest of the baby's face and ears. Avoiding the eye area, dry carefully with clean cotton wool.

5   Check that the baby's nails are short. Carefully cut any long or jagged nails straight across with blunt-ended nail scissors.

6   Wash the baby's hair by leaning him or her over the bath, still wrapped in the towel. To do this you need to use one hand to hold the baby, and the other for washing the hair. Support the baby's head and shoulders in your hand, tucking the legs securely under your arm. Using your other hand, gently cup water over the head – you do not generally need shampoo for young babies. Dry the head gently by patting with a towel. A baby's head must not be left wet as the baby will quickly become cold. Place the baby back on the mat.

7   Remove the towel and the nappy. Clean the nappy area as you usually would when changing a nappy, and dispose of the nappy and soiled toiletries as usual. Lay a towel out ready for after the bath.

8   Lay the baby in the crook of your arm so that the head and neck are supported. Use your hand to hold the arm and shoulder furthest from you. Use your other hand to support the baby's bottom as you lower him or her into the bath. You can then let go of the bottom half of the baby – you now have a hand free for washing. Ensure that you still have a secure grasp with your remaining hand.

9   Gently cup water over the baby with your hand, using stroking movements to massage the skin clean. You may gently use a flannel or sponge, but avoid rubbing. Ensure that you pay close attention to skin creases in the thighs, neck, arms and under arms that can trap sweat and bacteria leading to soreness.

10 Some babies enjoy bathing more than others. If babies are happy, it is good practice to allow them to splash and kick for a short while before ending the bath. However, young babies get cold quickly, so do not prolong this.

11 Support the bottom half of the baby as before. Ensure you have a secure hold as the baby will be slippery. Lift the baby out and lay him or her on the mat. Wrap the baby in a warm towel without delay.

12 You must pat the baby's delicate skin dry (don't rub), paying close attention to the skin creases as before.

13 Apply any lotions necessary and put on a clean nappy. Dress the baby and gently brush the hair with a baby brush if appropriate (use a wide-toothed comb for Afro-Caribbean hair). Settle the baby somewhere safe before cleaning up.

14 Put everything away. Drain the water away first, as this can be hazardous. You should clean the baby bath out, ready for the next use. Put clothes in the appropriate place ready to be laundered. Wash your hands, even if you have been wearing gloves.

Wrap babies in a warm towel.

Did you know?

Babies can drown in a very small amount of water – just 5 cm – so you must always supervise them very closely around water, and never leave them alone. This applies to *any* water, including that in the bath, water tray and even puddles. You cannot be too careful in this respect.

Topping and tailing

As with bathing a baby, you should ideally watch an experienced practitioner top and tail a baby before you carry out the task yourself. The process of topping and tailing requires the same skills as bathing a baby, but you do not need to follow all of the same steps. Basic guidelines are given below:

- Make preparations following steps 1 and 2 of how to bath a baby. Prepare the equipment, the room and yourself.

- Undress the baby and clean the eyes, face and ears, following steps 3 and 4.

- Use additional dampened cotton wool to wash the baby's hands, cleaning in between the fingers. Pat the hands dry gently with a towel. Check the baby's nails, following step 5.

- Following step 7, remove the baby's nappy and clean the nappy area.

- Follow step 13, putting on a clean nappy, dressing the baby, brushing the hair and settling him or her her safely elsewhere.

- Clear up and wash your hands, following step 14.

Toiletries

Each child needs to have their own flannel and toothbrush and a clean towel. When it comes to using soaps, lotions, oils, toothpaste, sunscreens and so on, it is important to ensure that the products selected meet children's individual needs. Practitioners can check this with parents and carers. Failing to check may mean that practitioners use the wrong product for a child's skin or hair type, or use something that a child is allergic to. There are products designed specifically for the delicate skin and hair of babies, including soft, baby hairbrushes and toothbrushes.

Tooth care

A child's first set of teeth, known as milk teeth, usually start to appear during the first year. Cleaning the teeth should become a habit from the time a baby has their very first tooth. Even before then you can introduce babies to a baby's toothbrush (designed to be soft and small) so that they become familiar with it – they will naturally take it to their mouth to explore it.

Very gently clean the first tooth with the brush, morning and evening, so that the habit is formed.

Link Up!

For full details of tooth care, see Learning Outcome 6, Unit EYMP 3 Promote children's welfare and well-being in the early years

Care of the nappy area

Wet and dirty nappies are uncomfortable for babies and they can cause a baby's skin to become sore and inflamed. To avoid this, practitioners should change a baby's nappy as often as necessary. It is usual to change nappies every three to four hours to coincide with mealtimes and in between if the baby is awake and uncomfortable. Babies should always be settled down to sleep in a clean nappy. Many settings establish a routine of changing nappies at regular times to ensure that no child is left feeling uncomfortable. In addition, practitioners will change babies should they become aware that they have a wet or dirty nappy.

It is good practice for key workers to change their key babies' nappies as much as possible, as changing is a time for closeness, talking and play. The key worker will also be more likely to notice any changes that may be cause for concern (see page 462). Many settings require practitioners to make a note of the times that children are changed and whether they have been wet or dirty. This also helps key workers to spot patterns revealing cause for concern, and ensures that all children are changed at appropriate times. In addition, a written record allows practitioners to accurately inform parents and carers about the changes their baby has received. It is essential for key workers to talk with parents and carers about their child's individual nappy changing requirements, and the families' preferences.

Baby changing areas must:

■ Be located in a separate area, right away from food preparation and eating areas.

Changing is a time for closeness, talking and play.

■ Be warm and draught-free.

■ Be stocked with the necessary equipment/ toiletries (these may be provided by the setting or brought in by parents and carers), and a changing mat. Settings often have a mat on top of a changing unit. However, the mat can be placed on another suitable flat surface, or on the floor.

■ Have hygienic facilities for the safe disposal of dirty nappies (the content of which is referred to as 'stools') and wet nappies. There must also be a container for the storage of soiled clothes ready to be laundered. There must be facilities for the

thorough cleansing of surfaces and changing mats after each baby has been changed.

Types of nappy

There are two types of nappies, as described below:

■ **Reusable nappies**
Although shaped nappies are available, reusable nappies are generally made from a rectangle of absorbent terry towelling. Such nappies are folded to fit individual babies and fastened with nappy pins (these have been designed with a safety feature to ensure that they do not come undone). There is a range of nappy folding techniques to suit babies of different sizes, and some methods are more suited to boys or girls. It is best to learn how to fold nappies from an experienced practitioner who can demonstrate on one nappy while you follow along using another. A disposable nappy liner may be used inside of the nappy. These help to keep babies comfortable as they remain dry (keeping wetness away from a baby's skin) but let wetness through to the nappy. Disposable liners can be flushed down the toilet along with stools. Whether or not a liner is used, plastic pants are placed over the nappy – these are available in various sizes. For reuse, terry nappies must be thoroughly rinsed out. They should then be placed in a nappy pail (a bucket with a close fitting lid) filled with sterilising solution, and be left to soak. They can then be fully laundered.

■ **Disposable nappies**
These days, disposable nappies are not only available in a range of sizes, but also especially shaped to be suitable for boys or girls, although unisex nappies are still available. Used nappies must always be hygienically disposed of. Some settings have a nappy unit that automatically seals a nappy into a plastic wrapping as it is placed inside. In other settings, practitioners will place soiled nappies in plastic bag and tie the bag closed. The bag will then be disposed of in the appropriate bin, and the bin lid will be replaced.

Parent's preferences of nappy should be discussed and followed. In some cultures, a cloth may be placed under young babies instead of a nappy.

Cause for concern

Changing nappies gives practitioners the opportunity to detect any cause for concern in the nappy area of a baby's body. Details of some such concerns, along with concerns about infection and irregular bowel movements or urination, are given in the table below.

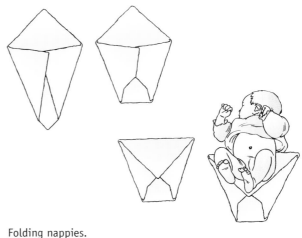

Folding nappies.

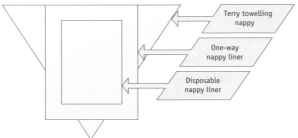

Using a nappy liner.

Changing nappies

The changing area should be suitable as previously described. It is important that all the necessary equipment is at hand so that you will not need to leave the nappy area. In the interests of safety,

Table CYPOP 6.1: Causes for concern

Cause for concern	Possible explanation and what to do
Baby passing stools very frequently. Stools are loose in consistency, and may be watery	The baby may have diarrhoea caused by infection. In a group setting, a child with diarrhoea should be sent home as soon as possible. Parents and carers will need to seek medical advice if diarrhoea persists.
Baby passing hard stools, which may be green in colour, or failing to pass stools regularly	The baby may be constipated. It is important to make parents and carers aware of this. Initially, giving a weaned baby fruit may be sufficient to solve the problem.
Blood can be seen in stools or streaks of blood are on the nappy	The baby may have an injury. Or, sometimes a small amount of blood is passed with hard stools when a baby is constipated. This information should be passed on to parents and carers who will need to seek medical advice.
Bruising or other marks on the skin of the nappy area	The baby may have been injured in an accident, or they may have been injured intentionally. If you do not know how the marks occurred, you may need to ask parents or carers, and/or log the accident.
Soreness/redness, a rash, blisters. This is very painful, and a baby may cry when a nappy is changed. Untreated soreness can quickly progress to a rash/blistering	The baby may have nappy rash or an allergy to the nappy/nappy liner, or in the case of reusable nappies, the detergent used for laundering. Or, the baby may have an infection such as thrush. Report to parents and carers, and ensure that nappies are changed frequently – at least every two hours and when necessary in between. Make sure that the baby's bottom is thoroughly dried after cleaning. Creams should be used sparingly (if appropriate). Sometimes special creams are prescribed by a doctor.
Failure to urinate regularly	The baby may not be drinking enough liquid. Offer frequent drinks and report to parents and carers.
Strong-smelling urine, which may be dark in colour	The baby may have a urine infection. Offer plenty of fluids, and report to parents and carers who will need to seek medical advice.

you must NEVER LEAVE A BABY UNATTENDED ON A CHANGING MAT. You MUST NOT LOOK AWAY, EVEN FOR A MOMENT. If you do need to leave the area for any reason, YOU MUST TAKE THE BABY WITH YOU.

1   Wash your hands and put on protective clothing – latex gloves and an apron.

2   Place the baby on the changing surface. If the changing mat is not on the floor, it is safest to keep one hand on the baby throughout the changing process. If the baby is happy, talk playfully and make eye contact. Soothe the baby with your voice if he or she is unhappy.

3   Undress the bottom half of the baby, gently pulling clothes well out of the way before you remove the nappy. Sometimes a nappy leaks a little, so check that clothes have not become wet or dirty. If they have, remove them.

4   Clean the nappy area thoroughly but gently. The method chosen for this will depend on the baby's requirements – you may use wet wipes or other lotions, or water and cotton wool. Ensure that the area you have cleaned is left dry to prevent soreness. Then apply any lotions in line with parents' or carer's wishes.

5   Give the baby time to move his or her legs around while the nappy is off, sometimes called 'kicking free'. This helps to make nappy changing an enjoyable experience. However if the baby is distressed, you should finish the changing process so that you can offer comfort.

6   Put a clean nappy on and redress the baby, using fresh clothing if necessary. Settle the baby safely elsewhere before clearing away.

Engaging with babies and young children in a respectful manner

It is important to ensure that all babies and children are allowed their dignity while care needs are attended to, and to ensure that they are touched in a gentle and respectful manner. See Unit EYMP 3, Learning Outcome 6 for further details. Also see the section 'Respect and sensitivity during everyday care routines' in Learning Outcome 2 of this unit.

Link Up!

Unit EYMP 3 Promote children's welfare and well-being in the early years

Ask Miranda!

Q How can I bond with babies when attending to their care needs?

A **Take your time and really make the most of the one-to-one opportunity to engage in eye contact with babies, to talk to them and to be close to them. This also helps babies to enjoy the process, which is important as a good deal of their physical contact with others takes place when care needs are met.**

Personalised physical care tailored to needs

As children grow up they can begin to care more for their own physical care needs such as:

■   toileting

■   washing

- bathing

- washing hair

- applying sun screen/lotions/oils.

It is good to encourage children to care for themselves because:

- it promotes independence

- it promotes self-reliance and confidence

- it promotes a positive self-image and self-esteem

- it also helps to protect children from abuse or exploitation. Children are vulnerable when someone else cares for physical needs such as toileting or washing their bodies.

Good practice

It is important to stress that younger children should not be rushed into caring for themselves until they are ready. Individual children will be ready at different times. Children's ages, needs and abilities must all be taken into account.

Procedures and processes that protect babies, children and adults

When attending to physical care needs, practitioners must follow their setting's procedures and processes for promoting good hygiene. This protects both adults and children from cross-infection. Procedures and processes that promote hygiene include:

- washing your hands before and after nappy changing, washing and toileting

- wearing disposable gloves for nappy changing (and toileting if necessary)

- wiping the changing mat thoroughly with disinfectant spray

- keeping soiled laundry away from clean clothes and washing it thoroughly

- keeping the bathroom area clean and well stocked with soap, toilet paper and paper towels.

It is essential that settings also adopt '**safe working practices**', that is, procedures to ensure the following:

- Children are protected from abuse during care routines such as toileting and nappy changing. (Babies and younger children are entirely dependent and unable to make a disclosure, which increases their vulnerability.)

- Children are not subject to abuse or exploitation at any time they are present in the setting.

- The adults who work with children are suitable according to regulatory requirements.

- The adults who work with children and who may become vulnerable to accusations of improper behaviour are protected.

Link Up!

You'll find further information about these procedures and processes in:
Unit CYP 3.4 Support children and young people's health and safety
Unit EYMP 3 Promote children's welfare and well-being in the early years

key term

Safe working practices ways of working that keep both the practitioner and the baby, child or young person they are working with protected and safe from harm.

LEARNING OUTCOME 2

...being able to provide routines for babies and young children that support their health and development

In this section you'll learn about providing routines and how to treat babies and young children with respect during those routines. You'll also learn about the principles of effective toilet training. This links with Assessment Criteria **2.1, 2.2, 2.3.**

Routines for babies and young children

When caring for babies and young children, there's a lot to do! Well planned routines are essential. Not only do these routines help the practitioner to ensure that they fit in everything that needs to be done, they also provide an important structure to each day for the babies and young children. Most are happier and feel more emotionally secure when they have settled into a good routine, and in particular their sleep pattern is generally much improved. Routines need to take into account the individual needs of the babies and young children you work with, and activities such as play and going for a walk in the fresh air will be fitted around a core structure of repetitive everyday physical needs including the following:

■ **Nappy changes**
As you've learned, practitioners usually plan to change nappies at certain times, such as after meals and before naps. They'll also change nappies in between times if they become aware that a baby is wet or dirty.

■ **Bathing and washing**
As previously mentioned, bath-time is sometimes part of the morning routine, and sometimes part of the evening routine. It's important to be organised

and have everything ready so the baby doesn't become cold.

■ **Dressing**
Organisation is the key to ensuring that babies and children have plenty of clean clothes available as they may get through a couple of changes during the day, particularly if a baby brings up a feed or a nappy leaks.

■ **Rest, naps and night-time sleep**
Regular routines are much more conducive to good-quality sleep and this impacts on a baby or child's mood and experience when they are awake. During waking hours, it's important to provide a good balance of physically stimulating play and activities (see Learning Outcome 3), interspersed with quieter, more restful opportunities, such as sharing a book together. The latter are also helpful for winding down in preparation for a daytime nap.

■ **Feeding/mealtimes/snacks**
Babies and young children need to be fed nutritiously as regular intervals – you'll learn more about this in Learning Outcomes 5 and 6.

Respect and sensitivity during everyday care routines

Because these tasks are repeated so frequently when children are young, they are an important part of their overall experience of life and their knowledge of interacting with adults. Practitioners must remember this and ensure that they attend to children's care needs sensitively.

For children to have a positive experience, it is important that practitioners do not rush when attending to care needs. Sometimes you may need to remind yourself of this. Practitioners working in busy group settings with several babies to attend to must remember to take their time with each child, avoiding the 'treadmill approach' of simply dealing with one task after another without engaging with the individual babies or children concerned. Every child must be and must feel respected during care routines. This is achieved through affectionate and appropriate touch, speech and gesture.

During care routines adults can do the following:

- **Make the most of one-to-one time**
  Care routines are a great time to bond and play with babies and children on a one-to-one basis. Approaching care routines playfully also helps children to enjoy them. While babies are changed or fed, they are lying or sitting in front of their carer. It is an ideal time to make eye contact and to talk.

- **Let children know they are cared for and respected**
  You can do this by attending to care needs at a child's pace, and by using respectful, affectionate touch, speech and gesture.

- **Use the experience as a learning opportunity**
  For instance, it is never too soon to talk with babies and children about care routines. While washing a child's hands for instance, you can say 'We'll rub some soap in to make your hands nice and clean...'.

- **Encourage independence**
  Children will eventually take responsibility for all of their own care needs. It is the job of practitioners to encourage this.

For information on routines that provide opportunities for learning and development and using routines to encourage self-care, see Learning Outcome 6, Unit EYMP 3 Promote children's welfare and well-being in the early years

Toilet training

Children can only become clean and dry, or 'toilet trained', when they have control over their bowels and bladder. There is no point in trying to toilet train a child until this time. Babies have no bowel or bladder control – they will often wet or dirty their nappy soon after feeding, but they may also do so at any other

Babies and young children need regular rest, naps and night-time sleep.

time. Bowel and bladder control develops at different times in different children. It often occurs between the age of about 18 months and 3 years. Most children are dry and clean during the daytime by the time they are 3.

Frequent accidents can be expected at first as children may not notice until the last minute that they need to go to the toilet. Sometimes, children may wait too long to go, particularly if they are absorbed in an activity. Initially, adults generally need to remind children to go to the toilet. The best way to do this is to build visits to the toilet into the day-to-day routine. It makes sense to ask children to go to the toilet before meals and snacks as they will be going to the bathroom to wash their hands in any case. You should also take them to the toilet before and after naps.

It's important that toilet training does not become an issue of conflict between children and adults. To avoid conflict and stress, it is best to take a relaxed approach, waiting until the individual child is showing definite signs of being ready for training before attempting the process. Although children may have control as early as 18 months, many children will be into their second year before they show signs of readiness. Some will be older. The signs include:

- children saying they are about to soil or wet their nappy

Ask Miranda!

Q What about night-time/sleep-time bladder control?

A This takes longer to develop. Many children still have accidents at night until the age of 6 or 7, and some continue to do so beyond this age. Some disabled children may develop bowel and bladder control much later and may continue to use nappies. A few may never develop control.

Build visits to the toilet into the daytime routine.

- children telling a carer that their nappy needs changing

- children showing interest in the toilet or potty, or in other children's use of them

- children showing reluctance to wear a nappy

- children saying that they want to wear pants

- children being able to tell adults that they need to use the toilet, verbally or with signs.

Equipment for toilet training

Ensure that you have the right equipment for toilet training before you begin the process as follows:

- **A child-sized toilet or potty, or a child's toilet seat that fits inside a normal toilet seat**
  It is advisable to introduce children to these prior to training, so have them in the bathroom. Children who already use the toilet or potty can be good role models, helping other children to understand their use.

- **Soft toilet paper**

- **Plenty of spare clothes**
  Children may wet through everything they are wearing, including socks and shoes.

- **Materials for cleaning up both children and the environment after accidents.**

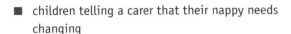

Good practice

Here are some good practice guidelines for toilet training:

- Plan your approach to training in consultation with parents and carers. Some may ask your advice but others may be clear about the approach they would like to take.

- Be relaxed about training, and do not rush children. If you do, children may become anxious or toilet training may become a battle. Praise children for using the toilet or potty. Deal with any accidents without fuss, and in private, getting children into clean clothes as soon as possible. Do not make children feel guilty, bad or embarrassed about having accidents by showing disapproval.

- It's helpful to give children plenty of fluids and fibre in their diet to prevent hard stools, which can be uncomfortable to pass and lead to a negative association with going to the toilet.

- Most libraries stock children's books that show characters using the toilet or potty. There are several that show children learning the skill and being praised. These can be useful to read with children who are toilet training, particularly if they do not have another child as a role model.

467

LEARNING OUTCOME 3

FOCUS ON

...being able to provide opportunities for exercise and physical activity

In this section you'll learn about the importance of exercise and physical activity for babies and young children. You'll also learn how to support babies and young children's exercise and physical activity. This links with Assessment Criteria **3.1, 3.2.**

Plenty of floor space is a key consideration in meeting the needs of babies and young children.

The importance of exercise and physical activity

You learned about the importance of exercise and physical activity in Unit EYMP 3. Babies and young children need plenty of opportunities for exercise and physical activity within a balanced routine that also promotes periods of rest and daytime naps as required.

▶▶Link Up!◀◀

Unit EYMP 3 Promote children's welfare and well-being in the early years

Supporting babies and young children's exercise and physical activity

Plenty of floor space is a key consideration in meeting the needs of babies and young children. They must have space:

■ for exercise and physical activity

■ to develop mobility

■ to explore their environment safely.

Babies and young children need more clear floor space than older children because of the way that

they play and learn. Practitioners need to give this special consideration when planning the layout of the setting, as explained in more detail in Learning Outcome 4.

In addition to providing appropriate space, practitioners can encourage babies and young children to exercise, develop mobility and explore their surroundings by:

■ providing appropriate resources, equipment and experiences for the developmental stage of babies and children

■ joining in play with babies and young children

■ praising babies and young children when they exercise, explore or engage in activities that develop mobility

■ helping babies yet to crawl to explore their environment by moving them periodically and changing the resources within their grasp.

Resources and activities to promote exercise and physical activity

Selecting appropriate resources and activities to promote exercise and physical activity depends on your knowledge of:

■ patterns of physical development and

■ the current stage of physical development of the individual children that you work with.

This knowledge enables you to provide opportunities for babies and young children to consolidate and enjoy their existing physical skills, while providing them with the opportunity and challenge to practise the skills they are likely to master next. This is illustrated in the following Practical example.

There is more information in Unit CYPOP 1 Learning Outcome 2, where in the 'Play-based activities tailored to support needs, learning and development' section, the activities that promote exercise and physical development are indicated with the abbreviation 'PD'.

Unit CYPOP 1 Work with babies and young children to promote their development and learning

Practical example

Julietta selects resources

Julietta is a childminder. She hasn't cared for a baby for a while, but she recently began working with 9-month-old Cole. He often gets onto his hands and knees, and is likely to crawl very soon. To encourage him, Julietta sorts out a selection of toys she has had packed away that are suitable for his age. She's particularly pleased to find some items that will travel across the floor, including two balls with bells inside and a largish, brightly coloured car made from durable, chunky plastic. She also makes a mental note of the fact that she has a baby walker trolley tucked away too – that could be very useful in two or three months' time.

Question

What other toys or resources would promote exercise and physical activity for Cole at this stage in his physical development?

LEARNING OUTCOME 4

FOCUS ON

...being able to provide safe and protective environments for babies and young children

In this section you'll learn about the health and safety policies and procedures that cover health, safety and protection of babies and young children. You'll also learn about environmental safety features and supervision for babies and young children, and about current advice on minimising sudden infant death syndrome in everyday routines for babies. This links with Assessment Criteria **4.1, 4.2, 4.3, 4.4.**

Policies and procedures for health, safety and protection

Settings caring for babies and young children must comply with the relevant laws and regulations, which will have been interpreted by individual settings within their health and safety and child protection policies.

Link Up!

These are outlined in Learning Outcome 1, Unit CYP 3.4 Support children and young people's health and safety

Organisational issues

In order to ensure the health and safety of babies and young children, practitioners need to give careful consideration to room arrangement.

Babies and young children need to have plenty of clear floor space. Very young babies will need room to lie out comfortably on baby mats placed on the floor

and there should be sufficient space for them to roll around. They will also spend some time in their baby chairs. As babies start to crawl, they need plenty of room to manoeuvre and explore.

When babies first start to walk, they will frequently fall over – when they are moving around in an open area there is less chance of them injuring themselves on furniture. As they grow into busy toddlers, children often enjoy moving around a room quite quickly, making the most of the space they have to play in. They have not yet developed the concentration span necessary to spend very long in one place doing one activity. Practitioners need to ensure that the layout of the setting accommodates plenty of clear floor space. It makes sense to keep furniture to the minimum. The stability of the furniture chosen is important as babies will use it to pull themselves to standing position and will hold onto it for support when they first start to walk.

Floor space must also be allocated to the equipment that is needed by this age group – high chairs and cots take up quite a lot of space in group settings.

High chairs and other equipment take up a lot of space.

Supervising babies and young children

Babies and young children need constant and close supervision. They must not be left unsupervised at any time. In addition, much adult time is spent attending to their physical care needs. Practitioners will be making up feeds, feeding, changing nappies and so on. Babies and young children also need to have the time and attention of adults to meet their emotional needs. To allow for this, regulations stipulate that there must be a higher ratio of adults to young children than is required for older age ranges.

Did you know?

The required ratios for day care settings in England are: children under 2 years: one adult to three children, children aged 2 years: one adult to four children. These ratios are the accepted minimum standards. Many settings exceed them.

There is more information about levels of supervision in Learning Outcome 2, Unit CYP 3.4 Support children and young people's health and safety

Assessment of hazards and risks

Risk assessments are a vital part of keeping babies and children safe. There is information about how and why you should conduct risk assessment in CYP 3.4, Learning Outcome 2. A good understanding of babies and young children's development also informs the assessment process.

A balanced approach to risk management

Practitioners should take all reasonable precautions to ensure that babies and young children are safe. However, it is important that opportunities for development are not restricted. Practitioners have to accept that all young children will incur minor injuries as they play and develop. As long as young children move around and use equipment, they will occasionally have minor accidents leading to grazes, bumps and bruises. But to deny them the opportunity to move freely and play would be wrong – it would

limit their experiences and ultimately affect their development.

Health and safety policies held by settings will explain how the organisation manages risk assessment. Practitioners can take the opportunity to explain in the policy that risk assessment should ensure that all reasonable precautions are taken without restricting opportunities for development.

Safe practices must still allow young children to move and play freely.

Responsive care

It is important to have responsive, reflective and knowledgeable adults caring for babies and young children. 'Responsive care' is the term used to describe how practitioners identify and respond to the care needs of children. This is extremely important with this age group as they do not generally have the language to explain to adults what they need – practitioners must interpret this for themselves. This is a skill based on practitioners' knowledge of:

■ the development pattern of babies and children

■ the individual baby or child.

For instance, a baby may cry for a number of reasons. The practitioner needs to find out what is wrong so that they can attend to the child. The practitioner will look for signs accompanying the crying in order to work out what the baby needs. They will consider what they know about babies and young children in general, as well as what they know about the specific child. They will want to find out if the baby is any of these things:

- **Tired**

  Are they rubbing their eyes or yawning? Are they blinking heavily and slowly? When did they last sleep? Do they often sleep around this time?

- **Hungry**

  When did they last have a feed? Did they take all of their feed? Are they ready to start weaning – perhaps they seem to be hungry again a short time after feeding, and are they right age to begin weaning?

- **Lonely**

  Are they alone? Do they need a cuddle or someone to play with? In the case of a baby who cannot crawl yet, do they need to be repositioned closer to other children for company?

- **Bored**

  Have they been in the same position or playing with the same toy for some time? Have they got access to resources or activities likely to stimulate them at their stage of development?

- **Unwell**

  Are they displaying any signs or symptoms of illness? Are they the right age to be teething, and are they showing any signs of this (dribbling, red cheek, inflamed gums)?

- **In need of a nappy change**

  A quick check will reveal whether they are wet or dirty.

- **Frightened**

  Have they been startled by a sudden or loud noise? Have they seen a stranger? Do older, mobile children scare particular younger babies when their play becomes boisterous or too close?

- **Frustrated**

  Are they experiencing difficulty with a task? Are they frustrated because they cannot reach a toy they have dropped? Or are they hungry but

struggling to feed themselves effectively – has most of the food ended up on the floor?

Effective practitioners are constantly using their **responsive care** skills.

key term

Responsive care how practitioners identify and respond to the care needs of children.

Ask Miranda!

Q How can I develop my responsive care skills?

A These skills are informed by experience – the more time you spend with babies and young children, the more 'tuned in' you will become to recognising their care needs. It is eventually a very natural, intuitive part of a practitioner's role, and a key way in which practitioners notice when a baby or young child is hurt, unwell or in need of protection. Reflection is also a key part of developing responsive care skills.

▶▶ Link Up ◀◀

For more on reflection, see Unit SHC 32 Engage in personal development in health, social care or children's and young people's settings

Safety features and equipment

There are many pieces of equipment that help adults to keep babies and young children safe and secure. While it is essential to use safety equipment when it is required, practitioners must ensure that they do not restrict the movement of babies and young children unnecessarily. For instance, while reins may be used to take 2-year-olds on a short walk, such walks should not be used to replace time spent running around and exploring freely outside. The following diagram shows the safety equipment that may be used.

Toys and equipment

Care must be taken when choosing toys and equipment for all children. See Unit CYP 3.4 Learning Outcome 1 for information on how to choose equipment safely. This explains the safety marks you should look for before purchasing any toys or equipment. Many children's products are not suitable for children under 3 – you must always read the safety labels closely. It's also important to keep toys and equipment safe and hygienic.

To prevent cross-infection, toys used by young babies should be sterilised between each use as infants will put everything into their mouths. Highchairs and changing mats must also be cleaned thoroughly after each use. As children grow, toys can be cleaned at the end of each day. To keep their clothes in a clean and hygienic condition, babies and young children need to wear protective garments when they are engaged in activities that could be messy.

This may include:

- bibs worn at feeding and meal times

- aprons worn during activities such painting or playing with sand/water/modelling clay and so on.

Unit CYP 3.4 Support children and young people's health and safety

Handing back to parents and carers

The person collecting a child needs to be given the appropriate information that they need in order to continue with the child's care. The information they need includes:

- whether the child has taken a milk feed or eaten a meal (if so, how much was consumed and when; if not, when they were last offered food)

- when the child last had a drink

- whether the child has slept, when, and for how long

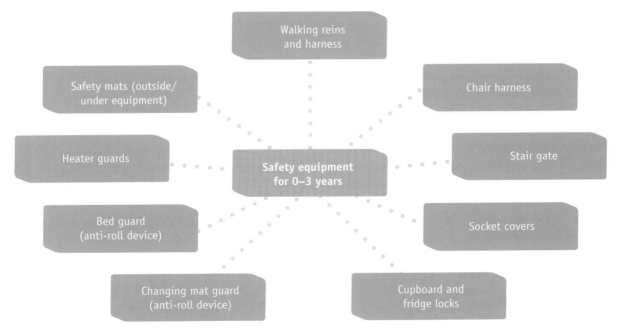

Safety equipment for children between 0–3 years.

- whether the child has been generally happy and well throughout the session – if not, further details should be supplied

- brief information about an activity the child has done today or a toy they enjoyed. (Remember that many children in the age range will not have the language to tell parents and carers about their day.)

Many settings provide this information in a short, written daily report.

It's important to pass on information needed in order to continue with a child's care.

Sudden infant death syndrome

Sudden infant death syndrome (SIDS) is the term used to describe the sudden and unexpected death of an infant that is initially unexplained. Some deaths are later explained at a post-mortem examination. Deaths that cannot be explained at post-mortem are generally registered as sudden infant death syndrome. A specific cause is identified in less than half of sudden infant deaths. The babies usually die peacefully and without distress in their cots during the day or night-time, but sudden infant deaths can occur during any period of sleep – when babies are in their prams or in the arms of a parent or carer for instance.

SIDS can affect any babies, but those that are premature and have low birth weight are more at risk, as are boys and babies born to mothers who are very young. SIDS is most common in babies' second month and the risk reduces as babies grow. Almost 90 per cent of sudden infant deaths occur by 6 months. SIDS is uncommon in babies under 1 month and in babies over 1 year. SIDS is more common in families who smoke heavily or live in difficult circumstances. It is uncommon in Asian families although the reason for this is not yet known.

On average, 300 babies currently die from SIDS every year in the UK. This figure is an improvement on the death rates before a 'reduce the risk' campaign in 1991. This shows how important it is to follow the guidelines issued by the Foundation for the Study of Sudden Infant Death Syndrome (FSIDS) for reducing the risk of SIDS. The guidelines are as follows:

- Parents should stop smoking in pregnancy (fathers as well as mothers).

- No one should be permitted to smoke in the same room as a baby.

- Babies should be placed on their backs to sleep (not on their front or sides).

- Babies should not be allowed to get too hot.

- Babies' heads should be kept uncovered. They should be placed to sleep with their feet at the bottom of the cot to prevent them from wriggling down under the covers.

- Medical advice should be sought promptly if a baby is unwell.

- It is safest for babies to sleep in a crib or cot in their parents' bedroom for the first 6 months.

- It can be dangerous to share a bed with a baby.

- It is very dangerous to sleep together with the baby on a sofa, armchair or settee.

- Settling a baby to sleep with a dummy (day and night) can reduce the risk of cot death, even if the dummy falls out while the baby is asleep.

- Breastfeed babies where possible. Establish breastfeeding before starting to use a dummy.

Did you know?

FSID has a freephone helpline (**0808 802 6868**) for parents and professionals seeking advice on safe baby care. The Helpline also supports bereaved families. Advice for parents and professionals can also be found at **www.fsid.org.uk**

Good practice

Sleeping babies must be checked on frequently, and in daycare settings, a record of these checks must be kept. It's also sensible to have a baby-room thermometer on the wall of play and sleep areas.

Practical example

Sonia's sleep log

Sonia is the team leader of the baby room at a children's centre. She keeps a log near the sleep room door. When her staff put a baby to bed, they record the time. They then check the baby every 10 minutes and log the time of the check on the form. They also record what time the baby gets up. Additional information can also be recorded, such as when the baby actually fell asleep and whether they slept soundly.

Question

Why has Sonia introduced this system?

LEARNING OUTCOME 5

FOCUS ON

...being able to provide for the nutritional needs of babies under 18 months

In this section you'll learn how to meet young babies' nutritional needs in line with government advice, and how to plan a programme of weaning. You'll also learn how to prepare formula feeds effectively, and how to evaluate different types of formula commonly available. This links with Assessment Criteria **5.1, 5.2, 5.3.**

Regulations for food handling

The Food Safety Act 1990 and the Food Hygiene Regulations were introduced to protect people from food poisoning. Under the Act:

- all staff who handle or serve food must have a Basic Food Hygiene Certificate

- the person in charge has responsibility for ensuring safety

- it is illegal to cause illness to people through contamination of food if the contamination was avoidable

- it is illegal to contaminate food on purpose or knowingly.

General food preparation and storage guidelines are given on page 374.

The nutritional needs of babies under 18 months

In order to have a balanced diet, babies should receive the recommended nutrients each day. The nutritional needs of babies and children vary according to their age, height and weight. Until the age of 4 to 6 months, babies will be fed exclusively on either breast milk or formula milk.

Supporting breast-feeding

Breast milk naturally contains all the nutrients that babies need in the correct proportions at the right stage. It is also convenient – there is no need to prepare bottles, the milk is already the right temperature and it is free of charge. Colostrum is the name given to the first milk that is produced. This contains maternal antibodies produced within the mother's body. They are passed on to the baby through the milk and can protect them against some infections. There is less risk of infection occurring in the feeding process when babies are breast-fed. The milk itself does not contain germs. Some mothers want to continue breast-feeding their baby when they start attending a setting. Practitioners should discuss the mother's needs with them, following their setting's guidelines. The mother may wish to express her breast milk and supply it in a feeding bottle so that practitioners can bottle feed the baby with breast milk. In this case:

- all equipment must be sterilised as described below

- bottles should be clearly labelled with the date and the baby's name

- expressed breast milk must be stored in the fridge and used within 24 hours

- expressed breast milk may be kept in the freezer for up to three months by parents and carers at home, but it must be thoroughly defrosted before use

- at a workplace crèche, a mother may be able to come and breast-feed her baby when necessary. Settings can provide a comfortable, private area where mothers can breast-feed or express milk.

Preparing formula feeds

There are two stages to preparing a formula feed for babies – the cleaning and sterilising of equipment, and making up the formula.

Breast milk naturally contains all the nutrients that babies need.

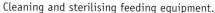

Cleaning and sterilising feeding equipment.

Sterilising equipment

When making up formula for babies under 1 year old, all of the equipment that will be used must be thoroughly cleaned and sterilised. This is to kill germs that may still remain after the usual washing and drying of dishes. The same applies to all feeding equipment (such as bowls and spoons) used for this age group. The equipment used will be:

■ bottles

■ teats

■ bottle caps

■ measuring spoons

■ plastic knife

■ plastic jug

■ bottle brush

■ teat cleaner

■ sterilising unit with sterilising tablets or liquid *or* a steam sterilising unit.

Before sterilising, the equipment must be cleaned. It must be rinsed, washed and rinsed again (see the diagram on page 476). A bottle brush must be used to clean the bottles. A much smaller version of this, known as a teat cleaner, should be used on the teat. At one time salt was used to clean teats, but this is *no longer considered good practice* as there is a risk of increasing the salt intake of a baby if residue remains in the teat. *Never use this method.*

The equipment can now be sterilised. There are different methods of sterilising. The traditional method is to make up a sterile solution by mixing either sterilising tablets or sterilising solution with water, according to the manufacturer's instructions. The equipment is then submerged in a sterilising unit for a specified time (see below). However, steam sterilising units are also now available. They come with manufacturers' instructions for use.

Making up the formula

It is very important to make up formula, correctly otherwise babies could become ill.

The diagram on page 478 shows the procedure that should be followed. There are some important things to remember:

■ Only use boiled water to make up feeds.

■ Clean and disinfect the kitchen surface you're working on before you start.

■ Always measure the formula powder out carefully. Formula that is too strong is dangerous to babies' health. Formula that is too weak means that babies will not get the nutrients they need. Never use more powder than necessary. Do not pack the powder down into the scoop, do not use heaped scoops and do not add extra scoops of powder. You must level the scoop off with a sterilised knife, as shown in the diagram.

You will need to cool the formula before it can be given to a baby. An effective way to do this is to stand the bottle in a jug of cold water for a few minutes. Then shake the bottle and test the temperature of the milk by putting a few drops on the inside of your wrist (this is a sensitive area). It should feel just warm.

1 Check that the formula has not passed its sell-by date. Read the instructions on the tin. Ensure the tin has been kept in a cool, dry cupboard.

2 Boil some fresh water and allow to cool.

3 Wash hands and nails thoroughly.

4 Take required equipment from sterilising tank and rinse with cool, boiled water.

5 Fill bottle, or a jug if making a large quantity, to the required level with water.

6 Measure the exact amount of powder using the scoop provided. Level with a knife. Do not pack down.

7 Add the powder to the measured water in the bottle or jug.

8 Screw cap on bottle and shake, or mix well in the jug and pour into sterilised bottles.

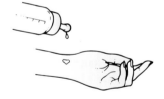

9 If not using immediately, cool quickly and store in the fridge. If using immediately, test temperature on the inside of your wrist.

Preparing a feed.

10 Babies will take cold milk but they prefer warm food (as from the breast). If you wish to warm the milk, place bottle in a jug of hot water. Never keep feeds warm for longer than 45 minutes, to reduce the chance of bacteria breeding.

Note: whenever the bottle is left for short periods, or stored in the fridge, cover with the cap provided.

Good practice

Recently, guidelines about the storage of prepared feeds have changed. The advice now is that to achieve best practice, you should make up feeds at the time they are required whenever possible, whereas previously it was considered equally acceptable to make up bottles in advance and store them in the fridge. The purpose of the new advice is to minimise the risk of food poisoning. Here's the current advice to parents from the NHS:

Feeding away from home

If you need to feed your baby while you are away from home, you can take a measured amount of milk powder in a small, dry container, plus a flask (or bottle) of hot water that has been boiled and an empty, sterilised feeding bottle. This will enable you to make up a fresh feed as and when you need it.

However, the water must still be hot when you use it so that any bacteria in the milk powder are destroyed. Remember to cool the bottle under cold running water before you start to feed your baby. Alternatively, you could use ready-to-drink infant formula milk.

If you are unable to follow the above advice or if you need to take a feed to another location, such as a nursery or a child minder's house, you should prepare the feed at home and cool it at the back of the fridge. Take it out of the fridge just before you leave and transport it in a cool bag with an ice pack.

You should use the feed within four hours, or if you reach your destination within four hours, take it out of the cool bag and store it at the back of the fridge. Do not store the feed for more than 24 hours. However, this length of time is no longer considered to be ideal, particularly for young babies. Wherever possible it is always safer to make up a fresh feed.

Current advice from the NHS about feeding away from home.

Types of formula

If making up a feed at the time it is required is not practical (e.g. because the baby and carer will be out), it's possible to use cartons of ready-to-drink formula.

However, these are quite an expensive option. All this means that for many families formula feeding has lost one of its primary attractions – convenience.

You should always use the brand of formula milk agreed upon with the parents unless a doctor or health visitor advises otherwise. Changing brands of formula may upset a baby's stomach.

Bottle-feeding babies

The amount of milk that should be offered to babies depends on their weight. The formula will have directions, which you should follow. As a general guide, over each 24-hour period, babies need 150 ml of milk for each kilogram of their weight.

At first, babies who are bottle-fed should be fed when they are hungry. This is known as 'feeding on demand'. However, babies should soon settle into a routine where they are fed at regular intervals. The routine will vary from baby to baby, but generally, new babies need about eight feeds a day, given at approximately four-hour intervals. Adults can calculate how much milk babies need at each feed by:

- dividing the amount of food needed in 24 hours (see above) by the number of feeds per day.

Practitioners should bottle-feed babies in accordance with current best practice and the wishes of parents and carers.

How to bottle-feed

Bottle-feeding is a time for bonding and closeness, and so ideally a baby's key worker should feed the baby as often as possible. It is important to establish a comfortable and calm environment in which to feed a baby. You must not rush the feeding process. Use the time to talk to the baby, and to hold the baby's gaze with eye contact.

1   Gather together everything you will need – bottle, bib and muslin cloth – and wash your hands thoroughly.

2   Before feeding, CHECK THAT YOU HAVE THE RIGHT BOTTLE FOR THE RIGHT BABY – a child with an

allergy could become seriously ill or even die if they are given the wrong bottle.

3   YOU MUST ALWAYS BE ABSOLUTELY SURE THAT YOU HAVE THE RIGHT FEED. Babies can experience wind if the flow of the teat is too slow, as they will take air into the stomach as they are forced to suck too hard. However, if the flow of the teat is too fast, a baby may choke. Check the flow of the teat by tilting the bottle – the milk should steadily fall from the teat in drops. It is the size of the hole in the teat that controls the flow. Teats with holes of differing sizes are available to suit the needs of differing babies. As a general rule, young babies need a slower flow of milk than older babies.

4   Warm and test the temperature of the milk as described above.

5   Put a soft bib on the baby, and sit together somewhere comfortable. Some settings may have suitable soft furniture to sit on, or you may sit on the carpet.

6   Hold the baby in a semi-reclining position with one arm, so that the head is resting in the crook of your arm. The baby's head should be higher than the rest of the body.

7   Hold the bottle at an angle with your opposite hand so that the teat fills with milk, and allow the baby to latch on to the teat (take the teat into his or her mouth). Babies often curl their hand around your fingers as you hold the bottle. Continue to tilt the bottle further as the baby drinks the milk.

8   Go at the baby's pace. Some babies like a break or two during their feed.

9   Wind a baby during this time (as well as at the end of their feed). After a short break, offer the baby the bottle again. Younger babies generally require breaks more frequently than older babies.

10 Wind can be uncomfortable for babies, and because a baby's mobility is limited, it can be difficult for a baby to pass wind in order to release the air in the stomach. You should always wind a baby after feeding. To do this, hold the baby on your lap in a sitting position, the body leaning slightly forwards. Gently rub the back. Sometimes babies will bring up a little of their feed. You can anticipate this by having a muslin cloth (or other suitable material) to hand to clear up with. The bib helps to protect the baby's clothes. Some babies tend to bring up more feed than others. Some may have been prescribed drops to take in advance of their feed to help them keep their milk down.

11 After feeding, gently clean the baby's face and settle the baby in a new position. You should not clear away until the baby is settled. However, do not leave bottles unattended within the reach of other children – they may put the teat in their mouth and perhaps even drink left over milk that is not for them.

12 In line with the procedures at your setting, record the relevant details of the feed, as parents will need this information when they collect the child. It is usual to record the date and time of the feed, how much milk was taken and any difficulties – if the baby was more than a little sick afterwards, for instance.

Hold the bottle at an angle so that the teat fills with milk.

Babies sometimes need specialised feeding equipment, such as teats with a fast or slow flow, or with a special angle. These should be used in consultation with parents, carer and, if necessary, medical professionals. Information about the requirements should be documented and shared with all those who feed babies within the setting.

The importance of weaning

Weaning is the term used to describe the process by which babies are introduced to solid foods. The most up-to-date guidance from the Government (which has recently changed) states:

> 'Health experts agree that around six months is the best age for introducing solids. Before this your baby's digestive system is still developing and weaning too soon may increase the risk of infections and allergies. Weaning is also easier at six months. If your baby seems hungrier at any time before six months, they may be having a growth spurt and extra breast milk or formula milk will be enough to meet their needs ... solid foods should never be introduced before four months.'
>
> If you decide to wean at any time before six months, there are some foods that should be avoided as they may cause allergies or make your baby ill.

Current weaning advice from the NHS.

Did you know?

It is dangerous to introduce babies to solids before the age of 4 months because their kidneys are not mature enough to handle natural salt in weaning foods, and their digestive system and bowels are not yet developed enough to handle solid foods.

key term

Weaning the process by which babies are introduced to solid foods.

You'll learn more about allergies and food that makes babies ill on page 482.

The main aims of weaning are:

- to gradually decrease nutritional dependence on milk, and to introduce sufficient nutrients to meet the health needs of growing babies (such as iron)

- to introduce new textures and flavours

- to introduce bowls and spoons, allowing babies to join in socially at mealtimes

- to establish acceptance of healthy eating patterns and habits.

Practitioners should discuss weaning with parents and carers and agree a joint approach.

Families are sometimes anxious about weaning, but they can be reassured that in the early days children will still be getting most of their nutrients from milk as solids will be introduced gradually. At this stage the main priority is to get children used to flavours and textures, and to remain relaxed about feeding so that mealtimes do not become battlegrounds.

A weaning plan

Always check the most up-to-date guidelines, as these do change. The following is in line with current NHS guidelines for babies from 6 months of age:

- Establish a relaxed atmosphere. Make sure that babies are not too tired or too hungry before introducing solids. Some babies respond well to having some milk to settle them before they are offered solids.

- Sterilise all feeding equipment, including bowls and spoons. A broad, flat plastic spoon is best with most babies.

- At first babies should be offered a small amount of bland, warm food of a loose or sloppy consistency. The food should be free from salt, gluten and sugar. Baby rice and banana are both ideal, and they can be mixed with warm milk from the baby's bottle. Half to a full teaspoon of food is enough to start with.

- Babies may refuse the food at first because the experience is new. But the same food can be offered again the following day. It is good practice to give babies the opportunity to get used to one taste over two or three days before a new taste is introduced. This also means that adults can easily identify a food that may upset a baby's stomach.

- Puréed fruits, vegetables and bland baby cereals are all good foods for early weaning. (Give cereals only once per day.) Gradually babies will begin to take more spoonfuls of food. As the amount of solids taken increases, the amount of milk given should decrease. By about the fifth week of weaning, one of the baby's milk feeds should be replaced entirely by solid food. Cooled, boiled water can be offered to drink at this mealtime.

- As babies become interested in their feeding spoon, have an extra one for them to hold at feeding times, and allow them to help. This is the first step towards independence at mealtimes. Protect clothing and flooring well so that you can relax about this as learning to feed is generally a messy affair!

- Remember that mealtimes should be a positive social experience. Always supervise young children's eating in case of choking, and be particularly aware when new textures and lumps are introduced.

- When a baby is used to eating vegetables, other foods should be introduced, such as puréed or mashed-up meat, fish and chicken, lentils, pulses, mashed rice, noodles or pasta and dairy products, such as yoghurt, fromage frais or custard – select the varieties that are full-fat but contain lower amounts of sugar.

- Babies gradually learn to manage lumps, and then they can be offered harder foods such as peeled apple cubes and bread crusts. Babies can chew these with their hard back gums. They are ideal 'finger foods' for babies to feed to themselves.

From about 9 months, the NHS advise that babies should be offered:

- Three to four servings of starchy food each day, such as potato, bread and rice.

- Three to four servings of fruit and vegetables. Vitamin C in fruit and vegetables helps to absorb iron, so give fruit and vegetables at mealtimes.

- Two servings of meat, fish, eggs, dhal or other pulses.

- By now a baby should be learning to fit in with the family by eating three minced or chopped meals a day as well as milk. Babies may also like healthy snacks such as fruit or toast in between meals.

From 12 months, children can drink full-fat cow's milk instead of formula.

Special dietary requirements and information

Some babies and children have specific dietary and/or food preparation requirements.

These can relate to the milk a baby drinks as well as the food taken – some babies may have soya milk, for example. The special requirements may be due to allergies or medical conditions or they may be related to culture, ethnicity or religious beliefs. So it is essential that all dietary requirements are fully understood, and that the carer's instructions on the needs of their child are carefully followed. These must be documented and the information must be shared with appropriate colleagues.

For further information on special dietary requirements, see Learning Outcome 5, Unit EYMP 3 Promote children's welfare and well-being in the early years

Unsuitable foods

The following table explains which foods are unsuitable for babies and children at different ages, and the reason for this.

Table CYPOP 2.2: Unsuitable foods

Details of food	Details of age restriction	Reason
Salt Must not be added to babies' food. It is not allowed to be added to baby foods on sale in the UK. Limit the intake of food high in salt, such as cheese, bacon, sausages. Do not give processed foods not intended for babies (such as breakfast cereals), as these may be high in salt.	Up to 6 months, babies should have less than 1g of salt. From 7 months to 1 year, they should have no more than 1g. (Formula and breast milks contain the right amount of salt.)	A baby's immature kidneys cannot cope with more than the recommended amount of salt.
Sugar Do not add sugar to food or drinks. Sour fruit such as rhubarb can be sweetened with alternatives such as mashed banana or formula/breast milk.	This is advisable for all babies and young children.	Sugar can encourage an unhealthy sweet tooth and cause tooth decay as teeth come through.
Honey	Do not give honey until babies are at least 1 year old.	Honey can contain a bacteria that produces toxins in immature intestines, causing serious illness.
Wheat-based foods and other foods containing gluten including bread, wheat flour, breakfast cereals and rusks **Nuts and seeds** **Eggs** **Fish and shellfish** **Citrus fruit and citrus juice**	Avoid these five foods until a baby is 6 months old. Only ground or flaked nuts should be given to children under 5. Many settings have a no nut policy due to the commonality of nut allergies among children. Egg white and yolk must always be cooked to a solid consistency to prevent food poisoning.	These foods can cause allergic reactions, so it is advised that they are not introduced before the age of 6 months. GPs may advise introducing certain foods even later if food allergies run in the family.
Full-fat cow's milk **Goat's and sheep's milk**	Avoid until the baby is 1 year old (all milk must be pasteurised).	It does not contain enough iron and nutrients to meet the needs of younger babies.
Semi-skimmed milk	Avoid until the age of 2 years.	Can be introduced then if a child is a good eater with a varied diet.
Skimmed milk	This is unsuitable for children under 5.	It does not contain sufficient nutrients.
Squash, fizzy drinks, flavoured milk, herbal drinks, diet drinks, tea and coffee	These are unsuitable for babies and toddlers.	These are not recommended for one or more of the following reasons: they may contain sugar or caffeine, they may cause tooth decay or fill babies up, leading to a poor appetite and poor weight gain.
Low-fat foods, including yoghurt, fromage frais, cheese and fat spreads	Avoid until the age of 2 years.	It does not contain sufficient nutrients for younger babies and children.

LEARNING OUTCOME 6

...understanding how to provide for the nutritional needs of young children from 18–36 months

In this section you'll learn how to plan meals for young children that meet their nutritional needs. You'll also learn about food allergies and intolerances, and about the importance of following carers' instructions on the needs of their child. This links with Assessment Criteria **6.1, 6.2.**

Plan meals for young children that meet their nutritional needs

Meals planned for young children should meet their nutritional needs in line with the current guidelines from the Government.

Link Up!

You can read more about current Government guidelines in Unit EYMP 3 Promote children's welfare and well-being in the early years

As you know from Learning Outcome 3 and your learning about child development, between the ages of 18 months and 3 years young children are very busy! Most will naturally be very active, and you will be supporting opportunities for physical activity and exercise. Children also rapidly grow and develop physically during this phase of life.

To fuel all of this, young children need to receive a 'nutrient-dense diet' (see opposite) and also plenty of fruit and vegetables.

Did you know?

Nutritional guidelines are always subject to change, so it's essential to keep yourself up to date. Reading professional early years magazines and journals is a great way of doing this.

A nutrient-dense diet

Foods that are 'nutrient dense' are both high in calories and high in nutrients such as vitamins, protein and minerals. (The functions of these are outlined in full in Unit EYMP 3.) Young bodies need the calories to give them enough energy for all that activity, and the nutrient protein helps with growth. Young children have small stomachs, so it's important not to fill them up with foods that won't give them the nourishment that they need.

Foods that are high in calories but low in nutrients, and foods that are high in calories and also high in saturated fats, should only be offered to young children as very occasional treats. This includes fried foods and pastry-based foods such as pies and sausage rolls, snacks such as biscuits, crisps, sweets and chocolate, and sweet desserts or puddings. Sugary drinks should also be avoided – they are often

Young children need a nutrient-dense diet and plenty of fruit and vegetables.

laden with calories and they are also bad for young children's teeth. It's best to offer milk or water. Plenty of water also helps to avoid constipation.

Good practice

It's good practice to introduce young children to a range of new tastes and consistencies. Don't overwhelm them – just put a small helping on their plate and praise them if they try a little. If a child doesn't like a taste, wait a few days, then introduce it again – often familiarity is all that's needed, and after trying a taste a few times, a child will grow to like it. Never force a child to eat everything on their plate, or to try a food if they're not keen – this can put them off trying any new foods at all and turn mealtimes into a battleground. It's much better to stay relaxed. It can also be helpful for them to see other children and members of their family eating and enjoying foods that are new to them.

Sharing and responding to dietary information

In order to ensure that children have a good balanced diet, parents and carers need to be aware of what their children have eaten when they are with you. It's good practice to work in partnership with parents on the design of a menu because, as you've already learned, it's beneficial for young children to eat similarly to when they are at home. Always let parents or carers know if a child has not eaten well, so they can monitor this and also offer extra food if a child is hungry later. Ask parents to let you know if a change in appetite occurs at home so that you are equally prepared.

As you learned in Unit EYMP 3, it's important that you respect and follow instructions from parents and carers on the needs of their child in relation to nutrition and mealtimes. These may be due to personal preferences, cultural requirements or food allergies or intolerances. You may like to revisit Unit EYMP 3 to recap this essential information – remember that food allergies can seriously harm the health of young children.

Unit EYMP 3 Promote children's welfare and well-being in the early years

How are things going?

▶ Progress Check

1 What actions would you take to engage with babies and young children in a respectful manner while carrying out physical care? (1.1)

2 What actions can you take to support exercise and physical activity for babies and young children? (3.2)

3 What is meant by taking a 'balanced approach' to risk management? (4.3)

4 Why is it advisable to wean babies at 6 months of age and not before? (5.1)

5 Describe the process of making up a formula feed hygienically? (5.2)

6 What are the advantages of a 'nutrient-dense' diet for young children? (6.1)

Are you ready for assessment?

CACHE

In preparation for assessment of this Unit, you may like to collect together meal plans that you have completed for babies and young children, to use as evidence.

Edexel

In preparation for assessment of this Unit, you may like to collect together meal plans that you have completed for babies and young children, to use as evidence.

City & Guilds

In preparation for assessment of this Unit, you may like to collect together meal plans that you have completed for babies and young children, to use as evidence.

UNIT 5

Understand how to set up a home-based childcare service

LEARNING OUTCOMES

The learning outcomes you will meet in this unit are:

1 Understand how to set up a home-based childcare service

2 Understand how to establish a safe and healthy home-based environment for children

3 Understand the importance of partnerships with parents for all aspects of the home-based childcare service

4 Understand the principles of development of routines for home-based childcare

5 Understand how to provide play and other activities for children in home-based settings that will support equality and inclusion

6 Understand how home-based childcarers can support the safeguarding of children in their care

7 Understand the principles of supporting positive behaviour in home-based childcare settings

INTRODUCTION

Some aspects of providing a service in a home-based setting are unique to the home environment. However, many of the principles and practices of providing care for children at home are the same as in a group setting. Because of this, there are many links to other units in this section. You're advised to follow these as part of your study towards this unit.

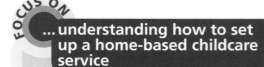

LEARNING OUTCOME 1

FOCUS ON

... understanding how to set up a home-based childcare service

In this section you'll learn about legislation, regulatory bodies, policies and procedures. You'll also learn about confidentiality, marketing, financial planning and services of support for your home-based childcare business. This links with Assessment Criteria **1.1, 1.2, 1.3, 1.4, 1.5, 1.6.**

Legislation and regulation

In the UK, anyone wishing to become a childminder for children under the age of 8, **must become registered**. However, registration for childminders caring for children over the age of 8 (who are regarded as 'older children'), and for nannies, is voluntary.

Each of the home countries has a different regulatory body. The regulatory bodies in each home country are responsible for their registration procedures, and each issue their own set of standards which potential childminders are required to meet before they can become registered. Here are the regulatory bodies in each of the home countries, along with the web addresses you need to find out about their standards:

- England: The Office for Standards in Education (Ofsted) **www.ofsted.gov.uk**
- Scotland: Social care and social work improvement Scotland (SCSWIS) **www.scswis.com**
- Wales: The Care and Social Services Inspectorate for Wales (CSSIW) **http://wales.gov.uk/cssiwsubsite/newcssiw/?lang=en**

Have a go!

Using the web addresses provided above, go online and find out about the registration processes in your home country. You can also download or request a paper copy of the relevant standards for registration.

- Northern Ireland: Your own local Health and Social Services Trust **http://www.northerntrust.hscni.net/**

Policies and procedures

The purpose of policies and procedures is to set out in writing how you will work in practice to meet the requirements of the legislation and regulations that apply to you as a childminder. Your regulatory body will want to see your policies (if you are registered), and you should also make these available to parents and carers. It's best to use straightforward language so that parents are clear about your ethos and work practices. Key policies and procedures will include:

- accidents, illness and emergencies
- behaviour
- safeguarding
- equal opportunities.

The Childminding Associations in the UK are fantastic sources of advice, and they have guidelines to support childminders with creating policies and procedures:

- National Childminding Association (for England and Wales): **www.ncma.org.uk**
- Scottish Childminding Association: **www.childminding.org**
- Northern Ireland Childminding Association: **www.nicma.org**

Have a go!

Have a go at devising a behaviour policy. You can refer back to Unit CYP 3.2, Learning Outcome 5, which includes guidelines on the key things to cover in a behaviour policy. Try to keep the language user friendly.

Link Up!

CYP 3.2 Promote child and young person development

Good practice

To make sure that policies and procedures are effective, it's good practice to review them regularly – at least once a year. At this time, you should check that the policies and procedures still reflect current legislation and regulations, as these are updated from time to time. You should also consider whether the ways of working outlined in the policies and procedures have worked effectively in practice.

Confidentiality and data protection

Confidentiality and data protection are covered in Unit SHC 1, Learning Outcome 4.

Did you know?

Sometimes parents may talk about their lives openly in the childminder's home, and others who live there may hear. It's important for a childminder's family to understand that they shouldn't pass on any information.

Link Up!

Unit SHC 1 Promote communication in health, social care or children's and young people's settings

Good practice

For childminders, it's essential to ensure that confidential documents cannot be accessed by others living on the premises, so it's advisable to have a lockable box or lockable filing drawer. Confidentiality applies to electronic files as well as paper-based information. So if others in the home use the same computers, it's essential to ensure that sensitive files are password protected. Sometimes, childminders find themselves under pressure from others to talk about things they know about families through their work. Neighbours and the parents of other children you care for can be quite curious! However, you must not be drawn into discussing any personal information.

You must not be drawn into discussing any personal information.

Practical example

Fiona's dilemma

Fiona is a part-time childminder for two parents, Jane and Nicole. On Mondays, both of their children attend, and Nicole's child comes on Fridays also. Jane and Nicole don't know each other well these days, but they attended the same school years ago. Nicole has started to ask Fiona things about Jane's life. At first she asked which house she lives in (she already knew the street), then what job her partner did. Fiona said they might only seem like little details, but she can't talk about Jane's business. Now Nicole is starting to tell Fiona things she knows about Jane instead. This gossiping makes Fiona uncomfortable and she feels she should interrupt.

Question
What do you think Fiona should say to resolve the situation without offending Nicole?

Starting your own business

Anyone who's starting up their own business, in any line of work, will need to do some business planning and organising. Some key areas to think about are shown on the diagram on page 491.

Marketing
Marketing is the term given to the process of letting your potential customers know that you're going to be offering a service. Your aim is to encourage parents and carers looking for childcare to get in touch. Hopefully some of the interest that marketing attracts will translate into childminding bookings for places. When you're first starting out as a childminder, you need to be organised about this, so you need to draw up a marketing plan.

You also need to think about your budget. There are some low-cost/free ways to advertise, but you'll also need some printed materials to display and to send out when parents get in touch with you. A flyer or leaflet designed on a home computer will be fine, and/or some business cards or postcards (ideal for shop window advertising). These can be ordered from a printer – from the high street or online – quite cheaply. Keep it simple and eye-catching. You'll want to include:

- your name and the name of the service if it has one (e.g. Happy Days Childminding)

- days and hours of service

- the fact that you are registered and insured

- the area you live in and phone number/email (don't put your actual address)

- the area in which you will drop off/collect children at schools/pre-schools

- your qualifications/training and experience (e.g. 'five years' nannying experience').

A brief statement that says something special about the service you're offering is also a good idea. On a business card, a few words are all you'll have space for. To help you to come up with a marketing statement, imagine there are three childminders advertising in the shop window. Why should parents be interested in you? What are the unique selling points that make your service stand out? You'll need to choose your own, but here are some examples:

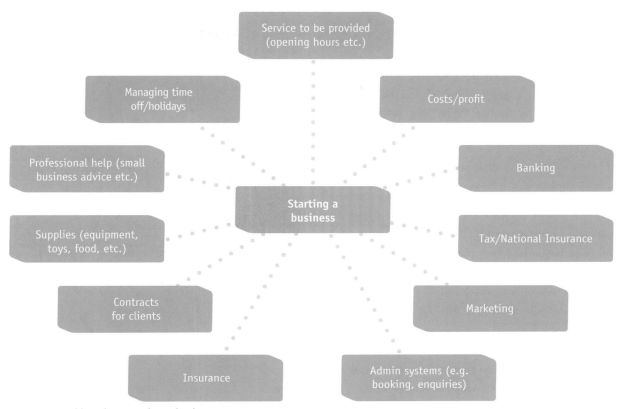

Areas to consider when starting a business.

- creative activities a speciality

- homely atmosphere

- a large garden for children to play in

- flexibility in terms of hours/days (e.g. early mornings, Saturdays)

- age range of children allows siblings to attend together

- individual attention/one to one work

- regular visits to the nearby park

- happy, settled children are your main priority.

Where to advertise

Think about where you can advertise within budget. Places where there are children and families and places where there are employees or people doing training courses are all a good bet, for example newsagents/local shop windows, schools, pre-

Did you know?

Often parents will call you first and ask for some information in the post. If they like the sound of your service, you have the days free that they require and the cost is within their budget, the next step is for them to come for a visit and a chat.

schools, community centres, libraries, health centres (especially where ante-natal classes and baby clinics are held), hospitals, job centres, recruitment agencies, personnel departments of large local employers, estate agencies, colleges, universities and so on. There's usually a small charge for notices in windows, but the display of notices on boards inside buildings is generally free.

Did you know?

A good tip: Boxed business adverts in local papers can be expensive. But it's much cheaper to advertise by the line in the 'jobs' listing. You can advertise your service here – it doesn't matter that it's not a job! And people looking for a job will see it; people who may have children who they need minding.

Financial planning

All small businesses must think carefully about their financial planning. Your childminding service won't be a successful business unless you handle the finances in an organised way so that you can make a profit. Key things to consider are:

- what your set-up costs will be – how much will you need to spend on toys, safety equipment, resources and so on to kit out your service

- cost of the training you need (e.g. first aid, child protection, food hygiene)

- on-going expenses including insurance and Childminding Association membership, food and drink, toiletries, cleaning materials, transport costs, wear and tear on home, extra heating/power costs

- on-going admin costs including stationery, postage, receipt book, account book

- professional costs such as an accountant

- how much you will charge (in line with the local going rate) for your basic rate, and how much for any additional services (such as unsociable hours or retainers to keep places held)

- when and how payment will be due (e.g. weekly by cash or cheque, monthly by standing order) and how/when you will invoice parents

- if/how much parents will pay when child is absent due to planned holidays or sickness

Think carefully about your financial planning.

- how much money you need to draw from the business each week to support yourself and your family)

- how you will make arrangements to pay your tax and National Insurance.

Sources of support and information

The previously mentioned Childminding Associations will be a big support. If you are thinking of joining a childminding network, you will also receive support there. Business Link will advise on all aspects of setting up and managing a small business. You can contact them and access advice via **www.businesslink.gov.uk**. Enter your postcode and you will be directed to your local service.

Good practice

To protect both you and the parent, it's advisable to always issue childcare contracts for each child. These should detail the days and time booked, fees payable and when they are due, any additional costs agreed (such as penalties for late collection), holiday arrangements (yours and theirs), what happens if you or a child are unwell and how much notice should be given to terminate the booking. This should be signed by you and by the parent – keep a copy for yourself and issue a copy to the parent.

LEARNING OUTCOME 2

FOCUS ON

...understanding how to establish a safe and healthy home-based environment for children

In this section you'll learn about the key components of a healthy and safe home-based environment, and the principles of safe supervision. You'll also learn about ensuring that equipment is suitable and safe, obtaining guidance on risk assessment and how to store and administer medicines. This links with Assessment Criteria **2.1, 2.2, 2.3, 2.4, 2.5.**

Safety in the home-based childcare service

Health and safety is covered fully in Unit CYP 3.4, and hygiene is also covered in Unit EYMP 3, Learning Outcome 4. Refer back to these as part of your study for this unit. However, there are some additional points which relate particularly to maintaining a safe environment in the home rather than a setting, for you to consider alongside. These are given opposite and on page 494.

Link Up!

Unit CYP 3.4 Support children and young people's health and safety
Unit EYMP 3 Promote children's welfare and well-being in the early years

Items that could cause harm

The home environment needs special attention in terms of keeping everyday household items that could cause harm away from children. Think about how you will safely store:

- medication and tablets (including vitamins, etc.)

- cleaning products

- alcohol

Did you know?

Many of the standards from your regulatory body will be concerned with safeguarding children, both in the home and off-site (when you go on walks, trips and visits). You must maintain these standards at all times.

- cigarettes

- matches, lighters

- gardening tools

- maintenance tools (DIY, car, decorating, etc.)

- plastic bags

- sharp objects (knives, scissors, etc.)

- poisonous plants

- glass objects (vases, etc. in the case of younger children)

- pet food.

Keep cleaning products out of the reach of children.

Good practice

In the home, it's important to make sure that others living with you know not to leave out items that could harm children. It's very easy to take aspirin for a headache and leave the tablets on the table, or to leave the scissors out after using them. The consequences could be very serious. Also make sure that you use safety gates as necessary. These are useful to prevent children from wandering into rooms alone as well as stopping them from accessing the stairs. You may have a gate at the kitchen door for instance.

Hygiene and waste disposal

- Have a proper system in place for what waste goes in what bin. Disposable nappies should be tied up in a plastic bag, then disposed of in an outdoor bin with a lid as soon as possible – never put them in a kitchen bin.

- Never change nappies or have a potty in the kitchen.

Storage and preparation of food

- If you store pet food in the fridge, it must be kept covered and stored towards the bottom, just above any raw meat.

Good practice

The kitchen can be a potentially hazardous place. Make sure that any sharp implements are out of reach, as well as equipment such as toasters and food processors, and make sure that any required safety features such as hob guards and cupboard locks are in place. Dish cloths and tea towels must be kept scrupulously clean, and surfaces must be frequently wiped over with antibacterial spray. Do not allow pets on the worktops. Avoid leaving pet food out.

- Never use food that has gone past the sell-by date.

- Ensure that frozen food is fully defrosted before cooking it.

Care of animals

Childminders must ensure that any animals on the premises are safe to be in the proximity of children and do not pose a health risk:

- Never leave children alone with pets or animals that could harm them.

■ Keep animals in good health, including keeping vaccinations up to date, worming regularly and keeping them free of fleas and ticks.

■ Keep animals clean.

■ Dispose of any animal waste immediately and safely, and clean the area with antibacterial product afterwards. Never exercise dogs in your garden, even when children are not there, and keep litter trays away from children's areas and out of their reach.

■ Make sure that sand trays are covered to stop animals getting in – cats in particular seem to regard them as giant litter trays!

■ Don't leave pet food out – dispose of remains after the animals have been fed and clear the floor area with antibacterial product after feeding to avoid bacteria multiplying. Remains of pet food can also attract pests. Keep food bowls out of children's reach.

■ Keep grooming brushes and so on out of children's reach, and don't leave pets' toys where young children can get hold of them. A toddler won't understand that the interesting squeaky toy on the floor shouldn't go in their mouth as well.

Using equipment according to manufacturer's guidelines

■ It's important to use equipment according to manufacturer's guidelines to ensure that it's used safely. However, you'll sometimes be using equipment provided by parents – the child's pram or buggy for instance. Make sure that you're shown how to fold these out properly, using all of the safety catches. This is not always as easy as it sounds to get the hang of! If you need to ask parents to show you more than once, that's fine – they probably had to have a couple of practice goes themselves.

■ Make sure that you observe the age guidelines given, not just for toys but for equipment. Sometimes weight guidelines are given instead/as well. It's dangerous to put a child in a car seat that's too big for them, or to put a toddler in a highchair that's intended for babies. Check equipment regularly for good working order and to ensure that there are not broken bits or sharp edges that could be hazardous, just as you would check toys and resources.

Response to illnesses

Make sure that parents understand your policies (including whether they have to pay when their child is absent due to illness). In the home, you may have medication and so on used by your family, but you must NEVER give children anything that has not been given to you by the parent/carer. You must get their written permission and follow the usual guidelines about administering medication and documentation.

Medication guidance is given in Learning Outcome 6, Unit EYMP 3 Promote children's welfare and well-being in the early years

Safe supervision

Generally, the younger children are, or the more challenging an activity, the closer the level of supervision will need to be. For some activities, it's safe for children to work and play independently as long as an adult keeps a **general**, watchful eye on things – children can approach them if they need assistance. Other activities would be unsafe without

Keep animals clean and in good health.

close direct support from an adult – when a newly walking toddler is playing in the garden, for example, or when an older child is learning to use woodworking tools. The levels of supervision required can change as problems occur, the mood of children changes, or children master skills. Practitioners learn through experience to adjust the supervision they give.

Also see 'Monitoring risk levels' in Learning Outcome 3, Unit CYP 3.4 Support children and young people's health and safety, for details of how to be responsive in terms of the levels of supervision you provide

Safety equipment

- Never buy second-hand safety equipment, even if it has a kite mark. It is particularly unsafe to buy car seats or safety helmets second-hand, as these must be thrown away if they have actually been involved in an accident because any damage, such as cracking inside, affects them.

- You may have equipment such as a buggy stored away, perhaps from when your own child was young. But does it still meet current safety guidelines? Is it still in tip-top condition and working order?

Safety equipment is covered in full in Learning Outcome 2, Unit EYMP 3 Promote children's welfare and well-being in the early years

Risk assessment

You should risk assess your home in the same way as a setting would do, and document the risk assessment. Remember to consider how children will be kept from leaving the premises (both the house and the garden) and how intruders will be prevented from entering. Electrical safety such as unprotected sockets and protection from fires and hot radiators are also particularly important to home-based childcare, as group settings have often been purposely designed to ensure that sockets are positioned halfway up the wall and so on. It can help to get down to a child's level and consider hazards from their height – what will they be able to reach?

Risk assessment is covered in Learning Outcome 2, Unit CYP 3.4 Support children and young people's health and safety

Current guidance on risk assessment

The Health and Safety Executive give up-to-date advice on risk assessment, and say that it needn't be over-complicated. You can download their guidelines from **www.hse.gov.uk**. You can also get advice from the Child Accident Prevention Trust at **www.capt.org.uk**. National Childminding Associations will also advise.

Never buy second-hand safety equipment.

...understanding the importance of partnerships with parents for all aspects of the home-based childcare service

In this section you'll learn about the importance of partnership with parents and carers. You'll also learn about how such partnerships are set up and maintained. This links with Assessment Criteria **3.1, 3.2.**

The importance of forming partnerships with parents and carers

The importance of forming a partnership with the parents and carers who use your service is covered in Unit EYMP 1, Learning Outcome 3.

▶▶Link Up!◀◀

Unit EYMP 1 Context and principles for early years provision

Forming and maintaining partnerships with parents and carers

Forming and maintaining partnership relationships with parents and carers is covered in Unit SHC 1 and Unit CYP 3.5, Learning Outcome 2.

▶▶Link Up!◀◀

Unit SHC 31 Promote communication in health, social care or children's and young people's settings
Unit CYP 3.5 Develop positive relationships with children, young people and others involved in their care

 **Good practice**

All practitioners should be aiming to establish friendly yet professional relationships with parents and carers. Because of the home environment and the fact that you will spend more one-to-one time with parents than practitioners do in group settings, it's perhaps a bit harder for home-based practitioners to strike the right note and to maintain professionalism. But in your approach, try to reflect the fact that you're providing a professional service to families. Otherwise there may be resentment if you need to be assertive – if parents repeatedly bring a child late, for instance, or forget to call you when their plans have changed and they decide not to bring the child in.

Did you know?

Professional relationships are built on trust and respect. Good professional standards and a friendly manner will help these to be established.

Professional relationships are built on trust and respect.

Practical example

Hazel's professionalism

Hazel moved across the country to live in a new town recently, as her husband needed to move for work. She's been childminding there for three months. She gets on well with the parents, especially one of the mums, Sasha. Hazel's really pleased about this, as since she's living in a new area and working from home, she hasn't made many friends. When Sasha comes in the morning, she tells Hazel how her son has been overnight, and always says 'How are you?' It gives Hazel the chance to talk to someone about how much she misses her family, whom she previously lived close to and how she regrets having left her old home.

Question

What's your opinion about Hazel's relationship with Sasha?

Have a go!

Periodically – once every six months perhaps – some childminders like to issue their families with a brief questionnaire about how they feel the service is meeting their needs. They also ask for any new suggestions. Have a go at drawing up a short survey for your own service. It's a great way to ensure that you support families appropriately.

LEARNING OUTCOME 4

FOCUS ON

...understanding the principles of development of routines for home-based childcare

In this section you'll learn about the factors that routines are based upon. You'll also learn about adapting routines to meet different children's needs and how to ensure that each child is welcomed and valued in the home-based setting. This links with Assessment Criteria 4.1, 4.2, 4.3.

Routines

Routines are important because they give children a sense of security, and enable you to structure each day to ensure that you fit in appropriate learning opportunities. Routine times for meals, snack and naps are also part of meeting children's physical needs. However, routines should also be flexible enough to respond to children's changing needs, and to take advantage of spontaneous learning opportunities. A flexible approach also enables you to follow and respond to children's interests – if they become particularly engaged in a certain activity, for instance, you may extend it.

Routines should be based on the following:

■ **Meeting a child's needs**

All children's individual needs should be met. This requires 'responsive caring' as well as an organised approach.

■ **Agreements with parents**

Parents will have preferences about how and when certain routine tasks are carried out.

■ **Participation of children**

Children's preferences should be taken into account.

Routines are covered in Unit EYMP 3, Learning Outcome 6 and Unit CYPOP 2, Learning Outcome 2.
Unit EYMP 3 Promote children's welfare and well being in the early years
Unit CYPOP 2 Care for the physical and nutritional needs of babies and young children

The diagram below shows activities that will be built into routines within the home-based setting:

Supporting children's homework

The purpose of homework is to reinforce what children are learning in school, and to involve parents and key carers in children's learning and education. Sometimes children's homework is to talk with an adult about what they've learned at school today. This is really valuable, and it's good practice for you to get into the habit of doing this casually each day, even when it hasn't been set as 'official homework'.

To support children's homework effectively, you should:

■ provide a quiet area and a table, with a good source of light

■ ensure that children have everything they need before they start – pens, pencils, ruler, rubber, scissors and so on – this prevents them from breaking off frequently to get things, which can sometimes be a deliberate avoidance technique

■ ensure that children doing homework aren't pestered or distracted by other children

■ agree in advance when children will do their homework (e.g. half an hour's play and a snack

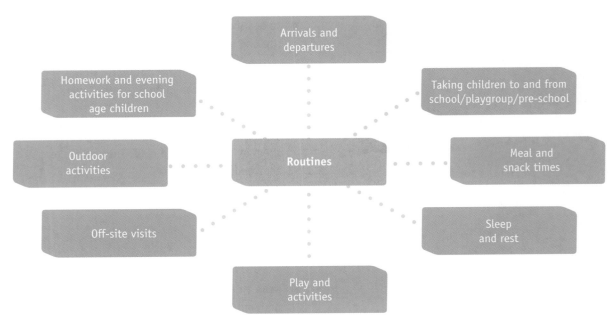

Routines.

when they get in from school, then it's homework time. Make it a nutritional snack as this will aid concentration.)

■ talk with children about how their homework connects with learning at school

■ don't have the TV on, although background music is fine for older children if they prefer to have it on

■ try to support children in the methods they're learning – teaching them another way to do something will confuse them (e.g. long division)

■ support children if they're stuck but don't give *too* much help. Try to support them in working out the answer for themselves (e.g. using the dictionary)

■ try to avoid homework becoming a chore by demonstrating a positive attitude towards it. (Avoid saying things like, 'I hate to tell you this Josh, but it's homework time I'm afraid...')

Support children's homework by providing a quiet area and a table, with a good source of light.

Reading homework

From Reception to Year 2, reading homework tends to have priority. Children will bring home a school reading book every day, and schools usually advise that the child and an adult read their book together every night. Many schools ask that a reading record is filled in to track the reading that's done. Homework is crucial to reading development, as school staff simply don't have adequate time within the school day to hear children read on a one-to-one basis often enough to give them sufficient reading practice. It's best for children to read little and often, so a great deal of time doesn't need to be set aside in order to fit it in each day.

Did you know?

Research has shown that supporting children with reading is the single most important thing a parent or carer can do to help their child's education.

Supporting reading

You can support reading in the following ways:

■ Take a lively, fun approach – you want to foster a lifelong love of reading and books.

■ Pause to talk about the content – what's happening and the pictures on the page.

■ Have plenty of books available, and encourage younger children to look at books and support them in 'pretending to read'. They might 'read' to their teddy for instance.

■ Take children to the library regularly to select books.

■ If children's first language isn't English, you can borrow dual-language books as well.

■ Keep an eye out for books that follow children's preferences and interests (e.g. animals, fairies, football, etc.).

Aim to foster a lifelong love of reading and books.

Ask Miranda!

Q I'm a bit apprehensive about helping older children with their maths homework. I didn't like maths when I was at school, and I don't know how much I remember.

A **This is quite a common concern. Schools are aware of this, and often produce their own guides on how to support children with the two key subjects – maths and English. You can contact the school to request a guide. These guides often include information about the method the school is using to teach certain tasks, such as division. But much of children's maths homework will be concerned with tasks that relate to everyday life and will be very familiar to you.**

Ensuring that each child is welcomed and valued

One of your main priorities as a practitioner will be to help children to settle into coming to your home and being cared for by you, and making them feel welcome and valued. Starting to come to you is a transition in a child's life. Guidance on supporting children with transitions is provided in Learning Outcome 6, Unit CYP 3.2.

However, there's an additional key point for home-based workers to consider. In a group setting, much can be done to help children to feel a sense of belonging to the setting, and to promote a sense of ownership of it. (The latter is particularly important for older children, who will hopefully come to feel as if it is 'their' out-of-school club.) This is traditionally done through a number of strategies, such as giving children their own named coat peg, giving them their own tray in a set of drawers that has their photo on, displaying their artwork and so on.

A childminder needs to think carefully about how to promote belonging, because the key strategies used by group settings aren't a natural fit in the home environment. In addition, the home environment clearly belongs to the childminder and will naturally be very personalised.

Have a go!

What can you do in your home setting to promote a sense of belonging and ownership?

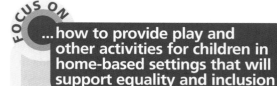
LEARNING OUTCOME 5

FOCUS ON

...how to provide play and other activities for children in home-based settings that will support equality and inclusion

In this section you'll learn about the importance of play to learning and development and the need for an inclusive approach. You'll learn about providing a challenging and enjoyable learning environment, and what can be learned through observation. You'll also learn about equal treatment and equal access, and about how to access other resources available to support children's play. This links with Assessment Criteria 5.1, 5.2, 5.3, 5.4, 5.5.

The importance of play to learning

Play is the primary way for children to learn, and it is also their favourite occupation! By providing challenging and enjoyable play opportunities, you will ensure that children both learn and have a great deal of fun.

▶▶▶**Link Up!**◀◀◀

How play is linked to learning and taking an inclusive approach is covered in detail in Learning Outcome 2, Unit CYP 3.1 Understand child and young person development

Equality and an inclusive approach

You must always promote equality by taking an inclusive approach to your work. This entails:

- treating children as individuals who are respected, valued and accepted regardless of social or ethnic

Have a go!

Think about the activities that you have offered over the last week. What opportunities were there for children to a) explore and make discoveries for themselves, b) problem solve and test their thinking, c) be creative and express their ideas and feelings?

Provide opportunities to be creative and express ideas and feelings.

background or abilities or health status (this is their legal right)

- being a positive role model

- challenging stereotypes and offensive remarks and attitudes appropriately

- acknowledging that children have rights and responsibilities.

Working with disabled children and their families

It's essential that you also know how to meet the needs of disabled children and their families. You're advised to read Unit CYPOP 6, even if you haven't selected this as one of your options for this qualification.

Link Up!

Inclusion is covered in full in:
Unit SHC 33 Promote equality and inclusion in health, social care or children's and young people's settings
Unit CYP 3.2 Promote child and young person development
Unit CYP 3.7 Understand how to support positive outcomes for children and young people
Unit EYMP 4 Professional practice in early years settings

Link Up!

Unit CYPOP 6 Support disabled children and their families and those with specific requirements

Library books are a good source of positive images.

Good practice

How well do you promote positive images of people? Books are full of images and stories about people. One easy way to promote positive images is to pay attention to what's portrayed in the books you select whenever you go to the library. Over time, this is a great way to cover a diverse range of positive images. For instance, keep an eye out for books that feature a range of ethnicities, stories that show girls taking on leadership or adventurous roles, and books that feature strong images of characters who happen to be disabled, rather than books that just focus on their disability.

Play in the home environment

You will of course provide children with bought toys and resources, but don't feel under pressure to try to replicate a nursery or pre-school in your home. Parents have chosen a home setting, so for the vast majority, that isn't what they are expecting. It's a good idea to think about floor space though, so you may want to push furniture back to the edges of the room for some of the time.

You can give children wonderful holistic play experiences with everyday domestic routines and domestic items – see the Practical example on page 548 for details of the treasure baskets. Children also love to play with plenty of low cost items you'll have around – from empty cereal boxes to plastic bottles that can be filled with rice or pasta to make shakers. Dens can be made with some blankets thrown across a table. Saucepans and wooden spoons make fantastic drums! Activities such as washing up the tea set (or even their own unbreakable dishes and cutlery) in the sink and bathing baby dolls in the bath are usually popular too. Chalk is great outside for mark-making but also for drawing out hopscotch grids, numbered circles to jump on and trails to follow.

Everyday domestic routines are learning opportunities.

Everyday tasks such as setting the table help with mathematical development (sequencing), and junk mail is great for emergent writing (lots of 'forms' to fill in) and for playing Post Office imaginary games. Helping with putting out the washing is good for fine manipulative skills, and activities such as making up pairs of socks is a great practical way to use sorting skills for a real purpose. Jobs in the garden are also learning opportunities – watering the plans, planting seeds and harvesting vegetable and flowers are all good experience. You can also involve children in food preparation and cooking in the kitchen, and they can also make their own modelling clay and gloop (corn flour paste, water and colouring).

Observing children

Observing children's play helps you to assess the progress of their development, which in turn helps you to plan for meeting their play needs, in light of what they're likely to learn next. It also helps you to recognise individual children's play preferences, so you'll be able to provide activities that they'll enjoy and feel motivated to participate in. This improves

engagement. Another key function of observation is to assist you in identifying any areas of development in which children might need extra support.

Observation and assessment is covered in full in Unit CYP 3.1, Unit CYP 3.2 and Unit EYMP 2.

Unit CYP 3.1 Context and principles for early years provision
Unit CYP 3.2 Promote child and young person development
Unit EYMP 2 Promote learning and development in the early years

Other resources

In addition to your own resources and materials, you can also give the children in your care the opportunity to benefit from those available at the following:

- **Libraries**
  In addition to books, resources available include CDs and DVDs, and in some libraries, related story sacks. Most libraries also plan regular story sessions and some related activities, such as arts and crafts. Many libraries have a special scheme that allows childminders to take out extra books on each visit, and to have them over a longer period.

- **Drop-in facilities**
  Group play sessions that you can drop into on a 'stay and play' basis, often held in children's centres. This provides an excellent opportunity for the child to experience a whole new set of resources, and to socialise with peers at the same time, while remaining under your supervision.

- **Toy libraries and equipment loan schemes**
  Here, you can borrow toys, games and equipment. If you belong to a childminding network, you may run an equipment loan scheme between you.

- **Scrap stores**
  See below.

Scrap stores

Scrap stores are wonderful places which collect unwanted items from businesses (often manufacturers) and make them available to those working with children for a small charge. Cellophane, paper, card, lollipop sticks, fabric, wool and foil are all usually in abundance. There will be lots of interesting shapes and sizes. For instance, if a manufacturer uses white cardboard discs in their product, they may donate strips of card with circular holes.

Scrap stores often provide ideas on what you can do with it all too. Most scrap stores do not permit children though for safety reasons – there are lots of large heavy rolls of paper and so on about, so you'll need to arrange a time to go without them. Make sure that you find out about your nearest scrap store – you'll get resources extremely cheaply, and it's a very green way of working too, as everything has been recycled.

Have a go!

Why not do an internet search for a scrap store near you?

LEARNING OUTCOME 6

FOCUS ON

…understanding how home-based childcarers can support the safeguarding of children in their care

In this section you'll learn about safeguarding children and the possible signs, symptoms and indicators of abuse. You'll also learn about the regulatory requirements that affect home-based childcare and the procedures to be followed. This links with Assessment Criteria 6.1, 6.2, 6.3, 6.4.

Duty of care to safeguard

You have an important responsibility to safeguard the children that you work with and to play your part in protecting them from abuse.

Link Up!

Full information about safeguarding children is given in Unit SHC 34 Principles for implementing duty of care in health, social care or children's and young people's settings

Regulatory requirements for safeguarding children

Whatever your home country, your regulatory body's standards for home-based children will include a section on safeguarding children. It's extremely important that you familiarise yourself with this, as it will tell you exactly what's expected of you. You must also understand the process of reporting abuse in your area, in terms of who you should contact directly. You must also understand the procedures to be followed should you yourself be accused of causing harm or abusing a child.

For example, the Welfare Requirements (which apply in England) state that in regard to specific legal requirements:

> 'An effective safeguarding children policy and procedure must be implemented. This must include the procedure to be followed in the event of an allegation being made against a member of staff. The provider must ensure that all members of staff understand the safeguarding policy and procedure. Providers must refer to paragraphs 3.8–3.9 of the *Statutory Framework for the Early Years Foundation Stage* for details of how to record and make available all of their policies and procedures.
>
> All providers must notify any child protection agency (usually local children's services or the police) previously identified by the Local Safeguarding Children Board (LSCB), without delay, of allegations of abuse as above.
>
> Registered providers must inform Ofsted of any allegations of serious harm or abuse by any person living, working, or looking after children at the premises (whether that allegation relates to harm or abuse committed on the premises or elsewhere), or any other abuse which is alleged to have taken place on the premises, and of the action taken in respect of these allegations. Registered providers must inform Ofsted of these allegations as soon as is reasonably practicable, but at the latest within 14 days of the allegations being made. A registered provider who, without reasonable excuse, fails to comply with this requirement, commits an offence.'

The Welfare Requirements – specific legal requirements.

In reference to the statutory guidance to which providers should have regard, the Welfare Requirements state:

> 'All providers should follow the guidance set out in the publication "What to do if you are worried a child is being abused" published by DCSF. This includes guidance on information sharing and confidentiality.
>
> All practitioners should have an up-to-date understanding of safeguarding children issues and be able to implement the safeguarding children policy and procedure appropriately. Policies should be in line with LSCB local guidance and procedures. Staff should be able to respond appropriately to any significant changes in children's behaviour; deterioration in their general well-being; unexplained bruising, marks or signs of possible abuse; signs of neglect; comments children make which give cause for concern.'

The Welfare Requirements – statutory guidance.

Signs and symptoms and indicators of abuse

Part of safeguarding children is to keep them safe when they are with you of course, but another aspect of this duty is to be aware of the signs and symptoms that indicate abuse, and to know what to do if you suspect that a child may be being abused.

Good practice

It's good practice for childminders to ensure that parents and carers see their policy on child protection as part of the induction to your service. They will then understand the steps that you have to take should you be concerned about their child being harmed or abused at any point.

It's important to acknowledge that child abuse occurs within all groups of society, so you must never assume someone couldn't be abusing their child because they seem 'respectable' or they have 'a good job' or seem 'so nice'.

Link Up!

Full information about what to do if you suspect a child may be being abused is given in:

Unit SHC 34 Principles for implementing duty of care in health, social care or children's and young people's settings

Unit CYP 3.3 Understand how to safeguard the well-being of children and young people

Good practice

It's your absolute duty to report concerns, however uncomfortable it may be. You don't have to be 'one hundred per cent sure' – you just have to be *concerned*. It's then up to the authorities to investigate and to decide whether action needs to be taken.

Did you know?

Vulnerable children can't stop abuse themselves. They need adults to recognise signs and report the signs so they can be protected.

LEARNING OUTCOME 7

FOCUS ON

...understanding the principles of supporting positive behaviour in home-based childcare settings

In this section you'll learn about the typical behaviours exhibited by children linked to stages of development and key events in their lives. You'll also learn about how the ground rules for behaviour and expectations are developed and implemented. This links with Assessment Criteria **7.1, 7.2.**

Children's behaviour

Children's behaviour is in a large part due to their:

■ age and stage of development

■ the events in their lives.

Age and stage of development

All children of the same age won't behave in exactly the same ways, but there are some common behaviour traits that you are very likely to see. Development-linked behaviour for children in each age range is shown in the development tables in Unit CYP 3.1.

Have a go!

Refer back to the development tables in Unit CYP 3.1. Starting from page 83, track children's unfolding behaviour patterns throughout the months and years, by following the segment of the tables colour coded, all the way through to page 101.

Life events

As you learned in Unit CYP 3.1, Learning Outcome 5 and Unit CYP 3.2, Learning Outcome 6, transitions in children's lives can have a significant impact on behaviour. These might include:

■ a new child starting at the setting

■ the birth of a new sibling

■ a change in routine

■ stress in the family at home

■ illness.

Other factors

Other factors that commonly impact on behaviour are outlined in Unit CYP 3.2, Learning Outcome 5. These include:

■ tiredness

■ illness

■ jealously

■ anger.

Unit CYP 3.1 Understand child and young person development
Unit CYP 3.2 Promote child and young person development

Jealousy can impact behaviour.

Regulatory requirements for behaviour

Whatever your home country, you must familiarise yourself with your regulatory body's standards relating to behaviour. For example, the Welfare Requirements (which apply in England,) state that in regard to specific legal requirements:

'Providers must not give corporal punishment to a child for whom they provide early years provision and, so far as it is reasonably practicable, shall ensure that corporal punishment is not given to any such child by any person who cares for, or who is in regular contact with, children, or any person living or working on the premises. An early years provider who, without reasonable excuse, fails to comply with this requirement, commits an offence.

A person shall not be taken to have given corporal punishment in breach of the above if the action was taken for reasons that include averting an immediate danger of personal injury to, or an immediate danger of death of, any person (including the child).

Providers must not threaten corporal punishment, nor use or threaten any form of punishment which could have an adverse impact on the child's well-being. Physical intervention should only be used to manage a child's behaviour if it is necessary to prevent personal injury to the child, other children or an adult, to prevent serious damage to property, or in what would reasonably be regarded as exceptional circumstances. Any occasion where physical intervention is used to manage a child's behaviour should be recorded and parents should be informed about it on the same day.'

The Welfare Requirements – specific legal requirements.

Ground rules and expectations

Children need to know what the rules and boundaries are so that they know what's expected of them. Try to tell children what to do in a positive way, rather than telling them what not to do. This not only makes things clear for them, it's a lot more positive and pleasant than saying, 'no' or 'don't' or 'stop' frequently. For instance, 'Please walk in the kitchen' is much better than 'Stop running around'. 'Please stay at the table while you're eating' is much better than 'Don't get down with food in your hand'.

Good practice

Depending on the age of the children, it's a good idea to involve them in setting some simple, positively phrased ground rules for your service, as suggested in Unit CYP 3.2. This is the focus of the Practical example below.

Link Up!

Unit CYP 3.2 Promote child and young person development

Managing typical behaviour types

You are likely to come across instances of the following:

- tantrums
- aggressive behaviour
- upsetting verbal remarks.

Strategies for dealing with these are given in Unit CYP 3.2. You're also likely to come across separation anxiety. Guidance for helping children to settle is given on pages 243–244.

Link Up!

Unit CYP 3.2 Promote child and young person development

Our rules:

- We respect other people by being polite and not hurting anyone.
- If you have a problem with a friend and you feel angry or upset, tell Daniel.
- Please share and take turns.
- Look after the toys and ask before you borrow someone's own things.
- We all help with tidying up.
- We only run and jump about outside.
- We eat and drink at the table.
- We play safely.
- We stay close to Daniel when we're out, and cross the roads safely all together.

Example rules.

Practical example

Daniel's boundaries

Daniel has recently begun childminding for three children aged 7–10 years after school. They've decided to draw up some rules together. Daniel has encouraged them to think about how they think they should behave towards each other, and what type of rules will help them to respect the environment and other people's property. They've also had a think about rules to keep them safe. They've come up with the following list, which they've typed out on the computer and put on the fridge with magnets. You can see the list above.

Question
Why is Daniel's approach beneficial?

How are things going?

▶ Progress Check

1 Explain the importance of confidentiality and data protection. (1.3)

2 What key details would you include on a marketing flyer? (1.4)

3 What sources of support can you go to when setting up your home-based service? (3.1)

4 Where can you obtain current guidance on risk assessment? (2.4)

5 What are the procedures relating to administering medicines? (2.5)

6 What can you do to ensure that children feel welcomed and valued? (4.3)

7 Explain the importance of play to children's learning. (5.1)

8 Give an example of how you can use everyday household routines and household items to support children's play and learning. (5.2)

9 Where can you access other resources? (5.5)

10 In your own locality, to whom must you report concerns of harm or abuse to children? (6.3)

11 Explain how you might involve children in setting ground rules. (7.2)

Are you ready for assessment?

CACHE

In preparation for assessment of this Unit, you may like to collect together all the policies and procedures you have devised for your service, to use as evidence.

Edexel

In preparation for assessment of this Unit, you may like to collect together all the policies and procedures you have devised for your service, to use as evidence.

City & Guilds

You may complete the optional Assignment 080. This has six tasks. It entails completing the tables provided, preparing reports/presentations, answering questions, creating a resource file (of local amenities and resources), role play and developing/reviewing policies. You can prepare by researching amenities and resources in your area online, and via a visit to the library. You'll find it helpful to collect relevant leaflets, flyers, press cuttings etc whenever you come across them, throughout your studies.

UNIT 6

Support disabled children and young people and those with specific requirements

LEARNING OUTCOMES

The learning outcomes you will meet in this unit are:

1 Understand the principles of working inclusively with disabled children and young people and those with specific requirements

2 Be able to work in partnership with families with disabled children or young people and those with specific requirements

3 Be able to support age and developmentally appropriate learning, play or leisure opportunities for disabled children or young people and those with specific requirements

4 Be able to evaluate, support and develop existing practice with disabled children and young people and those with specific requirements

5 Understand how to work in partnership with other agencies and professionals to support provision for disabled children and young people and those with specific requirements

INTRODUCTION

The terminology of inclusion is used throughout this unit. Practitioners should be aware of, and have the ability to use, the appropriate terminology of inclusion. Impairments, special educational needs, professionals, strategies and equipment all have various terms given to them. You should learn those that are appropriate to the children you work with. You should ensure that you use language that is acceptable and not outdated terms that are now considered inappropriate or in some cases offensive.

LEARNING OUTCOME 1

FOCUS ON

...understanding the principles of working inclusively with disabled children and young people and those with specific requirements

In this section you'll learn about legal entitlements to equal opportunities, working inclusively and models of provision. You'll learn about the social and medical models of disability, advocacy and the personal assistant role. You'll also learn about the importance of encouraging participation. This links with Assessment Criteria **1.1, 1.2, 1.3, 1.4, 1.5.**

Legal entitlement of disabled children and young people

Thanks to legislation that has been gradually brought in over the years, disabled children and young people now have significant legal rights. Both settings and individual practitioners must be aware of these entitlements, and work in ways to ensure that disabled children and young people's rights are promoted at all times.

Key pieces of legislation/requirements include:

- UN Convention on the Rights of the Child

- *Every Child Matters*

- Disability Discrimination Act 1995 and 2005

- Equality Act 2010.

You can read about these in Unit SHC 33, Learning Outcome 2. Settings must also comply with the **Special Educational Needs** Code of Practice 2001 (see opposite), and the requirements of frameworks that apply in the home country. For details of the Welfare Requirements that apply in England, see page 513.

Link Up!

Unit SHC 33 Promote equality and inclusion in health, social care or children's and young people's settings

Special Educational Needs Code of Practice 2001

The Special Educational Needs Code of Practice (SEN Code) was implemented in 1994 and revised in 2001. It applies to schools and early years settings. Children with special educational needs are identified as children who learn differently from most children of the same age. They may need extra or different help to learn. The SEN Code sets out procedures to be followed in order to meet the requirements of children with special educational needs.

Under the SEN Code, early years settings (even those in which there are currently no children with special educational needs) must:

- adopt the recommendations of the SEN Code

- train staff to identify and manage children with special educational needs

- devise and implement a Special Educational Needs policy in line with the SEN Code – this must explain how the setting promotes **inclusion**, which means how it includes children with disabilities and/or special educational needs within the mainstream setting. (You should be familiar with how inclusion works within your setting and your local area, and the reasons for this.)

- appoint a Special Educational Needs Co-ordinator (SENCO), who will have particular responsibility for overseeing the setting's practice with regard to meeting the needs of children and adhering to the SEN Code.

In addition, settings will implement graduated action and intervention working with children with special educational needs, known as Early Years Action and

Early Years Action Plus. You'll learn about these in Learning Outcome 3.

The five fundamental principles of the SEN Code are shown below:

Table CYPOP 6.1: The five fundamental principles of the SEN Code

A child with special educational needs should have their needs met.
The special educational needs of children will normally be met in mainstream schools or settings.
The views of children should be sought and taken into account.
Parents have a vital role to play in supporting their child's education.
Children with special educational needs should be offered full access to a broad, balanced and relevant education, including an appropriate curriculum for the Early Years Foundation Stage and the National Curriculum.

key terms

Special educational needs children with special educational needs learn differently from most children of the same age. These children may need extra or different help from that given to other children. *(National Occupational Standards)*

Inclusion/Integration children with disabilities or special educational needs belonging to mainstream settings. *(National Occupational Standards)*

Did you know?

A Government Green Paper on special educational needs is expected in 2011. This means that changes are likely in regard to what is currently required of settings under the SEN Code of Practice 2001.

Welfare requirements

You were introduced to the Welfare requirements that apply to early years settings in England in Unit CYP 3.4, Learning Outcome 1. In regards to equal opportunities, the requirements state that:

- all providers must have and implement an effective policy about ensuring equality of opportunities and for supporting children with learning difficulties and disabilities

- all providers in receipt of Government funding must have regard to the SEN Code of Practice.

The policy on equality of opportunities should include:

- information about how the individual needs of all children will be met

- information about how all children, including those who are disabled or have special educational needs, will be included, valued and supported, and how reasonable adjustments will be made for them

- a commitment to working with parents and other agencies

- information about how the SEN Code of Practice is put into practice in the provision (where appropriate)

- the name of the Special Educational Needs Coordinator (in group provision)

- arrangements for reviewing, monitoring and evaluating the effectiveness of inclusive practices

- information about how the provision will promote and value diversity and differences

The individual needs of all children must be met.

- information about how inappropriate attitudes and practices will be challenged
- information about how the provision will encourage children to value and respect others.

Unit CYP 3.4 Support children and young people's health and safety

The medical model of disability

Did you know?

The **medical model of disability** is still promoted in some cultures. You'll learn more about this in Learning Outcome 4.

The social model of disability

There is a worldwide organisation called the Disabled People's Movement. The British Council of Disabled People (BCODP) is a branch of this, formed in 1981. The BCODP believe that disability is not an inevitable consequence of a person's impairment, but that disability arises from the negative way in which disabled people are treated by society. They believe that disabled people are disabled by society's structure, its attitudes and its lack of access, which exclude disabled people from activities that non-disabled people take for granted. It is believed that society should change to meet the needs of disabled people. This gives disabled people rights and choices. This is known as the '**social model of disability**'.

key terms

Medical model of disability the medical model reflects the traditional view that disability is something to be 'cured', treating the child as a sick patient.

Social model of disability the social model considers that it is society that needs to change and that disabled people have rights and choices. *(National Occupational Standards)*

The Disability Discrimination Act supported the Social Model of Disability by giving disabled people (children and adults) rights regarding the way they receive services, goods and facilities.

Models of provision

There are two models of provision for disabled children and young people:

1. service-led
2. child- and young person-led.

Service-led provision fits in with the medical model of disability. The service (or setting) decides what they think is the best way to offer services and to meet the needs of disabled children and young people. Whatever the service decides is what the children and young people will get. This prioritises the organisation's needs and dictates both the opportunities available and the overall experience children and young people have of being in the provision.

Child- and young person-led provision promotes the social model of disability. Disabled children and young people are encouraged to express their views and to make decisions about the way in which they experience the service, and how their needs are met. The child or young person is at the centre of the provision – this means that their needs, interests, strengths and participation are the priority, rather than

Disabled children and young people should be encouraged to express their views and to make decisions.

the organisation's own needs. This is referred to as the provision being **'child-/young person-centred'**.

key term

Child-/young person-centred provision occurs in services where children/young people's needs, interests, strengths and participation are the priority, rather than the organisation's own needs.

Principles of inclusive working

You were introduced to inclusive practice in Unit SHC 33, Learning Outcomes 1 and 3, which included an introduction to identifying and overcoming barriers to participation. You may like to re-read this information now.

Unit SHC 33 Promote equality and inclusion in health, social care or children's and young people's settings

The following principles are central to inclusive working:

■ **Respect**

Respect should be shown to disabled children and young people, and their families, at all times. They should never be patronised or spoken down to. Respect underpins all of the other principles, for example there is no point consulting disabled children and young people if you don't respect and value what they say in response.

■ **Empowerment**

Disabled children and young people may experience times in their lives when they are expected to be passive receivers of services, as you learned in the section on the medical model of disability above. So it is particularly important that practitioners empower disabled children and young people to express their views, make decisions and to be in control of what they do and what happens in respect of meeting needs. This is part of a child-/young person-centred approach (see below).

■ **Enablement**

This is about the practical things that you do to enable empowerment, such as the ways you find to consult children and young people about the purchase of new equipment, or how you consult them about the effectiveness of the adaptations made to an activity.

■ **Empathy**

Being empathetic means understanding someone else's feelings and point of view. This informs the way in which you go about your practical work and

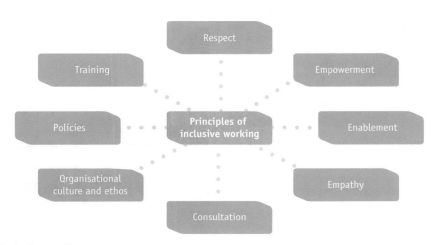

The principles of inclusive working.

your interactions with others. For instance, empathy helps practitioners to ensure that disabled children and young people's dignity is maintained when their physical care needs are met. Empathy is completely different to sympathy. It most certainly is not about feeling or acting in pity for disabled people. Empathy fits in with the social model of disability. Sympathy fits in with the undesirable medical model.

- **Organisation culture and ethos**
  Organisation should have a culture and ethos which promotes inclusive working as a matter of course. This means that services will be child- and young person-led. Also see the 'Models of provision' section above.

- **Policies**
  The organisational culture and ethos should be underpinned by inclusive policies that promote the legislation and requirements that apply in the home country.

- **Training**
  Practitioners should have access to high-quality training on inclusion and matters relating to disability.

Dignity must be maintained when physical care needs are met.

A child-/young person-centred approach

For all practitioners, taking a child-/young person-centred approach is a key part of inclusive working.

The approach is similar to that of the child-/young person-centred provision that you learned about above. The practitioner will prioritise the needs, interests, strengths and participation of the disabled children and young people they work with. Examples of how this may be achieved on a day-to-day basis include:

- asking a child which member of staff they'd like to work with them as their personal assistant (PA) on a group outing

- asking a young person how they'd like to adapt a game so they can fully participate

- consulting a child when evaluating activities to understand how effectively their needs were met and how this can be improved in the future.

Advocacy

You were introduced to advocacy in unit SHC 31, Learning Outcome 3. You may find it helpful to refer to the information now to refresh your memory.

Advocates have an extremely important role to play in ensuring that the voice of disabled children and young people is heard. Part of the advocate's role is to ensure that children and young people have accurate and appropriate information to help them make informed choices. Frequently, an advocate only needs to work with a child or young person for a short time.

Advocates are often trained volunteers working for organisations. However, professional advocacy will

Some young people may attend local self-advocacy groups.

be made available if children or young people need help to ensure that their views are represented at a time of crisis or a time of major change (such as a proposed move to a new residential centre). In this case, the advocate will be in contact with other professionals involved and through these links will be kept up to date with the latest information and developments.

Self-advocacy is the term used to describe the process of a disabled young person or adult making their own views known on matters that affect them. Some independent organisations and charities set up local self-advocacy groups. These aim to support young people and adults in gaining the skills they need to represent themselves. Group facilitators will also provide practical advice and support for members during the self-advocacy process.

key term

Self-advocacy the process of a disabled young person or adult making their own views known on matters that affect them.

The personal assistant role

Personal assistants, also known as PAs, are workers who support disabled children, young people or adults in an enabling, empowering role. They provide practical support to enable the disabled person they are working with to achieve the things they want to do, but with which they require help. The emphasis is firmly on empowering and enabling the disabled person, rather than making decisions for them.

A PA will provide practical care support if necessary, such as assistance with toileting, washing, eating and getting in and out of transport. But there can be many different responsibilities, depending on the needs of the child, young person or adult. For instance, a PA may do any of the following:

■ Describe the physical environment, the choice of activities and the members of the peer group present to a child with a visual impairment.

■ Accompany a young person with learning difficulties on outings to places they want to go – to the cinema, bowling and so on – enabling them to become more independent from their parents.

PAs support disabled children or young people in an enabling, empowering role.

■ Carry out fine manipulative movements under the instruction of a young person who has limited mobility in their hands, enabling them to execute their jewellery-making designs.

■ Take a child who is a wheelchair user on a shopping trip into town so they can choose a birthday present for a family member without them seeing what it is.

The importance of encouraging participation

It's important that practitioners encourage disabled children and young people to participate within the setting. This means much more than simply ensuring that they can take part in all activities.

There should be a genuine commitment to encouraging and empowering disabled children and young people to be actively involved in what happens at the setting – this includes the decision-making processes. It's also important to prioritise opportunities for the children and young people to choose what they want to do and to take on responsibilities.

As you've learned, a key feature of the medical model of disability is non-disabled people making the decisions for disabled people and deciding what will happen to them. The strategies outlined above are key ways for practitioners to ensure that they promote the social model of disability, rather than the medical model.

LEARNING OUTCOME 2

FOCUS ON

...being able to work in partnership with families with disabled children or young people and those with specific requirements

In this section you'll learn about the concepts and principles of partnerships with parents and carers. You'll also learn about the different types of support and information that they may require. This links with Assessment Criteria **2.1, 2.2, 2.3**.

Concepts and principles of working in partnership with parents and carers

As you've learned, families are generally the primary carers of children – they know their children best. Practitioners should recognise this and form partnerships based upon it. It is important to respect and value the role of parents and carers. Practitioners working with children or young people who are disabled or have specific requirements should be informed by families' knowledge and experience. Remember that having good knowledge about a specific impairment or requirements is helpful, but it does not tell you much about an individual child.

For example, a practitioner may be very well informed about Down's syndrome, but although there will be some general commonalities (i.e. similarities) between children with Down's syndrome, each child is an individual, just like all other children. Therefore, children with Down's syndrome will develop at different rates and have differing abilities. Some may have additional impairments or requirements. They will have different likes and dislikes, different personalities and different learning styles. They will respond differently to activities and experiences.

Parents and carers know all of these personal details about their child. When a good partnership is established, this information can be effectively shared and the quality of the practitioner's work with that child will be better as a result.

Did you know?

The partnership with parents and carers is a two-way street. Families may need a range of support and information, which the practitioner can help to provide.

The impact of having a child or young person with a disability or specific requirements

In Unit CYP 3.1, we discussed how early years workers are often the first to identify problems with children's learning or development and the first to raise these issues with parents and carers. In other cases, parents or carers may already be aware of a disability or special educational need, but if the child is young or recently disabled, they may still be adjusting to this news. (Remember that children who are born non-disabled may become disabled later in life through the onset of an illness or condition, or an accident.) It's important for you to understand how having a child or young person with a disability or specific needs can impact on parents, carers, siblings and members of the wider family such as grandparents, aunts and uncles, as it is likely that a family will need social and emotional support.

Link Up!

Unit CYP 3.1 Understand child and young person development

It is often a shock for family members to be told that a child or young person has a disability or specific requirements, and so the matter must be handled with honesty and sensitivity. A traumatic time may follow, and family members may go through a range of emotions similar to those that are experienced by the bereaved (i.e. people who are grieving for a loved one who has died). These emotions may include the following:

■ **Disbelief**

For example, a parent may think that the practitioner, doctor or specialist is mistaken.

■ **Denial**

For example, a grandparent may be convinced the child will grow out of it or catch up.

■ **Grief**

For example, a father may grieve for the child he has 'lost' – the one he imagined would be perfect, whose future he had thought about.

■ **Self-blame**

For example, a mother may think it was her fault – she must have done something wrong during pregnancy. Was she too active? Did she eat the wrong things?

■ **Aggression**

For example, a parent may feel angry, cheated out of the child he or she imagined. A sibling may feel angry about the extra attention their brother or sister needs.

Practitioners need to be supportive and understanding, even if parents and carers find it hard to accept what they are saying at first. The setting must be a non-judgemental environment where family members can feel safe to express their feelings, whatever they are, and find support.

Families of disabled children and young people or those with specific requirements can also feel isolated and ill-informed. Practitioners should liaise closely with SENCOs, who will know about local services and national sources of support and information for parents and carers, including organisations, parents' groups, professionals, books and leaflets. They will also know (or be able to access) information about training in practical skills that the family may want

Family members should feel it is safe to express their feelings.

to explore, such as learning to use sign language or Makaton, or use of a speech board. They will also be able to advise families on finding out about both the child/young person's and the family's legal rights. These details should be passed on when appropriate.

However, some parents will already be aware of their child's disability/impairment or specific requirements, and may feel quite differently. In the case of Down's syndrome, for instance, the condition will have been identified at birth (or perhaps during pregnancy) and the family will have had some time to adjust to this. Parents and carers may already be well informed about the syndrome and may have received support from professionals and organisations. They may even be 'expert parents', with wide-ranging knowledge of their child and the disability or special educational need. If so, they may be well-placed to offer support to other parents who find themselves in a similar situation.

Finances

The material and personal resources available to families of disabled children and young people and those with specific requirements will also vary, and so the experience of the families is likely to differ. We know that free services for those without a statement of special educational needs depend on local policy. Some families may be able to pay for additional specialist support, respite care or equipment for their child, while others will not. Some parents or carers may have a good support network of extended family, while others may be isolated. Practitioners can keep to hand information such as leaflets about benefits and contact numbers of organisations and services that provide related advice. This is demonstrated in the following Practical example:

Practical example

Adrian offers support

Adrian is the out-of-school club key worker for 7-year-old Naomi, who is disabled. When Naomi's mum comes to collect her, Adrian observes that she seems to be anxious. He asks how she is. Naomi's mum explains that her sister, who regularly babysat for Naomi, will be moving out of the area for work reasons. As a single parent, she relied on this to give her the occasional, much needed break. She's worried that she doesn't qualify for any financial funding to help pay for a babysitter, and she can't afford to pay for it alone. Adrian asks whether she'd like the details for the local Citizen's Advice Bureau, which may be able to advise her. Naomi's mum is grateful for the offer, and Adrian fetches her a leaflet that he keeps on file. It includes the Bureau's phone number and opening times.

Question
Why is it so important for Naomi's mum to receive this support?

Differing needs
Families have differing needs. It's the job of practitioners to be aware of the needs of families and to tailor the support they offer to them accordingly so that needs are effectively met. The types of support and information you may offer are summarised in the following diagram:

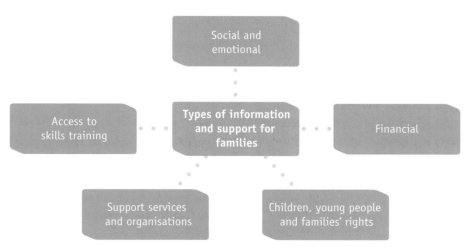

Types of support that you may offer to families of disabled children/young people and those with specific requirements.

Parent Partnership Services

Parent Partnership Services is an organisation which provides support and advice about education to parents with children or young people who have special educational needs. Their remit is to provide accurate information on the full range of options available to parents. This is important, as the choices may have complex implications for the child, and there may be some disagreement between local authorities and the parents or children/young people about the education that will be received. Parent Partnership Services help parents to make informed decisions, but they remain neutral (they do not take sides). The service can provide families with an independent parental supporter.

Have a go!

Find out more about Parent Partnership Services by visiting **www.parentpartnership.org.uk**

LEARNING OUTCOME 3

FOCUS ON

...being able to support age and developmentally appropriate learning, play or leisure opportunities for disabled children or young people and those with specific requirements

In this section you'll learn about engaging disabled children and young people, and how to encourage them to express their preferences and aspirations. You'll learn how to assess children or young people's learning, play or leisure needs and how to respond to identified barriers. You'll also learn how to develop and implement a plan to support a child or young person's learning, play or leisure needs. This links with Assessment Criteria **3.1, 3.2, 3.3, 3.4, 3.5.**

Engaging with disabled children and young people

To engage effectively with disabled children and young people, you should follow the same good practice guidelines for engaging with all children. This is because, as you learned in Learning Outcome 2, while knowledge about certain medical conditions or the implications of a disability has its uses, it does not tell you much about an individual child or young person.

As long as you're communicating in ways that meet any speech, language and communication needs experienced by disabled children and young people (see Unit EYMP 5), you should mainly be focusing on getting to know that child or young person as an individual, and forming a relationship. As you learned in Unit CYP 3.5, spending time together, working in partnership with parents and carers, and being aware of an individual child or young person's interests and preferences, will have the biggest impact on how well you engage with them. These things are of course particularly important for the practitioner in the key worker role.

Link Up!

Unit CYP 3.5 Develop positive relationships with children, young people and others involved in their care

Unit EYMP 5 Support children's speech, language and communication

Good practice

It takes time to get to know anyone well, but this can particularly apply to some children and young people who experience difficulties with social and emotional development. Settings need to support key workers in taking the time to work closely for extended periods with key children who find it challenging to form relationships.

The expression of preferences and aspirations

In Learning Outcome 1, you learned about the danger of disabled children and young people becoming passive recipients of services, as promoted in the social model of disability. To challenge this, it's extremely important that practitioners encourage disabled children and young people to consider and express their preferences and aspirations. (An aspiration is a desire or ambition to achieve something.)

This empowers children and young people to be independent, to have control over what happens to them, and to take responsibility for their own lives. It also helps to foster ambition, which can benefit children and young people hugely throughout their lives. Once preferences and aspirations are established, they can influence future planning (see opposite) as well as the practitioner's own practice when supporting the child or young person.

Did you know?

Aspirations come in all shapes and sizes. They may include an activity a younger child would like to do, somewhere an older child may like to go, or a career a young person would like to follow.

The way in which preferences and aspirations are expressed will vary greatly according to individual children and young people's methods of communication. Some may talk with you about these, while others may indicate their likes and dislikes non-verbally. For instance, they may use these methods:

■ **Sign language or Makaton**
See pages 418–419.

■ **Communication boards or picture cards**
See pages 418–419.

■ **Gesture/body language/facial expression**
For example, by pointing to what they want, nodding or shaking their heads (some may make larger movements to indicate yes or no, perhaps with their leg or arm), either moving towards or away from you or an activity, showing interest/disinterest in their face. Also see pages 418–419.

■ **Touch**
Children or young people may pull your arm when they want you to go with them or to participate with them, or they may pat your arm to get your attention. Some may squeeze your hand when you are talking to let you know that they agree or disagree.

It may be a case of interpreting the behavioural signals you receive from a child or young person, as illustrated in the Practical example on page 523.

Assessing learning, play or leisure needs

Assessing children and young people's learning, play or leisure needs enables you to identify where there

Practical example

Elenka expresses preferences and aspirations

Four-year-old Elenka has learning difficulties, and her social and emotional development is delayed. She speaks a few words, but rarely instigates interaction with her peers or the practitioners at her pre-school. Her key worker, Julia, is aware that Elenka generally prefers to play away from the hustle and bustle of the group, because during free play, she will often take a toy that has interested her off into a quiet corner. But today, Julia notices that Elenka is very interested in a game outside. A small group of children riding on toys are queuing up in front of another child. He's pretending to fill their 'cars' up with petrol before waving them on their way. Elenka eventually sits on a spare ride-on toy. She inches a little towards the game, but remains firmly on the edge of the activity. Another practitioner comes outside and calls the children in for snack time.

Question
What might Elenka aspire to do? How can Julia support this in the future?

are obstacles or barriers that need to be overcome. The general principles and methods of assessment that you learned about in Unit CYP 3.2 apply. The assessment process is informed by:

- observations made by the practitioner

- information received from parents and carers and other professionals who may be working with the child

- preferences of the child or young person.

Also see information on the Common Assessment Framework in Unit CYP 3.6, Learning Outcome 1.

Unit CYP 3.2 Promote child and young person development
Unit CYP 3.6 Working together for the benefit of children and young people

Assessment and intervention frameworks for children with special educational needs

Under the SEN Code, two models of graduated action and intervention are recommended to early years settings working with children with special educational needs:

- **Early Years Action**
  This is the initial stage in which children's special educational needs are identified. The setting should then devise interventions (strategies) that are additional to or different from those provided under the setting's usual curriculum.

- **Early Years Action Plus**
  This is the stage in which practitioners feel it is appropriate to involve external specialists/professionals. They can offer more specialist assessment of the child and advise the setting on strategies.

Early Years Action

Practitioners working in the early years are often the first to notice that a child may be experiencing difficulties with their learning and/or development,

Encourage young people to consider and express their preferences and aspirations.

although sometimes it is a parent or carer who first expresses a concern about their child. When it is suspected that a child is having problems, practitioners need to make focused observations of the child to see whether they can identify specific difficulties. These observations should be documented.

The SEN Code explains that practitioners will have cause for concern when, despite receiving appropriate early education experiences, one or a combination of the following criteria applies to a child:

■ makes little or no progress, even when practitioners have used approaches targeted to improve the child's identified area of weakness

■ continues working at levels significantly below those expected for children of a similar age in certain areas

■ presents persistent emotional and/or behavioural difficulties that are not managed by the setting's general behaviour management strategies

■ has sensory or physical problems and continues to make little or no progress despite the provision of personal aids and equipment

■ has communication and/or interaction difficulties, and requires specific individual interventions (one-to-one) to learn.

Once it has been established that a child meets one or more of the above criteria, practitioners should do the following:

■ Arrange a time to meet with parents or carers to discuss the concerns and to involve them as partners in supporting the child's learning. The practitioner should explain the role of the setting's SENCO, and discuss the involvement of the SENCO with the parents or carers. The practitioner should ask the parents and carers for their own observations of their child's learning and, if appropriate, for information about health or physical problems, or the previous involvement of any external professionals such as speech therapists. Parents are the prime source of information in many cases.

■ Meet with the SENCO. Practitioners should make available as much helpful information as possible (e.g. observations, assessments, health details).

■ The practitioner and SENCO should work together, liaising with the parents and carers to decide on the action needed to help the child progress in light of the observations made. The SEN Code states that action should 'enable the very young child with special educational needs to learn and progress to the maximum possible'.

■ An Individual Education Plan (IEP) should be devised for the child (explained on page 525).

The practitioner and SENCO should work together.

Developing plans to support learning, play or leisure needs

Plans to support learning, play or leisure needs can be devised for children and young people in many different ways. For instance, a Saturday morning sports club might draw up a 'play plan' to identify the goals a disabled child has and how the staff will support the child in achieving them. Or a youth club may agree a 'participation plan' with a disabled teenager to outline what they want to achieve and the support they'll receive to enable equality of access to activities and outings. However, most early years settings use the IEP method of planning which, as you learned above, is required if graduated action and intervention is in place under the SEN Code.

An IEP should concisely record three or four short-term targets set for a child, and detail the strategies that will be put in place. The IEP should only record that which is additional to or different from the general curriculum plan of the setting. The IEP should be discussed with parents, carers and the child concerned.

IEPs should be working documents, kept continually under review. They are primarily for checking the effectiveness of strategies implemented and the progress made towards targets. Reviews should take place as necessary in consultation with parents and carers. But they should occur regularly – at least three times each year. The SEN Code states that reviews need not be 'unduly formal', but a record of them must be kept in the IEP. New targets and strategies decided on at review must also be recorded.

Settings will have adopted a set of documents to complete throughout the stages of Early Years Action and Early Years Action Plus. The blank documents may have been bought or the SENCO may have devised them. The diagram on page 526 shows the information that will be recorded on the IEP.

Strategies to support children and young people in achieving targets may include:

- extra adult support for some activities

- provision of special equipment

- provision of different materials

- staff training and development

- allowing extra staff time for planning interventions

- allowing extra staff time for monitoring progress.

Implementing plans to support learning, play or leisure needs

It's important that all practitioners working with a child or young person are aware of the strategies planned to support them. This enables a consistent approach to the implementation of plans.

Good practice

It's good practice to reflect on how well you fulfil your own role and responsibilities when you implement plans to support learning, play or leisure needs. Think about how effectively you carried out support strategies, and whether you can develop this in the future.

Link Up!

There is more on reflective practice in Unit SHC 32 Engage in personal development in health, social care or children and young people's settings

Have a go!

Ask your supervisor whether it's possible for you to be given permission (from a child's parents or carers) to have a look at a child's IEP. Ask the SENCO to explain to you how it was drawn up, how it is implemented and how it is monitored.

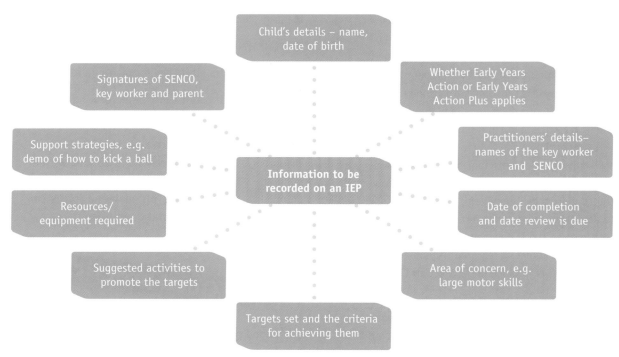

Child's details – name, date of birth

Whether Early Years Action or Early Years Action Plus applies

Signatures of SENCO, key worker and parent

Practitioners' details– names of the key worker and SENCO

Support strategies, e.g. demo of how to kick a ball

Information to be recorded on an IEP

Resources/ equipment required

Date of completion and date review is due

Suggested activities to promote the targets

Area of concern, e.g. large motor skills

Targets set and the criteria for achieving them

Information recorded on an IEP.

Early Years Action Plus

The decision to implement Early Years Action Plus (that is to involve external support services and professionals) is generally taken in consultation with parents or carers at a meeting to review a child's IEP. At this stage, a Common Assessment Framework (CAF) assessment will also be carried out. The SEN Code identifies that the implementation of Early Years Action Plus is likely to be triggered when, despite receiving support tailored to their needs, a child:

■ continues to make little or no progress in specific areas over a long period

■ continues working at a level substantially below that expected of children of a similar age

■ has emotional difficulties that substantially interfere with the child's own learning or that of the group, despite an individual behaviour management programme

■ has sensory or physical needs and requires additional equipment or regular specialist support

■ has on-going communication or interaction difficulties that are a barrier to learning and social relationships.

The type of support services available to settings under Early Years Action Plus varies according to local policy. You should find out about the provision made in your local area by your Local Education Authority (LEA). Your LEA's support services or local health or medical services may be able to provide support and help in terms of assessment, advice on IEPs, and strategies, activities, equipment and perhaps specialist support for some activities.

At the Early Years Action Plus stage, reviews should continue – external specialists should be consulted as part of the review while they are involved with the child.

Link Up!

For more on CAFs, see Learning Outcome 1, Unit CYP 3.6 Working together for the benefit of children and young people

School Action and School Action Plus

The same procedures will be followed in schools. The terms 'School Action' and 'School Action Plus' are then used.

Statutory assessment

In some cases, children do not make the expected progress despite the intervention of Early Years Action Plus. At this stage it is appropriate for the parents, carers, practitioner, SENCO and external professionals to meet to discuss whether a referral should be made to the LEA requesting a statutory assessment of the child. If it is agreed, an application for assessment is made.

The LEA will require all relevant documentation including observations, IEPs and assessments. These are considered and the LEA decides (within 26 weeks) whether the child should be made the subject of a Statement of Special Educational Needs. The statement is legally binding – it sets out a child's needs and outlines what special educational provision must be made to meet them. The LEA concerned is then legally obliged to provide this for the child. This applies to all LEAs in England. The nature of the provision will depend on the child's need, but some examples of provision include:

- a transfer to a specialist setting

- a place at a mainstream setting with additional one-to-one support

- a place at a mainstream setting with additional resources and equipment

- support of an educational or clinical psychologist

- a home-based programme, such as Portage (see page 531).

Statements for children under the age of 5 must be reviewed by the LEA every six months. Because of the time it takes to go through the stages of intervention, most children are not referred for statutory assessment until they are over the age of 5, by which time they will have started school.

Critical success factors

The SEN Code identifies 'critical success factors' by which settings can assess the success of their provision for children with special educational needs. These consider:

- practice, management and resources deployed to ensure all children's needs are met

- early identification

- children's wishes taken into account

- practitioners and parents/carers working in partnership

- multi-disciplinary approach

- interventions based on best practice and reviewed regularly.

LEARNING OUTCOME 4

FOCUS ON

...being able to evaluate, support and develop existing practice with disabled children and young people and those with specific requirements

In this section you'll learn about overcoming barriers to access, becoming an agent of change and using policies and procedures to challenge behaviour that is discriminatory, abusive or oppressive. You'll also learn about the impact of disability within different cultures, and systems for monitoring, reviewing and evaluating services. This links with Assessment Criteria 4.1, 4.2, 4.3, 4.4, 4.5.

Overcoming barriers that restrict access

To ensure that everyone within the setting has equal opportunities to access the provision, practitioners must identify barriers to access, and take action to overcome them. Full details are given in Unit SHC 33, Learning Outcome 3. It's a good idea to re-read this information as part of your study towards this unit.

Link Up!

Unit SHC 33 Promote equality and inclusion in health, social care or children's and young people's settings

Monitoring, reviewing, evaluating and challenging existing practice

As you learned in Unit SHC 34, it's important for you to be a reflective practitioner, and to evaluate and improve your own practice in all areas. This includes the way in which you and your setting work with

disabled children and young people and those with specific requirements. Key factors to consider include:

■ how well environmental barriers are identified and overcome

■ how well attitudinal barriers are identified and overcome

■ how well institutional barriers are identified and overcome

■ how well the setting's equality and inclusion policies are implemented in practice

■ whether the approach is child-/young person-centred

■ whether effective partnerships have been established with parents and carers

■ how well individual children or young people's individual needs are met – the children or young people will be best placed to give feedback on this. (For children or young people who are unable to express this, you should analyse their responses to the current provision.)

Practitioners have a duty to take action if improvements are necessary. It's a matter of professional and personal ethics – you must find the appropriate way to challenge any practices that are inappropriate or otherwise fail to come up to scratch. Taking action is known as becoming an **'agent of change'**. You can read more about this below, and also in Unit SHC 33, Learning Outcome 3 (see from 'Supporting the promotion of equality and challenging discrimination' onwards).

key term

Agent of change someone who takes action to challenge existing practices

Did you know?

If there hadn't been agents of change in the past, we would still be shutting disabled people out of sight in our society today.

Link Up!

Unit SHC 33 Promote equality and inclusion in health, social care or children's and young people's settings
Unit SHC 34 Principles of implementing duty of care in health, social care or children's and young people's settings

Past agents of change made inclusive settings a reality.

Using policies and procedures to challenge, review, monitor and evaluate

The purpose of a setting's equality and inclusion policies and procedures is to set out how they will, at the very least, meet the minimum equality and inclusion requirements dictated by law. In this case, settings will be breaking the law if they fail to work in line with the policies. Of course, it is hoped that all settings will go further, and develop policies and procedures that reflect the very best practice. In this case, there may be elements of the policies and procedures that would not affect the setting's compliance of law should they fail to meet them. It would, however, be poor professional practice. Policies and procedures are a public declaration of what the setting undertakes to do, and as such, settings have a clear duty to live up to them. If they don't, they will not be fulfilling the service they have promised to families.

If you feel an aspect of practice is failing to live up to the policies and procedures expressed by the setting, you are in a strong position to raise the issue and by doing so to instigate change, because what should be happening will be clearly expressed on the page for all to see. The 'Parents and carers' section on page 65 of Unit SHC 33, also gives an example of how a policy may be used to challenge a discriminatory request.

Link Up!

Unit SHC 33 Promote equality and inclusion in health, social care or children's and young people's settings

If you are concerned about an aspect of the setting's practice, you should not wait to raise the issue. However, routine annual reviews of policies and procedures are another important way for settings to review, monitor and evaluate how well settings are doing, and what they should do to improve. Reviews should consider:

1. whether policies and procedures still meet legal requirements (these continually evolve)

2. whether policies and procedures still meet best practice benchmarks

3. whether policies and procedures are effectively facilitating equality and inclusion for all families at the setting

4. how effectively policies and procedures are delivered in practice.

The impact of disability within different cultures

Disability is viewed differently within different cultures, with some promoting the medical model of disability. This greatly impacts on the experience of both disabled children and young people and their families. It's important for practitioners to be aware of this, and to be sensitive to cultural views when working with families.

Good practice

It's good practice for settings to consult with disabled children, young people, those with specific requirements and their families, when reviewing, monitoring and evaluating the quality of the provision. They are best placed to comment on how equality and inclusion is experienced at the setting.

Have a go!

You can read an interesting article about cultural perceptions of disability here **www.disabilityworld.org/01-03_02/ employment/rethinking.shtml**

LEARNING OUTCOME 5

FOCUS ON

...understanding how to work in partnership with other agencies and professionals to support provision for disabled children and young people and those with specific requirements

In this section you'll learn about the roles and responsibilities of partners that are typically involved with disabled children and young people and those with specific requirements. You'll also learn about examples of multi-agency practice. This links with Assessment Criteria **5.1, 5.2.**

Roles and responsibilities of partners

A number of professionals may work in partnership with practitioners to support disabled children, young people, those with specific requirements and their families. As you learned in Unit EYMP 3, multi-agency and integrated working provides strong benefits in terms of inclusion and equal opportunities. This is because families who experience disability are likely to need several different types of support. This may include support from the following:

- **Social workers**
  See page 256

- **Doctors, paediatricians, consultants and nurses**
  See page 369

- **Health visitors**
  See pages 369 and 256

- **Speech and language therapists**
  See pages 256 and 370

- **Physiotherapists**
  See page 370

- **Psychologists**
  See pages 257 and 371

- **Personal assistants (PAs)**
  See page 517

- **Specialist play workers**
  See page 257

■ **Voluntary agencies and services**
See page 257

■ **Advisors**
See page 258

■ **Learning support assistants**
Assistants who support the learning of children or young people within educational establishments are given various titles – they might also be called 'special needs assistants', 'SEN TAs' (special educational needs teaching assistants). Their role is to work under the direction of the class teacher to support a child or young person's learning, in line with the child's Individual Education Plan (IEP). Many learning support assistants will contribute to the devising of the IEP, and assist in monitoring a child or young person's progress. This is valuable, as the learning support assistant will usually spend the most time working with the child or young person in school, and will support them in carrying out the learning activities specified on the IEP.

Learning support assistants work under the direction of the class teacher.

■ **Portage workers**
Portage is a home visiting service for pre-school children who have developmental or learning difficulties, physical disabilities or other special educational needs. They support families by suggesting a programme of activities and daily routines that will encourage development. They teach parents and carers new skills to enable them to carry out the suggestions, and to help them to make learning fun for their child. There is a focus on taking goals that may take a long time for the child to achieve – walking and talking, for example – and breaking them down into smaller steps. This helps families to support their child's learning, while helping them to notice and celebrate progress. Portage workers visit families regularly to monitor progress and to set new goals.

Unit CYP 3.6 Working together for the benefit of children and young people
Unit EYMP 3 Promote children's welfare and well-being in the early years

Examples of multi-agency working
Multi-agency working is covered in full in Unit CYP 3.6 – several Practical examples are given in Learning Outcome 1.

Unit CYP 3.6 Working together for the benefit of children and young people

How are things going?

▶ Progress Check

1. Explain the differences between: a) service-led provision, and b) child- and young person-led provision. (1.2)

2. Describe: a) the social model of disability, and b) the medical model of disability. (1.3)

3. What types of support and information might parents and carers require? (2.1)

4. Explain why practitioners should encourage disabled children and young people to express their preferences and aspirations. (3.2)

5. What is the purpose of an individual education plan? (3.4, 3.5)

6. What is an 'agent of change'? (4.2)

7. How can policies and procedures be used to challenge discriminatory behaviour? (4.3)

8. Outline the roles of: a) a social worker, b) a PA and c) a learning support assistant. (5.1)

Are you ready for assessment?

CACHE

In preparation for assessment of this Unit, you may like to reflect on instances when you have been involved in multi-agency and partnership working, making notes in your reflective journal.

Edexel

In preparation for assessment of this Unit, you may like to reflect on instances when you have been involved in multi-agency and partnership working, making notes in your reflective journal.

City & Guilds

In preparation for assessment of this Unit, you may like to reflect on instances when you have been involved in multi-agency and partnership working, making notes in your reflective journal.

Learning Outcomes 2, 3 and 4 must be assessed in real work environments.

UNIT 7

Promote creativity and creative learning in young children

INTRODUCTION

Creativity and creative learning are extremely important, because they can positively influence all aspects of children's learning and development. Practitioners can use some interesting techniques to support children's creativity and creative learning, and can even nurture their own creativity at the same time. It can be very rewarding for practitioners to both provide, and work in, a stimulating, vibrant, creative environment that promotes innovation and offers inspiration.

LEARNING OUTCOME 1

FOCUS ON

...understanding the concepts of creativity and creative learning and how these affect all aspects of young children's learning and development

In this section you'll learn about the differences between creative learning and creativity, and about current theoretical approaches to creative learning and creativity in childhood. You'll also learn about critical analysis of how creative learning and creativity can support children's development. This links with Assessment Criteria **1.1, 1.2, 1.3.**

Creativity and creative learning

There is some ambiguity about the difference between creativity and creative learning. This is because the term 'creativity' means different things to different people, as you'll no doubt experience in your career. There are also conflicting theories about creativity and creative learning, with experts disagreeing about where creativity comes from, whether it can learned, and if so, how. We'll take a look at some of the theories below, but first we'll define exactly what we mean when we refer to creativity and creative learning in this unit.

Creativity

'**Creativity**' refers to the traditional creative arts. The traditional creative arts are shown on the diagram below.

key term

Creativity play and exploration related to the traditional creative arts.

So in this context, a child is using their creativity – or in other words, being creative – when they are:

a) engaged in an activity that relates to the traditional creative art forms

b) expressing themselves through that activity.

Play, exploration and discovery are key to creativity, not just for children, but for adults too. It is highly valued by many professional artists, who will play with ideas and/or explore the materials relating to their art form to discover a new way of working or to develop a concept for a new piece of work. Because children are intrinsically motivated to play and explore, this means that we can give them rich opportunities to be highly creative by providing the right environment. Here are some examples.

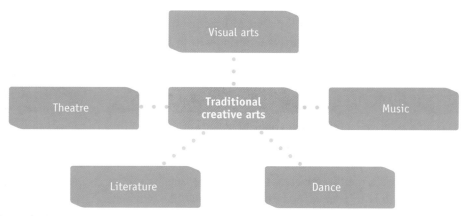

The traditional creative arts.

■ **Visual arts**

This area of the traditional arts includes painting, drawing and so on, as well as three-dimensional works, such as sculpture and design. So examples of children being creative in this context include:

- mark-making in any way (e.g. with a paintbrush or making finger trails in a tray of sand)
- exploring malleable materials (e.g. modelling clay or corn flour paste).

■ **Music**

This area of the traditional arts includes playing instruments and singing. So examples of children being creative in this context include:

- banging on some pots and pans with a wooden spoon
- singing songs or rhymes, or humming their own made-up tunes.

■ **Dance**

Examples of children being creative in this context include:

- a toddler swaying instinctively when music is played

Dance is an area of the traditional arts.

- any creative physical movement (e.g. pretending to be a lion and crawling along on all fours with a swagger).

■ **Literature/theatre**

The area of literature is about the writing of fiction. It is linked closely to theatre, which is about acting out the written word, as well as improvisation. So examples of children being creative in this context include:

- imagining what might happen next when a storybook is read to them
- retelling a story they know or making up their own (this could involve role play, puppets and so on and can include assigning character traits to dolls and figures, and giving them something to do, for example the little girl figure is unwell so she's going to the doctor)
- imaginary play/role play and dressing up, particularly when items such as long pieces of fabric are used creatively to make a sari or a cape or a skirt, as opposed to 'off the peg' dressing-up costumes such as a nurse's uniform
- representation of objects in play (e.g. a piece of string becomes a snake or a wedding ring, a cardboard box becomes a car or a house).

Link Up!

The main focus of creativity for young children will be on the *process* rather than the *product* – you can read more about this in Unit EYMP 1 Context and principles for early years provision

Creative learning

'Creative learning' refers to the process of developing the skills of imaginative thinking and problem solving. These skills are used across all of the curriculum areas, and in recent years have been increasingly valued in mathematics, science and design. You'll learn more about this in Learning Outcome 2.

The process of developing the skills of imaginative thinking and problem solving includes encouragement of the skills used in 'divergent thinking'. Divergent thinking is a name given to the thought processes or methods that are used to generate creative ideas by exploring many possible solutions. You may use divergent thinking yourself. For instance, when planning a theme for children, you may start by thought-storming related ideas. You can encourage children to develop imaginative thinking and problem solving skills by providing them with an environment that supports the exploration of a wide range of stimuli, allowing for connections between these to be made by children and then applied.

key term

Creative learning the development of the skills of imaginative thinking and problem solving.

Although creativity and **creative learning** are quite different, many creative activities will in themselves promote creative learning. For instance, a child making a skirt from a piece of fabric will need a way to keep it on. They may try tying the fabric in a knot, or using sticky tape, before successfully using a clothes peg from the home corner. This is an example of imaginative and divergent thinking.

The difference between creativity and creative learning

In summary, the difference between creativity and creative learning is that creativity refers to play and exploration related to the traditional creative arts, while creative learning is about developing the skills of imaginative thinking and problem solving, which can be applied throughout all curriculum areas.

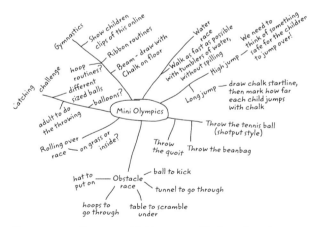

You may use divergent thinking yourself when thought-storming ideas.

Theoretical approaches to creativity and creative learning

As is usually the case when it comes to theoretical approaches, there's some disagreement between experts as follows:

■ **Nature vs nurture**

The nature versus nurture debate that you learned about in Unit CYP 3.1 also applies here. Some believe that children are born with a talent or gift for a specific creative art or that they are born with a predetermined creative personality, which makes them naturally inclined to think creatively.

■ **A form of intelligence?**

Some theorists, including the prominent Howard Gardner, believe that creativity is a form of intelligence that centres around making associations between different things, and that it can be measured to a certain extent. This is commonly referred to as a cognitive theory. In all, Gardner has identified eight forms of intelligence that he believes should be fostered in children. These are Linguistic, Musical, Logical-Mathematical, Visual-Spatial, Bodily-Kinesthetic, Interpersonal, and Intrapersonal. He believes each child has their own individual pattern of capability that spans the eight intelligences, and that first-hand experiences should be provided by adults across each of the domains.

■ **Personality traits**

Some studies have found that a high IQ is not necessarily linked to high levels of creativity, and that certain personality traits that promote divergent thinking are more important. These traits include curiosity, persistence, a willingness to take risks, and a tendency towards non-conformity.

■ **An attitude?**

In *Teaching for Creativity*, theorists Robert Sternberg and Wendy M. Williams say that creativity is as much a decision about and an attitude toward life as it is a matter of ability. They believe creativity is easy to spot in young children, but harder to find as they grow up because their creative potential has been suppressed by a society that encourages intellectual conformity. Sternberg and Williams believe that activities such as expecting children

Robert Sternberg and Wendy M. Williams say that creativity is easy to spot in young children.

to colour within the lines in a colouring book suppress children's natural creativity.

■ **Lateral thinking**

This term was first used by Edward De Bono to describe the process of solving problems through an indirect and creative approach. Lateral thinking is about reasoning that is not obvious or predictable and is outside of the processes that are used to come to a logical conclusion. De Bono promotes the idea of planning to meet children's need to think creatively, but others who believe that children's thoughts cannot be creative if they can be predetermined in this way disagree with this approach.

■ **Social models**

Some theorists subscribe to the social model that promotes the environment and the adults in children's lives as the key factors in shaping creativity and creative learning. They believe that a child's level of creativity is derived from their experience of these two things. Within a setting, this would mean that practitioners have an important role to play in modelling creativity and creative learning. Many settings promote this model, and you will learn practical techniques that relate to it in Learning Outcomes 2 and 3.

■ **The unconscious mind**

The old adage that if you have a problem you should 'sleep on it' may well be good advice. Recent research has linked the ability to both be creative and to think creatively with getting sufficient good-quality sleep. There is much still to be learned about this. However, one of the earliest creativity theorists, Graham Wallas, was the first to suggest such a link. He believed that creativity is a process that includes an 'incubation' period in which the unconscious mind works away at a problem before the conscious mind becomes aware of the solution. Also see 'Extended and unhurried periods of time' on pages 542–543.

Unit CYP 3.1 Understand child and young person development

How creativity and creative learning support young children's wider development

Creativity and creative learning can support children's emotional, social, intellectual, communication and physical development. Examples include the following:

■ **Emotional development:**
 – expressing oneself through creative activities relating to visual arts, music, dance and literature/theatre
 – expressing oneself through design
 – gaining confidence through the development of thinking and problem-solving skills
 – experiencing both success and failure when trying out own ideas and through this developing tenacity and perseverance, which can lead to increased self-reliance.

■ **Social development:**
 – learning and using skills to contribute own imaginative ideas to a group (e.g. during role play or shared art work) and to listen to, understand and respond to the imaginative ideas and leads given by others

– developing the ability to be creative and to engage in creative learning within social boundaries and environmental limitations (e.g. it is fine to draw on the ground outside with chalk but unacceptable to paint on the carpet inside).

- ■ **Intellectual development:**
  - learning and using the skills of imaginative thinking, divergent thinking and problem solving. This includes the skills to question and make choices, identify problems, generate a number of imaginative solutions, try out and apply ideas.

- ■ **Communication development:**
  - learning and using the language associated with thinking and problem solving
  - responding to creative questions and asking creative questions (see Learning Outcome 2)
  - singing and rhyming
  - using language for expression in role play
  - learning and using the language associated with storytelling
  - learning and using the language associated with behaviour and emotions.

Singing is creatively expressive and also contributes to language development.

- ■ **Physical development**
  - using large motor skills – moving imaginatively and in new ways during music and movement sessions,

when role playing (e.g. slithering along the floor like a snake) and when dancing, and so on
  - using fine motor skills – controlling mark-making implements such as paintbrushes and pencils, handling small objects such as sequins and beads when creating artwork, fastening zips, buttons and so on when dressing up.

Early years frameworks

Creativity and creative learning opportunities will also promote creative aspects of the early years framework that applies in your home country. In England, this area of learning is called Creative Development. The outline of the educational programme which must be provided for the area states that:

Children's creativity must be extended by the provision of support for their curiosity, exploration and play. They must be provided with opportunities to explore and share their thoughts, ideas and feelings, for example, through a variety of art, music, movement, dance, imaginative and role-play activities, mathematics, and design and technology.

The following early learning goals express what most children following this educational programme are expected to be able to do by the end of their reception year:

- ■ Respond in a variety of ways to what they see, hear, smell, touch and feel.

- ■ Express and communicate their ideas, thoughts and feelings by using a widening range of materials, suitable tools, imaginative and role-play, movement, designing and making, and a variety of songs and musical instruments.

- ■ Explore colour, texture, shape, form and space in two or three dimensions.

- ■ Recognise and explore how sounds can be changed, sing simple songs from memory, recognise repeated sounds and sound patterns and match movements to music.

- ■ Use their imagination in art and design, music, dance, imaginative and role play and stories.

LEARNING OUTCOME 2

Link Up!

Further resources to support creativity and creative learning are given in the resources table on page 346 of Unit EYMP 2 Promote learning and development in the early years

FOCUS ON

...being able to provide opportunities for young children to develop their creativity and creative learning

In this section you'll learn how to promote creativity and creative learning in your own practice. You'll also learn about children's need for extended and unhurried periods of time to develop their creativity. This links with Assessment Criteria **2.1, 2.2**.

Promoting creativity and creative learning

As you learned in Learning Outcome 1, many experts now agree that creativity and creative thinking skills can be successfully nurtured and developed throughout life. There are a number of ways for you to promote creativity and creative learning in your practical work with children. We'll look at the key techniques in turn.

Providing an environment that promotes creative exploration and play

As well as the provision of the physical environment, this includes a positive attitude to appropriate risk-taking and innovation, and acceptance of a certain amount of untidiness and noise. You'll learn more about this in Learning Outcome 3.

Providing options and allowing choice

To support creative activities, you need to provide a wide range of resources and materials for children to explore and use in their creative pursuits, for example a varied collection of natural materials such as fir cones, shells and pebbles, and a wide range of art/craft resources such as tissue paper, cellophane and corrugated card.

Modelling creativity and creative thinking

One of the most effective and powerful ways for you to promote creativity and creative learning is to ensure that children see you being creative and using creative thinking skills within the setting. The goal is to model techniques rather than to give children prescriptive instructions which could hamper their creative development and undermine their confidence. So you may paint your own picture alongside a child, for instance, using the paintbrush in a dabbing motion to allow a child to see a different way of mark-making, which they can try for themselves if they want to. You can model creative learning skills by thinking aloud. For example, you may say 'It's starting to rain and I haven't brought my umbrella. I wonder how many ways I can think of to stay dry when I pop out to buy a sandwich at lunch time...'

Model techniques rather than giving children prescriptive instructions.

Do you feel that you are a creative person? Do you feel confident in your creative thinking abilities? If not, why not read one of the many books for adults on developing your creativity? It's likely to benefit you in many areas of life.

Emphasising process over product

As you learned in Unit EYMP 1, Learning Outcome 2, you should always value the creative processes of children ahead of the end product. Creative expression from young children rarely looks 'tidy'.

Unit EYMP 1 Context and principles for early years provision

Providing inspiration

Everyone needs inspiration to be creative, and the more children are exposed to a wide range of experiences, the more inspiration they will have to draw on. Visits and visitors can be invaluable. It's fantastically inspiring for children to see a dancer perform, hear a brass band in the park, to go to the theatre or to hear an accomplished storyteller. Galleries and museums generally make no charge for young children and may have many extra activities aimed at stimulating the minds of their young visitors. Trips unconnected to the traditional arts can be just as inspiring – for example handling animals at a city farm or visiting the coast. Children should also be exposed to a diversity of cultures and ways of thinking. It's good for them to see the different approaches that people take to specific problems and to everyday life. You can also provide inspiration through visual stimulus in the setting – via pictures on the wall for instance. There's more about this in Learning Outcome 3.

Supporting language development

We need to help children to develop the vocabulary to express themselves in conversation and in role play. Language relating to feelings, behaviour and action should be promoted. You can expose children to this language by modelling it yourself. An effective method is to provide a running commentary on events in real life, in story books or on television, for example 'Look, Jacob's rubbing his eyes and yawning, I think he must be tired. Yes, he's snuggling up with his teddy and having a cuddle with his Mum. What do you think?' Children also need support to develop the language of thinking and problem solving – opportunities to hear and respond to creative questions, and also to ask their own creative questions, is helpful here (see below).

Expose children to a wide range of experiences, such as the theatre.

Using creative-thinking questions

Asking children questions that encourage them to think creatively is perhaps one of the most effective ways of all for practitioners to promote creative learning, and it can be applied to any activity or experience right across the curriculum, whatever age range you are working with. It really is worth developing this as an area of strength. Try using the following types of questions:

■ What if?

■ What will happen next?

■ How can we change?

- Why?

- Why not?

Pay attention to the way in which skilled colleagues ask questions and learn from the reaction that they get from children. There's more about the use of questions to support children's learning in Unit EYMP 2, Learning Outcome 4.

Unit EYMP 2 Promote learning and development in the early years

Practical example

Lucien's questions

Lucien works in a pre-school. He's making modelling clay for the group with 4-year-old Ruby. Lucien says, 'This clay is a bit too dry to knead. What can we add to the mixture to solve the problem?' Ruby says, 'A little bit more water.' Lucien replies, 'Good idea, let's try it.' It works. Lucien asks, 'What do you think would have happened if we added a lot of water?' Ruby doesn't know. Lucien realises that she's picked up from making modelling clay before that water should be added in small quantities, but that she doesn't know the reason for this. Lucien breaks off a section of the clay for Ruby and says, 'How can we find out using this piece of dough?'

Question
How is Lucien supporting Ruby's creative learning?

Building self-confidence and self-reliance

As you learned in Learning Outcome 1, it's important that children develop the confidence to express themselves, and gain the self-reliance and self-esteem that comes from believing that they can think and learn effectively and solve problems for themselves – these are beliefs that will nurture them throughout their lives. Notice and praise children's creativity and creative learning – let them know you value their expression, ideas and thoughts, and that you believe they are good at conveying them. Part of the creative process is to fail – not all ideas will be good ones, and not all creative techniques will work. Be accepting of children's mistakes, and help them to move on with their confidence intact.

Encouraging collaboration

This links with providing inspiration. Collaboration can drive creativity and creative learning to a new level. You will have experienced this yourself, perhaps in a meeting when the ideas are flowing, and one person's suggestion triggers you to have a related idea – this is known as the 'cross-fertilisation of ideas'. You can encourage young children to develop these skills by giving them opportunities to collaborate with one another, perhaps to build a den or to make a giant collage for the wall. Young children can also collaborate with older children and adults as this will facilitate role modelling, but adults should not take over the activity. As children mature, it's valuable for them to have the opportunity to collaborate with creative professionals who have refined their processes

Collaboration can drive creativity and creative learning to a new level.

and exude creativity, creative thinking and a passion for their art. This is why visual artists, writers, dancers and musicians are often invited to work within schools for a limited period on special projects.

Encouraging idea generation

You can promote imaginative, divergent thinking and problem-solving skills by encouraging children to come up with lots of ideas. When working with young children, these will often be connected with what the group might do, or how to do something. For instance, if a child floats a large piece of corrugated card in the water tray, you could encourage the children at the water tray to suggest as many ways as possible to sink it. Imaginative ideas should be valued as much as practical ones, for example, one child may suggest weighing it down with pebbles, while another may suggest putting out some bread and waiting for a duck to land on it. As mentioned above, collaboration can also lead to enhanced idea generation.

Encouraging children to imagine other viewpoints

The ability to look at situations from new angles is a key part of divergent thinking and problem solving. Understanding the feelings and thoughts of others also supports creative collaboration, as this depends on those involved exchanging and accepting one another's creative ideas. You can encourage children to describe how the characters they meet in books may be feeling or what they might be thinking. This will be based on events, how the characters look, what they say and do. There will also be naturally occurring opportunities to talk about differing viewpoints within the group, particularly when there is a disagreement between children. If a child imagines how another person (or animal) feels, they are likely to have their own emotional response, and they may use their own creativity to express it.

Finding wonder and excitement

When children respond to the activities and experiences that you provide with wonder and excitement, this often indicates that creativity and/or creative learning is taking place. Different children will be drawn to different aspects of creativity, and it is part of a practitioner's role not only to help children to experience a full range of opportunities, but also to help them to find what excites them and gives them that creative spark. Highly creative people working in the traditional arts are often intrinsically motivated to practise their art, just as a child is intrinsically motivated to play. An artist rarely describes painting as a chore for instance, and it is enjoyment and satisfaction that has driven them to put in the many hours it takes to become accomplished.

Did you know?

There's a saying that relates to creative collaboration: 'A good idea is best shared'.

Extended and unhurried periods of time

Creativity and creative learning cannot be rushed. Creative ideas and insights take time to develop. When children first participate in an activity or experience, they are likely to do something familiar, something they have done before. They need extended, unhurried periods to really get into activities and experiences, and to engage at a deeper level. This is when new connections and new explorations and discoveries tend to be made.

Time is also important when it comes to creating new ideas. Often, children (and adults) will only begin to think creatively once all the obvious suggestions have been made, or all the most common ways of doing something have been tried. It takes time to work through all of these and to move into the deeper, richer, more imaginative stuff.

Ask Miranda!

Q Won't children become bored if activities aren't changing frequently?

A **Young children will be accessing creative activities and experiences as part of their free play, so opportunities to engage for extended periods will be offered within an environment that also facilitates moving on to the next thing when children are ready. In fact, an important part of making creative connections for young children is joining and mixing up what is on offer to them – taking some water to the sand tray, for instance, or taking a car to the drawing table and subsequently drawing a road.**

It's helpful to allow children the opportunity to revisit creative activities and experiences throughout the day, and to also make them available at a follow-up session, ideally the next day. Many visual artists and writers say they need time for their ideas, thoughts and concepts to 'percolate' (mature) over a period of consecutive work sessions. Many feel that their unconscious minds work on problems they have encountered in their practice while they do other things, allowing them to return to their work with new insight at a later time. Recent research suggests that there are links between creativity, creative learning and sleep. It seems that sleep helps us to process our learning and to gain a better understanding of the problems we have encountered during the day. So the

opportunity to revisit activities and experiences after sleep could be extremely beneficial.

Recent research suggests that there are links between creativity, creative learning and sleep.

Promoting creativity across the curriculum

As you learned in Learning Outcome 1, creative learning opportunities should be embedded in all areas of the curriculum framework followed in your home country. This should be in addition to opportunities for creative play and exploration related to the traditional creative arts.

We'll take the Early Years Foundation Stage, which applies in England, as our example. The table on page 544 gives an example of a learning activity or experience that may be provided in each of the six areas of learning and development – you'll notice that some of these overlap as children's learning is never compartmentalised and all of the areas are interlinked. An example of ICT is included, which like creative learning, should also be used to support learning right across this curriculum.

Adult-led opportunities such as those shown in the table should be offered within a programme that also promotes child-led creative and creative learning activities and experiences. You'll learn more about supporting creative and creative learning activities and experiences through the provision of resources in Learning Outcome 3.

Table CYPOP 7.1: Creative learning opportunities that may be provided in each of the six areas of learning and development

Area of learning and development	Activity/experience
Personal, social and emotional development	Pausing part way through a story to discuss how the characters are feeling and what they might be thinking in light of events, their expressions and their behaviour.
Communication, language and literacy	Coming together at circle time and thinking up questions to ask a dancer who is due to visit the setting and dance with the children. These are written down by an adult.
Knowledge and understanding of the world	What will happen if we water one plant and not the other? Let's try it and see...
Problem solving, reasoning and numeracy	We've built a tower next to our sunflower with the Mega® Bloks – it's ten blocks high. What else can we use to measure it?
Physical development	Developing fine motor skills when using tools to shape malleable materials.
Creative development	What will happen if we plot a course for a programmable robot, then place it in a shallow tray of sand? Will it leave footprints? Let's try it and see...

Link Up!

For more information on curriculum frameworks, see:
Unit EYMP 1 Context and principles for early years provision
Unit EYMP 2 Promote learning and development in the early years

Have a go!

Think of a further three activities to promote creativity and creative learning for each of the areas of learning that apply to the curriculum framework followed in your home country.

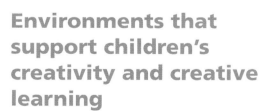

LEARNING OUTCOME 3

FOCUS ON

...being able to develop the environment to support young children's creativity and creative learning

Environments that support children's creativity and creative learning

In Learning Outcome 2, you learned about ways in which practitioners can promote creativity and creative learning in their practical work with children. We're going to build on that knowledge in this

In this section you'll learn about the features of an environment that supports creativity and creative learning. You'll also learn about monitoring and evaluating the effectiveness of the environment in supporting children's creativity and creative learning. This links with Assessment Criteria **3.1, 3.2.**

section, because environments that support creativity and creative learning depend on two key factors:

1. **The practices and attitudes held by staff, which set the all-important tone and atmosphere of the environment**

   Environments that support young children's creativity and creative learning promote exploration and play without undue limitations. Boundaries are of course necessary, but in a creative environment the atmosphere supports acceptable risk-taking, doing things in unconventional ways, making mistakes and a certain level of both untidiness and noise during sessions. Flexibility and a willingness to go with the flow of children's ideas is also necessary. For instance, imagine that a child spontaneously dips the wheels of a toy vehicle into some paint and drives it around a sheet of paper, making a track. In an unsupportive environment, the child may get into trouble for getting paint on the toys. But in a supportive environment, a practitioner may take the child's lead, and enable him or her to do the same thing outside with a huge sheet of paper and ride-on toy.

2. **The physical environment provided**

   In a creative environment, children will be given access to a wide range of materials and resources. They will have many varied opportunities to be creative and to think creatively during child-initiated and adult-initiated activities. Children will be surrounded by inspirational materials/ works/people that have the potential to stimulate creativity.

Did you know?

To establish a creative environment, a good understanding of creativity and creative learning and a willingness to support them is crucial among staff. Negative attitudes or wariness can present a barrier to creativity within a setting. You'll learn more about this in Learning Outcome 4.

Common features of environments that support creativity and creative learning

So, what might you expect to find in an environment that supports young children's creativity and creative learning? Let's look at different areas of the setting in turn.

Displays

You'd be likely to find plenty of visual and sensory inspiration on display. This might include interest tables as well as displays of the children's own individual work. There may also be a large piece of artwork that children (and perhaps adults) have collaborated on. Interesting and inspirational visual artwork from a variety of artists may also be provided – there could be paintings, prints, photographs, posters, postcards, wall hangings, stained glass, sculptures, ornaments and so on. These inspirational items will be rotated over time so that the visual stimuli available maintain a fresh quality. If items such as paintings are not rotated regularly, children and adults alike will tend to stop noticing them.

Link Up!

For more information on displays and interest tables, see Unit EYMP 1 Context and principles for early years provision

Role play

Role-play areas are likely to feature real objects and artefacts to enrich imaginary play. There may be real pasta 'cooking' in the saucepans of a home corner, for example, and a real telephone to play with (disconnected!). Creative environments will change the focus of imaginary areas regularly, providing ever-expanding opportunities to bring the real world in. For instance, if the area is a corner shop, real cans and packets of food can be sold, along with real fruit and vegetables. A price-labelling gun can be borrowed, and actual money can be used. If the area is a post office, real junk mail can be made available, and so on. In Learning Outcome 1, you learned how 'off the peg' dressing-up outfits can inhibit creativity in imaginary play, so creative environments are likely to provide lengths of fabric and so on, which encourage creative use. You can also provide real items such as hats, handbags and bangles.

Small-world toys

Small-world toys are common in most settings, but within creative environments they will be presented in exciting ways to maximise potential creativity. For instance, the train set may be set out with construction materials such as corrugated card and tape. If an adult models making their own tunnel for a train to pass through, children are likely to follow suit. Mark-making resources and a large sheet of paper may be provided with the cars so that children can draw their own roads – much more creative than tipping the cars out onto a ready-made play mat. If Lego® bricks are available they may make garages too. A farmyard may be set up in a tray of real soil and turf, and sand, water and shells may recreate a sea-bed in which to play with small-world marine life creatures.

Music

In a creative environment, musical instruments will be made available during free play, not just under close adult supervision at 'music time'. This is likely to inspire children to move and think imaginatively.

They might dance along while they play perhaps, or imagine that they are part of a marching band, or that they are a musician performing on stage or on the television. Instruments might inspire a music shop imaginative area, where the customers come to 'try and buy', or even a bandstand area in the playground. Children might make or devise their own simple instruments (e.g. plastic bottles filled with pasta can become shakers and pots and pans can become a drum kit with the addition of a wooden spoon). There will also be opportunities to hear recorded music from around the world, and live music played by musicians (perhaps a staff member plays the guitar, or a parent comes to play the keyboard).

Stories

A well-stocked, inviting book corner will be ready and waiting to whisk children off on an imaginary journey into another world, to meet characters and situations both familiar and new. Meanwhile, non-fiction books will stimulate creative learning. Children will explore and handle books freely outside of the set 'story time', and books will be rotated regularly. **Story bags** will add interest and extend learning, as will a range of sensory books. Imaginative extension activities will stimulate creativity and creative thinking further – see page 348 of Unit EYMP 2 for a practical example of this. Practitioners will be skilled at reading aloud to children, making story time a rich, engaging experience. There will be opportunities to visit the

Role-play areas are likely to feature real objects and artefacts to enrich imaginary play.

Children may be inspired to dance along as they play.

local library, and to hear skilled storytellers (who tell and develop stories from memory in a performance style).

key term

Story bags/story sacks a collection of items relating to a particular story, which are used to enhance storytelling and/or to extend learning (e.g. a Goldilocks story bag may contain three different-sized teddies, three different-sized bowls and spoons).

▶▶**Link Up!**◀◀

Unit EYMP 2 Promote learning and development in the early years

Physical movement

A wide range of sounds – from music to animal noises – will inspire creative movement. Props such as ribbon and floaty scarves will be available, alongside role-play resources such as masks (children may make these themselves), fringed waistcoats and skirts that twirl when children spin. There will be exposure to a range of dance genres, accessed via video clips, the internet, pictures and stories. There will also be opportunities to see live dance, for example via a visiting professional or a visit to the local school to see older children perform.

Mark-making

Mark-making will often be purely creative, and materials to support it will be varied and plentiful. This will include pencils, crayons, felt-tipped pens, charcoal, chalk and paint, and there will also be opportunities to make marks in sand, foam, corn flour paste and so on. Alongside these, creative opportunities will be provided for children to develop emergent writing skills by mark-making for real purposes. These opportunities will be well integrated into all other areas of the setting. For instance, in the home corner children may use notebooks and pencils to create their own shopping lists, in an imaginary shop area they may mark-make on point-of-sale

cards or price tags with wide and narrow felt-tipped pens. In the music area, they may experiment with making marks on blank sheet music paper (which can be printed for free from many online sites). Outside they may chalk all over the playground, and 'paint' the walls with water (not paint!), paintbrushes and rollers.

Art, craft and design

Art, craft and design resources will be interesting, varied and plentiful. There will be opportunities to use natural and recycled objects as well as manufactured supplies. Many opportunities will be child-led and purely inspired by the materials – free collages for instance, or models made from clay. There will be access to varying sizes of base materials such as paper and card. This enables children to choose the scale of their work, and also gives them the room to collaborate with peers and/or adults.

Free space

There will also be some free space in creative environments. Children can use this as they wish. They can get out new resources, or use the space to bring together items from around the setting that they'd like to explore together in one place. This supports joined-up thinking and discovery. However, it's important to understand that children's freedom to choose and mix up resources won't be limited to this one dedicated free space – it just helps to ensure that there is room

Creative opportunities to mark-make for real purposes will be provided.

Practical example

Tansy's treasure basket

Tansy is a student on placement in a nursery toddler room. She's recently learned about heuristic play – a term first used in the 1980s by child psychologist Elinor Goldschmeid to describe what happens when babies and children explore the properties of real objects (as opposed to toys). For babies and toddlers, this play centres on a 'treasure basket' filled with a diverse collection of objects, which babies can explore from the time they are able to sit up unaided. Tansy makes her own treasure basket. She gathers both natural and manmade objects from the real world, including a whisk, a large pebble, a sponge, a hairbrush, a wooden spoon, a metal sieve, a cardboard tube, a square of fun fur and a woollen glove. She checks that the items are clean. She leaves the basket on the playroom floor, then moves away. She watches from a distance as children discover the basket and explore the items.

Question
What is the advantage of Tansy moving away so that the children discover the basket for themselves?

within the overall layout for extra, spontaneous things to happen in the environment. The movement of both children and resources between activities adds vibrancy and excitement to the creative environment, while a lack of space is likely to inhibit some aspects of creativity and creative learning, for example creative movement.

Age appropriateness
As you've learned, environments that support creativity and creative learning provide access to a range of resources, materials and real objects and artefacts. A key difference between bought toys and gathered items is that the gathered items do not come with safety marks or age guidelines. So it's up to practitioners to make sensible, safe judgements about what materials are suitable for children in the light of their age and stage of development. However, this doesn't mean that any age group need be excluded from exploring a range of materials that promote creativity and creative learning, as the Practical example above shows.

Monitoring and evaluating the effectiveness of the environment
To successfully monitor and evaluate how effectively an environment supports children's creativity and creative learning, practitioners can analyse the observations they make of children's play and the assessments they make of children's learning. This can include target area observations. This means that rather than focusing on a target child, the practitioner observes a particular area of the setting for a length of time and records the play that happens there, whichever children come and go.

Signs that children are well supported include the following:

■ Good progress is made in the relevant area of learning in the curriculum framework that applies to the setting's home country (as described in Learning Outcome 1). In England, this area of learning is Creative Development.

■ Children show high levels of engagement in their play – they are focused and immersed.

- Children are engaged in activities for a good length of time – as you learned in Learning Outcome 1, children may spend extended periods engaged in the pursuits of creativity and creative learning. Remember, though, that some children may move busily around the setting while engaged on one idea, so physically staying in one place is not the sole indicator of the length of engagement.

- Children respond positively to the environment – they show signs of wonder and excitement.

- Children are curious – they ask questions about how things work, why things happen, and so on.

- Children respond well when asked questions intended to inspire creative thinking.

You can of course also ask children how they feel about certain aspects of the environment.

LEARNING OUTCOME 4

FOCUS ON

...being able to support the development of practice in promoting young children's creativity and creative learning within the setting

In this section you'll learn about evaluating and reflecting on your practice in promoting creativity and creative learning, and how to support others in developing their own practice in this area. You'll also learn about developing a programme of change to the environment to enhance creativity and creative learning. This links with Assessment Criteria 4.1, 4.2, 4.3.

Evaluating and reflecting on your own practice

In Learning Outcome 3, you learned about strategies for monitoring and evaluating how effectively environments support children's creativity and creative learning. These strategies will also help to reveal how well practitioners are supporting children's creativity and creative learning – you may

like to review them now. But there is more you can do.

Reflection and observation

As you know from Unit SHC 32, reflection brings many benefits. But as it can be hard to be objective about your own practice in supporting creativity and creative learning, observation can be a valuable tool. It's helpful to have someone record you or to record yourself as you work with children, either using a video camera or an audio recorder. (Make sure that you have written permission from your supervisor and children's parents or carers first.) Alternatively, you can ask a colleague to make a written observation of you for a period of time. You can then analyse the recordings or observation notes at your leisure.

To do this, you can refer to the practical techniques that promote creativity and creative learning, which you learned about in Learning Outcome 2. Reflect on how well you:

- provide children with options and allow choice

- model creativity and creative thinking

- emphasise process over product

- provide inspiration

- support language development

- make use of creative thinking questions

- build children's self-confidence and self-reliance

- encourage idea generation

- encourage children to imagine other viewpoints

- provide opportunities that result in wonder and excitement.

It can also be helpful to ask colleagues to give you feedback on how they feel you do in terms of supporting children's creativity and creative learning. If you do this, ask for both strengths and weaknesses to be shared.

Link Up!

Unit SHC 32 Engage in personal development in health, social care or children and young people's settings

Did you know?

Creativity thrives on trial and error. Regularly experiment with new ways of working by introducing new activities or resources, or make alterations to your old ones. Monitor children's responses. Repeat things that go well. If something doesn't work, simply try something else next time.

Supporting others to develop their practice

We've established that the skills of staff are crucial to the promotion of children's creativity and creative learning. But some practitioners may not feel confident about their ability to support children in this area. Adults who feel they are not strongly creative themselves sometimes worry that a lack of creative expertise or flair will let them down. However, when working with young children, adults do not need to be accomplished in creative fields, as the

Good practice

You can improve your own practice by learning more about creativity. There are plenty of books dedicated to the subject of promoting children's creativity, and even more on how to promote your own creativity and creative thinking skills. As you've learned, the most effective practitioners develop their own creativity as well as children's. There are an increasing number of short courses and seminars on promoting creativity – some focus solely on theory, while others introduce activity ideas and practical techniques. You can also learn from skilled colleagues, and visits to other settings are a wonderful way to become inspired and pick up tips.

creative process will be emphasised rather than the end product of creative endeavours. How well adults can paint or dance is nowhere near as important as modelling taking part. Explain this to reluctant adults, then allow them to build up their confidence gradually. While it's important to monitor progress, space and time is needed as the pressure of being watched is likely to hamper creativity further.

Some practitioners feel uncomfortable with the concept of promoting creativity and creative learning. Certain creative techniques may go against their own values – becoming more tolerant of untidiness during play sessions, for instance, or allowing children to experiment in certain ways. A good example of this (relating to a child dipping the wheels of a vehicle in paint) is given on page 545. Adults who have a tendency to be risk adverse and those used to a very structured approach may fear that children's behaviour will decline and that the setting will become wild or out of control. It's important for practitioners to talk through these concerns.

All settings must find the right balance between promoting creativity and establishing clear and

It's important for practitioners to talk through concerns about promoting creativity.

consistent boundaries. When practice is being developed, this will involve some trial and error. The crucial thing is for practitioners to keep talking, acknowledging when things are working and when changes made fall short of the mark and need to be re-examined. The more development work that needs to be done, the more gradual changes will need to be. It can help to plan some in-house staff training sessions, looking in turn at different areas of practice

(such as role modelling) or different areas of the setting (such as the imaginary area). The team can discuss what good practice is in these areas, and how it can be achieved over time in gradual steps. It can be effective to consider the observations gathered within the setting at these sessions – there may be video or audio clips of good practice for instance, which everyone can learn from.

Developing a programme of change

If it is identified that the current environment needs to be improved in order to enhance creativity and creative learning, it will be necessary to develop a programme to introduce the changes. Some people – children as well as adults – find change stressful, so it is important not to overwhelm when there is a lot to do. Gradual change also allows practitioners to see the impact of each step they take, and to tweak things as they go if necessary.

When drawing up a programme, it's important to be specific about each aspect of change that will be implemented. The following diagram shows factors to be agreed upon and recorded for each aspect of change:

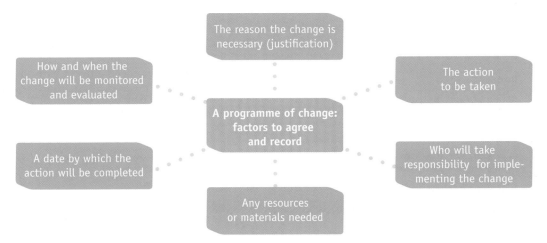

Factors to be agreed and recorded for each aspect of change.

How are things going?

▶ Progress Check

1. What are the key differences between creativity and creative learning? (1.1)

2. How can creativity and creative learning support the following aspects of children's development: a) emotional, b) social, c) intellectual and d) physical? (1.3)

3. Why do young children require extended and unhurried periods of time to develop their creativity? (2.2)

4. What are the key features of an environment that supports creativity and creative learning? (3.1)

5. Explain ways in which you could evaluate the effectiveness of the environment in meeting young children's needs for creativity and creative learning. (3.2)

6. Explain ways in which you could support others to develop their practice in promoting creative learning and creativity. (4.2)

Are you ready for assessment?

CACHE

In preparation for assessment of this Unit, you may like to reflect on your own practice in promoting creativity and creative thinking, making notes in your reflective journal.

Edexel

In preparation for assessment of this Unit, you may like to reflect on your own practice in promoting creativity and creative thinking, making notes in your reflective journal.

City & Guilds

In preparation for assessment of this Unit, you may like to reflect on your own practice in promoting creativity and creative thinking, making notes in your reflective journal.

Learning Outcomes 2, 3 and 4 must be assessed in real work environments.

REFLECTIVE PRACTICE

SHC 31

For one day, pay close attention to all the information you are given verbally by families and colleagues. How much of it is confidential? You may be surprised at how much verbal information comes your way that it would be inappropriate to disclose outside of the setting. This might include information about a child's recent upset at home, for instance, or even a change in their sleeping or eating patterns. Also take note of how much confidential information you give to families and colleagues. This might include details about children's achievement or health, or well-being. Think about how well you have handled this information, and make notes in your reflective journal.

SHC 32

Turn to page 38 and recap the reflective analysis techniques. Now think about your own reflective practice. Are you effectively using a range of techniques? If not, plan how you will begin to expand the scope of your reflective practice.

SHC 33

Have a think about the toys and equipment you select when you are setting up a room ready for free play. Do you consider whether you have, across your whole choice, promoted positive images of people and/or reflected the cultures of children and young people? Make notes in your reflective diary. If necessary, also think about how you can address this in the future.

SHC 34

As we've discussed, it can be emotionally difficult to exercise the duty of care, particularly if a practitioner feels that they are breaking the trust and confidentiality of a parent with whom they have worked in partnership, and may know well.

Imagine a colleague is in this position. She knows that she must exercise her duty of care and formally raise her concerns, but she feels upset about doing so. As a supportive friend and colleague, what would you say to her?

Write this down in full in your reflective journal. If you are ever in a similar position yourself during your career, you can return to your own words of support.

CYP 3.1

Return to the information on learning and development theories in Learning Outcome 2, and spend some time considering each one. Which of the influences can you recognise in your own practice? You may be surprised how many links there are. Even if you haven't been aware of the theories until now, the chances are you've been influenced by them considerably. This is because the techniques associated with some theories have been passed down through the years in the practice of those working with children.

CYP 3.2

Think about a time when you found a child's inappropriate behaviour challenging to deal with, and take a moment to reflect. Can you pinpoint what triggered the behaviour? What specifically did you find challenging? With this in mind, return to the techniques and behaviour strategies for promoting positive behaviour and managing challenging behaviour. Which approaches may have been useful? Make notes in your reflective diary.

CYP 3.3

Turn to the 'safe practice' bullet points on pages 179–181. Reflect on each bullet point in turn, asking yourself how safe your working practices are. Where could you improve? What strategies might help you to do so? Note your answers in your reflective journal.

CYP 3.4

Obtain copies of the health and safety documents used within your setting, including the health and safety policy, accident forms and risk assessments. Look through them carefully. Do you fully understand the purpose and content of each document? Make notes in your reflective journal. Ask your workplace supervisor to explain anything you're unsure about.

CYP 3.4

On page 245 you were given a list of behaviour indicators that can be used to evaluate your effectiveness in building relationships with children and young people.

Think of a child or young person that you have worked with regularly. Go through the behaviour indicators, asking yourself how they apply to your relationship with the child or young person you have selected. For instance, does the young person you have in mind approach you regularly to tell you things? Make notes in your reflective journal.

When you've considered all the indicators, analyse your findings. What do they tell you about your effectiveness? What can you do to improve your practice? For instance, you may decide to show more interest in the young person's interests, so they are more likely to tell you about things that are important to them in this area.

CYP 3.6

Have a think about the terms, jargon and abbreviations (e.g. EYFS), that you have picked up in your study/work. Consider whether these would make sense to someone who isn't a practitioner – a parent for example. In a report you can provide a glossary of terms by way of explanation. But how well do you explain the terms or use alternative language when you are sharing information with non-experts verbally? What could you do to improve this? Make notes in your reflective journal.

CYP 3.7

In Learning Outcome 4, you learned that a good indicator of whether children and young people have picked up stereotypes is how they assign roles in their imaginary play. You were encouraged to monitor this in your setting. Take the time now to reflect on what you've observed. In light of your findings, is it necessary to do more to promote positive images of people? Make notes in your reflective diary on how this could be achieved.

EYMP 1

Re-read the information about different approaches to working with children in Learning Outcome 1. Now think about your current setting. How many of the influences can you identify? How do these directly impact on the learning and development of the children you know?

EYMP 2

Take one plan that you have devised and already implemented. Ask yourself the questions in the section 'Reflect on your own practice in supporting children's learning and development' on page 355, consulting appropriately. Note your answers in your reflective journal.

EYMP 3

Take another look at your current setting's health and safety policy. Consider the procedures outlined for preventing cross-infection, and through reflective analysis, evaluate your own practice. Is it consistently of high standard? Do you ever cut corners? Make a note in your reflective diary of anything you need to work on, and develop a plan of action for doing so.

EYMP 4

Using the reflective analysis techniques that you learned in Unit SHC 32, conduct a review of your effectiveness in promoting diversity, inclusion and participation, paying close attention to your anti-bias practice. Make notes in your reflective diary. If improvements are necessary, think about how you can make them happen. Could you shadow someone with more experience of promoting diversity, inclusion and participation perhaps?

EYMP 5

Turn to the 'Evaluating the effectiveness of the support provided for children' bullet points on page 423. Reflect on each bullet point in turn, asking how well you support children's development in each of the areas. Where could you improve? What strategies might help you to do so? Note your answers in your reflective journal.

CYPOP 1

You've learnt how important it is to acknowledge and talk about feelings with young children. Have a think about how well you calm, comfort and reassure babies and children in ways that also encourage them to express their feelings. Make notes in your reflective diary, and identify ways in which you can build on this in the future. Some play with puppets, perhaps?

CYPOP 2

Have a think about the way in which you provide physical care for babies and young children during everyday routines. Do you show them respect and sensitivity? Is your approach unhurried? Do you engage them and take advantage of the opportunity to bond? Make notes in your reflective diary. If necessary, also think about how you can address these issues in the future.

CYPOP 5

Make a list of the everyday domestic routines you utilise for play and learning purposes. Now make a list of the domestic items you utilise as play objects. How well are you doing in these areas? Is there something new you could introduce? Make notes in your reflective diary.

CYPOP 6

Turn to the 'monitoring, reviewing, evaluating and challenging existing practice', bullet points on page 528. Reflect on each bullet point in turn, asking yourself how well you and your setting work with disabled children and young people and those with specific requirements. Where could you improve? What strategies might help you to do so? Note your answers in your reflective journal.

CYPOP 7

Turn to the reflection and observation bullet points on page 549. Reflect on each bullet point in turn, asking how well you use each of the techniques to promote children's creativity and creative learning. Where could you improve? What strategies might help you to do so? Note your answers in your reflective journal.

APPENDIX 1

ANNEX A: NATIONAL SERVICE FRAMEWORK FOR CHILDREN, YOUNG PEOPLE AND MATERNITY SERVICES – STANDARDS

Standard 1: Promoting Health and Wellbeing, Identifying Needs and Intervening Early

The health and wellbeing of all children and young people is promoted and delivered through a co-ordinated programme of action, including prevention and early intervention wherever possible, to ensure long-term gain, led by the NHS in partnership with local authorities.

Standard 2: Supporting Parenting

Parents or carers are enabled to receive the information, services and support which will help them to care for their children and equip them with the skills they need to ensure that their children have optimum life chances and are healthy and safe.

Standard 3: Child, Young Person and Family-Centred Services

Children, young people and families receive high quality services which are co-ordinated around their individual and family needs and take account of their views.

Standard 4: Growing Up into Adulthood

All young people have access to age-appropriate services which are responsive to their specific needs as they grow into adulthood.

Standard 5: Safeguarding and Promoting the Welfare of Children and Young People

All agencies work to prevent children suffering harm and to promote their welfare, provide them with the services they require to address their identified needs and safeguard children who are being or who are likely to be harmed.

Standard 6: Children and Young People who are ill

All children and young people who are ill, or thought to be ill, or injured will have timely access to appropriate advice and to effective services which address their health, social, educational and emotional needs throughout the period of their illness.

Standard 7: Children and Young People in Hospital

Children and young people receive high quality, evidence-based hospital care, developed through clinical governance and delivered in appropriate settings.

Standard 8: Disabled Children and Young People and Those with Complex Health Needs

Children and young people who are disabled or who have complex health needs receive co-ordinated, high quality child and family-centred services which are based on assessed needs, which promote social inclusion and, where possible, which enable them and their families to live ordinary lives.

Standard 9: The Mental Health and Psychological Wellbeing of Children and Young People

All children and young people, from birth to their eighteenth birthday, who have mental health problems and disorders have access to timely, integrated, high quality multidisciplinary mental health services to ensure effective assessment, treatment and support, for them and their families.

Standard 10: Medicines for Children and Young People

Children, young people, their parents or carers, and healthcare professionals in all settings make decisions about medicines based on sound information about risk and benefit. They have access to safe and effective medicines that are prescribed on the basis of the best available evidence.

Standard 11: Maternity Services

Women have easy access to supportive, high quality maternity services, designed around their individual needs and those of their babies.

APPENDIX 2

Extract of the EYFS profile documentation for Communication, language and literacy

The profile provides examples of attainment evidence that may be observed.

Scale points 1–3 describe the attainment of a child who is still progressing towards the early learning goals in this scale (the actual early learning goals are expressed in scale points 4–8).

Linking sounds and letters (LSL)
(Communication, language and literacy)

For scale points 1–3, assessment should be made on the basis of the child's attainment in their preferred language. For some children, this may be a recognised sign language or Picture Exchange Communication symbol system. Assessments of scale points 4–9 should be in English (or BSL or sign-supported English) reflecting the child's emerging competence in the language.

Scale point	**1** Joins in with rhyming and rhythmic activities
The child takes an active part in singing and rhyming activities, joining in with some of the words and moving to the music.	Pip enjoys singing along to the rhymes on the CD. She claps in time to her favourites. While the class say *Humpty Dumpty* with the practitioner, Sehmaz pats her knees and nods her head in response to the rhythm. Jack and Becky sit holding hands and move backwards and forwards to the song *Row, row, row your boat*. Sasha echoes the practitioner's clapping to her name.

Scale point	**2** Shows an awareness of rhyme and alliteration
The child is aware of rhyme in songs and poems and sometimes distinguishes sounds of personal significance from others or notices when words begin with the same sound.	Rosie carries on with an action (touching her knee), thinking the end of a song would rhyme. She laughs when the last word is changed. 'Clap your hands together, one, two, three, put your hands upon your … head.' When listening to the tongue twister *Six sizzling sausages* Sarah laughs and says 'They're all 's' like me.' When listening to rhyming text such as 'Don't put your finger in the jelly, Nelly,' Helen says 'They're the same.'

Scale point	**3** Links some sounds to letters
The child hears some sounds and links them to specific letters, for example the letters in his or her name, and is able to recognise a few of them.	A small group of children are suggesting all the objects they can think of beginning with the sound 'd' – door, dog, doll, drink. Suddenly Donna smiles and says 'd' for Donna.' Karen spots a capital K on the cover of a big book. 'Look, it's the same as at the beginning of my name, it's a 'k'.' Bailey is fishing for magnetic letters in the water tray. He finds the letter 'm' and says 'mummy'. Izzy is in the role play area making party invitations for her friends Rosie and Lawrence. After using non-standard marks for the invitations she writes 'r' for Rosie and 'l' for Lawrence on the envelopes.

Scale point **4**	Links sounds to letters, naming and sounding letters of the alphabet
Across a range of activities, the child is able to name and sound letters of the alphabet, recognising more letters than not. The child needs to be able to accurately link the letter shape with its sound and name.	Victoria brings in some objects to go on the interest table. 'I've brought a doll, a dog and a picture of my dad,' she explains. The children play the game 'Noisy Letters'. The practitioner gives each child a letter, and the children attempt to find the other child(ren) who have been assigned the same letter by saying their letter sound out loud. Whilst pretending to be a teacher, Abigail uses the practitioner's pointer to point out correctly letters of the alphabet as she names them. In a later observation the practitioner observes her sieving letters in the sand tray correctly identifying the sounds. The practitioner uses these observations to correlate the sounds and names of the letters she knows.
Scale point **5**	Hears and says sounds in words
When sounding out simple CVC words, the child hears and says sounds in the word.	Danya takes the model of the cat out of the box. When asked to do so, she is able to say the sounds in order 'c-a-t'. Paul is in the role play area which is a pizzeria. He asks Sharon for a pizza with cheese on. As Sharon writes his order, Paul says 'Cheese, that's 'ch-ee-z'.' Will and Jess are working in the creative area painting pictures for each other. Jess asks Will 'How do you do your name?' Will says 'W-i-ll'.
Scale point **6**	Blends sounds in words
The child is able to blend sounds together in the order in which they occur to say simple CVC words.	The children are playing the 'Robot' game. The practitioner says 'r-e-d' and Evie says 'red'.
Scale point **7**	Uses phonic knowledge to read simple regular words
The child uses his or her phonic knowledge to read a range of simple CVC words, some of which are new to them. Scale point 7 cannot be achieved without LSL scale points 4, 5 and 6.	While reading a book in the book area, Craig encounters an unfamiliar word. When the practitioner suggests separating the short vowel sounds within the word, Craig is able to correctly identify the word 'M- e-g' and says 'Meg'. Amina spells out the words 'jam' and 'eggs' from the recipe card when taking part in a baking activity. Alice and Connor help the practitioner set up for a car boot sale. They both match labels to the objects and Alice correctly chooses the word 'sheep' and matches it with the toy sheep.
Scale point **8**	Attempts to read more complex words, using phonic knowledge
The child attempts to read more complex words, sometimes with adult support.	Walking round the sea life centre Jack noticed the sign 'crabs' and says 'We haven't seen the crabs, yet.' Whilst the teacher is labelling a lost property jumper box, Areeb says 'J-u-m-p-er. Is that for our jumpers?' In Santa's grotto, the children are wrapping presents. John reads from a list the word 'handbag' and says 'I need one of those for mummy's present.'

Scale points 4–8 describe the attainment of a child in the context of the early learning goals. They are not hierarchical and a child may achieve them in any order.

Scale point	9	The child has achieved all the early learning goals for linking sounds and letters. In addition, the child uses a knowledge of letters, sounds and words when reading and writing independently
In his or her independent reading and writing, the child uses a range of strategies when tackling unfamiliar words, including fluent and appropriate use of phonic knowledge.		While writing a story, Yan realises that he does not know how to spell 'beanstalk'. 'I can do the 'bean' bit' he says, and then sounds out the rest of the word phonetically as he writes. 'St-or-k – but 'ork' doesn't look right – I know, it's st-alk, stalk!' he says, and writes down the correct spelling of the word. When writing, Melissa writes about going to the beach. She sounds out b-ea-ch but writes b-ee-ch.

Scale point 9 describes the attainment of a child who has achieved scale points 1–8 and developed further, working consistently beyond the early learning goals.

GLOSSARY

Agent of change someone who takes action to challenge existing practices.

Alternative and Augmentative Communication (AAC) this refers to any device, system or special method of communication that helps individuals who have communication difficulties to communicate more easily and effectively. *(National Occupational Standards)*

Assistive technology (AT) technology used by disabled people to perform functions that might otherwise be difficult or impossible.

Best-practice benchmarks widely agreed as the most up-to-date thinking and practice against which you can measure what you are doing – not minimum standards. Benchmarks can be statutory/regulatory or based on other requirements or research. *(National Occupational Standards)*

Bilingual someone who speaks two languages.

Child protection the measures taken to keep children and young people safe from abuse and harm caused by others.

Child-/young person-centred provision occurs in services where children/young people's needs, interests, strengths and participation are the priority, rather than the organisation's own needs.

Compliance children co-operating with requests. *(National Occupational Standards)*

Concentration span the period of time that an individual child is able to focus completely on one activity or task.

Continuing professional development ongoing training and professional updating. *(National Occupational Standards)*

Creative learning the development of the skills of imaginative thinking and problem solving.

Creativity play and exploration related to the traditional creative arts.

Cross-curricular balance the provision of opportunities across each area of learning included in the early years framework of the relevant home country.

Disclosing/disclosure the process of passing on confidential information in certain circumstances, in line with confidentiality procedures.

Duty of care term used to describe the responsibility to act at the level of 'a reasonable parent' when *in loco parentis*.

Excessively risk adverse prone to avoiding risk altogether.

Excessive risk taking taking inappropriate risks.

Expected development rates the approximate age at which most children will achieve key developmental milestones.

Fine motor skills (sometimes called 'small motor skills') the delicate, manipulative movements that are made with the fingers.

Formative assessment initial and on-going assessment. *(National Occupational Standards)*

Gross motor skills (sometimes called 'large motor skills') whole-body movements, such as walking.

Hazard an item or situation that may cause harm.

Impairment a condition that is not usually experienced by a child or young person at the current age or stage of development.

Inclusion/Integration children with disabilities or special educational needs belonging to mainstream settings. *(National Occupational Standards)*

Inclusive practice the practice of embracing diversity and ensuring that everyone can participate.

In loco parentis being responsible for a child or young person's safety and welfare instead of their parents.

Key worker a person appointed to take a special interest in the welfare of a particular child.

Learning styles styles people prefer to use when learning and that help them to learn best, such as seeing, hearing or doing. *(National Occupational Standards)*

Medical models of disability the medical model reflects the traditional view that disability is something to be 'cured', treating the child as a sick patient.

Multilingual someone who speaks three or more languages.

Need to know basis the process of only disclosing confidential information to those allowed to have access to it and at times when they have reason to be informed.

Neonate newly born baby.

Ofsted The Office for Standards in Education, Children's Services and Skills, which inspects and regulates care and education for children and young people.

Planning cycle constant cycle of planning, implementing, reviewing/evaluating. *(National Occupational Standards)*

Play agenda what a child wants to achieve in their play.

Processes, practices and outcomes how you do things, what you do and what you achieve. *(National Occupational Standards)*

Reflective practice/reflecting the process of thinking about and critically analysing your actions with the goal of changing and improving occupational practice. *(National Occupational Standards)*

Reflective practitioner a worker who uses reflective practice regularly.

Reflexes physical movements or reactions that neonates make without consciously intending to do so.

Regressed moved backwards.

Responsive care how practitioners identify and respond to the care needs of children.

Safeguarding umbrella term describing measures taken to keep children and young people safe from a wide range of dangers.

Safe working practices ways of working that keep both the practitioner and the baby, child or young person they are working with protected and safe from harm.

Self-advocacy the process of a disabled young person or adult making their own views known on matters that affect them.

SENCO Special Educational Needs Coordinator.

Sequence of development rates the expected order in which most children will achieve key developmental milestones.

Social models of disability the social model considers that it is society that needs to change and that disabled people have rights and choices. *(National Occupational Standards)*

Special educational needs children with special educational needs learn differently from most children of the same age. These children may need extra or different help from that given to other children. *(National Occupational Standards)*

Story bags/story sacks a collection of items relating to a particular story, which are used to enhance storytelling and/ or to extend learning (e.g. a Goldilocks story bag may contain three different-sized teddies, three different-sized bowls and spoons).

Summative assessment assessment that summarises findings and may draw overall conclusions. *(National Occupational Standards)*

Sustained shared thinking occurs when a practitioner uses language to encourage children to explore an activity, event, idea or concept on a deeper level.

Synthesising ideas the process of gathering different ideas from different sources. These are reflected upon, and in a considered way they are blended or joined together to form a new idea.

Times of transition times when children are moving onto a new stage in their lives or development (e.g. when children leave the baby room or start school).

Weaning the process by which babies are introduced to solid foods.

INDEX

ACKNOWLEDGEMENTS

Eve Thould – thank you for being so fantastic! (Miranda Walker)

The author and the publisher would like to thank the following for permission to use or adapt copyright material:

p68 A Dictionary of Law, E. A. Martin, 1994, published by Oxford University Press; p174 © NSPCC 2011; p191 © Kidscape website, www.kidscape.org.uk; p234 © Meningitis Trust 2011; pp259, 321, 397, 398, Department for Education © Crown copyright 2010; p295 © Learning and Teaching Scotland; p296 Welsh Assembly Government © Crown copyright 2008; p296 Department for Education, Northern Ireland © Crown copyright 2010; p323 Early Years Foundation Stage © reprinted under Crown copyright PSI License C2008000256; p324 DfE Learning and Development © reprinted under Crown copyright; p332, Appendix 2, © Qualifications and Curriculum Development Agency; pp372, 481, Reproduced by kind permission of the Department of Health © 2011; pp378, 382, Food Standards Agency © Crown copyright 2011; pp457, 479, www.nhs.uk content provided by

content supplied by

NHS choices ; Appendix 1 Department of Health © Crown copyright 2009.

Many thanks to the parents, children and staff at Little Hoots Preschool, Bishops Cleeve and Monkey Puzzle Day Nursery, Cheltenham

PHOTO ACKNOWLEDGEMENTS

www.**heathergunnphotography**.co.uk pp22, 30, 40, 43, 45, 87 (top), 88 (top), 94 (bottom), 95, 96 (top, bottom), 97, 99, 114, 129, 130, 133, 141, 144, 164, 173, 180 (top, bottom), 197, 203, 236, 237, 243, 244, 245, 254, 264, 265, 267, 278, 279, 284, 291, 299, 304, 305, 309 (top), 310 (left, right), 313, 331, 334, 338, 342, 347, 352, 353, 356, 360, 362, 363, 374, 393, 403, 408 (right), 414 (right), 415, 419, 421, 422, 435, 436, 437, 438, 439, 446, 449, 450, 452, 466, 467, 468, 470, 471, 474, 480, 484, 519, 524 (bottom), 537, 538, 539, 542, 543, 546 (left, right), 547, 551; **Alamy:** © Angela Hampton Picture Library / Alamy p190; © Brownstock / Alamy p501; © Catchlight Visual Services / Alamy p257 (left); © Christina Kennedy / Alamy p408 (left); © Daniel Atkin / Alamy p103; © David Hoffman Photo Library / Alamy p276; © jacky chapman / Alamy p504; © Medical-on-Line / Alamy p182; © moodboard / Alamy p514; © Paul Doyle / Alamy p516 (left); © Picture Partners / Alamy p15; © Picture Partners / Alamy p459; © Stephen Hale / Alamy p496; © thislife pictures / Alamy p497; PhotosIndia.com LLC / Alamy p59; **fotolia:** © Christian Schwier – Fotolia.com p195; © darko64 – Fotolia.com p156; © darko64 – Fotolia.com p239; © igor kisselev – Fotolia.com p106; © Irina Vorontsova – Fotolia.com p364; © jörn buchheim – Fotolia.com p366; © Michael Ireland – Fotolia.com p169; © michaeljung – Fotolia.com p128; © Monart Design – Fotolia.com p13; © moodboard – Fotolia.com p163; © Olga Sapegina – Fotolia.com p489; © Pavel Losevsky – Fotolia.com p47; © pershing – Fotolia.com p248; © photocreo – Fotolia.com p201; © pressmaster – Fotolia.com p98;

© rnl – Fotolia.com p91 (top); © Sergey Galushko – Fotolia.com p302; © Serhiy Kobyakov – Fotolia.com p476; © Tomasz Trojanowski – Fotolia.com p68; © Yuri Arcurs – Fotolia.com p36; **Getty:** Abel Mitja Varela/ Getty Images p431; B2M Productions/Getty Images p492; Blend Images/Getty Images p241; blue jean images/Getty Images p503; Christopher Futcher/ Getty Images p153; jo unruh/Getty Images p349; K.Hatt/Getty Images p500; Marcy Maloy/Getty Images p329; Peter Cade/Getty Images p535; Photodisc/ Getty Images p194; Ruth Jenkinson/Getty Images p455; Science Photo Library/Getty Images p256; Tetra Images/Getty Images p429; Tracy Morgan/ Getty Images p495; Vanessa Davies/Getty Images pp309 (bottom), 325, 386; **Connie Handscombe** p84 (bottom); **iStockphoto:** pp16, 19, 20, 23, 25, 35, 52, 55, 56, 57, 60, 61, 62, 63, 67, 69, 74, 77, 79, 89 (top, bottom), 91 (bottom), 92 (bottom), 100 (top, bottom), 101, 136, 146, 147, 150, 157, 161, 168, 199, 205, 206, 211, 214, 215, 216 (left, right), 218, 220, 221, 224, 227, 229, 234 (top left, right), 240, 249, 251, 260, 262 (bottom), 272, 287, 289, 293, 297, 300, 320, 326, 327, 328 (right), 332, 350, 359, 367, 383, 392, 396, 406, 411, 414 (left), 417, 425, 428, 434, 441, 444, 458, 461, 487, 494, 502, 511, 513, 516 (right), 524 (top), 531, 533, 540; **Daisy Lawson** p90; **Tallulah Lawson** pp84 (top), 85 (top); **Elliott Loader** p81; **John Birdsall MR/PA Photos** pp283, 517; **Photolibrary.com:** Photolibrary.com/ John Warburton-Lee Photography p72; Photolibrary.com/All Canada Photos p368; Photolibrary.com/ Floresco Productions p307; **Rex Features:** Canadian Press/Rex Features p290; Design Pics Inc/Rex Features p328 (left); Garo/Phanie/Rex Features p262 (top); Image Source/Rex Features p48; Richard Sowersby/ Rex Features p286; Stewart Cook/Rex Features p508; **SCIENCE PHOTO LIBRARY:** CHRISTIAN DARKIN / SCIENCE PHOTO LIBRARY p102; JOTI / SCIENCE PHOTO LIBRARY p529; CECILIA MAGILL / SCIENCE PHOTO LIBRARY p288; D.AUCLAIR,PUBLIPHOTO DIFFUSION / SCIENCE PHOTO LIBRARY p433; JIM VARNEY / SCIENCE PHOTO LIBRARY p104; LIFE IN VIEW / SCIENCE PHOTO LIBRARY p257 (right); **Martin Sookias** pp87 (bottom), 88 (bottom), 92 (top), 93, 94 (top), 222, 230, 233; **Izabelle Wastell** pp83, 85 (middle, bottom); **Izabelle Wastell and Alasdair Laing** p86